10-21-92 $ 375.00   (5 vols)

GREAT EVENTS
FROM
HISTORY II

GREAT EVENTS FROM HISTORY II

Human
Rights
Series

Volume 5
1982-1991

Edited by

FRANK N. MAGILL

SALEM PRESS

Pasadena, California   Englewood Cliffs, New Jersey

Library of Congress Cataloging-in-Publication Data
Great events from history II. Human rights series / edited by Frank N. Magill.
    p.   cm.
    Includes bibliographical references and index.
    1. Human rights—History—20th century—Chronol-
ogy. I. Magill, Frank Northen, 1907-   .

K3240.6.G74   1992
341.4′81′0904—dc20
ISBN 0-89356-643-8 (set)   92-12896
ISBN 0-89356-648-9 (volume 5)   CIP

LIST OF EVENTS IN VOLUME V

LIST OF EVENTS IN VOLUME V

GREAT EVENTS
FROM
HISTORY II

THE U.N. PRINCIPLES OF MEDICAL ETHICS INCLUDE PREVENTION OF TORTURE

Categories of event: Prisoners' rights; health and medical rights
Time: December 18, 1982
Locale: United Nations, New York City

The U.N. Principles of Medical Ethics transformed isolated national ethical codes into an internationally unified humanistic voice

Principal personages:

THOMAS PERCIVAL (1740-1804), a general practitioner in Manchester, England; author of a code of conduct that formed the basis for the code of medical ethics of the American Medical Association

BENJAMIN RUSH (1745-1813), a committed revolutionary, called an "American Hippocrates" because of his extensive lecturing on medical ethics

HIPPOCRATES (C. 460 B.C.-C. 377 B.C.), the Greek physician generally called "the father of medicine"

HAMMURABI (C. 1810 B.C.-1750 B.C.), known for his *Code of Hammurabi*, a collection of Babylonian laws

Summary of Event

The story of human civilization is the meandering story of the invincible will of the human race to assert its natural right to live with dignity. The dynamics of the struggle to survive and to thrive have provided the protagonist of the story, the human race, with a vibrant resilience otherwise called the will to survive. The dynamics between a tradition of torture and the history of the evolution of medical ethics, a body of codes of professional conduct developed by individuals and groups within the medical profession and voluntarily practiced by them in word and spirit, demonstrates how the human will to survive has worked its way toward an increasingly fuller and more coherent realization of the right to live with dignity.

The code of Hammurabi, the earliest of the ethical codes of medical practitioners, protected the natural rights of human beings in the crude spirit of "an eye for an eye and a tooth for a tooth," a spirit that condemns the inhuman and the cruel in humanity only to introduce a remedy as bad as the disease. According to this code, a surgeon, for example, who destroys his patient's eye in an operation must lose his hands much the same way as a builder whose faulty construction of a house results in the death of the householder's child must lose his own child. The code does not mention prisoners, since prisons are a relatively recent reformatory social institution, replacing the original harsher punitive measures of death, mutilation, banishment, transportation, flogging, and branding. The prevailing cruelty of the Babylonian society of Hammurabi's days generated a cruel code of ethics.

Hippocrates, the renowned physician of the fifth century B.C., has been called the "father of medicine." He responded to the prevailing institutionalized cruelty of his age in a different manner from Hammurabi, giving the human will a different mode of survival and a new way of asserting its right to live with dignity. His code counsels physicians to use their skill and learning on their patients with kindness. One of the ways the physician can choose to be kind is to make sure that he or she does no harm to the patient in cases in which the patient cannot possibly be helped. The code captures this injunction in its phrase "above all, do no harm." Further, the Hippocratic oath strongly urges physicians to keep under complete control their possible amorous proclivities toward patients. It also admonishes physicians to keep secret any knowledge that they gain concerning their patients "which ought not to be spread abroad." Above all, Hippocrates wants physicians to apply these tenets with an uncompromising professional egalitarianism to all, "be they free or slave." The Hippocratic oath's professionalism in the conduct of physicians and care of their patients promoted not only the physical health but also the autonomy of the patient, combating the inhumanity of the forces of cruelty and leading the human will to triumph over the social institutions of evil.

The code's unfailing devotion to the propagation of the quintessential existential rights of humans, especially in its enunciations of the interrelationship between the doctor and the patient, made the Hellenistic Hippocratic oath the overarching proclamation in the body of literature on medical ethics. The early Christians modified it only to eliminate its invocation to pagan deities, which they replaced with the Christian God the Father and Jesus Christ. Medieval Arabs admired the oath in its Arabic translations by Avicenna and Averroës, although they found the pagan ideals of the Greek philosopher-physician in conflict with their Islamic theology. They found the oath flexible enough, however, for them to incorporate Islamic ethics without changing the oath in spirit. Medieval Jews followed suit. The humanism of the Renaissance, with its new enthusiasm for Greek and Latin works, showed a deep appreciation for the oath.

Benjamin Rush, an eighteenth century American physician, drew heavily upon the works of Hippocrates for his extensive lectures on medical ethics. His contemporary, Thomas Percival, based his 1803 *Code of Medical Ethics* on a mixture of Hellenistic background and Christian morality, extending the same humanistic temperament to his brief observations on new issues of medical ethics emerging as a result of advances in medical research. Percival's code formed the core of the medical ethics discussed at the first meeting of the American Medical Association in 1847. In spite of its revisions in 1903, 1912, 1947, and 1980, the American Medical Association's medical code retained the fundamentals of the Hippocratic oath as adapted and interpreted by Percival.

The political events of the mid-twentieth century heralded a new evil and threat to medical well-being and health, the evil of institutionalized torture of political prisoners. Dictatorial regimes in South Asia, Africa, and Latin America used the traditional repertoire of torture methods but also added to it the sophisticated insights the medical profession could offer. These nations were not the only transgressors—

torture was practiced practically worldwide to varying degrees. Some politicized medical and health-care professionals volunteered to assist in torture, with various motives, and many others were coerced into using their skill. Medical practitioners acted to "rejuvenate" the tortured, so that torture could be prolonged until the tortured person "confessed," and advised torturers on how to inflict pain and damage while leaving the least possible evidence of torture, making the burden of proof almost impossible to meet for humanitarian agencies working on behalf of the rights of the tortured. Some even signed false documents attributing natural causes to deaths resulting from torture. In some countries, psychiatrists were used to interpret political dissidence as "delusions," commit the "deluded individuals" to psychiatric hospitals, and administer drugs for the person's "treatment."

This retrogression of the rights of humans to an autonomous selfhood became a matter of concern to the World Medical Association, an association of national medical associations. In its 1975 "Declaration of Tokyo," the World Medical Association expressed the collective conscience of medical professionals and called upon colleagues not to use their medical knowledge against the natural laws of humanity and to desist from providing "any premises, instruments, substances, or knowledge to facilitate the practice of torture or other forms of cruel, inhuman, or degrading treatment or to diminish the ability of the victim to resist such treatment." The United Nations broadened the scope of the Declaration of Tokyo after elaborate consultations with the World Health Organization (WHO), the World Medical Association, and the Council for International Organizations of Medical Sciences, an international nongovernmental scientific organization jointly established by WHO and the United Nations Educational, Scientific and Cultural Organization. Finally, it consolidated all suggestions into the *U.N. Principles of Medical Ethics Relevant to the Role of Health Personnel, Particularly Physicians, in the Protection of Prisoners Against Torture*, which was formally adopted by its General Assembly's thirty-seventh session on December 18, 1982.

Impact of Event

The six principles contained in the U.N. document concerning medical ethics are rather unlike their predecessors in that they target a specific group of people (prisoners) and address the ethical problems related to a particular category of social pathology (torture). For example, the second principle specifically denounces the practice, active or passive, by health personnel, particularly physicians, of torture or other cruel, inhuman, or degrading treatment or punishment. The principles are also like their predecessors, as they are the intramural directives of medical professionals without the extramural legal authority of law. In the absence of a legal backing, they may seem to be the beautiful words of an angel beating its luminous wings in the void. In reality, they offer extensive moral support—local, national, and international, of professionals and of the laity—for those medical personnel who are coerced into the abuse of medical ethics under the threats of torture or inhuman and degrading acts either from their employers or from their national dictators. Further, presence of such international moral support was hoped to be an effective deterrent to those in the medical profession who may have been tempted to volunteer for the transgression of their professional ethics.

An authoritarian regime cannot afford to exist without ties to the world outside, which is becoming progressively interdependent for economic, technological, scientific, and many other reasons. In such an increasingly interconnected world, consciousness raising can be stronger than the power of legal implementation. Realizing this, the United Nations has publicized the document extensively. In the resolution to which the principles are attached, the General Assembly calls upon all governments to give the resolution and the principles the widest possible distribution, in particular among medical and paramedical associations and institutions of detention or imprisonment. It also requests that intergovernmental and nongovernmental agencies, especially WHO, do the same. Such acts of consciousness raising attempted to make the U.N. Principles of Medical Ethics a more efficacious force than they may appear.

Consciousness raising within the medical profession has led to more soul-searching at the national, continental, and local levels, resulting in the formation of smaller groups espousing the same cause. These local, national, and even international groups may not succeed in preventing dictators from trampling on human rights, but they do shine their little lights on the moral darkness so created by dictatorships. As the number of such lights increases and their light gets stronger, moral darkness is bound to diminish. The United Nations resolution on medical ethics is a part of such light.

Bibliography

Against Torture: An Amnesty International Briefing. London: Amnesty International Publications, 1984. Examines torture in the 1980's comprehensively, suggesting how victims, their families, and national and international groups can prevent it. It reproduces a one-page 1975 document, the *Declaration Against Torture: United Nations Declaration on the Protection of All Persons from Torture.*

American Medical Association. Judicial Council. *Current Opinions of the Judicial Council of the American Medical Association.* Vol. 4. Chicago: American Medical Association, 1984. Replaces previous editions of *Current Opinions* and supersedes *Opinions and Reports of the Judicial Council*, compiled in 1958 and revised in 1979. It treats all aspects of medical ethics, such as social policy issues, confidentiality, and advertising.

Burns, Chester R., ed. *Legacies in Ethics and Medicine.* New York: Science History Publications, 1977. A collection of essays designed for use in the classroom by teachers of history, philosophy, and religion. Explores the problems of medical ethics in relation to ethics in general, religion, and secularism.

Catholic Church. Archdiocese of São Paulo (Brazil). *Torture in Brazil: A Report.* Translated by Jaime Wright and edited by Joan Dassin. New York: Vintage Books, 1986. A "shocking report on the pervasive use of torture by Brazilian military governments 1964-1979, secretly prepared by the archdiocese of São Paulo," with a section on "Medical Assistance to Torture."

McCabe, Joseph. *The History of Torture: A Study of Cruelty, the Ugliest Impulse in Man.* Girard, Kans.: Haldeman-Julius, 1949. Traces the origins of torture and its movement to the West. Criticizes the West for claiming moral superiority while perpetrating torture in the name of Christianity.

Philosophy and Practice of Medical Ethics. 3d impression. London: British Medical Association, 1986. Published in 1984 as *The Handbook of Medical Ethics*, a self-help type of manual for doctors to work out on their own medical ethical questions, both contemporary and future. "Ethical Codes and Statements" is a useful compilation of documents on medical ethics.

United Nations. General Assembly. Council for International Organizations of Medical Ethics. *Principles of Medical Ethics Relevant to the Protection of Prisoners Against Torture.* Geneva: CIOMS, 1983. A synopsis in English, French, Russian, Chinese, and Arabic of the U.N. General Assembly's resolution of December 18, 1982.

Abdulla K. Badsha

Cross-References

The United Nations Sets Rules for the Treatment of Prisoners (1955), p. 935; Amnesty International Is Founded (1961), p. 1119; The U.N. Covenant on Civil and Political Rights Is Adopted (1966), p. 1353; Brazil Begins a Period of Intense Repression (1968), p. 1468; A Medical Group Helps Gather Evidence of Torture in Greece and Chile (1974), p. 1747; The Helsinki Agreement Offers Terms for International Cooperation (1975), p. 1806; The Declaration of Tokyo Forbids Medical Abuses and Torture (1975), p. 1829; The United Nations Issues a Declaration Against Torture (1975), p. 1847; Zia Establishes Martial Law in Pakistan (1977), p. 1898; Soviet Citizens' Group Investigates Political Abuses of Psychiatry (1977), p. 1909; Misuse of Psychiatry Is Addressed by the Declaration of Hawaii (1977), p. 1926; Commission Studies Ethical and Legal Problems in Medicine and Research (1980), p. 2090; Amnesty International Adopts a Program for the Prevention of Torture (1983), p. 2204; Argentine Leaders Are Convicted of Human Rights Violations (1985), p. 2280.

THE UNITED NATIONS RESPONDS TO PROBLEMS OF THE HOMELESS

Category of event: Homeless people's rights
Time: December 20, 1982-1988
Locale: United Nations, New York City, and Washington, D.C.

The United Nations declared 1987 as the International Year for Shelter for the Homeless, focusing worldwide attention on the plight of the homeless

Principal personages:
 ARCOT RAMACHANDRAN (1923-   ), the executive director of the United Nations Centre for Human Settlements
 RONALD V. DELLUMS (1935-   ), a Democratic member of the United States House of Representatives
 JAMES W. ROUSE, chairman and chief executive officer of the Enterprise Foundation
 R. PREMADASA (1924-   ), the prime minister of Sri Lanka, the sponsor of the concept of the International Year of the Homeless

Summary of Event

On December 20, 1982, the General Assembly of the United Nations proclaimed 1987 as the International Year for Shelter for the Homeless (IYSH). In its resolution, the General Assembly expressed serious concern that, despite the efforts of governments at national and local levels and of international organizations, the living conditions of many people continued to deteriorate in both relative and absolute terms. In response, the resolution set forth two principal objectives for activities before and during the year: to improve the shelter and neighborhoods of some of the poor and disadvantaged by 1987, and to demonstrate by the year 2000 ways and means of continuing to improve shelter for these groups.

The General Assembly urged governments to prepare national shelter strategies. It designated the Commission on Human Settlements (established in 1977) to act as the United Nations' intergovernmental body responsible for organizing the year, and it assigned the United Nations Centre for Human Settlements (Habitat) responsibility for coordinating the programs and activities of other organizations and concerned agencies.

The concept of the IYSH was first introduced to the General Assembly in 1980 by R. Premadasa, the prime minister of Sri Lanka, who described the problems faced by homeless persons worldwide. The resolution declaring the IYSH followed after reports were prepared by the Commission on Human Settlements and the Economic and Social Council in 1981.

The importance of shelter acknowledged by the IYSH proclamation was not a new notion for the United Nations. The Universal Declaration of Human Rights, unanimously adopted by the General Assembly on December 10, 1948, in Article 25 established that "Everyone has the right to a standard of living adequate for the health and well-being of himself and of his family, including food, clothing, [and] housing . . ." The Universal Declaration has gained almost universal acceptance. Its clauses have been incorporated in decisions by United Nations organs and agencies, in international treaties, in national constitutions, and in national legislative and court decisions.

The 1966 International Covenant on Economic, Social, and Cultural Rights stands as the preeminent treaty that incorporates the right to housing. In 1976, this international covenant became a legally binding multilateral treaty when ratified by the required thirty-five countries. As of March, 1990, ninety-four countries had become parties to this treaty. Thus, the declaration of the IYSH constituted a major step taken by the international community to implement the prior recognition of the importance of the right to shelter. Significantly, however, the United States steadfastly refused to ratify the covenant. President Jimmy Carter signed this international covenant in 1977, but the Senate had not given its advice and consent to ratification by 1991.

From 1983 to 1987, many programs were instituted to further the goals set by the IYSH. On October 8, 1987, Arcot Ramachandran, the executive director of Habitat, chronicled these activities in his briefing to nongovernmental organizations. He indicated that some of the most important successes during the first phase of the IYSH involved a sensitization in regard to shelter issues. The IYSH established 139 national focal points and more than six hundred demonstration projects around the world to improve shelter conditions. In support, the World Bank agreed to increase its loans to developing countries up to one billion dollars a year and to give higher priority to housing infrastructure and services. Habitat also assisted eighty-five developing countries in implementing shelter programs and organized ten subregional IYSH meetings to facilitate exchange of information on projects.

Ramachandran also described some of the actions taken by governments at the national level. These included programs focusing on services, self-help, and low-income housing projects. Many nations gave high priority to increasing access to affordable building materials and housing finance. Urban development projects, though, met with uneven success because of lack of resources and technical and personnel problems. Disturbing as well was the lack of commitment of national governments to improve management of their cities. Ramachandran concluded that without the involvement of the communities or the concerned people themselves, the shelter programs would fail.

To generate the needed nongovernmental involvement, Habitat organized four regional meetings. In April, 1987, a global forum was held in Nairobi, Kenya. More than four hundred nongovernmental organizations (NGOs) participated. The forum adopted a plan of action which included measures to develop the relationships between NGOs and community-based organizations, ways to strengthen the relationships with governments, proposals for increasing media attention to the problems of the homeless, development of regional NGOs to facilitate links between locally based NGOs and aid agencies so as to improve fund-raising mechanisms, and plans for creating national and regional NGO networks for greater exchange of information and experiences.

Despite the U.S. Senate's refusal to ratify the International Covenant on Economic, Social, and Cultural Rights which contains the right to housing, NGOs and community-based organizations in the United States worked independently of the federal government to implement the IYSH objectives. Their efforts culminated, most significantly, in 1988 with the introduction of the "National Comprehensive Housing Act" (H.R. 4727) in the House of Representatives by Congressman Ronald V. Dellums (D-Oakland, Calif.).

The act would "provide an affordable, secure and decent home and suitable living environment for every American family. . . ." While functioning primarily as a visionary model against which to measure less ambitious legislation, the act provided for the first time a comprehensive legislative mechanism for acting on a right to housing for all citizens. It backed up its grand statement of purpose with an appropriation of $55 billion annually (with adjustments for inflation) to create, within ten years, a permanent supply of nonprofit housing in sufficient quantity to provide all persons with decent, affordable housing. Adoption and implementation of the act by Congress would fulfill the objectives of the IYSH for the inhabitants of the United States by the turn of the century.

Congressman Dellums based the act on *A Progressive Housing Program for America*, written in 1987 by the Institute for Policy Studies' Working Group on Housing. The IPS working group recognized, as did Habitat's Ramachandran, that statements of policy and declarations of rights amount to little more than wishful thinking unless backed by the financial resources and political will of national governments. The group consequently fashioned a program premised on the necessity of a significant reordering of national funding priorities.

If adopted, the Dellums legislation would substantially alter the housing delivery system in the United States. The IPS program acknowledged the inability of the private sector to produce housing affordable to low-income households without substantial subsidies. The program called upon the federal government to facilitate production by providing direct capital grants to local nonprofit and public-agency developers. This would eliminate expensive reliance on private credit and ensure than the housing would be protected permanently from the speculative effects of the private market.

The National Housing Task Force, a group primarily composed of developers, bankers, and government officials, came to much the same conclusion as the IPS working group. Chaired by developer James Rouse of the Enterprise Foundation, the task force's 1987 report, "A Decent Place to Live," proposed that the federal government renew its commitment to housing based upon "the clear understanding that housing for poor people cannot be produced by the private sector acting alone." The task force recommended that the federal government establish a new system for the delivery of affordable housing. Under the recommendation, the government would provide matching grants to state and local governments and nonprofit groups to help develop, renovate, and conserve low-income housing.

Impact of Event

The IYSH was regarded by many as a success because it focused world attention on a problem that most people would prefer to ignore. During its tenth session, in April, 1987, the Commission on Human Settlements adopted twenty-two resolutions and an agenda to guide policies and programs for shelter strategies. At that time, fifteen countries pledged more than $2 million in support of the activities of Habitat and the IYSH. This was in addition to $1.5 million pledged earlier by thirty-one other countries.

Despite this, the fact remained that one-fifth of the world's population did not have adequate shelter. About one hundred million people had no shelter at all. Every day more than fifty thousand people, most of them children, died of malnutrition and disease. Many of these deaths are attributed to lack of adequate housing.

Perhaps the greatest value of the IYSH was that as a result of IYSH activities some lessons were learned regarding what was needed to make shelter a reality for all people. These lessons were summarized by Ramachandran in his briefing to NGOs. First, an integrated approach to shelter issues in the overall scheme of economic and social development is necessary. Second, pressure on the world's largest cities has to be reduced by placing a greater emphasis on the role of smaller cities. Third, strategies must be adopted that will facilitate helping people to help themselves. Fourth, security of tenure with respect to land must be provided. Fifth, urban management and community participation in all projects has to be strengthened, as do industrial development and employment-generating strategies. Sixth, systems furthering resource conservation, environmental protection, health, and social development have to be increased.

The most important factor in securing adequate shelter for the homeless is conspicuously absent from Habitat's list. Governments must declare housing a national priority, and adequate financial, physical, institutional, and human resources must be allocated for the realization of this right. A 1990 report prepared by the Habitat International Coalition, an organization comprising NGOs from throughout the world, stresses the need for finances. It also identifies the need for democratic participation so that groups and communities can make their needs known and have them satisfied.

In the United States, community-based groups and NGOs made the economic resource commitment the linchpin of their national efforts. As part of its national campaign preceding the 1988 presidential election, the National Jobs with Peace Campaign featured the IPS program and the Dellums legislation as the centerpiece of its housing platform. Although Dellums' H.R. 4727 failed to pass in the House of Representatives, he reintroduced it in 1989 as H.R. 1122. It became the standard for subsequent legislation addressing national housing policy.

Bibliography

Appelbaum, Richard P. *A Progressive Housing Program for America.* Washington, D.C.: Institute for Policy Studies, Working Group on Housing, 1987. This technical document was drafted over a three-year period by the IPS working group, fifteen individuals from throughout the United States including social scientists, nonprofit housing developers, lawyers, and housing activists. Meant for students of national housing law and policy as well as professionals and government officials working on housing-related matters. The work includes a lengthy explanation, supported by extensive data, of the national housing crisis. Also presents a detailed description and explanation of the program itself, which served as the basis for Dellums' National Comprehensive Housing Act. Has a comprehensive bibliography.

"Commission on Human Settlements Stresses Need for Global Strategy for Shelter to Year 2000." *United Nations Chronicle* 18 (July, 1989): 47-58. This article describes the activities of the Commission on Human Settlement's meeting in April, 1987. It is followed by a series of articles dealing with the issue of homelessness. These include case studies of housing development projects and a review of actions taken by the U.N. Economic and Social Council.

Gilderbloom, John I., and Richard P. Appelbaum. *Rethinking Rental Housing.* Philadelphia: Temple University Press, 1988. Chapter 9 is based upon "A Progressive Housing Program for America." The authors present the proposal in the context of their in-depth social and political critique of national housing policy.

Human Rights: A Compilation of International Instruments. New York: United Nations, 1988. This paperback book contains the texts of sixty-seven conventions, declarations, recommendations, resolutions, and other instruments concerning human rights adopted by the United Nations and other international organizations. Included are the Universal Declaration of Human Rights and the International Covenant on Economic, Social, and Cultural Rights.

Institute for Policy Studies, Working Group on Housing, with Dick Cluster. *The Right to Housing: A Blueprint for Housing the Nation.* Washington, D.C.: Institute for Policy Studies, 1989. This is a popularized booklet version of the IPS Working Group's *A Progressive Housing Program for America.* It contains a clear and cogent description and analysis of the housing crisis in the United States as well as the progressive housing program, illustrated by numerous real-world examples.

"IYSH Proclaimed." *Habitat News* 5 (April/May, 1983): 11-12. This article reviews the activities in the United Nations that resulted in the resolution declaring the IYSH. It also describes the endeavors undertaken under the auspices of the IYSH during 1983 and 1984.

Ortiz, Enrique. *The Right to Housing: A Global Challenge.* Mexico City: Cuadernos de Dinámica Habitacional, 1990. Describes the problem of lack of housing worldwide and outlines the legal basis for the right to housing. Attempts to define the obligations of governments, the international community, individuals, and communities with respect to this right. Outlines the international campaign for housing rights of Habitat International Coalition.

Connie de la Vega
Michael Rawson

Cross-References

The United Nations Adopts the Universal Declaration of Human Rights (1948), p. 789; Cubans Flee to Florida and Receive Assistance (1960's), p. 1044; A U.N. Declaration on Hunger and Malnutrition Is Adopted (1974), p. 1775; An APA Report Discusses the Homeless Mentally Ill (1984), p. 2226; The Stewart B. McKinney Homeless Assistance Act Becomes Law (1987), p. 2326.

NIGERIA EXPELS WEST AFRICAN MIGRANT WORKERS

Categories of event: Workers' rights and immigrants' rights
Time: 1983
Locale: Nigeria and neighboring countries

Nigeria declared that illegal aliens were a threat to its national security and public morals and in January, 1983, abruptly expelled an estimated two million migrant workers

Principal personages:
ALHAJI SHEHU SHAGARI (1925-), the president of Nigeria from October, 1979, until ousted by the military on January 1, 1984
NNAMDI AZIKIWE (1904-), Nigeria's first president (1963-1966), a strong critic of the expulsion
ALHAJI ALI BABA, the minister of internal affairs for Nigeria who announced the decision to expel "undocumented" aliens
JERRY RAWLINGS (1947-), the president of Ghana from June to September, 1979, reinstated in 1982

Summary of Event

Migration across state borders has been a feature of West African history for centuries. The region's ethnic mosaic contains numerous, long-settled communities whose places of origin lie outside the borders of their current countries of residence. Africa's colonially imposed borders divide many ethnic, linguistic, and cultural communities. Prompted by such factors as drought, deforestation, the changing fortunes of national economies, repressive political conditions, and the survival of historic trade and nomadic routes that cut across contemporary state boundaries, modern migrations have often taken place with little regard for the formalities of immigration laws. Well-established migrant communities existed in West Africa throughout the twentieth century, and few faced significant barriers to integration into their host countries. On occasion, however, migrants have been subject to expulsions, sometimes for crimes committed but often as a political expedient.

Beginning in the mid-1970's, Nigeria was the destination of much of the migration in this African subregion. Buoyed by the export of more than a million barrels of high-quality oil per day, Nigeria's economy expanded rapidly during the 1970's. Millions of migrants from Ghana and other neighboring countries flooded into Nigeria, attracted by the opportunities offered by its booming economy. In contrast, many of the migrants' home economies faced high inflation and the burdens of debt. Thousands of professionals from farther afield (the United Kingdom, the Philippines, India, and Poland, for example) joined the influx of foreign labor into Nigeria.

In the early 1980's, however, Nigeria's economic situation suffered a major setback. The country responded to the world glut in oil by cutting daily production well below one million barrels by 1983. Government revenues plummeted, international indebtedness became a significant problem, the inflation rate soared to more than 25 percent, and an estimated 20 percent of the work force was unemployed. The country's ambitious development plans were scaled back drastically; import controls, foreign exchange restrictions, and other emergency measures were adopted; and many public- and private-sector employees worked for months without pay.

The economic collapse fueled antiforeigner sentiments in Nigeria. Foreigners were perceived by the general public as taking jobs from Nigerians, hoarding and smuggling consumer goods and currency, and generally sabotaging the economy. Workers' organizations repeatedly charged that employers were taking advantage of cheap foreign labor while Nigerians were facing growing unemployment and destitution.

On January 17, 1983, the minister of internal affairs for Nigeria, Alhaji Ali Baba, announced the government's decision to expel all "undocumented" West African aliens from Nigeria. These "illegal" aliens, estimated to number at least two million, were given two weeks to leave the country. The order was amended on January 25 to allow skilled aliens (such as nurses, secretaries, masons, teachers, and carpenters) an additional four weeks to regularize their stay or leave. In addition, foreigners employed by federal and state government institutions and enterprises, and citizens of Cameroon and Chad who had entered Nigeria prior to 1963, were exempted from the expulsion.

Official reasons for the expulsion included the charge that religious riots among Islamic sects in Kano, Kaduna, Sokoto, Maiduguri, and elsewhere, which began in 1980, involved and had been instigated by foreigners from the neighboring states of Cameroon, Chad, Mali, Niger, and Upper Volta. The chief instigator, Mallam Muhammed Marwa, was a Cameroonian. Another major charge was that the growing rates of robbery, prostitution, and indigence in Nigeria were largely the result of the influx of illegal Ghanaian migrants. The Nigerian government argued that illegal aliens were a threat to public security and morality and declared that it "cannot, and will not, fold its hands and allow such unwholesome developments to continually plague the nation."

Although there was some truth to the charges of the involvement of aliens in the religious disturbances, armed robbery, and prostitution, and that aliens were among the ranks of the unemployed, it is generally conceded that the charges were exaggerated. The vast majority of the rioters, criminals, social undesirables, and indigents were Nigerians.

In the weeks following the expulsion order, according to Nigerian government estimates, at least 1.2 million aliens left Nigeria. These included 700,000 Ghanaians, 150,000 Chadians, 120,000 Cameroonians, 18,000 Beninoise, and 5,000 Togolese. Other estimates place the total number of aliens who left near 2 million. The legality of the expulsion was not in question: Nigeria had the sovereign right to expel illegal immigrants. What caused consternation among Nigeria's neighbors and in the wider world were the facts that no warning was given to the neighboring states that would have to cope with a massive return of their migrants, that the time period of two weeks did not allow for structures and provisions to be put in place to assist returning migrants, and that no internal procedures had been established in Nigeria to allow for an orderly departure of the expelled aliens. The results were widespread fear and suffering among the expelled aliens, strained political relations between Nigeria and its neighbors, especially Ghana, and, outside of Nigeria, general condemnation of the expulsion.

World reaction was universally negative. The United States State Department charged that the expulsion violated "every imaginable human right." Pope John Paul II declared the expulsion had resulted in the "worst human exodus in this century." Other international condemnation was expressed in such terms as "heartless," "inhumane," and "unworthy" of a country that was among the leaders of Africa.

The expulsion was seen by many as a violation of the spirit, although not the letter, of the protocol on the free movement of citizens of the member states of the Economic Community of West African States (ECOWAS). Nigeria had been the leading force behind the establishment, in 1975, of this economic association of sixteen West African states. Intending to create eventually a fully-fledged common market, the ECOWAS member states had by 1979 agreed to the right of their citizens to travel freely within the community without visas and to remain for up to ninety days in another member state. Nigeria had argued strongly in favor of ratification of this protocol and, along with other community states, had been lax in enforcing the ninety-day limitation on the undocumented stay of ECOWAS citizens. The expulsion was seen as a direct blow to the spirit of the ECOWAS. There was also criticism of the preferential treatment received by non-black, Asian, and European migrants in comparison to the treatment of black, fellow West African aliens.

The Nigerian government, surprised at the strength of the aversion to the expulsion, defended its decision, declaring that no United Nations human rights provisions had been violated and that no country could allow the flagrant violation of its laws to go unchallenged. To the extent that it could be judged, public opinion in Nigeria was largely in favor of the expulsion. Certainly, the Nigerian media were unanimous in support of the decision. The point was made repeatedly that Nigerians and other illegal immigrants in countries such as France, the United Kingdom, and the United States received short shrift from legal authorities and often suffered imprisonment prior to deportation. It was also pointed out that when Nigerians had suffered expulsions from Ghana, Zaire, the Congo, Gabon, Equatorial Guinea, and Sierra Leone, no such international condemnation was forthcoming.

One of the noted critics within Nigeria was Nnamdi Azikiwe, the country's first president. He argued that "efforts could have been made to repatriate these people under more humane conditions," and he saw the expulsion as a "mortal blow" to the philosophy of African cooperation and unity.

Whatever the official reasons, it was broadly believed that the dramatic decline in Nigeria's economic situation was the prime reason for the expulsion. Many perceived the expulsion as a cynical political ploy by President Alhaji Shehu Shagari and his National Party of Nigeria (NPN) to curry favor with the electorate ahead of the upcoming 1983 elections. Worsening economic conditions weakened the NPN's reelection bid, and the expulsion move was seen as an effort to take advantage of growing antiforeigner sentiments among Nigeria's millions of unemployed and un- deremployed.

There also may well have been an element of delayed retaliation for the prior expulsion of Nigerians from Ghana. In November, 1969, the Ghanaian government issued the Aliens Compliance Order, which gave aliens two weeks to regularize their status or be expelled. Aliens were accused of causing a growing tide of criminal activity and undermining the economy and public morals. The vast majority of as many as half a million aliens expelled from Ghana in 1969 and early 1970 were Nigerians. Relations between Ghana and Nigeria always had been competitive and at times had been openly hostile. Ideological differences pitted a generally conserva- tive, capitalist Nigeria against often-radical, socialist-oriented Ghanaian regimes. Regional leadership aspirations, fluctuating economic fortunes, and national chauvi- nisms also underlay this fractious relationship. The Ghanaian government charged that the expulsion was an attempt to destabilize its new, radical regime, led by Jerry Rawlings.

The economic impact of the forced departure of migrant workers was noticeable in several areas. In Lagos and other cities where many aliens had been employed as cooks, drivers, and gardeners, and in other domestic service, the impact was imme- diate. Finding replacements was difficult and required the payment of higher wages. The construction and hotel industries and the docks were also hard hit by the loss of skilled artisans, clerks, stewards, and cargo handlers. No appreciable alleviation of the overall unemployment situation among Nigerian workers, or of the other mal- adies of the Nigerian economy, was evident.

Impact of Event

The expulsion order came as a surprise. Neighboring countries were not con- sulted, transportation was not arranged, and relief agencies were not forewarned. Reportedly, even the Nigerian ministry of external affairs and the police responsible for enforcing the order learned of the decision through the media. This precipitous expulsion, without preplanning, of an estimated two million people resulted in sig- nificant hardships. There were numerous reports of robbery and mistreatment of the aliens while they waited for transportation to arrive and borders to open. There were also reports of inflated prices for food and transportation and extortion by airport and border officials. Many deportees were forced to sell their property at giveaway prices in order to buy food. The crowding of thousands of aliens at the border for more than a week produced hunger and outbreaks of malaria and cholera. The re- turning aliens were at times subject to brutal crowd control, and some were victims of road and rail accidents. No large-scale harassment of aliens by the Nigerian au- thorities or the general public took place. In fact, there were reports of employers and communities covering up the presence of illegal aliens. In sharp contrast to the widespread profiteering among transporters, the Nigerian Transport Owners Asso- ciation made two hundred large trucks available to help evacuate deportees stranded at the docks. The association expressed both support for the government's decision and sympathy for the plight of the expelled migrants. The roundup and prosecution of illegal aliens who defied the expulsion order was desultory and soon halted. Governments and ordinary citizens of other nations rapidly mobilized to assist Ghanaians passing through on their way home.

An estimated sixty to one hundred deaths were attributed directly to the expulsion exercise. Although much lower than originally speculated, the death toll underscores the hardships suffered. The Nigerian government and media claimed that much of the suffering could have been avoided if the borders of neighboring states had not been closed. They blamed especially the government of Jerry Rawlings in Ghana for precipitating the border closures of Benin and Togo. Ghana's border had been closed since September, 1982, to prevent smuggling and because of fear of external subversion. On the announcement of the expulsion order, Benin and Togo also closed their borders, fearing that a flood of Ghanaian refugees would be trapped within their countries.

International assistance was forthcoming, although most donors were slow to react to the appeals from Ghana and the other affected states. Libya sent medical supplies and several aircraft to help with the evacuation. Denmark and the United Kingdom also sent medical supplies. The United States committed 720 tons of food supplies. Denmark, Luxembourg, Norway, Sweden, and Switzerland sent blankets, food, and tents. Italy provided a broad range of emergency assistance. International relief agencies, including the United Nations Children's Fund, Oxfam, the World Council of Churches, the Salvation Army, the Red Cross, and Christian Aid, also rendered assistance to the returning migrants. An offer by the Nigerian government of some financial assistance to Ghana was rejected as "blood money."

The Ghanaian government established a National Relief Committee, which chartered ships and buses to transport its citizens from Lagos, coordinated relief supplies, and processed the returnees in regional centers. Plans were made to incorporate them into the national reconstruction exercise that the Rawlings government had initiated upon its takeover in September, 1982. Economic conditions in Ghana were far worse than in Nigeria, however, and the reabsorption of approximately one million people was difficult. In fact, significant numbers of Ghanaians returned to Nigeria later in 1983, and some suffered another expulsion in April, 1984.

Bibliography

Aluko, Olajide. "The Expulsion of Illegal Aliens from Nigeria: A Study in Nigeria's Decision-Making." *African Affairs* 84 (October, 1985): 539-560. Examines how and why the expulsion decision was made, how it was implemented, and its consequences. Especially strong in exploring the impacts on the decision of the global and domestic economic situations, subregional relations, the history of hostility between Nigeria and Ghana, internal instability, and growing crime. Concludes that the decision making process was autocratic and defective. Many references to Nigerian sources.

Brown, M. Leann. "Nigeria and the Ecowas Protocol on Free Movement and Residence." *The Journal of Modern African Studies* 27, no. 2 (1989): 251-273. Explores the expulsion of aliens in the context of Nigeria's commitments to ECOWAS. Points out Nigeria's leadership in the establishment and financial support of the community. Argues that popular discontent with perceived "burdens" of ECOWAS membership, along with immediate and specific socioeconomic and political considerations, resulted in Nigeria's decision to ignore the spirit of West African cooperation and unity enshrined in the ECOWAS protocol regarding the free movement of people.

Brydon, Lynne. "Ghanaian Responses to the Nigerian Expulsions of 1983." *African Affairs* 84 (October, 1985): 561-585. An analysis of the economic and political factors that prompted Ghanaians to migrate to Nigeria and significant numbers of them to return to Nigeria after their expulsion. Provides concise political histories of Ghana and Nigeria and relations between them. Explores the human impact of the expulsion by means of interviews with a small number of returnees. This "participants" viewpoint contributes to a broader appreciation of the expulsion.

Gravil, Peter. "The Nigerian Aliens Expulsion Order of 1983." *African Affairs* 84 (October, 1985): 523-537. Points out the historical importance of migration to the development of major countries around the world. Details the political events surrounding the expulsion order and the numbers of Ghanaians and other West Africans affected. Official reasons and statistics in support of the expulsion are analyzed and questioned. The author sees the expelled aliens as victims of scapegoating and stereotyping. Many useful references.

Ojo, Olatunde J. C. B., D. K. Orwa, and C. M. Utete. *African International Relations.* London: Longman, 1987. A wide-ranging introduction to the international relations of African states. Contains concise, informative essays on the regional, continental, and global relations of Africa. Solid background material for a generalist interest in the broad political and economic environment within which the expulsion occurred.

Hashim Gibrill

Cross-References

The United Nations Adopts the Universal Declaration of Human Rights (1948), p. 789; The United Nations High Commissioner for Refugees Statute Is Approved (1950), p. 855; The Organization of African Unity Is Founded (1963), p. 1194; Civil War Ravages Chad (1965), p. 1273; The Secession of Biafra Starts a Nigerian Civil War (1967), p. 1365; The OAU Adopts the African Charter on Human and Peoples' Rights (1981), p. 2136.

THE NATIONAL COMMISSION AGAINST TORTURE
STUDIES HUMAN RIGHTS ABUSES

Categories of event: Prisoners' rights; atrocities and war crimes
Time: January, 1983
Locale: Chile

Beginning in 1983, the National Commission Against Torture courageously worked to end the mistreatment of prisoners and detainees by the Pinochet dictatorship in Chile

Principal personages:

AUGUSTO PINOCHET (1915-   ) the commander of the Chilean army and dictator of Chile (1973-1989)

PEDRO CASTILLO YÁÑEZ, a thoracic surgeon and president of the National Commission Against Torture

RAÚL CARDINAL SILVA HENRÍQUEZ (1907-   ), the cardinal archbishop of Santiago and a leading advocate of human rights during the Pinochet dictatorship

SALVADOR ALLENDE (1908-1973), the Marxist president of Chile (1970-1973) and head of the Popular Unity coalition of leftist parties

Summary of Event

On September 11, 1973, a military coup headed by General Augusto Pinochet Ugarte overthrew the constitutionally elected Chilean government of Marxist president Salvador Allende Gossens. The Allende presidency had polarized Chile. Terrorism from the political left and right had undermined the democratic traditions of the nation. Poor economic management on the part of socialist planners, resistance to government policies by Chilean industrialists, agriculturalists, and businesspeople, and economic pressure against the Allende regime by the United States had created turmoil in the country. Inflation soared, real personal income declined, and shortages of basic commodities afflicted the nation. The coup left Allende dead in the presidential palace, the military in power, and Chile under a regime of torture and political assassinations.

A superficial calm descended upon the country. As many as five thousand opponents of the coup were tortured, executed, or "disappeared," including leftist politicians, union leaders, and student activists. Fearing for their lives, thousands more went into exile. Pinochet and his supporters promised to rid Chile of the communist menace, claiming that Allende's supporters had conspired to murder military and political leaders who opposed the Marxists and impose a thoroughgoing communism upon the nation. The coup had foiled the plot, said Pinochet, and now he would safeguard Chile from the Left. What actually emerged was a military and police state which, by crushing the Allende camp, temporarily won the toleration and sometimes the support of the middle and upper classes.

By 1977, the dictatorship felt secure enough to begin loosening its grip on the nation. In that year, to appease European critics and under pressure from the administration of Jimmy Carter in the United States and his emphasis upon human rights, Pinochet abolished the Dirección Nacional de Inteligencia (DINA), the infamous security bureau that had been involved in the kidnapping, torture, and murder of the regime's perceived opponents since the coup. Meanwhile, the economy improved, as the socialist measures of the Allende period were reversed under the guidance of a group of University of Chicago-trained economists, who emphasized the free-market and monetarist policies of Milton Friedman. The resulting economic recovery won Pinochet further support from the middle class, although unemployment remained above 15 percent and the country's foreign debt was mounting ominously. To consolidate its gains and legitimate its rule, the regime held a plebiscite on September 11, 1980, in which the new constitution received the approval of two-thirds of the voters. The new charter permitted General Pinochet to retain power until 1989, when an election would determine if he would continue as president until 1997.

The calm imposed by the dictatorship was superficial, and when the worldwide recession of the early 1980's plunged Chile into depression, discontent and resistance mounted. The regime had never abandoned its weapons of kidnapping, torture, and assassination. In fact, shortly after abolishing DINA, Pinochet had formally created the National Information Center (CNI), which carried on its predecessor's brutal tasks under the broad mandate of national security. Soldiers and police still paid nocturnal visits to outspoken critics of the regime or suspected subversives, who disappeared into the CNI's interrogation rooms. Under state-of-emergency decrees, the CNI secret police and torturers could hold a detainee incommunicado for up to twenty days before beginning any of the niceties of legal process.

The dictatorship's security forces inflicted physical and psychological torture. On March 8, 1982, for example, Enzo Ivan Antonio Riffo Navarette, a young carpenter from Santiago, was abducted by the CNI and tortured for sixteen days. He reported to investigators from Amnesty International that his tormenters beat him and applied electrical shocks to his face, genitals, and anus. At one point, they told him he was to be executed, whereupon a guard pointed a pistol at his head and pulled the trigger. He discovered that the weapon was empty, but the trauma intimidated him. A young woman arrested by the CNI in early 1981 suffered seventeen days of torture. Bound naked to a metal bed, she received powerful electrical shocks on her face, chest, and genitals, and four men raped her. The torturers also told her that her boyfriend had been killed and forced her to lie facing a decomposing corpse. To intimidate her further, the torturers kept her blindfolded almost the entire time she was at the torture center, locked her in a room filled with rats, and threatened to rape her with a dog.

As opposition to Pinochet's dictatorship mounted and the economic crisis deepened, hundreds of other victims experienced similar outrages. Blindfoldings, beatings, and electrical shocks were routine. Security agents often threatened to torture or rape the detainee's family members. Many reported that doctors had assisted the security forces, giving the detainees physical examinations upon arrival, advising the torturers when to stop to avoid killing the captives, and giving injections of sodium pentathol and other drugs to break down the prisoners' resistance. Often one security agent acted the part of sympathetic guard, commiserating with the prisoners and encouraging them to reveal any information to avoid additional abuse.

Not all the Chileans could be intimidated. Some possessed such international or moral stature that the regime feared to silence them. They courageously organized themselves to protest the dictatorship's violation of human rights and to assist the victims of its terror. In so doing, they received support from other nations and from international organizations such as Amnesty International that were also working to end torture and political imprisonment in Chile.

Although many Catholic leaders had strongly opposed Allende's ideology and policies and welcomed the coup, afterward parts of the church became a bulwark in defense of human rights. On October 6, 1973, less than a month after Allende's death, the ecumenical Committee of Cooperation for Peace in Chile, directed by Catholic Bishop Fernando Ariztía and Lutheran Bishop Helmut Frenz, began providing humanitarian assistance to those abused by the regime. Under pressure from the dictatorship, the cardinal archbishop of Santiago, Raúl Silva Henríquez, abolished the committee in late 1975 but then organized the Vicariate of Solidarity the following January to carry on the same work. It gave legal assistance to prisoners, helped exiles, provided medical and psychological care to victims, and issued a broad spectrum of newsletters to publicize the state of human rights in Chile. By helping protect other human rights groups, the vicariate became the focus of moral resistance to the regime. Meanwhile, Bishop Frenz of the Evangelical Lutheran Church established the Christian Churches' Social Assistance Foundation (FASIC), which provided medical and psychiatric care for those tortured and imprisoned and their families. FASIC also pressed the regime to exile rather than imprison individuals condemned by the tribunals. Many Lutherans objected to Frenz's activism, however, and formally separated from the church. This ambivalence also marked Chilean catholicism.

Other groups also formed. Lawyers established the Chilean Human Rights Commission in December, 1978, in reaction to the regime's excesses. By the late 1980's, it had more than thirty-five hundred members, with 128 subgroups spread throughout the country. The National Commission for Juvenile Rights, founded in 1977 in Valparaíso, sought to protect Chilean youth from human rights violations. Activists created another organization concerned with the young in 1979, the Foundation for the Protection of Minors Harmed by the State of Emergency.

Equally important were the heroic actions of individual Chileans in hiding suspects from DINA and the CNI, caring for the tortured, and publicly opposing the regime's brutality. By 1975, for example, the regime had several torture centers in the vicinity of Santiago. Priests and nuns gave sanctuary to suspects hiding from the CNI and sometimes helped them escape the country. Lawyers volunteered time and expertise to file *recursos de amparo* (similar to writs of habeas corpus) on behalf of those sequestered by the security forces. Doctors examined and treated those released after interrogation and torture and compiled affidavits attesting to the criminal actions of the police.

Some physicians actively cooperated with the torturers, and the Chilean College of Medicine, the country's medical association, refused until 1982 to investigate and denounce such abuses. Dr. Pedro Castillo Yáñez, a thoracic surgeon, chose to assist human rights organizations, providing medical care for the victims. The regime had removed him in 1975 as chair of the Department of Surgery at the University of Chile because he had publicized the location of secret torture centers and reported that some Chilean doctors were assisting in the torture of detainees. The CNI placed him under surveillance in May, 1981, and then arrested him, along with fellow physicians Patricio Arroyo and Manuel Almeyda. The secret police claimed that the doctors had been involved in the bombing of a naval officers' club and that Castillo operated a secret clinic for terrorists at his Andean vacation home. The doctors received immediate wide support from Chilean and international human rights organizations, and the pressure secured their release after more than a month's detention. Later that year, Castillo and other activist physicians launched a campaign to force the Chilean Medical College to discipline members who assisted in the abuse of prisoners.

In 1982, the regime arrested 1,789 people for political reasons, nearly double the number from the preceding year. Within this context, the Chilean Human Rights Commission sponsored a national seminar in January, 1983, about torture in the country. As an offshoot of that seminar, participants recommended the formation of an organization to deal exclusively and specifically with allegations of torture, and in that manner the National Commission Against Torture was born. Its membership included representatives from a wide spectrum of Chilean society, including religious, artistic, and scientific figures and human rights and labor activists. They chose Pedro Castillo Yáñez as president of the commission.

Impact of Event

Creation of the National Commission Against Torture brought the wrath of the dictatorship down upon Castillo and some of his associates, but in the long term, the commission, working with other Chilean and international organizations, focused attention upon the barbarisms committed by the regime and helped prepare the nation for democracy. When the security forces abducted and tortured a Chilean, the commission publicly denounced the violation of human rights. It organized conferences and seminars and helped mobilize pressure against the regime for the release of individual detainees. The commission also produced and distributed videotapes dramatizing the effect of torture on the victims and on society.

On May 11, 1983, Chileans from all classes and political persuasions participated in a national day of protest. They kept their children home from school and clanged pots and pans in the streets, reminiscent of the homemakers' protests against the Allende government on the eve of the 1973 coup. Trying to quell the opposition, the regime killed two protesters and arrested two hundred others. A month later, hundreds of thousands joined in another national day of protest, and the following months saw more demonstrations. More deaths and arrests followed.

Security forces cracked down on those suspected of fomenting the demonstrations, particularly anyone connected with two Marxist organizations committed to the violent overthrow of the regime, the Movement of the Revolutionary Left (MIR) and the Manuel Rodríguez Popular Front. The secret centers of the CNI and other security forces stepped up their activity, and the National Commission Against Torture and other human rights organizations responded courageously.

On November 11, 1983, the crowning protest occurred against the regime's use of torture and violation of civil and human rights. Distraught over the detention of two of his children and his inability to learn their whereabouts, Sebastián Acevedo sat down in front of the Concepción cathedral and immolated himself. From his ashes came the "Sebastián Acevedo" Movement Against Torture, committed to nonviolent demonstrations. On December 15, two hundred members of the movement gathered in front of CNI headquarters in Santiago, where they were brutally beaten by the police. Undeterred, their protests against the torturers continued.

Pressure mounted on Pinochet to resign, but he refused to relinquish power until 1989. Instead, he declared a new state of emergency on November 6, 1983, which lasted until June 15, 1985. In July, 1985, members of Chilean Anti-Communist Action, a right-wing terrorist group, bombed the head office of the Chilean Human Rights Commission, and shortly thereafter, security officers arrested Pedro Castillo and sent him into internal exile on a deserted island in southern Chile, where he remained for three months until released.

Lawyers and judges had no power to coerce the security forces into ending the reign of terror as long as the military supported the dictatorship. Although the demonstrations shocked the armed forces and many officers privately wished Pinochet would step aside, the military refused to overthrow the government. Perhaps if Chilean politicians had offered a viable alternative as a transition to democracy, the generals might have acted. The regime, however, had outlawed political parties, and clandestine organizations were so divided among themselves that they offered no solution to the nation's crisis. In August, 1985, all the principal political parties agreed to support a National Accord, which demanded an end to the dictatorship and the restoration of democracy. In mid-November, 1985, half a million Chileans demonstrated in Santiago against the regime, but still Pinochet clung to power.

Pinochet declared that he would step aside only if defeated in the constitutionally mandated referendum in 1989. In that election, a majority of Chileans voted to turn him out of office. The dictatorship ended, and the Christian Democratic candidate, Patricio Aylwin, was elected president. Pinochet, however, retained control of the military.

Bibliography

Amnesty International. *Chile, Evidence of Torture.* London: Author, 1983. Presents the results of AI's 1982 investigation conducted in Chile. The report includes the victims' paraphrased accounts of their torture as well as medical and psychological assessments of the veracity of the allegations. The investigators concluded that torture continued to be a serious problem in Chile.

Cassidy, Sheila. *Audacity to Believe.* London: Collins, 1977. A moving narrative by an idealistic young British doctor arrested and tortured by DINA in 1975 for giving medical treatment to a wounded Marxist leader. Her account provides a graphic view of life for female detainees and the heroic charity of priests and nuns.

"Confessions of a State Terrorist." *Harper's* 270 (June, 1985): 15-17. Excerpts of an interview with Andrés Antonio Valenzuela Morales, a member of the Chilean air force's intelligence service who fled Chile after becoming disgusted with his participation in torture and murder. His description of the psychological impact of such crimes upon the perpetrators is harrowing. When interviewed, Valenzuela was hiding in France, convinced that Chilean secret operatives would soon kill him.

Labin, Suzanne. *Chile: The Crime of Resistance.* Richmond, Surrey, England: Foreign Affairs, 1982. Originally published in French in 1980, this work defends the Pinochet regime on the grounds that if the country had fallen under communist control, the repression would have been much worse. An interesting if not altogether convincing counterweight to the other listed works, it focuses on the coup and the first years of the Pinochet dictatorship.

Loveman, Brian. *Chile: The Legacy of Hispanic Capitalism.* 2d ed. New York: Oxford University Press, 1988. The final chapter, "Dictatorship," lays out in detail how the regime's use of torture fit into the context of its other policies. Also provides a good explanation of the pressures on the government that enabled activists to form the National Commission Against Torture and other human rights organizations.

Politzer, Patricia. *Fear in Chile: Lives Under Pinochet.* Translated by Diane Wachtell. New York: Pantheon Books, 1989. Presents a series of interviews conducted in 1983 and 1984 with a variety of Chileans, from Pinochet enthusiasts and a soldier to a clerical radical, a union activist, and a woman from a squatter neighborhood. The book is impressionistic but gives a vivid picture of life under the dictatorship.

Smith, Brian H. "Old Allies, New Enemies: The Catholic Church as Opposition to Military Rule in Chile, 1973-1979." In *Military Rule in Chile: Dictatorship and Oppositions*, edited by J. Samuel Valenzuela and Arturo Valenzuela. Baltimore, Md.: The Johns Hopkins University Press, 1986. For many years, the Catholic church and the Chilean military had supported each other because of their mutual interest in maintaining peace and social order. Smith describes the church's growing opposition to the regime, which evolved into such activities as the Vicariate of Solidarity.

Stover, Eric. *The Open Secret: Torture and the Medical Profession in Chile.* Washington, D.C.: American Association for the Advancement of Science, 1987. A report by the Committee on Scientific Freedom and Responsibility of the AAAS, based on the author's investigations in Chile during 1984 and 1985. Straightforward and easily digested, it concludes that a number of Chilean physicians cooperated in the torture of detainees and that the Chilean Medical College refused to investigate or discipline them until 1982.

Timerman, Jacobo. *Chile: Death in the South.* Translated by Robert Cox. New York: Alfred A. Knopf, 1987. Imprisoned and tortured by the Argentine military during the "dirty war" of the 1970's, journalist Timerman offers moving witness to the trauma of Chile, based on his visit to the country in the mid-1980's. Most chapters conclude with a "testimony," citing a victim's account of torture and suffering at the hands of the dictatorship.

Kendall W. Brown

Cross-References

The United Nations Sets Rules for the Treatment of Prisoners (1955), p. 935; Papa Doc Duvalier Takes Control of Haiti (1957), p. 1009; The Chinese Cultural Revolution Starts a Wave of Repression (1966), p. 1332; Brazil Begins a Period of Intense Repression (1968), p. 1468; An Oppressive Military Rule Comes to Democratic Uruguay (1973), p. 1715; Allende Is Overthrown in a Chilean Military Coup (1973), p. 1725; A Medical Group Helps Gather Evidence of Torture in Greece and Chile (1974), p. 1747; Khmer Rouge Take Over Cambodia (1975), p. 1791; The United Nations Issues a Declaration Against Torture (1975), p. 1847; The Argentine Military Conducts a "Dirty War" Against Leftists (1976), p. 1864; The U.N. Principles of Medical Ethics Include Prevention of Torture (1982), p. 2169; Argentine Leaders Are Convicted of Human Rights Violations (1985), p. 2280; Voters in Chile End Pinochet's Military Rule (1989), p. 2540.

BARBIE FACES CHARGES FOR NAZI WAR CRIMES

Category of event: Atrocities and war crimes
Time: February, 1983
Locale: Lyon, France

Klaus Barbie, head of the Gestapo in Lyon, France, during World War II, was extradited to France, where he was tried and convicted of crimes against humanity

Principal personages:

KLAUS BARBIE (1913-   ), the former head of the Lyon office of the Nazi Gestapo, also known as the "Butcher of Lyon"

SERGE KLARSFELD (1935-   ), a French lawyer and anti-Nazi activist who helped organize Barbie's prosecution

JACQUES VERGES (1925-   ), a controversial French attorney known for defending unpopular causes, who served as Barbie's lawyer

PIERRE TRUCHE, the chief government prosecutor in Barbie's trial

Summary of Event

Early in World War II, German armies overran northern France, forcing the government of Marshal Henri Philippe Petain to sign an armistice pact with the Nazi regime. Under this armistice, northern and western France remained under German military occupation, while Petain's government, relocated from Paris to Vichy, would observe military neutrality in the war but would retain authority over the southeastern part of the country. In 1942, in response to Allied army successes in North Africa, German and Italian forces swept southward through Vichy France, eventually bringing the entire national territory under Nazi occupation.

Wherever German armies consolidated their control, the official agencies of the German government and of the Nazi Party quickly set up operations. The most notorious of these were the black-shirted "defense echelon," or Schutzstaffel (SS), and the infamous state secret police, or Gestapo. Klaus Barbie served as head of the Gestapo in the French city of Lyon from the date of the German invasion, November, 1942, through 1944. During this period, he was responsible for the deaths of some four thousand French citizens and the deportation of some seventy-five hundred others, including women and children, mostly to their deaths. His personal involvement in torture, his reputation for brutality and sadism, especially in the treatment of Jews and French Resistance fighters, and his forced deportation of forty-four Jewish children, aged three to thirteen, to their deaths at Auschwitz brought him the nickname "The Butcher of Lyon."

Under traditional rules and laws of war, the establishment of military security in occupied territory often requires the occupying forces to maintain order and to conduct ordinary administrative business. In addition, the occupying administration legitimately may be required to execute a counterinsurgency against local resistance fighters. In occupied France, the collection of intelligence regarding and eventual neutralization of the Resistance fell largely to the Gestapo. This sort of counterinsurgency activity is itself bound by certain rules and norms, codified in international treaties such as the Geneva Convention. Among these norms are rules regarding respect for the human rights of civilians and noncombatants, the treatment of prisoners and incarcerated civilians, and prohibiting torture and other forms of physical or mental abuse.

Barbie was directly and personally involved in the violation of these norms. His crimes included supervision of and participation in the torture, sometimes to death, of prisoners during interrogation, and the execution of captured civilians. These tortures included protracted beatings to extract information, suspension of prisoners by the thumbs until death, extended immersion in ice water to the point of near drowning, flaying and subsequent application of ammonia to the wounds, sexual tortures, and the use of spiked manacles. Sometimes these tortures were inflicted while family members were present. Such acts are considered criminal violations of laws of war under both international and municipal law. They fall under the jurisdiction of both military tribunals and civilian courts. Barbie was convicted *in absentia* of these crimes in 1952 and 1954, and was twice sentenced to death.

Following the German defeat in the war, however, Barbie was able to exploit his knowledge of French and other European intelligence sources to render himself useful to U.S. occupying forces. The U.S. government at the time was preoccupied with the threat of communism in France and elsewhere. During the occupation, French communists had been at the heart of the Resistance, and in the context of the emerging Cold War, U.S. intelligence agencies feared the possible influence of these communist heroes in postwar French politics. Barbie's extensive files on and knowledge about communist networks, gathered during his counterinsurgency efforts against the Resistance, provided the bargaining chips he needed to ensure his safety from prosecution for his war crimes. With the help of U.S. intelligence agencies, he was spirited from Europe and allowed to resettle in Peru under an assumed name, Klaus Altmann. He later moved to Bolivia, where he remained safe from extradition back to France. After several years, the statute of limitations in France ran out on his sentences.

In Peru and Bolivia, Barbie was involved in local profascist activities, drug trafficking, and financial swindles. He served as a lieutenant colonel in the Bolivian army and was involved in the torture and killing of persons opposed to the Bolivian military government. He developed close ties with local intelligence and police agencies affiliated with successive military governments and assisted them in establishing concentration camps for opponents of the regime. He sold arms to international drug traffickers, some of whom were also affiliated with South American intelligence and security agencies. When these military regimes were replaced in the 1980's with democratic governments, Barbie's police agency contacts could no longer protect him from extradition. He was deported to France in 1983.

Amid heavy publicity, Barbie was tried in French court for "crimes against humanity." The specific crimes for which he was convicted included ordering and participating in the torture and execution of hundreds of Jews and Resistance fighters from November, 1942, to 1944, and ordering the deportation of hundreds of French Jews and Resistance fighters to the Auschwitz death camp. The Nazis had set up the death camps initially as slave labor camps and later employed them in an effort to exterminate systematically the entire population of European Jews, along with Gypsies, communists, homosexuals, and others deemed by the Nazis to be either socially corruptive elements or threats to the Nazi vision of world Aryan supremacy. The name given by the Nazis to this campaign of purification by extermination was the "final solution." The program was deemed genocidal, and thus a crime against humanity, by postwar international legal tribunals. It was for participating in this "final solution" that Barbie's war crimes fell under "crimes against humanity" in French law.

Barbie's defense attorney, Jacques Verges, sought to discredit some of the prosecution's witnesses and raised the issue of atrocities committed by Israel, by France in Algeria, and by the United States in Vietnam to suggest that his client was being used as a scapegoat to expiate the imperialist and colonialist crimes of Europeans in the Third World. Barbie himself admitted fighting a vigorous campaign against the Resistance but denied participating directly in the "final solution." He excused his crimes as the products of a war context and argued that he simply had been following orders and policies dictated by his superiors. He argued that laws are enforced only by the victors in war, and that he was being prosecuted because his country lost the war. He was nevertheless convicted and sentenced to life imprisonment.

The specific crimes for which Barbie was convicted stemmed from three separate incidents and several individual cases. In total, 340 separate charges were filed against him; he was found guilty of all. The charges included having participated in the torture and execution or deportation to their deaths of some 60 French Resistance fighters and individual Jews; organizing the roundup and deportation to their deaths of 86 Jews from a French Jewish organization office in February, 1943; arranging a last-minute death convoy of 650 people, the majority of whom were Jewish women and children, just before the liberation of Lyon by Allied troops; and the deportation to their deaths in Auschwitz gas chambers of 44 Jewish children and seven adults from the Izieu home for children outside Lyon.

Impact of Event

The life in exile, arrest, trial, and conviction of Klaus Barbie highlighted several human rights issues in addition to those brought back to the surface by revelations of his crimes. Barbie was convicted both of war crimes (in 1952 and 1954) and of crimes against humanity (in 1987). One of the most important human rights breakthroughs of the twentieth century has been the recognition that individuals are criminally and legally responsible for their own actions and decisions even when following orders or carrying out prescribed policies. This is true in wartime as well as peacetime. Soldiers and officials have a right and a duty to refuse illegal orders. Barbie's defense, that he was only following prescribed policies, is no longer recognized as a legitimate defense against accusations of having committed war crimes. The establishment of international human rights tribunals, the legal enforcement of war crimes codes in national civilian and military courts, and the incorporation; through treaties and other mechanisms, of internationally recognized standards of human rights into the legal codes of most nations have dramatically reduced the force of Barbie's argument that only war victors enforce war crimes laws. The inculcation into the members of the world's armed forces of such central human rights notions was provoked largely by the obvious inhumanity of the particular crimes perpetrated by Nazis such as Klaus Barbie.

Barbie's trial also underscored the nature of criminal participation in crimes against humanity, especially the crime of genocide, or the intended extermination of an entire people. Barbie's case reinforced earlier judgments that even simple active cooperation, such as ordering deportations to death camps, in a genocidal program can constitute criminal behavior.

In addition, Barbie's case raised disturbing issues regarding the willingness of postwar Western governments, especially that of the United States, to condone or overlook even horrible human rights violations by their clients and human "assets." Not only had Barbie been employed by the U.S postwar occupying forces, but he had been smuggled out of France and hidden by human rights-violating Latin American governments that were themselves sustained directly by the United States as part of Cold War regional policy. Barbie's continued activities in exile illustrated the international collaboration among right-wing movements and governments concerned with stopping communism no matter what human rights cost needed to be paid and underscored the tremendous costs of the Cold War for human rights on both sides of the Iron Curtain. Finally, the case resurrected long-standing guilt feelings in European countries over their own populations' complicity in the Holocaust against the Jews, since it became clear during the trial that many local citizens of Lyon had either cooperated or collaborated with Barbie's Gestapo (while many resisted, some paying with their lives).

Bibliography

Bower, Tom. *Klaus Barbie, the Butcher of Lyon.* New York: Pantheon, 1984. Good general introduction to and overview of the Barbie case. Accessible to the general reader. Covers the basic issues and facts well.

Epstein, Helen. *Children of the Holocaust.* New York: Putnam, 1979.

Lowrie, Donald A. *The Hunted Children.* New York: W. W. Norton, 1963. Both books document the stories of child victims of the Holocaust. Powerful and evocative discussions of the impact of genocide against children. Contain first-person narratives and documentation from Nazi and other sources.

Kahn, Annette. *Why My Father Died: A Daughter Confronts Her Family's Past at the Trial of Klaus Barbie.* New York: Summit Books, 1991. Disturbing and moving personal account by the daughter of a Jewish French Resistance leader who was executed under Barbie only a few months before the liberation of France by Allied forces. Traces the human impact of the occupation through the postwar era.

Morgan, Ted. *An Uncertain Hour: The French, the Germans, the Jews, the Barbie Trial, and the City of Lyon 1940-45.* New York: Arbor House/William R. Morrow, 1990. Good general chronicle of the Barbie case and the impact of his trial in France. Contains much personal and anecdotal information and testimony.

Paris, Erna. *Unhealed Wounds: France and the Klaus Barbie Affair.* New York: Grove Press, 1986. Paris is a Canadian journalist who lived for a decade in France as a French citizen and knows the country's political secrets. She places the Barbie affair in the context of the evolution of the history of French political factions, especially the ideological divisions between Left and Right that date back before the Revolution, and shows how the trial of Barbie led to the resurfacing and re-definition of old political divisions.

Ryan, Allen A. *Klaus Barbie and the United States Government: A Report to the Attorney General of the United States.* Washington, D.C.: United States Department of Justice, 1983. Definitive report provided by the U.S. Justice Department lawyer assigned to document the postwar ties between American intelligence operatives and Klaus Barbie. The report clearly demonstrates the U.S. government's role in arranging Barbie's escape from Europe, despite French efforts to apprehend him, and Barbie's role in providing anti-Soviet and anticommunist intelligence for occupying forces. Ryan's excellent research led to an official apology by the U.S. government to France.

Larry N. George

Cross-References

Legal Norms of Behavior in Warfare Formulated by the Hague Conference (1907), p. 92; Hitler Writes *Mein Kampf* (1924), p. 389; Nazi Concentration Camps Go into Operation (1933), p. 491; Nazi War Criminals Are Tried in Nuremberg (1945), p. 667; Eichmann Is Tried for War Crimes (1961), p. 1108; The Statute of Limitations Is Ruled Not Applicable to War Crimes (1968), p. 1457.

OPPOSITION LEADER BENIGNO AQUINO
IS ASSASSINATED

Category of event: Atrocities and war crimes
Time: August 21, 1983
Locale: Manila, the Philippines

The assassination of Benigno Aquino transformed him into a nationalist martyr and mobilized a massive reaction against the rule of Ferdinand Marcos

Principal personages:
>BENIGNO "NINOY" AQUINO, JR. (1932-1983), the leader of the Philippine liberal opposition who was assassinated on August 21, 1983, when he returned to the Philippines from exile
>FERDINAND MARCOS (1917-1989), the dictator of the Philippines from 1965 until 1986
>CORAZON AQUINO (1933-), married Benigno Aquino in 1954 and became president of the Philippines in 1986
>IMELDA MARCOS (1929-), the wife of Ferdinand Marcos
>GENERAL FABIAN VER (1920-), the head of the Philippine secret police and army
>RICHARD HOLBROOKE (1942-), the assistant secretary of state for East Asia during the Jimmy Carter Administration
>JAIME SIN (1928-), a cardinal of the Catholic church who mobilized the church to support Benigno Aquino

Summary of Event

Benigno "Ninoy" Aquino knew that his return to Manila from three years of exile in the United States was fraught with danger. President Ferdinand Marcos and his wife, Imelda, had warned Aquino that his life was threatened. Defense Minister Juan Ponce Enrile had asked him to delay his return. The supreme court of the Philippines had declared that his alleged crimes of "subversion, murder, and illegal possession of firearms" still warranted punishment by a firing squad. Aquino, however, knew that Ferdinand Marcos' health was deteriorating, and he feared that Imelda Marcos or General Fabian Ver would try to take over the government. He believed that only he could avert a bloody civil war between the military and the radical masses.

Using false passports and scheduling a complex and secret itinerary, Aquino arrived from Taipei, Taiwan, on China Airlines on August 21, 1983. Special agents had alerted General Ver of the "secret arrival." Armed military men surrounded the plane. Three uniformed soldiers escorted Aquino into a movable passenger tube and, instead of proceeding through to the waiting room, directed him out the service door and down the exterior service stairs. Before he reached the bottom of the stairs that led to the tarmac, Aquino was shot in the back of the head. The soldiers threw his body in a van and disappeared.

Aquino's assassination was the bloody conclusion of a rivalry between Aquino and Marcos. The government's flagrant attempts to cover up for the perpetrators included kidnapping, murder, intimidation, and falsification of evidence. Marcos' policies of retribution and economic exploitation of the country frightened the middle class and traditional ruling families. They mobilized around Ninoy's wife, Corazon Aquino, and drove Marcos out of power.

Ninoy was the major liberal critic of Marcos and a contender for the presidency. It was widely believed that Marcos had declared martial law in 1972 in order to prevent Ninoy from running for the presidency. Within hours of the proclamation of martial law, Ninoy was arrested and charged with subversion. He endured years of prison confinement and was many times isolated and abused. After several abortive military trials, he was convicted in 1977 and sentenced to death by firing squad. International appeals and local political movements saved him. In 1978, he campaigned from jail. His party, *Lakas ng Bayan* (Strength of the Country), was known by its acronym, *Laban* (Fight). The symbol for the party, a closed fist with thumb and pinky extended, formed the letter *L*. This gesture became famous as a visual statement against Marcos and his government. Because of ill health, Aquino was finally allowed to leave the Philippines with his family. He spent three years in the United States preparing for his return and for renewed political struggles.

Aquino's support was drawn from many sectors of the Philippines and from his international connections. He began his career as a newsperson covering the Korean War; his close relationship with foreign journalists helped him to achieve international notoriety during his imprisonment and exile. While working at the *Manila Times*, he attended the prestigious law school of the University of the Philippines, and he became famous for his oratorical ability and charismatic leadership.

After his graduation, Ninoy married Corazon and started a career in politics. At the age of twenty-two, he became the youngest mayor in the Philippines. At the same time, he successfully managed a sugar plantation, increasing its productivity and providing good treatment for its workers. At twenty-eight, he became the youngest governor in the Philippines in his home province of Tarlac. His firm administration brought prosperity and stability to the area. He achieved national popularity when he became the youngest member of the Philippine congress in 1967. He availed himself of the "privilege hour," in which one could speak about anything with full immunity, and focused his impressive oratorical skills on attacking the Marcoses. He revealed Marcos' intent to declare martial law, castigated Marcos for lifting the writ of habeas corpus after the Plaza Miranda bombings in 1971, and revealed Marcos' corrupt practices. Aquino's own modest life-style contrasted greatly with the opulence of the Marcoses. Most flagrant of all of his denunciations were his attacks on the president's wife for using public funds for lavish and wasteful projects, especially the Philippine Cultural Center, which he characterized as "Imelda's Pantheon."

Aquino's incarceration in Forts Magsaysay and Bonifacio from 1972 to 1980 enhanced his reputation as a martyr for international human rights. Written in self-defense at his military trial in 1977, his *Testament from a Prison Cell* (1977) was both a documentary of Marcos' abuse of power and Ninoy's own vision for a free society. This society was to incorporate democratic institutions with Christian policies of social justice. His political program was greatly influenced by the experience of his Christian conversion in 1975, while he was on a hunger strike in jail. His newfound ideology found deep support among the liberals in the Filipino church and from the Filipino people.

In 1980, Ninoy suffered a severe heart problem that necessitated surgery. Instead of facing the possibility of having Aquino die in a Manila hospital, Marcos allowed him to leave the country for medical care in the United States. For the next three years, Aquino traveled extensively to organize Filipino exile groups and to publicize the problems in the Philippines. Soon after he recovered from his heart operation, he spoke before the Asia Society. His oft-quoted speech ended with a ringing declaration of his commitment to helping his countrymen oppose authoritarian rule in order to support freedom: "I have carefully weighed the virtues and the faults of the Filipino, and I have come to the conclusion that he is worth dying for."

Officials of the Carter Administration, especially Assistant Secretary of State Richard Holbrooke and congressmen Stephen Solarz and Donald Fraser, had been sympathetic to Aquino. Ronald Reagan, who had been a special guest at the opening of Imelda Marcos' Philippine Cultural Center, directed his administration to support Ferdinand Marcos. For Reagan, the security of American military bases in the Philippines took priority over human rights and the welfare of Aquino and the opposition. Realizing that his influence on United States policies had become limited, Ninoy decided to return to the Philippines.

The adverse reaction to Aquino's assassination was overwhelming and maintained its momentum until 1986, when Corazon Aquino became president. Millions of people gathered for the funeral procession. Archbishop Jaime Sin's homily further expressed the Catholic church's regard for Benigno Aquino and underlined the need to seek peace and justice through a change in government. The government's clumsy attempts to cover up the perpetrators with a show trial that exonerated General Ver further outraged the population. The success of Corazon's People's Power movement drove the Marcoses, General Ver, and their close followers into exile. With the major witnesses absent, a new investigation of the assassination could not reveal the real perpetrators, but a 172-page report in 1990 did set the record straight: The alleged Communist gunman, Rolando Galman, was innocent, and the military men who had surrounded the plane were guilty of conspiracy to commit murder.

Impact of Event

A self-conscious nationalist who was proud of his family's anti-imperialist traditions, Ninoy became a Filipino martyr in the tradition of José Rizal. Like Rizal, Ninoy was willing to die for his country and the freedom of his people. His prison experiences—writings, political organization, hunger strike, solitary confinements, and abusive interrogations—were obviously similar to other famous international cases of conscience and resistance such as those of Nelson Mandela, Andrei Sakharov, and Martin Luther King, Jr.

Ironically, Ninoy admired the autocratic and authoritarian rule of leaders such as Kemal Atatürk of Turkey, Lee Kuan Yew of Singapore, and even General Park Chung Hee, who had placed South Korea under martial law in 1972. Ninoy, however, became a symbol of the People's Power movement in the Philippines. The success of this nonviolent and democratic overthrow of an autocratic ruler provided great hope and inspiration to democratic and human rights movements throughout East Asia. Democratic movements in Taiwan, South Korea, and even China looked for lessons in the Philippine experience. Largely through the success of nonviolent protest, martial law in Taiwan and in South Korea was abrogated in the mid-1980's. Only in China was the democracy movement aborted. The Philippine symbol of personal sacrifice and political accomplishment, however, remained greatly admired in East Asia.

Ninoy's international reputation and popularity resulted in tremendous attention from journalists and human righis organizations. Domestically and internationally, the problems of the Philippines were studied and reports about them were circulated. Under Marcos, there was very little outside interest in the Philippines, and much of the critical information available was censored by the government or by multinational businesses. Nevertheless, a large number of domestic human rights monitoring groups kept a close account of abuses. In addition to many church and lay organizations, the Free Legal Assistance Group (FLAG) became well regarded for its reports and struggles on behalf of human rights issues.

As a result of this newfound openness and interest, the administration of Corazon Aquino has been scrutinized. A 1991 report by the International Commission of Jurists concluded that there had been significant improvements, but there were still many abuses. The military and intelligence agencies still engaged in widespread torture.

Benigno Aquino's assassination alarmed the Filipino citizenry to the point where they became conscious of the need to develop and monitor policies of social justice in order to further the attainment of human rights for all. This establishment of a new standard to measure political success was Benigno Aquino's greatest domestic and international legacy.

Bibliography

Amnesty International. *Report of an Amnesty International Mission to the Republic of the Philippines, 22 November-5 December, 1975.* 2d ed. London: Amnesty International Publications, 1977. By a major human rights organization that publishes regularly on human rights in the Philippines. The focus is primarily on civil and political rights rather than the broader topics of economic, social, and environmental rights. Also see Amnesty International's annual reports on human rights abuses throughout the world.

Aquino, Ninoy. *Testament from a Prison Cell.* Los Angeles: Philippine Journal, 1988. This limited edition of five thousand copies is Aquino's major political testimony and forms his political legacy to the Filipino people. Written in 1977 for his defense at the military trial that accused him of subversion and murder, the volume outlines Aquino's countercharges and his political philosophy.

Bonner, Raymond. *Waltzing with the Dictator: The Marcoses and the Making of American Policy.* New York: Times Books, 1987. Focuses on Ambassador Stephen Bosworth and his relations with Marcos. Important study of the state department's activities in Manila.

Burton, Sandra. *Impossible Dream: The Marcoses, the Aquinos, and the Unfinished Revolution.* New York: Warner Books, 1989. Provides a dramatic and personal description of the government's cover-up of Benigno Aquino's assassination and the politicization of Corazon Aquino.

The International Commission of Jurists. *The Failed Promise: Human Rights in the Philippines Since the Revolution of 1986, Report of a Visit.* Geneva: Author, 1991. An extensive assessment of Corazon Aquino's "Unfinished Revolution." The conclusion praises Aquino for having rescinded most of the decrees that formed the basis for martial law, but the administration is still criticized for not adequately protecting the human rights of all of its citizens.

Karnow, Stanley. *In Our Image: America's Empire in the Philippines.* New York: Random House, 1989. A well-documented study of U.S.-Philippine relations. Provides an excellent discussion of the decisionmaking process in Washington, D.C., during the Reagan Administration. Karnow, an outstanding journalist on East Asian affairs, has personally interviewed the Marcoses, General Ver, Benigno Aquino, Corazon Aquino, Juan Ponce Enrile, and other political leaders in both the Philippines and the United States.

Lawyers Committee for Human Rights. *Out of Control: Militia Abuses in the Philippines.* New York: Author, 1990. Argues that Marcos' legacy of the militarization of the Philippines has not been adequately reformed by the Corazon Aquino Administration.

Leary, Virginia A. *The Philippines: Human Rights After Martial Law.* Geneva: International Commission of Jurists, 1984. Investigates the abuses of the armed forces and the police and provides excellent documentation of the abuse of economic and social rights and a legal critique of the criminal law and the judicial system. The report provides a unique survey of the abuse of tribal people.

Simons, Lewis M. *Worth Dying For.* New York: William Morrow, 1987. Simons, a journalist in Asia, received the Pulitzer Prize for International Reporting for articles that exposed the corruption of the Marcoses. Detailed report on the investigation of the assassination. Good reporting on the events that followed the assassination.

Richard C. Kagan

Cross-References

The Philippines Ends Its Uprising Against the United States (1902), p. 7; Marcos Declares Martial Law in the Philippines (1972), p. 1680; The United Nations Issues a Declaration Against Torture (1975), p. 1847; Sakharov Is Awarded the Nobel Peace Prize (1975), p. 1852; Biko Is Murdered by Interrogators in South Africa (1977), p. 1887; Carter Makes Human Rights a Central Theme of Foreign Policy (1977), p. 1903; Marcos Flees the Philippines (1986), p. 2286.

AMNESTY INTERNATIONAL ADOPTS A PROGRAM FOR THE PREVENTION OF TORTURE

Categories of event: Civil rights and prisoners' rights
Time: October, 1983
Locale: London, England

Amnesty International's Campaign Against Torture, which was begun in 1972, culminated in the adoption of the 12-Point Program for the Prevention of Torture

Principal personages:
PETER BENENSON (1921-   ), a London lawyer who founded Amnesty International
MARTIN ENNALS (1927-   ), the secretary-general of Amnesty International who proposed the first statute against torture
SALVADOR ALLENDE (1908-1973), the president of Chile whose government was overthrown by a military coup

Summary of Event

Amnesty International's campaign against torture began almost incidentally in 1965, almost four years after AI's founding by Peter Benenson. Two publications on prison conditions, one on South Africa and the other on Portugal and Romania, contained evidence that physical and mental pain were being applied against prisoners. The South African report indicated no official guidance on prisoners' torture; wardens were allowed to devise their own means of interrogation, such as burying prisoners up to their necks and then urinating into their mouths. By contrast, the report on Portugal showed a well-organized system of torture. For example, when thirty-one students were arrested in 1965, they were subjected to the "statue" treatment, which involved having the prisoner stand and preventing him or her from sleeping more than ten minutes at a time. The Romania report was primarily of historical value since the prisons were empty of political detainees at the time that the information was released. Nevertheless, the methods employed by prison guards in the 1950's were worth noting if only for their originality. One method required that the prisoner be stripped naked and forced to walk barefoot around a cell for six hours at a time.

In 1968, Amnesty International's membership rose to include twenty national sections, and its funds increased to $23,000. Because it now had the resources to take on a new mission, Amnesty International began to address the problem of worldwide torture itself. The secretary-general of Amnesty International, Martin Ennals, presented a new statute that would streamline the administration to enable it to cope with what he called its "mammoth objective": the abolition of torture. This action was taken primarily in response to the Greek coup of 1967, which brought a right-wing military *junta* to power. As soon as this dictatorship took over the country, six thousand people were arrested. Reports to Amnesty International told of ill-treatment of these prisoners. The standard initial torture was the *falanga*, which involved beating the soles of a prisoner's feet with a stick or pipe and then forcing him or her to run through a gauntlet of heavy blows. A special report on these atrocities, prepared by two lawyers who visited Greece, Anthony Marreco and James Becker, was published in 1968. That same year, Amnesty International published a hundred-page booklet entitled *Torture in Greece* which not only verified the data included in the Marreco-Becker report but actually showed that the earlier document had underrated the extent of torture in that country. For example, prisoners were forced to stand on one foot at attention for several hours, with intermittent beatings. Because of these publications, the military *junta* was ousted from the Council of Europe. In 1975, one year after the *junta* had been ousted, twenty-four soldiers were tried and convicted on charges of torture. This trial was important to Amnesty International because it provided a rare look into the torture methods and the training of torturers.

In December, 1972, Amnesty International began a worldwide "Campaign for the Abolition of Torture." In 1973, the United Nations General Assembly followed suit by passing a resolution formally denouncing torture. This resolution asked all nations to "adhere to existing international instruments forbidding the practice of torture." The United Nations passed a declaration against torture and other cruel, inhuman, or degrading punishment in 1975.

The 1972 Amnesty statute was followed a year later by the publication of the first edition of an international survey on torture. This country-by-country report concluded that torture was deliberately used by many nations, often employing the services, either directly or indirectly, of police, soldiers, doctors, civil servants, judges, and scientists. The survey devoted little space to torture methods in communist countries, where torture was unnecessary because the huge secret police forces made opposition almost impossible. Instead, the survey concentrated on Africa, Central and South America, the Middle East, and Asia. The worst offenders, the survey charged, were Chile, Brazil, Paraguay, and Turkey.

The latest reports came from Chile, where President Salvador Allende had been overthrown in September, 1973. Some of the allegations of torture and maltreatment included cases of burning with acid or cigarettes, of electrocution, and of psychological threats, including simulated executions and threats to families of the prisoners. An unknown number of women were raped or subjected to having insects forced up their vaginas. Pregnant women were often beaten until they aborted. An Amnesty delegation concluded that torture in that country had reached "animalistic levels."

Shortly after Brazil was taken over by a military coup in 1964, Amnesty International became flooded with reports of torture of political prisoners. In 1972, Amnesty published a ninety-page document which gave the names of 1,081 people who had been tortured, as well as the names of 81 torturers. The report also revealed the existence of an advanced school of torture, run by the army. The most original method of torture to emerge from this school was the *pau de arara* (the "parrot's perch"). After his or her arms and legs had been tied together, the prisoner was suspended from an iron bar under the knees and beaten, whipped, or shocked with electrodes.

Brazil's neighbor, Paraguay, was another South American country where atrocities were committed by a military regime. President Alfredo Stroessner, the general who had come to power in 1954, frequently employed torture during the 1960's as a means of interrogating suspected communists. Professor Luis Resck, who was adopted by Amnesty as a prisoner of conscience, was arrested, beaten, and ill-treated a total of thirty-six times.

In 1972, an Amnesty investigation of the atrocities committed in Turkey produced another prisoner of conscience, a woman. The Turkish government declared that no prisoners had been ill-treated and even permitted the mission to interview one of them, a twenty-three-year-old woman named Ayse Semra Eker, who had been seized in the street. Eker's statement revealed a strain of sexual sadism in the torturers. After beating her arms and legs with an axe handle, a police officer inserted a truncheon with an electric wire attached to it into her vagina and passed current. Eventually, she was released, but she could not menstruate for four months. Amnesty International's 1973 *Report on Torture* asked if Ayse Eker's torture could be justified; it concluded that there are countries that think that it can.

The annual reports that were published by Amnesty throughout the remainder of the decade found that many governments subscribed to U.N. human rights declarations and resolutions on paper only. Physical methods of torture were still openly used in the 1970's in dictatorships in Spain, Iran, and Iraq. The Amnesty reports also discovered clandestine torture being used in Third World nations such as Uganda and Ghana. A particularly disturbing trend that emerged at this time was the development of psychiatric and medical techniques designed to control a prisoner's behavior.

By 1983, it became clear that more formal measures were needed to deal with the worldwide problem of torture. The continued use of old methods of torture as well as the invention of new ones in countries such as Guatemala, Syria, and Rwanda led, in October, to Amnesty's adoption of its 12-Point Program for the Prevention of Torture.

The twelve points are as follows. (1) law enforcement personnel must never employ torture; (2) incommunicado detention should not become an opportunity for torture; (3) prisoners must be held in a publicly recognized place; (4) all prisoners must be told of their right to lodge complaints about their treatment; (5) all reports of torture must be independently investigated; (6) evidence obtained through torture should not be invoked in court proceedings; (7) acts of torture must be categorized as punishable offenses under criminal law; (8) torturers should be prosecuted, and there should be no "safe haven"; (9) training procedures of all prison officials must make it clear that torture is a criminal act; (10) victims of torture and their dependents should be entitled to compensation; (11) all nations should intercede with governments accused of torture; and (12) all governments should ratify international instruments containing safeguards and remedies against torture.

Impact of Event

Since its birth in 1961, Amnesty International has repeatedly demonstrated to its critics that ordinary people really can save from torture men and women they have never met. The publication of Amnesty International's 12-Point Program for the Prevention of Torture in its 1984 book-length report *Torture in the Eighties* helped to mobilize worldwide reaction against torture. Although Amnesty has no scientific way to measure its effectiveness, its stand on torture has clearly struck a nerve in people everywhere. In a number of countries—Argentina, Bolivia, Chile, Colombia, El Salvador, Guatemala, Honduras, and Mexico—human rights organizations have been formed to combat the use of torture. In the United States alone, more than five hundred groups have formed to help Amnesty International stop torture. In 1984, largely as a response to Amnesty's annual reports on worldwide torture, the U.S. Congress passed and the president signed into law an American commitment against torture that requires diplomats to report regularly on human rights abuses overseas and to take specific steps to end them.

Following the publication of *Torture in the Eighties*, thousands of young people all over the world adopted Amnesty's cause as their own. In September, 1988, a group of socially aware rock stars including Bruce Springsteen, Sting, Peter Gabriel, Tracy Chapman, and the band U2 generated millions of dollars for Amnesty International through their benefit tour entitled "A Conspiracy of Hope: Concerts for Amnesty International." Accompanying the tour were victims of repressive governments, including a Chilean torture victim and a survivor of Cambodia's Khmer Rouge regime.

Probably the most important measure of the effectiveness of Amnesty's war against torture is the number of governments that have gone to great lengths to improve their image. As a direct result of Amnesty's publications, a number of nations have abolished torture, Portugal, Equatorial Guinea, Democratic Kampuchea, and Rhodesia among them. Other nations, such as Guatemala and Peru, have tried to discredit Amnesty by accusing the organization of being part of a communist conspiracy. Some nations, such as Turkey, have even gone as far as hiring public relations firms in America to change the way that the world views them as a result of Amnesty's stand against torture. These acts of desperation on the part of the offending nations demonstrate that the most powerful weapon for preventing the use of torture is the mobilization of international opinion and pressure. This has always been, and will continue to be, the primary goal of Amnesty International.

Bibliography

Amnesty International. *Torture in the Eighties.* London: Amnesty International Publications, 1984. Despite the broad title, this book actually covers only the first three years of the decade. Still, it provides an in-depth look into the ill-treatment of prisoners in Africa, the Americas, Asia, Europe, and the Middle East.

Barber, James David. "The Fight to Stop Torture." *USA Today* 116 (November, 1987): 29-31. This article picks up where *Torture in the Eighties* leaves off, with a close look at the ways in which some nations defend and justify their use of torture. The article ends by paraphrasing Amnesty's 12-Point Program for the Prevention of Torture.

Larsen, Egon. *A Flame in Barbed Wire: The Story of Amnesty International.* New York: W. W. Norton, 1979. This text can be considered as the standard history of Amnesty International. Even though this is an unauthorized history, the book is filled with case histories and photographs.

Morley, Jefferson. "Inhuman Bondage." *Rolling Stone* 19 (June, 1986): 55-56+. This objective examination of Amnesty International's efforts on behalf of the victims of torture is of importance because it shows how the organization's image has changed through the years.

Moskin, J. Robert. "Bringing Light into Dark Cells." *Town and Country* 140 (October, 1986): 236-239+. This long overview of Amnesty's activities since 1961 is a good introduction to the organization. The article also explains how Peter Benenson founded the organization.

Power, Jonathan. *Amnesty International: The Human Rights Story.* New York: McGraw-Hill, 1981. The author, a columnist for the *International Herald Tribune*, drew from his journalistic travels for this biased but thorough history of Amnesty International. This text is of particular interest because of the photographs that are scattered throughout the book.

Alan Brown

Cross-References

Nazi War Criminals Are Tried in Nuremberg (1945), p. 667; The United Nations Sets Rules for the Treatment of Prisoners (1955), p. 935; Eichmann Is Tried for War Crimes (1961), p. 1108; Amnesty International Is Founded (1961), p. 1119; The United Nations Issues a Declaration Against Torture (1975), p. 1847; A Lawyers' Union Demands Justice and Political Reform in Syria (1978), p. 1967; China Publicizes and Promises to Correct Abuses of Citizens' Rights (1978), p. 1983; The United Nations Issues a Conduct Code for Law Enforcement Officials (1979), p. 2040; A Paraguayan Torturer Is Found Guilty of Violating the Law of Nations (1980), p. 2106; The OAU Adopts the African Charter on Human and Peoples' Rights (1981), p. 2136.

JACKSON BECOMES THE FIRST MAJOR BLACK CANDIDATE FOR U.S. PRESIDENT

Category of event: Racial and ethnic rights
Time: November 3, 1983
Locale: Washington, D.C.

Jesse Jackson's candidacy brought minority-rights issues to the forefront of American politics

Principal personages:
JESSE JACKSON (1941-   ), a civil rights activist and candidate for the U.S. presidency
WALTER MONDALE (1928-   ), the 1984 Democratic candidate for president
GERALDINE FERRARO (1935-   ), the first female vice-presidential candidate in U.S. history
MARTIN LUTHER KING, JR. (1929-1968), the moral and political leader of the Civil Rights movement
CORETTA SCOTT KING (1927-   ), the wife of Martin Luther King, Jr., also a civil rights activist
RONALD REAGAN (1911-   ), the president of the United States from 1981 to 1989

Summary of Event

The society of the United States in the 1980's reflected a history of distinctly different opportunities for African Americans and white Americans. African Americans had faced slavery, and even after emancipation had experienced discrimination in education, housing, employment, voting, and other aspects of social life. Throughout World War II, black soldiers fought for the "double V," meaning victory against America's enemies abroad and victory against racial oppression within American society. President Harry S. Truman integrated the U.S. armed forces in 1948, and by 1954 the U.S. Supreme Court had declared, in *Brown v. Board of Education*, that "separate but equal" schools were inherently unequal and unconstitutional. Rising expectations gave birth to the U.S. Civil Rights movement, led by Martin Luther King, Jr. Defeating segregation was the highest priority of the Civil Rights movement. Black and white civil rights workers were beaten, imprisoned, and killed during this struggle, but peaceful demonstrations, sit-ins, freedom rides, and boycotts were the main tactics used to achieve the movement's goals. Dr. King was assassinated in 1968. Supporters, such as Jesse Jackson, continued his work and carried the fight for racial equality into the political arena. Militants, such as Malcolm X, predicted that equality would be won either by the ballot or by the bullet.

Politics was viewed as the key to equality. In 1971, Jackson ran for mayor of Chicago against powerful Richard J. Daley. Jackson lost the mayoral election but managed, on a technicality, to unseat Daley's delegation to the 1972 Democratic Convention. Jackson tried to organize a "Liberation Party," formed of blacks and liberal whites, to elect a black president. Black Democratic Congresswoman Shirley Chisholm declared her candidacy with the Democratic Party but lost to George McGovern and destroyed Jackson's effort to run a black for president as the Liberation Party's candidate. Jackson gave McGovern his support but received little help for black causes from him.

Republican abolitionist Frederick Douglass became, in 1888, the first African American to be nominated by a major political party for president. His largely symbolic campaign unsuccessfully protested the rise of white supremacy and resulting disenfranchisement and virtual reenslavement of millions of blacks following the Tilden-Hayes Compromise and the rise of rigid Jim Crow racial segregation in virtually all areas of life.

The Civil Rights Act of 1964 and affirmative action programs opened broader opportunities for millions of blacks. As a result, the black middle class expanded considerably. The black underclass, however, was little affected by these programs. They remained ill-educated, poorly housed, underfed, and without proper medical care. White resentment of black gains led to a backlash, heralded by charges of reverse discrimination. Attacks on programs designed to assist blacks became common. Jackson became convinced that the best way to combat these injustices was to influence government policy by running for president.

Voter apathy hurt blacks politically. Jackson observed that during the 1980 presidential election, Ronald Reagan won Alabama by 17,500 votes, but that there were 27,200 unregistered blacks. Reagan similarly won Arkansas by 5,000 votes, with 85,000 unregistered blacks. The story was common nationwide, convincing Jackson that Reagan had won with support of a coalition of the rich and the registered. Jackson believed that if he ran for president it would provoke hundreds of thousands of black unregistered voters to register. Jackson proclaimed that when more blacks registered, the hands that once picked cotton would pick the president.

Some black leaders, such as Benjamin Hooks of the National Association for the Advancement of Colored People (NAACP) and Coretta Scott King, widow of Martin Luther King, Jr., believed that Jackson's presidential candidacy would split the Democratic vote, producing a white backlash at the polls. Jackson disagreed and declared that Dr. King had taught him to seize opportunities. Blacks were distressed by the erosion of past gains and by rapidly deteriorating conditions within black communities. Jackson planned to use the eighteen million eligible black voters as a base upon which he would build a coalition of the rejected. This coalition would include the six million Hispanic, half million Native American, forty million poor white, and millions of female voters. Jackson called this the "Rainbow Coalition." Jackson intended to include all who had formerly been excluded from the political process. This was a peaceful human rights revolution, using the ballot, not the bullet.

"Run, Jesse, run," chanted encouraging crowds when Jackson formally announced his candidacy in November, 1983. He was the first black male seriously to seek presidential nomination with either the Democratic or Republican party. Those watching his candidacy predicted that, win or lose, increased voter registration would be one benefit he brought to the Democratic party. Jackson electrified minority groups. Many thought that the Jackson candidacy signaled the long-sought fulfillment of the American dream of inclusion for all Americans. They gave Jackson overwhelming support. More than 90 percent of the black clergy endorsed Jackson within two months after he announced his candidacy. They claimed that this registered their discontent with Democratic candidates who had accepted their votes but had done little to reciprocate that support after winning elections. Jackson's campaign captured the imaginations of Puerto Ricans, white liberals, women, Native Americans, the unemployed, left-wing activists, and the poor.

Jackson had little money to mount a national campaign, and many white voters did not know what he stood for. Jackson had called for arms reductions by the United States and the Soviet Union, removal of cruise missiles from Europe, normalizing diplomatic relations with Cuba, an end to U.S. intervention in Central America, protection of U.S. industry from unfair foreign competition, and protection of U.S. jobs and small farms. He also called for increased spending for the domestic war against drugs and urban crime, improved education for America's youth to make them more competitive in the international labor market, and the revitalization of America's inner cities.

In December of 1983, a U.S. reconnaissance plane was shot down on a routine mission over Syria. The pilot was killed and the navigator, Lieutenant Robert Goodman, was taken prisoner. U.S. president Ronald Reagan failed to secure his release. Jackson declared, "Whoever can act, should." In an unprecedented move, he journeyed to Syria without official U.S. support to plead for Goodman's release. After considerable discussion, President Hafez al-Assad of Syria released Goodman to Jackson's custody. Jackson and Goodman were given "heroes' welcomes" by President Reagan at the White House. All of the publicity surrounding this case gave Jackson broad national media coverage. Most Americans subsequently recognized Jackson's name and positively associated him with patriotic duty. This gave Jackson's candidacy visibility it could not afford to buy. Critics argued that Jackson had interfered in the conduct of American foreign affairs, despite Reagan's obvious pleasure with his success.

Jackson's relations with the Arab and Third World nations were excellent. At the same time, two serious incidents cost him much of his Jewish support. First, an off-the-record comment to a *Washington Post* reporter, calling New York City "Hymie Town," caused many Jewish groups to accuse Jackson of being anti-Semitic. Second, his refusal to denounce Nation of Islam minister Louis Farrakhan, who referred to Judaism as a "gutter religion," added to Jewish voters' fears.

At the National Democratic Convention in San Francisco in July, 1984, Jackson secured approximately three hundred delegates. Walter Mondale, the Democratic Party's front-runner, had two hundred black delegates who supported him, and this eroded Jackson's bargaining power. Walter Mondale won the party's presidential nomination, and Geraldine Ferraro won the vice-presidential nomination. Jackson gave this ticket his support, but it was defeated by Ronald Reagan.

Jesse Jackson's candidacy undoubtedly contributed to the large black voter turnout in the 1984 election. An estimated three million blacks voted in the Democratic primaries, and Mondale received more than ten million black votes during the 1984 election. Almost ninety percent of black voters supported Mondale in the November elections, providing evidence that Jackson's candidacy captured the hearts and minds of millions of neglected citizens.

Jackson ran a stronger campaign in 1988, but he again failed to capture the Democratic Party's nomination. He remained, however, a source of hope and inspiration for millions of minority group members and the poor. He encouraged them to struggle for personal excellence and full human rights through the fulfillment of the promises contained in the Declaration of Independence and the Constitution.

Impact of Event

Jesse Jackson's bid for nomination as the Democratic Party's 1984 presidential candidate moved African Americans and other minorities closer to the realization of self-determination. He symbolized black efforts to achieve equity and parity in all areas of American life. His campaign forced the United States to address issues of concern to blacks such as social justice, or equal legal protection of civil rights; economic justice, or workers' rights and restoring jobs for Americans in America; political justice, or freedom of assembly and proportional representation; freedom of the press; and freedom of religion. Jackson dramatically increased black voter registration as well as active minority voting. This gave blacks more bargaining power and leverage.

Jackson's campaign informed millions of Americans that blacks had limited constitutional or legal protection. In fact, he noted that the Constitution defined an African American as three-fifths of a person. The Dred Scott case had declared that blacks "had no rights which a white man must respect," and in 1896 *Plessy v. Ferguson* had legally established the principle that "separate but equal" and apartheid color caste systems were the law. Although the *Brown v. Board of Education* decision subsequently reversed this, and the Civil Rights movement made some gains, Jackson declared that the United States was still a nation divided by race, gender, and class barriers.

Emotionally loaded terms such as "reverse discrimination" and "preferential treatment," he warned, had been used to slow or halt desegregation efforts. Although progress had been made and most forms of overt racial segregation and injustices had been eliminated, obvious differences persisted. There was still one white attorney for every 680 whites and one black attorney for every 4,000 blacks; one white physician for every 649 whites and one black physician for every 5,000 blacks; and one white dentist for every 1,900 whites and one black dentist for every 8,400 blacks. Less than one percent of all engineers, chemists, physicists, and geologists were black. Even more surprising, at the time less than one percent of all elected and appointed officials were black, even though a few mayors of large cities served as very visible signs of political progress. There were no black senators and only one black governor, even after over two decades of affirmative action.

In terms of education, only 3.6 percent of American school children were bused in order to balance school systems racially, a small figure considering the huge public outcry. Daily, 55 percent of American children were bused to school without comment. Outrage was provoked only when busing was used to integrate schools.

In New York City, it cost more than $40,000 a year to keep a person in jail. For less than $20,000, that person could attend college for four years, then graduate, work, pay taxes, and help society. America had more black men in prison than in college, and Jackson's campaign asked why. His campaign also asked America to develop a new focus and new set of national priorities that would help all Americans to enjoy a full measure of human rights. Good health care, good housing, a good education, and a good job were all declared human rights, not privileges, by Jackson. He asked that all concerned people demand that these rights be universally available for Americans. Jackson asked that the United States put human needs ahead of military needs, especially in the post-Cold War era.

When Jesse Jackson declared his candidacy on November 3, 1983, in Washington, D.C., most experts believed that he was doomed to fail. In 1984, however, he won 21 percent of the total Democratic primary votes and 11 percent of all the Democratic convention delegates in San Francisco. In 1988, he finished second only to Michael Dukakis. His image had changed so dramatically during this brief time span that some analysts believed he was the most qualified Democratic candidate in 1988.

Jackson ventured abroad twice during his 1984 campaign, once to negotiate the release of U.S. Navy navigator Lieutenant Robert Goodman from Syria. Less remembered is the fact that in 1984 Jackson obtained freedom for forty-eight Cuban-American prisoners held in Cuban jails. During these negotiations, he even persuaded Fidel Castro to attend church for the first time in decades. This improved church-state relations in Cuba remarkably. Jackson consistently offered peace and justice plans for troubled nations in Central America, Southern Africa, and the Middle East.

Jackson maintained throughout his campaign that he was a public servant doing his best against great odds. He asked the public to be patient with him as he developed and served. He stated, "God is not finished with me yet." The American people were not finished with him either. His campaigns for human rights continued and had already illustrated the progress, as well as the lengths still to go, in attaining human rights for all Americans.

Bibliography

Barker, Lucius, and Ronald Walters, eds. *Jesse Jackson's 1984 Presidential Campaign.* Urbana: University of Illinois Press, 1989. An excellent collection of scholarly essays that analyze Jackson's contest, his constituents, the voters, the convention, and Jackson's impact on American politics.

Chaplik, Dorothy. *Up with Hope: A Biography of Jesse Jackson*. Minneapolis, Minn.: Dillon Press, 1986. Provides young children with the story of Jesse Jackson's life up to the 1984 presidential campaign. Also contains a short history of the Civil Rights movement and other famous black leaders.

Colton, Elizabeth. *The Jackson Phenomenon*. New York: Doubleday, 1989. Jackson's former press secretary provides an insider's version of Jackson's campaign for the U.S. presidency. One of the author's ancestors was Andrew Jackson's law partner and campaign manager and among the largest slave holders in the South.

Faw, Bob, and Nancy Skelton. *Thunder in America*. Austin: Texas Monthly Press, 1986. A balanced, somewhat critical account of Jesse Jackson's 1984 presidential candidacy, from a journalistic perspective.

Hatch, Roger D. *Beyond Opportunity: Jesse Jackson's Vision for America*. Philadelphia, Pa.: Fortress Press, 1988. Attempts to describe Jackson's vision for a new America where blacks can move beyond mere survival to prosperity and success within a democratic-capitalistic framework. Emphasizes human rights issues and discusses controversies associated with Jackson.

Jackson, Jesse L. *Straight from the Heart*. Philadelphia, Pa.: Fortress Press, 1987. A collection of original speeches delivered by Jesse Jackson. The speeches outline his basic belief that "right is might." Contains his views on race, peace, corporate culture, and human rights.

McKissack, Pat. *Jesse Jackson: A Biography*. New York: Scholastic, 1989. A biography which presents Jackson as an irrepressible idealist who refused to let assassination threats stop him. A story of courage and bravery for youth.

Reynolds, Barbara A. *Jesse Jackson: The Man, the Movement, the Myth*. Chicago: Nelson-Hall, 1975. One of the earliest full biographies of Jesse Jackson. It looks at his relationship with Dr. King, Operation Breadbasket's attempt to develop jobs for blacks, and Operation PUSH's efforts to create minority businesses and inspire black children to excel in school.

Wilkinson, Brenda. *Jesse Jackson: Still Fighting for the Dream*. Morristown, N.J.: Silver Burdett Press, 1990. A complete biographical sketch suitable for junior high school students and teenagers. Covers his life and achievements well.

Dallas L. Browne

Cross-References

Truman Orders Desegregation of U.S. Armed Forces (1948), p. 777; *Brown v. Board of Education* Ends Public School Segregation (1954), p. 913; Congress Passes the Civil Rights Act (1964), p. 1251; Congress Passes the Voting Rights Act (1965), p. 1296; Martin Luther King, Jr., Is Assassinated in Memphis (1968), p. 1419; Chisholm Becomes the First Black Woman Elected to Congress (1968), p. 1451; The Supreme Court Rejects Racial Quotas in College Admissions (1973), p. 1697; Wilder Becomes the First Elected Black Governor (1989), p. 2517.

SIKHS IN PUNJAB REVOLT

Categories of event: Revolutions and rebellions; indigenous peoples' rights
Time: 1984 and continuing
Locale: Punjab, India

Growing discontent among some sectors of the Sikh population in India culminated in an armed insurrection in Punjab that was put down by the Indian army but led to continued violence

Principal personages:

INDIRA GANDHI (1917-1984), the prime minister of India at the time of the 1984 uprising, later assassinated by Sikh bodyguards

JARNAIL SINGH BHINDRANWALE (1947-1984), a Sikh leader of the Golden Temple insurrection of 1984

RAJIV GANDHI (1944-1991), the prime minister who succeeded Indira Gandhi and reached some accords with Sikh rebels, assassinated in 1991

HARCHAND SINGH LONGOWAL (1932-1985), the president of the Akali Dal at the time of the 1984 uprising

JAGMAL SINGH CHAUHAN (1927-), the creator of the idea of Khalistan; self-declared president of Khalistan in exile

Summary of Event

The Sikhs are a religious group that composed approximately 2 percent of the total population of India as of 1991. The majority of the Sikhs live in the province of Punjab, but followers of the Sikh faith are also scattered across northern India and in several other nations, such as the United States, the United Kingdom, and Canada. Since virtually all Sikhs are linguistically and culturally Punjabi, the identity of the Sikhs as a religious group has become intertwined with a sense of separate social identity as well.

Sikhism originated in the fifteenth century A.D., when its founder, Guru Nānak, gathered a group of disciples (*sikhs*) who rejected the ritualism and caste hierarchy of Hinduism in favor of social equality and a mystical devotion to a single deity. A succession of ten gurus led the Sikh community (the *panth*), which quickly acquired converts from various sectors of society, particularly from among the Hindu lower castes. Repression by both Hindu and Muslim governments led the Sikhs to develop a firmly militant identity, symbolized by the sword which all carried and the highly visible turban which proclaimed the Sikh faith. A secret brotherhood, the *khalsa* or "pure," led the Sikh community in this militancy.

Sikhs, Muslims, and Hindus in fact coexisted peacefully in many villages and locales in India even at the height of government repressions and communal tensions. The British colonization of India, however, drove a new wedge between the

Sikhs and other Indians in that the British recognized the martial valor of the Sikhs and enlisted them in large numbers into the armed services, in which they are still represented in disproportionate numbers. As the indigenous movement against colonialism progressed, Sikhs were also alienated from the Hindu majority by the latter's usage of specifically Hindu rhetoric in framing the anticolonial struggle. The common Hindu claim that the Sikhs were but a caste or sect of Hinduism particularly offended many in the Sikh community, which explicitly stated social equality and independence as axioms. Sikh identity eventually coalesced around a movement called the Akali Dal, "the army of the faithful," which became the major political mouthpiece of the Sikhs and became a key political party in the region by the end of the twentieth century.

After India gained independence in 1947, Punjab was divided between Pakistan and India, with virtually all the Sikhs ending up on the Indian side. They shared Indian Punjab with Hindus, who were a majority in that state. In the 1950's, a movement began to divide the state of Punjab again, this time along linguistic lines, with Punjabi and Hindi speakers to have their own territories. This was a recognized principle in the Indian constitution. The new state of Punjabi-speaking Punjab, established in 1966, had a Sikh majority.

The idea that the Sikhs of Punjab should form an entirely separate and independent nation had been around since the time of partition, when the creation of the sovereign Muslim state of Pakistan provided an immediate example. Jagmal Singh Chauhan proposed a Sikh nation called *Khalistan*, which he formally declared in 1980, establishing himself as president-in-exile. Although the notion of a sovereign Sikh nation aroused the support of only a minority of Indian Sikhs, it had a romantic appeal for many overseas and served as a rallying cry for political agitation in the 1980's. Combined with separatist movements in the far northern, eastern, and far southern areas of India, the plea for Khalistan helped create a mood of fear that the Indian state might risk disintegration.

The discontent of the Sikhs focused on several areas. Religious questions, such as control over the *gurdwaras* (Sikh temples) and independence from Hinduism, were key for some groups, while issues of resource allocation, such as the distribution of river waters between Punjab and Haryana, were more important for others. Incidents such as the Asian Games episode of 1982, in which Sikhs were humiliated by not being allowed into New Delhi during the event (to forestall possible violence), were highly publicized by Sikh leaders. Crucial for the grass-roots momentum of the Sikh movement was the fact that the state of Punjab had been undergoing rapid modernization, which created a class of highly educated individuals and transformed the countryside within a generation. Punjab became one of the wealthiest regions of the nation. One source of malaise was the continuing sentiment that the central government, while relying on Punjab's flourishing economy, neglected the people of this state in favor of the mostly Hindu electorate of the central plains.

One man who was able to tap the frustration of many Punjabi Sikhs was Sant Jarnail Singh Bhindranwale. (*Sant* is a respect term connoting a holy person.) Bhindranwale, an uneducated individual of agricultural origins, acquired a substantial following among some elements of the Sikh population which was enhanced by his involvement in a series of violent actions against Hindus. Sikh youths killed in retaliatory incidents were celebrated as martyrs, and frustration with the methods of civil disobedience that had been tried before gave way to enthusiasm for violent uprising among some sectors of the population. It should be noted that the great majority of Sikhs condemned these violent actions but supported the overall goals of the movement.

Demonstrations in the early months of 1984, centering on incidents such as the public burning of the Indian constitution and the attempt to block all roads in Punjab, led to the imposition of President's Rule in Punjab and the banning of the All-India Sikh Students Federation, which had been accused of involvement in several incidents. In May, Sant Harchand Singh Longowal, president of the Akali Dal, called for the blockade of grain from Punjab as a means of bringing the central government to its knees. Thousands of police were deployed in Punjab, and terrorist episodes increased dramatically.

Bhindranwale had meanwhile gathered a group of armed Sikh militants in the Golden Temple of Amritsar, the holiest shrine of the Sikhs. He issued a list of demands to the central government from this stronghold. Prime Minister Indira Gandhi imposed a curfew on the entire state, prohibiting all traffic and putting restraints on journalism. In a move called Operation Bluestar, she ordered the Indian Army to take the Golden Temple complex from the Sikh insurgents. Four days of fighting (June 3-7, 1984) left five hundred to more than one thousand dead, including Bhindranwale. The government cites the lower figure, while Sikh sources claim the higher number of casualties.

The fact that the Indian Army would invade the sacred Golden Temple complex turned many Sikhs across Punjab and north India more firmly against the central government. On October 31, 1984, Prime Minister Indira Gandhi was assassinated by two of her Sikh bodyguards. Sikh-Hindu rioting broke out in most major Indian cities. Thousands were killed, wounded, or rendered homeless. Accusations of government complicity in anti-Sikh actions further inflamed Sikh alienation and militancy, as did the election campaign of Rajiv Gandhi, which many felt purposely played on anti-Sikh sentiment.

Rajiv Gandhi was elected prime minister in a landslide victory, reaching limited accords with Sikh rebels. Violent incidents between Sikhs and Hindus continued, however, and Sikh separatism remained a potent force in Indian politics as late as 1991. In 1988, a second major confrontation took place at the Golden Temple of Amritsar.

Impact of Event

The immediate human rights impact of the Sikh uprising of 1984 was the large number of Sikhs killed. In addition to at least five hundred killed during the Golden Temple confrontation itself, several thousand more died in Hindu-Sikh rioting after the assassination of Indira Gandhi and up to fifty thousand more fled their homes.

A second area in which the Sikh movement affected human rights related to the crackdown of the central government deemed necessary to forestall further separatist action by the Sikhs or by other groups (for example, the Kashmiris). The imposition of President's Rule in Punjab and elsewhere, the restrictions on the press imposed during peak moments of the crisis, and increasing numbers of arrests and of imprisonments without trial all contributed to a sense of crisis with regard to India's vaunted democracy. Especially problematic was government's unwillingness to investigate accusations related to human rights abuses. Citizens' groups, such as the People's Union for Civil Liberties and Citizens for Democracy, carefully monitored these developments along with several international agencies.

Perhaps the most difficult problem for the future was the increasing Hindu solidarity prompted by this and other agitations on the part of geographically, ethnically, or religiously peripheral groups. This revitalized solidarity was expressed not only in political terms through the continuing rise of the major Hindu party, the Bharatiya Janata Party, but also in populist movements such as that which began attempts in the early 1990's to build a Hindu temple on the site of a Muslim mosque at Ajodhya. This reaction, while understandable as an attempt to reintegrate a nation whose cohesion appeared threatened, will have the long-term effect of further polarizing groups who feel excluded from or subordinated to the Hindu nationalist identity. The Indian Army's incursion into the Golden Temple precinct in 1984, however necessary from a governmental standpoint, carried indelible symbolic value for those who had previously relied on India's claim to protect all religions equally.

At issue are not only human lives and rights, then, but the continued existence of democratic, multiethnic, secular India. This state has had some success in protecting human lives and rights in the past, certainly by most Third World standards. Whether it will be able to continue to do so in the future is a matter of some concern. The brutal assassination of Rajiv Gandhi in 1991 led many Indians to a rethinking of all of these issues.

Bibliography

Fox, Robin. *Lions of the Punjab: Culture in the Making.* Berkeley: University of California Press, 1985. An anthropological view of the formation of modern Sikh identity from colonial times to the present. Heavily theoretical; most useful for readers with some background in modern social sciences debates.

Gupte, Pranay. *Vengeance: India After the Assassination of Indira Gandhi.* New York: W. W. Norton, 1985. This book by an experienced journalist covers reactions to Indira Gandhi's assassination, the backlash against the Sikhs, and Rajiv Gandhi's rise to power. Most useful for its region-by-region coverage and its revealing anecdotes that express the strains and tensions in contemporary India.

Jeffrey, Robin. *What's Happening to India? Punjab, Ethnic Conflict, Mrs. Gandhi's Death, and the Test for Federalism.* London: Macmillan Press, 1986. This excellent survey of the events leading up to the Golden Temple incident and Indira

Gandhi's assassination focuses on the roles of media and modernization. Concludes with a discussion of Indian federalism as a way of coping with regional discontent.

Kapur, Rajiv. *Sikh Separatism: The Politics of Faith*. Boston: Allen & Unwin, 1986. Traces the evolution of Sikh identity, its shift to a militant stance, and its role in the communal troubles of the early 1980's. Straightforward narrative makes this an appropriate volume for the general reader.

McLeod, W. H. *The Sikhs: History, Religion, and Society*. New York: Columbia University Press, 1989. A useful and learned introduction to the world of the Sikhs, including chapters on doctrine, history, literature, and politics. Appropriate for the general reader.

Cynthia Keppley Mahmood

Cross-References

Canada Invokes the War Measures Act Against Separatists in Quebec (1970), p. 1543; The Emergency Provisions (Northern Ireland) Act Is Passed (1973), p. 1720; Tamil Separatist Violence Erupts in Sri Lanka (1980's), p. 2068; Basques Are Granted Home Rule but Continue to Fight for Independence (1980), p. 2079; Indira Gandhi Is Assassinated (1984), p. 2232; Muslims Riot Against Russians in Kazakhstan (1986), p. 2298; The Palestinian *Intifada* Begins (1987), p. 2331; Ethnic Riots Erupt in Armenia (1988), p. 2348; Ethnic Unrest Breaks Out in Yugoslavian Provinces (1988), p. 2386; Kashmir Separatists Demand an End to Indian Rule (1989), p. 2426; Lithuania Declares Its Independence from the Soviet Union (1990), p. 2577.

NEW YORK STATE IMPOSES THE FIRST
MANDATORY SEAT-BELT LAW

Category of event: Health and medical rights
Time: July 12, 1984
Locale: Albany, New York

In 1984, New York became the first state to require the use of automobile safety belts through a law mandating them for children under age ten and for all front-seat occupants

Principal personages:
MARIO CUOMO (1932-   ), the governor of New York
ELIZABETH DOLE (1936-   ), the United States secretary of transportation
VINCENT J. GRABER (1931-   ), a New York assemblyman and chair of the Assembly Transportation Committee
NORMAN J. LEVY (1931-   ), a state senator of New York and chair of the Senate Transportation Committee
JOHN A. PASSIDOMO (1920-   ), the New York commissioner of motor vehicles and a strong proponent of seat-belt use

Summary of Event

During the economic boom years following World War II, the automobile secured its place in American culture. By the late 1940's, an estimated eighty-five million vehicles thronged the American highways, and as the suburbs spread, the automobile became the dominant mode of transportation. The population shift to the suburbs that marked the decades following World War II increased reliance upon individual modes of transportation. Efforts at improving highway safety, widely accepted as desirable and necessary, focused on three major areas: highways, automobile design and manufacture, and driver skill and competence. Along with the increase in miles driven came the establishment of the interstate highway system, providing safer roads and easier travel. Also, standardized road markings and traffic signals and signs made streets and highways safer.

As improvements in the roads brought safer travel, improvements in the design and equipment of automobiles themselves increased their safety. Standard hydraulic brakes, improved headlights, shatter-resistant glass, turn signals, and more reliable suspension systems improved cars' performance in accidents. A further safety factor involving drivers resulted from a demographic coincidence. Low birth rates during the Depression meant that relatively few young and inexperienced drivers would begin their driving during the 1950's. Along with these changes came increased weight, power, and speed of automobiles, permitting more devastating crashes when automobiles collided.

Road safety during the time may be illustrated by the occurrence of deaths per 100 million miles driven. During 1933, when thirty-four thousand people died on the nation's highways, the death rate was eighteen per 100 million miles. By 1956, the figure had been cut to under six, a 66 percent reduction. The great increase in the number of miles driven, however, meant that the annual fatalities nationwide had increased to more than thirty-six thousand. By the 1960's, when the baby boomers began driving, the number of highway deaths annually was to climb to more than fifty thousand.

It is not surprising that seat belts should have received serious attention as a safety device. Relatively cheap, they had been used for many years to reduce injuries and deaths during airplane crashes and were routinely used by racing drivers for the same reason. They effectively prevented bodies from exiting a vehicle during a crash and also prevented injuries from passengers hurtling around inside a vehicle. In 1956, Ford Motor Company introduced safety belts as standard equipment on mainline models. Although the cost of the addition was minimal, the additional safety they provided did not improve sales. Of drivers who purchased vehicles with seat belts, fewer than 20 percent actually wore them. Still, their potential for saving lives and reducing injuries, and consequently reducing liability expenses, became widely recognized.

State legislatures and executive branches, concerned with the economic burdens imposed on state budgets by accidents, began passing laws requiring safety belts in state-owned vehicles. New York, under the administrations of governors W. Averell Harriman and Nelson Rockefeller, led the way in adopting these measures. In 1961, a New York law required all automobiles sold in the state to be equipped with anchors for safety belts. By 1967, all models manufactured in the United States were required to have safety belts as standard equipment.

Laws requiring that children be belted in were widely adopted by states during the early 1980's. New York's law required children under age six to be secured by seat belts. Penalties were minimal, however, and the laws were often unenforced. Studies on public compliance produced discouragingly low figures. Seeking to lower liability costs, insurance companies sponsored advertising campaigns encouraging the use of belts, but with minimal results. According to National Safety Council estimates, only 10 to 15 percent of passengers regularly wore seat belts.

By 1984, Western European nations and Canada had adopted laws requiring seat-belt use by drivers and passengers, and while compliance was uncertain and varied, estimates for compliance ranged as high as 85 percent in Sweden and 90 percent in England. In Ontario, the compliance rate increased to 59 percent shortly after the law was enacted. A comprehensive study of the law in Great Britain detailed a 25 percent reduction in traffic deaths during the first year following its enactment. The only measure in the United States that had approached these results was the 1972 law lowering the legal speed to fifty-five miles per hour. Within a year, it had reduced automobile fatalities by more than 20 percent. The results of foreign experience with seat-belt laws suggested that a law would increase the number of wearers and therefore save lives and costs.

In the United States, New York, Illinois, and Michigan were seriously considering instituting a similar requirement, but New York took the lead. The picture was clouded somewhat by the federal Transportation Agency, which issued a ruling that by 1989 all automobiles manufactured in the United States had to be equipped with passive restraint systems, either automatic seat belts or airbags. An exception would be made if a large majority of the states passed laws requiring the use of seat belts. Proponents of the laws feared that their passage might save lives but at the same time discourage better safety technology.

More serious opposition came from the familiar libertarian view that government had no business regulating a matter of personal choice. Gradually, the consensus view that public interest in keeping down medical costs, in saving insurance dollars, in protecting citizens from preventable death and maiming injuries, and in reducing the social costs of welfare and social security to survivors prevailed. Proponents were able to point out that billions of dollars and a large number of lives would be saved by a relatively inexpensive measure. In this instance, education had done much of the work, and the law encouraged people to do what they already knew they should.

By June 5, 1984, two key New York legislators announced agreement in principle on a mandatory seat-belt law. This agreement followed by one week the defeat of a bill favored by Governor Mario Cuomo that would have raised the state's legal drinking age from nineteen to twenty-one. Although this measure seemed to the governor the most effective way of reducing highway deaths, he quickly supported the seat-belt law as a wise step. State Senator Norman J. Levy, chair of the Senate Transportation Committee, and Assemblyman Vincent J. Graber, chair of the Assembly Transportation Committee, announced that they were close to an agreement on reconciling their respective legislative proposals and expressed their determination to enact the first legislation of its kind in the nation. The Assembly's version provided for stronger penalties and required that all passengers be belted. Senator Levy, whose bill was less rigorous, estimated that the law could prevent many serious injuries and save 350 to 400 lives each year if 50 percent of New Yorkers complied. Automobile manufacturers favored such measures, because of their apprehension over costly new mandates from the federal government. On June 7, *The New York Times* published an editorial supportive of the law, stressing the possible economic benefits and rejecting libertarian opposition.

On June 19, the two legislators announced their agreement on specific measures in the law. The bill required drivers, front-seat passengers, and all passengers under age ten to wear seat belts. Violations were punishable by a fine of fifty dollars. The bill was to go into effect on December 1, 1984, but violators were allowed a month's grace period before fines were to be imposed. People with medical conditions that made the use of safety belts dangerous or inconvenient were to be treated as exceptions. Other exceptions included drivers and passengers of limousines and taxicabs and passengers in all vehicles weighing more than eighteen thousand pounds. In addition, automobiles manufactured before 1966 were exempted from the law.

Governor Mario Cuomo signed the bill into law on July 12, stressing its possible benefits. Senator Levy predicted that it would save four hundred lives and seventy thousand injuries annually if everyone complied. Governor Cuomo estimated that the law would lower medical costs and property losses associated with accidents by $240 million annually. Both criticized the transportation secretary's ruling that linked seat-belt laws to requirements for passive restraints like airbags and took the position that airbags or other passive restraints should be federally mandated regardless of the states' position on seat belts.

Impact of Event

The New York law requiring the use of seat belts had diverse and far-reaching effects, some of them unanticipated and most of them difficult to measure. Other states quickly followed New York's lead; New Jersey and Illinois became the second and third states to enact seat-belt laws. Before two years had passed, more than twenty-five states had adopted mandatory seat-belt laws. Acceptance was not without some retrogression. Faced with organized opposition, Nevada and Massachusetts repealed their laws before the end of 1986.

Following the law's passage, safety-belt use in New York increased dramatically. During December, 1984, before penalties were in effect, usage increased from below 20 percent to 40 percent. January compliance reached 67 percent, but this figure gradually diminished throughout the year, declining to approximately 50 percent at the end of 1985. Public officials responded with educational campaigns aimed at improving compliance. In areas where educational campaigns were combined with vigorous enforcement, compliance reached very high levels. In Elmira, for example, the compliance rate in late 1985 stood at 80 percent.

Although the saving of lives did not reach the most optimistic projections, it appeared that during the first year hundreds of lives were saved and thousands of serious injuries were prevented. During December, 1984, highway deaths statewide were 84, compared with 104 during December, 1983. During the first three months of 1985, traffic fatalities statewide decreased 27 percent (to 184 from 252 during the previous year's first quarter). Thus, the law's effects in bringing about greater highway safety were similar to those found elsewhere—as in Great Britain, for example, where the law reduced traffic fatalities by 25 percent. Fears that the use of safety belts in accidents involving fire, explosions, and submersion of vehicles might decrease chances of survival proved to be groundless.

In general, the law did not have the expected effect of preventing adoption of other measures designed to improve automobile safety. Governor Cuomo's proposal to raise the legal drinking age from nineteen to twenty-one was enacted into law in 1985. Federal mandates for passive restraint systems, previously delayed, were not delayed further as had been feared. The safety-belt law seemed if anything to intensify the efforts of insurers and consumer groups on behalf of airbags, which, combined with safety belts, provided a much greater margin of safety, particularly to drivers. Among American manufacturers, Chrysler Corporation pioneered by providing driver's-side airbags as standard equipment on all of its models. In the New York Assembly, serious consideration was given to a measure extending the law to school buses, but this was deemed impractical.

On the other hand, some unexpected results were explored and studied. Statistics on use of seat belts by back-seat passengers, not required by the law, revealed disturbing trends. Belts alone did not appear to improve chances of survival among rear-seat passengers, and, indeed, some studies showed higher death rates among those who were wearing safety belts. A study in England suggested that as drivers began to use seat belts they became complacent about their own safety and endangered the lives of pedestrians and cyclists. A subsequent study in Nova Scotia reached conclusions that refuted those of the British study. In the legal area, defense attorneys for insurance companies and drivers began seeking lower compensation for victims of accidents who were not wearing safety belts at the time of their crashes. As safety belts lowered the death rate, particularly among young adults, the point was made in the popular press that they had contributed to the shortage of organs for transplant operations.

On balance, the use of safety belts mandated by law reduced both deaths and serious injuries. It should be noted, however, that the laws were adopted during a period of decreasing rates of traffic fatalities. During the period 1980-1983, U.S. traffic fatalities decreased 17 percent, while mileage driven increased 8 percent. Nationwide, 56,300 people died in highway accidents in 1980, compared to 42,600 in 1983. The 1966 death rate of 5.72 per 100 million miles dropped to 2.47 by 1985. Because of seat-belt laws and other safety measures affecting automobiles and drivers, the death rate continued to decline throughout the late 1980's. During the period when seat-belt laws were being adopted, some of the lives saved were probably the result of more rigorous attempts to suppress drunk driving and to other safety improvements in automobile design.

Bibliography

Evans, Leonard. *The Effectiveness of Safety Belts in Preventing Fatalities.* Warren, Mich.: General Motors Research Laboratories, 1985. Pioneer study in the ways safety belts work. Evans gives statistical results of numerous kinds of automobile crashes and provides careful statistical analysis. Data and conclusions strongly support the use of seat belts.

Evans, Leonard, and Richard C. Schwing. *Human Behavior and Traffic Safety.* New York: Plenum Press, 1985. A collection of papers presented at a General Motors-sponsored symposium on traffic safety. Among the numerous studies are two carefully documented articles on seat-belt use in England and Newfoundland. Overall, the articles center on the driver's role in safety rather than on automobile design.

Highway Safety Literature. Transportation Research Board, National Research Council. 1973-   . An annual publication that includes abstracts, articles, papers, and reports relating to traffic safety. Numerous abstracts relating to seat-belt studies appear in the 1985-1986 volumes. Indexed.

Insurance Institute for Highway Safety: Status Report. A periodical published by The Insurance Institute of Washington, D.C., that features short articles advocating the use of seat belts and proposing numerous other safety measures. Strongly pro-safety, it is critical of manufacturers for delaying safety measures relating to manufacture of automobiles. Contains several favorable articles on the New York law.

The New York Times. 1984-1986. Remains the most valuable and accessible source of information on the New York seat-belt law. For the three years 1984-1986, it published more than a hundred news stories, articles, and editorials on the subject. Strongly prosafety, the newspaper gave front-page coverage to stories relating to the law and lent editorial support at critical times.

Stanley Archer

Cross-References

The Pure Food and Drug Act and Meat Inspection Act Become Law (1906), p. 64; Nader Publishes *Unsafe at Any Speed* (1965), p. 1267; The Motor Vehicle Air Pollution Control Act Is Passed by Congress (1965), p. 1310; Manville Offers $2.5 Billion to Victims of Asbestos Dust (1985), p. 2274; A. H. Robins Must Compensate Women Injured by the Dalkon Shield (1987), p. 2342; A Jury Awards Monetary Damages to the Estate of a Smoker (1988), p. 2381.

AN APA REPORT DISCUSSES
THE HOMELESS MENTALLY ILL

Category of event: Homeless people's rights
Time: October, 1984
Locale: Washington, D.C.

The American Psychiatric Association (APA) released a comprehensive report that described possible causes for and solutions to the problem of the growing number of homeless mentally ill

Principal personages:
KENNETH DONALDSON, a former mental patient who was the plaintiff in the Supreme Court case *Donaldson v. O'Connor*
RUBY ROGERS, a former mental patient who was the plaintiff in the Supreme Court case *Rogers v. Okin*
BRUCE ENNIS, the staff attorney for the New York Civil Liberties Union who was instrumental in changing the commitment laws for the mentally ill during the 1970's
JOYCE BROWN (1947-   ), a homeless mentally ill woman in New York who challenged the commitment laws and won her right to remain on the streets in 1987
H. RICHARD LAMB (1929-   ), the chairperson of the American Psychiatric Association Task Force on the homeless mentally ill

Summary of Event

In colonial America, the homeless mentally ill were often transported from one village to another, in the hope that someone might care for them in another town. By the nineteenth century, this practice had given way to housing the mentally ill in large hospitals or asylums. Although these places were originally designed to provide treatment for the mentally ill, after a while the asylums became more like warehouses, in which the mentally ill simply existed. Conditions in these hospitals did not improve over time. In the 1970's, these same hospitals began to discharge their patients, some of them to the streets of America rather than to proper homes.

Deinstitutionalization of the nation's mental hospitals was a complex process with various causes. Conditions within the hospitals were deplorable, but this fact became widely publicized only after World War II. In 1955, antipsychotic drugs were administered to patients for the first time. These produced dramatic and what were thought of at the time as beneficial effects. With the help of these drugs, it was thought that those on the "back wards" might be able to function outside the hospital. In the early 1960's, several books were published which questioned the very concept of mental illness. In *The Divided Self: A Study of Sanity and Madness* (1960),

Ronald Laing wrote that schizophrenics had devised an intelligible way to confront an impossible living situation in their so-called craziness. Laing wrote that since this craziness was perfectly understandable, the psychosis of schizophrenia might even be a higher form of sanity than sanity itself. In *The Myth of Mental Illness: Foundations of a Theory of Personal Conduct* (1961), Thomas Szasz declared that people who had been labeled as mentally ill merely had problems with living. Sociologist Erving Goffman suggested in *Asylums: Essays on the Social Situation of Mental Patients and Other Inmates* (1961) that many of the symptoms which plagued the mentally ill, such as apathy, were the result of being kept within the hospital.

These books had particular influence on the mental health bar, which came into existence during the 1970's. Bruce Ennis led the group of lawyers who systematically brought suits throughout the United States to establish the rights of the mentally ill. In *Donaldson v. O'Connor*, the Supreme Court decided that a mentally ill patient had the right to treatment. In *Rogers v. Okin*, the Court granted patients the right to refuse treatment. One of the results of these cases was that in order to avoid liability in either of these instances, doctors found it easier to let patients leave the hospital than to attempt to get them to submit to proper treatment. When these patients were released from the hospitals, the mental health bar and particularly Bruce Ennis worked hard to change involuntary commitment laws, which might force former patients to return to institutions. Ennis succeeded in getting states to narrow the standards by which a mentally ill person could be committed involuntarily. The standard throughout the United States became that a person could be committed to a mental hospital against his or her will only if he or she posed a danger to himself or herself or to others. As a result of these new laws, many mentally ill people who formerly were committable were left to their own devices, which in some cases meant living on the streets.

A final reason for the deinstitutionalization of the nation's mental hospitals was the assumption by the federal government of some of the financial costs involved in hospitalization. In 1963, Congress passed the Community Mental Health Centers Construction Act with the intention that these new centers would take over the treatment and care of the patients being discharged from hospitals. In addition, those discharged became entitled for the first time to Social Security disability benefits. These funds would enable them to live in the community after leaving the hospital. This was the hope behind deinstitutionalization; the reality was quite different.

Many discharged patients went to live with their families. When this arrangement proved unworkable for some of the mentally ill, they found their way to single room occupancy hotels. When many of these were demolished in the early 1980's in the wake of urban renewal, many of the former patients turned to the streets. At this point, the government cut back on the benefits to which they had been entitled. Most problematic and troubling of all was the fact that during this period, this group, made up mostly of the chronically mentally ill, found little care offered at the community mental health centers. Those who worked in the centers did not want to deal with this population, whom they found too chronic, too resistant, and simply too difficult. Thus, "bag ladies" and disheveled men yelling at voices only they could hear began to appear more frequently in the streets.

It was in this context that the American Psychiatric Association (APA) formed a task force on the homeless mentally ill in the early 1980's. Dr. H. Richard Lamb, professor of psychiatry at the University of Southern California School of Medicine, led the group of nine members. Thirty professionals, including doctors, nurses, social workers, and one lawyer, contributed to the task force's final report. The report, published in October, 1984, detailed many aspects of the problems of the homeless mentally ill.

Most of the contributors attributed the increase in the population of homeless mentally ill to deinstitutionalization. The population of mental hospitals had gone from 559,000 in 1955 to 150,000 in 1980. Given the mobility of the homeless population, the task force found it hard to determine how many homeless people had been patients in these hospitals and how many were currently mentally ill. The task force's studies, which have been subject to some criticism, concluded that roughly 40 percent of the homeless were mentally ill. Figures concerning the size of the group ranged from 250,000 to more than a million.

The contributors to the task force report did not generally question the premises underlying deinstitutionalization. They said that the problem with the movement was the way in which it was implemented. They found that the community mental health centers had not planned effectively for the care of former mental patients. Lamb went even further by suggesting that the homeless mentally ill were in that situation because of their mental illness. He claimed that the chronically mentally ill who composed this group tended to form hostile dependent relationships with others. They feared the subsequent intimacy, needed to deny that dependence, and thus had a tendency to drift. This theory explained why living with families, as the discharged mentally ill originally did, or even attempting to seek any kind of treatment, if available, was fraught with difficulties. Lamb encouraged mental health professionals to begin to accept these dependency needs when dealing with this group.

Most members of the task force, when they spoke of any change in the involuntary commitment laws, spoke of these changes in terms of creating some kind of laws for commitment not to hospitals but to community care. The task force noted that twenty states had such laws at the time of their writing in 1984. Many believed that the general narrow standard of dangerousness by which a person could be involuntarily committed was inhumane, in that a person could be so psychotic that he or she could not properly meet basic needs or know whether he or she was in need of treatment.

The task force urged that many different groups assume more responsibility for the care of the homeless mentally ill. It urged that the mental health profession, particularly those in the community mental health centers, attend to the needs of this group more sensitively and carefully than it had done before. It urged lawyers to help in the enactment of more humane commitment laws. Finally, it urged the federal government to provide more funding for the homeless mentally ill.

Impact of Event
It is difficult to pinpoint a direct impact of the task force's report on the homeless mentally ill. Few observers since the report refer to it in their writing. Estimates indicate that the population of the homeless mentally ill has grown, rather than diminished, since the report. Nevertheless, there have been significant events regarding the homeless mentally ill since the task force's report appeared.

In 1987, Congress made an effort to assume its responsibilities to this group by passing the Stewart B. McKinney Homeless Assistance Act. This act provided for a broader range of housing, health care, multiservice centers, employment programs, and self-help groups than previously. The act required the mental health profession to assume more of a role than it previously had played. In some areas, such as St. Louis, Missouri, such attempts have been successful.

Problems remained concerning involuntary commitment laws. By 1991, only Kansas had broadened its laws beyond the standard of dangerousness. In 1985, Edward Koch, then mayor of New York City, began to send out police to round up the homeless mentally ill during the winter. Mayor Koch granted the police emergency powers to commit those rounded up to mental hospitals, from which they eventually would be released to community care. In 1987, Joyce Brown successfully challenged this law. Hospitalized and diagnosed as a paranoid schizophrenic in 1984, this young black woman had taken up residence on the streets of New York by 1986. In 1987, several citizens called the authorities and complained that she was shouting obscene epithets at men and urinating and defecating on the sidewalks. Police picked her up and committed her to Bellevue Hospital. She won her release later in court and then proceeded to speak on several talk shows and at Harvard on her right to remain free in the community, if not on the streets. She was found again, yelling more insults to men, a year later.

Some people argued that the solution to the problem of the homeless mentally ill was to change the commitment laws and rehospitalize this group. Others objected to the involuntary incarceration of the blameless. Many of the homeless mentally ill themselves indicated strongly that they preferred to live, if not to die, on the streets rather than return to a hospital.

In many ways, the problems of caring for the homeless mentally ill remained as intractable as they were when the task force issued its report. The major problem remained finding someone to assume responsibility for them. Mental health professionals as a group disliked dealing with the chronically mentally ill, who for the most part made up this population. Some lawyers tried to change the commitment laws, mainly at the behest of families of the mentally ill. Others brought right-to-shelter cases, which achieved neither positive results nor favor with the public. The public would just as soon ignore these living reminders of the nation's poverty and pain. That left the government, which faced its own fiscal problems, and instead of creating new programs cut back on those already in place. Estimates of the homeless mentally ill centered on one million in 1990. Unless solutions to their problems are found, it is conceivable that American society will revert back to the practice of colonial America, transporting these people who are largely incapable of caring for themselves from one city to the next in the hope that someone else will be responsible, and someone else will care.

Bibliography

Cohen, Neal L., ed. *Psychiatry Takes to the Streets: Outreach and Crisis Intervention for the Mentally Ill.* New York: Guilford Press, 1990. A collection of interesting and well-written essays. Valuable insights on deinstitutionalization. Not all of the essays deal with the homeless mentally ill. No mention of the APA task force.

Goffman, Erving. *Asylums: Essays on the Social Situation of Mental Patients and Other Inmates.* Garden City, N.Y.: Anchor Books, 1961. A collection of essays describing the phenomenon of institutionalization, whereby a mental patient acquires symptoms not because of illness but because of being incarcerated in what the author defines as a total institution. The book encouraged the move toward deinstitutionalization.

Isaac, Rael Jean, and Virginia C. Armat. *Madness in the Streets: How Psychiatry and the Law Abandoned the Mentally Ill.* New York: Free Press, 1990. A forceful and thorough account of how the mentally ill became homeless. Offers a clear indictment of the role psychiatry and the law played in this crisis. The authors say that any civil rights the mentally ill may enjoy merely disguise their neglect. The authors support redesign of commitment laws. No mention of the APA task force.

Johnson, Ann Braden. *Out of Bedlam: The Truth About Deinstitutionalization.* New York: Basic Books, 1990. An impassioned account describing the homeless mentally ill by a social worker who works with them. Highly critical of the mental health profession, which has refused to care for this group, and the mental health bureaucracy, which is too far removed from its clients. Contains a history of deinstitutionalization similar to the account of Isaac and Armat. No mention of the APA task force.

Laing, Ronald D. *The Divided Self: A Study of Sanity and Madness.* London: Tavistock Publications, 1960. Laing is a British psychologist who suggests here that those who have been proclaimed "mad" have created an understandable and intelligible world in reaction to a mad existence. There is then a real sanity in alleged madness, which gives rise to the question whether mental illness or insanity really exists.

Lamb, H. Richard, ed. *The Homeless Mentally Ill: A Task Force Report of the American Psychiatric Association.* Washington, D.C.: American Psychiatric Association, 1984. Comprehensive collection of essays addressing the problem of the homeless mentally ill. Much discussion about the failures of deinstitutionalization as implemented and how this group needs care in community settings. Although the report makes many recommendations, it makes few practical suggestions.

Ropers, Richard H. *The Invisible Homeless: A New Urban Ecology.* New York: Insight Books, 1988. A well-written and thoughtful book using economic, social, and political theories to explain the homeless mentally ill. Mentions the task force and is critical of some of its conclusions. Deals mainly with the problem in Los Angeles, California, but refers to other parts of the country. A balanced account which challenges those with more psychological explanations.

Szasz, Thomas S. *The Myth of Mental Illness: Foundations of a Theory of Personal Conduct.* New York: Hoeber-Harper, 1961. The author's thesis is that those who have been called mentally ill merely have problems in living; thus, there is no such thing as mental illness. The libertarian views expressed influenced psychiatric and legal professions toward deinstitutionalization.

Jennifer Eastman

Cross-References

The First Food Stamp Program Begins in Rochester, New York (1939), p. 555; The Geneva Convention Establishes Norms of Conduct in Warfare (1949), p. 808; Legislation Ushers in a New Era of Care for the Mentally Disabled (1963), p. 1206; Incarcerated Mental Patients Are Given a Right to Treatment (1971), p. 1622; The United Nations Declares Rights for the Mentally Retarded (1971), p. 1644; Congress Responds to Demands of Persons with Disabilities (1973), p. 1731; The Declaration of Tokyo Forbids Medical Abuses and Torture (1975), p. 1829; The United Nations Issues a Declaration Against Torture (1975), p. 1847; The United Nations Responds to Problems of the Homeless (1982), p. 2174; The Stewart B. McKinney Homeless Assistance Act Becomes Law (1987), p. 2326.

INDIRA GANDHI IS ASSASSINATED

Categories of event: Indigenous peoples' rights and political freedom
Time: October 31, 1984
Locale: New Delhi, India

Revenge was the immediate motive for the two men who shot and killed Indian Prime Minister Indira Gandhi, but a complex chain of historical events made the murder almost inevitable

Principal personages:
JARNAIL SINGH BHINDRANWALE (1947-1984), the foremost leader of those Sikhs calling for the establishment of an independent state in the Punjab
INDIRA GANDHI (1917-1984), the daughter of India's first prime minister, Jawaharlal Nehru; was unable to manage the Sikh separatist movement in the Punjab
HARCHAND SINGH LONGOWAL (1932-1985), a leader of the moderate wing of the Akali Dal, the largest Sikh political organization
BEANT SINGH (?-1984), a member of Indira Gandhi's elite personal bodyguard who participated in her assassination and was killed on the spot by her other security officers
SATWANT SINGH (?-1989), a bodyguard of Indira Gandhi who participated in her murder; tried and hanged January 6, 1989

Summary of Event

Indira Gandhi, in effect, signed her own death warrant when she ordered the Indian army to execute "Operation Bluestar" in the first days of June, 1984. Bluestar involved putting the entire state of Punjab under martial law, but, more important, it called for soldiers to invade the precincts of the Golden Temple, the most sacred shrine of the Sikhs located in the Punjabi city of Amritsar.

In January of the same year, a charismatic Sant (a Sikh holy man) named Jarnail Singh Bhindranwale occupied parts of the Golden Temple with more than one hundred of his followers. They began to collect a cache of weapons and vowed that they would not leave the temple until the government of India allowed the Sikhs their own state in the Punjab.

From January until May, Indira Gandhi's administration tried to ignore Jarnail Singh Bhindranwale and his private army. The increasing militancy of this army of extremists expressed itself in a wave of assassinations of more moderate Sikhs and Hindus. Public pressure mounted for some kind of strong action, and the press criticized Indira Gandhi for her seeming weakness. In May, the general staff of the Indian army began to plan a response to the militant takeover of the Golden Temple. They gave it the code name Operation Bluestar.

Bluestar envisioned a surprise attack on the militants in the Golden Temple. The army also expected that its soldiers would require only small arms to achieve their mission. From the start, everything went wrong. The Golden Temple itself was crowded with innocent pilgrims unaware of any danger. As many as one thousand of the visitors were caught in the crossfire. The militants put up stiff resistance, forcing the army to employ tanks and heavy artillery. More than one hundred soldiers and uncounted numbers of pilgrims and militants died in a battle that lasted through June 4 and June 5. The Golden Temple compound itself sustained serious damage. For example, a library containing many early copies of the Sikh holy book, *The Shri Guru Adi Granth Sahib*, was reduced to ashes.

Jarnail Singh Bhindranwale died during the assault. A number of his associates, however, managed to escape during the battle. They formed the core of an expanding army of rebels. These rebels continued to assassinate their opponents within the Sikh community as well as indiscriminately massacre Hindu residents of Punjab or other non-Sikhs who happened to be passing through the area on trains and buses.

Indira Gandhi tried to avoid the practical consequences of the Bluestar disaster. Although her closest advisers told her to transfer the Sikhs in her personal bodyguard, she refused to take any action that would appear to accentuate communal tensions.

At about 9:00 A.M. on the morning of October 31, 1984, Mrs. Gandhi left her residence and began to walk across the walled garden that separated her home from her office. On the way, two of her guards, Beant Singh and Satwant Singh, approached her and opened fire with their automatic weapons. At least sixteen bullets pierced her body. Beant Singh was killed immediately by other members of the security forces. Satwant Singh was later hanged for his role in the assassination.

One needs to understand parts of India's religious background to understand fully Indira Gandhi's assassination. The Sikh religion is rooted in the preaching of ten "gurus" (teachers), the first of whom was Nānak (1469-1539) and the last Gobind Singh (1666-1708). The word "sikh" itself means disciple or student. The early Sikh leaders asserted that there was only one god and combined their monotheistic beliefs with a social doctrine rejecting any hierarchy based on caste in favor of a single community (the *Khalsa*; literally, "the pure") in which all believers were equal.

The earliest gurus advocated pacifism, but the Sikh movement became involved with the Punjab region's resistance to the revenue exactions of the Mughals, a Muslim dynasty that ruled parts of India from the sixteenth through part of the eighteenth century. Sikhs began to equate that empire's attempts to suppress the tax rebellion with religious persecution. In response, the Sikh religion became increasingly militaristic. Guru Gobind Singh added to the rise in militarism by decreeing that every "true" Sikh undergo a special baptism and take the name Singh, which translates as "Lion." As marks of their status, every male was supposed to carry a sword, wear clothes suited to a warrior's life, and avoid such things as alcohol, that might diminish a fighting man's prowess in battle.

As the authority of the Mughal empire began to disintegrate in the eighteenth century, the Sikhs of the Punjab region were able to establish their own independent states. The empire of Ranjit Singh (1792-1839) brought together those petty kingdoms. Shortly after the death of Ranjit Singh, the expanding British empire came into conflict with the Sikhs. In two wars, the British narrowly defeated them, but during those conflicts the Sikhs won the admiration of the British military. The British classified the Sikhs as one of India's martial races, which meant that Sikhs had a privileged place in Britain's Indian army.

The British actually worked to enhance the importance of Guru Gobind Singh's religious reforms. Before Gobind Singh, the Sikhs had been barely distinguishable from other popular religious movements in the Punjab. Gobind Singh's emphasis on such things as baptism and a prohibition on the trimming of a male's hair and beard served to distinguish his followers. The British army recruited only men who had undergone the baptism and adhered to Gobind Singh's rules.

During the Revolt of 1857, also known as the Mutiny, Sikhs remained steadfastly loyal to the British. The support of Sikh troops was especially crucial during the siege of Delhi. Considered not only martial, but also trustworthy, the Sikhs formed one of the largest components of the British Indian army. After Indian independence in 1947, the proportion of Sikhs in the military (around 25 percent) considerably exceeded their numbers in India's general population (less than two percent).

When the British decided to give up their Indian empire in 1947, they reluctantly agreed to divide the subcontinent between a Muslim nation, Pakistan, and a predominantly Hindu India. Although one of the cardinal doctrines of the Sikhs is "We are not Hindu, we are not Muslim," the Sikh community's leaders agreed to be counted as Hindus at the time of partition, believing that it would be advantageous to be part of the larger state of India. This brought considerable hardship to the Sikhs. Many of them lived in the western Punjab, the region which would go to Pakistan. As they moved eastward toward the new border, they encountered many Punjabi Muslims headed west, toward Pakistan. What some saw as a forced migration raised tensions and escalated ill feelings between groups. Many incidents of violence occurred during this period.

In 1947, a minority of Sikhs did not agree with the policies of their leaders. A few believed that the Sikhs should have joined Pakistan. Others believed that the Sikhs would be better off having their own nation. By the 1950's, the Sikhs were politically divided. Even the moderates began agitating for a "Punjabi Suba," a distinct province with a Punjabi-speaking majority. In 1966, Indira Gandhi's government seemed to accede to that demand. The hill tracts of northern Punjab that had a Hindi-speaking majority were separated into a new state, Himachal Pradesh, with its capital at Simla. The Hindi-speaking areas of southern Punjab were turned into the state of Haryana. The state of Punjab was much reduced in size, although it did have a Sikh majority of fifty-two percent. Punjab and Haryana were supposed to share a common capital at Chandigarh. Many Sikhs, both moderates and extremists, decided that these changes did not meet their demands. Harchand Singh Longowal, the moderate leader of the Akali Dal, the largest Sikh political organization, began to agitate for the transfer of Chandigarh to Punjab alone.

Despite the political turmoil, Punjab's economy in the 1960's and 1970's boomed. The "Green Revolution" particularly benefited farmers who had the capital to invest in new strains of grain seed and chemical fertilizers. Even without those resources, Punjabi farmers experienced a rising standard of living. The income of the average Punjabi peasant household was more than twice that of farmers elsewhere in India. The government invested considerable sums in the region to build roads, irrigation works, and small industries. In the 1980's, however, the boom ended. The burden fell most heavily on small peasant producers. In their frustration, these peasants began to listen to the voices of political radicals such as Jarnail Singh Bhindranwale.

At the same time, Indira Gandhi's government began to discuss plans that called for the numbers of any given community in the military to match their proportion of the total population. For the Sikhs, this would have meant a reduction in their membership from twenty-five percent to less than two percent. Many Sikhs depended on military service as a means of earning cash income, which in turn allowed them to enter into business ventures. The plan would have caused them great economic hardship. The mere mention of the idea further alienated the Sikhs and persuaded increasing numbers of them that only in their own state could they be truly secure.

The increased agitation favored the radicals, whose takeover of the Golden Temple was supported by a significant number of Sikhs. In choosing confrontation over negotiation, Indira Gandhi failed to win back the loyalty of the majority of Sikhs. The assault on the Golden Temple served only to inflame the religious component of Sikh radicalism and led not only to Indira Gandhi's death but also to the deaths of uncounted Indians.

Impact of Event

Shortly after Indira Gandhi's death, a wave of violence broke out against the Sikhs in Delhi. Busloads of young thugs were brought into Sikh neighborhoods and allowed to rape, kill, and pillage. The police made no attempt to interfere. Although the Sikhs fought back, they were outnumbered, and many died. The government's official count of the dead was twelve hundred, but most observers believed that figure was far too low.

In the wake of the violence, many claimed that the killings had been orchestrated by officials in the Congress Party. Rajiv Gandhi, who was sworn in as prime minister on the night of his mother's murder, promised an inquiry into the rioting. It was only in April, 1985, that he appointed a commission of inquiry, headed by Justice Misra. The committee met and investigated for two years before it finally released a report. The report did not name any individual culprits. No leader of the Congress Party was indicted, and the public, especially the Sikhs, claimed that the commission had covered up the truth.

Rajiv Gandhi attempted to forge an alliance with the moderate Sikhs. He agreed to Harchand Singh Longowal's request that Chandigarh would serve as capital of the Punjab state only and not be shared with Haryana state. In 1985, Longowal was assassinated. Rajiv Gandhi no longer had a Sikh leader of any significance with whom to negotiate.

In the years since 1984, murder and massacre became endemic in the Punjab and the areas immediately adjacent to it. Militants bombed buses and stopped trains, pulling off all non-Sikh passengers and brutally killing them. The Punjab was placed under a state of emergency, but the violence continued. No easy solution to the conflicting demands of the Sikhs and the government of India seemed likely to appear.

Bibliography

Brass, Paul R. *The Politics of India Since Independence.* Cambridge, England: Cambridge University Press, 1990. An overview of the structures of the Indian political system as well as of the interplay of parties and personalities. Unavoidably, the author passed up certain important topics but gives a lively survey of the problems and potential of Indian democracy.

Cunningham, Joseph D. *A History of the Sikhs.* New Delhi: S. Chand, 1972. Originally written in 1849 by a British officer who fought in the Sikh wars. Contains many interesting observations on the character of the independent Sikh kingdoms, especially on the empire of Ranjit Singh.

Fox, Richard G. *Lions of the Punjab: Culture in the Making.* Berkeley: University of California Press, 1985. This work by an anthropologist describes the emergence of a distinct Sikh community in the Punjab. The general reader may wish to pass over Fox's theoretical discussions of culture, but his comments on the many ways in which British policy contributed to Sikh separatism are highly relevant to understanding the political situation in the 1980's and 1990's.

Hart, Henry C., ed. *Indira Gandhi's India.* Boulder, Colo.: Westview Press, 1976. A collection of essays discussing Indira Gandhi's impact on Indian politics, especially on the position of the Congress Party. Several authors deal with her increasingly authoritarian and paranoid style of leadership which contributed to her ultimately fatal confrontation with the Sikhs.

McLeod, W. H. *The Evolution of the Sikh Community.* New Delhi: Oxford University Press, 1975. McLeod is one of the best Western scholars on Sikh religion and history. His writing is very engaging, bringing out many interesting and uncommon insights into a discussion of the Sikh faith.

Singh, Khushwant. *A History of the Sikhs.* 2 vols. Princeton, N.J.: Princeton University Press, 1963-1966. Khushwant Singh is one of modern India's most celebrated novelists as well as a historian. Singh's own status as a member of the Sikh community gives his work an interesting perspective.

Gregory C. Kozlowski

Cross-References

The Defense of India Act Impedes the Freedom Struggle (1915), p. 156; Soldiers

Massacre Indian Civilians in Amritsar (1919), p. 264; El Salvador's Military Massacres Civilians in *La Matanza* (1932), p. 464; India Gains Independence (1947), p. 731; The Sudanese Civil War Erupts (1955), p. 941; The Iraqi Government Promotes Genocide of Kurds (1960's), p. 1050; Sikhs in Punjab Revolt (1984), p. 2215; The Palestinian *Intifada* Begins (1987), p. 2331; Kashmir Separatists Demand an End to Indian Rule (1989), p. 2426.

LETHAL GAS KILLS THOUSANDS IN BHOPAL, INDIA

Category of event: Health and medical rights
Time: December 2-3, 1984
Locale: Bhopal, India

The release of lethal gas in Bhopal affected thousands of Indians and raised many questions about the production of toxic chemicals in developing countries

Principal personages:
> WARREN ANDERSON (1921-   ), the president and chief executive officer of Union Carbide at the time of the Bhopal tragedy
> RAJIV GANDHI (1944-1991), the interim prime minister of India
> HAREESH CHANDRA, the head of forensic medicine at Gandhi Medical College, the first specialist to perform autopsies on Bhopal victims

Summary of Event

In economic terms, India is a country of contrasts. By the end of the twentieth century it had become one of the world's largest industrial powers. It had a large corps of well-trained scientists and engineers working in a variety of technologically advanced enterprises. India sold its electronic goods, including stereos and, more recently, computers, in Southeast Asia. It exported automobiles and railroad cars to East Africa. At the same time, it remained primarily an agrarian country. Eighty-five percent of India's nearly one billion people still lived in villages and were directly engaged in the production of food.

India's agricultural economy experienced rapid development during the "Green Revolution" of the 1960's. This involved the introduction of new breeds of rice and wheat that were more productive and more resistant to drought and certain types of plant diseases than were the old varieties. Chemical fertilizers increased the yield of both food and cash crops. In addition, pesticides were used to reduce loss to insects. India became self-sufficient in terms of food production and even exported grain.

The combination of centrally planned technological development and the desire to maintain high agricultural productivity led the Indian government to enter into a cooperative venture with Union Carbide, a multinational corporation based in the United States. In 1969, Union Carbide was encouraged to build an insecticide manufacturing plant in the city of Bhopal, located about three hundred miles to the south of New Delhi.

One of the Bhopal plant's products was Methyl-isocyanide (MIC), a chemical widely used in pesticides applied to cotton and sugar cane, two of India's most important cash crops. Chemically, this mixture is related to cyanide, and in its concentrated form it is deadly. The mixing and storage of MIC ought to take place under tight control. One of the attractions for multinational companies that invest in Third World nations, however, is that government supervision of safety measures is often not as strict and effective as in Europe or the United States. Indeed, some European nations had banned MIC completely.

Late on the night of December 2 and in the early hours of December 3, 1984, a series of events brought the lax supervision at Bhopal to the rest of the world's attention. Even in the 1990's, the exact sequence of events remained unclear. Both the government of India and Union Carbide have acted to minimize the appearance of their own culpability, so any account of what really happened is certain to be speculative.

In its liquid state, MIC reacts violently to ordinary water. Its temperature rises quickly until it reaches a boiling temperature of about 125 degrees Fahrenheit. At that point, MIC vaporizes. On December 2, 1984, water that was being used to clean a series of pipes connecting the mixing and storage tanks entered one of the tanks holding MIC. The chemical's temperature rose rapidly. The temperature of a neighboring tank, however, was being deliberately increased through the introduction of nitrogen to make it possible to move the chemical vapor to the manufacturing area. Control-room technicians at first assumed that the rising heat of the first tank was a result of that operation. At about 11:30 P.M., a number of the plant's workers started to complain of eye irritation, one of the earliest signs that MIC vapor was present.

At midnight, some of the plant's personnel discovered the water running into the MIC tank and shut it off, but by then the chemical reaction could not be stopped. Several safety devices were supposed to go into operation if MIC vaporized. A series of safety valves was supposed to channel the MIC gas into a scrubbing tower, where it would be doused with caustic soda, which would reliquefy it. A flame tower would then ignite and burn off any of the gas unaffected by the caustic soda. Several of the valves burst, allowing much of the vapor to escape. The scrubbing tower was shut down for maintenance, and the flame tower was unable to keep pace with the flow of the MIC vapor. About forty-five metric tons of MIC escaped.

All these things happened during the plant's night shift. The plant manager, the engineers, the chemists, and most of the higher-grade technicians were at home. The men in charge of the plant that night were not among its most expert employees. They did not, at the beginning, understand what was happening. When they detected some MIC vapor in the air, most of them donned protective gas masks and suits. Thus, they did not experience the full force of the gas. They hesitated for several hours before calling in their supervisors, thinking that the problem was minor and would soon rectify itself.

Chemical factories are usually built away from densely populated areas. In India, municipal governments found it almost impossible to control settlement. Poor people tended to move onto any piece of unoccupied ground near a city. Unable to afford even mud huts, they built makeshift dwellings from bits of wood and tin or threw old cloth over flimsy frames of sticks. Street peddlers, day laborers, people who run donkey carts, and others who survived on a few rupees a day preferred the cities to the villages, because their opportunities to work for cash were greatly enhanced. They saved their hard-earned money by living in impromptu tenements.

Tens of thousands of people lived in such squatters' settlements near the Bhopal plant. They suffered the most from the discharge of the massive cloud of MIC gas.

Had the gas escaped during the daytime, the damage would have been greatly reduced. The sun would have caused the vapor to rise more quickly into the atmosphere and disperse. Also, if it had been a warm night, the gas would have moved skyward rapidly. The night of December 2-3, however, was cool and cloudy. A haze created by the day's emissions of vehicle exhaust and the smoke from thousands of cooking fires still hung over the city, trapped by the low ceiling of clouds. The MIC did not rise but stayed close to the ground. The night breezes allowed it to waft into the thousands of shacks and tents inhabited by Bhopal's poorest residents. It even reached some of the middle-class neighborhoods of the city.

MIC gas affects the soft tissues of the eyes, nose, throat, and lungs. It causes choking, uncontrolled tearing, shortness of breath, and even in small quantities, suffocation or heart failure. Thousands of sleeping people woke up with those symptoms. Many began running, but, since none of them knew what the problem was, some ran toward the plant. Others tried to find buses or headed for the railroad station.

Animals were affected by the same symptoms. Bhopal's slum dwellers kept cows and water buffalo to provide milk and dung. Many of the inhabitants had donkeys and horses because they made a living as carters. Packs of stray dogs were also common in the affected area. Panic gripped man and beast alike. Shouts, screams, coughs, bellows, neighs, and barks created a hellish noise. Hundreds fell to the ground writhing in pain. Fathers and mothers lost track of their children or each other. Some families despaired of escape, sat down, and died together.

When the first casualties reached clinics and hospitals, few doctors and nurses were on duty. These medical professionals had no idea about the cause of the victims' symptoms. They assumed that their new patients were having some sort of allergic reaction but had no idea of the source of their complaints. Not until several weeks later did doctors find countermeasures that gave some relief.

In the early hours of the morning of December 3, police and government officials began to suspect that the Union Carbide plant was the origin of the disaster. They telephoned the plant manager, who was still at home and unaware of the unfolding tragedy. He denied that his factory was the culprit, saying that its safety measures were absolutely foolproof. Rumors began to circulate wildly. Was it a sneak attack by Pakistan, India's enemy? Had a warplane crashed? Was the Indian army somehow connected to it? For several months afterward, executives of Union Carbide maintained that the incident was the result of sabotage.

The full impact of the disaster revealed itself over the next several days. In the short term, hospitals were overwhelmed and unable to give anything more than first aid. Handling the bodies of the victims also proved a daunting task.

Bhopal had a large Muslim population who by custom were supposed to be buried. The local Muslim religious authorities were forced to give their permission to open up graves that had already been occupied, an uncommon act, just to keep pace with the numbers of the dead. Hindu practice required cremation, but stocks of wood were soon exhausted. Many bodies were heaped up, splashed with gasoline, and set afire. It was not always possible to tell who was a Muslim and who a Hindu, so some of the former were cremated, while some of the latter were interred. For that reason, no accurate count of the dead was ever taken. The official estimate of twenty-five hundred dead was challenged almost immediately. Critics contended that many victims left Bhopal by train or bus and died in their hometowns or villages, without their deaths being reported as resulting from the gas leak.

Impact of Event

Critics of Rajiv Gandhi's government and of the United States have claimed that the actual death toll at Bhopal was closer to fifteen thousand than to twenty-five hundred. Although the Indian government announced that twenty thousand people, many of them children, had been injured, critics held that the figure was closer to one hundred thousand. A few respectable academics and journalists argued that the gas leak was not an accident at all but an intentional experiment in chemical warfare. They contended that Union Carbide conspired with the governments of India and the United States to hush up the true nature of the disaster.

Environmentalists the world over reacted strongly to the events in Bhopal. They pointed to the deadly effects of pesticides on the farmers who use them. Every year, many thousands of individuals die from misuse of these chemicals; Bhopal merely highlighted the problem. They also raised the problems posed by long-term exposure to pesticides, not only for agriculturalists but also for millions of people who consume foodstuffs treated with toxic substances. Those concerns were highlighted on August 11, 1985, when a Union Carbide plant in Institution, West Virginia, had a smaller leak of MIC gas. Only 135 people suffered minor reactions, but these individuals lodged a class-action suit against Union Carbide for the sum of $88 million.

Attorneys from the United States arrived in India within a few weeks of the tragedy and offered to represent Bhopal victims in American courts, since Union Carbide was incorporated there. Their clients sued for a total of $100 billion. In May, 1986, however, a U.S. judge ruled that claims against Union Carbide must be heard in the courts of India. This decision favored the company, since damage awards in India have never come close to the sums awarded in American courts.

On February 14, 1989, Union Carbide proposed a final out-of-court settlement with the victims. Dismissal of all criminal charges against Union Carbide employees, including Warren Anderson, the company's chief executive officer, was approved in exchange for payments totaling $470 million. In 1990, the Indian government went to the Indian supreme court and asked that it vacate its approval of the settlement. Until negotiations could resume, the government of India agreed to pay survivors and the injured the sum of two hundred rupees (about twenty dollars) per month. As litigation continued, many thousands of individuals continued to suffer from residual effects of the poisoning. Although environmentalists still campaigned against insecticides with a No More Bhopals slogan, the gas leak resulted in few direct changes. The Bhopal plant was permanently closed, but many others scattered throughout the world continued to produce pesticides from similar and equally lethal chemicals. Questions about the location of many such factories in developing countries were still occasionally asked, but only a few scientists and journalists remain concerned about the answers received.

Bibliography

Banerjee, Brojendra Nath. *Bhopal Gas Tragedy: Accident or Experiment.* New Delhi: Paribus Publications, 1986. Banerjee's book is full of righteous indignation. It is disjointed and highly repetitive. Also, American readers unfamiliar with books printed in India may be disturbed initially by the work's frequent misprints and misspellings. Nevertheless, the work represents opinions common among serious Indian intellectuals. Those who find Banerjee's views disturbing should probably give them serious thought.

Britannica Book of the Year. Chicago: Encyclopaedia Britannica, 1985-   . Relevant articles appear under the listing of "Bhopal" and elsewhere. Although the reports given in the yearbooks are brief, they are very instructive. *Britannica*, from the first relevant year, took a stance that minimized Union Carbide's culpability. The constant repetition of cautions about prejudging the facts of the Bhopal catastrophe should trouble the reader as much as Banerjee's diatribes against multinationals and his eagerness to find conspiracies everywhere. Taking a middle ground between Banerjee's book and *Britannica* will probably give readers an appreciation of the Bhopal event.

Galanter, Marc, and Gary Wilson. *The Legal Aftermath of the Bhopal Disaster: A Collection of Press Clippings and Other Materials.* Madison: University of Wisconsin Law School, 1986. Among American lawyers, Galanter is unequaled in his sense of how the courts of India work within the context of their society. This is a useful volume, as it highlights the differing perspectives of the victims, their almost self-appointed representatives, and the judiciary and the governments of India and the United States.

Iyer, Pico. "Clouds of Uncertainty." *Time* 124 (December 24, 1984): 24. Twenty days after the gas leak, the correspondent of a major international magazine confronts new facts and tries to place them in context. Journalists were able to emphasize the human tragedy while avoiding serious questions about the possible exploitation of developing nations.

_____. "India's Night of Death." *Time* 124 (December 17, 1984): 8-13. Reading a single correspondent's weekly reports about Bhopal is most instructive. Reporters were forced to change their stories on a week-to-week basis. Therefore, any student of Bhopal should choose to follow any well-known periodical's day-by-day or week-by-week coverage.

Gregory C. Kozlowski

Cross-References

Congress Passes the Occupational Safety and Health Act (1970), p. 1585; Toxic Waste Is Discovered at Love Canal (1978), p. 1961; Superfund Is Established to Pay for Hazardous Waste Cleanup (1980), p. 2084; Indira Gandhi Is Assassinated (1984), p. 2232; Manville Offers $2.5 Billion to Victims of Asbestos Dust (1985), p. 2274.

TUTU WINS THE NOBEL PEACE PRIZE

Categories of event: Racial and ethnic rights; peace movements and organizations
Time: December 10, 1984
Locale: Oslo, Norway

Bishop Desmond Tutu received the Nobel Peace Prize in 1984 in recognition of his role as the chief moral spokesperson against apartheid in South Africa

Principal personages:
DESMOND TUTU (1931-   ), the Anglican bishop of the Johannesburg diocese
PIETER WILLEM BOTHA (1919-   ), the prime minister of South Africa from 1981 to 1989
RONALD REAGAN (1911-   ), the president of the United States from 1981 to 1989
BALTHAZAR JOHANNES (JOHN) VORSTER (1915-1983), the prime minister of South Africa from 1966 to 1978

Summary of Event

Bishop Desmond Tutu's Nobel Peace Prize was awarded in recognition of his lifelong opposition to apartheid, the system of racial separation in South Africa under which the white minority owned more than 87 percent of the total area of the country. South Africa's five million whites enjoyed the best housing, employment, and schools while denying the nation's twenty-two million blacks a voice in the government. The country's white minority goverment branded Bishop Tutu as a subversive, a troublemaker, and a traitor. To the liberal whites, blacks, and clergy of South Africa, on the other hand, he stood as a freedom fighter and an apostle of racial equality.

Tutu first became aware of the needs of underprivileged people as a boy growing up in the western Transvaal gold-mining town of Klerksdorp. When he was twelve, his family moved to Johannesburg, where his mother found employment as a cook in a school for the blind. While his mother worked at the school, Tutu found a role model in a controversial Anglican priest named Father Trevor Huddleston. Tutu, even though still a boy, was so impressed by Huddleston's dedication and compassion that he decided to devote himself to a life of service.

Tutu also acquired firsthand knowledge of the problems of deprived people when he was growing up. While he was attending high school in a black township outside Johannesburg, he had to support himself by caddying at an all-white golf course. At the age of eighteen, he had to abandon his plan to attend medical school because his father, who was a teacher, could not afford the tuition. After graduating from Bantu University and the University of Johannesburg, he became a high-school teacher. He and many other teachers, however, resigned from Munsieville High School in Krugersdorp after the government introduced the inferior state-run system of "Bantu education" in 1957.

Guided by the memory of Father Huddleston's work on behalf of South Africa's oppressed people, Tutu decided that he could do the most good for South Africa's blacks as a churchman. He was ordained at St. Petersburg's Theological Seminary in 1960, the year of the Sharpeville massacre, in which more than seventy blacks were killed and two hundred injured in a peaceful protest against apartheid. After doing graduate study in England, Tutu set out to spread God's word, "whether it's convenient or not." He lectured at the Federal Theological Seminary and at the National University of Lesotho before returning in 1972 to England, where he administered scholarships for the World Council of Churches. He returned to South Africa in 1975 to become the first black Anglican dean of Johannesburg. As dean, Tutu was expected to live in a large mansion in an exclusive all-white suburb. He spurned Johannesburg's posh suburban deanery, however, so that he could live with the masses in Soweto.

Tutu first became involved in the politics of his country during his first year as dean. In the spring of 1976, Tutu encouraged the rebellious youth of Soweto to convert their violent outbursts into peaceful demonstrations. In a letter written on May 6, 1976, Tutu apprised the prime minister of South Africa, Balthazar Johannes Vorster, of the severity of the situation, but his warning was ignored. The validity of Tutu's words was borne out on June 16, 1976, when six hundred blacks were killed during the Soweto riots.

In 1978, Tutu assumed the position that catapulted him to prominence as an ardent champion of the freedom struggle in South Africa. As secretary of the South African Council of Churches (SACC), Tutu became the spiritual leader of thirteen million Christians. During Tutu's seven-year tenure, the SACC filled the void left by the banning of the main African nationalist parties. Legal and financial aid was given freely to detainees, victims of apartheid, and families of political prisoners. Tutu openly sponsored the aims of the banned African National Congress, South Africa's largest black underground organization, which fought against apartheid and for universal suffrage. In the grand tradition of Mohandas Gandhi, he also led many peaceful antigovernment demonstrations, warning the government that violence was inevitable unless Pretoria shared power with South Africa's black majority. He and many of his followers were jailed on numerous occasions.

On two monumental occasions in 1979, Tutu intentionally crossed the fine line that he constantly had walked with the authorities while serving as secretary of the SACC. Tutu outraged government officials with his opposition to the Group Areas Act, under which blacks were shifted from urban areas to desolate tribal lands. Following a visit to one of these squalid refugee camps, Tutu lashed out at the government, likening the camps to the Nazis' "final solution." In that same year, Tutu began speaking out at home and abroad against foreign investment in South Africa. In the fall, he was almost banned from participating in social and political activity in South Africa when, in a television interview, he asked the people of Denmark to refrain from buying coal from his homeland. Even though the government retaliated by withdrawing his passport, Tutu continued to attack South Africa's segregationist policies by supporting a nationwide school boycott and by warning that the arrest of protestors would lead to an outbreak of rioting.

Tutu's finest hour, though, took place in 1981. After the Anglican church issued a statement declaring apartheid a heresy, the government counterattacked by appointing a commission of inquiry into the affairs of the SACC to determine whether it was a subversive organization that had sponsored terrorist activities in South Africa. Testifying before the all-white commission in a government office building in Pretoria, Tutu delivered a major public denunciation of apartheid and an exposition of the theology of liberation. Brandishing an old leather-bound Bible in his hand, he said that the Bible was the most radical of books because it taught that all people were created in the image of God. In the end, the commission recommended no action against the council of churches.

Despite the fact that he was frequently denied the right to travel abroad in his last years as secretary of the SACC, Tutu persisted in his role as a proponent of racial equality and nonviolence. His constant message to the international community was that economic pressure had to be brought on South Africa if change were to be brought about without violence. By 1984, Tutu had been so successful in his campaign to disinvest South Africa that the Pretoria government described his citizenship as "undetermined" and allowed him to travel only on temporary documents. In September, 1984, he was given special permission to visit the United States for three months so that he could serve as a visiting professor at the General Theological Seminary in New York City. Ironically, it was during his visit to a country that had refused to disinvest in South Africa that the Nobel Committee chose him as the 1984 Nobel peace laureate. Upon hearing the news on October 16, 1984, Tutu told reporters that if change did not occur soon, a bloodbath would be inevitable. He added, though, "We don't want that bloodbath. We are trying to avoid it."

Impact of Event

It is not surprising that the reaction in South Africa to Bishop Tutu's Nobel Prize was mixed. In Pretoria, government officials ignored the Nobel announcement altogether. President Pieter Botha also chose not to express his feelings and released a "no comment" response from his office. The acknowledgment of the reward was much more hostile from the Afrikaans-language newspaper *Beeld*, which gave vent to the anger of the supporters of apartheid: "To South Africans who have so often read about his vicious verbal attacks, Bishop Desmond Tutu . . . must be one of the strangest recipients yet to receive a Peace Prize." The Organization of African Unity, on the other hand, took the opposite stance, calling Tutu's award "an urgent reminder to the racist authorities of Pretoria that their inhuman regime is doomed." At the Johannesburg airport, hundreds of supporters gave Tutu a hero's welcome, cheering and waving antiapartheid signs.

News of Tutu's prize also had an impact on the Anglican church itself. At the time that the decision was made to award the peace prize to Tutu, the white and black diocesan electors in Johannesburg were considering him as a candidate for bishop. Because the electors were clearly divided along racial lines, the national Anglican hierarchy decided to intervene. Thus, on November 3, 1984, Desmond Tutu left the South African Council of Churches to become the first black Anglican bishop of Johannesburg, the largest diocese in South Africa.

Bishop Tutu's peace prize had a positive effect on world politics as well. Being a Nobel Prize winner provided Tutu with a platform from which he could force those nations taking part in what U.S. president Ronald Reagan had called "quiet diplomacy" to become more vocal in their protest against apartheid. During the week preceding his acceptance of the Nobel Prize in Oslo, Tutu visited President Reagan, who defended his policy of condemning apartheid while keeping U.S. business interests in place in South Africa. While he was in New York, Bishop Tutu also gained the support of former President Jimmy Carter, who likened the mentality of the white South Africans to that of the Ku Klux Klan. By the time Bishop Tutu's three-month tenure as visiting professor at the General Theological Seminary had ended, thirty-one demonstrators had been arrested in the daily rallies being held outside the South African embassy in Washington, D.C. The demonstrations then spread to eight major cities across the United States. As a result of the pressure that Tutu's call for economic pressure had placed on the United States, President Reagan decided in 1985 to order a ban on imports of krugerrands, the gold pieces that were one of South Africa's major exports. After the United States began to withdraw investments from South Africa, other nations rapidly followed suit. Tutu had successfully shifted the focus from himself to the problems of his fellow blacks in South Africa.

Although the full impact of Tutu's peace prize cannot be measured, there is no doubt that the worldwide attention that his Nobel Prize speech received had long-term consequences for his homeland. The reforms that were set in place by President Frederik Willem de Klerk in the late 1980's, culminating in the release from prison of Nelson Mandela in 1990 and the lifting of economic sanctions by the United States in 1991, resulted in large part from the campaign that Tutu waged for economic pressure. Although Tutu alone was not responsible for the erosion of apartheid in his homeland in the 1990's, his receipt of the Nobel Prize certainly contributed to the demise of apartheid by putting his nation's problems in the spotlight.

Bibliography

"Bishop Tutu: 'Person of the Year.'" *Christian Century* 102 (January 2, 1985): 3-4. This article not only provides the positive and negative reactions to Tutu's prize but also discusses the impact that the prize could have on disinvestment in South Africa.

Canine, Craig. "A Parable—and a Peace Prize." *Newsweek* 104 (October 29, 1984): 89. Canine effectively describes the process by which Tutu was selected by the Nobel Committee. He also includes the immediate reactions of Tutu himself, of the South African government, and of Tutu's black countrymen.

Davis, Stephen M. *Apartheid's Rebels.* New Haven, Conn.: Yale University Press, 1987. Although the book does not discuss Tutu's contributions in enough detail, it does explain Tutu's connection with the African National Congress.

Hammer, Joshua. "Urging Nonviolent Change in His Tortured Land, South Africa's Desmond Tutu Wins the Nobel Prize." *People* 22 (December 17, 1984): 185-186. Hammer's article is a short but informative introduction to Tutu's life, work, and philosophy. Unlike other articles, this one stresses the human side of Tutu, even going so far as to describe his appearance.

Howell, Leon. "Antiapartheid Bishop Awarded Peace Prize." *Christian Century* 101 (November 14, 1984): 1054-1055. Even though this article is predictably biased in favor of Tutu, it does argue convincingly for disinvestment in South Africa.

Magnuson, Ed. "Fresh Anger over Apartheid." *Nation* 124 (December 16, 1984): 46-47. This article focuses on the effect that Tutu's peace prize had on President Reagan and on the protest movement in Washington, D.C. It is a fascinating look into the politics behind disinvestment.

"A Nobel Peace Prize for South Africa's Warrior for Peace." *Ebony* 40 (January, 1985): 80-82. Although this article includes most of the same biographical information as the other articles, it stands out because of the large number of photographs that illustrate various aspects of Tutu's life and career.

Ostling, Richard. "Peace: Proud and Sad." *Time* 124 (October 29, 1984): 62. This refreshingly objective portrait of Tutu examines the "tricky tightrope" that he has walked while trying to appease the white establishment and black militants.

Sparks, Allister. *The Mind of South Africa.* New York: Alfred A. Knopf, 1990. In a chapter dealing with the activities of the church in South Africa, Sparks concentrates on Tutu's 1981 confrontation with the government's commission of inquiry into the "subversive" activities of the South African Council of Churches.

Alan Brown

Cross-References

South Africa Begins a System of Separate Development (1951), p. 861; Lutuli Is Awarded the Nobel Peace Prize (1961), p. 1143; The United Nations Votes to Suppress and Punish Apartheid (1973), p. 1736; A World Conference Condemns Racial Discrimination (1978), p. 1993; The United Nations Issues a Declaration on South Africa (1979), p. 2008; Black Workers in South Africa Go on Strike (1987), p. 2304; Mandela Is Freed (1990), p. 2559; De Klerk Promises to Topple Apartheid Legislation (1991), p. 2606.

GORBACHEV INITIATES A POLICY OF *GLASNOST*

Category of event: Civil rights
Time: 1985
Locale: Moscow, Union of Soviet Socialist Republics

The discouragement of open discussion and the disregard of human rights was the traditional position of the Communist Party of the Soviet Union until Mikhail Gorbachev launched the policy of glasnost

Principal personages:
MIKHAIL GORBACHEV (1931-   ), the president of the Soviet Union and general secretary of its Communist Party
JOSEPH STALIN (1879-1953), the Communist leader of the Soviet Union (1924-1953)
NIKITA S. KHRUSHCHEV (1894-1971), the Communist leader of the Soviet Union (1958-1964) who initiated social reforms that provided a model for *glasnost*
YEGOR LIGACHEV (1920-   ), a member of the Politburo and secretary of the Communist Party of the Soviet Union central committee who vigorously opposed *glasnost*
BORIS YELTSIN (1931-   ), the first freely elected president of the Russian republic

Summary of Event

After the announcement on March 11, 1985, of the death of General Secretary Konstantin Chernenko on the previous day, Mikhail Gorbachev at the age of fifty-four became the youngest leader of the Soviet Union since Joseph Stalin. It was revealed by top party officials that Gorbachev had provided leadership for the Politburo and the Secretariat during Chernenko's final days. The Soviet Union was in the midst of a severe economic crisis in which the very legitimacy of the government was questioned. Each Soviet leader since the 1917 Bolshevik Revolution had promised radical social changes and restructuring to resolve problems. Gorbachev believed that immediate social reforms, including *glasnost* (openness), were necessary to revitalize the economy and to prevent the further economic and political decline of the Soviet Union and a resulting loss of global power. There was a growing awareness by the Soviet government under Gorbachev's leadership that serious economic problems would be remedied only by extensive political reforms and democratization.

The word *glasnost* was derived from the Russian adjective *glasnyi* (public disclosure). In April, 1985, Gorbachev began to use the term *glasnost* to mean full public disclosure of significant national issues concurrent with exposure and critical evaluation of governmental performance, including weaknesses. The concept of *glasnost* was considered a necessary component of democratization in the Soviet Union, as it encouraged public awareness, debate, and discussion and an informed and intelligent citizen body. In 1988, *Pravda* expressed the meaning of *glasnost* to include freedom of speech, freedom of the press, and open comparison of ideas; the making available to citizens of any information they needed to participate in the discussion and solution of state life; openness and accessibility of all organs of power to citizens; opportunities for citizens to make suggestions to the government; consideration of public opinion in the making of decisions; and the publication of adopted decisions.

Glasnost and political reforms in Soviet society were prompted by the shrewd, energetic, and innovative leadership of Gorbachev and by major transitions in various economic, cultural, and demographic conditions. In contrast to the passive political culture of the primarily rural peasant society of Stalin's period, the Soviet Union witnessed in the 1980's the arrival of an outspoken, intelligent, professional urban middle class. After the expansion of telecommunications to a national audience, the Soviet people demanded full disclosure of significant policy decisions and major national disasters (the Chernobyl nuclear accident, for example). Gorbachev's adoption of *glasnost* was influenced primarily by the stagnant Soviet economy. *Glasnost* was thought of by Gorbachev as the catalyst for necessary economic changes and *perestroika* (restructuring) for a society that had had only 2 percent economic growth for the 1980's. Gorbachev's open articulation of the problems of the Soviet system and the critical need for *glasnost*, social reforms, and an extended sphere of legitimate private activity, freedom, and human rights was an ironic affirmation of what had been expressed in the past three decades by numerous human rights activists and dissidents.

Gorbachev's policies of social reform, human rights, and *glasnost* were launched in a society that had a history of deep-rooted hostility to openness and the protection of human rights. The concepts of individualism and inalienable rights were not part of the traditional Russian political vocabulary. In the decades prior to Gorbachev's leadership, the traditional position of the Communist Party of the Soviet Union (most notably expressed in the 1977 Soviet constitution) lacked an understanding of natural or human rights and instead emphasized obligations citizens owed to the state. The Soviet government often did not comprehend Western allegations of Soviet human rights violations.

Under Joseph Stalin's leadership (1924-1953), Soviet citizens were confronted by the arbitrary imposition of terror and the denial of basic human rights by a totalitarian government. Stalin justified coerced collectivization and pervasive human rights abuses as necessary to the economic transformation of the Soviet Union. Nikita Khrushchev's leadership (1958-1964) and somewhat unsystematic social reforms served as the most immediate historical precedents for Gorbachev's policy of *glasnost*. The major components of Khrushchev's social initiative included sharp criticism of Stalin's flagrant violations of human rights, a reduction in abusive state authority, and a gradual improvement in the respect for basic human rights.

Many of the gains made in the protection of human rights under Khrushchev, however, were reversed under Leonid Brezhnev's leadership (1964-1982). Restriction of political and religious activities, particularly those of dissidents, were justified by Brezhnev as the necessary promotion of state and party interests over individual rights. The climax for the reversal of reforms occurred upon the expulsion of the novelist and political dissident Aleksandr Solzhenitsyn from the Soviet Writers' Union in 1969 and his arrest and loss of citizenship in February, 1974. Brezhnev's foreign policies did provide some hope for human rights activists because of an accelerated emigration of Soviet Jews and the Soviet government's promised compliance with the human rights provisions of the 1975 Helsinki Accords.

In the period prior to Gorbachev's promotion of *glasnost*, the Soviet government used a variety of strategies to harass the members of social reform and human rights activist groups and to impede their free assembly, association, and speech. Political, religious, and ethnic dissidents were subjected to political trials, accused of anti-Soviet agitation, malicious hooliganism, and treason, sentenced to internal exiles, prisons, and psychiatric hospitals, or even deported from the Soviet Union. Prisoners of conscience confronted restricted religious freedom (even simple prayer was considered a serious break with prison regulations), extreme isolation, and severed communication ties with their families.

The Soviet government for several decades prior to Gorbachev's leadership was committed to a policy of harassment and imprisonment of religious rights activists. Persecuted religious rights activists included Jews, members of the Russian Orthodox church, Catholics, Muslims, and Baptists. Members of such religious groups were often arrested for innocent spiritual activities, including the participation in congregational services during religious holidays and the publication and distribution of religious literature. In particular, Jewish dissidents and "refuseniks" (Jews who had been denied permission to emigrate from the Soviet Union) who persisted in the teaching of Jewish religious values and the Hebrew language were often accused of anti-Soviet slander and Zionism and sentenced to hard labor.

As early as the April 23, 1985, meeting of the central committee of the Soviet Communist Party, Gorbachev began to use an elementary understanding of *glasnost* as a political strategy that identified particular issues to be addressed, encouraged citizen support of the government, and provided critical oversight of the state bureaucracy. In an ironic development, the future leader of the Communist Party's conservative opposition to Gorbachev's policy of *glasnost*, Secretary Yegor Ligachev, was promoted to full Politburo membership by Gorbachev at the April meeting. The development of Gorbachev's interpretation and application of the concept of *glasnost* evolved through various major policy statements expressed in the Soviet Communist Party program printed in October, 1985, the report presented by Gorbachev to the Twenty-seventh Communist Party Congress in February, 1986, Gorbachev's book *Perestroika: New Thinking for Our Country and the World* (published in 1987), and his historic speech delivered to the Nineteenth All-Union Conference of the Communist Party on July 1, 1988.

A fundamental objective of *glasnost* was the exposure of the Soviet bureaucracy's natural tendency toward corruption, mismanagement, and lack of innovation. The Soviet military newspaper *Krasnaya Zvezda* on July 11, 1986, openly criticized several Uzbekistan Communist Party officials who had protected their sons from military combat in Afghanistan. Instead of relying upon the Communist Party to promote public disclosure and discussion, Gorbachev articulated the critical need for the continuous support of the Soviet people and their demands for open dialogue. Throughout 1985, 1986, and 1987, Gorbachev sponsored open public debates in workplaces and communities in an effort to inquire about grievances of the Soviet population and to promote democratization in the Soviet Union through the expansion of the channels of citizen access to government.

Gorbachev's policy of *glasnost* greatly reduced state censorship over literary works and the flow of information and permitted controversial problems in the Soviet Union, including alcohol and drug abuse, crime, housing and consumer goods shortages, unemployment, prostitution, and national accidents, to be openly and critically discussed by the mass media. The Chernobyl nuclear accident of April, 1986, was a landmark in the development of Gorbachev's implementation of *glasnost*, since Western analysts criticized the Soviet government for not promptly alerting the Soviet people or global leaders about the nuclear disaster. After the Chernobyl accident, the Soviet leadership became prompt in reporting information on a variety of major accidents throughout 1986, including the sinking of the passenger ship *Admiral Nakhimov* on August 31, 1986, and the sinking of a Soviet nuclear submarine off the coast of New York on October 3, 1986.

The previously censored novels by Boris Pasternak and Anatoly Rybakov were finally published in the Soviet Union in 1987. Although banned for decades for alleged anti-Soviet biases, Nikolai Gumilev's poems and Vladimir Nabokov's novels were printed in 1987. The proreligious film *Repentance* (1987) which was very critical of Stalin's implementation of terror, had its premiere in Moscow in January, 1987. In addition, former political prisoners and dissidents were allowed to publish an autonomous journal of political commentary on the Soviet Union entitled *Glasnost*. The previously jammed radio broadcasts of the British Broadcasting Corporation and Voice of America were finally approved for transmission to the Soviet audience.

Impact of Event

A variety of complex domestic and global consequences resulted from Gorbachev's initiation of the policy of *glasnost*. The most significant and successful changes developed in the area of human rights, and not necessarily in the promotion of *perestroika*. Under Gorbachev's leadership, *glasnost* gradually expanded in scope, intensity, and purpose to include a transformation of social relations, the recognition and respect of basic human rights and freedoms, and "rethinking" in Soviet foreign policy. Gorbachev's call in 1986 for a genuine revolution in the minds and hearts of people stimulated the proliferation of voluntary associations (an estimated thirty thousand in 1986) and the emergence of a pluralistic society in the Soviet Union.

A series of dramatic events that promoted *glasnost*, social reform, and human rights were openly reported by the Soviet government throughout 1986. On February 11, 1986, human rights dissident Anatoly Shcharansky was given his freedom and permitted to emigrate to Israel after nine years of imprisonment. In May, 1986, many Georgian Muslims who had been exiled from Georgia and stripped of their basic civil rights by Stalin in 1944 were granted permission to return to their homeland. In July, 1986, a Soviet Human Rights Commission was instituted to analyze humanitarian problems and educate Soviet citizens about their human rights. On November 5, 1986, Gorbachev articulated a much more liberal and efficient emigration policy designed to promote a greater sensitivity to the reunification of family members and the personal needs of individuals.

The most striking release of a political prisoner occurred on December 16, 1986, when Gorbachev personally telephoned Andrei Sakharov, the nuclear physicist, Nobel Peace Prize winner, and articulate human rights activist, informed him that his seven-year exile in Gorky was over, and requested him to continue his patriotic work in Moscow. Gorbachev's direct authorization of Sakharov's freedom and open acknowledgment of the Soviet government's unethical treatment of the human rights activist was a novel act for a Soviet leader. Several hundred other human rights activists and dissidents were soon released.

Gorbachev's recognition that the historical window of opportunity remained open to implement *glasnost* and comprehensive social reforms, including the protection of human rights, was expressed by him at the January and June, 1987, meetings of the Central Committee. At the meetings, Gorbachev articulated that citizens had the right to evaluate critically and openly the performance of the Soviet leadership in resolving problems. The creation in the spring of 1988 of an All-Union Center for the Study of Public Opinion was another indication of the Soviet government's efforts at *glasnost* and democratization.

Rising democratic and free-market expectations were often unfulfilled, however, and open frustrations were expressed by the Soviet people and some of the more outspoken, radical leadership. Boris Yeltsin, the first freely elected president of the Russian republic, demanded immediate comprehensive democratic reforms, including the establishment of extensive popular elections, independence for the Soviet republics, and the implementation of market-economy principles. Several Soviet liberals, including former Foreign Minister Eduard Shevardnadze, created the Democratic Reform Movement in July, 1991, to save *glasnost* and *perestroika* and to accelerate democratic processes.

Gorbachev's policy of *glasnost* entailed multiple risks to his leadership. He faced explosive ethnic uprisings, demands by several republics for independence, and a backlash by the bureaucracy, conservative party members, and the military. On August 19, 1991, a coup was initiated by hard-line Communist leaders of the interior and defense ministries and the Komitet Gosudarstvennoi Bezopasnosti (KGB). By

August 21, 1991, however, the coup had collapsed, and Gorbachev reclaimed his constitutional authority.

Bibliography

Copeland, Emily A. "Perestroika and Human Rights: Steps in the Right Direction." *The Fletcher Forum of World Affairs* 15 (Summer, 1991): 101-119. This scholarly article provides a critical examination of the historical development of Soviet human rights policy. Useful for its informative discussion of the relation between ideological factors and social reform in the Soviet Union. Especially helpful is its critical analysis of Soviet foreign policy and human rights. Contains an extensive list of scholarly references.

Doder, Dusko, and Louise Branson. *Gorbachev: Heretic in the Kremlin.* New York: Penguin Books, 1991. Offers a detailed historical account of the intellectual and political context that shaped Gorbachev's articulation of the policies of social reform, *glasnost, perestroika*, and "new thinking" in foreign policy. Especially useful is its analysis of the role of the intelligentsia and *glasnost* and the complexities of Soviet politics. Contains a list of references and an index.

Gorbachev, Mikhail. *Perestroika: New Thinking for Our Country and the World.* New York: Harper & Row, 1987. In this philosophical and historical work, Gorbachev articulates in detail the theoretical blueprint for comprehensive changes through his policies of *glasnost, perestroika*, democratization, and "new political thinking." This work provides insight on Gorbachev's critical assessment of the political and ideological causes of the fundamental problems confronting the Soviet Union. The updated edition includes the major statements articulated by Gorbachev at the 1988 All-Union Conference of the Communist Party of the Soviet Union.

Nove, Alec. *Glasnost' in Action: Cultural Renaissance in Russia.* Boston: Unwin Hyman, 1989. This scholarly work focuses on the historical context that preceded Gorbachev's initiation of the policy of *glasnost* and the significant cultural aspects of *glasnost.* In particular, the chapters on religion, morality, literature, and the media provide detailed substantive information on the implementation of the policy of *glasnost.* The appendix contains a useful guide to Soviet publications.

Sheehy, Gail. *The Man Who Changed the World.* New York: HarperCollins, 1990. This political-biographical study of Gorbachev uses numerous interviews of individuals associated with the Soviet leader to develop an analysis of his political behavior. Contains a list of references, a bibliography, and an index.

Toscano, Robert. *Soviet Human Rights Policy and Perestroika.* Lanham, Md.: University Press of America, 1989. This scholarly work uses a philosophical and historical approach to examine the development of Soviet human rights policy. It focuses on human rights and Gorbachev's initiation of "new thinking" in Soviet foreign policy and promotion of *perestroika.* Offers extensive references.

White, Stephen. *Gorbachev in Power.* Cambridge, England: Cambridge University Press, 1990. Offers a highly scholarly, sophisticated, and comprehensive critical analysis of the first five years of Gorbachev's political leadership. Especially useful is its detailed examination of the social, political, and economic context of Gorbachev's leadership and promotion of social reforms. The chapter focusing on *glasnost* is very informative. Contains a list of references and an index.

Mitchel Gerber

Cross-References

Bolsheviks Deny All Rights to the Russian Orthodox Church (1917), p. 202; Lenin and the Communists Impose the "Red Terror" (1917), p. 218; Lenin Leads the Russian Revolution (1917), p. 225; Stalin Begins Purging Political Opponents (1934), p. 503; Stalin Reduces the Russian Orthodox Church to Virtual Extinction (1939), p. 561; Khrushchev Implies that Stalinist Excesses Will Cease (1956), p. 952; Soviet Jews Demand Cultural and Religious Rights (1963), p. 1177; The Moscow Human Rights Committee Is Founded (1970), p. 1549; Solzhenitsyn Is Expelled from the Soviet Union (1974), p. 1764; The Helsinki Agreement Offers Terms for International Cooperation (1975), p. 1806; Sakharov Is Awarded the Nobel Peace Prize (1975), p. 1852; Soviet Citizens' Group Investigates Political Abuses of Psychiatry (1977), p. 1909; Soviets Crack Down on Moscow's Helsinki Watch Group (1977), p. 1915; Soviet Farmers Are Given Control of Land and Selection of Crops (1989), p. 2471; Gorbachev Agrees to Membership of a United Germany in NATO (1990), p. 2589.

MINNESOTA PARENTS ARE GIVEN BROADER CHOICES IN PUBLIC EDUCATION

Category of event: Educational rights
Time: 1985-1991
Locale: St. Paul, Minnesota

Leading the nation's school-choice movement, Minnesota lawmakers gave parents the right to send their children to any public school in the state

Principal personages:

RUDY PERPICH (1928-   ), the three-term democratic governor of Minnesota during the 1970's and 1980's

TOM NELSON, the chairman of the finance division of the Minnesota State Senate Education Committee and later commissioner of education

JOE NATHAN (1948-   ), an educator, author, and major creative force in the Minnesota choice movement

RANDY PETERSON, a state senator and finance division chairman after Nelson

DAN LORITZ, a member of the Minnesota Department of Education, later Perpich's deputy chief of staff

RUTH RANDALL, a former Minnesota commissioner of education

BETSY RICE, legal counsel to the Senate Education Committee

CONNIE LEVI, a Republican state representative who introduced choice legislation in the Minnesota House of Representatives

GENE MAMMENGA, a lobbyist for the Minnesota Education Association and opponent of school-choice options

BARBARA ZOHN, a former president of the Minnesota Parent-Teacher Association and an assistant at the Minnesota Department of Education

Summary of Event

Growing concern over diminishing standards in American public education during the latter decades of the twentieth century led to greater interest and innovation in educational reform. Public schools were run by state departments of education, and the impetus for change most often came from the state or even local level. Such was the case in the development of public-school choice options in Minnesota from 1985 through 1991.

Traditionally, schoolchildren in the United States have been assigned to schools on a geographical basis. Attendance at a school outside one's neighborhood or school district required special permission from both schools or districts and was granted only for extraordinary circumstances. As early as 1955, Nobel Prize-winning economist Milton Friedman suggested the development of systems whereby parents and children would be given greater choice among schools. Several school districts in the nation, most notably Cambridge, Massachusetts, and East Harlem in New York City, initiated choice options in the late 1970's and early 1980's, with impressive results in student achievement.

Beginning in 1971, school districts in Minneapolis and later St. Paul offered options among different types of schools at the elementary level. During the early 1980's, a number of suburban and rural Minnesota districts created wider options for failing secondary-school students to decrease their dropout rates. In 1985, Minnesota's Democratic governor, Rudy Perpich, proposed a nine-point program, entitled "Access to Excellence," that included several of the choice options that would be enacted over the following years. His program and his strong advocacy of a broader approach to education, with many options, were instrumental in establishing Minnesota as a leader in the school-choice phenomenon.

Minnesota's choice program actually consisted of four separate programs, each with its own objectives and history. The Post-Secondary Enrollment Options Act was enacted in 1985, allowing high-school juniors and seniors to take classes at public and private colleges and universities and state vocational schools, at public expense and for credit at both levels. State senator Tom Nelson, chairman of the finance division of the Senate Education Committee, was instrumental in seeing Perpich's bill through the senate; in the house, Representative Connie Levi, a Republican, crossed party lines to sponsor the legislation. Major lobbying pressure also came from Dan Loritz, a strong Perpich supporter in the state department of education.

In 1987, the legislature passed acts establishing the High School Graduation Incentives Program and Area Learning Centers. The former offered options to students between the ages of twelve and twenty-one who were having difficulty in school and were in danger of dropping out. It offered them a chance to try a new school or district to complete their education. The latter program established nontraditional educational settings that provided year-round schooling. Also in 1987, a law was passed requiring all school districts in the state to decide whether they would allow students to leave the district.

The program that received the most attention among school-choice advocates and was the cornerstone of Perpich's educational initiative was the Open Enrollment Options Act. Authored by state senator Randy Peterson, Nelson's successor as chairman of the finance division of the Senate Education Committee, it covered, during the 1989-1990 school year, those school districts with more than one thousand students, expanding to include all districts in the state the year after. Under this program, any of the state's more than seven hundred thousand public-school students were given the right to attend any public school in the state. The only exceptions were cases in which the chosen school was not able to accommodate the student or in which such choices would violate existing racial desegregation guidelines, primarily in the metropolitan districts of Minneapolis-St. Paul and Duluth. In the Open Enrollment Program, state funds would follow students to chosen schools. School districts were given the option to participate; by 1990, almost all districts had chosen to do so. The law further stipulated that schools could not choose among students according to record or performance; in cases where more students chose a school than could be accommodated, a random selection process had to be utilized.

The Open Enrollment Program manifested Perpich's desire to bring the forces of free enterprise into the education marketplace, which traditionally had been a controlled state monopoly. He believed that open enrollment, along with the other options available, would improve educational standards, increase competition, enhance parental involvement, empower teachers and administrators, and decrease transfers to private schools. Minnesota, since 1983, had offered tax deductions for private-school tuition, but the choice options enacted did not involve vouchers applicable to private and parochial institutions, as was the case with a contemporary and well-publicized program in Milwaukee, Wisconsin. Barbara Zohn, former president of the Minnesota Parent-Teacher Association and later an assistant at the Department of Education, applauded choice as a way of encouraging diversity among schools and school programs. Many of the proponents of choice argued that students all had different educational needs, and allowing them to attend the schools where their needs would best be met made perfect sense. Following the program's passage, Peterson oversaw the implementation of open enrollment in the 1988-1989 school year.

In 1991, continuing the momentum, Perpich's successor, Arne Carlson, signed into law the Charter Schools Act, which allowed licensed teachers to create teacher-run, outcome-based schools. Such schools would be deemed public and would be run by the state but would be relatively autonomous and would very likely expand the level of competition.

Student participation in the programs steadily increased from their inception. For the 1989-1990 school year, six thousand students entered the Post-Secondary Enrollment Options Program, eighteen hundred entered the High School Graduation Incentives Program and five thousand chose interdistrict transfers. Many used two or more options simultaneously. These figures do not include the thousands who chose new schools within a residential district. Although critics charged that only a small number—less than 1 percent—of Minnesota students were entering choice programs, proponents argued that the programs would increase awareness and accountability among educators and self-reliance and empowerment among students and parents.

In rural areas, choice options led administrators to create magnet schools to attract dwindling student populations. Throughout the state, an adjunct issue to choice itself was that of publicity and the importance of informing minority families, especially those whose primary language was not English, of the options available. A December, 1990, report by Joe Nathan and Wayne Jennings of the University of Minnesota, "Access to Opportunity," which utilized detailed questionnaires given to more than fourteen hundred students in the various programs, indicated that students were benefiting in terms of attendance, attitude, and achievement but recommended more sophisticated means of disseminating information about the programs.

Impact of Event

The various options that constituted the Minnesota school-choice programs had a strong impact on education and educational policy both in Minnesota and nation-wide. The programs increased discussion and controversy over fundamental educational premises and social ramifications. The Minnesota Education Association, led by Gene Mammenga, and the Minnesota Federation of Teachers generally opposed the legislation. Many critics believed that parents and students simply would not make wise and well-informed choices. Others argued that increased competition would lead to elitism and segregation and that low-income and minority students would still end up with inferior educations. Some feared a period of turmoil marked by school failures and the eventual adoption of superficial advertising techniques. Many who approved of public-school choice noted that its power was limited and warned educators and parents not to abandon other, more essential reforms. The issue of nonacademic transfers was raised, and the Minnesota legislature deferred to the Minnesota High School Athletic Association to reconcile school choice with athletic recruitment.

Nevertheless, the record indicated the relative success of the choice programs. Students who would not have been graduated began to stay in or even return to school under the new options. Few requests were turned down for geographical or racial reasons. Authorities and observers did not notice any tendency toward polarization, nor did the politics of public-school choice immediately grow to include public subsidies for private education, as some had feared. Partially in response to the new programs, from 1985 to 1990 the number of advanced placement courses offered in the state quadrupled, and the number of schools offering dual credit with the University of Minnesota increased from one to twenty-four. Although public-school choice did not prove to be a panacea, it clearly addressed problems faced by thousands of Minnesota students.

On the national scene, the Minnesota programs were watched closely by state and federal governments and an educational establishment increasingly interested in public-school choice. In 1986, the National Governors' Association endorsed public-school choice across party lines. Five years later, it sponsored an influential report on the subject, *Time for Results*, coordinated by Joe Nathan. Following the lead of Minnesota, other states embarked on choice programs. Nebraska, Iowa, Arkansas, Ohio, and Washington were among the most notable; by 1989, thirty states had choice plans passed or proposed on the legislative agenda.

In January of 1989, the administration of outgoing President Ronald Reagan held a White House Workshop on Choice in Education, and in the following months the U.S. Department of Education sponsored five regional conferences on the subject. President George Bush immediately embraced choice as a cornerstone of his educational philosophy. Media attention on the issue focused on Minnesota, and public and private agencies began publishing literature on choice including guidelines, listings, and worksheets. In December of 1990, the Department of Education opened the Center for Choice in Washington, D.C., to increase public awareness. In September of 1991, President Bush proposed legislation providing up to $230 million for the design and implementation of school-choice programs.

Public support for choice remained high. A December, 1988, poll of the Minnesota Education Association reported 60 percent approval of choice, despite the association's official opposition. Gallup polls consistently indicated support for public-school choice by a two-to-one margin on the national level. As the century entered its final decade, more and more people became aware of the possibilities and limitations of public-school choice, and more and more leaders and institutions worked to improve education by increasing options. Much of the impetus for this reform came from the experience of the Minnesota educational system.

Bibliography

Chubb, John E., and Terry M. Moe. *Politics, Markets, and America's Schools.* Washington, D.C.: Brookings Institution, 1990. Chubb and Moe, political scientists at the Brookings Institution and Stanford University respectively, examine the issues confronting American education and the school-choice option from the perspectives of economic and political theory. This dense study, full of statistics, tables, and theoretical models, has attracted great attention.

Coons, John E., and Stephen D. Sugarman. *Education by Choice: The Case for Family Control.* Berkeley: University of California Press, 1978. This volume, written before the widespread emergence of the school-choice movement, examines its philosophical and intellectual origins and underpinnings. The prose is accessible to the lay reader, and the authors, law professors, focus on the welfare of the child and the social institutions designed to guarantee it.

Darling-Hammond, Linda, and Sheila Nataraj Kirby. *Tuition Tax Deductions and Parent School Choice: A Case Study of Minnesota.* Santa Monica, Calif.: Rand, 1985. This is a deeply empirical study of parent attitudes and behavior regarding tax deductions for private-school tuition. Although predating the emergence of public-school choice and not squarely focused on the same issues, the research, from telephone interviews of school administrators and parents of public- and private-school students, deals exclusively with Minnesota and gives interesting insights into how income, geography, occupation, family structure, and other variables affect decision making.

James, Thomas, and Henry M. Levin, eds. *Public Dollars for Private Schools: The Case of Tuition Tax Credits.* Philadelphia: Temple University Press, 1983. This relatively early volume is an anthology of essays by prominent economists and educators on various aspects of the tuition tax-credit debate. On the whole, the essays are well documented, pragmatic, and analytical, though several explore more theoretical questions.

Lieberman, Myron. *Privatization and Educational Choice.* New York: St. Martin's Press, 1989. This book, written in an often-technical vernacular of economic theory, focuses on the government's role in education and the various aspects of voucher plans. Lieberman effectively incorporates statistical information and case studies, including a chapter on the Office of Economic Opportunity experience in the mid-1960's.

_____. *Public School Choice: Current Issues/Future Prospects.* Lancaster, Pa.: Technomic, 1990. A detailed examination on all aspects of the subject of school choice, as the issue stood in 1990. Lieberman strives to maintain an objective viewpoint and a healthy skepticism in conveying and evaluating the various data and claims at a time when the choice debate was gaining momentum nationwide. Includes appendices of practical documents and approaches.

Nathan, Joe, ed. *Public School by Choice: Expanding Opportunities for Parents, Students, and Teachers.* St. Paul, Minn.: Institute for Learning and Teaching, 1989. This is an anthology of articles by proponents of public-school choice, many of whom have been deeply involved in the programs in Minnesota, Cambridge, East Harlem, and Milwaukee. The programs are described in detail. The anthology as a whole is very much in favor of choice. Includes a foreword by Perpich.

Rinehart, James R., and Jackson F. Lee, Jr. *American Education and the Dynamics of Choice.* New York: Praeger, 1991. Rinehart, an economist, and Lee, an educator, join to present a probing and theoretical examination of contemporary trends in American education, the movement toward school choice, and the dilemmas it presents. The authors attempt to render the complex material clearly and concisely for the lay reader, with fair success.

Barry Mann

Cross-References

Students Challenge Corporal Punishment in British Schools (1911), p. 109; Spanish Becomes the Language of Instruction in Puerto Rico (1949), p. 801; *Brown v. Board of Education* Ends Public School Segregation (1954), p. 913; Eisenhower Sends Troops to Little Rock, Arkansas (1957), p. 1003; Head Start Is Established (1965), p. 1284; Congress Enacts the Bilingual Education Act (1968), p. 1402; The Supreme Court Endorses Busing as a Means to End Segregation (1971), p. 1628; The Supreme Court Rejects Racial Quotas in College Admissions (1973), p. 1697; Congress Enacts the Education for All Handicapped Children Act (1975), p. 1780; Southern Schools Are Found to Be the Least Racially Segregated (1975), p. 1786.

THE FIRST FEMALE CONSERVATIVE RABBI IS ORDAINED

Categories of event: Women's rights and religious freedom
Time: May 12, 1985
Locale: New York, New York

The Rabbinical Assembly, the governing body of Conservative Judaism, decided after years of debate to admit women as rabbis and to ordain its first female rabbi, Amy Eilberg

Principal personages:
> AMY EILBERG (1954-   ), a Jewish Theological Seminary student who became the first female Conservative rabbi
> GERSON D. COHEN (1924-1991), the chancellor of the Jewish Theological Seminary from 1972 to 1985
> DAVID NOVAK (1941-   ), a spokesman for the Union for Traditional Conservative Judaism

Summary of Event

In the middle of the nineteenth century, European nations became more democratic and began to separate the affairs of church and state. Consequently, Jews, who historically had been confined to living in ghettos, found themselves increasingly emancipated. Many newly freed European Jews wished to rebel against tradition completely and create a new religious authority. They founded the Reform movement and exported their ideas to the new world. They were so successful that by 1880, 91 percent of American synagogues considered themselves Reform.

Still, there were many Jews who reacted against this radical movement. These were not Orthodox Jews, who hailed mainly from Eastern Europe. These Jews were from Western Europe and America. They wanted to retain most of their traditional practices and beliefs but also to maintain some flexibility in adapting to modern life. They remained devoted to the use of Hebrew in the liturgy, the observance of dietary laws, and the Sabbath. In the United States, this movement became known as Conservative Judaism, referring to its effort to conserve the essence of traditional Judaism. In Europe, it is called the Historical Movement, because it considers itself the heir of the entire history of Judaism, which has changed over time and therefore can continue to do so.

In 1886, Conservatives formed the Jewish Theological Seminary of America. The articles of incorporation of this school say that it is dedicated to "the preservation in America of the knowledge and practice of historical Judaism as ordained in the law of Moses expounded by the prophets and sages in Israel in Biblical and Talmudic writings." In 1898, the Conservatives tried to merge with the Orthodox movement, but they failed. Two years later, the Orthodox movement barred the graduates of the Jewish Theological Seminary from becoming rabbis.

Seminary advocates reorganized their school to define themselves as traditionalists, yet separate from the Orthodox community. The alumni of the new Jewish Theological Seminary formed the Rabbinical Assembly of America. This organization became the worldwide governing body of Conservative Judaism.

In 1913, Conservatives founded the United Synagogue of America as an umbrella body for all congregations that were not Orthodox, yet maintained the essential elements of traditional Judaism. This covered a wide spectrum of independent congregations that remained free to define their practices within the framework of Jewish law. This plurality became an inherent source of conflict in the Conservative movement.

Through the years, Conservative Judaism made several amendments to its laws to accommodate modern life. In 1936, the Rabbinical Assembly voted to make it possible for a woman whose husband had abandoned her to get a legitimate religious divorce. It passed further liberalizations of divorce laws in 1952 and 1968. In 1960, the Rabbinical Assembly permitted the use of electricity on the Sabbath and Sabbath travel to the synagogue to attend services. From the 1920's to the 1960's, Conservative Judaism answered the needs of second-generation European Americans who wished to follow the religious traditions of their youth yet maintain fully American life-styles. Their children, the third generation, tended either to drift away from tradition or to demand it in a purer form.

An example of the latter phenomenon occurred in the Eilberg family of Philadelphia in 1969. Joshua Eilberg, a former Democratic representative, and his wife, Gladys, were Conservative Jews who were religious but did not observe kosher dietary laws. Gladys' mother was a Russian Jew, matriarch of a traditional Jewish family that had suffered attacks from Cossacks in the Ukraine. During the summer of 1969, the Eilbergs' fourteen-year-old daughter, Amy, became enamored of the strict practices of traditional Judaism when she participated in a program given by the United Synagogue Youth, the national Conservative youth organization. When Amy returned home, she declared that she would eat only food that was prepared according to kosher dietary laws. Her family soon followed her example and began to keep kosher. Eilberg maintained her passion for traditional Judaism in high school. When she was a senior, she attempted to have the date for the prom moved from Friday night because it conflicted with the Sabbath.

Eilberg was a freshman at Brandeis University in 1972 when she and other students protested rules that forbade the participation of women in synagogue services and that required women to sit apart from men. Because of the students' lobbying efforts, the Brandeis Jewish chapel made its Sabbath service fully egalitarian, welcoming participation and leadership from both men and women. It was then that Eilberg realized that she could try to find equality for women within the structure of the *halakah*, the traditional Jewish legal system.

In 1973, at the First National Jewish Women's Conference, Rachel Adler, a pioneering Jewish feminist, prayed wearing a prayer shawl and phylacteries, leather boxes that contain Scripture. This form of prayer had been practiced only by men, according to Jewish tradition. Eilberg followed Adler's example to protest the idea that her gender excluded her from the central activities of her religion. She began to lead services and read from the Torah, and she taught other women how to do this.

This experience made Eilberg decide to try to become a Conservative rabbi, though this was impossible for women at that time. She entered the Jewish Theological Seminary in 1976, and by 1978 had earned a master's degree in the study of the Talmud, a source book of discussions about Jewish law. She continued her study of the Talmud until she had met all the requirements for a doctorate except for her dissertation. She chose not to finish her degree then, preferring to work with people and not solely as an academic. Women were not yet allowed in the rabbinic training program at the seminary.

Eilberg decided to pursue her own course of study to prepare herself for the possibility that she might someday be ordained. She earned a second master's degree in 1984, this time from Smith College, in social work. Dr. Gerson D. Cohen, chancellor of the Jewish Theological Seminary, finally won his fight to have women accepted into the school's rabbinic training program in October, 1983. Eilberg enrolled in September, 1984, and was able to complete the requirements for ordination in one school year.

Meanwhile, the Conservative movement was in great turmoil over the ordination of women. In 1979, the faculty of the Jewish Theological Seminary voted to table the issue because it was too divisive. In April, 1983, two female Reform rabbis, Beverly Magidson and Jan Kaufman, attempted to gain entrance to the Rabbinical Assembly. The Reform movement had begun ordaining women in 1972. To become Conservative rabbis, Magidson and Kaufman would have to submit themselves to a vote at the annual convention of the more than eleven hundred Conservative rabbis from around the world. Their acceptance into the Assembly would require a 75 percent majority approval vote. Their bid for admittance into the Rabbinical Assembly was rejected, but a Conservative congregation in New York State hired Rabbi Magidson anyway. In May, 1984, the Rabbinical Assembly again barred Magidson and Kaufman from their organization by failing to give either of them a three-quarters majority vote.

Early in 1985, supporters of ordination for women tried a different tack. They submitted their resolution to the Rabbinical Assembly as a constitutional amendment. The Assembly votes on amendments through the mail, and these require only a two-thirds majority for passage. The resolution did not ask directly for the ordination of women. It requested instead that all graduates of the rabbinic training program of the Jewish Theological Seminary be automatically admitted into the Rabbinical Assembly. This would eliminate the need for a three-quarters vote of approval for each rabbinical candidate at the annual convention. As a secondary result, any woman who graduated from the training program would also become a member of the Rabbinical Assembly and, hence, a fully recognized Conservative rabbi.

The tactic worked. This amendment to the constitution passed by a 70 percent majority. The Rabbinical Assembly announced the result of its vote on February 14, 1985, at a news conference at the Jewish Theological Seminary in New York City. There, it introduced its first female rabbinical candidate, Amy Eilberg, who would graduate in May. On that occasion, Eilberg commented gratefully, "The long vigil is over." Then she stated that, "As of today, Jewish women need never again feel that their gender is a barrier to their full participation in Jewish life."

Impact of Event

In 1991, six years after Rabbi Eilberg's ordination, she estimated that there were between thirty and fifty female Conservative rabbis. She stated that the women rabbis "are not a homogeneous group. There are profound ideological differences between us." She said that some do not consider themselves "feminists," although they were among the first women to achieve the rabbinate. Some women struggled to raise families even while they worked in the pulpit of a synagogue and fought to have their religious authority recognized.

Eilberg spent only one year at a congregation. She had to work constantly, and this left her little time to spend with her husband, Dr. Howard Schwartz, a scholar of religion, and their infant daughter. She decided to abandon the pulpit when she heard her daughter's first words: "Bye bye, Ima-schul," which means, "Bye bye Mommy, synagogue."

Eilberg spent the next five years as a hospital chaplain. She declared that this work was "Wonderful. In all those years I was struggling [in school], I didn't have a specific picture of what I was called to do. I didn't know I was meant to be a pastoral care giver." As a chaplain, she could approach people as a helping figure, rather than as an authority. Consequently, Eilberg explained, "I experience less face to face resistance [than I would in a synagogue], although I do occasionally get thrown out of a room. My identity as a woman is an issue in a positive sense. I'm grateful that I'm not fighting all the time."

Not that there was not more fighting to do. In 1991, Eilberg revealed that the experience of female rabbis was "not dissimilar to what happens to women in law, medicine, and business." She claimed that sexism persisted in the Conservative movement, although in a subtler form. Women rabbis still found their religious authority questioned by traditional groups. They continued to be forced off political committees for espousing points of view different from those of the male majority. Women rabbis often failed to get preferred jobs and had applications dismissed with vague excuses, such as "You don't quite fit into our congregation."

Still, there were signs of hope. In 1991, the Rabbinical Assembly prepared a new manual for its members, with instructions on how to perform various religious ceremonies. The section on childbirth was expanded to take women more into account. The female rabbi assigned to write this section shared the task and the credit with other women so that it would have a comprehensive outlook. Rabbi Eilberg commented on this action, "It's women's way—it mutually empowers. We have our foot in the door. We are speaking in a different voice. Our authority is just beginning to emerge."

Bibliography

"Amy Eilberg Will Be Conservative Judaism's First Woman Rabbi." *People Weekly* 23 (April 29, 1985): 50. An accessible article on Eilberg's background and outlook. She describes working for ten years to achieve her goal. She took a self-directed course in preparation for the rabbinate until the Jewish Theological Seminary decided to admit women.

Cantor, Aviva. "Rabbi Eilberg." *Ms.* 14 (December, 1985): 45-46. A more in-depth article, focussing on Eilberg's background and philosophy. Cantor stresses the years that Eilberg struggled, completing years more study than an average male rabbinical candidate would. As a result, she was prepared when the Rabbinical Assembly voted to admit women into its ranks. An inspirational as well as informative article.

"End of a Vigil: A First For Jewish Women." *Time* 125 (February 25, 1985): 61. A short but accessible article outlining the Rabbinical Assembly's decision to accept women. Here, Eilberg admits that the question of female rabbis has caused tension in the Conservative movement. Also, Rabbi Pinchas Stolper, from the Orthodox Jewish movement, declares that, with this move, the Conservatives have irreparably separated themselves from Jewish tradition.

Gordis, Robert. "On the Ordination of Women." In *Understanding Conservative Judaism*. New York: Rabbinical Assembly, 1978. Gordis voices his opinion on the ordination of female rabbis, citing passages from the Torah. These arguments presaged the actual acceptance of women as rabbis. Gives interesting background. Other chapters explain different aspects of Conservative Judaism.

Greenberg, Simon, ed. *The Ordination of Women as Rabbis: Studies and Responsa*. New York: Jewish Theological Seminary of America, 1988. Eleven faculty members of the Jewish Theological Seminary give their opinions on the ordination of women based on interpretations of the *halakah*, or traditional Judaic legal system. This gives history of the reasoning behind the acceptance of women as rabbis. For advanced students.

Portnoy, Mindy Avra. *Ima on the Bima: My Mommy Is a Rabbi*. Rockville, Md.: Kar-Ben Copies, 1986. Although this book is written for Jewish children, it provides an excellent introduction to the duties of a rabbi for those people unfamiliar with Jewish religious tradition. It is one of the few books available on female rabbis. Contains a glossary that explains some Hebrew words and important Jewish holidays.

Pamela Canal

Cross-References

Presbyterian and Methodist Churches Approve Ordination of Women (1955),

p. 929; The National Organization for Women Forms to Protect Women's Rights (1966), p. 1327; The United Nations Issues a Declaration on Equality for Women (1967), p. 1391; The World Conference on Women Sets an International Agenda (1975), p. 1796; A U.N. Convention Condemns Discrimination Against Women (1979), p. 2057.

FRENCH GOVERNMENT AGENTS SINK
A GREENPEACE SHIP

Categories of event: Peace movements and organizations; atrocities and war crimes
Time: July 10, 1985
Locale: Auckland Harbor, New Zealand

French bombing of a Greenpeace ship heightened public awareness about the series of nuclear tests being conducted in the Pacific and raised questions regarding civil control over security services in France

Principal personages:

CHARLES HERNU (1923-1990), the head of the French Ministry of Defense at the time of the attack and one of those held responsible for it

PIERRE LACOSTE (1898-1989), the head of the French Intelligence Service responsible for carrying out the attack on the *Rainbow Warrior*

FRANÇOIS MITTERRAND (1916-), the president of France; French newspapers alleged that he sought to cover up his government's involvement in the attack

LAURENT FABIUS (1946-), the prime minister of France; directed that inquiries be undertaken and dismissed members of his government for their involvement

DAVID LANGE (1942-), the prime minister of New Zealand; opposed nuclear testing in the Pacific

Summary of Event

Shortly before midnight on July 10, 1985, two bombs ripped through the hull of the *Rainbow Warrior*, which was anchored in the harbor in Auckland, New Zealand. The first blast occurred near the engine room and created a hole large enough to drive a truck through. Water entered the *Rainbow Warrior* at the rate of six tons per second. The second blast came a minute later, near the propeller. It destroyed the ship's propulsion system. One member of the *Rainbow Warrior*'s fourteen-person crew, photographer Fernando Pereira, was killed.

The *Rainbow Warrior* was a thirty-year-old converted research trawler that Greenpeace had bought in 1977 with a grant from the Dutch branch of the World Wildlife Fund. Greenpeace itself was established in 1969 by Canadian environmentalists. It advocates direct and nonviolent action to bring attention to the world's environmental problems and is well known for its confrontational tactics.

The *Rainbow Warrior* was the flagship of Greenpeace's busy fleet of four protest vessels. Previously, it had sailed to Iceland, Spain, and Peru to protest commercial whaling operations. It had also sailed into Siberian waters to document illegal Soviet whaling operations. Other missions saw it bring attention to the Canadian slaughter of harp seal pups on icepacks, to American chemical dumping and offshore oil and gas development, and to the dumping of nuclear waste in the North Atlantic.

By using the *Rainbow Warrior* and its other vessels in this way, Greenpeace brought worldwide attention to the negative environmental impact of these actions and, on occasion, seemed to goad governments into taking corrective measures. For example, Peru closed down its whaling operations following the *Rainbow Warrior*'s 1982 campaign against whaling, and the European Parliament voted a ban on the dumping of radioactive waste at sea. Many also link the increased global concern for the fate of whales to Greenpeace's efforts. On the other hand, Greenpeace's aggressive tactics also brought the organization into recurring conflict with national authorities. On more than one occasion, the *Rainbow Warrior* or its crew were seized and had to either engineer a dramatic escape or rely on diplomacy to secure freedom.

In 1985, Greenpeace International decided to make the Pacific Ocean its priority for that year. The focus of its concern was with the continued use of the region as a nuclear testing area. The testing of nuclear weapons had begun in the Pacific only a few short years after the end of World War II. In May and April of 1948, Operation Sandstone was conducted at Eniwetok Atoll. The three nuclear explosions that were carried out as part of this test ranged in magnitude from eighteen to forty-nine kilotons. In comparison, the explosion at Hiroshima was thirteen kilotons and that at Nagasaki was twenty-one kilotons.

In conducting these early tests, officials routinely played down or ignored the potentially dangerous consequences that followed from exposure to high levels of radiation. By the late 1950's, the evidence of danger became increasingly difficult to dismiss, and public pressure began to build for a halt to the above-ground or atmospheric testing of nuclear weapons. In 1958, both the United States and the Soviet Union agreed to stop such tests and began negotiating a test ban treaty. As Cold War tensions between these states heated up, interest in arms control faded. In 1961, the Soviet Union announced that it would resume atmospheric testing. The United States quickly announced that it would also end its moratorium on these tests. Concern over how close the Cuban Missile crisis had brought the world to war reversed this trend and led to the signing of the 1963 test ban treaty which, while it outlawed the atmospheric testing of nuclear weapons, did permit their continued underground testing.

In 1968, the two superpowers took another step toward arms control by signing the Nonproliferation Treaty. By terms of this treaty, signatory states that possessed nuclear weapons would refrain from helping nonnuclear states to acquire such weapons. States that did not have nuclear weapons pledged not to attempt to develop them. France refused to sign this treaty (only in 1991 did it indicate a willingness to do so). France has steadfastly maintained that only a French nuclear force can guarantee French survival and sovereignty. To that end, it has asserted the right to engage in the acquisition of nuclear weapons and to test and improve the weapons in its nuclear inventory.

At first, France tested its nuclear weapons in the Sahara Desert. Its first test came on February 13, 1960. With the success of the Algerian revolution and the passing of

French colonial stewardship over North Africa in 1962, the French were forced to turn elsewhere to continue testing their nuclear weapons. It was for this reason that Charles de Gaulle established a French test facility in the Pacific in 1966. The site selected was Mururoa Atoll. French nuclear tests were conducted there in 1972 and 1973.

The centerpiece of Greenpeace's protest efforts in 1985 was to be the disruption of French activities in Mururoa, scheduled as the site of an October nuclear test. Unlike earlier protest activities noted above, this protest was planned in advance and was not spontaneous in nature. The *Rainbow Warrior* was in Auckland in preparation for that protest. Its disruption of the French nuclear test was to be the highlight of the protest effort.

Protest vessels and Greenpeace were no strangers to the French. According to the *New Statesman*, in 1966 a motorized sail ship was crippled en route to Mururoa by having sugar poured in its tanks. The following year, a mysterious illness struck a member of that same ship's crew. In 1972, another protest ship was sabotaged and yet another was crippled in the water after French officials boarded the ship to inspect it. With this history, it was not surprising that suspicion quickly fell upon the French, who denied any responsibility for the *Rainbow Warrior* bombing. Misgivings regarding the role of the French, however, were not easily erased. After three days of investigation, New Zealand authorities arrested a French-speaking couple who held false Swiss passports. Authorities were also able to identify others involved in the bombing as well as the vessel they had used. Both the vessel and the other suspects, who had actually done the bombing, managed to flee New Zealand before they could be arrested.

Uncharacteristically, French newspapers did not accept government denials about its involvement in the bombing but published information suggesting that a link existed. In early August, Prime Minister Laurent Fabius announced that Bernard Tricot, a former adviser to de Gaulle, would head an inquiry into the attack on the *Rainbow Warrior.* Tricot termed the evidence he was shown by New Zealand authorities as disquieting but not conclusive. He acknowledged that those under suspicion by New Zealand were French agents but asserted that they were innocent. Tricot also recommended that a more detailed study be conducted. With the debate over French complicity refusing to die, Fabius then asked Minister of Defense Charles Hernu to conduct the recommended study. To show his support for the nuclear program and to demonstrate his government's innocence, French President François Mitterrand went to Mururoa in September to witness a test of a French nuclear weapon.

Within days of his return, *Le Monde* added more fuel to the controversy by suggesting that high French government officials had ordered the bombing, or at least had known about it in advance. Implicated were Defense Minister Hernu, General Jean Saulnier, and Pierre Lacoste, head of the French intelligence service. *Le Monde* also charged that Mitterrand, while he had known nothing about the attack prior to its taking place, had been informed about French involvement about one week afterward. In late September, Fabius acknowledged that French agents had sunk the ship and blamed Hernu and Lacoste, both of whom were forced to resign.

The *Rainbow Warrior* affair came to an end in July, 1986, when United Nations Secretary-General Javier Pérez de Cuellar, who was brought in to mediate a settlement, announced his decision. He ruled that France should formally apologize to New Zealand, pay $7 million in damages, and refrain from taking any action that would threaten New Zealand's trade with the European Community. New Zealand was to turn over to France the two convicted French agents, who would spend three years in a French military jail.

Impact of Event

As in the past, Greenpeace planned to use the *Rainbow Warrior* to bring worldwide attention to an environmental danger. It succeeded in doing so not through its efforts but through the actions of the French government. The French decision to attack the *Rainbow Warrior* does not appear to have been a spontaneous one. Documents reveal that at least as early as July officials anticipated the environmental protest threat. Press reports also suggest that Hernu asked his chief adviser to keep an eye on protest activities and to keep them out of the French test zone.

The long-term significance of the French attack on the *Rainbow Warrior* can be found in several areas. First, the incident played a major role in the continued development of antinuclear feelings in the Pacific. Earlier that year, New Zealand had refused to allow a United States destroyer into its waters because the United States would not divulge whether it carried nuclear weapons. Mitterrand's trip to Mururoa was characterized by both Australia and New Zealand as provocative. Second, the attack needs to be viewed in the context of decolonization in the Pacific. The micro states of the Pacific have been among the last to receive their independence, and nuclear testing on or around them raises serious questions regarding their true territorial sovereignty and the quality of stewardship exercised by French colonial forces.

Third, the *Rainbow Warrior* affair is also important for what it indicates about French politics. Several themes stand out. One is the depth of the French commitment to achieving status as a great power through the acquisition and maintenance of a nuclear capability. The second theme centers on the role of the military in French politics. The government's response to the attack on the *Rainbow Warrior* demonstrated continued military influence. One of Mitterrand's first acts upon taking office in 1981 was to reorganize the French intelligence service by ridding it of many of its most ardent right-wing agents. Still, few seemed surprised when allegations surfaced regarding the possibility that these forces may have acted on their own in attacking the *Rainbow Warrior.* A further sign of the political importance of the military came when Fabius' September statement made no mention of trials or reprimands for those involved. Finally, in October, 1985, the new minister of defense announced the revival of the Eleventh Shock, an elite regiment known for its dirty tricks and right-wing sympathies.

On a more personal level, the French attack on the *Rainbow Warrior* had the effect of bringing into sharp focus the extent to which world politics was incompatible with concerns for human rights and environmental well-being. What was involved was not superpower Cold War intrigue in which spy fought spy. This was a deliberate act of sabotage, resulting in one death, that pitted a large state (France) against private citizens of other states and took place in the territorial waters of yet another state. Even the method by which the issue was resolved (by the United Nations) showed the lack of concern that world politics, as it is traditionally practiced, had for individual rights and protecting the environment. New Zealand was compensated by France for violations of its sovereignty but little of significance was done to compensate Greenpeace or the family of Fernando Pereira. France continued its program of nuclear testing and continued to receive clandestine help from the United States in developing a usable nuclear arsenal. The people of New Zealand have begun to protest nuclear proliferation by supporting their government's stance against permitting U.S. nuclear-armed vessels to dock in its harbors and by resisting U.S. attempts to pressure a reversal of this decision.

Bibliography

Fontanel, Jacques. "An Underdeveloped Peace Movement: The Case of France." *Journal of Peace Research* 23 (Spring, 1986): 175-182. French public opinion was generally supportive of Mitterrand's government. This article is helpful because it sheds light on French attitudes toward militarism and nuclear deterrence.

Gidley, Isobelle, and Richard Shears. *The Rainbow Warrior Affair.* Boston: Unwin Paperbacks, 1985. Far less useful as an account of the *Rainbow Warrior* affair than the volume by King. This is an attempt at popularizing history and relies heavily on reconstructed conversations. The real strength of the volume lies in its chapters on the political background of the Pacific Ocean.

King, Michael. *Death of the Rainbow Warrior.* New York: Penguin Books, 1986. A very readable account of the attack on the *Rainbow Warrior.* Its focus is on the individuals involved at the "ground level" rather than on the larger issues. Spends a great deal of time looking at the investigation by New Zealand authorities.

Macridis, Roy. "French Foreign Policy: The Quest for Rank." In *Foreign Policy in World Politics.* 7th ed. Englewood Cliffs, N.J.: Prentice-Hall, 1989. Written by one of the leading authorities on French foreign policy. Provides an excellent overview of post-World War II developments and a general context within which to put the attack on the *Rainbow Warrior.*

May, John. *The Greenpeace Book of the Nuclear Age.* New York: Pantheon, 1990. This work does not deal directly with the issue of nuclear testing in the Pacific. Rather, it examines nuclear accidents. It is worth consulting because it shows how Greenpeace approaches nuclear issues.

Thakur, Ramesh. "A Dispute of Many Colours: France, New Zealand, and the Rainbow Warrior Affair." *The World Today* 42 (December, 1986): 209-214. Although this is a short article, it is still valuable because of the paucity of book-length studies done on this subject. Covers such issues as nuclear-free zones, the Greenpeace foundation, nuclear weapons tests, and relations between France and New Zealand.

Touraine, Alain, et al. *Anti-Nuclear Protest: The Opposition to Nuclear Energy in France.* New York: Cambridge University Press, 1983. Written prior to the attack on the *Rainbow Warrior.* Looks at French antinuclear militants. Adopts a neo-Marxist perspective and is written for an academic audience.

Ullman, Richard. "The Covert French Connection." *Foreign Policy* 75 (Summer, 1989): 3-33. This looks at the various ways in which the United States secretly and illegally helped the French nuclear program. In doing so, it provides insight into both French thinking and the larger issues of nuclear strategy.

Weston, Bruce, ed. *Toward Nuclear Disarmament and Global Security.* Boulder, Colo.: Westview Press, 1984. This book is an excellent introduction to the field of disarmament. While it lacks an index, there are extensive bibliographic entries at the end of each section. Topics include confronting the nuclear crisis, rethinking basic assumptions, and opting for nuclear disarmament.

Glenn Hastedt

Cross-References

Legal Norms of Behavior in Warfare Formulated by the Hague Conference (1907), p. 92; The French Quell an Algerian Nationalist Revolt (1945), p. 651; The Zero Population Growth Movement Spurs Environmental Consciousness (1967), p. 1386; Leftists Rebel in France (1968), p. 1425; Toxic Waste Is Discovered at Love Canal (1978), p. 1961; Lethal Gas Kills Thousands in Bhopal, India (1984), p. 2238.

MANVILLE OFFERS $2.5 BILLION TO
VICTIMS OF ASBESTOS DUST

Categories of event: Workers' rights and consumers' rights
Time: August-December, 1985
Locale: Denver, Colorado

The accord reached between the nation's leading manufacturer of asbestos and victims of asbestos-related health problems brought to an end an almost twenty-five-year-old legal battle

Principal personages:

VANDIVER BROWN (1901-1983), the chief attorney for Johns-Manville Corporation in the 1930's

JOHN A. MCKINNEY (1923-), the chairman and chief executive officer of Manville Corporation at the time of the settlement

IRVING J. SELIKOFF (1915-), a doctor who in 1964 established the link between the inhalation of asbestos fibers and the contraction of asbestosis

WARD STEPHENSON (1921-1973), a Texas lawyer who brought the first successful product-liability case involving asbestos-induced illness

Summary of Event

The wonders of asbestos, the "magic mineral," have been known since the days of the ancient Greeks. Asbestos' great advantage is that it is fire-resistant, yet asbestos fibers are soft and flexible, making it relatively easy to fabricate into a desired product. Although relatively unimportant in antiquity, asbestos became extremely important during the Industrial Revolution in nineteenth century Europe and America. Because asbestos is incombustible, it became indispensable as an insulation material on furnaces, turbines, boilers, steam pipes, and ovens as well as an integral material in the shipbuilding and construction industries.

Unfortunately, asbestos, for all of its positive properties, contained a serious and deadly drawback. As early as the first century A.D., the Greeks mentioned lung problems afflicting slaves who wove asbestos fibers into cloth. This information was virtually ignored until 1906, when a British physician, H. Montague Murray, performed an autopsy on a worker who had spent fourteen years in an asbestos-textile factory. On the basis of slender slivers of asbestos found in the worker's lung tissues, Murray concluded that the worker's death was connected to his occupation.

Murray's discovery could have been devastating to the booming asbestos industry, especially for the Johns-Manville (J-M) Corporation, the world's largest manufacturer of asbestos. Thus, in 1929 the Metropolitan Life Insurance Company, at the request of several leading corporations within the asbestos industry (including J-M and Raybestos-Manhattan, the two largest firms), commissioned medical research to study the hypothesized link between asbestos and lung problems and to determine what, if anything, could be done to control or prevent serious health problems in asbestos-manufacturing plants.

The results of the study, done by Dr. Anthony Lanza and two colleagues, were reported to J-M in 1931. Lanza noted that more than half of the workers he had studied in an asbestos plant had developed asbestosis; that asbestosis was "clinically . . . milder than silicosis" (a condition already known to cause pulmonary problems to miners); that asbestosis could be fatal; and that asbestos dust control in conjunction with physical exams and X rays were important measures to monitor worker safety. Vandiver Brown, the head of J-M's legal department, suggested that, without altering the results of his study before publication, Lanza might emphasize two facts that were beneficial to the asbestos industry: that asbestosis was milder than silicosis and that, at the time, the state of medical and scientific knowledge was such that special precautions (for example, sharing the results of X rays and physical exams with infected workers) were unwarranted for the owners of asbestos plants.

The extent of scientific knowledge concerning asbestos dangers is vital to an understanding of the asbestos controversy and the subsequent legal settlement. In 1964, Dr. Irving J. Selikoff and his associates, studying asbestos-insulation workers at the behest of two labor unions, provided "incontrovertible evidence" that exposure to asbestos was extremely hazardous to health and that such hazards increased with prolonged exposure. This only reinforced what J-M already knew as a result of Lanza's research some thirty-five years before. By the early 1960's, J-M had become the subject of numerous wrongful-death and product-liability suits brought by asbestos workers and their family survivors—workers who suffered from asbestosis, mesothelioma, or a host of other pulmonary diseases.

J-M contested such suits, avowing that it did not know of the health consequences of prolonged exposure to asbestos dust. This was, of course, at complete odds with the Lanza study as well as several other studies done between 1931 and 1964. Moreover, it failed to acknowledge J-M's own role (through Vandiver Brown's memorandum to Lanza prior to publication of the latter's research) in suppressing scientific knowledge concerning the health dangers posed by exposure to asbestos. J-M further argued that the federal government should be held liable, since hundreds of thousands of workers had been exposed to asbestos in the nation's shipyards during World War II, and J-M was merely fulfilling government contract specifications requiring asbestos insulation throughout U.S. Navy vessels. Finally, J-M indicted the lawyers representing those who were exposed to asbestos, maintaining that large portions of successful monetary settlements went to the lawyers and not to the workers who brought suit. J-M asserted, in effect, that lawyers involved in an association such as the Asbestos Litigation Group (an organization of lawyers who shared legal strategy, court rulings, and medical evidence relating to asbestos) had become new "ambulance chasers."

By the late 1970's, J-M was facing more than fifteen thousand lawsuits. Until that time, J-M's numerous insurers had had little trouble paying damage awards won by successful litigants. One of the insurers, the Travelers Corporation, began to refuse payment on asbestos-related claims, and thus arose the "trigger date" controversy. The critical issue concerned which insurance firm would be held liable for settling claims: the insurer during the exposure of the victim, the insurer during the manifestation of the disease, the insurer during the filing of the lawsuit, the insurer during the judgment of the case, or some combination of these. This was an extremely important question to the various insurers who would ultimately pay damages, since asbestosis can appear decades after the initial exposure.

On August 26, 1982, Manville (J-M had changed its name in 1981 as part of a restructuring move) took the wholly surprising and unprecedented step of filing for bankruptcy under Chapter 11 protection, even though it held more than $2 billion in assets. It successfully argued before the bankruptcy court that asbestos suits (which then included punitive damages awards in the millions of dollars) had left Manville in a position of "equity insolvency," meaning that at some point in the future it would be unable to pay its debts as they came due. Obviously, a large percentage of its future debts would be caused by the more than sixteen thousand asbestos claims then awaiting litigation.

The significance of Manville's petition for bankruptcy was that all payments and awards to asbestos claimants were halted pending Manville's emergence from bankruptcy. This, in turn, placed a severe financial burden on those workers who were disabled or incapacitated from asbestos dust exposure and for whom cash settlements granted by judges or juries were crucial to survival.

Lawyers representing asbestos workers immediately appealed to bankruptcy judge Burton Lifland to deny Manville's petition, claiming that Manville's filing under Chapter 11 represented a callous attempt to deprive successful asbestos litigants of their monetary awards. Judge Lifland denied the appeal and ordered both sides in the case to effect a compromise.

Acrimonious negotiations began in late 1982, and the broad outlines of a compromise were reached in the winter of 1985. The complex compromise eventually agreed upon included the following terms: all claims brought by Manville's commercial creditors were settled with money and stock, and, most important, asbestos litigants would seek compensation from a fund totaling more than $2.5 billion generated by contributions made by Manville and its insurers. This would result in settlements of between thirty and fifty thousand dollars for the estimated forty to sixty thousand asbestos claims yet to be filed. This represented a mere pittance compared to the average total compensation of $385,000 won by individual claimants who went to trial between 1980 and 1982. Apparently worn out by incessant delays and legal squabbling, asbestos victims thought that it was better to receive some compensation than to risk getting nothing as a result of unfavorable legal rulings in the future.

The settlement ended this particular chapter in the scientific, legal, and moral battle diseased workers waged against Manville and other corporations in the asbestos industry. The latter continued to draw the ire of thousands of workers exposed to asbestos. The misery and suffering of those workers unquestionably played a part in the decision of the Environmental Protection Agency (EPA) to impose a comprehensive ban on asbestos by 1996. History suggested that Manville and the rest of the asbestos industry would wage a strong and determined fight to rescind the EPA mandate.

Impact of Event

Manville's bankruptcy and subsequent settlement with victims of asbestos-related diseases raised significant issues relevant to the consumer rights movement. When Manville declared bankruptcy in August of 1982, it was the richest and healthiest corporation to do so. The gist of Manville's bankruptcy petition was that it would not be able to make good on successful asbestos claims against it at some point in the future, although it held more than $2 billion in assets at the time it was granted Chapter 11 protection by the courts. Manville's action became known as an instance of "strategic bankruptcy," whereby a solvent enterprise protects itself against future liabilities, evading what some maintain is its corporate responsibility. Such action was perfectly legal under the liberal reforms granted under the 1978 Bankruptcy Reform Act. Manville's action may have set a precedent for other firms involved in the manufacture of potentially hazardous or toxic substances, especially those in the nuclear, medical, and chemical industries, possibly leaving affected workers no chance for compensation in the courts for injury or sickness.

By far the biggest losers in the settlement were Manville's shareholders, who lost 80 percent of the value of their stock. Shareholders' substantial equity losses (together with Manville profits) helped fund the $2.5-billion compensation claims pool for asbestos victims. Not surprisingly, shareholders were the only group to vote against the agreement.

It remained to be seen whether the settlement would remain intact. The estimates of future asbestos-related health cases and the continued financial health of Manville were fairly complex, but were estimates nevertheless. It is important to note that by the mid-1980's more than twenty million Americans had been exposed to asbestos through insulation materials in schools, homes, and office buildings. What if the number of future asbestos sufferers had been seriously underestimated? What if Manville (which moved out of asbestos manufacturing and into forest products in the 1970's) were to suffer a serious financial downturn in a volatile and competitive market? How would that affect its ability to pay the cash allotments granted to asbestos workers in the final settlement? The central question posed by the asbestos controversy and settlement remained: Of what real value were such payments to the thousands of asbestos workers who suffered severe health problems and died agonizing deaths as a result of their exposure to asbestos?

Bibliography

Brodeur, Paul. "The Asbestos Industry on Trial." *The New Yorker* 61 (June 10-July 1,

1985). This four-part series is essential reading for anyone wishing to understand the asbestos controversy. It is thoroughly documented and extremely well written and reads like a mystery novel that one cannot put down. Its greatest contribution is that it makes the complex medical, legal, and scientific jargon and arguments understandable to a nontechnical audience.

_____. *Outrageous Misconduct.* New York: Pantheon Books, 1985. Contains the four chapters that were excerpted in *The New Yorker* as well as seven other chapters. Provides more history and detail of Manville's role in preventing information about asbestos-induced disease from reaching workers. All the significant corporations, lawyers, corporate executives, and health officials are discussed in this book, one of the most widely cited works related to the topic. The last three pages provide a gripping and poignant reminder that the dizzying dollar figures and other statistics in the book often mask the human tragedy that is the asbestos controversy.

Calhoun, Craig, and Henryk Hiller. "Coping with Insidious Injuries: The Case of Johns-Manville Corporation and Asbestos Exposure." *Social Problems* 35 (April, 1988): 162-181. This is a first-rate academic treatment of the legal issues and complexities raised by the J-M bankruptcy. The authors argue for incentives to motivate corporate managers to provide full information about potentially dangerous products such as asbestos.

Delaney, Kevin J. "Power, Intercorporate Networks, and 'Strategic Bankruptcy.'" *Law and Society Review* 23 (1989): 643-666. Provides a brief sketch of the asbestos controversy and Manville's role in it. In addition, the article traces the history of bankruptcy legislation, details the negotiated settlement, and demonstrates the ways in which insurers, creditors, and the federal government constrained Manville's ability to act unilaterally during its tenure under Chapter 11 protection.

Selikoff, Irving. "Asbestos-Associated Disease." In *Asbestos Litigation,* edited by Wendell B. Alcorn, Jr. New York: Harcourt Brace Jovanovich, 1982. Useful reference to understand the studies of asbestos-associated disease as well as the kinds of cancers and pulmonary illnesses that result from asbestos exposure.

Vermeulen, James E., and Daniel M. Berman. "Asbestos Companies Under Fire." *Business and Society Review* 42 (Summer, 1982): 21-25. This piece serves as a highly readable and useful introduction to the controversy surrounding asbestos and the role of Manville in that controversy. It is primarily an overview, however, and does not capture the complexity of the controversy or (because of the publication date) the history of the eventual negotiated settlement.

Craig M. Eckert

Cross-References

Social Security Act Establishes Benefits for Nonworking People (1935), p. 514; Consumers Union of the United States Emerges (1936), p. 527; The World Health

Organization Proclaims Health as a Basic Right (1946), p. 678; The United Nations Adopts the Universal Declaration of Human Rights (1948), p. 789; Congress Passes the Occupational Safety and Health Act (1970), p. 1585; WHO Sets a Goal of Health for All by the Year 2000 (1977), p. 1893.

ARGENTINE LEADERS ARE CONVICTED OF
HUMAN RIGHTS VIOLATIONS

Category of event: Atrocities and war crimes
Time: December 9, 1985
Locale: Buenos Aires, Argentina

The conviction of the Argentine commanders in chief documented a program of state terrorism and demonstrated national determination to punish human rights violations

Principal personages:
JUAN PERÓN (1895-1974), the president of Argentina (1946-1955, 1973-1974) and founder of Peronism and the Peronista political party
JORGE RAFAEL VIDELA (1925-   ), the commander of the army and head of the first *junta* from 1976 to 1981
ROBERTO EDUARDO VIOLA (1924-   ), the commander of the army and head of the second *junta* in 1981
LEOPOLDO FORTUNATO GALTIERI (1926-   ), the commander of the army and head of the third *junta* from 1981 to 1982
RAÚL ALFONSÍN (1926-   ), the leader of the Radical Party; president of Argentina (1983-1989)

Summary of Event

In December, 1985, five commanders in chief of the Argentine military who had led the nation as members of governing military *juntas* from 1976 to 1983 were convicted for human rights violations of the Argentine Penal Code. The defendants' claim that they had been engaged in a war against subversion reflected an extreme reaction to the nature of Peronist politics in Argentine history.

In June, 1973, ex-President Juan Domingo Perón returned to Argentina from exile and four months later was elected president. His return unleashed a political maelstrom in the nation. From his ascension to power in 1943, Perón had positioned himself as a champion of the working and lower classes, which he referred to as the *descamisados*, the "shirtless ones." Perón nationalized basic industry, provided jobs and social programs for the working classes, and institutionalized his political following into the Peronist Party.

In opposition to his populist politics, the armed forces, backed by the Catholic church, overthrew Perón and sent him into exile in 1955. Over the next eighteen years, the military and civilian politicians practiced an exclusionary policy designed to proscribe Peronism. For the average Argentine, however, Peronism meant good wages, job security, and government support for labor. Consequently, the party remained vibrant and an essential element for any electoral and legislative success.

Over time, the mystique of Peronism broadened and took on confusing and even contradictory interpretations.

In the aftermath of the Cuban Revolution (1959), some followers proclaimed Peronism a revolutionary movement of national liberation, and various guerrilla groups began campaigns of kidnapping and terrorism to bring revolutionary change to Argentina. The two most significant were the Montoneros, founded in 1969, and the People's Revolutionary Army (ERP), founded in 1970. The Montoneros gained the attention of the nation with the kidnapping and execution of General Pedro Eugenio Aramburu, the head of the military coup of 1955. The ERP declared the province of Tucumán a "liberated zone" and attacked military garrisons in various provinces. Perón cultivated all interpretations of his politics so that by the time of his return, Peronism, in its different guises, drew support from disparate sources. Perón took office as president in October, 1973.

The average Argentine decried the social instability of the revolutionary violence, and upon his return, Perón also condemned the radical Left. With this encouragement, a secret right-wing Argentine Anti-Communist Alliance (AAA) opened its own terrorist campaign against suspected Leftists. In July, 1974, Perón died, and the presidency passed to his wife, María Estela Isabela Martínez de Perón. The new president declared a state of siege and authorized the armed forces to annihilate the subversion. The armed forces planned not only an antiterrorist campaign but also the overthrow of the government. On March 24, 1976, a *junta* of representatives of each of the armed forces, led by army commander Lieutenant General Jorge Rafael Videla, seized the government.

The military elite had concluded that Argentina was the key battlefield in a worldwide confrontation. The enemy was left-wing terrorism. From 1976 to 1983, four consecutive *juntas* implemented a dictatorship that has been described by Juan E. Corradi as "the most radical of all military experiments in Argentine history. It was determined to become more impersonal, autonomous, permanent, repressive, and deeply 'structural' than anything before."

Argentines were accustomed to military coups serving to bring order for the next round of civilian governments. They now experienced a tragic aberration from the norm. From 1976 through 1982, 340 secret detention camps were established, and anywhere from nine thousand to thirty thousand civilians "disappeared" as the armed forces attacked not only the guerrilla movements but any nonviolent, potential, or even imaginary opposition. Autonomous task forces raided homes, kidnapped, murdered, and tortured suspects with impunity. Normal security forces were prohibited from interfering with these actions, and there was a systematic denial from all levels of the state of any knowledge of the suspects.

Testimony from the trial of the various *junta* leaders offers terrifying personal scenarios. One woman described being forced to have her child in the back of a police car on the way to her next torture chamber. In one of the most poignant episodes, during the "Night of the Pencils" in September, 1976, seven secondary students who had supported a campaign favoring subsidies for school bus fares were kidnapped from their homes and tortured for "subversion in the classroom." Only three survived. University curricula were purged of such disciplines as oceanography, folklore, and psychology, and even Antoine de Saint-Exupéry's *The Little Prince* (1943) was banned as subversive literature. As defined by Videla, "A terrorist is not just someone with a gun or bomb, but also someone who spreads ideas that are contrary to Western and Christian civilization."

In 1975, many prominent political and religious leaders organized Argentina's Permanent Assembly for Human Rights and began to investigate more than two thousand cases of the disappeared. In 1977, mothers and other relatives of the disappeared began regular protest marches in the Plaza de Mayo.

In April, 1982, the armed forces tried to draw attention away from domestic problems by invading the Falkland Islands. In the short war with England, Argentine forces were defeated and the military government was undermined. Military leaders were charged by critics at home and abroad with human rights abuses and faced an increasingly united civilian political opposition. Moderates in the military created a transitional *junta* in June of 1982 and prepared the way for national elections and a return to civilian rule.

In October, 1983, Raúl Alfonsín, candidate of the Radical Party, won the election for president. Upon assuming office, Alfonsín decreed that all members of the first three military *juntas* must be brought to trial. He also created the National Commission on Disappeared Persons (CONADEP), which was ordered to investigate the disappearances and report to the government. CONADEP's findings were published in 1984 under the title *Nunca Mas* (never again). The report catalogued 8,960 disappearances, identified 340 clandestine detention centers, and concluded that human rights had been violated in a systematic way using state machinery.

On December 18, 1983, the members of the three military *juntas* were brought to trial, charged by State Prosecutor Julio Strassera with violations of the Argentine Penal Code by serving as "indirect perpetrators" in the criminal exercise of power using clandestine methods of repression beyond the borders of legality.

The first stage of the trial was held before the Supreme Council of the Armed Forces. In April, 1985, the proceedings were transferred to the Buenos Aires Federal Court of Criminal Appeals. Public Prosecutor Strassera introduced 711 charges against nine defendants, including Videla, Roberto Eduardo Viola (leader of the second *junta*), and Leopoldo Fortunato Galtieri (leader of the third *junta*). A twenty-thousand-page report, including three thousand statements and the presentation of more than eight hundred witnesses, attested to incidents of torture, rape, robbery, murder, and illegal detention. The prosecution charged the *junta* members with shared collective responsibility as indirect perpetrators of an organized power apparatus of state terrorism. Strassera emphasized that the trial was not a political trial. The accused were not being tried for having organized a coup or for overthrowing the constitution but rather for criminal violations of the Argentine Penal Code, which remained in force throughout the years of the *juntas*.

The defense council argued that the armed forces had been engaged in a legitimate war against armed subversives and that the commanders in chief were acting in due obedience to orders of the pre-*junta* civilian government to annihilate the enemy. If excesses occurred, the persons criminally responsible for the deeds should be on trial, and not the *junta* members. Ultimately, the defense argued that the trial was illegal.

On December 8, 1985, the federal court rendered its verdict. The court rejected the principle of collective responsibility and concluded that liability should be assessed individually. Five of the nine defendants were found guilty, and two, including Videla, received life sentences. Viola received seventeen years, and Galtieri was acquitted. All of the guilty parties were disqualified in perpetuity from holding public office, stripped of all rank, discharged from the armed forces, denied all entitlements, and ordered to pay court costs. In response to an appeal by the defense, the Argentine Supreme Court upheld the verdicts with only slight reductions of the sentences.

Impact of Event

In both political and legal terms, the significance of the trial of the Argentine commanders in chief is wide ranging. As noted by the Amnesty International report on the trial, it was unique in modern Latin American history as the only case of leading government figures who had presided over a period of gross violations of human rights being brought before a court of law to account for their misdeeds. In legal terms, the trial was unusual in the Latin American tradition of jurisprudence not only for the massive documentation and unprecedented nature of evidence presented but also for the variety of independent civil and military jurisdictions which had to be acknowledged and harmonized.

More significant in terms of human rights, the trial demonstrated that leading members of repressive regimes, without having been deposed by force, may be brought to justice before civilian courts for human rights violations within the context of national codes of criminal law. While setting aside the principle of collective responsibility, the decision of the court to assign individual responsibility under the provision of "indirect perpetrators" served notice that those who violate human rights by design, if not by direct participation, are by no means certain to escape legal prosecution.

Internationally, the trial of the Argentine commanders was viewed as a dangerous precedent by supporters of repressive governments in Chile, Brazil, and Uruguay. Following a return to civilian rule in Chile in 1990, President Patricio Aylwin named a Truth and Reconciliation Committee to investigate human rights abuses which occurred during the years of the Pinochet dictatorship (1973-1990).

In the four years following the sentencing, Argentine politics remained focused on this event. The average citizen combined the joy of a return to a civilian government with shame and horror as the trial exposed the atrocities of the generals. Some citizens pressed forward in their efforts to find the disappeared. Others chose silence. Many politicians sought some institutional reconciliation. In 1986 and 1987, the Argentine congress passed laws ending the introduction of any new prosecutions and exempting from trial all military subordinates below the rank of lieutenant colonel. In 1989 and 1990, President Carlos Menem granted controversial pardons to those convicted. Public opinion polls demonstrated that more than 80 percent of Argentines opposed the pardons. Former President Alfonsín labeled the day of the pardons the saddest day in Argentine history. Despite President Menem's conciliatory gestures, the "dirty war," the "disappeared," and the trial of the generals were continuing foci of political and personal debate in Argentina.

Bibliography

Amnesty International. *Argentina: The Military Juntas and Human Rights, Report of the Trial of the Former Junta Members.* London: Amnesty International Publications, 1987. An in-depth review of the background, proceedings, verdicts, and sentencing of the trial.

Argentina Comisión Nacional Sobre la Desaparición de Personas. *Nunca Mas (Never Again).* London: Faber & Faber, 1986. The published report of Argentina's National Commission on Disappeared People. Contains victims' personal accounts, photos, and diagrams of detention centers.

Guest, Iain. *Behind the Disappearances: Argentina's Dirty War Against Human Rights and the United Nations.* Philadelphia: University of Pennsylvania Press, 1990. Examination of specific cases of human rights abuses and international reaction, with focus on the forum of the United Nations.

Hodges, Donald. *Argentina's "Dirty War": An Intellectual Biography.* Austin: University of Texas Press, 1991. Intellectual history tracing the foundation of ideological conflicts in Argentine society which led to the "dirty war." Comprehensive and balanced.

Rock, David. *Argentina 1516-1982: From Spanish Colonization to Alfonsín.* Berkeley: University of California Press, 1985. Updated edition. An excellent general history of Argentina. Good for placing more contemporary events in historical perspective.

Simpson, John, and Jana Bennett. *The Disappeared: Voices from a Secret War.* London: Robson Books, 1985. Dramatic narrative accounts of individual cases of the disappeared.

Thornton, Lawrence. *Imagining Argentina.* New York: Doubleday, 1987. A moving and sensitive novel of a man and his family caught up in the "dirty war." Evocative and extremely well written.

Timerman, Jacobo. *Prisoner Without a Name, Cell Without a Number.* New York: Alfred A. Knopf, 1981. Personal account by the editor of *La Opinión* of his detention and torture for being a dissenter and Jew. This account called international attention to the situation in Argentina.

Roger P. Davis

Cross-References

Perón Creates a Populist Political Alliance in Argentina (1946), p. 673; The Declaration on the Rights and Duties of Man Is Adopted (1948), p. 755; The Organization of American States Is Established (1951), p. 879; The Inter-American Commission on Human Rights Is Created (1959), p. 1032; Brazil Begins a Period of Intense Repression (1968), p. 1468; The Inter-American Court of Human Rights Is Established (1969), p. 1503; An Oppressive Military Rule Comes to Democratic Uruguay (1973), p. 1715; Allende Is Overthrown in a Chilean Military Coup (1973), p. 1725; The Argentine Military Conducts a "Dirty War" Against Leftists (1976), p. 1864; The National Commission Against Torture Studies Human Rights Abuses (1983), p. 2186; Amnesty International Adopts a Program for the Prevention of Torture (1983), p. 2204; Voters in Chile End Pinochet's Military Rule (1989), p. 2540.

MARCOS FLEES THE PHILIPPINES

Categories of event: Political freedom, indigenous peoples' rights
Time: February 25, 1986
Locale: Manila, the Philippines

The February, 1986, People's Revolution forced Marcos to flee the Philippines, ending more than a decade of authoritarian government, economic mismanagement, and human rights abuses

> *Principal personages:*
> FERDINAND E. MARCOS (1917-1989), the president of the Republic of the Philippines (1965-1986), exiled to the United States in 1986
> BENIGNO "NINOY" AQUINO, JR. (1932-1983), a Philippine senator (1967-1972), imprisoned (1972-1980), exiled, and then assassinated
> CORAZON AQUINO (1933-), Benigno's wife, assumed presidency of the Philippines in the February, 1986, People's Revolution
> JUAN PONCE ENRILE (1924-), the secretary of national defense of the Philippines (1970-1986), allied with the Aquino forces to topple Marcos
> FIDEL RAMOS (1928-), the deputy chief of staff of the armed forces of the Philippines (1981-1986), allied with Aquino forces to topple Marcos

Summary of Event

In 1972, President Ferdinand E. Marcos imposed martial law in the Philippines, alleging a "national emergency" arising out of the country's communist and Muslim insurgencies, economic dislocations, and general civil disorder. The insurgencies posed no immediate military threat to the country, but Marcos faced the end of his term in office and was constitutionally prohibited from seeking reelection. The national emergency was his way of retaining power. Nine years of formal martial law and an additional five years of de facto authoritarian government resulted in a deterioration of the political order, the militarization of society, widespread human rights abuses, and economic collapse.

Upon declaring martial law, Marcos suspended the country's congress; he ruled by decree. Political opponents, including Senator Benigno "Ninoy" Aquino, were arrested. Three years into martial law, fifty thousand people had been imprisoned. Newspapers as well as television and radio stations were shut down.

Over the course of the martial law era, Marcos assumed most executive and legislative prerogatives within the country. Members of the judiciary served at his pleasure. Opposition newspapers and electronic media were sold to Marcos family members and friends. The media were subject to varying levels of censorship. Strikes were forbidden, and labor organizers, attorneys, civil rights workers, and dissident religious leaders were harassed and prosecuted. Citizens' right to a writ of habeas corpus was suspended.

The implementation of martial law and the necessity of combating the growing communist and Muslim insurgencies were used as the rationale for massive increases in military manpower and expenditure levels. The armed forces, 62,000 strong in 1972, grew to 230,000 by 1986. During the martial law decade, military budgets increased 257 percent; by 1986, the Philippines had Asia's fastest growing military, with annual expenditures of US $600 million. Military resources were concentrated in Manila to support the martial law government. In the countryside, a poorly paid and undisciplined army confronted insurgents in conditions of guerrilla warfare. Military abuses against the civilian population were pervasive.

The most blatant perpetrators of such abuses were the Civilian Home Defense Forces (CHDF), bullies and petty criminals recruited from the indigenous population and armed and paid by the Philippine government. Incidents of incommunicado detention, torture (including beatings, suffocation, electric shocks, rape, and mutilation), killings, and "disappearances" of civilians involving the armed forces of the Philippines and the CHDF were well documented by international organizations such as Amnesty International and Task Force Detainees of the Philippines (TFDP, a unit of the Association of Major Religious Superiors). Between 1976 and 1986, the CHDF was implicated in more than two thousand murders. Immediately preceding the February, 1986, People's Revolution, the city of Davao experienced an average of three to four murders per day, yet no one had been brought to justice in more than a year. During the late 1970's and early 1980's, TFDP documented an average of thirty disappearances a year.

The reversal of political development and cost in terms of human suffering imposed by the martial law era are rivaled in severity by the economic mismanagement of the period, in terms of long-term damage. In 1965, the Philippines was second to Japan in the region in terms of prospects for economic growth. When Marcos fled the country, the Philippines was in an economic shambles. Ownership and control of entire economic sectors of the country had been transferred to approximately two hundred Marcos family members and friends in what became referred to as "crony capitalism." Funds in the national treasury and aid from international sources were diverted from worthwhile ventures to kickbacks, showcase projects, and personal use. Moderate estimates suggest that Marcos and his associates transferred approximately US $25 billion into foreign bank accounts and real estate investments in their own names.

The foreign debt of the Philippines in 1969 was US $738 million; by 1986, the country's external debt was $26.5 billion. Debt service consumed sixty percent of the country's export earnings. This debt burden, mismanagement, corruption, and international factors such as the oil crises and the decline of prices for export commodities produced a negative average annual growth rate of three percent in the country's economy between 1984 and 1986. In 1965, twenty-eight percent of the population lived below the internationally established poverty level; by 1986 that figure had risen to sixty percent. An unemployment and underemployment rate of thirty percent in 1986 and malnutrition among seventy percent of Philippine school children are indicators of the human suffering that resulted from mismanagement and corruption. In 1985, the Catholic church reported that one hundred children in the city of Bacolod died each month from hunger and hunger-related illnesses, out of a population of about 250,000. The World Health Organization reported that the Philippines had the highest incidence of tuberculosis of any country in the western Pacific.

These political, economic, and social conditions coalesced to create a volatile political environment in the early 1980's. As the crony-run corporations collapsed and Marcos' associates fled abroad with their assets, the financial situation deteriorated. This, combined with international outrage at the human rights violations, concerns about the rising influence of the left in the country, and Marcos' failing health, made change in the Philippines inevitable. The most prominent member of the exiled opposition, Benigno Aquino, was assassinated at the Manila airport on August 21, 1983, while attempting to return home to participate in the process of political change. Most analysts regard the assassination as the beginning of the end for the Marcos regime. The official government investigation of the assassination and exoneration of the military officers accused of the crime did not convince the public of Marcos' innocence in the act.

To provide legitimacy for his continued exercise of power in the face of increasing domestic and international pressure to step aside, Marcos called a snap presidential election for February 7, 1986. A multiplicity of opposition groups (the Catholic church, the labor movement, civil rights activists, students and academics, and in the wake of the assassination and economic collapse, the middle class and the business community) united behind the candidacy of Corazon Aquino, widow of Benigno Aquino.

Both Marcos and Aquino claimed presidential victory in the election, which was characterized by many highly publicized incidents of cheating by Marcos partisans. It is estimated that 400,000 people in Manila alone, or ten percent of the electorate, were disenfranchised by having their names removed from electoral lists before election day. The Conference of Bishops of the Roman Catholic church charged the Marcos regime with a "criminal use of power to thwart the sovereign will of the people." A compliant Parliament validated Marcos' election. Aquino responded on February 16 by calling her supporters to participate in a nonviolent civil disobedience campaign.

On February 22, as the Marcos regime moved to eliminate its enemies among the military reform movement, Minister of Defense Juan Ponce Enrile and Acting Army Chief of Staff Fidel Ramos joined the Aquino opposition in demanding Marcos' ouster. In a three-day standoff between government and opposition military forces, as many as one million Aquino supporters, urged into the streets by Catholic church-sponsored radio, formed a human barrier between advancing government armored personnel carriers and tanks to protect the rebel forces in an unprecedented People's Revolution. Faced with the public outpouring of antipathy against his regime, his inability to rout the rebel military forces without bloodshed, and the United States' withdrawal of support, Ferdinand Marcos and his family consented on February 25, 1986, to be airlifted out of the presidential palace into exile in Honolulu, Hawaii.

Impact of Event

Corazon Aquino was perceived as personally incorruptible and provided an inspiring role model for government service. She restored representative government and the independence of the national judiciary. Citizens' right to a writ of habeus corpus was reinstated, more than five hundred political prisoners were released, and a presidential commission on human rights, under the leadership of Jose W. Diokno, was established to investigate allegations of torture under the previous regime. News media censorship was abolished, and workers' right to strike was restored.

Hundreds of corporations previously owned by the state or controlled by Marcos' cronies were returned to the private sector. The United States, Japan, and the international lending institutions supported the Aquino regime by facilitating the rescheduling of its debt and offering further financial support. The country's economy achieved an average annual growth rate of six percent between 1987 and 1990. This growth, however, was not translated into improved living conditions for most of the country's poor.

The Aquino government exhibited the uncertainties and divisions endemic to coalitions. The military reformers that joined forces with her party to end the Marcos government became dissatisfied with their president's indecisiveness and what they perceived as her softness toward the communist and Muslim insurgents. There were at least eight attempts of varying significance to overthrow the government, mostly led by disgruntled junior military officers.

Early in 1986, the Aquino government initiated dialogue with the communist and Muslim opposition, releasing their leadership from prison and offering them amnesty if they agreed to forsake armed struggle. These efforts at reconciliation failed with the Communist New People's Army and yielded mixed results with the Muslims. The left regarded the revolution in the Philippines as incomplete, lacking transformation of basic economic and social structures.

There was little success in affecting land reform, which is essential to eliminate the sources of rural poverty and dissent. As the disorder continued in insurgent areas, conservative elements within the Aquino government encouraged the maintenance of private militias, which were little more than vigilantes. This demonstrated the lack of government control. A year after the People's Revolution, as many as 260 of these armies flourished in the countryside.

The Philippines remains, in the early 1990's, a resource-rich but politically and economically troubled country. There is progress to be made before the political, economic, and social needs of its citizenry are adequately met.

Bibliography

Aquino, Belinda A. *Politics of Plunder: The Philippines Under Marcos.* Quezon City, Philippines: Great Books Trading, 1987. Details the corruption of the Marcos regime. Researched primarily from twenty-three hundred pages of documents retrieved from the plane carrying Marcos' personal possessions when he fled the Philippines. Bibliography and lists of articles accompanying the Marcos party.

Bonner, Raymond. *Waltzing with a Dictator.* New York: Times Books, 1987. Chronicles the United States government's involvement in Philippine politics, aimed at preserving access to military bases and containing communism. Describes Marcos' evisceration of democracy and plunder of the country. Polemic and journalistic style. Sources include CIA documents and interviews. Bibliography.

Bresnan, John, ed. *Crisis in the Philippines: The Marcos Era and Beyond.* Princeton, N.J.: Princeton University Press, 1986. Nine articles by established United States and Filipino scholars dealing with the social, political, and economic crises that precipitated the February, 1986, revolution. Has a suggested readings list.

Karnow, Stanley. *In Our Image: America's Empire in the Philippines.* New York: Random House, 1989. Well-researched, journalistic account of the United States' involvement in the Philippines, beginning with the period of colonization and concluding with the 1986 revolution. Provides maps, chronology, "Cast of Principal Characters," bibliographic information, and index.

Lyons, John, and Karl Wilson. *Marcos and Beyond: The Philippines Revolution.* Kenthurst, Australia: Kangaroo Press, 1987. Australian journalists provide detailed description of the revolution and its social and economic sources. Particularly good analysis of the communist and Muslim insurgency movements.

Mercado, Monina Allarey, ed. *People Power: The Philippine Revolution of 1986.* Manila, Philippines: James B. Reuter, S.J., Foundation, 1986. Pictorial and eyewitness accounts of the Benigno Aquino assassination, the 1983-1985 street demonstrations against the Marcos regime, and the 1986 electoral campaign and revolution. Maps and chronology.

Rosenberg, David A., ed. *Marcos and Martial Law in the Philippines.* Ithaca, N.Y.: Cornell University Press, 1979. Five Filipino and U.S. scholars analyze the rise of authoritarian government in the Philippines; included are discussions of the legal environment, press censorship, and the economic repercussions of the era. Fourteen appendices of legal documents and nongovernmental organizations' reactions to martial law.

Sterling, Seagrave. *The Marcos Dynasty.* New York: Harper & Row, 1988. Exposé of personal histories of Marcos family members from birth to exile in Hawaii. Bibliography, index, map, photographs.

Wright, Martin, ed. *Revolution in the Philippines? A Keesing's Special Report.* Harlow, Essex, England: Longman Group UK, 1988. Discusses the challenges faced by Corazon Aquino's government in the early part of her presidency. Particularly useful description of the various factions within the communist and Muslim opposition movements and the early coup attempts. Data on Philippine economic structure and text of 1987 constitution. Index, map, and bibliography.

M. Leann Brown

Cross-References

The U.N. Covenant on Civil and Political Rights Is Adopted (1966), p. 1353; Marcos Declares Martial Law in the Philippines (1972), p. 1680; The United Nations Issues a Conduct Code for Law Enforcement Officials (1979), p. 2040; Opposition Leader Benigno Aquino Is Assassinated (1983), p. 2198; Amnesty International Adopts a Program for the Prevention of Torture (1983), p. 2204.

WIESEL IS AWARDED THE NOBEL PEACE PRIZE

Categories of event: Humanitarian relief and political freedom
Time: December 10, 1986
Locale: Oslo, Norway

Elie Wiesel, a Jewish survivor of the Holocaust, received the 1986 Nobel Peace Prize for his words and deeds, which provided leadership essential to the support of peace and human rights

Principal personages:

ELIE WIESEL (1928-   ), a Holocaust survivor whose authorship and humanitarian acts were honored by the 1986 Nobel Peace Prize

EGIL AARVIK (1912-   ), the chair of the Norwegian Nobel Committee

CARL VON OSSIETZKY (1889-1938), a German journalist and pacifist who received the 1935 Nobel Peace Prize (awarded in 1936) and was mentioned prominently in Aarvik's presentation speech

Summary of Event

On October 14, 1986, Egil Aarvik, chair of the Norwegian Nobel Committee, announced that Elie Wiesel would receive the 1986 Nobel Peace Prize. The prize was formally given to Wiesel in ceremonies held at Oslo University's Aula Festival Hall on December 10, 1986. The factors that brought Wiesel to Oslo go back to events that occurred more than forty years earlier.

Born on September 30, 1928, Wiesel lived in Sighet, Romania, a town controlled by Hungary during much of World War II. In May, 1944, soon after Nazi Germany occupied the territory of the faltering Hungarian government, Sighet's Jewish population—including Wiesel, his parents, and his youngest sister, Tzipora—were deported to the death camp at Auschwitz, Poland. Caught in the Holocaust, Nazi Germany's systematic attempt to destroy the European Jews and millions of other people, Wiesel's mother and little sister perished at Auschwitz. Wiesel and his father were spared for labor. Late in January, 1945, they were force-marched from Auschwitz to Germany. Wiesel's father died at Buchenwald. Liberated in April, 1945, Wiesel was eventually reunited with his two older sisters. After living in France for a time, Wiesel settled in the United States and became an American citizen in 1963.

Wiesel could not forget the consuming fire that destroyed his pre-Holocaust Jewish world. Believing that he survived Auschwitz by chance, Wiesel felt duty-bound to give his survival meaning and to justify each moment of his life. Intensified and honed in silence, his memories have found expression in a life of dedicated service and remarkable authorship. He has led the United States Holocaust Memorial Council and protested on behalf of oppressed people everywhere—Soviet Jews as well as groups in Cambodia, Biafra, Bangladesh, Latin America, and the Middle East, among others. In addition, he has organized international symposia on human relations, taught throughout the world, and interceded with world leaders for the sake of human rights.

The Nobel Peace Prize citation commended Wiesel as a messenger to humanity. It stated that his messages about human dignity take "the form of a testimony, repeated and deepened through the works of a great author." The citation is sound, because Wiesel's writing desk is a foundation for his contributions to justice and peace. Wiesel's command of words, however, did not come easily. Although he intended early to become a writer, his Auschwitz survival conferred awesome responsibility upon him. That responsibility meant testimony, but determining what to say and how to express his message for maximum effect required painstaking care and time. Wiesel vowed to be silent about his Holocaust experiences for ten years. Not until 1956 did he publish his first book.

Written in Yiddish, that initial book, *Un di Velt Hot Geshvign (And the world remained silent)*, was a lengthy account of Wiesel's life in Auschwitz. Two years later, he radically shortened it to about one hundred pages, translated it into French, and published it as *La Nuit* (1958). *Night*, the English version, appeared two years later. Wiesel has observed that all of his other books are built around this, his best-known work. Although he dealt constantly with fundamental issues, Wiesel has not seen himself primarily as a philosopher. Nor has he identified himself as a theologian, despite the fact that religious themes, and questions about God in particular, appear frequently in his writings. Political theory has not been his chosen field either, even though his books are full of implications for politics. Instead, Wiesel has usually described himself as a storyteller.

To mention only a few of the nearly forty books that Wiesel has published between 1956 and 1991, novels such as *A Beggar in Jerusalem* (1970), *The Oath* (1973), *The Fifth Son* (1985), and *Twilight* (1988) have received international acclaim. So have his studies of biblical characters (*Messengers of God*, 1976) and later Jewish teachers (*Souls on Fire*, 1973) as well as his essays and dialogues in books such as *A Jew Today* (1978) and *From the Kingdom of Memory* (1990).

While the Holocaust is not usually placed center stage in his writings, it nevertheless shadows all the words Wiesel writes and informs all the messages he delivers. Central to those messages are four major themes. First, Wiesel stresses that the Holocaust is a watershed event that calls everything into question. "At Auschwitz," Wiesel states in *Legends of Our Time* (1968), "not only man died, but also the idea of man. . . . It was its own heart the world incinerated at Auschwitz." Like nothing else, Wiesel believes, the Holocaust shows that human thought and action need revision—unless one wishes to continue the same blindness that produced the darkness of *Night*. Second, language is linked with life and death. Be careful with words, Wiesel insists, because the wrong ones waste lives and the right ones save them. Third, no enemy of humankind is greater than indifference. Wiesel insists that indifference to evil is worse than evil itself. Along with passivity and neutrality, indifference always favors the killer, not the victim. Fourth, while life is imperiled by forgetting, it can be saved by remembering, and death and despair deserve no more victories. Humanity's moral task is to transform injustice—including God's—into human justice and compassion.

Using his own sorrow to prevent further suffering, Wiesel has worked for human rights and peace in many ways, but when Aarvik, the Norwegian Nobel Committee's chair, presented the prize, he emphasized the significance of Wiesel's writings and his role as a teacher who practices a humanitarian philosophy. Not hate and revenge but respect and understanding, not death and degradation but rebellion against evil— these themes in Wiesel's work, said Aarvik, are the ones that made Wiesel so worthy of the Nobel Peace Prize.

Fifty years earlier, Aarvik noted, the Nobel Peace Prize went to Carl von Os- sietzky, a German journalist and pacifist who denounced his nation's rearmament and consequently suffered Nazi imprisonment. Aarvik recalled how controversy swirled around Ossietzky's award. Not only Nazis took offense. Critics outside Ger- many thought the selection provoked Germany too much and failed to serve the cause of peace. What Nazi Germany did to Elie Wiesel and millions of his Jewish brothers and sisters, contended Aarvik, vindicated the Nobel Committee's decision to honor Ossietzky.

Elie Wiesel survived the death camps' abyss, but even more, Aarvik stressed, Wiesel turned his survival into an inspiring spirit of resistance that protests every- thing in violation of human rights. Aarvik suggested that their dedication to prevent the wasting of human life links Wiesel and Ossietzky. The Nobel Peace Prize, he added, is a fitting bond between them.

In Oslo, Norway, on December 11, 1986, Wiesel responded by delivering his Nobel lecture, "Hope, Despair and Memory." It explored how "if anything can, it is mem- ory that will save humanity." Wiesel affirmed that hope is possible—not without despair but beyond it. Remembering the victims of injustice, especially those who perished in the Holocaust, obliges one, he insisted, to "reject despair" and "invent a thousand and one reasons to hope."

Impact of Event

From time to time Wiesel has noted that Holocaust survivors have been too opti- mistic in thinking that their testimony would bring the world to its senses and put mass death to an end. As he did on October 14, 1986, the day his winning of the Nobel Peace Prize was announced, Wiesel has since reiterated that Holocaust sur- vivors have been "an example to humankind how not to succumb to despair, al- though despair often was justified." Wiesel added that the Nobel Peace Prize would give him an opportunity to "speak louder" and "reach more people" in defense of human rights. Those themes apparently reflected the thinking of the Norwegian No- bel Committee, because its chair observed how impressive it was that a man could experience so much destruction, hate, and suffering and still become "a spokesman for peace and conciliation." Chairman Aarvik's comments summed up the wide- spread international support that Wiesel's Nobel nomination had received, which included backing from previous Nobel laureates such as German political leader

Willy Brandt, India's Mother Teresa, and Poland's Lech Wałęsa.

Some dissenters found fault with Wiesel for failing to speak out boldly enough against Israel's policies toward the Palestinians. On the whole, however, public reaction to Wiesel's award was favorable, although it was acknowledged with serious respect more than exuberant celebration because the messages he brings are somber and challenging. He could have received the Nobel Prize in literature, some commentators pointed out, but the Nobel Prize for peace seemed particularly appropriate for Wiesel, whose life has united words and deeds so effectively. It was in keeping with Wiesel's character that, while in Oslo to receive the Nobel Peace Prize, he spent hours on the telephone encouraging Jewish refuseniks in the Soviet Union. Wiesel has long been dedicated to relieving the plight of Soviet Jews, and his efforts to win greater freedom for them have been considerable.

After winning the Nobel Prize, Wiesel continued to teach and write. A dozen of his books appeared between 1986 and 1991. No one can quantify the effect he has had on those who hear and read him, but Wiesel's voice makes sure that the abuse of human life will not be ignored or forgotten. To carry those concerns further, Wiesel used his Nobel Prize to establish in 1987 the Elie Wiesel Foundation for Humanity. Under its auspices, seventy-five Nobel laureates met in Paris in January, 1988, to discuss the threats and promises that will face humankind in the twenty-first century. In 1989 and 1990, the foundation sponsored a series of international symposia to explore the nature of hate and ways to move beyond it. Also included in the foundation's activities is the Elie Wiesel Prize in Ethics, which goes to the winners of an annual essay contest for college and university seniors in the United States.

Bibliography

Berenbaum, Michael. *The Vision of the Void: Theological Reflections on the Works of Elie Wiesel*. Middletown, Conn.: Wesleyan University Press, 1979. Writing from a Jewish perspective, Berenbaum explores the religious implications of Wiesel's work. He skillfully compares and contrasts Wiesel's views with those of other Jewish thinkers who have reflected on the religious significance of the Holocaust. This book not only sheds light on Wiesel but also helps its readers to comprehend the human predicament after Auschwitz.

Brown, Robert McAfee. *Elie Wiesel: Messenger to All Humanity*. Notre Dame, Ind.: University of Notre Dame Press, 1989. Brown is an important Christian thinker who has been substantially influenced by Wiesel. This highly recommended book is a comprehensive study of Wiesel's authorship. One of its fascinating contributions involves Brown's linking of Wiesel to biblical figures such as Job and Jeremiah.

Cargas, Harry James. *Harry James Cargas in Conversation with Elie Wiesel*. New York: Paulist Press, 1976. Cargas knows Wiesel well and has interviewed him often. Here he puts demanding questions to Wiesel, and Wiesel responds to them openly and in detail. This book is an excellent source for information about Wiesel's life and also for insight about his major concerns as a writer.

Hilberg, Raul. *The Destruction of the European Jews*. Rev. ed. New York: Holmes & Meier, 1985. Hilberg's book is the definitive work in English about the Nazi policy of genocide against the Jews. Its grasp of the formation and execution of that policy is as gripping as it is thorough. This work provides invaluable background to help one understand why the Holocaust is so important to Wiesel.

Moyers, Bill. *Beyond Hate*. New York: Public Affairs Television, 1991. Featuring Elie Wiesel and other significant humanitarians and scholars, this documentary includes coverage of a symposium in Oslo, Norway, which was sponsored in 1990 by the Elie Wiesel Foundation for Humanity. The film illustrates Wiesel's practical involvement in issues concerning ethics and human rights in particular.

Rittner, Carol, ed. *Elie Wiesel: Between Memory and Hope*. New York: New York University Press, 1990. Carol Rittner has worked closely with Elie Wiesel as the first executive director of the Elie Wiesel Foundation for Humanity. In this carefully planned book, she brings together leading Jewish and Christian interpreters of Wiesel's thought. These literary scholars, theologians, and philosophers explore all of Wiesel's writings, showing how his outlook has developed and changed, but in ways remained constant.

Rubenstein, Richard L., and John K. Roth. *Approaches to Auschwitz: The Holocaust and Its Legacy*. Atlanta: John Knox Press, 1987. This overview of the Holocaust and its legacy has four major parts. They concentrate on the Holocaust's historical roots, the rise and fall of Nazi Germany and its "Final Solution," responses to the Holocaust, and reflections on its aftermath and the future. The book draws on Wiesel's experience and authorship while providing background that places his life and work in a broad historical context.

Wiesel, Elie. *From the Kingdom of Memory: Reminiscences*. New York: Summit Books, 1990. This volume contains Wiesel's Nobel acceptance speech and his Nobel lecture, "Hope, Despair and Memory," as well as a variety of essays, reflections, and a moving series of dialogues. Its contents, many of them written after 1986, provide a representative sample of the themes, questions, and causes to which Wiesel has devoted his life.

_____. *Night*. New York: Bantam Books, 1986. Few books about the Holocaust are more widely read or better remembered than this memoir, which portrays Wiesel's year in Auschwitz and Buchenwald. For any reader who has not read Wiesel before, *Night* is the place to start.

John K. Roth

Cross-References

Hitler Writes *Mein Kampf* (1924), p. 389; Hitler Uses Reichstag Fire to Suspend Civil and Political Liberties (1933), p. 480; Nazi Concentration Camps Go into Operation (1933), p. 491; Nazi War Criminals Are Tried in Nuremberg (1945), p. 667; Israel Is Created as a Homeland for Jews (1948), p. 761; The United Nations Adopts the Universal Declaration of Human Rights (1948), p. 789; Eichmann Is Tried for

War Crimes (1961), p. 1108; Soviet Jews Demand Cultural and Religious Rights (1963), p. 1177; Conflicts in Pakistan Lead to the Secession of Bangladesh (1971), p. 1611; Palestinian Civilians Are Massacred in West Beirut (1982), p. 2164; The Palestinian *Intifada* Begins (1987), p. 2331; Iraq's Government Uses Poison Gas Against Kurdish Villagers (1988), p. 2397.

MUSLIMS RIOT AGAINST RUSSIANS IN KAZAKHSTAN

Categories of event: Indigenous peoples' rights; revolutions and rebellions
Time: December 17-19, 1986
Locale: Alma-Ata, Kazakhstan, Union of Soviet Socialist Republics

Glasnost *revealed to the Central Asians, Russians, and other Soviet citizens that Communist Party chiefs covertly protected oppressive feudal lords to maintain stability in the Soviet Union*

Principal personages:

MIKHAIL GORBACHEV (1931-   ), the president of the Soviet Union

DINMUKHAMED KUNAYEV (1912-   ), a protégé of Leonid Brezhnev who built a fiefdom in Kazakhstan employing relatives and cronies

LEONID ILICH BREZHNEV (1906-1982), the first secretary of Kazakhstan and later general secretary of the Communist Party

GENNADII V. KOLBIN (1927-   ), an ethnic Russian whose appointment in 1986 as Kunayev's replacement triggered three days of unrest in Alma-Ata

JOSEPH STALIN (1879-1953), the head of the Communist Party of the Soviet Union from 1924 to 1953

NIKITA S. KHRUSHCHEV (1894-1971), the Soviet leader who introduced the program that made the Kazakhs a Muslim minority in their own republic

YURI ANDROPOV (1914-1984), a Soviet ruler who singled out the republics for scrutiny and weeded out corrupt cadres

ALEXANDER II (1855-1881), a Russian emperor whose reforms led to the emancipation of Russian serfs and to the emigration of many peasants to Kazakhstan

Summary of Events

The riots in Kazakhstan in 1986 were the early signs of serious confrontations that occurred in the wake of Mikhail Gorbachev's 1985 reforms. The reforms were intended to root out corruption and to undo the illegal actions of previous leaders, especially Leonid Brezhnev. They revealed, however, that Russians were no longer welcome in some Soviet republics and that Islam and Pan-Turkism were serious issues with which to contend. Furthermore, frustrated non-Russian Soviet youth believed that Russians were given preferential treatment in employment, while the Soviet Union as a whole feared complete Russian domination of its affairs.

Kazakhstan was the second-largest republic in the Soviet Union, accommodating more than sixteen million inhabitants. Although it was originally a Muslim domain, Kazakhstan has been heavily settled by Russians, Byelo-Russians, Ukrainians, Germans, and Koreans. Kazakh was the official language of the republic. Modern Kazakhstan is the home of the Soviet space program and a testing ground for nuclear weapons.

Historically, after the demise of the Golden Horde and the fall of Tamerlane's empire in Turkistan, two Turko-Mongol domains appeared. One of them, the Uzbeks, claimed descent from the Golden Horde Khan Uzbek. They consolidated their position and settled as farmers in the Khiva and Bukhara regions. The Kazakhs, or "free people," ranged over the northwest persisting in their nomadic lifestyle as livestock breeders.

Before the Crimean War (1854-1856), the Caucasus Mountains and Iran to the west and the territories of Kazakhstan, Turkistan, and Afghanistan to the east served as buffers between Russia and the British Empire. Russian peasants, freed by the reforms of victorious czar Alexander II, overran the fertile lands of Kazakhstan, confiscating nearly one hundred million acres of land. Native Kazakhs were pushed up into the hills or into the harsh desert regions of the south and southwest, where most of them died. This marked the beginning of the distrust and dislike of Kazakhs for the Russians.

Although Kazakhstan joined the Russian empire in 1893, it was not until 1916 that the Kazakhs were approached for military conscription. The army of czar Nicholas II sustained high casualties on the German-Austrian front, and Central Asian forces were mobilized to work behind the lines. The Kazakhs rebelled against conscription for two reasons: The planned conscription coincided with the harvest, and Muslim tribespeople refused to risk their lives to benefit what they considered to be an infidel Russian tyrant. The ensuing four-month rebellion was the first sign of nationalist consciousness among the Muslims under czarist rule. Thousands of Kazakhs were killed in that conflict, and approximately one million sought refuge in Sinkiang, China. After the Russian Revolution, the Kazakhs suffered in poorly administered collective farms. Kazakh households declined from 1.2 million to 565,000. Their entire native leadership was purged.

Nikita Khrushchev determined that Kazakhstan would be a national showcase for agrarian reform in the mid-1950's. Leonid Brezhnev was appointed first secretary of Kazakhstan in 1954 with a mandate to effect changes. Unlike the farmland of the Ukraine, where abundant use of fertilizer was necessary, the Kazakh "Virgin Lands" could be sown after plowing. The ease of cultivation affected the Kazakh peasants; inexperienced urban youth were recruited to cultivate the land. Within two years Brezhnev, assisted by Dinmukhamed Kunayev, a Kazakh tribal chief, turned the Kazakh grazing lands into productive wheat and cotton fields. Increased use of machinery alienated the nontechnologically oriented Kazakhs, while the devotion of the land exclusively to cotton and wheat crops for the use of the greater Soviet Union destroyed Kazakhstan's economy and made the Kazakhs dependent on imports.

When Brezhnev left Kazakhstan in 1956, Kunayev became Kazakhstan's first secretary. In 1962, Khrushchev removed Kunayev from his post, but Kunayev was reappointed when Brezhnev became first secretary of the Soviet Union in 1964. Kunayev remained in his post even after Brezhnev's death in 1982 and consolidated his fiefdom through a network of loyal Russian communists, tribal nobility, and cronies. These bureaucrats found themselves with secure jobs, and no constitutional restraints or independent media to expose them. They rode roughshod over legitimate Kazakh needs and sentiments. Only Kazakh nationalists landed key governmental positions.

These relics of Brezhnev's policies were questioned by Yuri Andropov and later by Mikhail Gorbachev. After the introduction of *glasnost* (openness) and *perestroika* (restructuring), Gorbachev overhauled the *nomenklatura*: the Soviet Politburo, Secretariat, and Central Committee. He promised freedom of choice at most levels of society. In Kazakhstan, *glasnost* caused a confrontation between Gorbachev and Kunayev. From the outset, Gorbachev recognized the degree of Kunayev's entrenchment in Kazakhstan and the extent of the corruption. He knew that Kazakh officials had inflated statistics and fudged records so that Kunayev would look good. He also knew that Kunayev could mobilize the same bureaucrats and their families under the banner of nationalism and create difficulty.

Gorbachev moved carefully, criticizing Kunayev for Kazakhstan's stagnant economy in his political report in 1985 and removing Kazakh party officials. By February, 1986, Gorbachev had dismissed two-thirds of Kazakhstan's party committee and approximately five hundred party officials. Finally, despite its full Central Asian support, Gorbachev tabled Siberian water diversion legislation vital to Kazakhstan's economy. Funds requested by Kunayev were earmarked for other purposes, leaving the Central Asians to face the consequences of their earlier misguided irrigation projects.

On December 16, the Communist Party of Kazakhstan ousted Kunayev, replacing him with Gennadii Kolbin, an ethnic Russian. This transfer of power went against the Kremlin's tradition of first secretary appointments, whereby the office had been given to a Kazakh. Thus it was not so much the removal of the retiring Kunayev as the imposition of Kolbin that triggered latent sentiments rooted in cultural, religious, economic, and political deprivations visited upon the Kazakhs by the Soviets.

To prevent further Russian infringement, the Kazakhs in Alma-Ata reacted in what began as a peaceful demonstration. The demonstration turned into riots when Soviet troops attempted to disperse the crowd. Outbursts of nationalist feeling eventually swept through the city. Demonstrators armed with wooden sticks and metal rods stopped public transportation, beating Russian passengers and overturning buses. Demonstrators also burned a food store, smashed store windows, pillaged and looted displays, and destroyed the flowerbeds in front of the Communist Party headquarters. Soviet troops, supported by armored vehicles, responded by attacking the crowd with truncheons and water cannons. Approximately 250 soldiers were hospitalized. After that initial encounter, the demonstrators remained around the central committee building throughout the night. The troops deployed to monitor the crowds and keep the peace also remained in the area. The demonstrators renewed their assault on the government center the next morning. The troops again fought back, this time with water cannons and rubber bullets. Scores of demonstrators were killed and hundreds were injured.

By December 20, everything was back to normal. A confident Kolbin took Mikhail Solomentsev, a Politburo member and chair of the Communist Party committee on party discipline, on a tour of Alma-Ata. The visit underscored high-level concern regarding the growing Muslim population and its potential to cause disaster. In official Soviet reports, the riots were portrayed as the work of disgruntled hooligans. They were, in fact, far more organized and enjoyed the support of factory workers as well as some school and party agencies.

More shocking to the Kazakhs and the Russians than the demonstrations and the killings were Gorbachev's bold moves against despotism, nepotism, and rampant corruption. Gorbachev allowed the news of the riots in the Muslim republic to be broadcast nationwide, serving notice to other republican protégés that their activities, too, were being observed and that the myth that all was well in the republics belonged to the past.

Impact of Event

Before Sovietization, Central Asian society was nomadic. Tribal chiefs dictated the rules of conduct in social, political, and economic domains. Orders were carried out by the heads of the *oymak* (lineage), *boy* (clan), and *soy* (family). An individual's power was determined through blood relationship to the *khan* (prince) rather than by ability. Sovietization attempted to replace that feudal hierarchy with a more equitable socialist system. Great strides in this regard were made in the 1920's and 1930's, when *khujum* (assault on the traditional ways, especially seclusion of women), *dekulakization* (confiscation of riches by the state), and purges eliminated the *bays* (landlords) and the *khans*. The root of the problem, class distinctions among the Kazakhs, survived.

Kazakhs had long known that although they lived under the rules of a planned socialist economy their real ruler was Kunayev, who reigned like a medieval tyrant rather than an equitable first secretary. Because of their national and tribal sentiments, they ignored Kunayev's misuse of Kazakhstan's resources. After all, in the 1960's and 1970's, Kunayev's network of irrigation systems had provided food for most of the nation. Could a Russian inspire similar pride?

As *glasnost* progressed and people discussed their problems, it became apparent to the Kremlin that Kazakhstan's production statistics could not be substantiated and that fudging, coercion, extortion, and nepotism had been the norm in the republic. To meet strict quotas, and to avoid embarrassment, party officials had misused their offices, while those expelled from the party had assisted in corruption to regain admission. The most distressing aspect, however, was Kunayev's mismanagement of the Aral Sea, which virtually disappeared as a result of unsustainably heavy water use. The death of the sea affected the health and well-being of all those who drew on it for a living.

Calamities such as the Aral's slow death were the result of rapid industrialization at the expense of employing advanced technology and mechanization in agriculture. Only a sound plan backed by a strong economy could have averted disaster. Since

Kunayev did not have access to either, in the 1980's he took refuge in issuing inflated statistics and in promising relief through such grandiose schemes as the Siberian river diversion project. His magic, however, had lost its power. Kazakhs who saw no relief from standing in long lines wished him to be replaced by another native son. The Kremlin viewed the situation differently and opted for a nonnative who could suppress Kazakh nationalism. Kolbin had successfully alleviated similar problems in the Ulyanovsk region. There was reason to believe that he could create fair employment in the urban centers, decrease the length of lines for daily necessities, and respond sympathetically to the needs of the farmers. The appointment underscored Gorbachev's resolve.

Frustrated and faced with uncertainty, some youths took advantage of *glasnost* and joined the nationality movement. Others joined Sufi orders or thought of reviving Pan-Turkism. Whatever the direction, however, the revolt against the system signaled to the world that the Central Asians had been suppressed far too long, and that they would seek national, religious, and cultural freedom at any cost. Other republics appeared to resonate with Kazakhstan, suggesting the turmoil to come within the union of republics.

Bibliography

Bennigsen, Alexandre, and Marie Broxup. *The Islamic Threat to the Soviet State.* New York: St. Martin's Press, 1983. Studies Islam in an international setting and shows that both the Soviet Union and the People's Republic of China have high stakes in Central Asia. Includes appendices, bibliography, glossary, and index.

Bennigsen, Alexandre, and S. Enders Wimbush. *Muslims of the Soviet Empire: A Guide.* Bloomington: Indiana University Press, 1986. A well-organized, comprehensive study of Islam in the Soviet Union, with vital data on all the Muslim republics, including Kazakhstan. Includes maps, glossary, bibliography, and index.

_____. *Mystics and Commissars: Sufism in the Soviet Union.* Berkeley: University of California Press, 1985. Sufism has played a major role in shaping Islamic reaction to Soviet rule. This study discusses the history of Soviet Sufism, identifies its orders, and traces Sufi movements between Daghistan and Central Asia. Includes maps, notes, glossary, and index.

Dellenbrant, Jan Ake. *The Soviet Regional Dilemma: Planning, People, and Natural Resources.* Armonk, N.Y.: M. E. Sharpe, 1986. Focusing on the latter part of the Brezhnev era, this work examines central economic planning and the ramifications of Russian objectives for the republics. Includes notes, bibliography, and subject index.

Eklof, Ben. *Soviet Briefing: Gorbachev and the Reform Period.* Boulder, Colo.: Westview Press, 1989. A thorough study of *glasnost* and *zakonnost* (legality). Eklof puts Gorbachev's reforms into perspective, noting that reformists like Gorbachev grew up during the Khrushchev and Brezhnev eras.

Hosking, Geoffrey. *The Awakening of the Soviet Union.* Cambridge, Mass.: Harvard University Press, 1990. Chapter 5, "The Flawed Melting Pot," traces the roots of the kinship mentality revealed by Gorbachev's reforms in the Muslim republics, especially Uzbekistan and Kazakhstan. Includes notes and index.

Lieven, Dominic. *Gorbachev and the Nationalities.* London: Center for Security and Conflict Studies, 1988. Examines the conflict between Russian nationalism and Central Asian ethnic and religious mores. According to the author, the future of Central Asia and the prosperity of its people depend upon Russian decisions.

Murarka, Dev. *Gorbachev: The Limits of Power.* London: Hutchinson, 1988. An analysis of Gorbachev's political career, his rise to power, and his ability to meet challenges. The 1986 Kazakhstan riots are discussed in the context of Gorbachev's reforms. Includes appendices, notes, selected bibliography, and index.

Olcott, Martha. "Central Asia: The Reformers Challenge a Traditional Society." In *The Nationalities Factor in Soviet Politics and Society,* edited by L. Hajda and M. Beissinger. Boulder, Colo.: Westview Press, 1990. A comprehensive study of recent social, political, and cultural problems in the republics.

Rywkin, Michael. *Moscow's Muslim Challenge: Soviet Central Asia.* Armonk, N.Y.: M. E. Sharpe, 1982. Studies the nature and application of Moscow-based policies for the Central Asian republics. Although economically helpful, these policies have not affected Muslim loyalties. Includes maps, notes, selected bibliography, and index.

Iraj Bashiri

Cross-References

The Young Turk Movement Stages a Constitutional Coup in Turkey (1908), p. 98; Bolsheviks Deny All Rights to the Russian Orthodox Church (1917), p. 202; The Baltic States Fight for Independence (1917), p. 207; Finland Gains Independence from the Soviet Union (1917), p. 212; Stalin Begins Purging Political Opponents (1934), p. 503; The French Quell an Algerian Nationalist Revolt (1945), p. 651; Khrushchev Implies That Stalinist Excesses Will Cease (1956), p. 952; The Brezhnev Doctrine Bans Acts of Independence in Soviet Satellites (1968), p. 1408; Soviets Invade Afghanistan (1979), p. 2062; Gorbachev Initiates a Policy of *Glasnost* (1985), p. 2249; Ethnic Riots Erupt in Armenia (1988), p. 2348; Ethnic Unrest Breaks Out in Yugoslavian Provinces (1988), p. 2386; Lithuania Declares Its Independence from the Soviet Union (1990), p. 2577; Demise of the U.S.S.R. Paves the Way for Reforms in Former Soviet Republics (1991), p. 2618.

BLACK WORKERS IN SOUTH AFRICA GO ON STRIKE

Categories of event: Racial and ethnic rights; workers' rights
Time: 1987
Locale: South Africa

Newly formed black trade unions shook South Africa's apartheid-based economy with massive strikes

Principal personages:

PIETER W. BOTHA (1916-   ), the South African prime minister and leader of the ruling National Party

NELSON MANDELA (1918-   ), the leader of the African National Congress

JOE SLOVO (1926-   ), the South African Communist Party general secretary

Summary of Event

The Republic of South Africa is unique in a number of ways. Although it resembles other Western capitalist societies in terms of its economic structure, it has one glaring difference: In South Africa, the majority of the industrial working class is denied, on the basis of race, the most basic human rights, which generally exist to some extent even under dictatorships.

South African society is strictly divided into various "nations" by race. This policy of segregation, or "apartheid," has a vast social and economic impact on the black majority, particularly on industrial workers. In some ways, the destruction of black trade union organizations has always been one of the most important goals of the apartheid system. This is hardly surprising, since the apartheid system holds that the only reason for a black to be present in a white area is for the performance of labor.

During the 1960's and early 1970's, the South African economy grew rapidly, mainly on the basis of increased use of black labor. This gave black workers increased power, as they became indispensable in many sectors of the economy. For the first time, blacks were recruited into semiskilled and even skilled trades, as a white labor shortage made necessary the relaxation of numerous "job-reservation" rules. When a wave of strikes involving sixty thousand workers hit South Africa in 1973, the response by companies and the government was relatively mild. In addition, legislation was submitted to South Africa's parliament to give black workers the right to strike.

As the potential power of the black working class grew in the mid-1970's, white corporate South Africa was forced to watch as its power increasingly became challenged from below. Although unrecognized by most employers, black unions grew in membership despite their semilegal position. Real wages for black workers rose more rapidly than did white wages. Nor were the struggles purely economic, as millions of working days were lost to political strikes protesting the continued imprisonment of African National Congress leader Nelson Mandela and to South African Communist Party-sponsored May Day celebrations that drew huge crowds.

By 1986, more than 1 million days of work had been lost because of economic strikes, while another 3.5 million strike days could be attributed to political protests. The following year, however, was to see an escalation of the strike wave to historic levels. On May Day alone, 2.5 million working days were lost. More than 6.6 million days were lost in the year as a result of wage disputes. Further, the strikes in 1987 tended to last three times longer than those of the year before and were accompanied by massive membership growth for black trade unions.

This strike-filled year began with more than ten thousand retail workers out on a ten-week work stoppage that began in February. Of even greater significance were a forty-six-day strike against Mercedes-Benz and four different disputes involving postal workers. The former was important given the economic role and high profile of the auto company in the heavy-industry sector of the South African economy, while the latter had decidedly political overtones, as the postal strikes signaled the spread of union activism to the public sector.

A strike by twenty thousand railroad workers that began on April 22 and lasted until June 5 was yet another indication of spreading labor unrest among black workers. Perhaps the most notable struggle was that undertaken by the National Union of Mineworkers (NUM). Gold mines accounted for almost half of South Africa's foreign earnings, and the mining industry had always attempted to prevent, or at least limit, organization among miners, particularly black miners. During an August, 1946, strike, seventy-five thousand mine workers were forced back to work, at gunpoint with at least twelve deaths and more than a thousand injuries. In later years, the right-wing Mineworkers' Union represented white miners and attempted to preserve their privileged position in the mines. The cozy relation that existed between the all-white union and the employers meant that black miners were given low pay and excluded from many more-desirable mining jobs.

This relationship was shaken by the emergence of the NUM, the first black mine workers' union, in August, 1982. Although most workers were hesitant to risk their relatively well-paid positions by joining the new union, the NUM made significant inroads within the first two years of its formation. It was even to gain official recognition at some mines.

Still, when the NUM led South Africa's first legal strike by black miners in 1984, it fought stiff resistance from mining companies that resulted in the deaths of a number of strikers. Despite a difficult, uphill struggle, the black trade union was able to continue to combine growing industrial muscle with political opposition to the apartheid system. When on October 1, 1986, 250,000 black miners struck to mourn victims of a mining disaster, thousands of workers outside the mining industry joined the strike in sympathy.

The NUM was to launch its first campaign for a national wage agreement in 1987.

The resulting strike, which lasted from August 9 to August 30, involved at its peak 340,000 workers. Again, employers mustered bitter opposition, and after sixty thousand workers were fired in retaliation, the NUM was forced to accept an only slightly improved pay agreement. Still, the emergence of a national trade union for black workers in such a key sector of the economy clearly worried employers and government alike.

When challenged by a railroad strike, the government of Pieter Botha attempted to denounce the struggle as part of a revolutionary strategy devised by Joe Slovo and the South African Communist Party. By September, 1987, the Labour Relations Amendment Bill attempted to ban sympathy strikes. Although the counteroffensive by white businesspeople and government officials helped to contain the growing black trade union movement, it failed to crush it. In fact, it was generally conceded that the struggle was over the content of labor agreements with black workers and not an attempt to return to the days of refusing to bargain at all.

Nor were these new, independent black unions limited to a few isolated industries whose workers they represented. By the end of 1985, thirty-four of the most important black trade unions had united to form the Congress of South African Trade Unions (COSATU), which claimed 450,000 members. Formed in late November, 1985, the COSATU was influenced by the exiled leadership of the African National Congress and by the NUM, the most powerful of the industrial unions.

From the beginning, the new trade-union federation was overtly political in orientation. At the founding congress, there were calls for the nationalization of the mines and other key industries as well as for support for the international disinvestment campaign. Whether judged from a purely trade-union standpoint or from the broader view of political opposition to apartheid, the formation of the COSATU was a historic achievement.

Thus, the federation's "National Living Wage Campaign," which began in April, 1987, was a focus for wage-centered strikes and political agitation against the repression of black workers under apartheid. This labor offensive was turned back by massive resistance by employers and repression by the government, which invaded union headquarters and arrested labor leaders. In addition, many unions were drawn into factional warfare with more conservative black organizations, particularly the moderate United Workers Union of South Africa. Despite these defeats and difficulties, the strike wave that swept over South Africa in 1987 was certainly a turning point in the struggle for human rights in general and workers' rights in particular.

Impact of Event

The peculiar nature of apartheid-based oppression in South Africa had its origin, in large measure, in the desire for unlimited, cheap, and powerless black African labor. The tremendous prosperity of many white South Africans and the huge profits of industrial corporations depended on having a black working class forced to work under conditions and for wages that harked back to the worst abuses of the early Industrial Revolution. Thus, whatever racial or cultural prejudice contributed to the brutality of South Africa, there existed a powerful economic incentive to continue to deprive black Africans of their human rights.

Therefore, when hundreds of thousands of workers struck in 1987 for better wages or out of political sentiment, it was an attack at the heart of the apartheid system. The fact that black trade unions, independent of governmental control, established themselves in South Africa was a change that severely undercut the very basis of apartheid. On a day-to-day basis, almost all black laborers were powerless, but strikes and the unions that led them gave a collective expression of power.

This experience had a vital psychological impact on the black masses, and its practical significance was likewise great. The strikes of 1987 proved to both white employers and black employees that the old system of treating blacks as less than human was dying. Even the clashes that took place over the largely symbolic observation of May Day illustrated this change.

Although the South African government and employers had always scorned May 1 as a "socialist holiday," black workers by 1987 were walking off the job on that day to express their belief in a better, postapartheid future. These walkouts were more than mere expressions of abstract sentiment. They were expressions of the newly gained rights of black workers. The reality was that many corporations were unable to stop May Day observations. Of little significance in and of itself, this was an important sign that the complete control once exercised over the black labor force had been weakened.

The 1987 strikes were more than the normal labor-management conflicts that occur in many nations, inasmuch as they represented long-oppressed people demanding not only better wages but also human dignity and freedom. That so many of the major unions and the COSATU were sympathetic to or linked with Mandela's banned African National Congress and even Slovo's outlawed Communist Party was in itself a challenge to Botha's South African regime.

Perhaps the most meaningful aspect of the strike wave was that it presented a powerful potential alternative method of liberation that avoided the passivity of peaceful protest and the recklessness of armed guerrilla warfare. It opened up the possibility of a transition to a new South Africa that would grant all citizens the same human rights and dignity. Finally, it offered a model of organization that held the potential to overcome the factional disputes that continued to plague the antiapartheid movement.

Bibliography

Callinicos, Alex. *South Africa: Between Reform and Revolution*. London: Bookmarks, 1988. Although openly partisan in its approach, this book gives an excellent insight into the antiapartheid movement, with particular emphasis on labor. Contains reference notes and an index.

Cohen, Robin. *Endgame in South Africa*. Trenton, N.J.: Africa World Press, 1988. Brief but useful treatment of the role of ideology in the apartheid system of South Africa. Includes an index and a bibliography.

Holland, Heidi. *The Struggle: A History of the African National Congress.* New York: George Braziller, 1990. Popularly written. Holland chronicles the ANC's history from its formation in 1912. A very useful book for those who wish to go beyond Mandela and study the organization he led. With index and reference notes.

Leach, Graham. *South Africa: No Easy Path to Peace.* London: Methuen, 1986. Written by a British Broadcasting Corporation South African correspondent, this is a lively, very readable work for those just learning about the subject. Includes select bibliography and index.

Magubane, Bernard Makhosezwe. *The Political Economy of Race and Class in South Africa.* New York: Monthly Review Press, 1990. Both readable and scholarly. Magubane shows the interconnection between racial oppression and the growth of capitalism in South Africa. Contains reference notes and an index.

Minter, William. *King Solomon's Mines Revisited.* New York: Basic Books, 1986. A revealing and readable examination of the role Western interests played in the creation and maintenance of the South African apartheid system. Bibliography, index, and references.

William A. Pelz

Cross-References

Reformers Expose Atrocities Against Congolese Laborers (1903), p. 13; South Africa Begins a System of Separate Development (1951), p. 861; The Organization of African Unity Is Founded (1963), p. 1194; Zimbabwe's Freedom Fighters Topple White Supremacist Government (1964), p. 1224; The United Nations Votes to Suppress and Punish Apartheid (1973), p. 1736; Students in Soweto Rebel Against the White Government (1976), p. 1882; Biko Is Murdered by Interrogators in South Africa (1977), p. 1887; The United Nations Issues a Declaration on South Africa (1979), p. 2008; Tutu Wins the Nobel Peace Prize (1984), p. 2244; Namibia Is Liberated from South African Control (1988), p. 2409; Mandela Is Freed (1990), p. 2559; De Klerk Promises to Topple Apartheid Legislation (1991), p. 2606.

FIJI'S ELECTED GOVERNMENT IS OUSTED BY THE MILITARY

Categories of event: Racial and ethnic rights; political freedom
Time: 1987
Locale: Suva, Fiji

An elected coalition government headed by an ethnic Indian prime minister was brought down through two bloodless military coups to establish native Fijian rule

Principal personages:

TIMOCI BAVADRA, the first prime minister of Fiji of Indian ethnic origin
RATU SIR KAMISESE MARA, the first elected prime minister of Fiji after its independence in 1970
RATU SIR PENAIA GANILAU, the first governor general of Fiji after independence, later nominated as the first president of the Republic of Fiji
SITIVENI RABUKA, the leader of the two bloodless army coups in 1987

Summary of Event

The modern history of Fiji, a South Pacific island state, began with the advent of British colonial rule in 1874. The island of Fiji was handed over to the British by a group of Fijian chiefs led by Ratu Seru Cakobau; Fiji did not gain its independence until 1970. The multiethnic nature of Fijian society is a part of its colonial heritage. This pluralist society represents a tradition of interethnic mistrust, competition for power, and ethnic conflict, particularly between the two most populous groups, the indigenous Fijians and the Fijians of Indian ethnic origin. The latter group owes its presence to the importation of Indians as coolies and indentured laborers from colonial India by the British to work on sugar plantations.

In 1987, indigenous Fijians constituted about 46 percent of the island's population; the people of Indian descent began to outnumber them around the middle of the twentieth century and constituted about 48 percent of the total population in 1987. The less-numerous groups on the island included Europeans, part-Europeans, and Chinese. The main antagonism and hostility, however, existed between the native Fijians and the Indian Fijians. The lack of cultural and political integration among the population in Fiji was attributed by Fijian political analyst Victor Lal to the British policy of "benevolent apartheid" to further British colonial interests.

After its independence in 1970, Fiji adopted a political system based on the British model of a parliamentary form of government and an electoral system. In view of its ethnic plurality, however, coupled with the fact that since 1948 the Indian population had outnumbered the indigenous Fijians, a unique system of communal electoral representation was created to protect the dominant status of local Fijians and to give representation to a variety of contending factions and interests. This system of "communal roll" instead of "common roll" angered the Indian community, which began to perceive it as a device to keep Indians in an unequal position of political power and second-class-citizen status. While trying to accommodate itself to the new political system by integrating itself with the power structures, the Indian community continued its efforts to organize politically and to keep the pressure on for a "common roll," or general electorate. As a result of their separate demands, Indians began to be viewed as disloyal and power-hungry by the other Fijians.

Between 1970 and 1987, Fiji was ruled by the right-wing Alliance Party, mainly supported by the indigenous Fijians, under Ratu Sir Kamisese Mara as prime minister. In the fifth general elections held April 4-11, 1987, however, the long-reigning Alliance Party was defeated by an Indo-Fijian-dominated coalition. Dr. Timoci Bavadra led the coalition of the National Federation Party (NFP) and the Fiji Labour Party (FLP). The NFP had the strong support of Fiji Indians, and the FLP represented assorted racial groups. The NFP-FLP coalition won twenty-eight of the fifty-two seats in the house of representatives, while the Alliance Party, backed mainly by the indigenous Fijians, won twenty-four seats. The coalition, led by the new prime minister, Bavadra, included nineteen Indians, seven Fijians, and two others.

The defeat of the Alliance Party indicated, on one hand, the urban middle class's challenge to the conservative approach and influence of the Great Council of Chiefs, which was bent on perpetuating a system of tribal allegiance in Fiji and its paramount position within that system. Overall, however, the Indian Fijians had not won the confidence of the rank-and-file Fijians, who distrusted Indians and remained suspicious of their desire for political power and control in Fiji. The native Fijian population still believed in the traditional tribal ways and placed high respect and faith in the Great Council of Chiefs. The political legitimacy of Ratu Mara's government had not derived from electoral victory alone but also from the fact that he was a descendant of a traditional chiefly tribe. The majority of the native Fijian population was still rural, culturally traditional, and economically and educationally backward, while the Indian population, by and large, was more commerce-minded and had integrated itself into professions and the modern sector of the economy.

Not the least important among the factors complicating the political situation in Fiji was the continued external interference of the British in the internal affairs of Fiji after independence. Such interference was ostensibly done on behalf of the native Fijians, but in fact it was intended to perpetuate the British indirect control in Fiji and the influence of Western powers in the region to offset perceived Soviet influence. The office of the governor-general as the agent of the British in Fiji was a direct instrument used to interfere with internal Fijian politics.

The coming into power of the Bavadra government provided a cause for jubilation in the Indian community but was met with anger and resistance from native Fijians. In the existing climate of mutual suspicion and lack of national integration, the Great Council of Chiefs and other conservative elements could easily stir up already troubled waters. Soon after Bavadra's victory, an activist political organization, Tau-kei, was formed to mobilize the native Fijians to demand the constitutional guarantee of the right of native Fijians to political rule.

Beginning on April 23, 1987, street protests and noisy public demonstrations began against the Bavadra government. The protesters began to send petitions to the governor-general indicating their lack of confidence in the new government. The nature of the protests and demonstrations, however, was generally peaceful. The overt grievance of the protesters was that Indians wanted to rob native Fijians of their land and their way of life.

On May 14, 1987, at 10:00 A.M., a bloodless coup led by Lieutenant Colonel Sitiveni Rabuka took place in Fiji, as about ten soldiers attacked the parliament. Prime Minister Bavadra, his ministers, and other colleagues present in the parliament were arrested and detained. Meanwhile, Rabuka declared that he had seized power to "safeguard the Fijian way of life" from Indian dominance, political or otherwise. The military takeover was celebrated by jubilant Fijians, some of whom also began to harass and threaten the ethnic Indians in Suva and surrounding areas. Some began to demand that Indians should be expelled from Fiji. The coup sent waves of terror and panic among the Indians, who began to perceive their future in Fiji, their homeland, as bleak.

Following the coup, the political administration was handed over by Rabuka to civilian authorities under the former prime minister, Ratu Mara. Bavadra and his associates were released unharmed on May 19, 1987. Meanwhile, under a multiparty caretaker government under Ratu Mara, efforts were under way to find ways of reaching some form of political compromise whereby a system of communal proportional representation could be maintained while guaranteeing political supremacy of the local Fijians. Although the Indian community in general was dismayed by the overthrow of Bavadra's government, Bavadra personally became associated with the efforts under Ratu Mara for seeking a political compromise.

The first coup was followed by a second coup by Rabuka in September, 1987, which ended all political efforts to seek a multiracial compromise. The second coup was designed to establish clearly the supremacy and control of the native Fijians and the subordination of nonnative Fijians to formal secondary political status. Unlike the first coup, it led to a political restructuring and power shuffle in the government. Work on constitutional changes was initiated in order to safeguard permanently the political control and dominance of the native Fijians. The office of the governor-general was abolished, and Ratu Sir Penaia Ganilau, the former governor-general, resigned to become the first nominated president of the Republic of Fiji. Ratu Mara was nominated as the prime minister of Fiji. The new cabinet formed after the second coup included most of Ratu Mara's old cabinet associates, four members of the military, and some members of the Taukei movement. Rabuka became minister for home affairs in the new cabinet. The racial makeup of the cabinet was seventeen Fijians, two Indians, and two part-Europeans. Once again, civilian rule was restored by the military, but the democratic experiment had ended. The Western-style democratic process, based on equality of citizens, free electoral competition of political parties, and the right of the majority party to come into power, was replaced by a pseudo-parliamentary system controlled by traditional tribal chiefs and the hegemony of one group over others in a racially plural society.

Under the new political system in Fiji, steps were taken to ensure the racial and ethnic inequality by drafting a new constitution to safeguard the right of Fijians (by implication, Fijian chiefs) to political rule. A constitutional council was appointed to undertake work on the framing of a new constitution.

A draft of the amended constitution was presented in September, 1988. It called for the president and prime minister both to be Fijian and for a unicameral legislature with thirty-six Fijian members. This document was rejected by Indians, led by Bavadra, as militarist and racist. A later version, presented in late 1989, called for a bicameral legislature with the Senate consisting of appointed chiefs and an elected House with thirty-seven Fijians, twenty-six Indians, and five others. Before its implementation, the new law was to be endorsed by the Council of High Chiefs and the Great Council of Chiefs, both of which upheld the right of Fijian supremacy. More amendments were sought in 1990, as the constitution still had not been accepted.

Impact of Event

The most serious consequences of the 1987 coups in Fiji were borne by the local Indian population. Their long political struggle for equal political rights in Fiji, which they considered to be their homeland, ended in despair. Their future in Fiji became more uncertain and insecure in view of the new constitutional amendments initiated after the second coup to give the native Fijians a permanent right to political rule. Indians were further disconcerted by the already existing land-ownership laws, according to which more than 90 percent of the land was under permanent native Fijian control; Indians could only rent or lease land for residence or agricultural purposes. The fear of a possible Indian expulsion from Fiji and the memory of the nightmarish Indian and Asian experience of deportation from Uganda during Idi Amin's rule continued to haunt Fijian Indians.

After the coups, a number of Fijian Indians, mostly from the educated middle class, began to emigrate to Australia, New Zealand, and other Western countries. The prospects of migration were dim for those Indians who belonged to the rural, unskilled, and less-prosperous strata. The size of the Indian population declined after the coups, though Indians on Fiji remained slightly more numerous than native Fijians.

A possible explanation of the peaceful and nonviolent nature of the coups was that Fiji needed its Indians as much as they needed Fiji as their homeland. The Indian contribution to and integration in the educational, economic, and intellectual life of Fiji were great assets for the entire Fijian society. The sudden, significant withdrawal of Indian population could cause disruptions of the Fijian society.

The overthrow of the Bavadra government meant the end of the democratic process, the denial of political rights, and the denial to a people of a homeland. It also signified the victory of the tribal chiefs in perpetuating their interests and control over the native Fijians. The educated and urban native Fijian middle classes and the less-affluent Fijians, who under normal circumstances would have demanded economic justice and equal opportunities, had been silenced, and their attention had been misdirected.

Bibliography

Ali, Ahmed. *Fiji: From Colony to Independence, 1874-1970.* Suva, Fiji: University of the South Pacific, 1977. A chronological and analytical historical account of the politics and society in Fiji as a British colony and during the period surrounding its independence. The development of the multiracial and multicultural character of Fiji during this critical period and its implications for the future of Fijian society are discussed.

Lal, Victor. *Fiji: Coups in Paradise.* London: Zed Press, 1990. The best work available about the political history and the nature of group conflict in Fiji. The causes and consequences of the two military coups and the reversal of the democratic process are analyzed in depth. A sophisticated political examination of the historical, sociological, and economic reasoning behind the political moves to perpetuate the political insecurity and second-class status for Fijians of Indian ethnicity.

_____. "The Fiji Indians: Marooned at Home." In *South Asians Overseas: Migration and Ethnicity*, edited by Colin Clarke, Ceri Peach, and Steven Vertovec. Cambridge, England: Cambridge University Press, 1990. Discusses the events surrounding the coups of 1987 in Fiji and the struggle for political equality, status of insecurity, and future of the Fijian Indian community.

Mamak, Alexander. *Colour, Culture, and Conflict: A Study of Pluralism in Fiji.* New York: Pergamon Press, 1978. A sociological analysis of race and group consciousness in the multicultural and multiracial Fijian society. The historical and political reasons behind the lack of national integration and sense of nationalism are discussed.

Milne, R. S. *Politics in Ethnically Bi-Polar States: Guyana, Malaysia, Fiji.* Vancouver, Canada: University of British Columbia Press, 1981. A comparative study of multiculturalism and political polarity in the non-Western plural societies of Guyana, Malaysia, and Fiji.

Indu Vohra

Cross-References

The Iranian Constitution Bars Non-Muslims from Cabinet Positions (1906), p. 52; The Muslim League Attempts to Protect Minority Interests in India (1906), p. 87; The Statute of Westminster Creates the Commonwealth (1931), p. 453; The Atlantic Charter Declares a Postwar Right of Self-Determination (1941), p. 584; India Gains Independence (1947), p. 731; South Africa Begins a System of Separate Development (1951), p. 861; The Tamil Federal Party Agitates for Greater Language Rights

(1961), p. 1090; The United Nations Issues a Declaration on Racial Discrimination (1963), p. 1212; A World Conference Condemns Racial Discrimination (1978), p. 1993; Tamil Separatist Violence Erupts in Sri Lanka (1980's), p. 2068; Congress Formally Apologizes to Japanese Internees (1988), p. 2392; Kashmir Separatists Demand an End to Indian Rule (1989), p. 2426.

GOVERNMENT-SUPPORTED DEATH SQUADS QUASH JVP INSURRECTION IN SRI LANKA

Category of event: Atrocities and war crimes
Time: 1987 to 1991
Locale: Southern and central Sri Lanka

Rebellion by the Maoist Janatha Vimukthi Peramuna (JVP) led to the assassination of thousands of government supporters and the slaughter of thousands of suspects by government-supported death squads

Principal personages:
> S. SAMAN PIYASIRI FERNANDO (KEERTHI WIYAYABAHU) (c. 1957-1989), the leader of the military wing of the JVP who used the name of a colonial rebel leader against British rule
> UPATISSA GAMANAYAKE (c. 1948-1989), the second in command of the JVP during the 1980's
> RANASINGHE PREMADASA (1924-   ), the president of Sri Lanka elected in December, 1988
> RANJAN WIJERATNA (1931-1991), the Sri Lankan state minister for defense and an important strategist in the war against the JVP
> ROHANA WIJEWEERA (1943-1989), a leader of the JVP who led both the 1971 and the late 1980's insurrections

Summary of Event

Sri Lanka endured a large amount of civil strife in the 1980's. Two civil wars were fought throughout much of the decade. In 1987, the Janatha Vimukthi Peramuna (JVP) (People's Liberation Front) began an all-out war to gain power in Sri Lanka. Their campaign resulted in a bloody response by government-supported death squads and the suspension of constitutional rights and due process for nearly two years. The violence and human rights abuses shook the foundation of constitutional rule in Sri Lanka.

The JVP was the same organization that had led an insurrection against the government in 1971, in which ten to twenty thousand people died. The leaders of the 1971 insurrection were jailed but given amnesty in 1977. These included Rohana Wijeweera, the leader and organizer of the insurrection. After the amnesty, the JVP regrouped and organized as a legal political party, and its leader, Wijeweera, even entered the 1982 presidential elections, placing third out of six candidates. The party participated in legal politics until it was banned following ethnic riots in 1983. At that point, it went underground and began to prepare for the next insurrection. The arrival of Indian peacekeeping forces in the northern and eastern parts of the island to enforce a truce between the government and the ethnic minority Tamil guerrillas in 1987 was the catalyst for the revolt. Many Sri Lankans feared India and its intentions, and the government-invited arrival of Indian troops on Sri Lankan soil was seen by many as a serious threat to the sovereignty of the country. The JVP exploited this fear to gain support for its movement.

The JVP leadership espoused a Maoist ideology. Its appeal was to both male and female youths, especially in the southern province of Sri Lanka across the southern tier of the island. Among university students, there was strong sympathy for the JVP. At the height of the violence, from 1988 to 1990, the universities of Sri Lanka were closed down by supporters of the JVP. The JVP's appeal to the young was based on nationalism, the fear of Indian encroachment in Sri Lanka, and the offer of hope in a climate of few economic opportunities, rather than on the organization's Maoist ideology.

The JVP's main tactic was an assassination campaign against government supporters and anyone who did not oppose the Indian troops in Sri Lanka. Thousands were slaughtered in the uprising's first two years. At first, the Sri Lankan government was helpless to stop the JVP killings. By 1988, however, this began to change; the bodies of alleged JVP supporters began to appear at night across the southern districts of Matara and Hambantota. At times, the bodies would be found with signs on them listing their alleged crimes. Eventually, the killers began to burn their victims beyond recognition. The killings spread in 1989 to other parts of the island. Bodies began to appear in the Anuradhapura district in north-central Sri Lanka. Bodies began to appear in June, 1989, in the Kandy district in the central hill country, which had been spared much of the JVP violence. The killings became more gruesome, and the mutilation of bodies became more common. The deaths of victims became less an objective of the killers, while the terror created by leaving body parts in public places or sending them to victims' relatives became more important. In August, 1989, a ring of heads appeared overnight around a campus site where a University of Peradeniya official had been killed the day before. The police refused to allow the heads to be removed. In September, hundreds were killed in villages of low-caste people near the university, and their bodies were thrown in rivers. Often, security personnel would prevent relatives from retrieving the bodies, forcing them to leave the bodies for the public to view. By the end of the violence, more than ten thousand bodies appeared around the country. Some groups have estimated that the number of victims who disappeared during the violence may be more than one hundred thousand.

Although the government denied it, there was strong evidence to indicate that the killings were carried out by off-duty police and army personnel, assisted at times by government supporters. A few of the killers were captured. The son of a member of Parliament and seven police and army personnel were arrested in 1988 for the murder of three youths picked up at gunpoint on a crowded street in the city of Ratnapura. Most of the time, however, the government denied any involvement in the killings and fought to avoid investigating them.

The killings began to subside in November, 1989, after Rohana Wijeweera and Upatissa Gamanayake, the leaders of the insurrection, were captured. Wijeweera was the first to be captured and died within forty-eight hours of his capture. The official explanation of his death indicated that he was shot by a member of his politburo as he led security forces to a hideout. His body was cremated within hours of his death. Within weeks, the government claimed that all members of the politburo and the district leaders of the JVP had either been captured or been killed. Most of them died while in custody, and their bodies were burned, but not before they had "decided" to provide the government with important information to find other leaders.

The capture of the leadership was followed by a bloodbath by the death squads, as they sought out suspects and killed them on the spot. On one night in December alone, more than 170 bodies appeared across the southern district of Hambantota. What made the killings even more remarkable was that they were usually carried out at night, while strict government curfews were in effect and roadblocks dotted the roadways of the island. Remarkably, the security personnel at the roadblocks rarely noticed vehicles used to pick up thousands of victims. In a few instances, security men were killed when they tried to stop or arrest the death-squad members. Despite the destruction of the JVP leadership, the death squads continued killing for another two months with little decline in the number of victims. Even after that period, the death squads were active for nearly two more years at a much-reduced rate.

The killings were made easier by the existence of the Prevention of Terrorism Act (PTA), which was passed in 1979 to curb Tamil ethnic minority guerrillas in the north and east of the island. The act allowed security forces to search and arrest suspects without warrants or evidence. The police and army were allowed to take detainees to any site to interrogate them for up to eighteen months without notifying the courts or any other authorities. The act allowed suspects to be tried before a judge without a jury and for security forces to dispose of the bodies of suspects without autopsies or notification of next of kin. The act also allowed for press censorship of any reports of actions related to the Prevention of Terrorism Act. The PTA, along with other emergency regulations, allowed the government security forces to carry out any actions they wished.

Impact of Event

The death-squad activity in Sri Lanka resulted in the elimination of the JVP threat to the government. By mid-1991, JVP violence had been reduced to occasional attacks and arrests. The reign of terror, however, had a profound effect on Sri Lankan society. The exercise of violence by the police, military, and youths undermined the control of the security forces. Some of the death-squad killings appeared to have been personal vendettas cloaked as anti-JVP activity. In addition, the security forces no longer followed the rule of law to protect the constitution. Abuses by the security forces were relatively rare in the southern parts of the island prior to the JVP insurrection; afterward, criminal acts carried out by security force personnel became much more common. These acts included robberies, extortion, and rapes.

Sri Lankan students responded in defiant fear. Unrest at the universities where the

JVP had great support, such as Peradeniya, continued. Student protests took the form of boycotts of student government elections and the election of slates of candidates sympathetic to but not openly in support of the JVP's political positions. The respect for the legitimacy of the government also suffered. Many youths lost trust and faith in the older generation's ability to deal with the country's problems.

Perhaps the largest impact on the country was the brutalization of Sri Lankan society. The extensive violence in the country left many physical and psychological scars that would take years to heal. Students not only rebelled against authority but killed representatives of that authority. These included professors, businesspeople, and the families of security personnel. The once-peaceful Sri Lankan society became very violent. Violent crime, once a rarity, became common. Drug use and suicides climbed to near-record levels.

Police and military, who found that torture and violence against suspects could be very effective in controlling civil unrest, continued to use them to solve crimes. The government's unwillingness or inability to punish illegal activity by the security forces provided an umbrella of protection to the police and military. Attempts to punish wrongdoers were prevented or covered up. The death of an internationally known journalist provided strong evidence of the government's willingness to protect the death squads at all costs. The young journalist, Richard de Zoysa, a leftist who apparently was not connected to the JVP, was arrested at his home by men who claimed to be police on February 18, 1990, more than three months after the death of Wijeweera and the decline in JVP offensive operations. De Zoysa's mutilated and tortured body was found the next day on a beach south of Colombo. His mother, who had observed his arrest, identified a police officer as one of the group that arrested her son, but the government decided that there was not enough evidence to pursue the case. It also blocked an attempt in Parliament to appoint a commission to investigate the murder.

Sri Lanka, once a model of democracy, descended to the edge of authoritarian government. The willingness of the government to use extraconstitutional means such as murder and torture to protect itself left an undemocratic legacy that threatened the country's future.

Bibliography

Amnesty International. *Sri Lanka Briefing*. London: Author, 1989. Part of a regular series of reports produced by Amnesty International on human rights abuses in conflicts in Sri Lanka.

De Silva, Kingsley. "The Sri Lankan Universities from 1977 to 1990: Recovery, Stability, and the Descent to Crisis." *Minerva* 28 (Summer, 1990): 156-216. A leading Sri Lankan historian chronicles the rise of violent student activism in the Sri Lankan universities that led to the closure of the schools by JVP activists from 1988 to 1990.

Dubey, Swaroop Rani. *One-Day Revolution in Sri Lanka: Anatomy of 1971 Insurrection*. Jaipur, India: Aalekh, 1988. A historical account of the 1971 insurrection, with an update to 1987, just before the second insurrection intensified.

Ivan, Victor. *Sri Lanka in Crisis: Road to Conflict.* Ratmalana, Sri Lanka: Sarvodaya, 1989. A history of the events leading to the conflicts in Sri Lanka by a former politburo member of the JVP during the 1971 insurrection. The book focuses on the economic situation in Sri Lanka.

Kodikara, Shelton U. "The Continuing Crisis in Sri Lanka: The JVP, the Indian Troops, and Tamil Politics." *Asian Survey* 19 (July, 1989): 716-724. This analysis examines the relationship between the Tamil insurrection in Sri Lanka and the JVP revolt.

Marino, Eduardo. *Political Killings in Southern Sri Lanka.* Los Angeles: International Alert, 1989. Describes the JVP conflict, with a description and chronology of some of the killings in southern Sri Lanka and special emphasis on human rights issues.

Oberst, Robert C. "Political Decay in Sri Lanka." *Current History* 88 (December, 1989): 425-428, 448-449. An analysis of the JVP and Tamil conflicts and the Sri Lankan government's attempts to resolve them.

Robert C. Oberst

Cross-References

Soldiers Massacre Indian Civilians in Amritsar (1919), p. 264; The Tamil Federal Party Agitates for Greater Language Rights (1961), p. 1090; Zimbabwe's Freedom Fighters Topple White Supremacist Government (1964), p. 1224; Sri Lankans Promote Nationalism (1971), p. 1590; Zia Establishes Martial Law in Pakistan (1977), p. 1898; Tamil Separatist Violence Erupts in Sri Lanka (1980's), p. 2068; Sikhs in Punjab Revolt (1984), p. 2215;

THE SUPREME COURT RULES THAT LAWS CAN FORCE GROUPS TO ADMIT WOMEN

Categories of event: Women's rights and civil rights
Time: May 4, 1987
Locale: Duarte, California, and Washington, D.C.

The Supreme Court ruled that states and communities could enforce antidiscrimination regulations of nonintimate private clubs so long as First Amendment rights are respected

Principal personages:

LEWIS FRANKLIN POWELL, JR. (1907-   ), a justice of the Supreme Court from 1971 to 1987; a moderate Southerner who wrote the *Rotary* opinion

WILLIAM BRENNAN, JR. (1906-   ), a leading liberal of the Court from 1956 to 1990; in 1984 he developed the conceptual framework used by Powell

SANDRA DAY O'CONNOR (1930-   ), the first woman to be on the Supreme Court

MARY LOU ELLIOTT (1933-   ), a school administrator in Duarte who was one of the three women to join the local Rotary club in 1977

Summary of Event

In 1958, the Supreme Court explicitly ruled that the First Amendment implied a "freedom of association" (*NAACP v. Alabama ex rel. Patterson*). The Court prohibited Alabama from requiring a list of members of the civil rights group on the grounds that this would discourage people from joining. Six years later, in *Bell v. Maryland*, Justice Arthur Goldberg made a distinction between a public business and a private club, declaring that for the latter the Constitution gave each person the right "to choose his social intimates and business partners solely on the basis of personal prejudices including race." Likewise, in *Evans v. Newton*, Justice William Douglas wrote that in a group such as a private golf club, membership based on race or sex was a protected "expression of freedom of association."

Title II of the Civil Rights Act of 1964 made it illegal to discriminate on the basis of race, religion, or national origin in public accommodations (meaning businesses open to the public). Title II expressly exempted private clubs not open to the public, and in contrast to other parts of the 1964 law, it did not prohibit discrimination based on gender. Within a few years, the Court was faced with the complex task of deciding when a club should be treated as a business establishment, and, even more complicated, deciding at what point a state's involvement with a club would constitute "state action" that should be regulated by the equal protection clause of the

Fourteenth Amendment. In 1969, the Court examined the Lake Nixon recreation club of Arkansas, where as many as one hundred thousand white patrons a year purchased services after paying a "membership fee" of twenty-five cents. The majority of the Court decided that this was a place of "public entertainment" that could not exclude African Americans. In 1972, however, the Court decided that the Loyal Order of Moose in Pennsylvania was indeed a private club that might refuse to serve African Americans. In this controversial opinion, the majority ruled six to three that the issuance of a liquor license did not constitute the kind of state action that would come under the Fourteenth Amendment.

Meanwhile, those dissatisfied with Title II were able to convince many states and communities to pass public accommodations acts (PAAs) that went beyond federal standards. By 1983, twenty-eight states had passed PAAs that did not make exemptions for most private clubs, and twenty-six PAAs prohibited sex discrimination. Minnesota was one of the states with a broad PAA, and when the national organization of the U.S. Jaycees threatened to expel two chapters in Minnesota because they had defied the national bylaws by allowing women full membership, the local groups sought legal relief, arguing that the U.S. Jaycees were in violation of Minnesota's law. The national organization prevailed in the U.S. Court of Appeals on the grounds that associational freedom outweighed a state law and that the law was excessively vague in reference to public accommodations. On July 3, 1984, however, the Supreme Court reversed the lower court in *Roberts v. United States Jaycees,* deciding by a seven-to-zero margin that the law's application did not violate the freedom of association in this particular instance.

In the official opinion, Justice William Brennan recognized that the Fourteenth Amendment gave Minnesota "a compelling interest in eradicating discrimination against female citizens," justifying state regulations of private clubs so long as there was no "serious burden" on their rights to "intimate association" or "expressive association." The first principle referred to characteristics such as "relative smallness" and selectivity in membership; the second principle referred to the promotion of ideas and other activities protected by the First Amendment. Brennan noted that the two Minnesota chapters had about four hundred members each, that there were some three hundred thousand members nationwide, and that the requirements for membership were minimal. The organization, moreover, was for business and community-service training and not concerned with the promotion of any political or religious ideas. Since the Jaycees allowed women as associate members, they had failed to demonstrate that full membership for women would force the organization to change its mission or character. Justice Sandra Day O'Connor agreed with the outcome of the decision but disageed with Brennan's stress on intimacy. She argued that the key point was that the U.S. Jaycees had more of the characteristics of a "commercial association" than of a private association, and that the former could claim "only minimal constitutional protection."

The *Roberts* decision failed to answer a number of important questions. Some observers believed that a private club might have a better case if it totally excluded women from membership, in contrast to the Jaycees' policy of partial exclusion. More important, Brennan wrote that a smaller group such as the Kiwanis might enjoy constitutional exemption from state regulations, but the decision presented few guidelines about the degree of intimacy required for such protection.

In 1974, California amended its statutes to outlaw gender-based discrimination in "all business establishments of every kind whatsoever," giving no exemption to non-profit groups. Rotary International was a nonprofit corporation that had 19,788 local clubs in 157 countries, with local clubs having from twenty to four hundred members. The organization was moderately selective in membership requirements. Although the Rotary bylaws did not allow women to be members, in 1977 the local club of Duarte, California, because of a declining membership, voted to admit three women—Mary Lou Elliott, Dona Bogard, and Rosemary Freitag. After the international organization's board of directors terminated the charter of the Duarte club, the local group filed a complaint in the California Superior Court of Los Angeles, which ruled that Rotary International was not a business establishment. The Duarte club, however, won the decision in the state court of appeals, giving the Rotarians the choice of readmitting the club or ceasing operations in California. After the California Supreme Court denied a petition for review, the U.S. Supreme Court accepted the petition in order to decide if the appellate court's decision was a violation of Rotary International's First Amendment rights.

On March 30, 1987, the Supreme Court heard the opposing arguments. Judith Resnick, speaking for the Duarte chapter, argued that Rotary International was a "business-like organization" and that "the message to women is that we're second-class citizens, not part of the business community's leadership." Representing the Rotarians, William Sutter stressed that their goal was community service rather than career advancement and that they were more selective than the Jaycees.

On May 4, 1987, the Court, in a seven-to-zero decision, upheld the application of the California statute to the Rotarians. Justices Harry Blackmun and Sandra O'Connor did not take part in the decision because of conflicts of interest. Justice Lewis Powell wrote the opinion for the Court, using the theoretical framework that Brennan had presented in the *Roberts* case. First, Powell argued that individuals enjoyed a "zone of privacy" that allowed them to exclude people from many kinds of "intimate or private relationships," but that the Rotarians did not constitute one of these relationships. Second, individuals enjoyed the freedom to form associations that had the goal of expressing political or religious ideas, a freedom that must be respected. States, however, could regulate private clubs when necessary to serve a compelling state interest as long as they did not violate the two rights of intimate association and expressive association. In a footnote, Powell wrote that he was not making any judgment about the possible protection of other clubs and that each club's privileges would be decided by considering factors such as its size, selectivity, and purposes. Powell did not directly refer to O'Connor's theory about the special limits of business-related clubs, although her perspective appears to have colored the logic of his opinion.

Impact of Event

Very often, justices of the Supreme Court must attempt to reconcile competing values of the law, and this was certainly the challenge in the *Roberts* and *Rotary* decisions. The First Amendment freedom of association implies that an individual can decide to exclude some people in private relationships, while the Fourteenth Amendment and public accommodations laws create governmental interests in providing equal opportunities for commercial and professional activities. The conflict is especially apparent in private clubs, for it is generally recognized that these institutions present an important opportunity for making business contacts and for professional training. The New York City Commission on Human Rights published a study in 1975 that reported a survey of businesspeople in which two-thirds said that participation in private clubs was important to their success. In addition to such considerations, feminists maintained that exclusion tended to perpetuate stereotypes of gender inequality.

After the *Roberts* and *Rotary* decisions, observers expected that in the majority of states most business-related clubs would soon be forced to include women. In 1988, women who wanted to join private clubs won another victory in the case of *New York State Club Association v. City of New York*. This decision of the Supreme Court upheld a New York City ordinance that prohibited sex-based discrimination in social clubs of more than four hundred members when nonmembers were allowed to purchase meals. Since this case dealt with social clubs that had very limited connections to the business world, it appeared that there remained few significant limitations on the ways in which states and communities might apply their antidiscrimination laws to private clubs. Almost half of the states did not have such laws, but these were mostly smaller states that historically have tended to follow the examples of larger concentrations of population.

There were some libertarians who regretted the *Roberts* and *Rotary* decisions. They protested that the laws were overly broad and that they unjustly interfered with the personal liberty of individuals to form associations of their own choosing. Supporters of the decisions, however, noted that the Supreme Court had not taken away the rights of intimate association and expressive association. A group of men or women might form single-sex clubs when their goals presented a reasonable justification for a policy of exclusion. The Connecticut Supreme Court in 1987 ruled that the Boy Scouts of America had the right to bar women from leadership roles because the purposes of the organization included a need for role models, although after the decision the Boy Scouts changed their policy, in part to avoid costly legal battles. Not many women wanted to join such groups of special purpose anyway, but a growing number of professional women did want to have the right to join those private clubs that might help them to advance their businesses and careers.

Two years after the *Rotary* decision, there remained a number of large, prestigious clubs that did not admit women. The Bohemian Club of San Francisco was protesting a municipal antibias law on the grounds that it was not business oriented, but based on the *Rotary* precedent, few observers expected that such clubs would be able to prevail in court.

Bibliography

Abraham, Henry. *Freedom and the Court: Civil Rights and Liberties in the United States.* New York: Oxford University Press, 1988. This standard text provides a broad perspective of how the Court has interpreted issues of freedom and equality, with pages 488-494 giving a good summary of the topic of private clubs.

Burns, Michael. "The Exclusion of Women from Influential Clubs: The Inner Sanctum and the Myth of Full Equality." *Harvard Civil Rights-Civil Liberties Law Review* 18 (1983): 321-409. A well-documented treatment of how single-sex clubs prevent women from advancement and business opportunities. Burns attacks a narrow view of "state action" and argues that state and local laws should not exempt private clubs.

Marshall, William. "Discrimination and the Right of Association." *Northwestern University Law Review* 81 (Fall, 1988): 68-107. A theoretical discussion of how the freedom of association might conflict with the goal of equality in the public realm. Proposes a solution that allows freedom of expression but prohibits discriminatory actions.

Pavchinski, Alexa. "Social Clubs as Public Accommodations: Expressive and Intimate Association v. State Anti-Discrimination Legislation." *University of Florida Law Review* 40 (Fall, 1988): 1035-1077. Clear and excellent short summaries of the major cases that relate to the topic, arguing that although the Court has allowed some infringement on association freedoms, First Amendment rights have been respected.

Pompa, Lisa Tarin. "*Rotary International v. Duarte:* Limiting Association Rights to Protect Equal Access to California Business Establishments." *Pacific Law Journal* 19 (January, 1988): 339-426. Probably the best and most detailed analysis of the issues and facts of the *Rotary* case, arguing that the case reflected the changing roles of women in the United States.

Powell, Lewis, Jr. "*Board of Directors of Duarte International et al. v. Rotary Club of Duarte et al.*" *Supreme Court Reporter.* St. Paul, Minn.: West Publishing, 1990. The full and original text of Powell's opinion for the Court, with a short summary of all of the major facts of the case. The same text is found in *United States Reports* and *United States Supreme Court Reports, Lawyers' Edition.*

Rhode, Deborah. *Justice and Gender: Sex Discrimination and the Law.* Cambridge, Mass.: Harvard University Press, 1989. Written from a strong feminist point of view. Rhode provides an excellent treatment of all legal issues relating to gender equality. On the issue of private clubs, Rhode supports the views of Justice O'Connor and criticizes the emphasis on intimate rights. The bibliography is especially helpful.

Varela, Paul. "A Scout Is Friendly: Freedom of Association and the State Effort to End Private Discrimination." *William and Mary Law Review* 30 (Summer, 1989):

919-955. Written from a libertarian perspective, arguing that zealous reformers have produced vague laws and have gone too far in limiting the freedom of association. Varela provides a good summary of public accommodation acts in various states. His views can be contrasted with those of Rhode and Pavchinski.

Thomas T. Lewis

Cross-References

Rankin Becomes the First Woman Elected to Congress (1916), p. 190; The Nineteenth Amendment Gives American Women the Right to Vote (1920), p. 339; The U.N. Convention on the Political Rights of Women Is Approved (1952), p. 885; Canadian Bill of Rights Prohibits Sexual Discrimination (1960), p. 1079; Congress Passes the Civil Rights Act (1964), p. 1251; The National Organization for Women Forms to Protect Women's Rights (1966), p. 1327; The United Nations Issues a Declaration on Equality for Women (1967), p. 1391; The Equal Rights Amendment Passes Congress but Fails to Be Ratified (1972), p. 1656; Congress Votes to Admit Women to the Armed Services Academies (1975), p. 1823; A U.N. Convention Condemns Discrimination Against Women (1979), p. 2057; O'Connor Becomes the First Female Supreme Court Justice (1981), p. 2141.

THE STEWART B. McKINNEY HOMELESS ASSISTANCE ACT BECOMES LAW

Category of event: Homeless people's rights
Time: July 22, 1987
Locale: Washington, D.C.

The Stewart B. McKinney Homeless Assistance Act provided a substantial increase in federal funds for emergency support to shelter programs for the homeless

Principal personages:

MITCH SNYDER, the most prominent advocate for the homeless, lobbied Congress relentlessly for increased federal aid to the homeless

STEWART B. MCKINNEY (1931-1987), a Republican from Connecticut who was an activist within Congress for the cause of homelessness

RONALD REAGAN (1911-   ), the fortieth president of the United States (1981-1989)

Summary of Event

There have always been homeless people in the United States, but with the possible exception of the Great Depression era, homelessness had never achieved the status as a political issue that it did in the 1980's. The passage of the Stewart B. McKinney Homeless Assistance Act in the summer of 1987 represented the culmination of a decade of debate about homelessness, its causes, and the federal government's responsibility to respond to the problem. The prominence of the issue in the 1980's was the result of the visibility of homeless people on the streets of American cities.

The homeless of the 1980's were a different group both in size and in demographics from those who traditionally had been homeless. The Skid Rows of an earlier age were found in the largest cities in the nation and were populated largely by older, alcoholic, single, white men who lived in cheap residential hotels and provided unskilled day labor for local businesses. The "new homeless," although also plagued with alcohol and drug problems, were more likely to be younger and to be members of ethnic or racial minorities. Further, they were more likely to be completely lacking in shelter and employment of any kind. Consequently, they were more visible because they lived on the streets, in parks, and in subway and railroad stations. Finally, there were many more women and children among the new homeless. A 1987 report by the United States Conference of Mayors found that there had been a 25 percent increase in the number of families with children seeking shelter. In 1986, New York City provided shelter in welfare hotels for an average of thirty-five hundred families every month. During the 1980's, families were the fastest growing segment of the homeless population, and by the end of the decade constituted approximately 30 percent of the homeless. The visibility and changed nature of the homeless population was in large part responsible for the pressure placed on the federal government to respond to the problem.

The plight of the homeless became an important public issue because it captured the attention of the media. A study of the *Readers' Guide to Periodical Literature* for 1975 and 1986 found a marked increase in magazine attention to homelessness. In 1975, there were no entries on homelessness, where in 1986 there were forty-eight. There were movies, documentaries, and nightly news stories, especially during the winter months, telling the stories of individual homeless people or the problems encountered in particular cities. Mitch Snyder, an advocate for the homeless who led the Washington, D.C.-based Community for Creative Non-Violence, held several hunger strikes and protests to draw attention to the problem in the nation's capital. Around the country, religious and other private charities established or expanded emergency shelters and soup kitchens to serve the increased demand for these services.

During this period, Congress did allocate some increased aid, through existing housing programs, to the homeless. Beginning in 1982, the Subcommittee on Housing and Community Development of the House Committee on Banking, Finance, and Urban Affairs held a series of hearings on the problems of the homeless. These hearings eventually led to the proposal that became the McKinney Act. During the 1986-1987 winter, several events helped motivate Congress to act on emergency housing assistance. A United States Conference of Mayors study released the week before Christmas, 1986, announced a marked increase in the number of people seeking emergency shelter. The study found that a quarter of the demand was not satisfied with the existing provision of shelter and food by private charity groups. It called for Congress to provide federal aid to the overtaxed services of local governments and private groups. The National Coalition for the Homeless released a similar report that winter, demonstrating that families with children were the fastest growing group among the homeless. To encourage support for legislation, Mitch Snyder and actor Martin Sheen organized a "Grate American Sleep Out," encouraging members of Congress to spend the night on the streets of Washington, D.C. Some did, including Stewart B. McKinney, the ranking minority member of the House Subcommittee on Housing and Community Development and an active supporter of aid to the homeless.

There was debate and disagreement over several issues during congressional consideration of emergency aid legislation. The Ronald Reagan Administration and Congress argued over the number of homeless and whether that number warranted increased federal aid. The Department of Housing and Urban Development held that the number of homeless people was approximately one-quarter million and that existing funding and programs were adequate to serve this number. The position of advocates for the homeless, both inside and outside Congress, was that the number was substantially higher (some estimates went as high as three million) and that the federal government had an obligation to increase its help. Many congressional Democrats argued that the increasing number of homeless was the result of Reagan Administration policies that had cut federal housing programs by 70 percent, tightened eligibility requirements for welfare, and generally harmed the working poor. In its final report on the McKinney bill, the House subcommittee argued: "In a nation so blessed with natural resources and material wealth, as in the United States, there is no justifiable reason for the Federal Government to abdicate an appropriate role to assist these most needy citizens."

When the emergency aid package was first introduced in January of 1987, President Reagan threatened to veto the package as unnecessary and fiscally irresponsible. The bill passed with broad bipartisan support in both houses of Congress (65-8 in the Senate; 301-115 in the House) and was signed into law by the president on July 22, 1987. The bill was named after Stewart B. McKinney, who died on May 7, 1987, of AIDS, complicated by pneumonia that resulted from his participation in the "Grate American Sleep Out" in March.

The McKinney Act appropriated $442 million for homeless assistance in fiscal year 1987 and promised $616 million for 1988. The funds were to be channeled through a number of existing housing programs and provided housing assistance, subsidies for existing private and public shelter programs, funds for rehabilitation of abandoned buildings to provide increased shelter, and help for programs of health care, mental health, and assistance to the handicapped serving the homeless. It also created an Interagency Commission on the Homeless, made up of representatives of various federal agencies, with oversight responsibilities for programs assisting the homeless.

Impact of Event

The passage of the McKinney Act was important because it acknowledged the extent to which the needs of the homeless in the United States had reached emergency proportions and admitted a federal responsibility to respond to that emergency. In the short term, it certainly helped ease the burden of care that small private shelters throughout the country were experiencing in trying to meet the increased demands for aid. Even its short-term effect, however, was less than its supporters had hoped because the money authorized in the bill was never fully allocated. For example, in 1987, the bill called for the spending of $442 million, but in fact only $335 million was actually appropriated. This pattern continued in later years. Spiraling federal budget deficits through the 1980's made the intentions of the bill increasingly more difficult to fulfill. It is testimony to the importance attached to the issue of homelessness that such a spending bill passed at all, given the cuts in social programs then occurring.

With its focus on the provision of emergency assistance, the McKinney Act did little to provide any long-term solutions to the problem of homelessness. Its emphasis on shelter support meant that there was less attention to addressing the root causes of homelessness or to the provision of larger quantities of stable low-income housing. The problem of homelessness did not disappear as a result of the McKinney

Act, but the prominence of the issue of homelessness diminished. A study by the United States Conference of Mayors in 1990 found declining public concern about and support for aiding the homeless. The public had become weary of the issue and demonstrated a marked lack of sympathy for the plight of homeless people. As Congress and the president struggled with a burgeoning federal deficit that made increased funding for any social programs unlikely, the issue faded from the public agenda.

Bibliography

Belcher, John R., and Frederick A. DiBlasio. *Helping the Homeless: Where Do We Go from Here?* Lexington, Mass.: Lexington Books, 1990. This scholarly book's focus on the impact of the economic system on homelessness offers a useful counterpoint to other works, which tend to focus on anecdotal evidence and personal stories of the homeless. The authors argue that homelessness results from economic dislocation and offer policy solutions that address what they see as needed changes in the management of the economy. There is an interesting chapter on homelessness as a global problem.

Bingham, Richard D., Roy E. Green, and Sammis B. White, eds. *The Homeless in Contemporary Society.* Newbury Park, Calif.: Sage Publications, 1987. A set of essays on homelessness by scholars and public officials. The first part of the book offers essays on the causes of homelessness and demographic characteristics of the homeless. The second part discusses policy options and solutions. The essays are informative, are written for the general reader, and represent several different viewpoints on the issue. Lacks an index.

Hollyman, Stephenie. *We the Homeless: Portraits of America's Displaced People.* Text by Victoria Irwin. New York: Philosophical Library, 1988. A book of black and white photographs of the homeless across the United States. Highlights the diversity among the homeless by region, race, gender, family status, and age. A brief introductory essay discusses the problem and encourages awareness of and sympathy for the homeless. Some text accompanies the pictures, but for the most part the images are allowed to tell the story.

Hombs, Mary Ellen, and Mitch Snyder. *Homelessness in America: A Forced March to Nowhere.* Washington, D.C.: Community for Creative Non-Violence, 1982. Published by an advocacy group at the start of the first congressional hearings on the homeless in 1982 in order to "deepen awareness" of the problem of homelessness in the United States. It includes essays and photographs related to different aspects of homelessness. The authors are highly critical of federal policy toward the poor.

Kozol, Jonathan. *Rachel and Her Children: Homeless Families in America.* New York: Fawcett Columbine, 1988. Winner of the Robert F. Kennedy Memorial Book Award. A sympathetic narrative of homeless families, based on interviews with residents of New York City's notorious welfare hotels. Although he offers some suggestions for change at the end, the primary value of Kozol's work lies in its compelling portrait of the frustrations and tragedies in the lives of homeless people.

Rossi, Peter. *Without Shelter: Homelessness in the 1980's.* New York: Priority Press Publications, 1989. In this paper, commissioned by the Twentieth Century Fund, Rossi describes the rise of the "new homeless" of the 1980's. He offers much useful data and suggests short-term and long-term solutions to the problem of homelessness. Interesting introductory material provides a historical perspective on the problem.

Katy Jean Harriger

Cross-References

The First Food Stamp Program Begins in Rochester, New York (1939), p. 555; The United Nations Adopts the Declaration of the Rights of the Child (1959), p. 1038; Legislation Ushers in a New Era of Care for the Mentally Disabled (1963), p. 1206; The United Nations Responds to Problems of the Homeless (1982), p. 2174; An APA Report Discusses the Homeless Mentally Ill (1984), p. 2226; The United Nations Adopts the Convention on the Rights of the Child (1989), p. 2529.

THE PALESTINIAN *INTIFADA* BEGINS

Category of event: Indigenous peoples' rights
Time: December, 1987
Locale: The West Bank and the Gaza Strip

Beginning in the Jebalya refugee camp and later spreading to the rest of the Gaza Strip and the West Bank, Palestinians started the Intifada *(uprising) to resist the twenty-year Israeli military occupation*

Principal personages:

YITZHAK RABIN (1922-   ), the defense minister of Israel during the first two years of the *Intifada*

YITZHAK SHAMIR (1915-   ), the prime minister of Israel

YASIR ARAFAT (1929-   ), the leader of the Palestine Liberation Organization

Summary of Event

Protests in the Palestinian Jebalya refugee camp in the Gaza Strip during the second week of December, 1987, were severely repressed by the Israeli army, with heavy Palestinian casualties. These protests became the cornerstone of the *Intifada*, one of the most important political events in the history of the Palestinian-Israeli conflict. To understand the factors behind the *Intifada* is to understand the cumulative effect of Israeli policies on the Palestinians, who have been under occupation since 1967. In general, the Israeli government followed a strategy that brought the West Bank and the Gaza Strip under a firm grip through the use of three control mechanisms: infrastructure, labor, and market. Israel linked the West Bank and the Gaza Strip to its economy in several ways: by making the occupied territories a captive market wherein nearly 90 percent of annual imports were Israeli products; by linking the physical infrastructure of the West Bank and the Gaza Strip to Israel through roads and water and power grids; and by employing Palestinians as cheap and unskilled labor.

This process was accelerated after the Likud Party came to power in Israel in 1977. Freely elected mayors were dismissed and replaced by Israeli military officials. Land confiscation increased rapidly, and by 1987 more than 52 percent of the land was confiscated. Jewish settlements were built rapidly. Palestinian labor grew even more heavily dependent on the Israeli economy. Nearly 120,000 Palestinians, representing 54 percent of the West Bank labor force and 67 percent of the Gaza Strip's, commuted daily to work in Israel. The lopsided relationship became evident in other areas as well, most noticeably in poor health care services and inadequate education for Palestinians.

On August 4, 1985, Israeli Defense Minister Yitzhak Rabin introduced his "iron fist" policy. The policy turned the Palestinian population into virtual prisoners, requiring them to have permits to travel abroad. An increasing number of Palestinians were jailed, were placed under administrative detention without charge or trial, or were exiled. An estimated two hundred thousand Palestinians out of a population of 1.7 million had been arrested at one time or another before the uprising. Collective punishment, including extended curfews, school closures, and house demolitions, increased.

These practices, Palestinians believed, were designed to drive them out in the course of Israel's "creeping annexation" of the occupied territories. The critical turn in this perception took place in 1982, when Israel invaded Lebanon and drove the Palestine Liberation Organization (PLO) away. The PLO split into two factions and was rendered ineffective. Palestinians in Lebanon were under constant attack, as "the war of the camps" between 1985 and 1987 demonstrated. Anxiety, frustration, and humiliation simmered as conditions deteriorated. A series of incidents involving the Gaza Strip prepared the grounds for the *Intifada* to erupt there at the end of 1987.

On December 4, 1986, the Israeli army shot dead two Birzeit University students who happened to be from Gaza. On April 10, 1987, another Birzeit student, also from Gaza, was killed. On October 1, the Israeli army ambushed and killed seven Gaza men believed to be members of the Islamic Jihad movement. Five days later, four more Gaza men and a high-ranking Israeli prison official were killed in a shootout. Several days later, a settler shot a schoolgirl in the back. In the deteriorating situation, demonstrations became more frequent, and Palestinian youths pelted Israeli cars with stones. On December 7, a Jewish merchant was stabbed in the city of Gaza. On December 8, an Israeli military tank transporter slammed into a line of cars loaded with day laborers. Four Palestinians from the Jebalya camp were crushed to death, and seven others were injured. That night, ten thousand camp residents turned out in protest. The following morning, the burial procession turned into a spontaneous demonstration. The army responded by firing into the crowd. Another Jebalya resident was killed, marking the first casualty of the *Intifada*.

Protests engulfed the entire Gaza Strip, and by late December, West Bank refugee camps such as Balata, near Nablus, became involved; the same cycle of protest, repression, and death occurred again. December alone saw 288 demonstrations, two thousand arrests, twenty-nine killed, and a total of thirty-six curfew days. By mid-January, 1988, leaflets signed by the Unified National Leadership of the Uprising (UNLU) began to appear. These leaflets, called *bayanat*, contained communiques that gave direction to the population. The UNLU was made up of four activists representing four major groups within the PLO. The communiques called for specific acts of civil disobedience to be followed by the population. These ranged from confronting the military to forming popular committees.

The most visible acts of the *Intifada* were the constant demonstrations by Palestinians, which Israeli troops broke up with tear gas, rubber-coated or plastic-coated bullets, and sometimes with live ammunition. These confrontations were also accompanied by stone throwing; stones assumed symbolic status as the protesters' only defense. In response, Rabin allowed the Israeli army to use the "beating" policy, which led to thousands of brutal beatings, some of which were televised internationally. It was during demonstrations that most fatalities occurred. In April, 1988, for example, 416 demonstrations took place, and sixty-one Palestinians were killed.

Commercial strikes, which were introduced first in Nablus and were later endorsed by the UNLU, became another feature of the *Intifada*. Before the strikes became a daily routine, the Israeli military tried to break them by forcing merchants to reopen their shops. This "war of the shops" was won by the activists, and from March onward, shops were open for only three hours of the day.

Because curfews sometimes extended for weeks, the UNLU encouraged each neighborhood to establish its own popular committees for the distribution of food and other necessities. Agricultural committees provided a model for the "return to the land"; every available plot was cleared, plowed, and planted by neighborhood youths. Along with the promotion of cottage and national industry, such methods emphasized self-sufficiency and economic independence. Eventually, the UNLU called for a boycott of Israeli products except for those that had no Palestinian equivalent. After schools and universities were closed, education committees provided basic instruction, especially on the primary-school level. Health-care committees provided instruction in first aid and tended to the injured and the needy. Popular committees became an extension of the UNLU, and both were fully accepted and supported by the population. The UNLU and the popular committees became the political leaders of their community and formed an alternate political structure to that of the Israelis. Indeed, they assumed many features of the institutional structure of a state.

The Israeli military intensified its attack against the *Intifada* and its activists by tightening economic controls and increasing the use of force. More than two hundred thousand Israelis served in the West Bank and the Gaza Strip during the first two years of the *Intifada*. This was met with equal intensity on the part of the Palestinians. Whenever a lull in the *Intifada* took place, a new storm of protest would follow. The continuity of the *Intifada* led many to believe that the *Intifada* could not be stopped militarily, since it had grown from a demonstration into an active political movement calling for national self-determination.

Impact of Event

The *Intifada* transformed the Palestinians from refugees and "residents" in their own land to a society about to achieve its nationhood. Carried out largely by youths who were born under occupation, the *Intifada* shifted the center of political gravity to the West Bank and the Gaza Strip. It signaled Palestinians' impatience with the inability of the external forces, the PLO and the Arab governments, to bring about a just and peaceful solution to the Palestine question. Despite the enormous price that the Palestinians paid in deaths, injuries, and incarcerations, the *Intifada* represented a self-empowerment. It won them a new confidence and created a cohesiveness among the various sectors of the society that had not existed before.

The creation of the UNLU and the popular committees established an alternate political authority that gave the population directions to sustain the *Intifada* and to create institutional bases for a future state. Respected and supported by the population, the UNLU became the instrument for the political unification of the various factions and political trends within the PLO.

It was largely because of the *Intifada* and the demands of the UNLU that the PLO changed its political positions. The PLO declared its acceptance of two United Nations Security Council resolutions as bases for a political settlement, recognized Israel, and renounced the use of terrorism in a framework of a two-state solution. The PLO declared on November 15, 1988, through the Palestine National Council, the establishment of a Palestinian state, which was gradually recognized by a majority of the world's nations.

The *Intifada* had a strong impact on Israeli government and society as well. The perpetuation of military occupation became impossible. Many Israelis began to favor a two-state solution. The Israeli military expressed on several occasions that it could not stop the *Intifada*. A growing number favored negotiations with the PLO. The *Intifada* had serious implications for Israeli social structure, since many of Israel's Arab citizens participated in the uprising by providing political support, food, and medical and other aid to the protesters.

More serious for the Israeli government was the failure of its plans to annex the occupied territories through the infrastructural changes that it introduced after 1967. The *Intifada* had grave consequences for the Israeli economy. Merchants and others refused to pay taxes. Popular committees supervised the boycott of Israeli goods. Tourism, the construction industry, textile factories, agriculture, and other concerns that grew dependent on cheap Arab labor suffered after the outbreak of the *Intifada*. The use of Israeli reservists in the army caused more economic and social disruptions.

The outbreak of the *Intifada* and the way Israel treated the Palestinians had important global repercussions. Israel's control over the West Bank and the Gaza Strip was no longer viewed as a benign occupation. World public opinion was galvanized by images of youths confronting well-equipped soldiers. More people began to realize that a political solution to the Palestine question was necessary and urgent so that further conflict and bloodshed could be avoided.

Bibliography

Brynen, Rex, ed. *Echoes of the Intifada: Regional Repercussions of the Palestinian-Israeli Conflict.* Boulder, Colo.: Westview Press, 1991. Experts in various fields evaluate the Palestinian uprising in the context of Israel's violation of Palestinian rights during the occupation of the West Bank and the Gaza Strip and discuss the impact of the *Intifada* on political thinking in Israel and the surrounding Arab countries. The book also examines the impact of the *Intifada* on the superpowers.

Law in the Service of Man. *Punishing a Nation: Israeli Human Rights Violations During the Palestinian Uprising.* Boston: South End Press, 1990. Law in the Service of Man is an affiliate of the International Commission of Jurists. Based in the West Bank, it carries out legal research and provides legal service to the community. Its report is a thorough documentation of the violations of human rights of Palestinians under occupation and includes interviews and affidavits of victims.

Lesch, Ann Mosely, and Mark Tessler. *Israel, Egypt, and the Palestinians: From Camp David to the Intifada.* Bloomington: Indiana University Press, 1989. The authors discuss the impact of the Camp David agreements and the Israeli-Egyptian Peace Treaty on the Israeli relationship to the Palestinians in the West Bank and the Gaza Strip and how the unfolding relationship led to the Palestinian uprising in 1987.

Lockman, Zachary, and Joel Beinin, eds. *Intifada: The Palestinian Uprising Against Israeli Occupation.* Boston: South End Press, 1989. An excellent collection of more than thirty contributions by a host of international and local scholars, Palestinians and Israelis, who experienced the *Intifada.* The photographs and poems make more poignant the fact that the *Intifada* was a living experience. The book includes relevant articles on the meaning of the *Intifada* for Palestinian history, an evaluation of recent Israeli scholarship that challenges the official version of Israeli-Palestinian relations, an evaluation of the role of women and other groups in the *Intifada,* and its impact on Israel and the United States. An appendix includes translations of some communiques from the underground leadership.

Nassar, Jamal, and Roger Heacock, eds. *Intifada: Palestine at the Crossroads.* New York: Praeger, 1990. A sourcebook on the *Intifada.* Contributions include articles on its background, its major events, and its participants. There are articles that show its impact on local, regional, and international political developments regarding the Palestine question. A valuable effort is made to assess the impact of the *Intifada* on Palestinian society.

Schiff, Ze'ev, and Ehud Ya'ari. *Intifada: The Palestinian Uprising: Israel's Third Front.* Edited and translated by Ina Friedman. New York: Simon & Schuster, 1989. Two well-known Israeli journalists discuss the background and events of the *Intifada* from its start in the Jebalya refugee camp to the capture of members of the UNLU.

Mahmood Ibrahim

Cross-References

The Balfour Declaration Supports a Jewish Homeland in Palestine (1917), p. 235; Palestinian Refugees Flee to Neighboring Arab Countries (1948), p. 749; Israel Is Created as a Homeland for Jews (1948), p. 761; The United Nations Creates an Agency to Aid Palestinian Refugees (1949), p. 814; Israel Enacts the Law of Return, Granting Citizenship to Immigrants (1950), p. 832; Palestinian Refugees Form the Palestine Liberation Organization (1964), p. 1241; Arab Terrorists Murder Eleven Israeli Olympic Athletes in Munich (1972), p. 1685; Sadat Becomes the First Arab Leader to Visit Israel (1977), p. 1943; Sadat and Begin Are Jointly Awarded the Nobel Peace Prize (1978), p. 2003; Palestinian Civilians Are Massacred in West Beirut (1982), p. 2164.

ARIAS SÁNCHEZ IS AWARDED
THE NOBEL PEACE PRIZE

Category of event: Peace movements and organizations
Time: December 10, 1987
Locale: Oslo, Norway

Oscar Arias Sánchez received the 1987 Nobel Peace Prize for his efforts to achieve peace in Central America, specifically for the "Arias Peace Plan" signed by the five Central American presidents

Principal personages:

OSCAR ARIAS SÁNCHEZ (1941-   ), the president of Costa Rica and architect of the "Arias Peace Plan"

DANIEL ORTEGA SAAVEDRA (1945-   ), the president of Nicaragua

RONALD REAGAN (1911-   ), the president of the United States (1981-1989)

JOSÉ NAPOLEON DUARTE (1925-1990), the president of El Salvador

Summary of Event

The violence that gripped Central America in the 1980's was focused on two national tragedies: the war in Nicaragua between the Sandinista government and the United States-backed "contras," and the civil war in El Salvador between government and insurgent forces. Guatemala, too, experienced widespread political violence during the period. Only Costa Rica, with its tradition of peaceful democracy, seemed to avoid the bloodshed of the decade; even there, however, the turmoil of Central America took its toll in the form of incoming refugees.

All of these conflicts were rooted in the poverty and repression that plagued the region throughout the twentieth century. The 1980's, however, proved to be particularly tragic for the people of the region. It was a decade in which war and repression increased their toll on human life and produced a stream of refugees to countries both within and outside the region.

The immediate sparks to these events occurred in 1979, when Nicaraguan dictator Anastasio Somoza was deposed, and when a reformist civilian-military coup in El Salvador ended a long period of military rule. In both cases, it was hoped by many that the repression of the previous governments would give way to regimes more respectful of human rights. Whether the post-1979 governments in either El Salvador or Nicaragua fulfilled such promise remained controversial. In both countries, the violence of war severely jeopardized the human rights environment.

When Ronald Reagan assumed the presidency of the United States in 1981, the Sandinista National Liberation Front (FSLN) in Nicaragua, which had overthrown the Somoza dictatorship, was firmly in control (under the leadership of Daniel Ortega Saavedra) and was bitterly opposed by the Reagan Administration. The centerpiece of Reagan's anti-Sandinista policy became the training and funding of the "contras," a guerrilla army composed of Nicaraguan exiles dedicated to removing the FSLN from power. In El Salvador, Reagan sought to bolster the civilian government led eventually by José Napoleon Duarte, the Christian Democrat and winner of direct presidential elections in 1984. Increased numbers of U.S. military advisers were sent to El Salvador to sustain that government's efforts against the rebel Farabundo Marti National Liberation Front (FMLN), as were other forms of military and economic assistance. Given its pro-U.S. government and borders with both El Salvador and Nicaragua, Honduras became the recipient of a significant U.S. military presence and increased military and economic assistance. In general, Central America became a central focus of the Reagan Administration's foreign policy, and the United States became a key participant in the struggles in both El Salvador and Nicaragua.

By the mid-1980's, Central America had also become the focus for several international peace initiatives. In 1983 and 1984, the "Contadora Group"—composed of Mexico, Panama, Colombia, and Venezuela, and named for the Panamanian island on which they initially met—proposed a twenty-one-point peace plan to demilitarize and democratize Central America. By 1986, the Contadora process had come to an unsuccessful end, in part, it was argued, because of the opposition of the United States and some Central American governments.

For its part, the Reagan Administration appointed a bipartisan commission, chaired by former Secretary of State Henry Kissinger, to study the conflicts in Central America and to propose policy directions for the United States. The report of the Kissinger Commission, released in 1984, emphasized the interests of the United States in promoting economic development and regional security. Both the Contadora plan and the Kissinger Commission report stressed the need for greater attention to human rights throughout the region.

Indeed, human rights vied with security concerns as the yardstick by which to measure policies within and toward the region. Governments and rebels in both El Salvador and Nicaragua were accused (by different groups with different political objectives) of violating the human rights of innocent civilians throughout the 1980's. The United States accused the Sandinista government in Nicaragua of violating civil and political rights. The contras fighting that government, as well as Salvadoran government forces and paramilitary "death squads," received widespread criticism from human rights groups for such alleged acts as torture and assassination.

More than six thousand political prisoners, mostly peasants, were in Nicaraguan jails by 1986, according to some reports. There were also reports of disappearances and torture. Amnesty International criticized the Nicaraguan government for its policies of prolonged detention and keeping prisoners incommunicado, although it later noted that Sandinistas were actively pursuing investigation and prosecution of those responsible for human rights abuses. The opposition contras, on the other hand, were accused by Amnesty International of a continuous pattern of abuse toward prisoners, kidnappings of noncombatants, and assassination attempts.

In El Salvador, political killings had abated somewhat by 1987 in comparison to the early 1980's. The most prominent victim of this death squad activity had been Archbishop Oscar Romero, a moderate reformist who was assassinated during mass in March, 1980. The violence of that period produced tens of thousands of deaths and hundreds of thousands of refugees. Most of the deaths of this time were presumed to be the result of the armed forces and the death squads, although the left was not immune from such charges later in the decade, notably in the 1987 assassination of the president of the Salvadoran Human Rights Commission.

Fleeing El Salvador proved to be no panacea for refugees. The United States routinely deported Salvadorans, since accepting them would be tantamount to acknowledging their persecution by the very government the United States was supporting. While meaningful refuge could be found in Canada, the distance and difficulties—not to mention the profound cultural and climatic differences—limited the numbers that pursued it.

In February, 1987, following the end of the Contadora process and the lack of meaningful progress toward resolution of the conflicts, Costa Rican President Oscar Arias Sánchez proposed a peace plan to other Central American presidents. After lengthy negotiations and several modifications, it was signed by all five presidents on August 7, 1987, in Guatemala City, Guatemala.

Costa Ricans had been troubled throughout the 1980's by events elsewhere in Central America, particularly in neighboring Nicaragua. One claim pegged the number of refugees in Costa Rica at 250,000 in 1986. Costa Rica had actively opposed the Somoza dynasty and supported its overthrow but had come to oppose the Sandinista regime as well. Arias himself argued that the Sandinistas had betrayed the democratic principles of their own revolution. He was equally distressed by the Reagan Administration's support of the contras and its use of Costa Rican territory as a base of operations. Arias later argued that while Reagan saw the contras as part of the solution, he saw them as part of the problem. Thus Arias had profound domestic political and economic reasons for pursuing a workable peace plan in addition to the historical Costa Rican support of peaceful democratic processes.

The "Arias Peace Plan" contained eleven points calling for a cessation of hostilities, the democratization of governments throughout the region, and the cessation of assistance—whether from other Central American governments or from governments outside the region—to insurgent forces seeking to overthrow established governments. Under the plan, the signatories also committed themselves to resolving the educational, health, employment, and security problems of the refugees and displaced persons created by the regional crisis. In addition, the agreement emphasized that peace and democracy in the region required economic development and a significant lessening of its inequality and poverty.

In October of 1987, in a decision considered a surprise by some, the Norwegian Nobel Committee announced its decision to award the Nobel Peace Prize to President Arias in recognition of his role in designing the plan and achieving the compromise agreement. According to *Time*, the committee's chair stated that the award to

Arias was also designed to encourage the peace process in Central America.

Presidents Ortega of Nicaragua and Duarte of El Salvador welcomed the news and communicated their congratulations to Arias. President Reagan, whose administration had opposed the plan (in large part because of the provisions regarding foreign assistance to insurgent forces), congratulated the recipient but renewed his commitment to the contra forces seeking to overthrow the Sandinista government in Nicaragua. Just two days before the Nobel Committee's announcement, Arias had visited Washington to lobby for a postponement in any consideration of contra aid.

Arias received the award in ceremonies held in Oslo, Norway, on December 10 and 11, 1987. In accepting the prize, Arias emphasized the problems of human economic rights: "Behind the democratic awakening in Central America lie over a hundred years of cruel dictators, of injustice, of generalized poverty. . . . I receive this prize as one of five Presidents, who before the entire world have consecrated the wills of our peoples to change a history of oppression for one of freedom; to change a history of hunger for a destiny of progress; to change the weeping of mothers and the violent death of youth for hope, for the path of peace which we wish to travel together."

Impact of Event

The Arias Peace Plan did not bring to an end violence and repression in Central America. Nor did the plan end, over the short term, the Central American refugee problem. Nevertheless, in the years following the initial agreement, progress was achieved in the Central American human rights situation, most notably in Nicaragua.

In 1989, several follow-up agreements were reached by the Central American governments to further clarify and enforce the principles of the Arias plan. The governments presented a plan to deal with the region's estimated 1.8 million refugees and displaced persons, committed Nicaragua to presidential and legislative elections in 1990, developed plans to dismantle the contras, and sought to demobilize the FMLN in El Salvador.

On February 25, 1990, Violeta Barrios de Chamorro, leader of the United Nicaraguan Opposition, defeated Ortega in a presidential election. The peaceful transition of power to the opposition demonstrated Nicaragua's commitment to the principles of democracy articulated by the Arias Peace Plan. The Chamorro government initiated a series of measures which effectively demobilized the contras and reduced the size of the Nicaraguan army.

In El Salvador, talks between the government of Alfredo Cristiani and the FMLN were initiated, although fighting continued amid the dialogue. The murder of six Jesuit priests at a university in San Salvador in November, 1989, was followed by the government's stated resolve to bring to justice those accused of the crime within the military.

In both countries, and indeed throughout the region, the Arias plan's call for reduction in poverty levels, as a necessary prerequisite to durable democracy and peace in the region, was a more ambitious and less attainable goal. The Central American governments sought greater economic cooperation and a stronger Central American Common Market, but in general the prospects for dramatically reducing regional poverty levels did not appear promising.

From the perspective of human rights, one of the most significant outcomes of the Nobel award to Arias was that it drew attention to the Central American nation most respectful of human rights, Costa Rica. The absence of military forces and the presence of a highly participatory democratic political system, as well as its modest success in addressing poverty levels, made Costa Rica a model for its neighbors. The role of its president as a mediator in the region's vexing political conflicts enhanced the international image of the country.

The ending of the contra war, however, proved a somewhat mixed blessing for those Costa Ricans living near the Nicaraguan border. The *Washington Post* reported that in May, 1991, a father and his four young children were killed, allegedly by ex-contras involved in cattle rustling. Throughout the border region, killings, kidnappings, and robberies continued to rise more than a year after the end of the guerrilla war. Blame was placed on former contras, unwilling to return to Nicaragua, without work or money, but with the weapons to engage in criminal violence long after their political struggle had ended.

With the monetary award from the Nobel Peace Prize, Arias created the Arias Foundation for Peace and Human Progress, based in San Jose, Costa Rica. The foundation sought, through projects and workshops, to promote peace, development, and democracy, with special attention to the needs of the poor and oppressed.

Bibliography

Booth, John A. *The End and the Beginning: The Nicaraguan Revolution.* Boulder, Colo.: Westview Press, 1985. An effort to examine the 1979 Sandinista revolution and its aftermath in the context of prevailing social science theory concerning the causes and dynamics of revolution. The book examines the historical background to Nicaraguan politics, surveying developments from the nineteenth century to the 1980's. Accessible to the general reader. Includes index, references, figures, tables, and a list of abbreviations.

Gutman, Roy. *Banana Diplomacy: The Making of American Policy in Nicaragua, 1981-1987.* New York: Simon & Schuster, 1988. A critical investigation of the Reagan Administration policy in Nicaragua in the years leading up to the Arias Peace Plan. Meticulously researched piece of investigative journalism. Focuses on U.S. policymaking but extensively describes interactions with key Central American participants, including Arias. Endnotes, appendices, and index.

LaFeber, Walter. *Inevitable Revolutions: The United States in Central America.* New York: W. W. Norton, 1983. A critical interpretation of the involvement and intervention of the United States in the Central American region since the nineteenth century. Useful background for those with a specific interest in U.S. foreign policy toward this region. LaFeber is a prominent historian and critic of this policy.

Includes index and references.

Lowenthal, Abraham F. *Partners in Conflict: The United States and Latin America in the 1990s.* Baltimore, Md.: The Johns Hopkins University Press, 1990. Although concerned with U.S. policy not only toward Central America but toward the entire Latin American region, this book offers numerous insights into the problems of that region and suggestions for a more constructive role for the United States in regional affairs. Contains sober reflections on the prospects for Central America, even in light of the Arias initiative. Includes index and references.

Montgomery, Tommie Sue. *Revolution in El Salvador: Origins and Evolution.* Boulder, Colo.: Westview Press, 1982. Traces the origins of the Salvadoran civil war, with special attention to the historical legacy of inequality dating to the sixteenth century. Supportive of the efforts of revolutionary groups and critical of the oligarchy, the armed forces, and both Salvadoran and U.S. government policies. Includes index, illustrations, tables, and list of abbreviations. Comparable to Booth, *The End and the Beginning.*

United States. National Bipartisan Commission on Central America. *The Report of the President's National Bipartisan Commission on Central America.* New York: Macmillan, 1984. The so-called "Kissinger Report." This book seeks to provide an analysis of the social, economic, and political conditions of Central America and suggests a framework for U.S. policy toward the region. Emphasizes the link between economic development and regional security, and may be usefully contrasted with the Arias plan. Includes a foreword by commission chair Henry A. Kissinger and notes—of both endorsement and dissent—from other commission members. No references.

Woodward, Ralph Lee, Jr. *Central America: A Nation Divided.* New York: Oxford University Press, 1985. A classic survey of the history of the region since colonial times, providing useful, readable background to the key participants in today's crises. Particularly helpful for its extensive guide to the literature on the region.

Robert B. Andersen

Cross-References

U.S. Marines Are Sent to Nicaragua to Quell Unrest (1912), p. 137; El Salvador's Military Massacres Civilians in *La Matanza* (1932), p. 464; The Declaration on the Rights and Duties of Man Is Adopted (1948), p. 755; The Organization of American States Is Established (1951), p. 879; The Inter-American Commission on Human Rights Is Created (1959), p. 1032; The Inter-American Court of Human Rights Is Established (1969), p. 1503; Carter Makes Human Rights a Central Theme of Foreign Policy (1977), p. 1903; Indigenous Indians Become the Target of Guatemalan Death Squads (1978), p. 1972; Somoza Is Forced Out of Power in Nicaragua (1979), p. 2035; A Helsinki Watch Report Proposes Reform of Refugee Laws (1989), p. 2494; Sandinistas Are Defeated in Nicaraguan Elections (1990), p. 2564.

A. H. ROBINS MUST COMPENSATE WOMEN INJURED BY THE DALKON SHIELD

Categories of event: Consumers' rights; health and medical rights
Time: December 11, 1987
Locale: Richmond, Virginia

A federal judge's ruling in a bankruptcy case required the A. H. Robins Company to compensate 200,000 women harmed by the Dalkon Shield contraceptive intrauterine device.

Principal personages:

ROBERT MERHIGE, JR. (1919-   ), the United States District Court judge from Virginia who issued the 1987 order

MILES LORD (1919-   ), the United States District Court judge from Minnesota who accused A. H. Robins executives of corporate irresponsibility

E. CLAIBORNE ROBINS, JR. (1943-   ), the president of A. H. Robins beginning in 1978 and a member of its board of directors

E. CLAIBORNE ROBINS, SR. (1910-   ), the retired president and chief executive officer of A. H. Robins

HUGH DAVIS (1927-   ), a coinventor of the Dalkon Shield and the author of an initial study claiming a very high effectiveness rate for the device

ROGER TUTTLE (1930-   ), an attorney for A. H. Robins who revealed that he and other Robins employees had, on company orders, destroyed documents relating to the Dalkon Shield

Summary of Event

In the 1970's, the prestigious pharmaceutical firm A. H. Robins Company distributed a contraceptive intrauterine device (IUD) called the Dalkon Shield. Promotional materials described it as a superior IUD with a high birth control effectiveness rate. Amid controversy over the safety of birth control pills, the Dalkon Shield was marketed as a safe alternative form of contraception, appropriate even for women who had never given birth. Between 1971 and 1974, more than 2.5 million "shields" were implanted in women in the United States and more than 1 million of the IUDs were shipped abroad.

A. H. Robins, which produces such products as Robitussin and Dimetapp cough syrups, Chap Stick lip balm, and Sergeant's flea and tick collars, purchased rights to the Dalkon Shield in 1970. In 1971, the company began distributing the shield, a molded plastic, crab shaped device with "fins" on each side. When inserted into a woman's uterus, the device was intended to prevent pregnancy. A multifilament tail-string was attached to the bottom to aid in removal and to provide a check on expulsion.

In purchasing the rights to the Dalkon Shield, A. H. Robins recognized the demand for a safe, reliable form of birth control. Congressional hearings in 1970 exposed health risks associated with birth control pills. The controversy increased the demand for nonhormonal contraceptive methods, such as IUDs. The Dalkon Shield was portrayed by one of its inventors (and later by the Robins firm) as a "superior modern contraceptive," with outstanding effectiveness and safety, and thus seemed to fit the bill. A study published in 1970 by Hugh Davis, at the time a physician affiliated with Johns Hopkins and coinventor of the Dalkon Shield, reported that tests conducted on women who had used the Dalkon Shield yielded a low 1.1 percent pregnancy rate and a low expulsion rate. Later analyses of Davis' data indicated that his study underestimated both pregnancy and expulsion rates of the Dalkon Shield, but promotional materials circulated by the Robins firm continued to use the lower pregnancy rates cited in the original study. Further enhancing the attractiveness of the Dalkon Shield was the claim that its smaller version was safe for young women who had not yet had children. IUDs were previously viewed as appropriate primarily for women who had already had children, since their bodies were generally better able to tolerate intrauterine devices.

Almost from the beginning, physicians reported to Robins that the Dalkon Shield seemed to have a higher pregnancy rate than was claimed, that the device was difficult to insert and remove, and that it might be a cause of infections in women wearing it. Many women fitted with the device complained of excruciating pain upon insertion and painful cramping thereafter.

As early as 1972, Robins officials were told that the Dalkon Shield might be linked to spontaneous septic abortions, or miscarriages with associated infections, which are rare in industrialized countries. In March, 1973, an Arizona woman, who was wearing a Dalkon Shield when she became pregnant, died from a septic abortion. A. H. Robins has never specifically acknowledged that the Dalkon Shield's design may have contributed to sepsis in women who became pregnant while wearing it, but the company did notify doctors in October, 1973, that "serious consideration should be given to removing the device" once a woman becomes pregnant.

In February, 1975, the first case involving the Dalkon Shield was decided in favor of Connie Deemer. By that time, the product had been removed from the market but remained in the wombs of hundreds of thousands of women. In lawsuits across the country, women claimed that the Dalkon Shield caused a variety of health problems, including infertility (difficulty in conceiving), sterility (inability to conceive), pelvic inflammatory disease (infections of the uterus, ovaries, or Fallopian tubes), and perforations of the uterus. Some women were forced to undergo hysterectomies as a result of complications that they said were caused by the Dalkon Shield. Others miscarried fetuses or bore deformed children who were conceived with the Dalkon Shield in place.

In many of the lawsuits, women's health problems were attributed to defects in the design of the Dalkon Shield itself. In particular, some evidence implicated the Dalkon Shield's multifilament string as a cause of pelvic inflammatory disease infections, which can result in sterility or infertility. As early as 1970, A. H. Robins officials were warned by an employee that the string might have a "wicking" effect, causing it to transport bacteria from the vagina into the uterus, resulting in infection. Some later studies confirmed this wicking effect.

Because of the large number of women who had Dalkon Shields inserted in them, attorneys recognized the potential for a large number of lawsuits. Some attorneys even specialized in Dalkon Shield cases, taking on large numbers of clients who claimed that the IUD had harmed them. In Minnesota, where a large number of Dalkon Shield cases were filed, several such cases were assigned in 1983 to U.S. District Judge Miles Lord, who was considered to be a maverick with populist instincts. Judge Lord's involvement in the shield cases was significant for two reasons. Lord issued a document production order that permitted attorneys for the women to obtain documents from A. H. Robins. These documents would later prove useful in other cases brought by women against the company. In addition, Lord attracted nationwide publicity to the controversy over the Dalkon Shield, when on February 29, 1984, he lectured three Robins officers in open court. In his remarks, Lord charged the officials with corporate irresponsibility and beseeched them to track down women wearing the device so that the women could be urged to remove it. A federal disciplinary panel later that year ordered Lord to expunge from the court record his reprimand of Robins employees.

In October, 1984, A. H. Robins announced a $5 million program to pay for removal of Dalkon Shields from women still wearing them. In commercials, A. H. Robins informed women that it would pay medical bills for removal of the Dalkon Shield. One television commercial stated, "There is substantial medical opinion that continued use of the Dalkon Shield may pose a serious personal health hazard and it should be removed." The removal program occurred amid substantial adverse publicity, including testimony by a former attorney for A. H. Robins, Roger Tuttle, who revealed in the summer of 1984 that he and other Robins employees had destroyed documents relating to the Dalkon Shield. In addition, by the end of 1984, about twelve thousand women had brought claims or lawsuits relating to the shield. About one-third of these cases were unresolved at that time.

On August 21, 1985, as claims against A. H. Robins continued to mount, the company filed for Chapter 11 bankruptcy protection against creditors who, it was feared, could plunge the company into financial ruin. By 1985, Robins and Aetna Casualty and Surety, its insurer, had settled 9,500 injury suits at a cost of $530 million. New lawsuits were reportedly arriving at a rate of four hundred per month.

The bankruptcy case was assigned to Judge Robert Merhige, Jr. at the U.S. District Court for the District of Virginia. Judge Merhige had handled hundreds of Dalkon cases prior to taking on the bankruptcy case. Merhige was reputed to be a liberal judge and had rendered controversial decisions on such matters as school busing, women's rights, and the environment. On December 11, 1987, Judge Merhige ordered Robins to set up a trust fund of $2.48 billion from which would be settled the claims of nearly 200,000 women said to have been harmed by the Dalkon Shield.

Impact of Event

The bankruptcy reorganization of A. H. Robins had the effect of organizing individual claims by women across the United States into a single class-action format. Another well-known example of mass tort litigation being settled through bankruptcy proceedings involved several manufacturers of asbestos, including the Manville Corporation, which also filed for bankruptcy as a result of product liability claims. As part of his supervision of the A. H. Robins bankruptcy reorganization, Judge Merhige was given considerable authority to resolve the Dalkon Shield cases, which constituted most of the creditor claims against the company.

In 1987, Judge Merhige ordered Robins to institute a national advertising campaign notifying women of the class-action proceedings. More than 330,000 potential claimants responded. That number was then narrowed by the court to 196,000 claimants. While it was involved in the bankruptcy proceedings, A. H. Robins continued to reap a profit through the popularity of certain other products that it manufactured. The company's generally favorable financial picture prompted a bidding war by other pharmaceutical firms, eventually resulting in a takeover in 1988 by American Home Products. Members of the Robins family, who owned forty-two percent of the stock of the company, received nearly $300 million as a result of the deal with American Home Products. E. Claiborne Robins, Jr., and E. Claiborne Robins, Sr., agreed to donate $10 million of that amount to the Dalkon Shield victims' trust fund.

Upon acceptance of the buyout plan by American Home Products, Judge Merhige set up a Dalkon Shield claimants trust to administer the plan. Under the plan, women would be able to claim compensatory, but not punitive, damages. In 1988, 95 percent of women claimants who voted approved the plan. Several options were made available to claimants. Women with relatively minor claims could accept payment of $725. As of the end of 1989, about eighty thousand women had accepted this payment. Women with more serious injuries would be able to settle for predetermined settlement amounts corresponding to severity of injury and to amounts paid for similar injuries in prebankruptcy settlements. Women in a third category would be able to negotiate their cases on an individual basis.

Attorneys for some of the claimants filed an appeal claiming that the $2.5 billion trust fund was too small. Some women also contested court decisions that barred future individual lawsuits against senior Robins officials and Aetna Casualty and Surety. Their appeals were ultimately rejected in 1989.

Among the beneficiaries of the Dalkon Shield debacle were attorneys representing women claimants. Many attorneys represented large numbers of clients on a contingency fee basis whereby they received between 16 and 52 percent of any settlement. Standard contingency fees are between 20 and 33 percent.

A bankruptcy declaration such as the one made by A. H. Robins benefits a company facing large numbers of product liability claims by allowing it to concentrate on the immediate problem of settling those claims. Class-action litigation, such as the litigation in this case, has the advantage of preserving the time and resources of claimants who might otherwise need to bring individual lawsuits. The notification procedures implemented by the court made potential claimants aware of their rights to seek settlements for damages suffered. Women who wore the Dalkon Shield contraceptive device and who suffered from its various effects pointed out that the monetary compensation awarded could not restore either their health or the lives of their unborn children.

Bibliography

Breslin, Catherine. "Day of Reckoning." *Ms.* 18 (June, 1989): 46-52. Provides a personal account of harm caused by the Dalkon Shield intrauterine device and examines the impact of bankruptcy proceedings involving A. H. Robins on women harmed by the contraceptive device. The article also offers insight into efforts of various organizations formed to protect the rights of women who claimed that they were harmed by the Dalkon Shield.

Hargitai, Dianne, and Paula Span. "My IUD Nightmare." *Glamour* (October, 1985): 258-259, 329-334. The article includes both a personal account of medical problems, including a hysterectomy, which the author claims were brought on by pelvic inflammatory disease associated with wearing of the Dalkon Shield and a parallel history of the Dalkon Shield, from its initial distribution by A. H. Robins to the removal program following the filing of thousands of lawsuits by women claimants.

Mintz, Morton. *At Any Cost: Corporate Greed, Women, and the Dalkon Shield.* New York: Pantheon Books, 1985. A comprehensive account, written by a *Washington Post* business news reporter, of the acquisition and marketing of the Dalkon Shield by A. H. Robins and of the lawsuits brought by women harmed by the device. Covers the period through the mid-1980's. The author contends that A. H. Robins officials were aware of the potential danger of the contraceptive device from the beginning but were driven by the profit motive. The author calls for stricter legislation and for criminal prosecution of corporate officials who endanger lives.

_____. "At Any Cost: Corporate Greed, Women, and the Dalkon Shield." *The Progressive* 49 (November, 1985): 20-25. This article is adapted from Mintz's book of the same title. This briefer version provides a basic summary of the Dalkon Shield story.

Perry, Susan, and Jim Dawson. *Nightmare: Women and the Dalkon Shield.* New York: Macmillan, 1985. Traces the saga of the Dalkon Shield device through early 1985. Like the Mintz book, the account is comprehensive, based upon examination of thousands of documents. The authors claim that A. H. Robins officials were aware of problems with the device from the outset yet strongly promoted it. While comprehensive in its coverage, the book focuses in particular on the lawsuits that arose in Minnesota, including those heard by the U.S. District Court judge from Minnesota, Miles Lord.

Mary A. Hendrickson

Cross-References

The Pure Food and Drug Act and Meat Inspection Act Become Law (1906), p. 64; Sanger Opens the First Birth-Control Clinic in the United States (1916), p. 184; Sanger Organizes Conferences on Birth Control (1921), p. 356; Consumers Union of the United States Emerges (1936), p. 527; The International Organization of Consumers Unions Is Founded (1960), p. 1062; Nader Publishes *Unsafe at Any Speed* (1965), p. 1267; Commission Studies Ethical and Legal Problems in Medicine and Research (1980), p. 2090; The World Health Organization Adopts a Code on Breast-Milk Substitutes (1981), p. 2130; The U.N. Principles of Medical Ethics Include Prevention of Torture (1982), p. 2169; Manville Offers $2.5 Billion to Victims of Asbestos Dust (1985), p. 2274.

ETHNIC RIOTS ERUPT IN ARMENIA

Categories of event: Revolutions and rebellions; racial and ethnic rights
Time: 1988
Locale: Armenia and Azerbaijan, Union of Soviet Socialist Republics

An Armenian enclave within the Azerbaijani Republic was claimed by the Armenian Republic at the cost of considerable bloodshed over several years

Principal personages:
MIKHAIL GORBACHEV (1931-   ), the president of the Soviet Union, introduced *glasnost* and *perestroika*, movements that tolerated the expression of ethnic aspirations
JOSEPH STALIN (1879-1953), the commissar for nationalities (1919-1921) and general secretary of the Communist Party of the Soviet Union (1922-1953)
HENRY POGOSYAN (1932?-   ), an Armenian placed in charge of Nagorno-Karabakh in February, 1988, replacing a Russian
KAREN DEMIRCHIAN (1932-   ), the head of the Armenian Communist Party (1974-1988), under attack by the center in 1988 for failing to stamp out corruption in Armenia
SUREN ARUTYUNYAN, the first secretary of the Armenian Communist Party in 1988

Summary of Event

Armenia's history can be told largely in terms of conquests and subdivisions by foreign powers. In 1988, the Armenian diaspora extended over much of the Middle East and, indeed, much of the world. Of 5.4 million Armenians worldwide, approximately 4.7 million lived in the Armenian Republic, located in the Caucasus, a major region in the southwestern part of the Soviet Union. The largely Armenian region of Nagorno-Karabakh and the neighboring Muslim area of Nakhichevan were given to Armenia when the Soviets took power. Partly in response to protests from Turkey, Nakhichevan was then given to neighboring Azerbaijan because most of Nakhichevan's population was Azerbaijani. In 1923, Nakhichevan and Nagorno-Karabakh became autonomous regions within the Azerbaijan (or Azerbaidzhan) Republic.

Cultural and religious factors were not the only factors driving Soviet policy. In general, the Soviet Union did not consider religion as a factor in determining republic boundaries, since the Soviet government in the early days of the union wanted to obliterate religious influence in society. At the same time, the Soviet leadership was interested in good relations with neighboring Islamic countries as part of their policy on the "Eastern question" or the problems of peoples in less-developed countries.

It is also believed that when the republics were created in the 1920's, Joseph Stalin, the first commissar for nationalities and later the general secretary of the

Communist Party of the Soviet Union, wanted to ascertain that the republics would never unite against the central government. Stalin, himself of Georgian origin, was no stranger to the historic divisions among the Caucasian peoples. For this reason, it is believed that he consciously created republic boundaries designed to perpetuate long-term ethnic tensions in order to avoid a united front of the republics against the center. The new Soviet government hoped that ethnic differences would disappear as a united Soviet people evolved, a hope that has not been realized. To cement the union, Stalin dispersed industrial and agricultural production in such a way as to maximize interdependence among the republics and make it virtually impossible for any republic to survive alone. These two policies were especially significant as the Soviet Union tried to form a new, looser confederation among the constituent republics in the 1990's, only to discover that the republics' economic interdependence and border irregularities made the process of redefinition much more complicated than it might have been otherwise. Armenia and Azerbaijan were among the areas most affected by Stalin's policies of "divide and conquer."

A variety of policies have been pursued toward the many nationalities residing in the Soviet Union. In the early years, nationalism was strongly discouraged. Later, Russian nationalism was encouraged and nationalist views that were not contradictory to Russia were tolerated. Although the Soviet Union after Stalin was considerably freer, nationalist sentiments were discouraged. In the Nikita Khrushchev, Leonid Brezhnev, and Mikhail Gorbachev periods, the numerous nationalities were allowed to maintain their cultural traditions as long as those traditions did not threaten the union.

Armenia serves as an excellent case study of Soviet policy toward the nationalities. After World War II, the Soviet government extended an invitation to Armenians all over the world to come back to their Armenian homeland in the Soviet Union. At first, many responded to the call; some later regretted their decision. A certain amount of autonomy was allowed in Armenia. The autonomous Armenian Apostolic church, in particular, played a significant role as a symbol of independent Armenia and, later, as a supporter of Nagorno-Karabakh's union with Armenia. Like the other Caucasian republics, Armenia enjoyed gradual increases in its autonomy from Moscow beginning in the 1960's. Armenia submitted a number of requests to Moscow that Nagorno-Karabakh, which the Armenians call Artsakh, become part of Armenia, but nothing happened.

Greater liberalization occurred under Mikhail Gorbachev in 1985, marked by the gradual introduction of the policies of *glasnost* (openness), *perestroika* (restructuring), and democratization. National and ethnic sentiments throughout the Soviet Union came to the surface. Among these was the status of the region of Azerbaijan known as Nagorno-Karabakh, the majority of whose people were Armenian. The struggle of the republics for complete independence from, or in some cases greater autonomy within, the overall union became a major political force, as did some of the disputed boundary issues. In the north, for example, the three Baltic republics worked together and separately for the common cause of independence. In the south, although the three Caucasian republics, Armenia, Georgia, and Azerbaijan, were also natural allies in the struggle for independence or greater autonomy, the divisive issue of Nagorno-Karabakh prevented full cooperation. On the contrary, civil strife, bloodshed, and considerable unrest began in early 1988, when the issue first exploded. The reasons given for the outbreak of conflict in 1988 were several, one of the most serious of which was the accusation that Azerbaijanis were beating, raping, and killing Armenian nationals in Nagorno-Karabakh.

Pro-Armenia demonstrations began in Stepanakert, the capital of Nagorno-Karabakh, on February 11, 1988. They soon spread to Yerevan, the capital of Armenia. The 120,000 Armenians in Nagorno-Karabakh asked to be united with Armenia. On February 28, the demonstrations spread to Sumgait, an Azerbaijani city on the Caspian Sea, and exploded into rioting and violence. Perhaps coincidentally, the first major demonstrations on behalf of Nagorno-Karabakh erupted at a time when Karen Demirchian, the leader of the Communist Party of Armenia, was under attack from Moscow for not doing enough to curb corruption in Armenia. The proximity of the two developments allows the possibility that the Armenian communist leadership encouraged ethnic discontent in order to buttress its own position in Armenia vis-à-vis the central authorities in Moscow. On February 26, the Armenian Communist Party asked Moscow to establish a commission to study the problem of Nagorno-Karabakh.

The Nagorno-Karabakh issue quickly became the main agenda of Armenia. Violence erupted on a number of occasions, and both Armenians and Azerbaijanis lost their lives or were wounded. The Soviet military intervened several times to restore order, but its role was questioned by both Armenians and Azerbaijanis. In June, 1988, the Armenian Republic voted to annex Nagorno-Karabakh as part of Armenia, a resolution not recognized by Azerbaijan or the central Soviet government. In July, the Soviet government stated that Nagorno-Karabakh would remain part of the Azerbaijan Republic.

Demonstrations in Yerevan became virtually a daily event in the second half of 1988. In early December, 1988, Moscow sent troops with tanks to Baku to control the increasingly violent demonstrations. The Armenian earthquake of December, 1988, which killed at least twenty-five thousand people and left perhaps a half million without homes, deepened the sadness and discontent within Armenia and strengthened Armenians' resolve. Although attention temporarily shifted from the issue of Nagorno-Karabakh to coping with the earthquake's damage and fatalities, Nagorno-Karabakh continued to be a central concern of Armenians.

The unrest in Nagorno-Karabakh played a major role in the development of the All-Armenian National Movement (AAM), an outgrowth of the nationalist movement in Nagorno-Karabakh uniting approximately forty groups throughout Armenia. Its goal was an independent Armenia. The AAM also supported a cultural and religious renaissance for the Armenian people. In early 1990, Armenians and Azerbaijanis met to try to resolve their problems on neutral ground. They chose Riga, in the Latvian Republic, as their site. Talks continued intermittently. Demonstrations, often accompanied by violence, also continued, as the issue remained unresolved.

In the aftermath of the attempted *coup d'état* against Mikhail Gorbachev in August, 1991, both Armenia and Azerbaijan proclaimed their independence from the Soviet Union, as did a majority of the Soviet Union's republics. The conflict between Armenia and Azerbaijan continued to erupt intermittently, dismaying those who hoped that in the evolution of a new union old grievances could be put aside.

Impact of Event

The ethnic riots in Armenia are an important human rights issue for several reasons. The plight of the Armenians in Nagorno-Karabakh was another stage in the dramatic and sometimes tragic historic struggle of Armenia to survive as a nation. The struggle was also a microcosm of the nationalities' problems within the Soviet Union. There were numerous similar cases lying dormant across the gigantic expanse of the Soviet Union, threatening to erupt as the process of redefining the union proceeded. Nagorno-Karabakh was not an issue that would go away or be forgotten. It continued to gnaw at the peoples of the Caucasus and prevent their full cooperation in either forging a new union or seeking independent status. The violence affected both Armenians and Azerbaijanis and perpetuated the tense climate in the southern republics. The Armenians had a strong case for union with Nagorno-Karabakh on ethnic grounds, but the fact that the region was separated from Armenia by Azerbaijani territory complicated the issue, as did latent Muslim-Christian conflict in the region. There were numerous similarities to the Kosovo issue in Yugoslavia, which had also defied solution.

It frequently has been stated that, were it not for the Armenian-Azerbaijani clash, there would be a cooperative movement among Armenia, Azerbaijan, and Georgia toward formation of a Transcaucasus union. Such a hypothesis can be neither proven nor disproven, since the struggle remained a real one, unabated by attempts to find a compromise between the two warring republics. In the momentous events leading to the disintegration of the Soviet Union and the enormously complex struggle to construct a new political entity out of the remains of the old, the Nagorno-Karabakh issue did not emerge as a major agenda item for the central government. Furthermore, attempts by the central government to mediate politically or militarily were rebuffed by the two republics, each of which accused the center of favoring the other side in the conflict. For Gorbachev and the other national leaders, the Armenian-Azerbaijan conflict was a "no-win" situation on which they could not afford to stake their own careers.

The issue of Nagorno-Karabakh was further complicated by the hardships caused by the 1988 earthquake in Armenia, in which thousands died and perhaps one-half million were left homeless. Almost three years later, many Armenians survived in makeshift tents and shelters. Some have referred to this period as a kind of holocaust for Armenians.

No resolution of the Nagorno-Karabakh issue seemed likely in the years following the initial uprising. The union that Stalin built, with its ingrained ethnic conflicts and economic interdependence designed to perpetuate Soviet power, reaped a harvest of discontent in the Caucasus that threatened to cloud the future of the region for the foreseeable future.

Bibliography

Barnett, Anthony. "The Armenian Twist to Perestroika." *New Statesman* 115 (March 11, 1988): 26-27. Barnett explores the Armenian uprising over Nagorno-Karabakh in the context of Soviet policies since 1985. In particular, his article examines the differences between Gorbachev and his erstwhile, conservative rival Egor Ligachev on a variety of issues.

Barry, Donald D., and Carol Barner-Barry. *Contemporary Soviet Politics: An Introduction.* Englewood Cliffs, N.J.: Prentice-Hall, 1991. This well-respected text on Soviet politics has a chapter on the nationality problem that will provide a good background for the general problems of the multinational Soviet state and for the specific issues that affect Armenia, especially Nagorno-Karabakh.

Deats, Richard L. "Agony and Hope in Armenia." *Christian Century* 106 (January 25, 1989): 81-82. A brief historical overview that ties together Armenia's historic struggles, the Nagorno-Karabakh conflict with Azerbaijan, and the earthquake of December, 1988.

Hajda, Lubomyr. "The Nationalities Problem in the Soviet Union." *Current History* 87 (October, 1988): 317. An overview of the various nationality conflicts and aspirations, with a special focus on the events in Armenia and Azerbaijan in 1988.

Hofheinz, Paul. "People Power, Soviet Style." *Time* 132 (December 5, 1988): 36-38. Describes the development of the Nagorno-Karabakh conflict, with illustrations, just prior to the earthquake of 1988.

Hunter, Shireen T. "Nationalist Movements in Soviet Asia." *Current History* 89 (October, 1990): 325. In this essay, Hunter describes the various national movements, including the Azerbaijan National Front and the All-Armenian National Movement.

Rich, Vera. "Conflict Continues Between Armenians and Azerbaijanis." *Nature* 332 (April 7, 1988): 477. In this brief article, Rich analyzes and compares the socioeconomic status of Nagorno-Karabakh with that of Azerbaijan and Armenia. This is a useful article in light of charges about discrimination against Armenians in the region.

Sancton, Thomas A. "The Armenian Challenge." *Time* 131 (March 14, 1988): 32-34. Focuses on some of the specific events in the conflict, including the Sumgait riots and the demonstrations in Yerevan.

_____. "Defiance in the Streets." *Time* 131 (March 7, 1988): 41. Examines the outbreak of the conflict and the attempts by the central leadership of the Communist Party to resolve it.

Wilson-Smith, Anthony. "Explosive Protests." *Maclean's* 103 (January 14, 1990): 22. This article both updates the conflict and presents the Azerbaijani side in the events.

_____. "A Struggle for New Life." *Maclean's* 102 (April 24, 1989): 20-22. Wilson-Smith visits postearthquake Armenia to report on the impact of the earthquake, including its effect on Armenian life and on the struggle for Nagorno-Karabakh.

Norma C. Noonan

Cross-References

Armenians Suffer Genocide During World War I (1915), p. 150; The Baltic States Fight for Independence (1917), p. 207; Lenin and the Communists Impose the "Red Terror" (1917), p. 218; Lenin Leads the Russian Revolution (1917), p. 225; The Brezhnev Doctrine Bans Acts of Independence in Soviet Satellites (1968), p. 1408; Gorbachev Initiates a Policy of *Glasnost* (1985), p. 2249; Ethnic Unrest Breaks Out in Yugoslavian Provinces (1988), p. 2386; Lithuania Declares Its Independence from the Soviet Union (1990), p. 2577; Yugoslav Army Shells Dubrovnik (1991), p. 2612.

HUNGER BECOMES A WEAPON
IN THE SUDANESE CIVIL WAR

Categories of event: Atrocities and war crimes; nutrition
Time: 1988
Locale: The Sudan

*The success of the Sudan People's Liberation Army in its thirty-year conflict with
the army of the Republic of the Sudan led the Sudan government to obstruct and
withhold famine relief*

Principal personages:
SADIQ AL-MAHDI (1936-   ), the prime minister of the Sudan
HOWARD WOLPE (1939-   ), a member of the House Subcommittee on
  Africa
GEORGE THOMAS (MICKEY) LELAND (1944-1989), the chairman of the
  House Select Committee on Hunger
JULIA VADALA TAFT (1942-   ), the director of the Office of Foreign
  Disaster Assistance, US AID
CHARLES LA MUNIERE (1930-   ), the United Nations Disaster Relief
  coordinator

Summary of Event

Upon the arrival of the dry season in the southern Sudan in October, 1987, it
became clear that a massive disaster was imminent because of the lack of rain during
the growing season (May to October). The harvest was the poorest in almost one
hundred years, and more than ten thousand Dinka, mostly women and children from
the Bahr al-Ghazal, moved northward in late 1987 to seek food and famine relief.
The Dinka were closely associated with the African insurgent movement known as
the Sudan People's Liberation Army (SPLA), which since 1987 had achieved considerable military success in the south over the army of the Republic of the Sudan.
Unable to defeat the Dinka-dominated SPLA on the field of battle, the Sudan government found it more effective to destroy the opposition by denying food aid to
them when they were experiencing famine conditions, while at the same time arm-
ing their traditional enemies with automatic weapons. The Dinka who had sought
refuge in the towns of Meiram and Abyei found that the nongovernmental organizations, such as the United Nations Children's Emergency Fund (UNICEF) and the
Red Cross, were frustrated by government officials. The indigenous relief organizations, the Islamic African Relief Agency and the Islamic society, al-Da'awal Is-
lamiyyah, were closely associated with the government in Khartoum and provided
little assistance to the displaced Dinka. The groups were discouraged by government
officials in the southern Sudan who were losing control of the countryside.

Despite the obstruction of the government and the Islamic relief societies, the various donor agencies established the Western Relief Operation (WRO) in an attempt to support relief efforts in the western Sudan. The United States Agency for International Development (US AID) released to the Sudan government Relief and Rehabilitation Commission £S 14.7 million to help pay for food transport to the southern Sudanese, but these funds had no fiscal relevance outside the Sudan because the currency was externally worthless. Several of the nongovernment agencies, such as World Vision and Lutheran World Service, were expelled from the Sudan for continuing their humanitarian efforts. Given the attitude of the government in Khartoum, the principal Sudan government aid agency, the Relief and Rehabilitation Commission, demonstrated little interest in relieving the famine conditions that were escalating during the winter of 1987/1988 in the southern Sudan.

Market prices sharply increased in the southern towns and reached unprecedented heights by January, 1988. The government made no effort to facilitate the flow of information or famine relief aid into the southern Sudan despite the predictions of various donor agencies of thousands of Sudanese deaths if prompt action were not undertaken. The government of Sadiq al-Mahdi was apprised that there were serious food shortages in the southern Sudan brought about by drought, locusts, and of course the civil war. The price of sorghum in the Bahr al-Ghazal province rose to twenty times the amount in Khartoum. The southern Sudanese, particularly the Dinka, fled to the north and were looted by the *Murahileen*, the newly armed Arab Baqqara militias who were traditional enemies of the Dinka south of the Bahr al'Arab. The *Murahileen* militia had been armed by the government of the Sudan upon the advice of General Burma Nasr, former governor of Bahr al-Ghazal, whose forces had been consistently defeated by the Africans of the SPLA. The combination of crop failure and the *Murahileen* raiders resulted in the death by violence and starvation of tens of thousands of Nilotes (people from the Nile region), mostly Dinka.

The Dinka fled in two directions. One group, consisting of women and children seeking food and shelter, went north. The other, young males, fled to the east, into Ethiopia, to join the SPLA. Many perished during the long march.

The Red Cross, the Red Crescent, and US AID were quietly discouraged from participating in famine relief, leaving that to the Commission for Relief and Rehabilitation, the official relief agency of the Sudan government. The Sudan government was not about to restrain the militia, which they had armed, in their depredations among the northern Nilotes, nor were the ambassadors of the Western governments, despite pressure from the nongovernmental organizations and the private voluntary organizations, about to anger the government of the Sudan. The acting governor of the Bahr al-Ghazal, Darius Bashir, constantly informed the prime minister, Sadiq al-Mahdi, of the serious situation in the province and particularly in its capital, Wau, urging him to send food by any means available. In Khartoum, however, there was little sense of urgency on the part of the government or diplomats that a crisis was looming in the southern Sudan. The Sudan government, through its Commission on Rehabilitation and Relief, was in no hurry to provide supplies for those who were regarded as "rebels, bandits, and terrorists" by the Sudan government.

By February the situation in Wau had been somewhat alleviated by the arrival of 167 tons of food aid, carried by a convoy sponsored by World Vision despite the group's official expulsion from the Sudan. It was the last food to be received in Wau for many months to come. To the east, in Upper Nile Province, food supplies had virtually vanished except in Malakal, the capital of the Upper Nile, which had received 2,400 metric tons of cereals in March, 1987. Most of the cereal, however, was handed over to the army, merchants, and transport personnel. Those relief agencies still operating in Malakal had little to offer those who were starving. The army consumed much of the food aid, and the merchants generally hoarded stocks with the goal of driving up the prices and their profits. The transport personnel were well fed.

The result in the Upper Nile was similar to that in the Bahr al-Ghazal. Thousands of Nilotes from the Upper Nile moved north in search of food. The Commission for Relief and Rehabilitation reported that more than thirty thousand had arrived in Kosti by the end of February, 1988. They were greeted as a source of cheap labor, and many became essentially slaves in order to earn enough to live. Ironically, most of the food aid supplied by Western donors and private voluntary organizations, some sixty thousand tons, had been moving westward into Kordofan and Darfur, while nothing was being done for the displaced southern Sudanese. Kordofan and Darfur were, of course, the Muslim heartland of the Umma Party, whose leader was Prime Minister Sadiq al-Mahdi. It was no coincidence that he would use his influence with the donor agencies to send food aid to his people rather than to his enemies in the southern Sudan.

Further south, in the Equatoria Province, the situation was more localized but just as tragic. Displaced persons seeking food swarmed into the major towns of Yei and Juba in ever-increasing numbers. They expected to find not only food but also safety in the violent conflict between the armed forces of the Sudan army and its militia and the African insurgents of the SPLA. The flight of starving people to the principal centers in Equatoria was accelerated by the continuous victories of the SPLA. In March, 1988, the situation in the Sudan was characterized by thousands of people moving northward into Darfur, Kordofan, and Khartoum, eastward by the tens of thousands to Ethiopia, and southward from the Equatoria Province into the towns of Juba and Yei. By April, 1988, more than one-quarter million southern Sudanese, many described as walking skeletons, arrived in the refugee camps established in Ethiopia and administered by the SPLA. This huge flow of refugees into the Ethiopian camps at Itang, Dimma, and Fugnido overwhelmed the facilities of the SPLA and private voluntary organizations.

It is not known exactly how many perished on the eastward trek from the Bahr al-Ghazal to Ethiopia. Many who survived the long march died from lack of food and medical supplies in the refugee camps. There were conflicts as to whether the limited amount of food supplies should go to the local people or to the refugees walking into Ethiopia, who by June numbered more than ten thousand southern Sudanese per month. The United Nations High Commission for Refugees, which was providing the major source of funds for these refugee settlements in Ethiopia, was overwhelmed by the numbers of the destitute. In late 1988, the Organization of African Unity delegation visiting the Fugnido camp found that of the forty-three thousand refugees, sixty percent were orphans under the age of twelve who had lost their parents to famine or civil war. By the end of the year it was estimated by the British Minister for Overseas Development, Christopher Patten, that more than 700,000 southern Sudanese had arrived in Ethiopia and as many had died en route.

Impact of Event

The reaction of the United States government to this calamity was extremely mild, the State Department not wishing to antagonize the government of the Sudan. In late February, 1988, congressional leaders Howard Wolpe, of the House Subcommittee on Africa; Ted Kennedy; Thomas "Mickey" Leland, the Chairman of the House Select Committee on Hunger; and Paul Simon, of the Senate Subcommittee on Africa, all signed a joint letter to both Sadiq al-Mahdi, the prime minister, and John Garang, leader of the SPLA, condemning the unconscionable attitude of the Sudan government in refusing to allow donor agencies to provide food aid to those stricken in the southern Sudan. This was matched by a strident report in the British press in February, 1988, when twenty OXFAM trucks were commandeered by the Sudan army for combat against the SPLA. Since the British government had just announced an additional twenty million pounds sterling in foreign aid to be added to the twenty million pounds already pledged for famine relief, this incident created an embarrassment. The trucks were immediately returned, but the efforts of the donor agencies were severely curtailed.

By May, reports in the Western press described the situation in the southern Sudan as desperate. Continuous pressure was placed on Sadiq al-Mahdi, but these pleas were studiously ignored. The donor agencies, nongovernmental organizations, and private volunteer organizations were well aware of the impending disaster in the southern Sudan. By April there were more than 150,000 displaced people in Aweil alone, and by April, with no relief food in the whole region of the Bahr al-Ghazal, the starving began to die in large numbers. The Sudan government remained unmoved by reports from the South and frustrated any attempts by the donor missions to ship food into the northern Bahr al-Ghazal, which was torn by violence and ravaged by famine.

Under pressure from Western governments, Sadiq al-Mahdi agreed in June that he would guarantee the safety of the personnel of the International Red Cross who sought to make a survey of the famine needs in the South. These officials reported a mortality rate of thirty-five deaths per thousand per month in Safaha alone, compared to eight per thousand in the Ethiopian refugee camps. Adding to the misery were plagues of locusts which descended upon the few crops that had survived the drought.

The donor agencies found their allocations were curtailed by the reluctance to release local currency from their counterpart fund accounts (PL480 accounts, in which aid from the United States is converted to local currency, worthless on the world money markets but useful internally for a variety of assistance purposes). Sudanese trucking companies would not honor contracts with donor agencies unless they were reviewed with the promise of higher prices. There were interminable and complex negotiations over food aid and how to transport it, with most of the aid efforts mired in bureaucracy while the southern Sudanese starved.

Food began to arrive in August. Most of it was allocated to the army with the remainder confiscated by merchants in Meiram. The international community, led by Julia Taft of the Office of Foreign Disaster Assistance of the United States government, pleaded for direct intervention. Reports from donor agencies of high mortality rates in regions from the Bahr al-Ghazal to Kordofan brought Charles La Muniere, the United Nations Disaster Relief Coordinator, to Khartoum. The Office of Foreign Disaster Assistance of AID supplied one million dollars and released grain stored in the Sudan. It reached some of the stricken areas before the dry season in October, November, and December. Despite this relief, the number of southern Sudanese who died has been estimated as high as 500,000. Other estimates place the figure between 260,000 and 300,000. By December, 1988, food supplies were moving southward, but they were too little and too late.

Bibliography

Bonner, R. "A Reporter at Large: Famine." *The New Yorker* 65 (March 13, 1989): 85-96. A perceptive and informative analysis of the situation in the Sudan from a well-known investigative reporter.

Malwal, Bona. "One Hundred Thousand Leave Bahr el Ghazal." *The Sudan Times*, May 3, 1988. The author is a well-known journalist whose commentary on current affairs in the Sudan is widely read.

Minear, Larry. *Humanitarianism Under Siege.* Trenton, N.J.: Red Sea Press, 1990. A narrative of the difficulties of the humanitarian agencies in delivering food aid to the northern Bahr al-Ghazal.

"Sudanese Soldiers Commandeer Food Trucks, Oxfam Says." *Independent*, February 9, 1988. An account of the seizure of British vehicles by the Sudan army for their campaign against the insurgents.

U.S. Department of State. *World Refugee Report.* Washington, D.C.: Author, 1987. An official report on the number and condition of refugees in the southern Sudan.

Robert O. Collins

Cross-References

The Sudanese Civil War Erupts (1955), p. 941; Civil War Ravages Chad (1965), p. 1273; The Secession of Biafra Starts a Nigerian Civil War (1967), p. 1365; The Amin Regime Terrorizes Uganda (1971), p. 1600; Burundi's Government Commits Genocide of the Bahutu Majority (1972), p. 1668; Revolution Erupts in Ethiopia (1974), p. 1758; The Kenyan Government Cracks Down on Dissent (1989), p. 2431.

NEW YORK OPENS "SHOCK" INCARCERATION CAMPS FOR FEMALE PRISONERS

Category of event: Prisoners' rights
Time: 1988
Locale: Summit, New York

The first group of selected female prisoners entered an incarceration camp designed to reform them with intense physical and mental discipline

Principal personages:
WILLIAM BENNETT (1943-   ), the director of U.S. National Drug Control
MARIO M. CUOMO (1932-   ), the governor of New York
CHRISTOPHER J. MEGA (1930-   ), a New York state senator, chair of the Crime and Corrections Committee

Summary of Event

Female prisoners have tended historically to be a neglected and negligible group. Women have made up but a small part of the prison population in all countries. Because they have tended to be such a minority in the criminal justice system, their special needs as a specific group have not been met. Nonincarcerated women have sought to help female prisoners, but their treatment has gone through the same cycles as the treatment of male prisoners.

One of the ways in which female prisoners in New York State attained equal treatment with men occurred in 1988, when the first group of women entered the "shock" incarceration program in Summit, New York. The program was aptly nicknamed. Run on the model of armed forces boot camps, such incarceration camps were designed to break down the spirit of the inmates, thereby presumably also "shocking" them out of the bad habits and antisocietal conditioning that led them to crime in the first place. The concept involved rebuilding the inmates with strict discipline, rigorous physical exercise, and some educational and vocational training.

In a lengthy feature story in *The Village Voice* (May 22, 1990), reporter Jan Hoffman vividly described the experience of a few of the one hundred women who were sent to the Summit camp in 1990. The women were relatively young, for the program was limited to first-time, nonviolent felony offenders sentenced to a term of three years or less in prison. In 1989, the program accepted women from the ages of sixteen to twenty-six, but the age limit was later raised to twenty-nine. The overwhelming majority, more than 80 percent, were drug offenders. Other prisoners had been convicted of embezzlement, forgery, and burglary. If the inmates given the option of this six-month camp took it and made it through to graduation, they were immediately eligible for parole. If they were kicked out of the program, they started their sentence in prison all over again.

Some given the option chose not to participate. The discipline at these camps was severe. As Hoffman described it, the women's hair was trimmed severely, to within two inches of their heads. They were not allowed to use the pronoun "I" and instead referred to themselves as "this inmate." Inmates rose at 5:30 A.M. for one round of calisthenics, then spent several hours at hard labor, such as cutting down trees and transporting bricks. In addition to learning hundreds of new rules detailing every aspect of their daily routine, the women were subject to all sorts of mental and psychological discipline. Swearing, for example, was punished; a violator was made to wear a bar of soap with the words "Dirty Mouth" around her neck. Meals were to be eaten in silence, at breakneck speed, in eight minutes. Food not consumed had to be worn in a bag around the neck for three days.

The drill instructors and the superintendent noted that degradation was the point of such rules. Discipline was intended to help inmates overcome the greater problems out on the streets where they would, if successful, return. Everyone at the Summit camp, including the secretaries, was put through one month of such shock training so as to know what the inmates would endure.

Such boot camps were not unique to New York. Fourteen other states had them at the time, and others were considering them. New York's program, as Hoffman reported, was the biggest. In 1988, the Shock Incarceration Correctional Facility in Summit accepted its first group of sixteen women. New York's program had some features to recommend it over others, such as an emphasis, backed by resources, on rehabilitation. Inmates were given drug and alcohol counseling, group therapy, and high school classes. In one Summit shock group, for example, the average reading score reportedly increased 1.5 years. New York also had a follow-up parole program, After-Shock, with continued drug testing, curfews, weekly group meetings, and help in finding jobs.

Community leaders were divided over these shock camps. William Bennett, the "drug czar" of the Bush Administration, supported such incarceration camps as one solution to the crime problem. Politicians in general tended to be positive. According to an article in *The New York Times* (June 8, 1989), it was Governor Mario Cuomo's administration that proposed raising the age limit to twenty-nine and allowing inmates who had already been in state prison. The same article reported that the New York State legislature was told in January, 1989, that it could save $1.59 million for every hundred shock camp graduates, because the program so drastically reduced time spent in prison.

Although the financial saving was a prime attraction, supporters of such incarceration programs also cited humanitarian reasons: The chance to change the destructive habits of the inmates, to teach them self-respect and show them that they could succeed, was more constructive than locking them away and then returning them to the poor economic and personal conditions that had defeated them in the first place. Other community leaders were more cautious: Such severe discipline tactics, they pointed out, are prone to abuse. They also suspected that the humiliating treatment of the camp inmates may have served the less humanitarian and more human urge for revenge.

Broader issues were also at stake. In the group followed by the reporter from *The Village Voice*, a majority of the inmates were African American and Hispanic. The majority of the women in the New York State penal system as a whole were single mothers with children. Many women were themselves victims of domestic violence and suffered from low self-esteem. Finally, breaking a long historical pattern, women seemed to be committing more crimes and entering the criminal justice system at an alarmingly high rate. It seemed urgent to study the needs of women prisoners and to pinpoint their differences from male prisoners. Women as a group, and therefore female prisoners in particular, tended toward culturally conditioned behavior that is submissive, dependent, and self-doubting. With so many of the inmates at a place like the Summit Camp being women of color as well, the question of human dignity became doubly acute.

Impact of Event

With the persistently high crime rate in the United States, the problem of over-crowded prisons, the backlog of cases in the overworked court system, and wide-spread use of illegal drugs leading to crime, it was easy for a weary public not to question too closely what means were used to keep criminals off the streets or how prisoners were treated. The ways in which Western societies have tried to deal with lawbreakers have changed over the centuries, but in a cyclical fashion, with one of four major attitudes dominating at a time. Sometimes restitution to victims of crimes has been paramount; retribution has satisfied people in some ages; deterrence or rehabilitation seem more productive in others. The attitude in the United States has followed similar shifts, with growing emphasis in the late twentieth century on restitution to victims whenever possible, or restitution to society in general, as in the sentences of community service.

The shock incarceration camp for women in Summit, New York, incorporated a few such attitudes. On the positive side, it seemed to be intended as a therapeutic and rehabilitative program, giving inmates a chance to change and improve their lives, first by changing and improving themselves through personal discipline and a sense of accomplishment. Among the women tracked by Jan Hoffman in 1990, for example, one woman lost 56 of her 215 pounds. She was also, to her pride, made the leader of her platoon. Unquestionably, given the societal values prevailing at the time, for women especially, the opportunity to look and feel good about herself was an important first step in gaining control over other areas of her life. The means by which this particular inmate lost the weight is more problematic: hard physical labor combined with degrading sessions when she would step on a scale and be yelled at for being fat.

Such lack of human dignity in the process, no matter what ultimate human dignity is intended in the long run, may prove to be counterproductive. It is still too soon to say how the program affected the first group of women from Summit. As Hoffman pointed out, however, similar sorts of shock treatment have been tried, without clear positive results, such as the "Scared Straight" sessions of the 1970's, in which hardened criminals confronted juvenile offenders. New York Shock graduates, Hoffman noted, had proven slightly less likely than other inmates, as of the time her article was published, to revert to their former patterns of life.

For women prisoners, who most often come from homes that humiliated and degraded them, or who must abandon children for six months to go to a shock camp, such severe treatment may be particularly ineffective in the long run. Studies of prison culture show that women in prison have a distinct culture of their own, different from that of male prisoners. Incarcerated women tend to replicate the familial structure from the outside, building networks of mutual support and assistance. With the rising crime rate among women and the personality changes that drug offenders may undergo, even this female prison culture may vanish. It can only be hoped that what replaces it will be more humane and productive.

Bibliography

Adler, Freda. *Sisters in Crime: The Rise of the New Female Criminal.* New York: McGraw-Hill, 1975. Traces the changes in the pattern of female crime in America. Also discusses the psychosocial perspective on female criminal behavior. The epilogue speculates on future directions of crimes by women. References and index. A useful introduction to the topic.

Bowker, Lee H., ed. *Women and Crime in America.* New York: Macmillan, 1981. An anthology of twenty-four articles including theoretical work, reports on experiments, and data summaries. Leans toward a feminist perspective. Intended as a basic text for courses in women and crime; useful as an introduction and as a tool for further research. Tables.

Freedman, Estelle B. *Their Sisters' Keepers: Women's Prison Reform in America, 1830-1930.* Ann Arbor: University of Michigan Press, 1981. Provides a historical background to the subject. Three major sections of the book cover the response of white, middle-class women to female prisoners in the nineteenth century; the history of state prisons for women run by women; and the work of female criminologists. Appendices, notes, bibliography, index, and illustrations.

Price, Barbara Raffel, and Natalie J. Sokoloff, eds. *The Criminal Justice System and Women.* New York: Clark Boardman, 1982. An anthology of readings addressing the roles of women as offenders, victims, and workers in the criminal justice system. The four parts of the book examine theories about female criminality, women as crime victims, women as workers, and possibilities for changes in society and in the criminal justice system. Preface, postscript, and tables.

Simon, Rita James. *Women and Crime.* Lexington, Mass.: Lexington Books, 1975. A slender volume full of statistics on various aspects of female crime in the United States. Includes a review of the literature on women in crime, information on the treatment of women in the criminal justice process, and interviews with workers in the system. Tables, introduction, bibliography, and index. The appendix provides a comparative perspective on female arrest rates in twenty-five countries, from the early 1960's to 1970.

Watterson, Kathryn. *Women in Prison.* Garden City, N.Y.: Doubleday, 1973. An unusual and interesting perspective on the subject of women and crime. The author interviewed four hundred female prisoners and visited twenty-one jails and prisons for women to document their experience. The personal voices of the women interviewed make the impersonal subject vivid. Bibliography and photographs.

Shakuntala Jayaswal

Cross-References

The Pankhursts Found the Women's Social and Political Union (1903), p. 19; Women's Institutes Are Founded in Great Britain (1915), p. 167; The U.N. Convention on the Political Rights of Women Is Approved (1952), p. 885; The United Nations Sets Rules for the Treatment of Prisoners (1955), p. 935; *Gideon v. Wainwright* Establishes Defendants' Right to an Attorney (1963), p. 1182; Legislation Ushers in a New Era of Care for the Mentally Disabled (1963), p. 1206; Incarcerated Mental Patients Are Given a Right to Treatment (1971), p. 1622; Prisoners Riot in Attica (1971), p. 1633; The United Nations Issues a Declaration Against Torture (1975), p. 1847; The United Nations Issues a Conduct Code for Law Enforcement Officials (1979), p. 2040.

GOVERNMENT MANDATES COLLECTION OF DATA ON CRIMES AGAINST HOMOSEXUALS

Category of event: Gay persons' rights
Time: 1988-April, 1990
Locale: Washington, D.C.

The Federal Hate Crimes Statistics Act required the attorney general to collect information on all hate-motivated crimes, including those committed against gay men and lesbians

Principal personages:
GEORGE BUSH (1924-   ), the forty-first president of the United States, whose endorsement of the act seemed to mark a departure from his conservative views on gay rights
PAUL SIMON (1928-   ), a Democratic senator from Illinois; a prominent sponsor of the bill
KEVIN BERRILL, the director of the Anti-Violence Project for the National Gay and Lesbian Task Force and a chief lobbyist for passage of the act
URVASHI VAID, the executive director of the National Gay and Lesbian Task Force
JESSE HELMS (1921-   ), a conservative Republican senator from North Carolina

Summary of Event

The modern Gay Liberation movement was born in the 1960's. Its growth was ignited by a 1969 incident outside the Stonewall Inn in New York City, where homosexuals rebelled against police harassment. Since the birth of the movement, various local and national gay organizations have worked to document episodes of defamation, harassment, intimidation, assault, murder, vandalism, and other abuse directed at victims because of their sexual orientation. In 1978, when San Francisco mayor George Moscone and an openly gay city councilman, Harvey Milk, were murdered, members of the gay community nationwide pointed to the incident as another example of violence motivated by hatred or resentment of gay people.

The National Gay and Lesbian Task Force (NGLTF) was organized in 1972 to lobby, educate, and demonstrate for the rights and full equality of lesbians and gay men. In 1984, this group published the first national study focusing exclusively on antigay violence. More than two thousand lesbians and gay men in eight U.S. cities were surveyed. The results of the report revealed, for example, that 44 percent of those surveyed had been threatened with physical violence and 94 percent had experienced some type of victimization (from being spat upon or chased to suffering physical assault or police abuse) because they were homosexuals. The report also emphasized that fear of antigay violence profoundly affected the attitudes and behavior of the men and women surveyed. Most of them believed they might become victims of hate crimes in the future, and nearly half reported they had modified their behavior to reduce the risk of attack. For example, a person might avoid certain locations, or a couple might refrain from showing any affection in public, for fear of harassment or assault.

Other studies conducted in the 1980's by government agencies and academic researchers showed that the problem of antigay violence in the United States was widespread. Furthermore, the NGLTF held that the numbers in any study might greatly underestimate the seriousness of the problem, since many victims of antigay violence or harassment were afraid to report the incident for fear that such reporting might result in more abuse.

During the 1980's, in fact, lesbian and gay men's community organizations reported a dramatic increase in antigay violence and harassment. By 1990, the number of antigay episodes, from harassment to homicide, reported by local groups to the NGLTF had more than tripled since the task force's first official report six years earlier. The rise could have reflected better documenting of the antigay incidents, but records kept by several gay assistance groups and by police departments indicated that violence and victimization were indeed growing. The New York Gay and Lesbian Anti-Violence Project experienced, for example, a threefold increase in the number of clients it saw between 1984 and 1989.

When the acquired immune deficiency syndrome (AIDS) became a major health issue and a major media focus in the early-to-mid-1980's, the disease's initial association with the gay community caused even more antigay sentiment to be asserted. AIDS itself, even if not a cause of antigay violence, seemed to provide for many a new focus and justification for antigay prejudice. In a 1988 survey, gay men and lesbians reported that they had recently experienced violence or harassment that was AIDS-related, such as being called a "plague-carrying faggot." Although such antigay bias may not have been new, the increased visibility of lesbians and gay men in American society in the late 1980's was new. After the onset of the AIDS epidemic, the amount of media attention paid to gay rights issues increased dramatically. Although greater visibility could have led to greater understanding and acceptance, it also triggered more hostility toward lesbians and gay men, and made them more identifiable targets for harassment and violence.

The numerous surveys and studies carried out in the 1980's were a testament to the heavy prices paid by victims of antigay prejudice. The numerical measures in reports on antigay violence could only suggest, not quantitatively relate, the fear and anguish experienced by survivors of antigay-motivated assaults and those who shared their communities. Members of the country's gay communities believed they were suffering harsh setbacks in the earlier progress they had made toward equal rights and total acceptance. Gay activists called for greater study of antigay prejudice and violence and for an organized response from public officials, educators, and all people of conscience concerned with civil rights.

Since 1983, the NGLTF had been actively lobbying for passage of the Federal Hate Crimes Statistics Act. On May 18, 1988, the U.S. House of Representatives passed H.R. 3193, a bill requiring federal collection of statistics on crimes based on "homosexuality or heterosexuality," race, religion, and ethnic background. The victory in the House marked the first time a chamber of Congress had passed a piece of legislation recognizing the victimization of lesbians and gay men. An equivalent bill in the Senate was stymied by Senator Jesse Helms (R-N.C.), an opponent of human rights for gay people and other minorities.

Helms threatened to delay Senate business unless an amendment he drafted was added to the bill. The amendment stated that homosexuality threatened the strength of the American family unit, that state sodomy laws should be enforced, that the federal government should not provide discrimination protection on the basis of sexual orientation, and that school curricula should not condone homosexuality. Helms's efforts killed the measure.

The Hate Crimes Statistics Act was reintroduced in both the House (H.R. 1048) and the Senate (S. 419) on February 22, 1989. It again passed in the House by an overwhelming margin, but again languished in the Senate because of Helms's delaying tactics.

Gay groups shared a minor victory in 1988, however, when the Presidential Commission on the Human Immunodeficiency Virus Epidemic gave public acknowledgment to the problem of antigay violence in its final report, which stated that "increasing violence against those perceived to carry HIV, so-called 'hate crimes,' are a serious problem." Also during 1988, three major professional organizations—the American Sociological Association, the American Association for the Study of Social Problems, and the American Society of Criminologists—passed resolutions condemning antigay violence and calling for research on the problem. Furthermore, in June, 1989, the National Institute of Mental Health held a groundbreaking national research workshop on antigay violence cochaired by Kevin Berrill, director of the NGLTF's Anti-Violence Project, and Gregory Herek of the University of California at Davis. These workshops reflected a national willingness, concern, and need to express solidarity with and support for gay people who were being oppressed by the threat of violence and harassment from those who actively opposed their right to live openly as homosexuals.

In 1990, the hate-crimes bill finally passed both houses of Congress, after the third year of intense lobbying by the NGLTF and a wide array of religious, professional, law-enforcement, and civil rights organizations. Senator Helms's opposition was overcome by supporters of the bill, led by Senators Paul Simon (D-Ill.) and Orrin Hatch (R-Utah). The measure passed the Senate on February 8, 1990, by a vote of ninety-two to four.

On April 23, 1990, President George Bush signed into law the Hate Crimes Statistics Act, requiring the Department of Justice to collect data on crimes based on race, religion, sexual orientation, or ethnicity. Unlike most bills, this one was signed during a public ceremony to which more than twenty gay activists were invited. Notably absent was Urvashi Vaid, executive director of the NGLTF, who was not invited allegedly because she had heckled President Bush during a March 29, 1990, speech on AIDS. It was the first time gay activists had been invited formally to a presidential bill signing. During the ceremony, Bush declared his hopes for "a society blind to prejudice, a society open to all."

Impact of Event

Some high-ranking members of the Republican Party were concerned that Bush's signing of the bill might be perceived by his conservative supporters as an endorsement of homosexuality, and they feared that the president might alienate his own base. For many, the greatest significance of the act's passage was not its mandate to pursue hate-crime statistics, but the fact that it wrote "sexual orientation" into federal law for the first time. While Bush perceived the main issue as tolerance for homosexuals, gay lobbyists saw the signing as a positive step toward legitimacy for gay men and lesbians. "I was encouraged . . . that the Bush White House is not afraid to talk to or deal with gay and lesbian organizations," said Urvashi Vaid.

Of immediate concern was how the Hate Crimes Statistics Act would be implemented. The Federal Bureau of Investigation (FBI) was assigned this task, and the National Gay and Lesbian Task Force's Anti-Violence Project was invited to work with the FBI to discuss and plan implementation. The NGLTF continued to lobby for funding and took part in monitoring hate-crime law-enforcement training. Members worked closely with the FBI to develop hate-crime reporting guidelines and training materials. When Kevin Berrill and Urvashi Vaid took part in a 1991 press conference at the FBI to announce the agency's progress in implementing the Hate Crimes Statistics Act, it marked the first time that gay and lesbian activists had been invited to an official FBI event.

Many state legislatures followed suit after passage of the federal act. More laws to counteract antigay crimes were passed in 1990 than in any previous year. New legislation in Connecticut, the District of Columbia, Illinois, Iowa, Massachusetts, New Hampshire, New Jersey, and Vermont brought to twelve the number of states with hate-crimes laws that penalized crimes based on sexual orientation. In March, 1991, legislation addressing antigay violence and other crimes motivated by bigotry was pending in ten states.

The Immigration Reform Bill (which removed restrictions against gay men and lesbians entering the United States) and the Americans with Disabilities Act (which banned discrimination against people with AIDS and the HIV virus) were other important political victories for gay people that came in 1990 on the heels of the passage of the Hate Crimes Statistics Act. Following 1990's political successes, gay activists and lobbyists prepared to continue their struggle for equal rights in the 102d Session of Congress, where some thirty bills of interest to the lesbian and gay community were pending. Many believed that the 1991-1992 congressional sessions would be critical for gay activists to maintain gay rights gains.

The passage of the Hate Crimes Statistics Act left members of the gay community optimistic with regard to passage of the Civil Rights Amendments Act of 1991. The bill, reintroduced in Congress in 1991 for the ninth time, was intended to ban discrimination on the basis of affection or sexual orientation in housing, employment, federally assisted programs, and public accommodations. National Gay and Lesbian Task Force lobbyists pledged to get the act passed by the year 2000 by increasing grass-roots support, continuing to document antigay discrimination, and lobbying for congressional hearings.

Bibliography

Adam, Barry D. *The Rise of a Gay and Lesbian Movement.* Boston: Twayne, 1987. Useful for background on the modern gay rights movement, this introductory study includes chapter notes, a bibliography, and an index.

Herek, Gregory M., and Kevin T. Berrill. *Hate Crimes: Confronting Violence Against Lesbians and Gay Men.* Newbury Park, Calif.: Sage Publications, 1992. Includes a foreword by John Conyers, Jr., the lead sponsor in the House of Representatives for the Hate Crimes Statistics Act. Gives an overview of antigay violence and victimization. Academic and research findings are juxtaposed with survivor accounts. Addresses a number of social issues and concludes with implications for public policy.

Journal of Interpersonal Violence 5 (September, 1990). Coedited by Kevin Berrill, the issue is devoted to articles on the subject of antigay violence and represents the first major published body of information on violence against lesbians and gay men.

Kirk, Marshall, and Hunter Madsen. *After the Ball: How America Will Conquer Its Hatred and Fear of Homosexuals in the 90's.* New York: Doubleday, 1989. Offers a well-balanced overview of the accomplishments and failings to date of the gay revolution and assesses contemporary America's treatment of and beliefs about gay men and women. Discusses and offers ways to address the American crisis of "homohatred." Includes notes and a ten-page bibliography.

Mohr, Richard D. *Gays/Justice: A Study of Ethics, Society, and Law.* New York: Columbia University Press, 1988. Fourteen essays, including a useful introductory discussion on the social status of gays and attitudes about gays. Following are sections on privacy rights, civil rights protection against discrimination, the AIDS crisis, and the role of American education in fighting social injustices. Includes a thorough index.

Rice, Charles E. *Legalizing Homosexual Conduct: The Role of the Supreme Court in the Gay Rights Movement.* Constitutional Commentaries 1. Cumberland, Va.: Center for Judicial Studies, 1984. Introduction by Robert T. Donnelly, Justice of the Supreme Court of Missouri. A twenty-nine-page study on the role and influence of the U.S. Supreme Court in the legitimization of homosexual conduct in American society. Uses individual cases to examine how the Bill of Rights has been interpreted in reference to privacy rights, sodomy prohibitions, equal employment, and other concerns.

Timmons, Stuart. *The Trouble with Harry Hay: Founder of the Modern Gay Movement.* Boston: Alyson, 1990. A biography of Hay, an early gay activist credited with founding the modern gay movement and who organized the underground Mattachine Society (1950). His radical politics and theories provide a background for and perspective on the later achievements of gay rights groups. With bibliographic notes and index.

JoAnn Balingit

Cross-References

The World Health Organization Proclaims Health as a Basic Right (1946), p. 678; The Wolfenden Report Recommends Decriminalizing Homosexual Acts (1957), p. 991; Riots Against Police Harassment Launch the Gay Rights Movement (1969), p. 1479; A NIMH Task Force Recommends Legalizing Homosexual Behavior (1969), p. 1497; Homosexuality Is Removed from the APA List of Psychiatric Disorders (1973), p. 1741; The Civil Service Decides That Gays Are Fit for Public Service (1975), p. 1801; WHO Sets a Goal of Health for All by the Year 2000 (1977), p. 1893; An International Health Conference Adopts the Declaration of Alma-Ata (1978), p. 1998; The U.S. Court of Appeals Affirms the Navy's Ban on Homosexuality (1981), p. 2124.

ISRAEL CONVICTS DEMJANJUK OF NAZI WAR CRIMES

Category of event: Atrocities and war crimes
Time: April 18, 1988
Locale: Jerusalem, Israel

Demjanjuk's trial for atrocities committed at the Treblinka extermination camp continued the Nuremberg precedent of holding Nazi war criminals accountable for their violations of human rights

Principal personages:
JOHN DEMJANJUK (1920-   ), an SS auxiliary guard at the extermination camp at Treblinka in German-occupied Poland during World War II, known to inmates as Ivan the Terrible
ADOLF EICHMANN (1906-1962), the SS officer in charge of deporting Jews to extermination camps in Eastern Europe, convicted and executed by Israel for war crimes
ALOIS BRUNNER (1912-   ), an Eichmann deputy and SS officer who supervised deportations to extermination camps

Summary of Event

During World War II, the Nazi German government implemented a calculated policy of genocide by killing millions of human beings. Although victims included persons from many political and religious groups and numerous nationalities, Jews, Gypsies, and the handicapped were the primary victims of Nazi genocide. To accomplish their ends, the Nazis constructed killing centers and perfected mass murder on the assembly line.

The Treblinka extermination camp, which figured prominently in the trial of John Demjanjuk as it did in many Nazi war crimes trials, was one such killing center. One of the three camps of Operation Reinhard (the other two were Belzec and Sobibor) in eastern Poland, Treblinka opened in July, 1942. A revolt in August, 1943, destroyed parts of the camp, and the Germans closed it in November, 1943. Treblinka, as did the other two camps of Operation Reinhard, served only the purpose of mass murder. Every man, woman, and child arriving there was meant to be killed. Most were Jews; a few were Gypsies. A few young men and women were not immediately killed. They served the camp by sorting the belongings of those who had been murdered and by burning the bodies after any gold fillings had been extracted from the victims' teeth. Eventually, they too were killed. Only a handful, able to escape during the uprising, survived to testify. The number of people killed at the Treblinka camp has been estimated to be between 700,000 and 900,000.

The method of murder was relatively simple. The victims arrived by train, mostly in cattle cars. They were driven from the cars and the men were separated from the women. They were forced to undress and to surrender all their valuables. Those too old or too infirm to walk rapidly were shot, and their bodies were dropped into a ditch where a continuous fire consumed them. The others were driven naked toward the gas chamber facility, a large building whose interior was divided into chambers disguised as shower rooms. They were forced into the gas chambers, the doors were sealed, and carbon monoxide from a diesel motor was pumped into the chambers.

The Treblinka killing center employed a small staff. About twenty-five to thirty Germans, dressed in the uniform of the SS (*Schutzstaffel*), the elite German security unit, supervised all operations. They were supported by 90 to 120 Ukrainian auxiliaries (Soviet prisoners of war recruited and trained by the SS), without whose help the killing machine could not have been operated. A fluctuating number of Jewish prisoners, approximately five hundred to one thousand, performed all the necessary physical labor.

Demjanjuk was one of these SS auxiliaries. Born Ivan Demjanjuk in the Soviet Ukraine, he was drafted into the Soviet army in 1940. He was wounded but returned to active duty until captured by the Germans in May, 1942. He volunteered for and received training as an SS auxiliary at Trawniki, Poland. He was then posted to the extermination camps of Operation Reinhard and served at Treblinka until the camp closed in 1943.

After the war, Demjanjuk found refuge in Displaced Persons (DP) camps. In 1948, he applied for DP status, and in 1951 for an American immigration visa. He was ineligible for either because the operative definition of a displaced person given by the International Refugee Organization (IRO), later adopted by the United States Congress, specifically denied DP status to Nazi war criminals. Demjanjuk obtained both DP status and his American visa by lying about his wartime occupation. He entered the United States in February, 1952, settled in Cleveland, and became an auto worker. He was naturalized in 1958.

In the United States, criminal charges could not be brought against Demjanjuk because American courts have no jurisdiction to try persons who commit murder abroad. American law does require the denaturalization of those who lied in order to gain entry and citizenship and, after denaturalization, also requires their deportation if they had assisted Nazi Germany in persecuting civilians.

In 1977, the U.S. government instituted denaturalization proceedings against Demjanjuk, alleging that he was the SS auxiliary at Treblinka, known to the Jewish inmates as Ivan the Terrible, who had operated the diesel motor that fed lethal carbon monoxide into the Treblinka gas chambers and who had tormented, tortured, and shot Treblinka inmates. Demjanjuk denied that he had ever been at Trawniki or Treblinka. The government produced documents, expert witnesses, and Treblinka survivors to prove its allegations. The government's most important piece of evidence, in addition to the eyewitness identifications made by former Treblinka inmates and a former German Treblinka staff member, was Demjanjuk's Trawniki identity card.

This Trawniki card showed Demjanjuk's picture and signature and provided his name, nationality, family history, and such personal characteristics as a shrapnel scar on his back, the color of his hair and eyes, and the date of his birth, all of which matched the relevant information on his visa application. The authenticity of the Trawniki card was certified by an expert forensic documents examiner. A historian testified that the information on the Trawniki card conformed to the known facts of SS administration in occupied Poland.

Unable to deny that he was the man in the Trawniki photograph or that the personal data were accurate, Demjanjuk seized upon the fact that the Trawniki card had been obtained from Soviet archives to claim that it was a KGB forgery. He produced no credible reason for being singled out for persecution by the Soviet government and no evidence to support the forgery claim. Nor could he produce a plausible, or indeed even a consistent, alternative explanation of his whereabouts and activities during the war.

The federal district court found the government's case to be persuasive. In June, 1981, it revoked Demjanjuk's citizenship, a decision upheld on appeal. The government then instituted deportation proceedings against him. In May, 1984, an immigration judge concluded that Demjanjuk was deportable because he had assisted Nazi Germany in persecuting civilians and ordered him deported to the Soviet Union, a decision upheld on appeal.

In October, 1983, during the deportation proceedings but before Demjanjuk was ordered deported, Israel charged him with murder and other offenses in violation of its 1950 Nazi and Nazi Collaborators Law and requested his extradition. The U.S. government sought and received a certificate of extraditability from a federal district court. On February 27, 1986, United States marshals took Demjanjuk to Israel and turned him over to the proper authorities. On September 29, 1986, the government of Israel filed a twenty-four page indictment, charging Demjanjuk with having committed crimes against the Jewish people, crimes against humanity, war crimes, and crimes against persecuted persons.

The trial began on February 16, 1987, before a three-judge district court in Jerusalem. The Israeli prosecutors relied on documentary evidence, expert witnesses, and the testimony of Treblinka survivors. The principal documentary evidence was again the Trawniki card, once again authenticated by documents experts. A forensic anthropologist compared the photo appearing on the Trawniki card with a photo of Demjanjuk in prison, concluding that it was the same person. Historians testified about the Holocaust, Operation Reinhard and Treblinka, and the administrative procedures used by the Germans. The Treblinka survivors testified about their personal experiences at the camp, identified Demjanjuk as Ivan the Terrible, and recounted his specific acts of cruelty. As in the American proceedings, Demjanjuk relied largely on his own denial that he had ever been at Trawniki or Treblinka and the contention that the Trawniki card was a KGB forgery. Again Demjanjuk failed to offer credible evidence to refute the prosecution's case.

On April 18, 1988, after a fifteen-month trial, the court returned its verdict. For ten hours the judges read excerpts from their four-hundred-page opinion, reviewing, summarizing, and analyzing the documents and the testimony that led the court to find Demjanjuk guilty. The following week, the judges sentenced Demjanjuk to death. Demjanjuk appealed to the Supreme Court of Israel. That court heard Demjanjuk's appeal beginning in 1991. The appeal gained strength when, on June 5, 1992, a federal appeals court in Cincinnati, Ohio, ordered a reopening of the case involving Demjanjuk's extradition from the United States. The appeals court in Ohio asked to hear more evidence because of the possibility that the extradition order had been based on erroneous information.

Impact of Event

Israel has not been, and is not likely to become, the major forum for the trial of Nazi war criminals. Demjanjuk was only the second non-Israeli tried under the Nazi and Nazi Collaborators Law. The first, Adolf Eichmann, was tried in the early 1960's. Most Nazi war criminals have been tried in a large variety of international and domestic tribunals.

After World War II, the Allies established the International Military Tribunal (IMT) at Nuremberg to prosecute top-ranking German Nazis. In addition, each Allied power tried Nazi war criminals in its zone of occupation and extradited others to countries formerly occupied by Germany in which the crimes had been committed. Further, Austria and the two German states continued to prosecute Nazi war criminals.

By the 1950's, concern about Nazi crimes had waned, and many Nazis escaped trial. By the late 1970's, however, indifference to the Holocaust changed to renewed concern. Governments began to seek those perpetrators of Nazi crimes who had not been brought to justice. Some countries (Canada, Australia, and Great Britain, for example) made Nazi war crimes punishable under their domestic laws. The United States has relied on civil, not criminal, proceedings: It has sought to denaturalize those Nazi war criminals who had entered illegally and then to deport or, on occasion, to extradite them. The legal road to Demjanjuk's conviction for war crimes began in Cleveland, Ohio, in a civil denaturalization proceeding.

The Israeli trial of Demjanjuk, like the trials of Nazis in other forums, was a reminder to those still at large that they too could still be called to account. Under the Nuremberg precedent, international tribunals can be established to try war criminals. Moreover, under international law, every country has universal jurisdiction over crimes against humanity and war crimes, even if those crimes were not committed on their territory or against their citizens.

Justice, of course, has been neither swift nor sure for Nazi war criminals. Demjanjuk himself evaded the law for more than forty years. Other Nazi war criminals found refuge in dictatorships that refused to surrend them. Syria, as of 1991, continued to refuse the extradition of Alois Brunner, an Eichmann deputy. Still other war criminals died of natural causes in their old age without ever having had to answer for their crimes.

As Demjanjuk's trial illustrates, there is no statute of limitations for crimes such as those committed at Treblinka. The fact that Demjanjuk's past was discovered and that he was finally held accountable for his crimes serves as a warning to contemporary violators of human rights that they are not immune from prosecution for mass murder. The prosecution of Demjanjuk is another step in the development of an international system of justice wherein some crimes so offend norms of civilized behavior that perpetrators will be held accountable by international or domestic tribunals.

Bibliography

Arendt, Hannah. *Eichmann in Jerusalem.* New York: Penguin, 1977. Brilliant polemical essay on the Jerusalem trial, first published in *The New Yorker.* Includes a penetrating analysis of Eichmann as the technician of mass murder and a perceptive, but highly controversial, analysis of the Jewish leadership as unwilling instruments of the Nazi extermination program. Index.

Friedlander, Henry, and Earlean McCarrick. "The Extradition of Nazi Criminals: Ryan, Artukovic, Demjanjuk." *Simon Wiesenthal Center Annual* 4 (1987): 65-98. An account and analysis of the three cases in which the United States extradited war criminals to West Germany, Yugoslavia, and Israel.

Hilberg, Raul. *The Destruction of the European Jews.* Chicago: Quadrangle, 1961. Classic account based on an exhaustive study of the Nuremberg evidence and of the German documents captured by the Allies. Describes the processes and dynamics of the conception and execution of the Nazi program of extermination. A three-volume revised edition was published in 1985 by Holmes & Meier. Index and footnotes.

Reitlinger, Gerald. *The Final Solution: The Attempt to Exterminate the Jews of Europe, 1939-1945.* New York: Beechhurst, 1953. The earliest comprehensive account to be published after the war. Remains the best general history. Based on the Nuremberg evidence, it provides a description of the Nazi program of extermination and a detailed account of its country-by-country implementation. Index, footnotes.

Ryan, Allan A., Jr. *Quiet Neighbors: Prosecuting Nazi War Criminals in America.* San Diego: Harcourt Brace Jovanovich, 1984. Authoritative popular history of the illegal postwar immigration of Nazi war criminals to the United States and of the effort to denaturalize and deport them. This account by the former director of the Justice Department's Office of Special Investigation (OSI) also includes a description of the negotiations between American prosecutors and Soviet authorities that made Soviet legal assistance in war-crimes cases possible. Index, footnotes at end, and an appendix which includes photographs of the relevant documents and a list of cases filed by OSI.

San Jose Conference on the Holocaust. *The Holocaust: Ideology, Bureaucracy, and Genocide.* Edited by Henry Friedlander and Sybil Milton. New York: Kraus International, 1980. A comprehensive collection of twenty-seven scholarly essays covering various aspects of the Holocaust. Three essays cover the history of anti-Semitism, and three essays cover Jews and anti-Semites in Germany before Hitler. One essay analyzes the options open to Jewish leaders under Nazi rule. Several essays discuss the anatomy, the significance, and the postwar implications of the Holocaust. Index and footnotes.

Teicholz, Tom. *The Trial of Ivan the Terrible: State of Israel v. John Demjanjuk.* New York: St. Martin's Press, 1990. Written by a journalist who is also a lawyer, this is an accessible account of the Israeli trial of Demjanjuk with a background overview of the American denaturalization, deportation, and extradition proceedings against him. Index, selected bibliography, and a list of witnesses who testified in Jerusalem.

Earlean M. McCarrick

Cross-References

Hitler Writes *Mein Kampf* (1924), p. 389; Nazi Concentration Camps Go into Operation (1933), p. 491; Nazi War Criminals Are Tried in Nuremberg (1945), p. 667; The United Nations Adopts a Convention on the Crime of Genocide (1948), p. 783; Eichmann Is Tried for War Crimes (1961), p. 1108; The United Nations Issues a Declaration Against Torture (1975), p. 1847; A Paraguayan Torturer Is Found Guilty of Violating the Law of Nations (1980), p. 2106; Barbie Faces Charges for Nazi War Crimes (1983), p. 2193.

CANADA PASSES THE
TOBACCO PRODUCTS CONTROL ACT

Categories of event: Health and medical rights; consumers' rights
Time: June, 1988
Locale: Ottawa, Ontario, Canada

The Canadian Parliament attempted to discourage smoking by severely limiting advertising and significantly raising taxes on cigarettes and other tobacco products

Principal personages:
> BRIAN MULRONEY (1939-   ), the Canadian prime minister and leader of the Progressive Conservative government
> DAVID SWEANOR, an attorney for the Non-Smokers' Rights Association, an organization that fought a fifteen-year battle for the passage of such prohealth legislation
> BILL NEVILLE (1940-   ), the president of the Canadian Tobacco Manufacturers' Council and a vocal critic of the legislation

Summary of Event

In the years since cigarette smoking became a regular feature of polite society, the health effects of the practice have been debated. By the end of the 1970's, no responsible independent scientist or physician denied the ability of tobacco products to impair seriously or destroy the health of those who used them. In response to this consensus, many public laws limiting the locations where one could smoke were passed. Some of the most severe of these restrictions were incorporated in Canada's landmark Tobacco Products Control Act. The legislation, which passed the Canadian parliament in June, 1988, was designed both to decrease the number of new smokers starting the practice and to encourage current smokers to abandon the habit.

The first major restrictions on cigarette smoking were enacted in the United States, when the Ninety-Fifth Congress passed the Cigarette Labeling Act of 1965, which required all cigarette packages to carry a warning label that specified the general health risks associated with smoking. As a result of both the increasing explicitness of the warning and a ban on television and radio advertising (enacted in 1970), the number of smokers in North America declined during the 1970's. By the middle of the 1980's, Canada was ready to assume a world leadership role in the restriction of smoking.

In November, 1987, Prime Minister Brian Mulroney's Progressive Conservative government, in a rare event, received the support of all the parties in Parliament for the proposed Tobacco Products Control Act. The legislation, which passed with no effective opposition in June, 1988, contained four key planks. First, all tobacco advertising was phased out over a period of thirteen months. This included not only radio and television advertisements, which had been informally banned for more than fifteen years in some locations, but also all newspaper, magazine, and billboard advertisements. Second, the law prohibited any point-of-sale advertising and also forbade tobacco companies from sponsoring cultural events or sports contests as a means of promoting their products. The third principal element of the law was a requirement that all tobacco products carry large, explicit warnings on all packages. Also, each pack of cigarettes was required to contain a warning leaflet wrapped over the top one-quarter of the package. Further, this warning label could not be printed using colors that blended in with the general packaging of the product. The final element of the law was the application of a high tax on each pack of cigarettes sold in Canada. The specific purpose of the tax was to discourage the use of tobacco by making the habit very costly. The Tobacco Products Control Act became fully effective on June 1, 1991.

The premise underlying the legislation was labeled, alternately, progressive and paternalistic. Canada's vocal and highly organized Non-Smokers' Rights Association hailed the legislation and looked toward a decline in tobacco use throughout the country. The passage represented a continuation of the group's fight to make Canada the first smoke-free industrialized nation in the world. Representatives of the tobacco companies assailed the new law for its interference with smokers' and advertisers' free-speech rights through the limitations placed on advertising. It also pointed to the advertising restrictions as another example of the regulatory harassment to which they said the tobacco companies had been subjected.

The fear and ire of the tobacco companies reflected the effect of Canada's two-pronged attack. Although the cost of a standard package of cigarettes was approximately $2.10 (Canadian) in September, 1984, it stood at an average of $5.25 by March, 1991. Calculated over the course of one year, this increase meant that a one-pack-a-day smoker would pay $800 in new federal taxes and up to $1,700 per year when the provincial taxes were included. (The cigarette manufacturers were unable to increase prices by the full amount of the taxes.) These increases served to accelerate the pace at which smoking declined in Canada.

Before the new legislation, smoking in Canada had been decreasing by approximately 3 percent each year since the early 1980's. In 1989, it fell by more than 8 percent, and by July, 1990, it had fallen another 8 percent. The consequences of fewer smokers for the tobacco companies worked out to a 19.6 percent drop in cigarette consumption from February, 1990, to February, 1991. In addition, the tax increases were designed specifically to limit the number of young people developing the smoking habit. According to the 1991 Canadian federal budget, a 10 percent price increase was expected to reduce cigarette consumption by younger Canadians by as much as 14 percent and consumption by adults by between 4 and 9 percent. According to a Canadian governmental study, the rate of teenage smoking in Canada was cut in half between 1980 and 1989, while it remained relatively level in the United States. When Michael Wilson, a former finance minister, proposed a potential new tax, he estimated that the new levy would shrink the number of teen smokers in Canada by one hundred thousand.

The tobacco companies did not accept calmly the Tobacco Products Control Act and the threat it represented to their long-term corporate health. From June, 1988, when the law passed, the manufacturers, operating under the umbrella of the Canadian Tobacco Manufacturers' Council, an industry advocacy and lobbying organization, fought back against the new restriction. The tobacco industry pursued this fight using its own two-pronged attack. First, the manufacturers challenged the advertising restrictions in court. Citing the ban on all advertising and the rigid specifications for the warning labels, the firms claimed that their right to freedom of speech, as guaranteed by the Charter of Rights (1982), was violated. In a ruling handed down on July 26, 1991, Justice Jean-Jude Chabot agreed with the industry and removed the advertising ban, effective immediately. The industry also attempted to mobilize Canadian smokers into a lobbying organization. The Smokers' Freedom Society was organized to fight the parliament's measures to discourage and curtail smoking through taxation. In addition, the cigarette companies began inserting postage-paid protest cards on the inside of most packs of cigarettes. Bearing the message, "I am of voting age. I want you to stop unfair taxation of tobacco products in Canada. What are you going to do about it? I expect a reply," the cards were designed to intimidate Mulroney and his government into backing down in their support of the antismoking policies. In a reaction that reflected the deep feelings on both sides of the issue, the Canadian Council on Smoking and Health tried to pursue legal action to stop the cards, charging that they violated the Tobacco Products Control Act's stringent packaging specifications.

Impact of Event

The immediate consequences of the Tobacco Products Control Act were a significant increase in the cost of cigarettes and a resulting reduction of as much as 25 percent in the nation's per-capita use of cigarettes. Such reductions could provide long-term savings for the federal government, which provides all its citizens with health care through a socialized system. The decrease in the number of smokers could mean that the government may need to spend less on the treatment of emphysema, heart disease, and all the forms of cancer related to cigarette smoking. In addition, the added revenues generated by the higher taxes were spent to make smoking cessation programs more available to the general public.

In practical terms, the new taxes did not always help the Mulroney government. As the new levies took effect, a visibly significant increase in cigarette smuggling occurred. Those areas that bordered the United States, where the average cost of a pack of cigarettes remained around $1.60, reported increases in cross-border shopping as well as in smuggling, black-marketeering of American cigarettes, and burglaries and hijackings of Canadian cigarette dealers.

The resolution of the problem caused by the tobacco manufacturing companies' and the government's conflicting interests could be one of the most difficult balancing acts associated with the legislation. The former's free-speech rights in the advertisement of their products were poised against the latter's right and obligation to act in a manner that recognized the will of the majority of Canadians to have a less smoker-oriented culture. As a result, actions to limit the basic rights of those who sell or consume cigars, cigarettes, or other tobacco products have represented a dangerous and difficult path.

Perhaps more important than these obvious areas could be the eventual impact of the smokers' and nonsmokers' rights movements. The former believed that their rights of assembly and enjoyment were being reduced markedly and that they were being forced to contribute a disproportionate share of the government's operating expenses. The latter, which enjoyed a temporary success with the Tobacco Products Control Act, still pushed for the recognition of an absolute right not to absorb the extremely high health costs for those smokers who eventually develop one of the many deadly or debilitating diseases associated with smoking.

Bibliography

Diehl, Harold S. *Tobacco and Your Health: The Smoking Controversy.* New York: McGraw-Hill, 1969. Somewhat dated and occasionally limited by the partial tone. Valuable for both Diehl's conviction and the strength of his argument. His extensive background in the field of public health makes this a compelling, if somewhat polemical, work. A fine choice for the general reader. Contains a glossary, an index, and five useful appendices.

Goodin, Robert E. *No Smoking: The Ethical Issues.* Chicago: University of Chicago Press, 1989. Provides philosophical analyses of the ethical issues prompted by the existence of an industry dedicated to producing and selling a dangerous product. Goodin treats smoking as a political issue, one with a correct moral position. Index and comprehensive list of scientific studies.

Patterson, James T. "Smoking and Cancer." In *The Dread Disease: Cancer and Modern American Culture.* Cambridge, Mass.: Harvard University Press, 1987. A scholarly study of cancer in American society. This engaging, free-standing chapter examines the relationship between tobacco and cancer. The cigarette advertising question receives a thorough review. Contains a thorough index and references.

Tollison, Robert D., ed. *Smoking and Society: Toward a More Balanced Assessment.* Lexington, Mass.: Lexington Books, 1986. From a 1984 conference on the relationship between smoking and society. Examines the economic, health, psychological, and social aspects of tobacco use. Valuable to readers in search of specific data. Index and references.

Troyer, Ronald J., and Gerald E. Markle. *Cigarettes: The Battle over Smoking.* New Brunswick, N.J.: Rutgers University Press, 1983. This social monograph focuses on the cultural evolution of smoking, specifically its progress from immorality to mark of social sophistication to deviant behavior. Concerted attention is diverted toward the powerful groups with vested interests trying to destigmatize smoking. Rather technical in spots, but a valuable resource. Complete annotations and index.

E. A. Reed

Cross-References

The Pure Food and Drug Act and Meat Inspection Act Become Law (1906), p. 64; Congress Requires Cigarette Warning Labels (1966), p. 1338; Cigarette Advertising Is Banned from American Television and Radio (1970), p. 1527; The Canadian Charter of Rights and Freedoms Is Enacted (1982), p. 2158; A. H. Robins Must Compensate Women Injured by the Dalkon Shield (1987), p. 2342; A Jury Awards Monetary Damages to the Estate of a Smoker (1988), p. 2381; The U.S. Surgeon General Reports on Tobacco and Health (1989), p. 2455.

A JURY AWARDS MONETARY DAMAGES TO THE ESTATE OF A SMOKER

Category of event: Consumers' rights
Time: June 13, 1988
Locale: Newark, New Jersey

For the first time, a jury awarded damages to a cigarette smoker who suffered from health problems caused by long-term smoking

Principal personages:

ROSE CIPOLLONE (?-1984), a forty-two-year smoker whose addiction was so severe she could not stop smoking even after one lung was removed and she was dying of cancer

ANTONIO CIPOLLONE (?-1990), Rose's widower, who continued her lawsuit against the cigarette manufacturers after her death

H. LEE SAROKIN (1928-   ), the federal judge who presided over the trial of *Cipollone v. Liggett Group, Inc., et al.*

MARC EDELL, the principal attorney for the Cipollones

Summary of Event

Although there had been a number of unsuccessful attempts to sue tobacco companies for the illnesses their products caused, in June, 1988, the estate of Rose Cipollone won a $400,000 judgment against the Liggett Group, a cigarette manufacturer. Although the case was appealed, the judgment marked the first successful lawsuit against a tobacco company by a consumer.

In 1983, Rose Cipollone and her husband Antonio initiated legal action against the three cigarette companies whose products Rose had smoked at a rate of one pack a day. By that time, she had been smoking for forty-one years. During the first seventeen years of her habit, Cipollone had smoked Chesterfields, a brand produced by the Liggett Group, the fourth-largest cigarette manufacturer in the United States. In the late 1950's, she had switched to L&M, another Liggett brand, and in 1968 she began smoking Virginia Slims, a Philip Morris brand. Later she smoked Parliament, another Philip Morris product, before finally turning to Lorillard's True, a low-tar cigarette, in 1974.

In 1981, Mrs. Cipollone was diagnosed as having lung cancer. In spite of the diagnosis and the surgical removal of her right lung (the upper lobe in 1981 and the remainder of it in 1982), Cipollone continued to smoke. In spite of additional surgery, she died in 1984. Her husband continued the lawsuit against the firms after her death.

The case, *Cipollone v. Liggett Group, Inc., et al*, went to trial in January, 1988. Two hundred thirty-three prospective jurors completed a 108-question form as part of a jury-selection process that lasted eight days. Eventually, eleven members were impaneled, and from that group six (three men and three women) were drawn by lot to decide the case. Before the jury even received the case, Judge H. Lee Sarokin ruled that Philip Morris and Lorillard could not be held liable for any injuries Mrs. Cipollone might have received from their products, since she had begun using them after the first cigarette labeling law was passed in 1965. The law, which took effect on January 1, 1966, required that all cigarette packages bear a health warning that declared: "CAUTION: Cigarette Smoking May be Hazardous to Your Health."

Cipollone's attorney, Marc Edell, focused his attacks on the advertising of the cigarette companies and on some of their internal corporate memorandums. Among the ad campaigns Edell concentrated on was a long-running Liggett series that reassured Cipollone, "Play Safe—Smoke Chesterfields," and "The Mask Is Off in Cigarette Advertising," which went on to list all the package's ingredients: "1. Best Tobaccos, 2. Natural Sugars, 3. Costly Glycerol . . . NOTHING ELSE!" Later, the L&M campaign "Just What the Doctor Ordered" prompted her to switch to filter-tipped cigarettes, which the industry had been advertising as "safer." At the same time that consumers received such cheerful reassurances of cigarette safety, employees reported on the mounting evidence connecting smoking to cancer and other adverse health effects. A 1946 Lorillard chemist's letter revealed the company's awareness that scientists were reporting such links. In 1961, a consultant to Liggett reported that there were "biologically active materials present in cigarette tobacco" that were cancer causing, cancer promoting, poisonous, and "stimulating, pleasurable and flavorful."

The attorneys for the cigarette manufacturers focused their defense on three main points. Calling a number of medical experts to testify, the attorneys questioned what type of cancer killed Cipollone. The defense maintained that she suffered from atypical carcinoid, rather than small-cell carcinoma, the former a rare disease whose link to tobacco is not established and the latter a type of tumor common among chronic, heavy smokers. The defense also called advertising experts who testified that the only purpose of tobacco companies' advertisements was to persuade people who already smoked to switch brands, not to entice new people to take up the habit, as Edell had claimed. Finally, the attorneys for the defendants focused on Rose Cipollone's personality and her decision to smoke in the first place. The portrait painted for the jury was one of a well-read, intelligent, and decisive woman who made her own decisions. Sections of her deposition read into the record seemed to convince the jury that she enjoyed smoking even though she knew of the emerging links between smoking and cancer.

The jury received the case on June 7 along with seventy-two pages of specific instructions and the twenty specific questions required by the charges against the defendants. There were four basic claims to be considered against the tobacco companies: conspiracy, failure to warn users of known risks posed by products, fraudulent misrepresentation and concealment, and breach of an expressed warranty. Because Cipollone had not smoked cigarettes manufactured by the Philip Morris or Lorillard companies until after January 1, 1966 (when the required warnings first appeared), the failure to warn and expressed warranty claims were dismissed against those companies. Only Liggett faced the possibility of losing on all four claims.

In its verdicts, the jury rejected all the fraud, conspiracy, and concealment charges, thereby clearing Lorillard and Philip Morris completely. The Liggett Group was found to have breached its expressed warranties (implied by the "Play Safe" advertisements, among other things), and the jury also decided that the company should have warned customers of the possible health risks associated with its products before 1966. Although the jury decided that Liggett should pay damages to the Cipollone estate, it also found that Rose was personally responsible for 80 percent of her illness and fixed the award at $400,000.

The tobacco manufacturers appealed the verdict to the Third U.S. Circuit Court of Appeals in Philadelphia, Pennsylvania, which overturned the jury's award in 1990. The plaintiffs appealed that decision, and the U.S. Supreme Court reinstated the damage award in 1992.

Impact of Event

The immediate consequences of the jury's decision against the Liggett Group, in light of the small size of the award and the fact that it was overturned on appeal, seemed slight at first glance. The case, however, was profoundly important for a number of reasons. First, the judgment in favor of Rose Cipollone's estate was the first ever against a cigarette manufacturer for diseases caused by smoking. In prior cases, tobacco companies had deflected successfully any charge of responsibility for their customers' subsequent illnesses. Second, the fact that the jury held that advertising such as Liggett's, which suggested that its products were safe, constituted an implied warranty on cigarette safety and represented a major victory for the forces fighting the cigarette companies. Fifty cases similar to the Cipollone case were simultaneously pending in the federal courts, and the ruling significantly strengthened their chances for victory.

When the plaintiffs in the case announced their intention to appeal the ruling of the Third U.S. Circuit Court to the Supreme Court, the tobacco companies did not oppose the appeal. A broader and potentially even more dramatic threat to the cigarette makers existed in the state courts. Whereas Judge Sarokin and other federal judges held that the 1966 tobacco labeling requirement shielded companies from claims of damages caused after that date, a number of state courts held that the minimal warning did not provide a shield against such claims. The parties involved in similar cases looked to the U.S. Supreme Court to decide the shield issue once and for all. Should the decision go against the cigarette manufacturers, they would face the possibility of constant and financially ruinous litigation. Industry experts believed the cost of cigarettes would rise above the three-dollar-per-pack level if such a ruling were made. The Court announced in November, 1991, that the case was being held over. This may have indicated a four-to-four vote, with one vacant seat.

Moreover, the costs to the tobacco companies to fight the first lawsuits were quite high. In the *Cipollone* case alone, observers believed that the three companies named in the action spent at least $15 million on their defense, and that figure included none of the cost of appeals. The Cipollone estate's attorneys' fees were listed at slightly more than $2 million for the same period.

Finally, some experts believed that some of the tobacco industry documents that became public because of the trial could be used to mount a broad conspiracy suit against the cigarette manufacturers under the RICO (Racketeer Influenced and Corrupt Organizations) statutes. Although primarily designed for federal prosecution of organized crime, RICO permitted civil lawsuits against businesses or individuals who engaged in "a pattern of racketeering" through fraud and other acts. Although Cipollone failed to prove a conspiracy charge against the three companies originally, the standard of proof under a RICO action would be less severe. For an industry that is extremely conscious of its image, such a suit, even if wholly unsuccessful, could be extremely harmful. If such a case were to be successfully prosecuted, the tobacco companies, despite their size, wealth, and diversification, could be bankrupt and their assets seized because of the severe penalties provided for by the law.

Bibliography

Diehl, Harold S. *Tobacco and Your Health: The Smoking Controversy.* New York: McGraw-Hill, 1969. Somewhat dated. Valuable for the author's conviction and the strength of his argument, but occasionally limited by partiality. Suitable for the general reader. Glossary, index, and five appendices.

Goodin, Robert E. *No Smoking: The Ethical Issues.* Chicago: University of Chicago Press, 1989. A sometimes dense text. Goodin provides philosophical analyses of the ethical issues prompted by the existence of an industry whose product is, at the core, dangerous. He approaches smoking as a political issue that also contains a correct moral position. Contains an index and a comprehensive list of scientific studies.

Patterson, James T. "Smoking and Cancer." In *The Dread Disease: Cancer and Modern American Culture.* Cambridge, Mass.: Harvard University Press, 1987. This free-standing chapter is a scholarly study of cancer in American society. Examines the relationship between tobacco and cancer and reviews issues involved in cigarette advertising. Index and references.

Tollison, Robert D., ed. *Smoking and Society: Toward a More Balanced Assessment.* Lexington, Mass.: Lexington Books, 1986. The result of a conference addressing the relationship between smoking and society in 1984, this interdisciplinary and sometimes technical book examines the economic, health, psychological and social aspects of tobacco use. Its density and depth of information are valuable to readers in search of specific data. Fully indexed and referenced.

Troyer, Ronald J., and Gerald E. Markle. *Cigarettes: The Battle over Smoking.* New Brunswick, N.J.: Rutgers University Press, 1983. Focuses on the cultural evolution of smoking from immoral to socially sophisticated to deviant behavior. The powerful groups with vested interests trying to destigmatize smoking receive attention. Somewhat technical. Complete annotations and index.

E. A. Reed

Cross-References

The Pure Food and Drug Act and Meat Inspection Act Become Law (1906), p. 64; Congress Requires Cigarette Warning Labels (1966), p. 1338; Cigarette Advertising Is Banned from American Television and Radio (1970), p. 1527; A. H. Robins Must Compensate Women Injured by the Dalkon Shield (1987), p. 2342; Canada Passes the Tobacco Products Control Act (1988), p. 2376; The U.S. Surgeon General Reports on Tobacco and Health (1989), p. 2455.

ETHNIC UNREST BREAKS OUT IN
YUGOSLAVIAN PROVINCES

Category of event: Indigenous peoples' rights
Time: July-November, 1988
Locale: Yugoslavia

Centuries-old ethnic tensions and contemporary economic problems fueled political jockeying for position in the largest republic of Yuglosavia

Principal personages:
SLOBODAN MILOSEVIC (1941-   ), the president of the Serbian Republic and League of Communists, a Kosovar Serb catalyzing the unrest
RAIF DIZDAREVIC (1926-   ), the president of the Yugoslav state collective presidency; a Bosnian Muslim who resisted Milosevic
AZEM VLASI (1948-   ), a popular member of the Kosovar presidium
TITO (1892-1980), the postwar leader who created Yugoslavia's diffuse governmental structure and the autonomous Kosovo and Vojvodina provinces in Serbia

Summary of Event

Yugoslavia, the most clearly multiethnic state in East Central Europe, contains five major South Slavic groups: Serbs, Croats, Slovenes, Montenegrins, and Macedonians. It also contains more than a dozen non-Slavic groups, such as Albanians, Magyars, Turks, Czechs, Slovaks, Russians, Gypsies, Italians, Romanians, Vlachs, Poles, Germans, and Ruthenians. Hatred and discrimination among ethnic groups broke into open protests in 1988 among the Serbian, Albanian, and Montenegrin Yugoslavs. A chain reaction brought in nearly all other ethnic and nationalist groups and firmed federal republics' desires for independence.

Deep economic and political crises in Yugoslavia aggravated centuries-old ethnic tensions. Economic distress was largely a result of the country's political paralysis, which, in turn, derived from the decentralized political structure designed to accommodate the ethnic diversity. Leaders of the six republics and two autonomous provinces defended their own interests at the expense of Yugoslavia as a whole.

The tinder for the 1988 disturbances took the form of mutually exclusive Serbian and Albanian claims to authority in Kosovo. Serbs considered Kosovo their culture's cradle. There, in 1389, the Turks had defeated the Serbs and begun a domination of them that lasted into the mid-nineteenth century. Serbs believed that their numbers, traditions of statehood, and military prowess—particularly their participation on the Allied side in both world wars—entitled them to be at least first among equals in contemporary Yugoslavia. Instead, they argued, Tito had cheated them by establishing two autonomous provinces, Kosovo and Vojvodina, within Serbian territory.

On the other side were the Albanian Kosovars. They were the last Balkan people to acquire independence (in 1912). They formed a majority in Kosovo, an area that was part of Albania briefly during World War II. The Kosovars historically had been under Serbian control, though many believed Tito had promised that the region eventually could join Albania. Despite generous federal government spending in the region, Kosovar Albanians had high rates of unemployment and poverty. From later migrations and high Albanian birthrates (24.2 per thousand compared to 8.5 per thousand in Yugoslavia as a whole), the province by 1988 was nearly 90 percent populated by Muslim, non-Slav Albanians. Ethnic Albanians, then, claimed Kosovo on demographic grounds of majority rule. Serbs claimed it on historical grounds.

Serbian aspirations regarding Kosovo changed when Slobodan Milosevic became president of the Serbian League of Communists in May, 1986. Of Kosovar Serbian descent, he championed the Serbs when Kosovar Albanian police beat Serb demonstrators in his presence during a rally in April, 1987. He purged political opponents and dissenting voices in the Serbian mass news media and was elected president of the Socialist Republic of Serbia in May, 1987.

Milosevic found fertile soil for his appeals. Serbs had undergone political and cultural loss in the previous generation. The reformulated Yugoslavia after World War II had accorded Montenegro full republic status, though most Montenegrins considered themselves to be Serbs. Large numbers of Serbs were left in Croatia, Bosnia-Herzegovina, and Vojvodina. There they had no assured legal protection for their cultural, religious, or economic well-being. Serbs listed many ways their culture had been suppressed. The 1974 constitution, for example, permitted bureaucrats of other provinces to strengthen their statehoods at Serbia's expense. The names of centuries-old Serbian cultural institutions such as the Serbian National Theater in Novi Sad and the Serbian Cultural Center and Prosvjeta publishing house in Zagreb (Croatia) had been changed. The two million Serbians living outside Yugoslavia had no newspaper or other periodical oriented to them. In sum, the Serbian Academy of Sciences said, the religious, cultural, and political fate of Serbians had been better under the old Austro-Hungarian monarchy than it had in Yugoslavia.

Although Milosevic could not solve the Kosovo problem, he reunited many Serbians by working to undermine certain provisions of the 1974 constitution. Representatives of Vojvodina and Kosovo, which constituted one-third of the Serbian republic's territory, sat in the highest federal bodies and could veto any constitutional changes Serbia proposed. Inside Serbia, the two provinces' representatives could also veto Serbian legislation. Meanwhile, Serbia had no right to participate in the two provinces' assemblies. From late 1986 to early 1988, the Serbian government tried several ethnic Albanians for offenses ranging from membership in illegal separatist organizations to singing Albanian songs with alleged chauvinist sentiments, flying the Albanian flag, or giving children names expressing Albanian national identity. This Serbian attention was apparently driven by a belief that the separatists intended to create a Great Albania that would include Albania proper, Kosovo and parts of southern Serbia, western Macedonia, and southern Montenegro. Emigration by non-Albanians in the face of Albanian harassment was reported from all these areas.

The matchsticks in Kosovo in 1988 were, first, Serbian and Montenegrin claims that ethnic Kosovar Albanians were systematically harassing them out of the province through rapes, murders, and attacks on property, and second, Kosovar hopes of independent republic status. Unemployment running at 50 percent compounded the situation.

Beginning in July, hundreds of thousands of Serbs and Montenegrins demonstrated almost daily to protest Kosovo's purported mistreatment of minorities. The federal government sent a police unit to Kosovo to reinforce the federal paramilitary police unit there and gave the paramilitary police special powers. Serbians also campaigned to annex Kosovo and Vojodina into Greater Serbia. Vojvodina's leadership, although largely Serb, did not want to merge with Serbia. Kosovo's ethnic Albanian leadership also vehemently opposed annexation. In August, the collective state presidency announced that it was empowering its special federal police unit in Kosovo to maintain law and order. Serbian militia detachments deployed in Kosovar municipalities arrested dozens of alleged Albanian separatists.

In early October, some two hundred thousand nationalists staged protests in three Serbian cities. Approximately one hundred thousand protesters in Novi Sad, Vojvodina's capital, prompted the provincial party leadership to resign, a first for Yugoslavia. The party politburo, which had opposed joining Serbia, also resigned. In Titograd, Montenegro's capital, the interior minister ordered both local police and special antiriot and antiterrorist units (which included some federal militia personnel) to disperse crowds angered by suppression of students' public calls for multiparty elections. Riot police resorted to using clubs after repeatedly asking demonstrators to disperse. Rioters in Nikšic then attempted to get to Titograd to protest harsh methods the police had used. When a member of the Montenegrin League of Communists presidency could not calm the crowd, he resigned. Students initiated hunger strikes in Titograd and Nikšic. Disgruntled steelworkers and pro-Serbian nationalists were dispersed in Nikšic only after riot police used tear gas.

The president of the Yugoslav collective presidency, Raif Dizdarevic, a Bosnian Muslim, warned on October 9 that he would declare a state of emergency if the unrest did not stop. He conceded that the protesters grievances about the economy and about bureaucratic delay were justified, but he criticized Milosevic's inflaming of ethnic animosities. News reports said that army leaves were canceled and that reserves were being called up.

Other republics began reacting to the prospect of a Greater Serbia. Slovenia's party leadership on October 9 recommended using federal force to curb Serbian nationalist protests and warned against permitting Serbia to impose solutions, which would set a precedent that Slovenes would never accept. Croatia, which often allied with Slovenia, condemned Serbian nationals for pushing Yugoslavia toward violence and began independently buying arms from Hungary. Macedonia, Bosnia-Herzegovina, and Montenegro also criticized Serbian nationalism.

Next, the Serbian Communist Party tried to oust three top officials of Kosovo, including Azem Vlasi, perhaps the most popular Kosovar Albanian. The national party blocked the ouster, however, and went on to urge that senior state officials should no longer simultaneously hold party office. This setback for Milosevic triggered new demonstrations by the Serbs and Montenegrins in Kosovo, which caused resignations of Kosovo government officials. In response came the first major ethnic Albanian protests since 1981. Nearly one hundred thousand ethnic Albanian workers and students marched in Priština to the city's party headquarters to demand reinstatement of their leaders and Serbian respect for Kosovo's rights under the 1974 constitution.

In Belgrade, on November 19, a rally climaxed a series of protests organized in Serbian cities. Free transportation brought nearly one million Serbs to hear speeches in favor of proposed changes to the republic's constitution. Meanwhile, in Kosovo thousands of ethnic Albanians walked distances of up to fifty miles through rain and snow to attend demonstrations in Priština. Kosovo Albanians regarded Milosevic's constitutional amendments as an attempt to return Kosovo to colonial status. They denied that Serbians were being persecuted and claimed that the Slavs were leaving mainly for economic reasons. Finally, on November 23, the Kosovo provincial executive declared an immediate, indefinite ban on mass gatherings in Kosovo. Enough steam had escaped for the tempers to cool temporarily.

Impact of Event

Yugoslavia was forged in 1945 in the crucible of simultaneous war for national liberation and civil war. The country was created as a federation of six republics and two autonomous provinces headed by Tito. It was also a politically artificial attempt to quell centuries-old ethnic rivalries responding to the clarion call of self-determination.

National tendencies had been containable, generally, under four conditions: a strong leader, expanding prosperity, governmental legitimacy, and internal mutual security. All of these were coming apart by 1988. First, Tito died in 1980. Second, rising living standards were reversed shortly thereafter, and interethnic competition began for economic resources. Third, without Tito at the reins, the collective presidency was unable to undertake necessary market reforms. Consensus began eroding quickly. External respect for Yugoslavia diminished, as did much of the country's Soviet-opposing socialist self-image. Finally, several minorities began by 1988 to believe that their existence was endangered. Absence of Cold War anxieties within the great powers permitted the disturbances to occur without confrontational involvement in the civil strife. Yugoslavia's role as a strategic buffer between alliances was no longer essential.

Ethnic disturbances in Yugoslavia in 1988 moved beyond being local concerns, whether in Serbia or Macedonia, or assertions of self-determination, as in Croatia or Slovenia. The ways in which regional governments coped with ethnic protests and the growing inability of the federal government to address effectively either the regional tensions or the economic downturns set the stage in 1988 for friction among the republics. Given Yugoslavia's strategic position in the heart of the Balkans, widespread civil unrest inevitably spilled over into neighboring countries. The potential disintegration of Yugoslavia that the ethnic disruptions seemed to portend radiated unease about the future of human rights throughout the Balkans, even across the whole of Europe.

Milosevic advocated ending the interregional consensus rules adopted in the 1970's and urged other constitutional changes to dissolve the constitutional and political impasse frustrating Yugoslavia. Although he attacked opponents as bureaucrats, he sought a stronger federal government. Non-Serbians, however, rejected Milosevic's suggestions for reforms in Yugoslavia because they suspected Milosevic of scheming to expand Serbian sway and even to assimilate non-Serbs.

Milosevic, the leader of the League of Communists of Serbia, was behind the demonstrations and the annexation campaign. He was widely regarded as the most powerful figure in Yugoslavia outside the federal leadership. His hard-line Serbian nationalism appeared to endanger the fragile balances between Yugoslavia's many ethnic groups and between the central government and the republics. He actively resisted pressures for democratic reform and human rights.

Bibliography

Allcock, John B. "In Praise of Chauvinism: Rhetorics of Nationalism in Yugoslav Politics." *Third World Quarterly* 11 (October, 1989): 208-222. Since 1945, the author notes, the Communist leadership has tried to equate itself with unity and order while equating nationalist rhetoric with instability and divisiveness. Because Yugoslavs associated Communism with failure and because nationality meant different things in different republics, Yugoslavia had little unity language.

Biberaj, Elez. "Yugoslavia: A Continuing Crisis?" *Conflict Studies* 225 (October, 1989): 1-22. Examines two Yugoslav views of how to accommodate republics' and ethnic groups' interests: confederation, primarily supported by Slovenia and Croatia, with each unit enjoying full political autonomy, and increased centralization of federal government, supported by Serbia, with Serbia as senior partner.

Dragnich, Alex N. "The Rise and Fall of Yugoslavia: The Omen of the Upsurge of Serbian Nationalism." *East European Quarterly* 23 (June, 1989): 183-198. Serb protests gave vent to grievances that had been building since the 1981 Albanian riots. Since Serbian intellectuals preferred a Serb-dominated state over a "common" one, the 1988 Serbian outburst could be Yugoslavia's most important.

Kaplan, Robert D. "History's Cauldron." *The Atlantic Monthly* 264 (June, 1991): 93-103. Clear review of Balkan history, pivoting on Macedonia. Provides background on Serbian-Albanian tensions but argues that future competition among regional powers for sway in Macedonia will cause more torment than will other ethnic problems.

Larrabee, F. Stephen. "Long Memories and Short Fuses: Change and Instability in the Balkans." *International Security* 15 (Winter, 1990-1991): 58-91. Extensive notes. Argues that Yugoslavia's geopolitical integrity is essential for European security. Examines the array of ethnic groups pertinent to the stability of southeastern Europe. Notes the historical flashpoint of Macedonia and the contending claims of Greater Albania and Greater Serbia.

Magas, Branka. "Yugoslavia: The Spectre of Balkanization." *The New Left Review* 174 (March/April, 1989): 3-31. Uncompromisingly believes that Slobodan Milosevic opportunistically seized the Kosovo problem to impose renewed Serbian hegemony in Yugoslavia. The 1988 events made Milosevic a nationally known leader, the first since Tito.

Pipa, Arshi. "The Political Situation of the Albanians in Yugoslavia, with Particular Attention to the Kosovo Problem: A Critical Approach." *East European Quarterly* 23 (June, 1989): 159-181. Focuses on repression of ethnic Albanians in Serbia and Macedonia after the 1981 riots and Macedonian anxiety and Serbian outrage at appeals for a Kosovar republic. Criticizes Kosovars' intemperate nationalism but discounts assertions that Albanians persecute Serbs.

Rusinow, Dennison I. *The Other Albania: Kosovo, 1979.* 2 vols. Hanover, N.H.: American Universities Field Staff, 1980. Keen analyses of Kosovo instability. Pictures potential for violent irredentism on both sides before the 1981 and 1988 protests. Effectively portrays life, work, study, and politics in Yugoslavia's poorest province. Bibliography and index.

_____. "Yugoslavia: Balkan Breakup?" *Foreign Policy* 83 (Summer, 1991): 143-159. Knowledgeable analysis by a journalist resident in region for thirty years. Describes the interplay of major states' interests in the Balkans' ethnic stability that led to Yugoslavia's creation and how outside powers' inattention could hasten Yugoslavia's demise.

Kenneth L. Wise

Cross-References

A Hungarian Uprising Is Quelled by Soviet Military Forces (1956), p. 969; Basques Are Granted Home Rule but Continue to Fight for Independence (1980), p. 2079; Ethnic Riots Erupt in Armenia (1988), p. 2348; The Berlin Wall Falls (1989), p. 2523; Ceausescu Is Overthrown in Romania (1989), p. 2546; Albania Opens Its Borders to Foreign Nationals (1990), p. 2553; Yugoslav Army Shells Dubrovnik (1991), p. 2612.

CONGRESS FORMALLY APOLOGIZES
TO JAPANESE INTERNEES

Category of event: Atrocities and war crimes
Time: August 10, 1988
Locale: Washington, D.C.

In 1942, approximately 110,000 Americans of Japanese ancestry were interned by the United States government; in 1988, Congress apologized and paid reparations to the surviving internees

Principal personages:
WAYNE COLLINS (1912-   ), an attorney for the American Civil Liberties Union who kept the internees before the public via court cases
FRED KOREMATSU (1916-1986), one of the internees who challenged the internment order in the courts
MICHIKO NISHIURA WEGLYN (1926-   ), the individual who led the modern struggle for recognition of the wrong done to the Japanese-American community during World War II

Summary of Event

The Japanese attack on Pearl Harbor on December 7, 1941, not only brought the United States into World War II but also caused a tremendous outburst of prejudice and suspicion against persons of Japanese ancestry living in the United States. By law, Asian immigrants were barred from becoming naturalized U.S. citizens, although their children born in the United States were considered native-born citizens. The Japanese-American community, concentrated in the states of California, Washington, and Oregon, was made up of two basic groups: the issei, or noncitizen immigrants, some of whom had lived in the United States for many years, and the nisei, or native-born children of the immigrants.

In February, 1942, President Franklin D. Roosevelt issued Executive Order 9066, which allowed the United States Army to take whatever steps it considered necessary to protect strategic locations, even to the extent of removing civilians from areas deemed sensitive. In March, 1942, Congress passed Public Law 503, which gave further legal force to Roosevelt's order and which established the War Relocation Authority to handle the internment and to manage the camps, which were to be guarded by the Army. Under these two orders, evacuations of Japanese Americans began, eventually affecting approximately 110,000 people. Ten camps were established to house the evacuees: at Manzanar and Tule Lake, California; Poston and Gila, Arizona; Minidoba, Idaho; Heart Mountain, Wyoming; Granada, Colorado; Topaz, Utah, and Rohwer and Jerome, Arkansas.

Life in the camps was primitive. At the camps, an entire family or sometimes two families would be assigned an "apartment" of about twenty by twenty feet. Only minimal furniture was provided, and the first task for every family was to take the sacks of bed-ticking given them and stuff the sacks with straw to make mattresses. Food was provided in a mess hall, but the food was Army rations, which were difficult for infants to eat. Frank Kadowaki, one of the internees, remembered that "We were worried. We didn't know what our lives would be. We were surrounded by barbed wire, guards standing everyplace." This uncertainty was compounded by the fact that most families had sold all their possessions, including real estate, before going to the camps. The sellers received only a small fraction of the worth of their goods. Kadowaki described the process: "A lot of people had businesses and farms and they had to leave them. You couldn't take furniture. We just take spoon and fork. Can't even take cutting knife. During the war, burglar got in and stole everything we had left."

In 1940 and 1941, some five thousand nisei had been drafted into the United States Armed Forces. Many of these were discharged or assigned to routine duties after Pearl Harbor. Japanese Americans were declared to be ineligible for the draft in 1942, but protests from the nisei caused the Army to accept volunteers. In 1943, the 442d Regimental Combat Team was formed, and the Hawaii National Guard contributed the One Hundredth Infantry Battalion. Both these all-nisei units served in Europe. The 442d Regimental Combat Team became the most highly decorated combat unit in the history of the United States Army; its forty-five hundred members won more than eighteen thousand individual decorations for bravery, including one Congressional Medal of Honor and fifty-two Distinguished Service Crosses. Of course, many of the recipients of these awards lost their lives in winning the awards; the medals were presented to their parents, who were behind barbed wire under Army guard. During the entire war, there were no documented attempts at sabotage on the part of any Japanese American.

Immediately after World War II, Wayne Collins, a fiery lawyer dedicated to the defense of civil liberties, began to challenge the legality of the government's action in interning the Japanese Americans. He was especially active in the case of Fred Korematsu, a nisei who challenged the legality of the internment since it applied only to people of Japanese ancestry. Although they lost the case before the United States Supreme Court, Collins and Korematsu kept the issue before the public. Two other cases also provided a strong legal basis for further challenges to the treatment of the Japanese Americans. Gordon Hirabayashi and Minoru Yasui were arrested during the war for violating a curfew that applied only to persons of Japanese ancestry. Although the Supreme Court of the United States ruled unanimously that these arrests were legitimate, the idea was planted that racism and wartime hysteria were more the basis of the decision than were sound principles of constitutional law. By 1975, some progress was being made in redressing the Japanese-American grievances.

In 1975, President Gerald Ford issued a proclamation stating that the internment had been wrong. In 1980, Congress established the Commission on Wartime Relocation and Internment of Civilians to investigate the events of nearly forty years earlier and to interview survivors of the camps. By 1983, Fred Korematsu had had his conviction of failing to evacuate a restricted area overturned, and the congressional commission had reached findings whose conclusions were indicated by the title of the study: *Personal Justice Denied* (1983). Moreover, a class-action suit was pending in the courts seeking more than four billion dollars in reparations for Japanese Americans.

Against this background, in 1988 Congress began to debate the issue of paying reparations to the surviving internees. Some conservatives, such as Senator Jessie Helms (R-N.C.), argued that no payments should be made until the Japanese government made reparations for the attack on Pearl Harbor. It was pointed out, however, that those who were interned were not Japanese citizens but were mostly Americans of Japanese ancestry. Payments were not going to the Japanese government but to Americans who had been wronged by their own government. Syndicated columnist James Kilpatrick argued that in 1942, fears of a Japanese invasion were not unreasonable. In fact, immediately after Pearl Harbor the Japanese forces turned their attention to the Far East. By the end of December, 1941, General John DeWitt, military commander on the West Coast, had decided no invasion was likely. In May and June, 1942, the battles of the Coral Sea and Midway ended all possibility of a Japanese attack on the United States. The administration of President Ronald Reagan agreed with the sentiment of Representative Bill Frenzel (R-Minn.), who said, "It is time for an apology." Reagan stated, "No payment can make up for those lost years. What is most important in this bill has less to do with property than with honor. For here we admit wrong." On August 10, 1988, a bill became law offering a tax-free award of twenty thousand dollars to each survivor of the internment camps.

Impact of Event

The hostility, suspicion, and prejudice Asians had always faced in the United States contributed to the internment decision of 1942. There were some military considerations, and scrutiny of the issei would have been understandable, but as a group, Japanese Americans were not organized as political groups in the way people of German and Italian ancestry were. This made them all the more susceptible to abuse in a situation of war hysteria. There was also a public desire for revenge following the attack on Pearl Harbor. The passage of time made it clear that all these motives were wrong, however, and that clear historical understanding showed a debt was owed to Japanese Americans.

One proof of this debt was that the United States in 1942 acted against its own best information. The Federal Bureau of Investigation (FBI) had scrutinized the Japanese-American community for years and had noticed nothing disloyal or even alarming. A second proof was that people were singled out for internment based on their race alone. People were interned if they were only one-eighth Japanese by ancestry. There were no camps for German Americans despite the open support for Hitler displayed during the decade preceding the war by some German-American groups. Also, there were no internment camps in Hawaii, where there were many ethnic Japanese but where there was little prejudice.

The apology and the reparations were in line with the economic hardship suffered by Japanese Americans. The facts of this hardship have rarely been debated. The moral elements of the event have been more difficult to address. For decades before World War II, federal and state laws had denied citizenship to Japanese immigrants and had restricted their ownership of property. Japanese were viewed as isolated, devious, and impossible to assimilate. Indeed, the problems of assimilating immigrants of Asian ancestry would confront the United States throughout the twentieth century.

The attitude of the people affected by the apology and reparations is significant. One survivor stated that "we were among the few who knew what we were fighting for during World War II. We were fighting for our rights but also for our parents and our children. Our rights were not just threatened, they were not even recognized. The nation needs to recognize our loyalty." Another explained that "we had to rebuild not just our family economy, we had to rebuild our self-respect. What happened to us was like what happens to a woman who is raped. No amount of money can compensate but apologies would help the healing."

Others saw the impact of the reparations in a historical perspective. A child of internees commented, "This will be a fitting memorial for my parents; a memorial all Americans should be able to accept because this will be a memorial to freedom and democracy and human rights. When a right is taken away from one of us, it is taken from us all." Fred Korematsu summed up the meaning of the actions of the government perhaps best of all when he said, "No money can compensate but an apology is appropriate. The greatness of a country lies in how it treats the weak. An apology is one way of making sure this never happens to anyone ever again."

Bibliography

Bosworth, Allan R. *America's Concentration Camps.* New York: W. W. Norton, 1967. A good book for readers who want good information presented in a readable style. The author tells the story of the nisei by switching his viewpoint back and forth from the internment camps to the military units made up of nisei recruits.

Christgau, John. *"Enemies": World War II Alien Internment.* Ames: Iowa State University Press, 1985. This book deals with other ethnic groups and nationalities who were interned by the United States along with the Japanese Americans. The final section of the book deals exclusively with Japanese Americans. The book is well written, and each chapter tells a separate, complete story.

Collins, Donald E. *Native American Aliens.* Westport, Conn.: Greenwood Press, 1985. Although the overwhelming majority of Japanese Americans were loyal to the United States, about 7 percent, many of them naturalized, not native-born, citizens, chose to go back to Japan after the war. Few of these were motivated by disloyalty to the United States; most seem to have been overcome by the difficulties of life in the internment camps or to have been drawn back to Japan by family ties. This book tells the story of those who returned.

Gesensway, Deborah, and Mindy Roseman. *Beyond Words: Images from America's Concentration Camps.* Ithaca, N.Y.: Cornell University Press, 1987. Most histories of the experiences of Japanese Americans during World War II use words to recount their experiences. This book uses art. Many of the internees were artistically talented, and this book is a collection of paintings done by twenty-five such people. Brief selections from contemporary letters and documents accompany the pictures. In the case of this book, it is literally true that one picture is worth a thousand words. The bleak, crude, stark surroundings of the camps are highlighted by scenes of families carrying on with their lives as best they could under the circumstances.

Kikuchi, Charles. *The Kikuchi Diary: Chronicle from an American Concentration Camp.* Urbana: University of Illinois Press, 1973. This is an edited version of a diary kept by Charles Kikuchi from December 7, 1941, to August 31, 1942. During most of that time, the author and his family were interned at a race track in Southern California and lived in a converted horse stall. The book is especially articulate and shows a sophisticated use of irony.

Sundquist, Eric J. "The Japanese-American Internment: A Reappraisal." *The American Scholar* 65 (Autumn, 1988): 529-547. This well-written, thoughtful article allows a calm look at an emotion-laden subject. The pros and cons of the events of 1942 are discussed and a rationale presented as to why the apology and reparations were appropriate actions.

tenBroek, Jacobus, Edward Barnhart, and Floyd Matson. *Prejudice, War, and the Constitution.* Berkeley: University of California Press, 1975. A comprehensive analysis of the background, prejudices, wartime tensions, and government concerns that led to the internment of the Japanese Americans. The impact of the internment on civil rights is considered, and a good deal of discussion is devoted to how stereotypes about Asians contributed to the decisions made by the United States government.

Weglyn, Michi. *Years of Infamy: The Untold Story of America's Concentration Camps.* New York: William Morrow, 1976. This book is written by an internee who was sent as a teenager to the Gila Relocation Center in Arizona. It is not a personal reminiscence, however, but a thoroughly researched investigation into the official and quasilegal methods used by the United States to justify its actions toward the Japanese Americans. There is gripping material in this book.

Michael R. Bradley

Cross-References

Japan Protests Segregation of Japanese in California Schools (1906), p. 81; Japan Withdraws from the League of Nations (1933), p. 474; Nazi Concentration Camps Go into Operation (1933), p. 491; Japanese Troops Brutalize Chinese After the Capture of Nanjing (1937), p. 539; Roosevelt Approves Internment of Japanese Americans (1942), p. 595.

IRAQ'S GOVERNMENT USES POISON GAS
AGAINST KURDISH VILLAGERS

Categories of event: Atrocities and war crimes; racial and ethnic rights
Time: Late August, 1988
Locale: Kurdistan (northern Iraq and southeastern Turkey)

In August, 1988, Iraqi aircraft dropped lethal gases on Kurdish settlements in northern Iraq, killing thousands of Kurds and causing sixty thousand to flee into Turkey

Principal personages:
SADDAM HUSSEIN (1937-), the president of the Republic of Iraq during the gassing of the Kurds
TARIQ MIKHAYI AZIZ (1936-), Iraq's minister of foreign affairs
MASOUD BARZANI (c. 1935-), a leader of the Democratic Party of Kurdistan
SERBEST LEZGIN (c. 1940-), a local leader of Kurdish guerrilla forces, the *pesh merga*
RONALD REAGAN (1911-), the fortieth president of the United States (1981-1989), in office during Iraq's gassing of the Kurds; called for the resumption of chemical weapons manufacturing in the United States
GEORGE BUSH (1924-), the forty-first president of the United States; Ronald Reagan's vice president (1981-1989) who cast tie-breaking votes in the Senate to pass bills permitting the United States to resume manufacturing lethal gas
GEORGE SHULTZ (1920-), the U.S. secretary of state during the Reagan Administration; called for economic sanctions against Iraq
TURGUT OZAL (1927-), the prime minister of Turkey

Summary of Event

The Kurdish minority in the mountainous regions of northern Iraq, large portions of southeastern Turkey, parts of the southwestern Soviet Union, and Iraq's borders with Iran and Syria has sought autonomy since the early twentieth century. The European nations that signed the Treaty of Sèvres in 1920 did not honor a provision that granted autonomy to the Kurds. Rather, the former Ottoman Empire was divided among the five nations—Iraq, Iran, Turkey, Syria, and the Soviet Union—in which an estimated twenty million Kurds lived in the late 1980's.

The nations that became hosts to the Kurds sought to suppress their culture. The Kurdish language was not used in schools Kurdish children attended. Kurdish books and folk music were proscribed. Nevertheless, the Kurds represented a substantial percentage of the electorate, so national leaders were mindful that it was politically astute to cultivate members of the group. The gassing of Kurds by Saddam Hussein's forces in 1988 was not the first Iraqi attempt at Kurdish genocide. Similar attempts occurred in the 1960's. The 1988 incidents were a result of the Iran-Iraq War that raged from 1980 until 1988. In March, 1988, shortly before the war's end, Iranian forces swarmed across the border into Iraq and occupied Halabja, a largely Kurdish city.

Iraq had been using lethal gases—mainly cyanide, mustard gas, and nerve gas—against the human waves of infantry Iran was sending across its borders. Doing this violated the intent of the Geneva Protocol of 1925 forbidding chemical warfare. The United States and several European countries had been trying for years to broaden the provisions of this protocol to extend its prohibitions to the manufacture and storage of lethal gases. Although the United States was on record as opposing chemical warfare, under the Ronald Reagan Administration Vice President George Bush twice cast tie-breaking votes in the Senate that permitted the United States to resume the manufacture of such gases.

Although Bush was on record as opposing chemical warfare, the knowledge that the Soviet Union was developing gases caused the Reagan Administration to allow the resumption of production of poison gas, which had been halted in 1969 during the Richard Nixon Administration. Reports that Libya was greatly accelerating its production of lethal gases also caused the United States to act defensively.

Among the nations known to have chemical weapons in 1988 were the United States, the Soviet Union, France, and Iraq. The Central Intelligence Agency (CIA) believed that Burma, Cuba, Egypt, Ethiopia, Iran, Israel, Libya, North Korea, South Africa, South Korea, Syria, Taiwan, Thailand, and Vietnam had such weapons as well.

The use of lethal gases against the Iranians in occupied Halabja resulted in at least four thousand deaths, mostly among Kurdish inhabitants. The rebellious Kurd separatists were thorns in the sides of the Iraqis, so they did not look upon these deaths as losses of their own countrymen.

The Iraqis, amazingly, could not be called to account under the provisions of the Geneva Protocol because, in attacking Halabja, they were using lethal gases within their own borders. The gassing of the Kurds in this instance had to be regarded as an internal matter. Much of the world was horrified when it heard what had happened, but to interfere would have been to violate Iraq's sovereignty.

Not until some months later did Iraq do something that was deemed to violate the Geneva accord. On the morning of August 25, 1988, Iraqi warplanes dropped poison gas on the Kurdish town of Mesi in the mountains of northern Iraq, close to the Turkish frontier. This raid killed more than nine hundred people.

Among those who escaped across the border into Turkey were people who told stories of being exposed to a gas that smelled like rotting onions. They described how the gas burned their skin, eyes, and lungs, and how many people had collapsed, never to rise again. Those who escaped had sores that oozed. Their skin was scorched and badly discolored, and their hair fell out.

At about the same time, Iraqi warplanes dropped bombs armed with lethal gases on several other villages in the vicinity. In Butia, some people survived by drinking large quantities of milk, which absorbed some of the poison, and by running. More than sixty thousand Kurdish refugees poured over the border into Turkey. Refugee camps were set up, even though Turkey, which was dependent upon Iraq for its oil and did $2.4 billion in annual trade with the country, rejected the call for a United Nations inquiry into the gassing, saying that its own investigation, involving forty doctors and 205 other health officials, had uncovered no evidence of chemical warfare in northern Iraq.

The Iraqis, who denied officially that they were gassing the Kurds, were, in effect, punishing those who sided with Iran during the Iran-Iraq war. They sought to annihilate the Kurdish guerrillas, the *pesh merga*—literally "those who face death"—and the Kurdish nationalists who struggled for the establishment of an independent Kurdistan.

Despite Iraqi protestations of innocence, Iraq's foreign minister, Tariq Aziz, in 1986 told a group of United States congresspeople that Iraq's continued existence was being threatened. He said that if Iraq possessed nuclear weapons, it would surely unleash them against its enemies. Chemical weapons have been called the nuclear weapons of the poor.

The Kurds, a non-Arab Muslim people, constituted almost a fifth of Iraq's population of seventeen million. Masoud Barzani, a leader in the Democratic Party of Kurdistan, and Jellal Talibani, a leader in the Patriotic Union of Kurdistan, officially accused the Hussein government of practicing genocide against the Kurds in Iraq, an accusation the Western world believed.

With the gassing of the Kurdish villages, U.S. secretary of state George Shultz called for immediate action. Within hours, the U.S. Senate voted economic sanctions against Iraq. The Senate also became more amenable to pressing for a worldwide ban on the manufacture and stockpiling of chemical weapons, although the idea met with resistance from those who realized that such a ban was virtually unenforceable, since chemical weapons could be made easily from readily available materials.

Meanwhile, the Iraqi government offered amnesty to the nearly sixty thousand Kurds who had fled from Iraq. These Kurds had to decide by October, 1988, whether to return to their homeland or to risk being stateless. Knowing that because of their support of Iran during the war the government in Baghdad regarded them as traitors, Kurds suspected the amnesty offer, which attracted few takers.

The leader of the Kurdish guerrillas, Serbest Lezgin, said that he would return with his men only under orders from Kurdistan's separatist leaders. Meanwhile, Turkish prime minister Turgut Ozal, who faced election on September 25, 1988, wanted the matter settled. He needed the votes of Turkish Kurds, yet he could not risk offending Iraq by speaking openly of the atrocities that had caused hordes of refugees to flee into his country. His silence on that issue agitated his Kurdish constituency, weakening his chance of reelection.

Impact of Event

An obvious issue that arose from Iraq's gassing of the Kurds was whether a large, discrete ethnic minority had the right to self-determination. The Kurdish case was complicated by the fact that five nations—Iraq, Iran, Turkey, Syria, and the Soviet Union—were involved. A further complication was that an amalgamation of Kurds from those five nations would have resulted in a nation of some twenty million people, creating a sovereign entity with a considerably greater population than Iraq and more than twice the population of Syria.

Given the agitation that had characterized the Kurds for much of the twentieth century, the countries that would have been affected by allowing self-determination became understandably nervous. The resulting nation likely would have been stronger than Iran, which had been weakened considerably by war from 1980 until 1988. The Soviet Union, although much larger than the resulting autonomous Kurdish nation might be, had its own problems with separatist movements and would not have welcomed Kurdish independence. Turkey, with a large and widespread group of Kurds living within its borders, stood to lose territory and population if autonomy were granted.

On the other hand, the Kurds, particularly those in Iraq, suffered such incredible atrocities that it was clear that Iraq had renewed its efforts at genocide against them. For those Kurds, it was hardly overstating the case to say that autonomy appeared to be synonymous with survival.

That genocide occurred in northern Iraq was evident to Western governments. For various reasons, however, they did not rush to condemn Iraq. France remained circumspect, condemning chemical warfare but, despite the evidence, not accusing Iraq categorically of using it. Iraq still owed France several billion dollars for armaments it had bought from the French during the Iran-Iraq war. The British held back because they did not wish to give the appearance of marshaling their prestige against Iraq, an act that might have been construed as siding with Iran to enlist its help in gaining the release of British hostages held in Lebanon.

An important economic factor that inhibited the expression of Western outrage against Iraq's aggression was the expectation of Britain, France, and Italy that they would be beneficiaries in the reconstruction of Iraq after its eight-year war with Iran. Several Arab countries—Egypt, Saudi Arabia, and Jordan—supported Iraq because they considered any threat to that nation's sovereignty as a threat to their own.

Because the problems the Kurds faced did not lend themselves to simple solutions, they could be expected to continue well into the future. The Gulf War of 1991 resulted in Iraq's losing some of the support it received from other countries after the gassing of the Kurds in 1988, but the political situation remained sufficiently complex that the Kurds' future remained in doubt.

Bibliography

Karsh, Efraim. *Saddam Hussein: A Political Biography.* New York: Free Press, 1991. Although this book, one of a spate of books about Saddam Hussein and the war occasioned by his invasion of Kuwait in 1990, focuses largely on that conflict, it provides detailed information about Iraqi persecution of the Kurds and enumerates Hussein's political need for pursuing such tactics. Good bibliography and comprehensive index.

Khalil, Samir. *Republic of Fear: The Politics of Modern Iraq.* Berkeley: University of California Press, 1989. Khalil's analysis of the Kurdish situation is intelligent and balanced. This book shows the political development of a provincial leader whose hold on power is tenuous at best. The historical framework within which Khalil places the Saddam Hussein regime is indispensable to those who desire a deep understanding of his administration. Well documented; useful and comprehensive index.

McLeod, Scott. "The Cries of the Kurds." *Time* 135 (September 19, 1988): 33. Among the earlier articles to report the Iraqi raids on Kurdish villages in the northern, mountainous part of the country, this report provides details about how many people were affected by the atrocity and tells of the establishment of a Turkish refugee camp in Ortaköy capable of accommodating seven thousand people. Tells about George Shultz's protest to the Iraqi foreign affairs minister.

Marshall, Eliot. "Chemical Genocide in Iraq?" *Science* 241 (September 30, 1988): 1752. This article offers substantiation of the claim that Iraq had a chemical weapons plant that a West German firm helped build. It enumerates the economic sanctions imposed on Iraq by the United States after the gassing of the Kurds. Although the article is brief, it offers important specifics.

Smolowe, Jill. "Where Is the Outrage?" *Time* 135 (September 19, 1988): 36. Deals with the political complexities that caused some Arab nations to side with Iraq when news of the gassing of the Kurds became public and that caused some Western nations to attempt to remain neutral or at least noncondemnatory in the matter. Details economic reasons why right occasionally cannot triumph over human rights violations as egregious as this one. Nations are not free agents and often ignore ugly realities to protect their financial interests.

Watson, Russell, with John Barry. "Letting the Genie Out of the Bottle." *Newsweek* 113 (September 19, 1991): 30-31. Offers valuable information about the worldwide manufacture and stockpiling of chemical weapons. Identifies types of gas used against the Kurds. Recounts Secretary of State George Shultz's efforts to invoke some of the provisions of "Nuremberg law" to hit Iraq with charges of crimes against humanity. Points to the loophole in the Geneva Protocol of 1925 that made Iraq not subject to its provisions in its gassing of Kurds in Halabja in March, 1988.

R. Baird Shuman

Cross-References

Legal Norms of Behavior in Warfare Formulated by the Hague Conference (1907), p. 92; Germany First Uses Lethal Chemical Weapons on the Western Front (1915),

p. 161; The United Nations Adopts a Convention on the Crime of Genocide (1948), p. 783; The Iraqi Government Promotes Genocide of Kurds (1960's), p. 1050; Khomeini Uses Executions to Establish a New Order in Iran (1979), p. 2013; Iraq Invades and Ravages Kuwait (1990), p. 2600.

BENAZIR BHUTTO BECOMES THE FIRST WOMAN ELECTED TO LEAD A MUSLIM COUNTRY

Categories of event: Women's rights and political freedom
Time: November, 1988
Locale: Pakistan

For the first time since the seventh century A.D., *when the prophet Muhammad founded Islam, a woman was elected to be the legal and formal head of government in a predominantly Muslim country*

Principal personages:

BENAZIR BHUTTO (1953-   ), the daughter of Zulfikar Ali Bhutto and prime minister of Pakistan (1988-1990)

ZULFIKAR ALI BHUTTO (1928-1979), the founder of the Pakistan People's Party and president of Pakistan (1972-1977)

MOHAMMAD ZIA UL-HAQ (1924-1988), the chief of the army staff, chief martial law administrator, and president of Pakistan (1977-1988)

GHULAM ISHAQ KHAN (1915-   ), the president of Pakistan elected in 1989

NUSRAT BHUTTO (1934-   ), the wife of Zulfikar Ali Bhutto and nominal leader of the Pakistan People's Party after his death

Summary of Event

Pakistan is a very new country, having been created in 1947 as a result of the partition of the British Indian Empire. The movement to establish the country, which began in the late nineteenth century, was predicated upon the demand for a separate homeland for the Muslims of the Indian subcontinent. Accordingly, Islam was from the beginning a decisive force in the development of Pakistan's political institutions and practices. Islam was not the only factor shaping Pakistan's politics. Another significant influence was the legacy of Western civilization implanted over two centuries of rule by the British.

Pakistan was thus confronted with two powerful forces which were not always in harmony. On one hand, Islam imparted a strong spiritual foundation to the way people thought, interacted with each other, and were to be treated in the larger social and political contexts. In juxtaposition to this were the Western traditions of, among other things, secularism and democratic decision making.

In Islam, the totality of life is encompassed by spiritual commitment. Governments in Islamic countries may draw distinctions between religion and the law of the state, but to the Muslim, such distinctions have little significance. In Islamic societies, people are more likely to be guided by duty and obligation, as determined by religious forces, than by the pursuit or exercise of rights. In relations between men and women, for example, women can expect protection, an obligation of men rather than a right of women.

The British political legacy included, among other things, the notion that as far as political influence is concerned, all people are more or less equal. Basic political decisions should be made by a broadly representative body. The legal system should be neutral and dispassionate, with a goal of equal justice. Individuals enjoy fundamental rights which should be vigorously protected against abuse by government.

Efforts to wed the system of Islamic philosophical and spiritual requirements to the practical political and institutional experiences of the British period proved very frustrating for Pakistan. Martial law was imposed first in 1958 and then again in 1969, in both cases after the failure of constitutional government. The greatest catastrophe occurred in 1971, when the country was dismembered by the secession of its eastern portion, which became Bangladesh. Martial law was imposed for a third time.

A new government and a new constitution emerged out of this bitter experience and held out the promise of a more open and democratic political environment for Pakistanis. After some initial success in popularizing government, Zulfikar Ali Bhutto's Pakistan People's Party began to experience substantial opposition, especially from conservative political interests representing the traditional landed aristocracy and the Ulema, or Islamic clergy. Bhutto attempted to neutralize opposition by such measures as prohibition of alcoholic beverages and closing of nightclubs.

This was not enough. In 1977, Bhutto's elected government was dismissed by the military on the grounds that political instability in the country required temporary establishment of martial law. The commander of the army and chief martial law administrator, General Zia ul-Haq, promised that elections would be held on schedule or soon thereafter and that civilian rule would be restored. Ten years later, this had still not come to pass. People with large landholdings or financial resources thrived during this period, but others fared less well. The working class and professionals, such as lawyers and physicians, were particularly disenchanted with military rule.

There was more to the situation than Zia's concern for maintaining political order, however. He had his own agenda, which called for the Islamization of virtually every aspect of Pakistani society. An immediate worry for the general and his associates was the probability that an election would return Zulfikar Ali Bhutto to power. Bhutto's Pakistan People's Party (PPP) was the most popular and influential political party in the country. Even after Zia had Bhutto executed, Bhutto remained a powerful political force, since in death he became a martyr and symbol of antigovernment sentiment.

After Bhutto's death, the leadership of the PPP fell, nominally at least, to his widow, Nusrat Bhutto. She was, however, in poor health and not politically skilled. The dominant role in party affairs, therefore, was played by Bhutto's daughter Benazir. Zulfikar Bhutto did have sons, but they had opted for violent action against the government, preventing them from participating directly in the political process. During the decade-long period of martial law, the PPP and all opposition groups and politicians were harassed and persecuted by the military government. Many opposition leaders spent considerable time in jail or under house arrest, including Benazir Bhutto.

Resistance to the military rule of General Zia continued to manifest itself in various ways. Several opposition parties banded together in the mid 1980's to form the Movement for the Restoration of Democracy (MRD). The composition of the MRD reflected a wide spectrum of political opinion ranging from conservative religious organizations to parties advocating socialism. It was held together by hostility toward Zia and his government. Under the leadership of Benazir Bhutto and the PPP, open and direct opposition to Zia often took the form of public demonstrations, sometimes of a fairly violent nature. The efforts of MRD, however, were not successful in forcing changes in government policy or in effecting the removal of General Zia.

By 1988, the confrontation between the political opposition and the government of General Zia had reached a stalemate. Pakistan was faced with political gridlock. Zia's Islamization program was going nowhere, his efforts to promote political change were manifestly self-serving, and the political opposition was becoming more frustrated and restive. The situation was changed on August 17, 1988, when a plane crash took the lives of General Zia, the American ambassador, and several American and Pakistani generals.

Following the accident, the machinery of government moved with surprising dispatch. The president of the senate, Ghulam Ishaq Khan, was next in line of authority. He appointed Benazir Bhutto, as the leader of the largest political force, as acting head of government. Elections were held in November which confirmed Bhutto and the PPP, making Benazir Bhutto not only one of the few women heads of government, elected or otherwise, but the first ever chosen by popular election in a Muslim country.

Benazir's tenure in office was stormy from the beginning. The coalition involved in the opposition movement against the Zia government disintegrated. Many former allies of the PPP began vigorously opposing it. The opposition enjoyed considerable success in frustrating Bhutto's efforts. Provincial governments in Punjab, Baluchistan, and North-west Frontier Province showed an independence of mind, refusing to take directions from the central government. The political right, as allies of General Zia and supporters of his Islamization program, refused to accept the idea of a woman running the political affairs of the country. Benazir Bhutto was also embarrassed by the behavior of her husband, who seemed indifferent to public opinion. Her government was handicapped by its own ineptitude. It was never able to come up with a legislative agenda and enacted no important legislation.

Serious problems of civil disorder and violence continued to occur, especially in the major port city of Karachi, which suggested to those unsympathetic to the government that, once again, the country was out of control. In the end, Benazir Bhutto and her government were brought down by the same man, Ishaq Khan, who had installed her. As president, replacing Zia ul-Haq, Ishaq Khan announced that Bhutto's government had demonstrated it was incapable of governing. Bhutto was formally removed from office by order of the president on August 6, 1990. Ishaq Khan then asked opposition parties to form an interim government until new elections could be held. Elections were held on October 24, 1990, and the PPP suffered a serious defeat. Relegated to opposition status, with political power in the hands of their enemies, Bhutto and the PPP found themselves facing charges of corruption and misuse of office.

Impact of Event

Pakistan apparently has matured since its creation. Judicial processes are more independent and less in service to political power, and the military, at least as of 1991, seems content to remain on the sidelines. Benazir Bhutto's removal from office was endorsed by popular vote, so there was no sense that there had been a violation of the public trust. Those unsympathetic to the Bhutto family and the PPP, finding themselves in power, issued calls for investigations into official corruption during the previous government. Bhutto's husband was jailed briefly but she, and most PPP officials, avoided persecution and continued to be politically active. The spirit of Islamization was as strong as ever, however, and the new government under Nawaz Sharif announced the establishment of the Sharia, or Islamic law, as the highest law of the land.

The elevation of Benazir Bhutto to the prime ministership of Pakistan is an important milestone in the evolution of the political rights of women, but the substantive significance of this event should not be exaggerated. Her election does not indicate a significant change in the pattern of male-dominated politics or dramatic improvement in the lot of women in Pakistan in particular or the Muslim world in general. Benazir Bhutto came to office because of her link to her martyred and highly popular father and the sudden (and fortuitous) death of General Zia.

Benazir Bhutto's experience fits a pattern found in other South Asian countries. On several occasions women have occupied high political office, but in each case they have inherited political leadership roles from their fathers or husbands. The first and most significant was Indira Gandhi, who benefited from the fact that her father was Jawaharlal Nehru, the towering figure in Indian politics following independence in 1947. In Sri Lanka and Bangladesh, the women who were chosen to lead their governments were in both instances wives of former government leaders. Bangladesh became the second Muslim country with a woman leader.

During her brief tenure in office, Benazir Bhutto's government did little to reverse the pattern of arbitrary political authority that has characterized Pakistan since its inception. Human rights conditions in a broad sense were better because the military withdrew from active governance. For a brief period, the fact that a woman occupied the prime minister's chair, a woman whose own politics reflected a liberal cast of mind, resulted in an environment in which authoritarian and religious fundamentalist values were less in evidence. In the long run, Benazir Bhutto had little enduring impact on the specific question of women's rights, which were retrenched under renewed Islamization efforts of the successor government. Specifically, Islamization calls for the fullest implementation of Islamic laws and traditions as they govern all aspects of life. As concerns human rights, Islamic law accords to women a socially inferior status to that of men. For example, strict adherence to tradition demands that two women are required to bear witness in legal proceedings whereas only one man is required.

Advancing the cause of human rights in Third World countries such as Pakistan requires changes in social customs and mores. Indira Gandhi was able to sustain a lengthy and effective political career because of her ability to project herself as a symbol of mother India. Other women, such as Benazir Bhutto, have a much more tenuous grasp on political power and are not likely to remain in office long. Improving human rights in general and rights of women in particular is likely to be a slow process.

Bibliography

Burki, Shahid Javed. "Pakistan Under Zia, 1977-88." *Asian Survey* 28 (October, 1988): 1082-1100. This is a favorable assessment of Zia's impact on the political and economic development of Pakistan.

Hayes, Louis D. "From Confrontation to Accommodation." *Asian Thought and Society* 15 (October, 1990): 298-308. The departure of General Zia introduced a period of political development in Pakistan marked by greater institutional effectiveness than had generally been the case in the past. This article suggests a maturing of the political process and concludes that the failure of the Benazir Bhutto government does not suggest a reversion to type.

_____. "Islamization and Education in Pakistan." *Asia Pacific Community* 27 (Winter, 1984): 96-105. A detailed description and evaluation of Zia's Islamization reforms and their impact on education. Specific reference is made to the consequences of these reforms for women's education. Reforms would have reduced opportunities and created separate institutions for women from primary through university education.

_____. *The Struggle for Legitimacy in Pakistan.* Boulder, Colo.: Westview Press, 1984. This is a general survey of Pakistan's efforts to establish political institutions that are accepted as legitimate by politicians and citizens alike. The fate of leaders such as Zulfikar Ali Bhutto is testimony to the difficulty of this struggle.

Kurin, Richard. "Islamization in Pakistan: A View from the Countryside." *Asian Survey* 25 (August, 1985): 852-862. Zia's Islamization program is seen as largely irrelevant in the context of the daily lives of rural people, who believed that they were good Muslims already and did not need government programs to assist them.

Weiss, Anita M. "Benazir Bhutto and the Future of Women in Pakistan." *Asian Survey* 30 (May, 1990): 433-445. Written while Bhutto was still in office, this is an evaluation of her efforts to enhance the status of women by relaxing some of the restrictions imposed by Zia and by strengthening government programs for women.

_____. "Women's Position in Pakistan: Sociocultural Effects of Islamization." *Asian Survey* 25 (August, 1985): 863-880. An assessment of the impact of the government's programs to change Pakistan's institutions to make them conform to Islam. These efforts are seen as the result of a combination of factors: a response to traditional political forces, an effort to sustain a feudal economy, and government's ignorance of women's role in society.

Louis D. Hayes

Cross-References

The Muslim League Attempts to Protect Minority Interests in India (1906), p. 87; India Gains Independence (1947), p. 731; Conflicts in Pakistan Lead to the Secession of Bangladesh (1971), p. 1611; Zia Establishes Martial Law in Pakistan (1977), p. 1898; Zulfikar Ali Bhutto Is Hanged Despite Pleas from World Leaders (1979), p. 2018.

NAMIBIA IS LIBERATED FROM
SOUTH AFRICAN CONTROL

Categories of event: Political freedom and indigenous peoples' rights
Time: December 22, 1988
Locale: United Nations, New York City

On December 22, 1988, the Namibian people secured a plan for independence that ended more than one hundred years of colonial domination and paved the way for black majority rule

Principal personages:
SAM NUJOMA (1929-   ), the president of the South West Africa People's Organization
JOSÉ EDUARDO DOS SANTOS (1942-   ), the president of Angola
FIDEL CASTRO (1926-   ), the premier of Cuba
FREDERIK W. DE KLERK (1936-   ), the president of South Africa
CHESTER CROCKER (1941-   ), the U.S. undersecretary of state for African affairs

Summary of Event

On December 22, 1988, Angola, Cuba, and South Africa met at the United Nations for the final signing ceremony of a complex regional agreement that included a Namibian independence plan. Chester Crocker, undersecretary of state for African affairs of the United States, played an important mediating role in this historic compromise, although many observers were critical of the terms Crocker negotiated.

Germany had ruled the area now known as Namibia (then called South West Africa) from 1884 to 1914. South Africa captured the territory from Germany and dominated it for seventy-three years, beginning in 1915 (officially since 1921). During this time, the political and economic rights of the Namibian people, the black majority, were denied.

Prior to European conquest of this southwest African territory, various ethnic groups, mainly the Ovambo, the Nama, the Herero, the Damara, the San, the Kavango, and the Tswana, lived in the area. The Germans, who claimed most of Namibia except for Walvis Bay, Namibia's only deep sea port, had to fight and kill large numbers of Nama and Herero in order to establish their claim of 1884. In 1915, during World War I, South Africa invaded, taking the area from the Germans. In the years that followed, South Africa, too, had to use force to stop the rebellions of African Namibians who resisted South African claims to rule the country.

For a short time, the international community recognized the right of South Africa to govern South West Africa. Like other countries with mandates to govern under the jurisdiction of the League of Nations, however, South Africa was instructed to convert its governance of the mandate territory to a United Nations trust territory governed in preparation for independence. South Africa refused to govern the country as a trust and began to consolidate its control of all territory affairs.

Most African trust territories assumed statehood in the early 1960's. The territory's African allies argued that South Africa's introduction of apartheid into Namibia was a violation of the principles of the United Nations charter. The South Africans not only introduced racially discriminatory labor and living laws but also created the Native Nations Act, which created so-called "homelands" for each ethnic group and attempted to prevent all Africans in the territory from uniting as a single group. On October 27, 1966, the United Nations General Assembly adopted a resolution that revoked South Africa's mandate because of maladministration.

In 1967, the United Nations appointed an eleven-person Council for South West Africa to administer the territory, which it renamed Namibia. On June 21, 1971, the International Court of Justice declared South Africa an illegal presence in Namibia and ruled that South Africa should withdraw from Namibia immediately. The court's finding, in part, spurred a new round of Namibian resistance. Church organizations circulated petitions, workers embarked on a general strike, and the South African government responded by detaining and torturing hundreds. The full number of those executed is unknown. The South West Africa People's Organization (SWAPO), whose members fought internally and in exile to liberate their country, helped to organize the 1971 resistance.

In 1957, a group of migrant workers had formed the Ovamboland People's Congress (OPC) to address workers' issues such as discrimination in job salaries, hiring, promotion, and working conditions. The Ovambo are the largest ethnic group in Namibia. (Exact population numbers of any Namibian group are unknown, because prior to independence there was no national census.) In 1960, the OPC was renamed the South West Africa People's Organization (SWAPO). SWAPO was constituted to fight South African racist policies and external control of Namibia, although it continued to fight for workers' rights. Peaceful protests against South Africa often ended in deaths and injuries. By 1963, SWAPO leaders, living in exile, were committed to armed struggle to free their country. Sam Nujoma headed the organization and traveled the globe to obtain support for the freedom struggle in Namibia. SWAPO became Namibia's internationally recognized government-in-exile.

South Africa's efforts to counter indigenous support for SWAPO throughout the years of illegal occupation of Namibia prompted a multitude of reports of human rights violations. The reported violations included torture, assassinations, mass murder, imprisonment in cramped and squalid conditions, administration of depressant drugs and electric shocks, intimidation, harassment, denial of civil liberties, and economic disruptions. South Africa even used fighter bombers against the Nama to enforce subjugation. The governing Namibian authorities also attempted coercion through the education system. The school curriculum for those few black children allowed access to an (inadequate) education was a vehicle for discrediting SWAPO and building support for South African colonialism.

One of the most feared tools of the South African government was the paramilitary Koevoet (sometimes referred to as Takki Squads or Etango). Koevoet was renowned for its unrestrained use of terror against any village or individual it targeted. Beatings, torture, robbery, rape, and murder were part of its daily tool kit. This three-thousand-member unit, trained in brutality, for years inflicted arbitrary terror on the Namibian population. It demanded a role in the election process and postindependence police force before it would honor the regional settlement negotiated on December 22, 1988. Neither the South African government nor the United States government would act forcefully to eliminate Koevoet's role in the 1988 independence process.

Namibia's economic rights were also violated during its long colonial history. Despite proclamations by the international community that all transnational corporate (TNC) operations in Namibia were illegal, some TNCs continued to extract the mineral wealth of Namibia. Moreover, under Southern African jurisdiction, TNCs were never forced to establish or maintain codes of conduct for their black workers. In addition to exporting Namibia's physical resource base, TNCs did little to develop Namibia's human resource base.

The regional package signed in December, 1988, linked Namibia's fate to the actions of others in neighboring states. According to the package, if the Angolans agreed to various conditions (such as requesting Cuban troops to leave Angola), then the Namibians could have independence elections. This infuriated many Namibians. To the relief of many, however, the regional agreement's terms for Namibia were based on U.N. Security Resolution 435, adopted in 1978. In accordance with this resolution, the United Nations oversaw the election process leading to independence for Namibia, which was achieved on March 21, 1990. The South Africans would have preferred to install their own government or at least to conduct the elections.

Impact of Event

Independent Namibians designed one of the most democratic constitutions in the world. Following the elections of the negotiated independence agreement, the victorious representatives from the competing political parties formed a constitutional convention and quickly wrote a new constitution. After public discussion and some modification, the constitution was approved. The Namibian constitution guaranteed the human and political rights of all Namibians "regardless of race, colour, ethnic origin, sex, religion, creed or social or economic status." Apartheid laws and any other practices of racial discrimination were made illegal. The Namibian constitution offered women the opportunity, rare in Africa, to use their national constitution to claim equal rights with men. Police squads were eliminated and external donors helped to train a professional civilian police force and military. In 1991, the government was in the process of drafting a labor code respectful of the rights of workers as well as owners.

Namibia's new legal system guaranteed due process and a speedy trial. Competing newspapers published daily and were free to criticize the government. Affirmative action programs for black Africans and women were implemented to bring qualified individuals from these categories of people into the government and the private sector and to give them access to education. English was declared the official language. Afrikaans, the colonial language of South Africa, was available in the schools only as an elective.

Sam Nujoma, the former head of SWAPO, was elected Namibia's first president. The president's term of office was set at five years, with a two-term limit. Namibian political power was distributed by the constitution among the president, the National Assembly, the prime minister, the cabinet, the Supreme Court, and regional officials (scheduled to be elected in 1992).

Bibliography

Africa Contemporary Record, 1968-   . The chapter on Namibia in each of the annual editions provides a useful overview of the country's changing political and economic affairs. Any library with a good African collection should own this annual, which is often the initial research source consulted by students of African affairs.

Baker, Pauline. "United States Policy in Southern Africa." *Current History* 86 (May, 1987): 193-195, 225-227. Baker provides an insightful look at the Reagan Administration's foreign policy initiatives and programs in the South African arena, including Namibia. Her analysis includes attention to the multiple avenues for foreign policy conduct, including foreign aid, funding of destabilizing rebel groups, the use of U.N. Security Council vetoes, and coordination of multiple state relations in the region.

Green, Pipa. "Cutting 'The Wire': Labor Control and Worker Resistance in Namibia." *Association of Concerned Africa Scholars Bulletin* 22 (Winter, 1987): 27-36. This is a terse but rich piece on trade union movements and worker-state relations in Namibia shortly before independence.

Landis, Elizabeth S. *Namibian Liberation: Self-Determination, Law, and Politics.* New York: Episcopal Churchmen for South Africa, 1982. Landis, an attorney and former senior political officer in the Office of the United Nations Commissioner for Namibia, provides a historical overview of Namibia's quest for liberation that is clearly sympathetic to SWAPO's struggle and provides details often neglected in other accounts.

Rotberg, Robert I. "Namibia and the Crisis in Constructive Engagement." In *Africa Crisis Areas and U.S. Foreign Policy*, edited by Gerald J. Bender, James S. Coleman, and Richard Sklar. Los Angeles: University of California Press, 1985. Rotberg provides a balanced view of the Reagan Administration's Southern African regional policies and their consequences for Namibia. This piece was published before the negotiated settlement and therefore reflects the perspectives held by many analysts before the historic compromise was concluded.

Seidman, Ann. *The Roots of Crisis in Southern Africa.* Trenton, N.J.: Africa World Press, 1985. Seidman's prose is clear and efficient in presenting the complexities of domestic and international politics and economics of the countries in the Southern African region, including Namibia. Seidman demonstrates that the Namibian economy and the political struggle surrounding that country largely are a result of South African and U.S. foreign policies in the region. The book is especially useful in considering multinational corporation activities in Namibia and the possibilities for regional relations in a postindependence Namibia.

Singini, Richard E. *Namibia: A Summary of Facts and Figures, Vol. 1, No. 2.* Lusaka, Zambia: United Nations Institute for Namibia, 1984. This compilation of facts and figures for many sectors of Namibian society (education, mining, employment, population, and housing) provides excellent baseline data (mostly 1981 statistics) for understanding Namibia in its final phase of colonial occupation.

UN Chronicle 26 (March, 1989). This issue of the *UN Chronicle* is devoted to the agreement on Namibia. It notes the specifics of the complex regional agreement that included independence for Namibia and identifies the tasks facing the United Nations civil servants responsible for implementing elections and the process of Namibian independence. No political analysis of the regional agreement is offered. An abbreviated chronology of Namibia's road to independence is also included.

United Nations. *Namibia: A Unique UN Responsibility.* New York: United Nations Department of Information, 1983. This thirty-eight-page booklet and map offers a wide-ranging introductory view of the involvement of the United Nations in the path to Namibia's independence.

Eve N. Sandberg

Cross-References

The League of Nations Is Established (1919), p. 270; The Atlantic Charter Declares a Postwar Right of Self-Determination (1941), p. 584; South Africa Begins a System of Separate Development (1951), p. 861; The Organization of African Unity Is Founded (1963), p. 1194; The United Nations Imposes an Arms Embargo on South Africa (1977), p. 1937; The United Nations Issues a Declaration on South Africa (1979), p. 2008.

AMNESTY INTERNATIONAL EXPOSES THE CRUELTY OF THE DEATH PENALTY

Category of event: Prisoners' rights
Time: 1989
Locale: London, England

Pursuing its campaign against capital punishment, Amnesty International published When the State Kills, *advocating total abolition of the death penalty and reporting on one hundred governments' use of it*

Principal personages:
>RANDALL DALE ADAMS, the U.S. death row inmate released after the documentary film, *The Thin Blue Line,* revealed his erroneous conviction
>CHRISTIAN BRODA (1916-   ), the former minister of justice of Austria, the architect of the 1983 Sixth Protocol to the European Convention on Human Rights abolishing the death penalty
>THOMAS HAMMARBERG (1942-   ), the Executive Committee chair during Amnesty International's 1977 international conference in Stockholm on the abolition of the death penalty

Summary of Event

When the State Kills . . . The Death Penalty: A Human Rights Issue (1989) revealed the ancient legacy of Amnesty International's worldwide campaign against the death penalty by citing the earliest recorded parliamentary opposition, Diodotus' claim in 427 B.C. Greece that execution was not an effective deterrent. Sixteenth century critics of capital punishment objected to the widespread penalties of burning, beheading, hanging, and drawing and quartering that were imposed for more than two hundred offenses. Preindustrial societies in the Middle Ages substituted banishment or mutilation for execution, and the first prisons opened in the sixteenth century.

Reformers such as Jeremy Bentham successfully worked to reduce the number of capital offenses in England to four by 1861. In 1863, Venezuela became the first country to abolish the death penalty. The Netherlands ended capital punishment for most crimes in 1870, Sweden for all crimes in 1921, and the United Kingdom in 1965. Executions in the United States declined from 1,666 in the 1930's to 191 in the 1960's, before the Supreme Court halted all use of capital punishment from 1972 to 1976.

In an attempt to become more humanitarian, the United States was the only country to introduce electrocution, poison gas, and lethal injection as methods of execution. The Amnesty report, however, showed that all methods of premeditated state killing resemble unacceptably barbaric torture:

If hanging a woman by her arms until she experiences excruciating pain is rightly condemned as torture, how does one describe hanging her by the neck until she is dead? If administering 100 volts of electricity to the most sensitive parts of a man's body evokes disgust, what is the appropriate reaction to the administration of 2,000 volts to his body in order to kill him? If a pistol held to the head or a chemical substance injected to cause protracted suffering are clearly instruments of torture, how should they be defined when used to kill by shooting or lethal injection?

Malfunctioning electric chairs in the United States have caused head coverings to catch fire, have prolonged suffering, and have resulted in one failure that required postponement until a second execution date. Saudi Arabia conducted public executions, using a sharp sword to behead religious offenders or medium sized stones to kill those convicted of sexual crimes.

After 1948, developing international human rights law progressively imposed greater restrictions on judicially imposed executions. Article 3 of the Universal Declaration of Human Rights affirmed the right to life, and the 1949 Geneva Conventions circumscribed military punishments in wartime. The International Covenant on Civil and Political Rights draft Article 6 limited the death penalty to only the most serious crimes. Article 4 of the American Convention on Human Rights forbade the extension of capital punishment to crimes for which it was not imposed at the time as well as reestablishment of the death penalty in states that abolish it. Both conventions also prohibited execution of pregnant women and those below the age of eighteen at the time of their offense. Pressed by Sweden and Austria, the United Nations began collecting data and publishing reports. The General Assembly resolved that the number of capital offenses should be progressively restricted and affirmed the desirability of abolishing capital punishment in all countries.

Nearly forty states nevertheless continued to execute for crimes other than murder—Iran and Saudi Arabia for adultery, China for embezzlement and pornography, seven governments for rape, fourteen for robbery or armed robbery, and seven for drug trafficking. Twelve U.S. states had sentenced more than twenty-five young prisoners to death, and three of these were executed for offenses committed when they were below eighteen years of age.

Internationally mandated rules of fair criminal procedure did not eliminate arbitrary executions or completely protect the innocent. Governments prosecuted unrepresented defendants in secret proceedings of specially created courts with partisan judges from whose decisions there was no appeal. "In Turkey, for example," the Amnesty report states, "death sentences have been imposed after mass trials (with sometimes more than 1,000 defendants). . . . In one such trial in 1986 the judge ruled that confessions extracted under torture could be used in evidence." Summary execution immediately after trial renders meaningless any right to petition for clemency when unstable new governments, as in Liberia, hasten to eliminate potential rivals for power. Despite the extensive procedural guarantees and opportunities for appeal in U.S. courts, researchers discovered 350 miscarriages of justice in capital cases since 1900, resulting in at least twenty-three erroneous executions.

Founded in 1961, Amnesty International (AI) initially worked primarily on behalf of prisoners of conscience—individuals imprisoned for nonviolent political activity—and, as a second mandate, on behalf of all torture victims. In 1977, the year it won the Nobel Peace Prize, AI convened an International Conference in Stockholm which led in 1979 to publication of *The Death Penalty*, a handbook for the first global campaign against capital punishment. Thereafter, Amnesty actively opposed all executions, even of individuals convicted for violent offenses.

To publicize executions as human rights violations, AI began collecting and annually reporting the number of death sentences imposed and the number of individuals executed. The AI research provided a more complete record than did the U.N. secretary-general's periodic reports, based on surveys returned by fewer than one-third of the more than one hundred retentionist governments. Nevertheless, AI could record only a fraction of the executions actually conducted, since many went unreported or unacknowledged. During the 1980's, as many as sixty-seven countries imposed death sentences in a single year, and between thirty and forty-four governments were known to have conducted executions each year. The number of known executions in any given year ranged from a low of 769 to a high of 3,278, but there were certainly many more unacknowledged and unreported death sentences carried out by China, Iran, and other countries.

Abolitionists took heart, however, when on the average one government each year discontinued executions after 1976. European states led the way, first in national law and then in 1983 by adding Protocol 6 to the European Convention on Human Rights. The Council of Europe awarded its Human Rights Prize to Dr. Christian Broda, former minister of justice of Austria and architect of the Sixth Protocol. A similar protocol abolishing capital punishment was proposed for the American Human Rights Convention.

Thirty-seven states in the United States, however, reinstituted the death penalty. More than two thousand prisoners were soon sentenced to death, and frequent executions in four southern states raised the U.S. rate to eighteen per year. AI published a book-length attack on death penalty sentencing in the United States, attempting to counter the growing popularity of capital punishment. Conclusive evidence demonstrated that race, poverty, and mental retardation significantly affected the selection of those condemned to die. The Supreme Court, however, rejected statistical proof of racial disparities in affirming a highly questionable death penalty from Georgia. In other cases, new evidence led to the release of wrongly condemned individuals, including Randall Adams, the subject of *The Thin Blue Line*, a film documenting the criminal justice system's failure.

AI also singled out for special campaigns the governments with the highest execution rates: China, Nigeria, and Iran. Despite worldwide appeals for clemency, Pakistan's military government executed former Prime Minister Zulfikar Ali Bhutto in 1979. Following her 1988 election as prime minister, Bhutto's daughter Benazir arranged commutation of all remaining death sentences to life imprisonment.

AI also worked for new international human rights standards that would curtail use of the death penalty. At the United Nations, Amnesty supported procedural safeguards promulgated by the Economic and Social Council (ECOSOC) in 1984. The guidelines directed governments to provide fair trials, the right of appeal to a higher court, and opportunities to request clemency. The nonbinding ECOSOC safeguards also prohibited retroactive application of the death penalty and precluded execution of the insane. Throughout the 1980's, AI lobbied along with other nongovernmental organizations for an optional protocol to the International Covenant on Civil and Political Rights that would oblige ratifying governments to abolish capital punishment.

Ten years following its first campaign against the death penalty, AI launched another global abolition effort in 1989. *When the State Kills . . . The Death Penalty: A Human Rights Issue* presented the most compelling arguments and evidence against executions before surveying the law and practice in 180 countries. The nine-month campaign highlighted forty-one target countries with public opinion research, a week of actions against executions, specially produced videos, marches, vigils, letter writing, petitions, and resolutions by AI members and groups. More than one hundred leaders from twenty-six countries made public statements appealing for an end to executions. A former Nigerian chief judge, the mother of an American murder victim, and a number of academic and medical experts conducted lecture tours.

Impact of Event

Because there are so many allies in the campaign for abolition of the death penalty, there is no way to gauge AI's separate impact on revised norms, the fluctuating rate of executions, and shifting public opinion. New governments in Romania and Hungary which abolished the death penalty may have been reacting against communism rather than responding to AI's appeals. Could public opinion and political officials in the United States have become any more eager to extend the death penalty if AI had not campaigned in vain for abolition?

While not claiming credit, AI has enthusiastically noted continued progress on the legal front. In 1990, seven more countries became totally abolitionist. One more abolished the death penalty for ordinary crimes, two instituted moratoriums on executions, and two abolitionist governments defeated attempts to reintroduce capital punishment. By 1991, nearly half the countries of the world had abolished capital punishment either in law (forty-four totally, seventeen for ordinary crimes) or in practice (twenty-five with no executions for more than a decade). Ninety countries retained and used the death penalty. From 1976 to 1990, thirty-one countries abolished the death penalty, an average of more than one per year. After years of sustaining one of the highest rates of executions, South Africa instituted a moratorium, and the Soviet Union reexamined its practice.

Some major countries, such as the United States and China, however, moved against the trend. The U.S. Supreme Court limited death row inmates' right to habeas corpus appeals in federal court, reversed a recent precedent to allow victim impact statements, and authorized execution of the mentally retarded and those who committed offenses at ages as young as sixteen. The U.S. Congress extended capital punishment to noncapital offenses and also curtailed inmates' right to federal habeas corpus relief. After subjecting Democratic opponent Michael Dukakis to embarrassment for his coddling of dangerous criminals, President George Bush sought the death penalty for thirty-seven more federal offenses. Public opinion polls revealed broad support for capital punishment; gubernatorial candidates and legislators sought votes by proclaiming their commitment to swift and certain execution for heinous offenders.

AI could nevertheless find consolation in the successful quest for an international convention abolishing the death penalty. In 1990, the U.N. General Assembly opened for signature an optional protocol to the International Covenant on Civil and Political Rights that would abolish the death penalty in ratifying states. In addition, ECOSOC expressed concern about government practices incompatible with the 1984 procedural safeguards. While calling for improved implementation, ECOSOC also recommended further guidelines—the adequate assistance of counsel at all stages, mandatory appeals, a maximum age beyond which a defendant could not be executed, and elimination of the death penalty for the mentally retarded. The U.N. Sub-Commission on Prevention of Discrimination and Protection of Minorities also appealed to member states to stop using the death penalty against people under the age of eighteen. The General Assembly of the Organization of American States adopted for ratification a protocol to abolish the death penalty to the American Convention on Human Rights. The 1990 Eighth U.N. Congress on the Prevention of Crime and Treatment of Offenders, however, failed to adopt a resolution inviting retentionist countries to consider establishing a three-year moratorium on executions.

AI reported that despite the improved legal situation, in practice there were 2,229 known executions in thirty-four countries and at least 2,826 death sentences imposed in sixty-two countries during the 1989 campaign year. In the following year, AI learned that at least twenty-six countries had executed 2,029 prisoners and fifty-four governments had sentenced 2,009 to death. Whatever the ultimate impact of AI's second death penalty campaign, abolitionists will almost certainly need a third global effort to complete the task.

Bibliography

Amnesty International. *The Death Penalty*. London: Amnesty International Publications, 1979. Published after Amnesty's 1977 Stockholm Conference calling for abolition. Summarizes prevailing international law on the death penalty and provides country surveys of law and practice.

_____. *United States of America: The Death Penalty*. London: Amnesty International Publications, 1987. A thorough historical review and indictment of capital punishment in the United States. Details racial disparities; execution of the innocent, juveniles, and the mentally retarded; and procedural inequities. Highly readable account of prevailing national law, as interpreted by the U.S. Supreme

Court, and international standards prior to 1987.

Bedau, Hugo Adam, and Michael L. Radelet. "Miscarriages of Justice in Potentially Capital Cases." *Stanford Law Review* 40 (November, 1987): 21-179. The authors report on 350 erroneous convictions since 1900 in the United States, identifying 23 individuals mistakenly executed for crimes they did not commit and 22 other innocents reprieved at the last moment. Meticulously researched, the work demonstrates conclusively that procedural safeguards cannot eliminate the risk of erroneous convictions.

Gray, Ian, and Moira Stanley. *A Punishment in Search of a Crime: Americans Speak Out Against the Death Penalty.* New York: Avon Books, 1989. This collection of forty-two statements against capital punishment includes effective testimony by prison wardens, prosecutors, and victims' family members whose surprising views were personally affected by their direct participation in the criminal justice system. In combination with the passionate objections voiced by successful defense counsel, abolitionists, religious leaders, and the wrongly condemned, the interviews provided Amnesty International U.S.A. with a compelling brief for the general reader.

Gross, Samuel R., and Robert Mauro. *Death and Discrimination: Racial Disparities in Capital Sentencing.* Boston: Northeastern University Press, 1989. A methodologically sophisticated analysis revealing the undeniable institutional racism affecting death penalty decisions. While acknowledging the statistical patterns revealed by social scientists, the U.S. Supreme Court has nevertheless insisted that defendants prove intentional discriminatory conduct in their own trials.

Hood, Roger. *The Death Penalty: A World-wide Perspective.* Oxford, England: Clarendon Press, 1989. The third in a series of reports to the United Nations Committee on Crime Prevention and Control, and the most valuable. The author frankly acknowledges the inadequacy of government replies to U.N. Secretariat questionnaires and relies instead on the comparatively less fragmentary research by nongovernmental organizations and scholars. Refreshingly frank, for a U.N. document, in discussing governments which have disregarded international safeguards in conducting arbitrary executions.

Rodley, Nigel. *The Treatment of Prisoners Under International Law.* Oxford, England: Clarendon Press, 1986. Includes a section on capital punishment within a systematic overview of international procedural guarantees for criminal defendants. Within five years of publication, the work became dated as a result of optional protocols banning capital punishment that were added to the European Human Rights Convention and to the International Covenant on Civil and Political Rights.

Howard Tolley, Jr.

Cross-References

Capital Punishment Is Abolished in Sweden (1921), p. 345; The United Nations

HUNGARY ADOPTS A MULTIPARTY SYSTEM

Category of event: Political freedom
Time: 1989
Locale: Budapest, Hungary

In 1989, as part of the new political movements sweeping East Central Europe, Hungary began to develop a multiparty system

Principal personages:

MIKHAIL GORBACHEV (1931-   ), the Soviet leader who permitted greater political freedom in Eastern Europe

KAROLY GROSZ (1930-   ), one of the last Communist leaders of Hungary, whose power was reduced in the summer of 1989

IMRE POZSGAY, a liberal Communist leader of Hungary who was promoted to the Politburo in May, 1988

JOZSEF ANTALL (1932-   ), a member of the Hungarian (Magyar) Democratic Forum and prime minister of Hungary

IMRE NAGY (1896-1958), the leader of the Hungarian Revolution of 1956, rehabilitated posthumously in 1989

JANOS KADAR (1912-1989), the leader of the Hungarian Communist Party for many years; carried out limited reforms

ARPAD GONCZ (1922-   ), the president of Hungary beginning in 1990

Summary of Event

Mikhail Gorbachev's policies of *glasnost* (openness) and *perestroika* (restructuring) had wide-reaching effects throughout East Central Europe. Among the countries that responded to the new liberalization in the Soviet Union with its own drive for liberalization was Hungary. Hungary had long been one of the leaders of change among the socialist states, but most of the change had centered on the economy. In 1989, political change came to the foreground, as new political groups and movements began to challenge the ruling Communist elite in Hungary. Although the Hungarian Workers Socialist Party (HWSP), the Communist Party, was more liberal than most other East European communist parties and had taken the initiative in introducing economic change and limited political reform, the party was seen as the cornerstone of a hated regime and so came under attack in 1989.

In May, 1988, Janos Kadar, the Communist Party general secretary in power since late 1956, was replaced by Karoly Grosz. Kadar was given the honorary title of party chair. A year later, in May, 1989, Kadar was removed as president of Hungary and released from the Central Committee. Kadar was the first casualty in the party's campaign to change its image and respond to mounting public criticism. Although Kadar had permitted liberalization of the economy and, in later years, even of the political system, he remained the symbol of the betrayal of the 1956 Revolution. Indeed, a few days before Kadar's retirement, Radio Budapest broadcast a speech by

Imre Nagy, the leader of the Revolution of 1956. A month later, on June 16, Imre Nagy was reburied with full honors in Budapest, and in July was fully rehabilitated, shortly after the death of Kadar.

Hungary had planted the seeds of a multiparty system in the mid-1980's. As early as 1985, 10 percent of the seats in the Hungarian parliament were held by independents, which was quite unusual for an East European state. A multiparty system began to develop in 1988, but the majority of parties were formed in 1989. In late 1988, Grosz and others working with him, especially Imre Pozsgay, were moving toward a more liberal regime that would permit the right of association, thus allowing other political parties to exist. The first formal opposition group was the Hungarian Democratic Forum, established in September, 1988. It and other groups were formed even before the formal legislation allowing them was passed. Not all parties were new. Some were resurrected from the period before World War II, such as the Smallholders and the Social Democrats. Between late 1988 and 1990, fifty-two parties were born. This may appear extraordinary, but was not atypical of Eastern Europe, where the desire to express one's political perspective was strong after decades without the right of political association.

Social ferment characterized Hungarian politics in 1989. Initially, it appeared that the HWSP, which had initiated many of the reforms in response to popular pressure, would be among the few communist parties to survive in Eastern Europe. The party moved boldly yet cautiously in its reforms, mindful of the Soviet invasion of 1956. When at last the leaders were certain that the Soviet Union would not intervene, it may have been too late. The new political groups grasped the initiative of change from liberal Communists such as Pozsgay, who was regarded as the Hungarian Gorbachev.

The opposition groups quickly gained strength, and as early as June, 1989, there was talk of multiparty elections in Hungary. New electoral laws were passed, and plans were made for elections in 1990. Initially, there were fears that the Communists, who had been important in the reform movement, would not tolerate electoral defeat. The process of accepting political competition accelerated as the months passed. In June, 1989, the Communist regime began a series of roundtable discussions with the opposition parties. Present at the meetings were liberals and conservatives, and those both for and against the present regime. Somewhat comparable to the roundtable discussions held in Poland, these were a first step in recognizing the existence of opposition groups. Also in June, the HWSP formed a collective leadership which included Karoly Grosz, Imre Pozsgay, Miklos Nemeth, and Rezso Nyers, thus effectively reducing Grosz's power in favor of the other three more liberal Communists. In October, 1989, the HWSP renamed itself the Hungarian Socialist Party. This was a somewhat futile attempt to distance itself from its communist heritage. It was probably a sign, too, that the Communists accepted the inevitability of multiparty elections in the near future and were preparing a new image for the polls. As part of the mounting changes, the country itself was renamed the Republic of Hungary (instead of the People's Republic of Hungary) in late 1989.

The two strongest parties that emerged from the fifty-two formed in 1988-1989 were the moderate Hungarian (Magyar) Democratic Forum (MDF) and the more liberal Alliance of Free Democrats (SDS), both of which were major contenders for power. Jozsef Antall, the leader of the Hungarian Democratic Forum, and Arpad Goncz, the founder of the Alliance of Free Democrats, emerged as two of the most important political leaders in the multiparty spectrum. Parliamentary elections were held in March and April, 1990. The clear victor in the two rounds of elections was the MDF, in coalition with the Smallholders and the Christian Democrats. Together they obtained 60 percent of the seats in the new democratically elected parliament. The SDS and its allied parties became the democratic opposition. Antall, the head of the MDF, was selected as prime minister. In July, 1990, Goncz, the elderly leader of the Alliance of Free Democrats, was elected president of the republic, a largely ceremonial post.

Although both the MDF and SDS were reform parties, they were different in approach and orientation. The SDS wanted rapid transformation toward a free market economy. The MDF moved more slowly and cautiously, fearful that rapid privatization might result in severe economic dislocation. About 40 percent of Hungary's population was living at, or below, the poverty level, and rapid change was thought to endanger an even larger segment of the population.

Impact of Event

The rise of a multiparty system in Hungary was part of the larger picture of Hungary's greater political freedom and increased independence from the Soviet Union. Hungary under Janos Kadar had been one of the more independent Eastern European states, while remaining part of the Soviet network in Eastern Europe. The events of 1989 allowed Hungary at last to become fully independent from the Soviet Union, a process attempted unsuccessfully in the 1956 Revolution.

The disintegration of the HWSP (Communist Party) was especially noteworthy, because in Hungary it was the HWSP that had sanctioned moderate reforms for some time. From the people's perpective, the Communist-led reforms were too little, too late. The people wanted freedom in all areas, which was not possible under Communist Party rule.

The emergence of the multiparty system is one of the success stories in the renaissance of Eastern and Central Europe. Seldom has a multiparty system emerged so quickly and been able to stage meaningful elections. In the Soviet Union, for example, the development of a multiparty system proceeded much more slowly. Hungary, however, is a small country, a significant portion of whose population is concentrated in the capital, Budapest.

Those who applauded the rise of the multiparty system also cautioned that the pace of reform had slowed after 1990. Hungary was inclined toward Western Europe but was handicapped by the legacy of an "eastern" (that is, communist-style) political and economic system. Hungary had already sought greater cooperation with Western Europe, especially Austria and Germany. Aspirations for a Western-style democracy with a smooth and efficient economy had so far outpaced reality. Overwhelming economic problems and a weak political and economic infrastructure represented alarming obstacles to reform. Hungary's people were disappointed that the transition was neither swift nor easy. The transformation of the economic system appeared to be a protracted struggle that could have the unintended consequence of further impoverishing a significant part of the population. Despite foreign economic aid, progress was slow. Hungary had a huge annual deficit and a large foreign debt. Inflation took its toll on personal savings, as in other Eastern European countries, and people were exhausted from the strain of working two jobs to make ends meet.

Some of the political winds of freedom had negative overtones, including strong nationalism and anti-Semitism. Because ethnic and religious tensions among the states of East Central Europe were already strong, Hungarian patriotism contained the seeds of international and internal discord. An issue that defied resolution was the status of the Hungarian minority living in Romania, people who endured great hardship and discrimination under Nicolae Ceausescu's regime. Although the Hungarian government was outspoken in its support of the rights of Hungarians living in Romania, it stopped short of offering them the free right to emigrate to Hungary, a country already struggling to provide a better standard of living for its people.

Most of the states of East Central Europe, Hungary included, hoped that their political changes would provide a miracle cure. The cure, although remarkable, was far short of miraculous and popular discontent was evident, especially in the low voter turnout that characterized the several opportunities Hungarians were offered to go to the polls during 1990. Thus, although they were noteworthy human rights achievements, the rise of the multiparty system and greater political freedom had not succeeded, in their first several years, in solving Hungary's myriad problems or engaging the loyalty and enthusiasm of the population, who remained politically disenchanted after years of unmet Communist promises.

Bibliography

Brown, J. F. *Surge to Freedom: The End of Communist Rule in Eastern Europe.* Durham, N.C.: Duke University Press, 1991. Brown is one of the preeminent specialists on Eastern Europe. This work contains a chapter on Hungary since 1956, with special attention to the developments in 1989.

Echikson, William. "Bloc Buster." *World Monitor* 2 (June, 1989): 29-35. In this article, the reader can trace the emerging democratic movement in Hungary and the fears expressed by Communists. The article focuses especially on Imre Pozsgay, the most liberal of the Communist leaders, who predicted that a multiparty system would develop.

Gati, Charles. *The Bloc That Failed.* Bloomington: Indiana University Press, 1990. In this work, Gati traces the gradual disintegration of the East European bloc. It is a general work on Eastern Europe, but there is considerable material on Hungary because of Gati's strong interest in, and knowledge of, Hungary.

Pataki, Judith. "Major Political Change and Economic Stagnation." *Report on East-*

ern Europe, 1990: Democracy in the Year One 2 (January 4, 1991): 20-24. In this Radio Free Europe report, Pataki gives an overview of Hungary's problems. It is a detailed, well-written, and gloomy description of Hungary's prospects. Especially noteworthy is her attention to low voter turnout in the several elections and referenda held during 1990, an indication of popular apathy.

_____. "New Government Prefers Cautious Change." *Report on Eastern Europe: Toward Democracy in Eastern Europe* 1 (July 13, 1990): 20-24. In this report, Pataki traces the policies of the new coalition government in Hungary, headed by the MDF and its allies.

Prins, Gwyn, ed. *Spring in Winter: The 1989 Revolutions.* Manchester, England: Manchester University Press, 1991. This interesting book of essays about developments in Eastern Europe in 1989 has an essay by Elemer Hankiss on Hungary. An excellent appendix by Sarah Humphrey chronicles major events of 1989 in each East European country.

Reisch, Alfred. "Hungary in 1989: A Country in Transition." *Report on Eastern Europe, 1989: A Year of Upheaval* 1 (January 5, 1990): 19-23. In this Radio Free Europe analysis, Reisch chronicles the developments in Hungary in 1989. The whole volume provides a good overview of Eastern Europe in 1989.

Rothschild, Joseph. *Return to Diversity: A Political History of East Central Europe Since World War II.* New York: Oxford University Press, 1989. This general history of Eastern Europe since 1945 contains considerable material on Hungary that will provided useful background for the student trying to understand the context of the events of 1989.

Simons, Thomas W., Jr. *Eastern Europe in the Postwar World.* New York: St. Martin's Press, 1991. Simons presents a highly readable history of events leading up to 1989 in Eastern Europe and presents a postscript of future possibilities. This work provides a good background for understanding the events of 1989.

Volgyes, Ivan. "For Want of Another Horse: Hungary in 1990." *Current History* 89 (December, 1990): 421-422, 433-435. Volgyes, an East European specialist, examines events in Hungary in 1990, including the parliamentary elections in which all fifty-two parties participated. He evaluates the strengths and weaknesses of Hungary. This article is strongly recommended for further reading on the problems of reform in contemporary Hungary.

Norma C. Noonan

Cross-References

A Hungarian Uprising Is Quelled by Soviet Military Forces (1956), p. 969; The Brezhnev Doctrine Bans Act of Independence in Soviet Satellites (1968), p. 1408; Gorbachev Initiates a Policy of *Glasnost* (1985), p. 2249; Solidarity Regains Legal Status in Poland (1989), p. 2477; Poland Forms a Non-Communist Government (1989), p. 2500; The Berlin Wall Falls (1989), p. 2523; Ceausescu Is Overthrown in Romania (1989), p. 2546; Soviet Troops Withdraw from Czechoslovakia (1990), p. 2570; Lithuania Declares Its Independence from the Soviet Union (1990), p. 2577.

KASHMIR SEPARATISTS DEMAND
AN END TO INDIAN RULE

Category of event: Indigenous peoples' rights
Time: 1989
Locale: Kashmir, India

The Kashmir separatist movement drew attention to the rights of the Kashmiri people to determine their own political allegiances

Principal personages:

SHEIKH MOHAMMAD ABDULLAH (1905-1982), the secular leader of Kashmir who unremittingly fought for the freedom of Kashmir within the Indian federation

JAWAHARLAL NEHRU (1889-1964), the first prime minister of independent India

RAJIV GANDHI (1944-1991), the grandson of Jawaharlal Nehru and prime minister of India (1984-1989)

FAROOQ ABDULLAH (1937-   ), the chief minister and prime minister of Jammu and Kashmir who resigned at the appointment of Jaganmohan as the governor of Jammu and Kashmir

JAGANMOHAN, the governor of Jammu and Kashmir, known for toughness in administration

MOHAMMAD FAROOQ, the religious leader of Kashmir, known for his harsh criticism of India's human rights violations in Kashmir

VISHWANATH PRATAP SINGH (1931-   ), the prime minister of India for a short time during the separatist movement, who resigned because of the difficulty of maintaining a coalition

BENAZIR BHUTTO (1953-   ), the first female prime minister of Pakistan as well as the first female head of state of an Islamic country

ROBERT M. GATES (1943-   ), a special envoy of the president of the United States sent to help India and Pakistan solve the Kashmir problem

Summary of Event

The physical beauty of the Kashmir region has been so peacefully integrated with the spirit of its people that, traditionally, they seemed to have lived in a nearly perfect autonomous world of their own, although the region lacks the minimal homogeneity that is crucial to a harmonious life. The line of its rulership has been equally heterogeneous: The Hindus ruled it until the fourteenth century, and the Muslims took over from them for the following five centuries. In 1819, the Sikhs started their rule, giving in to the British in 1846. The British later sold Kashmir to the Hindu maharajah, consequently reducing its autonomy to that of an independent satellite princely state functioning along with five hundred or more of its kind under the protectorate of British India.

When British India became independent on August 15, 1947, it was divided, based on the dominant religious affiliations of its regions, into two dominions, which later became the constitutionally secular but mostly Hindu India and the Islamic republic of Pakistan. The existing princely states, such as Kashmir, were allowed to opt to be part of India or of Pakistan or to stay independent, although some historians think that the last option was not clearly enunciated. The Kashmiri, wishing to retain their independence, followed the spirit of their popular leadership, especially that of the intensely secular Sheikh Mohammad Abdullah, who incessantly propelled the predominantly Muslim Kashmir into a confederation of India with reasonable guarantees for Kashmir's autonomy.

Sheikh Abdullah's leadership, however, faced challenges in the town of Poonch, in the southwestern corner of Kashmir. The oppressive rule of the maharajah had built a strong nucleus of animosity toward him and everything he stood for. Consequently, the leadership in Poonch gravitated toward Pakistan. Politically weak at the outset, this movement snowballed into an overpowering military operation from July to October 22, 1947, because of active support from the *pathans*, a tribal group from Pakistan's northwestern frontier province. Inspired by an old antagonism of a tribal nature but politically primed by a sense of fraternal obligation to help their kinsmen across the border, this impatient group invaded Kashmir from its western borders, threatening the future of the Hindu maharajah. The maharajah, Hari Singh, had no choice but to seek India's protection. On October 26, 1947, Kashmir legally became a part of India, giving India the legal right to fight against the *pathan* incursion, which India believed to be the work of Pakistan's governor-general, Mohammed Ali Jinnah.

On October 27, 1947, India sent its choice military force to Kashmir. A bloody warfare broke out between the people of Kashmir, strengthened by the armed tribal *pathans* as well as a growing number of infiltrating Pakistan army regulars on one side and by the remarkably well-equipped forces of the Indian army on the other. On December 31, 1947, Jawaharlal Nehru, the prime minister of the independent India, complained to the United Nations against the aggressive acts of Pakistan against what had become the legal soil of India. Pakistan, in a countercomplaint made on January 15, 1948, strongly questioned the legal validity of the maharajah's accession to India, as the decision was made by the maharajah without giving the people of Kashmir an opportunity to express their opinions. Pakistan argued that the accession was thus provisional, pending approval of the Kashmiri people. The categorical imperative to provide for the right of a group of people to choose its own country through a plebiscite conducted by the United Nations was recognized by Lord Mountbatten, governor-general of India, in his letter of acceptance of the accession addressed to the maharajah on October 27, 1947. The right of people to choose their country was also recognized by the prime ministers of the two countries in a series of telegrams exchanged between them. The United Nations also decided in favor of a plebiscite. Hostilities between the two countries continued until July 27, 1949, when the two countries signed what is known as the Delhi Agreement, in which they agreed to cease fire at their respective points of control, and, in effect, divide Kashmir into two parts. The north and west, composing a third of the undivided Kashmir, was claimed by Pakistan and called Azad Kashmir meaning "free Kashmir." The south and east, roughly two-thirds of the original princely state called Jammu and Kashmir, provisionally joined India. With time, India discovered legal grounds to renege on the plebiscite issue in Jammu and Kashmir. Pakistan, for its part, decided not to relinquish its control on Azad Kashmir, resulting in two more wars in 1965 and 1971. The animosity between India and Pakistan erupted into active hostilities at the slightest imbalance in their relations, jeopardizing the rights of the people of Kashmir to create a country of their own choice.

India was successful in stalling, if not eliminating, foreign criticism that it had violated any moral or natural rights of the people of Kashmir through the instrument of accession signed by their ruler. India was not as successful with the people of Kashmir, whose faith in Indian government progressively eroded as the Indian government aggressively asserted its sovereignty through a series of increasingly unfair but seemingly legal measures. The Jammu and Kashmir elections of 1987 are one example. It is an open secret that in these elections the right of the people to express themselves freely through voting was violated in favor of Rajiv Gandhi's Congress Party and its colluding partners in the National Conference, the first indigenous political party in Jammu and Kashmir. The National Conference had been fighting for the self-determination of its people. Political maneuvering resulted in the election of an ideologically neutral and administratively inept chief minister, Farooq Abdullah.

The success of the Gandhi-Farooq alliance, according to some Kashmiri Muslims, was a continuation of the Indian government's refusal to acknowledge Kashmiri political rights. Demonstrations began against what they viewed as Indian oppression. The Indian government read these demonstrations as a renewal of the preaccession movement to secede Kashmir from India. Consequently, on August 9, 1989, in the name of enforcement of law and order, India sent its army into the state. The army, in conjunction with the state governor, Jaganmohan, instituted controls prohibiting international press reporters and human rights group representatives from entering into Kashmir. The Indian army arrested, wounded, and killed many peaceful protesters; *The New York Times* reported at least six hundred killed as of June 2, 1990. The army's major attack, reminiscent of the Tiananmen massacre in Beijing, was directed against a group of mourners carrying the body of their preacher. Dozens of mourners were killed, and a "soft" demonstration of real grievances developed into a diehard movement for separation from India.

Impact of Event

The first and the most immediate, although probably short-lived, impact of the "separatist" movement was the negative effect it had on the tourist industry, the chief source of foreign earnings for the state. With long curfews in place, one of them lasting for sixteen days, and a variety of law-enforcement personnel—Indian army troops, the paramilitary Central Reserve Police Force, the Border Security Force, the Indo-Tibetan Border Patrol, National Security Guards, and various intelligence agencies—keeping track of the scores of "separatist" groups, Kashmir was anything but a holiday playground for the contemporary tourist.

The second and the more significant effect of the movement was the great damage done to the traditional goodwill that existed between the Hindus and the Muslims of the region. At the height of the movement, the extremists among the separatists killed prominent Hindu government officials, including the assistant director of information and the director of the government-run Srinagar Television Centre. These extremists created fright and terror in many other Hindus, just as the police created similar feelings in them. Thousands fled from their homes to improvised camps, depending on the hospitality of the Indian government. Such instances have not been without their opposites, in which Muslims have attacked the extremists in defending their Hindu neighbors. These instances grew in number with the increasing unpopularity of the extremists among Muslims. Amicability between Hindus and Muslims was bound to suffer irrevocable damage.

The third effect of the infighting, the most significant of all, was the potential for nuclear war. India and Pakistan, two of the nuclear powers of the Third World, may have locked themselves in to adversarial positions more to strengthen their coalition governments at home than to address the problem of the people of Kashmir. The United States special envoy, Robert M. Gates, along with the special offices of the Soviet Union, helped offset the threat of nuclear war by raising consciousness at the Indo-Pakistan as well as the international level. As the issue of separatism failed to be resolved, these effects cumulated. The peace and the rights of the Kashmiri people continued to be violated, and their very existence remained imperiled.

Bibliography

Akbar, M. J. *Nehru: The Making of India.* New York: Viking Press, 1988. An authoritative thematic biography of an avowed secularist, Jawaharlal Nehru. Written by a journalist and political analyst who became a secular politician. Illuminates the history of the Kashmir problem.

Bose, Tapan, Dinesh Mohan, Gautam Navlakha, and Sumanta Banerjee. "India's 'Kashmir War.'" *Economic and Political Weekly* 25 (March 31, 1990): 650-662. An investigative journalistic essay incorporating news analysis, interviews, and contemporary historical insights. The five appendices at the end of the essay provide factual support for the views developed in it.

Jalal, Ayesha. "Kashmir Scars: A Terrible Beauty Is Torn." *The New Republic* 203 (July 23, 1990): 17-20. Written by a scholar at the Harvard Academy of International and Area Studies and author of at least two major monographs on the period surrounding the births of India and Pakistan. Develops the concept of *bira-*

dari, or brotherhood, as a meaningful source for understanding the problems between these countries.

Lamb, Alastair. *The Kashmir Problem: A Historical Survey.* New York: Praeger, 1967. Covers the 1947-1966 period. The historian author explains the Kashmir problem to the nonspecialist in simple terminology.

Rushdie, Salman. *Midnight's Children: A Novel.* New York: Alfred A. Knopf, 1981. Gives a fictionalized account of the period of partition of India.

Singh, Balbir. *State Politics in India: Explorations in Political Processes in Jammu and Kashmir.* New Delhi, India: Macmillan India, 1982. A fairly comprehensive Marxist analysis of the politics of Jammu and Kashmir.

Suharwardy, A. H. *Tragedy in Kashmir.* Lahore, Pakistan: Wajidalis, 1983. Makes a unique contribution because of its singular perspective, innovative historiography, and characteristic style, possibly coming from the author's identity as a Kashmiri who has experienced life on both sides of the cease-fire.

Abdulla K. Badsha

Cross-References

The Muslim League Attempts to Protect Minority Interests in India (1906), p. 87; Gandhi Leads a Noncooperation Movement (1920), p. 315; Gandhi Leads the Salt March (1930), p. 447; India Gains Independence (1947), p. 731; Conflicts in Pakistan Lead to the Secession of Bangladesh (1971), p. 1611; Zia Establishes Martial Law in Pakistan (1977), p. 1898; Zulfikar Ali Bhutto Is Hanged Despite Pleas from World Leaders (1979), p. 2018; Tamil Separatist Violence Erupts in Sri Lanka (1980's), p. 2068; Sikhs in Punjab Revolt (1984), p. 2215; Indira Gandhi Is Assassinated (1984), p. 2232; Government-Supported Death Squads Quash JVP Insurrection in Sri Lanka (1987), p. 2315; Demonstrators Gather in Tiananmen Square (1989), p. 2483.

THE KENYAN GOVERNMENT
CRACKS DOWN ON DISSENT

Categories of event: Political freedom; atrocities and war crimes
Time: 1989
Locale: Kenya

Kenya's government became increasingly repressive, and in 1989 the government and opposition groups intensified their positions

Principal personages:
> DANIEL ARAP MOI (1924-   ), the Kenyan who succeeded to the presidency upon the death of founding president Jomo Kenyatta in 1978
> GITOBU IMANYARA, the editor of the *Nairobi Law Monthly* and an advocate of human rights
> JOSIAH M. KARIUKI (1929-1975), an opposition member of parliament who was assassinated
> NGUGI WA THIONG'O (1938-   ), a novelist, academic, and political exile
> OGINGA ODINGA (1911-   ), the leader of government opposition
> GIBSON KURIA (1947-   ), a lawyer, human rights advocate, and political exile
> TOM MBOYA (1930-1969), an early opposition leader who was assassinated by the Kenyatta government
> ALEXANDER MUGE (?-1990), an outspoken Anglican clergyman who died under mysterious circumstances
> ROBERT OUKO (1932-1990), a foreign minister who was assassinated, presumably for being a potential threat to Moi's power

Summary of Event

When Kenya's first president, Jomo Kenyatta, died in 1978, newspaper headlines pointed to a likely power vacuum. In a regime long dominated by Kikuyu tribal interests (21 percent of the population), the emergence of a Kalenjin (11 percent of Kenya's population) president, Daniel Arap Moi, prompted uncertainty about whether a non-Kikuyu could manage the system so long in the grip of a Kikuyu oligarchy. A strong sense of tribal identity in Kenya dates back to the colonial period and through the preindependence process of political organizing to confront the British. During the Kenyatta regime, Kikuyus exercised virtually complete political dominance, particularly at the expense of the second-most-populous group, the Luo. Moi's political success was in part attributable to his being a member of a smaller group.

A former British colony, Kenya arrived on the international scene depicting itself as a democratic, uniparty system. During Kenyatta's regime, however, democracy was limited at best, although there was competition in intraparty elections for parliament. An oligarchy emerged, consisting primarily of Kikuyus, especially members of Kenyatta's family. His nephews were foreign minister and high commissioner to London, his daughter was mayor of Nairobi, and his fourth wife headed extensive business holdings which were clearly facilitated by her position. Kenyatta himself owned hundreds of thousands of hectares of prime farmland.

By the last days of his regime, likely successors (or threats) to Kenyatta had been eliminated. Tom Mboya, a Luo who was minister of economic planning and development, was gunned down at midday on a Nairobi street in 1969. Demonstrations accompanied by a popular outcry led to the banning of opposing parties. In response, Parliament determined there had been a police coverup of the murder. Another political leader, parliamentarian Josiah Kariuki, a Kikuyu, was assassinated by the secret police in 1975, having been abducted from a downtown hotel in Nairobi. His crime was that he was attempting to develop an alternative power center through coalition politics.

The 1979 presidential election, held within a year of Moi's taking office, could be characterized as the opening salvo of opposition not only to Moi and his Kalenjin-dominated oligarchy but also to the growing repression that occurred in the later years of the Kenyatta regime. Half of the incumbents, including one-third of the former cabinet, were unseated in the election, which also saw the success of Raila Odinga, son of Oginga Odinga, a primary opposition leader. A 1982 coup attempt by the air force resulted in its dissolution, the conviction of more than six hundred, or one-third, of its members for mutiny, and the execution of twelve of them.

Moi's regime continued the same repressive behavior as Kenyatta's regarding opposition. For example, foreign minister Robert Ouko, a potential threat to Moi, was assassinated in February, 1990. Public outcry then resulted in a British investigating team looking into the death. Its report was sealed, delivered to the government, and had not been released as of mid-1991.

The Moi regime created a curiously self-described "African" electoral process for the 1988 elections in order to dampen opposition. Declaring the secret ballot inherited from the British colonial system to be "un-African and against the will of God," the ministry of national guidance decreed that voters would queue behind photographs of their preferred candidates. Only about one-third of the eligible voters chose to participate in this election, and political unhappiness subsequently grew. When Kenneth Matiba pointed out election irregularities, he was expelled from the party and his wife and daughter were beaten by police who came to his home.

The ranks of the clergy produced some of the most outspoken opposition. Several clergy members have been victims of violence. Alexander Muge, Anglican Bishop of Eldoret, died in an auto accident under mysterious circumstances in August, 1990. Three days earlier, he had been threatened with death by Moi's minister of labor. The Catholic Bishops of Kenya issued a statement in April, 1991, calling for political change, including freedom of expression.

Since gaining its independence in 1963, Kenya has had one legal political party, the Kenya African National Union (KANU), the party of Kenyatta and Moi. Whatever electoral democracy existed was exercised within the context of intraparty elections. A shadowy opposition movement, Mwakenya, emerged in the 1980's. It consisted primarily of intellectuals with a Marxist bent. It was not formally recognized as a party and had had little impact by mid-1991.

There were reports of several other alternatives to KANU. Oginga Odinga announced the formation of the National Democratic Party; however, it suffered from being perceived in some quarters as a Luo-dominated organization, continuing the tribal perspective of politics. Other opposition movements included the Union of Nationalists to Liberate Kenya, the United Movement for Democracy in Kenya (led by the novelist Ngugi wa Thiong'o in London), the Kenya Patriotic Front, and the Mhetili Nationalist Movement, consisting of university faculty dismissed at the time of the 1982 coup attempt.

The 1989 crackdown thus came in the wake of long and vigorous opposition to the two unresponsive regimes which dominated independent Kenya. The 1982 coup attempt set off a course of repressive practices. The government's ostensible concern over the unhappiness which precipitated the crackdown resulted in the establishment of a committee, chaired by vice president George Saitoti, to hear public complaints on the topic of election procedure reforms. Its announced charge included receiving proposals to dissolve parliament, since the parliamentary election was widely thought to have been rigged, holding multiparty elections, restoring judicial independence, and limiting the term of the president. No evidence had emerged by 1991 that this process would lead to meaningful reform.

Moi added jailings, censorship, and harassment to the occasional murder as a means of silencing dissent. The *Nairobi Law Monthly* has been confiscated or banned several times since its inception in 1987. Its editor, Gitobu Imanyara, has been jailed for various crimes including advocating multiparty elections. In the wake of unrest and dissent in the legal community, the International Bar Association cancelled a meeting planned for summer, 1990, in Nairobi. Internationally recognized dissident Ngugi wa Thiong'o, a Kikuyu author, was a faculty member at the University of Nairobi until barred from that position by the government. Parliamentarian Chris Kamuyu was arrested in October, 1990, for possessing a banned magazine. Gibson Kuria, a lawyer who has represented political dissidents, was jailed and subsequently took refuge in the United States embassy in mid-1990, prior to fleeing to the United States. He had received the Robert F. Kennedy Human Rights Award in 1988. His co-defendants Kenneth Matiba and Charles Rubia were former cabinet ministers. Those two and a fourth codefendant, Raila Odinga, were jailed without charge. Rubia was released without explanation in April, 1991; the others were still being held as of July, 1991. The rule of law underwent further erosion in 1988 when President Moi unilaterally amended the constitution to end judicial independence and extended the time an individual could be jailed without charges. Judges served only at the pleasure of the president. Moi announced on June 16, 1990, that debate on multipartyism had ceased.

Despite the dangers, the legal profession, including Paul Muite, president of the

Law Society of Kenya in 1991, vigorously came to the defense of human rights. For example, at Imanyara's trial, thirty-nine lawyers appeared at the defense table in a demonstration of solidarity. This behavior resulted in Muite's reportedly being placed under police surveillance.

Gitobu Imanyara's writings, as well as other media criticism, elicited countercriticism from the government. Imanyara's publication has been banned frequently. News vendors commented that one could be shot for possessing it. At the same time, citizens in Nairobi robustly criticized the regime in casual conversations, with no apparent fear of reprisal. One could only conclude that the general public did not take seriously the Moi regime's repressive tactics, presumably assuming that eventually the regime would give way to another system. In the meantime, only a few serious challengers suffered the wrath of the government.

There have been sporadic student riots, including one in July, 1990, in which twenty or more students were killed, many were wounded, and hundreds were arrested. Schools and universities opened and closed in response to the political temperature of the times. It is noteworthy that president Moi, like Kenyatta before him, served as chancellor of the University of Nairobi.

Impact of Event

The New York Times editorialized in October, 1990, to the effect that Moi would either have to respond to critics or face the fate which toppled uniparty regimes in Eastern Europe as a consequence of the global movement toward democracy. This prompted a retort from Kenya's ambassador in Washington to the effect that Kenya had never been communist, culminating in the following statement: "The only government critic who has died mysteriously was J. M. Kariuki." Clearly, at least one government official acknowledges that there have been political murders.

The events recited above put into context the dissent which began in earnest in 1989 and continued at least until mid-1991. Dissident politicians, clergy, students, and especially the legal community expressed themselves and in turn felt the wrath of the regime in various ways. A measure of Kenya's sensitivity to criticism is reflected in severance of diplomatic relations with Norway, the first such instance in peacetime for Norway. This arose as a result of Norway's protestations regarding treatment of dissident Koiga wa Wamwere, a former parliamentarian who took refuge in Norway and was arrested upon his return to Kenya in October, 1990.

All the dissent, it should be noted, did not have political roots. One cannot ignore the economic realities in Kenya, including estimates of 25-40 percent unemployment. Periodically, shantytowns of the unemployed were cleared by the government. These events resulted in hundreds of "homes" being demolished and demonstrations by the displaced poor. When the agriculture minister criticized one such event, Moi suspended him. Kenya's economic crisis was implicitly acknowledged by the Central Bank of Kenya when it reported that only one-sixth of six hundred thousand needed jobs were created in 1988. High unemployment and general economic stagnation characterized the system.

The ostensible "wave of democracy" sweeping across Eastern Europe in the early 1990's had little impact in much of Africa. The world's media focused upon Kenya as a site for potential democratic reforms possibly because it is more appealing to Western business and tourism, and is a more attractive base for media reportage, than are many of its sister states in Africa. The level, pervasiveness, and persistence of dissent suggested that there is a movement toward reform that cannot easily be dismissed.

It is certainly not possible in 1991 to predict Kenya's future, nor is it plausible to predict with certainty the overthrow of the present regime. Moi is more than sixty-five years old, and it has been rumored that he has cancer. On the other hand, African rulers of various degrees of demagoguery have clung to office into their eighties. The makings of revolution in Kenya are now more advanced than in many states where representative political systems have emerged. There is a fairly strong economic base with substantial international involvement. There is a growing middle class with resources and intellectual content and a vested interest in stability. The post-Cold War international climate has spawned expectations which are more pressing than in the recent past. No fewer than twenty-six African states have either held elections—of varying degrees of representativeness—between 1990 and mid-1991 or announced intentions to do so. As South Africa continues toward a more representative system, one can expect that pressures to democratize will be greater in all African systems.

The absence of the essential traditions of representative government portend a difficult transition for Kenya, as in most other uniparty states. Even given an adequate level of political will, which appears to be lacking, moving to a stable and reasonably representative system will be troublesome. It is axiomatic in the study of revolution that once the process is under way, it is rarely possible to repress or reverse. Revolution in Kenya is deeply implanted; repression is unlikely to quash it.

Bibliography

Amnesty International. *Kenya: Torture, Political Detention, and Unfair Trials.* London: Amnesty International Publications, 1987. Details the human rights violations perpetrated by the Kenyan government in Amnesty's detached, legalistic style. Murder, imprisonment without trial, torture, and related human rights abuses are described.

Berg-Schlosser, Dirk. *Political Stability and Development.* Boulder, Colo.: L. Reinner, 1990. In this monograph, Berg-Schlosser examines the connection between political stability and economic development, with Kenya as a case study.

Maren, Michael. "Kenya: The Dissolution of Democracy." *Current History* 86 (May, 1987): 212. Maren documents President Moi's reaction to opposition and elucidates the political climate which has evolved during Moi's tenure. He also explains the nature of opposition to the regime and describes how it has fared.

Sicherman, Carol. *Ngugi wa Thiong'o: The Making of a Rebel.* London: Hans Zell, 1990. Wa Thiong'o is a widely recognized playwright and novelist who gained increased international recognition when he was forced to flee Kenya after angering the government with his works.

Stamp, Patricia. "Kenya's Years of Discontent." *Current History* 82 (March, 1982): 115. Stamp examines the social and economic roots of the political problems in Kenya. She provides an anthropological perspective on tribal antagonisms and how they affected postindependence politics.

Richard A. Fredland

Cross-References

The Mau Mau Uprising Creates Havoc in Kenya (1952), p. 891; Civil War Ravages Chad (1965), p. 1273; The Secession of Biafra Starts a Nigerian Civil War (1967), p. 1365; Burundi's Government Commits Genocide of the Bahutu Majority (1972), p. 1668; Students in Soweto Rebel Against the White Government (1976), p. 1882; Amnesty International Adopts a Program for the Prevention of Torture (1983), p. 2204; The Berlin Wall Falls (1989), p. 2523; Ceausescu Is Overthrown in Romania (1989), p. 2546; Lithuania Declares Its Independence from the Soviet Union (1990), p. 2577.

OREGON LEGISLATES GUARANTEED BASIC HEALTH CARE FOR THE UNINSURED

Category of event: Health and medical rights
Time: 1989
Locale: Salem, Oregon

The Oregon Health Plan was a blueprint for providing health care to uninsured Oregonians who did not fit into categories covered by federal health programs

Principal personages:

JOHN KITZHABER (1947-   ), the president of the Oregon senate, who authored the Oregon Health Plan

ROBERT SHOEMAKER (1932-   ), the head of the first Oregon Committee on Health Insurance and Bioethics

PAIGE SIPES-METZLER (1952-   ), the executive director of the first appointed Health Services Commission

MARK GIBSON (1950-   ), an executive assistant to Senator Kitzhaber who assisted in constructing the Oregon Health Plan

Summary of Event

In his 1990 book *What Kind of Life: The Limits of Medical Progress*, Daniel Callahan explores the values of United States citizens that have led to a greatly inconsistent allocation of funding for basic health care from state to state. He begins with the moving case of Adam "Coby" Howard, a seven-year-old Oregonian who died while awaiting a bone-marrow transplant that would have given him a 50 percent chance of survival. Such transplants were funded until July of 1987, when the Oregon state legislature cut Medicaid funding for heart, liver, pancreas, and bone-marrow transplants. In January of 1988, Oregon's legislative assembly again turned down a plea to finance organ transplants for impoverished Oregonians. Callahan points out that Oregon had a $200 million surplus in its state budget at the time, that the transplant crisis was "provoked by a voter-inspired expenditure limit that need not have happened and could be reversed in the future," that millions of state dollars were wasted elsewhere, and that in Washington State and Canada such surgeries were funded. He concludes that the real issue, that of the values of United States citizens, was not being addressed. He maintains that although Coby Howard may not have had to die, "to come to that conclusion is to choose the smaller, more poignant truth over the larger, more penetrating one." He leads to Oregon state senator John Kitzhaber's contention that the United States will not indefinitely continue to have the ability to pay for an expanding health-care system or for all new technologies that promise to extend life. Callahan concludes that, ultimately, United States citizens need to change their values so that they develop a system that guarantees a minimally decent level of health care for all, perhaps at a cost of reining in some private demands for goods and services. He says that such a health plan would be a "decent and manageable one" and that such a plan "is not an impossible ideal."

In Oregon, Kitzhaber pursued this ideal. He began by researching health care in Oregon to get to the roots of the health-care problem in the state. According to research conducted by Kitzhaber's office, the health-care problem had multiple roots. Kitzhaber and his research assistants discovered that 450,000 Oregonians had no basic health coverage. Of these, 250,000 were women and children; many were workers and their dependents. Kitzhaber observed that, in the late 1980's, impoverished Americans were rationed out of Medicaid; many workers lost health coverage for themselves and their dependents because their employers could not afford rising health-care premiums, and the number of uninsured Oregonians was increasing at approximately 5 percent per year. Costs of uncompensated health care for these citizens made meaningful reform difficult.

In response to his findings, Senator Kitzhaber authored Senate Bill 27 (SB 27), Senate Bill 935 (SB 935), and Senate Bill 534 (SB 534). These three bills formed the core of the Oregon Health Plan, designed to bring all citizens into the health-care system and to provide them with basic health care. Instrumental in drafting the bills and working them through both the committee and the legislature was Oregon state senator Robert Shoemaker, who headed the first Oregon Committee on Health Insurance and Bioethics. In 1989, the bills constituting the Oregon Health Plan were signed into law. A supplemental senate bill (SB 1076) was passed on June 27, 1991. Together, these laws began to meet the objective of providing basic health care to all Oregon citizens.

Senate Bill 27 extended Medicaid coverage to all Oregonians below the federal poverty level and set up a process to define the priorities within a Standard Benefit Package. After the passage of SB 27, the eleven-member Health Services Commission was appointed to develop the first public process used to prioritize health-care services according to their benefit to the entire population. The Health Services Commission, headed by Executive Director Paige Sipes-Metzler, included five physicians, four consumers, a public health nurse, and a social services worker. The commission's initial report took eighteen months and twenty-five thousand volunteer hours to complete. In February of 1991, the commission submitted its list of priorities in health care. The list was to be made current every two years "to reflect the medical outcomes, findings, and emerging social values." In 1993, for example, the committee was scheduled to integrate mental health and chemical dependency services into the list.

Senate Bill 935 expanded health-care access to the working poor by requiring employers to provide the Standard Benefit Package to all permanent employees and their dependents. This portion of the Oregon Health Plan responded to the national trends in health-care coverage. According to a 1991 article from the *Philadelphia Enquirer*, companies with one hundred or more employees increasingly discontinued health coverage throughout the 1980's. For example, in 1982, 75 percent of employees had health-care benefits; in 1989, 48 percent of employees had health-care benefits. In 1982, 50 percent of employees had health-care benefits for their families; in 1989, the corresponding figure was 31 percent. SB 935 was designed to give employers time to comply voluntarily with the law and then to impose the law if employees did not receive health-care benefits for themselves and their families as designated in the Standard Benefit Package.

The Standard Benefit Package, as laid out in SB 935, covered all current Medicaid mandates, all major diseases of women, including those resulting from physical or sexual abuse, all major diseases of children, unlimited hospitalization, dental services, hospice care, prescription drugs, most transplants, physical and occupational therapy, routine physicals, and mammograms. Under the package, a Medicaid recipient and the recipient's children would receive continued health care even after the recipient got a job, received a nominal raise, or got a car. This part of the Oregon Health Plan surpassed federal health-care aid.

Senate Bill 534 established a high-risk pool "to cover those denied insurance because of a pre-existing medical condition." The primary objective of this part of the Oregon Health Plan was to reform the insurance system in such a way that employers of small businesses, particularly those with fewer than one hundred employees, could afford to provide health-care coverage for their employees.

Senate Bill 1076, enacted in 1991, added senior and disabled citizens to the Oregon Health Plan, integrated mental health and chemical dependency services to the prioritized list, restructured the small-group health insurance market, and added additional cost controls by modifying patterns of physicians' practices and monitoring the acquisition and use of medical facilities, technologies, and services.

According to Senator Kitzhaber, the public and private components of the plan were tied together by law in such a way that Oregon could not implement either part without a waiver of federal Medicaid rules. In the summer of 1991, Oregon applied to the Health Care Financing Administration (HCFA) for these federal waivers. The HCFA was scheduled to decide on these waivers by January of 1992. If the waivers were allowed, this comprehensive plan would cover an additional 120,000 Medicaid poor and 300,000 working poor. The Oregon Health Plan was scheduled to begin its five-year demonstration period on July 1, 1992.

Impact of Event

The Oregon Health Plan came about not only through hard work and idealism but also through painful decisions. Part of the funding for Oregon health care came in July of 1987, when the Oregon state legislature cut Medicaid funding for heart, liver, pancreas, and bone-marrow transplants. The money reallocated by the legislature was used to provide basic health care for twenty-five hundred low-income children and pregnant women. The choice the legislature faced was to spend $1.18 million for an anticipated thirty heart, liver, pancreas, and bone-marrow operations or to spend the money for basic health care for twenty-five hundred impoverished children and pregnant women. Many citizens, of course, questioned the need for such a choice, but within those voter-imposed budget constraints, a 1988 poll showed that 68 percent of approximately eight hundred volunteer respondents favored allocating the funds for prenatal care for women and for general medical services for children, 24 percent favored allocating the funding for transplant operations, and 8 percent believed that both should be funded. The reallocation of funding triggered statewide debate of the values involved in health care. The resulting decisions allowed some inequity in an attempt to provide wider access to basic health care.

In her book *The Politics of Public Health* (1989), Meredeth Turshen begins her discussion of U.S. health policies with the statement, "Equity and access are the first principles of justice." She maintains that the United States has fallen behind many countries not only in providing health care but also in continuing to debate whether health care is a right or a privilege. In fact, in 1978, the International Conference on Primary Health Care declared that "Governments have a responsibility for the health of their people which can be fulfilled only by the provision of adequate health and social measures." In the "spirit of social justice," the declaration restated the 1977 policy of the World Health Organization (WHO) of health for all by the year 2000.

Senator Kitzhaber realized that the Oregon Health Plan was not a panacea for solving problems of health care at a national level. He stated that more than 32 million Americans, "two-thirds of them workers and their dependents, the majority women and children, lack health insurance and therefore timely and consistent access to health care." According to Kitzhaber, even with the plan, thirty thousand Oregonians would still not be eligible for basic health care. Despite the limitations of the Oregon Health Plan, however, the plan was expected to help many Oregonians.

The Oregon Health Plan provided a possible model for extended basic health care, but it was not a solution without limitations. Thirty thousand Oregonians still fell outside the program. Moreover, poverty still meant certain death for those in need of transplants or other radical treatment that would have been covered under comprehensive private health plans. In Oregon, those citizens entitled by wealth retained sole access to such treatment, as the death of Coby Howard demonstrated. Finally, even the basic health service provided by the Oregon Health Plan stopped at the state border. Almost all proponents of public health care believed that the issue of health care was appropriately a national one and that the Oregon Health Plan was only a beginning.

Bibliography

Breckon, Donald J., John R. Harvey, and R. Brick Lancaster. *Community Health Education*. 2d ed. Rockville, Md.: Aspen Systems, 1989. This textbook presents a perspective from inside the medical profession. The authors discuss ethical issues in dealing with patients but deal only superficially with access to medical care.

Callahan, Daniel. *What Kind of Life: The Limits of Medical Progress*. New York: Simon & Schuster, 1990. Callahan's comprehensive book begins with an analysis of the case of Coby Howard's death and leads up to an analysis of the need of U.S.

citizens to reassess their expectations. This exceptionally well-researched book includes extensive graphs and charts and a thorough index.

Dougherty, Charles J. *American Health Care: Realities, Rights, and Reforms.* New York: Oxford University Press, 1988. Dougherty looks closely at inequities in national health care, enters the debate of whether health care is a right or a privilege, and explores several positions on the debate. He concludes that Americans have a right to health care. The book contains a selected bibliography.

Green, Lawrence W. *Community Health.* 6th ed. St. Louis: Times Mirror/Mosby, 1990. In this textbook, Green focuses on the history and demographics of health-care coverage and looks at national trends. The book contains numerous graphs and charts, bibliographies for each chapter, and a thorough index.

Greenberg, Selig. *The Quality of Mercy: A Report on the Critical Condition of Hospital and Medical Care in America.* New York: Atheneum, 1971. In chapter 11, Greenberg deals extensively with the need to establish medical priorities for basic health services. To illustrate his points, he looks at Boston's choice not to do heart transplants and Houston's choice to do them. Much of the argument has to do with the state of transplant procedures at the time the book was written.

Kunnes, Richard. *Your Money or Your Life.* New York: Dodd, Mead, 1971. In the final chapter, Kunnes explores national health insurance, community control of community health, and seizure of services. The book has several useful appendices, including one prepared by the Department of Health, Education and Welfare in 1970 that compares five proposals for national health insurance.

Pickett, George E., and John J. Hanlon. *Public Health: Administration and Practice.* 9th ed. St. Louis: Times Mirror/Mosby, 1990. These authors approach public health primarily from a management and marketing perspective, though they touch on the global issues of a right to health care.

Schorr, Daniel. *Don't Get Sick in America.* Nashville, Tenn.: Aurora, 1970. An excellent history of the issues involved in public health care. Schorr reviews the shrinking numbers of people covered by health insurance, the "trauma" of Medicare and Medicaid, the drive for health maintenance, the need to bring the poor into the health system, and the international practices surrounding these issues. The book is illustrated with photographs and with informational charts.

Turshen, Meredeth. *The Politics of Public Health.* New Brunswick, N.J.: Rutgers University Press, 1989. Turshen approaches globally the problem of access to health care. She concludes that, internationally, the United States is falling behind other countries in providing health care for its citizens. The book includes notes, an index, and an extensive bibliography.

Carol Franks

Cross-References

Great Britain Passes Acts to Provide Unemployment Benefits (1920), p. 321; The World Health Organization Proclaims Health as a Basic Right (1946), p. 678; The

United Nations Children's Fund Is Established (1946), p. 689; The United Nations Adopts the Declaration of the Rights of the Child (1959), p. 1038; Head Start Is Established (1965), p. 1284; Canada Develops a National Health Plan (1966), p. 1321; WHO Sets a Goal of Health for All by the Year 2000 (1977), p. 1893; An International Health Conference Adopts the Declaration of Alma-Ata (1978), p. 1998.

PROLIFE GROUPS CHALLENGE ABORTION LAWS

Category of event: Reproductive freedom
Time: 1989
Locale: The United States

Sixteen years after Roe v. Wade, *the Supreme Court decision in* Webster v. Reproductive Health Services *allowed states to set some restrictions on abortion*

Principal personages:
RONALD REAGAN (1911-   ), the president of the United States from
1981 to 1989
GEORGE BUSH (1924-   ), the president of the United States in 1989,
campaigned on an antiabortion platform
WILLIAM C. BRYSON (1945-   ), the acting solicitor general who wrote
the brief submitted by the Bush Administration in *Webster v. Reproductive Health Services*
RANDALL TERRY (1934-   ), the founder of Operation Rescue

Summary of Event

Seldom has a Supreme Court ruling been as controversial as that of *Roe v. Wade*. Prior to this decision, abortion regulation was left to the states. In 1973, however, the Supreme Court examined state abortion laws with respect to the right to privacy, a right which is not explicitly protected by the Constitution but which the Court had previously decided was implied by it. While *Roe v. Wade* recognized that states properly have interests in safeguarding health, in maintaining medical standards, and in protecting potential life, there was no case in which these rights were upheld by the Supreme Court. After *Roe*, and prior to 1989, state laws restricting abortion were consistently struck down.

Prochoice groups were satisfied with the Court rulings. Prolife groups, however, were left with a situation in which they could find few legal avenues through which to express their dissent. Perhaps partly for that reason, a small minority turned to civil disobedience. Randall Terry, founder of Operation Rescue, an organization that sought to shut down abortion clinics by blocking access to the facilities, reasoned that it was time for those who believed that abortion was murder to begin to act like it was murder.

Only a very few prolifers, however, were involved in tactics such as those of Operation Rescue. Most attempted to work within the few legal avenues available in the aftermath of *Roe v. Wade*. The first of these avenues was constitutional amendment. Since 1973, the right-to-life movement had held an annual march to Washington on the January 22 anniversary of *Roe v. Wade*, protesting the decision and calling for a constitutional amendment prohibiting abortion. They consistently failed to gather sufficient support for such an amendment. A second legal avenue was to lobby against congressional funding for abortion. This tactic often worked. It could not, however, be used to contest the legality of abortion, a very important goal for pro-lifers. A third possibility was to work for a change in the composition of the Su-preme Court. This avenue eventually led to a window of opportunity for prolife groups in 1989.

The Court majority in *Roe v. Wade* had been steadily eroding as a result of retire-ments and appointments to the Court by President Reagan. Only three of those who made up the seven-to-two majority in 1973 remained on the Court in 1989. On Janu-ary 9, 1989, this Court, which was clearly more conservative than the one that had adjudicated *Roe v. Wade*, decided to hear the case of *Webster v. Reproductive Health Services*. The *Webster* case involved a Missouri statute which stated that life begins at conception and that unborn children have interests in life, health, and well-being which can be protected. It forbade the use of public funds to counsel or encourage a woman to have an abortion, made abortions more difficult to obtain after twenty weeks of pregnancy, and forbade public hospitals and employees to perform or assist in abortions not necessary to save the life of the mother. The Missouri law also required a physician to perform and record tests on fetal gestational age, weight, and lung maturity if there was reason to believe that the mother was twenty or more weeks pregnant. The state claimed that a fetus of that age may be viable given modern technology. The state of Missouri was in effect arguing that the Constitution does *not* protect a fundamental right to abortion.

Webster v. Reproductive Health Services drew seventy-six *amicus curiae* (friend-of-the-court) briefs, more than any case in recent history. Among the groups urg-ing prolife action were the Christian Action Coalition (CAC), Americans United for Life (AUL), the National Right to Life Committee (NRLC), the U.S. Catholic Con-ference, the National Association of Evangelicals, and JustLife. Groups urging pro-choice action included Planned Parenthood, the American Civil Liberties Union (ACLU), the Religious Coalition for Abortion Rights (RCAR), the National Or-ganization for Women (NOW), and the National Abortion Rights Action League (NARAL).

The Bush Administration also submitted a brief. The administration position was that *Roe v. Wade* should be overruled and that Missouri should not be required either to fund abortion counseling or to use public employees or facilities to perform abor-tions. George Bush had campaigned on an antiabortion platform and was on record as favoring a constitutional amendment barring abortions except in the cases of rape and incest and to save the life of the mother.

Prolife and prochoice groups swung into action. Legal representatives for Re-productive Health Services contended that the right to choose an abortion is prop-erly among the fundamental freedoms protected by the Constitution. Acting Solici-tor General William C. Bryson directly contradicted that contention in the brief submitted for the Bush Administration. He stated that a supposed fundamental right to abortion can draw no support from either the text of the Constitution or from United States history. Prochoice historians argued that abortion should not be restricted in 1989 because it was neither uncommon nor illegal in the early nineteenth century. Prolife groups countered that slavery, child labor, and the disenfranchisement of women were also common and legal at that time.

Religious leaders tended to focus on the fundamental right to life, and thus sided with the prolifers. Not all religious persons were on the prolife side of the argument, however. Faith Evans, president of the Religious Coalition for Abortion Rights (RCAR), pledged at a press conference that the religious community would not allow restrictions and erosion of the rights guaranteed by *Roe v. Wade*. Mark Ellingsen, a Lutheran pastor in Salisbury, North Carolina, argued that human life should be defined not by biological viability but by the more specifically human characteristic of relationality. If this definition were to be accepted, no human rights would be denied in the case of an abortion because it is impossible for a fetus to be involved in a relationship. Finally, some churches, such as the United Methodists, seemed highly sensitive to the fact that women could be exploited by boyfriends, spouses, and even governments if the choice of whether or not to bear children were not firmly in their own hands.

On July 3, 1989, the Supreme Court ruling in the case of *Webster v. Reproductive Health Services* upheld Missouri's abortion restrictions. The Supreme Court would no longer be the primary locus of the abortion controversy. Power would now reside as well in state and national legislative bodies, and with the governors of the states.

With that expanded battlefront in mind, prolife activists in every state began developing strategies to limit abortion. They planned for the introduction of legislation which could include requiring doctors to give women detailed information about fetal development and possible complications from abortion; granting some veto power to the father of the unborn child; and prohibiting abortion for such reasons as the sex of the child, inconvenience, or financial difficulties.

One year after the *Webster* decision, in 1990, approximately three hundred bills in total had been introduced in most of the forty-four state legislatures holding sessions in that year. Pennsylvania was the first state to take legislative action, passing a bill which set limits on late abortion; mandated notification of husband, informed consent, and a twenty-four-hour waiting period before an abortion; and banned sex-selection abortion and the use of aborted fetuses for medical research. South Carolina and Michigan passed laws requiring parental consent before a minor's abortion. West Virginia passed a law setting limits on state-funded abortions. Indiana established subsidies for the adoption of special-needs children as an alternative to abortion.

Attempts to pass prolife legislation were not always successful, however. In Idaho, Louisiana, and Mississippi, restrictive laws were passed by the legislature but vetoed by the governor. Florida Governor Robert Martinez miscalculated badly in calling a special legislative session to bar public funding for abortion and to require fetal viability tests. Sixty-five percent of the electorate opposed the special session, and 71 percent favored leaving Florida's permissive abortion laws alone or even expanding them. Martinez's popularity rating plunged to 24 percent.

Impact of Event

Although the 1989 *Webster v. Reproductive Health Services* decision did not result in any drastic curtailment in the number of abortions performed in the United States, at least not in the short run, prolife groups rightly hailed it as a significant change of policy on the part of the Supreme Court, one that allowed them to have a greater share in the decision-making processes regarding abortion. With more legislative possibilities open to them than at any time since 1973, prolife groups began to suffer from internal divisions. Although the official policy of all major prolife groups was to oppose abortion even in cases of rape and incest, some groups were willing to compromise on that issue in order to get laws passed that would severely restrict the number of abortions performed each year. Doug Scott, director of public policy for the Christian Action Council (CAC), said that he would feel responsible for the other 99 percent of the abortions performed if he were not willing to work with the system on the 1-3 percent of all abortions which are done following rape or incest. Others sided with Nellie Gray, president of March for Life, who was opposed to any exceptions or compromises. Such thinking, she said, bargains some human lives away. How is it right, she asked, to say that we will defend babies, but not those babies who are conceived by rape or incest?

Still other prolifers believed that to applaud the *Webster* decision, and to scramble to pass more legislation along the lines of the Missouri statute that it upheld, was to skew the prolife position in an unfortunate direction. Kathleen Hayes, director of publications for Evangelicals for Social Action and JustLife, pointed out that while the *Webster* decision served to protect more of the unborn, it did little for their often-desperate mothers. It thus fell short, in her opinion, of being fully prolife.

In 1989, survey results showed that 69 percent of Americans believed that the lives of unborn babies should be protected, while 67 percent believed that a woman should have the right to choose to have an abortion. What the American public seemed to be opposed to was either abortion-on-demand or government control of a woman's reproductive capacity. The survey results explain why either side in this debate has been capable of winning a majority, depending on how the issue is phrased.

The abortion issue had become extremely polarized as a result of the Supreme Court decision in *Roe v. Wade*, which effectively removed abortion from the give-and-take of the legislative process. In other developed nations, in which the abortion issue was settled legislatively rather than judicially, political compromises had long since been worked out. Those compromises were remarkably similar to one another, and also remarkably similar to what most Americans seemed to want according to public opinion polls. The compromises attempted to balance compassion for pregnant women and concern for fetal life.

The abortion issue is morally complex. It involves concerns about life, choice, gender, responsibility, and dependency. *Roe v. Wade* did not do justice to the complexity of the moral issues involved, nor did it do justice to the complexity of American moral sentiment surrounding abortion. In the *Roe* decision, the Supreme Court allowed one important value, that of privacy, to upstage all others. In so doing, it closed the door for sixteen years on the business of weighing and deciding among competing interests and values. *Webster v. Reproductive Health Services* reopened the door.

Bibliography

Biskupic, Joan. "Abortion Protagonists Gird for Crucial Court Test: No Matter What the Outcome, a New Flurry of Activity Seems Certain in Congress, State Legislatures." *Congressional Quarterly Weekly Report* 47 (April 8, 1989): 753-758. The best single article on *Webster v. Reproductive Health Services*, and the most comprehensive. Describes the case and its history, and tells where individual congresspersons, the Supreme Court, the administration, and the states stood on the eve of the decision. Also includes abortion statistics from the Alan Guttmacher Institute.

Dellinger, Walter. "Day in Court: No One Wins if *Roe* Is Restricted." *The New Republic* 200 (May 8, 1989): 11-12. Expresses the prochoice side of the debate. Written from a secular point of view.

Glendon, Mary Ann. "A World Without *Roe*: How Different Would It Be?" *The New Republic* 200 (February 20, 1989): 19-20. Written by a professor of law at Harvard University, this is by far the most insightful article concerning the problems with *Roe*. Glendon analyzes how *Roe v. Wade* blocked the normal legislative avenues for debate and discussion on difficult issues.

Hayes, Kathleen. "Fully Pro-Life." *Sojourners* 18 (November, 1989): 22. Written from a prolife position which is both nuanced and morally sensitive.

Lawton, Kim A. "Could This Be the Year? Supreme Court Observers Say the 1973 *Roe v. Wade* Decision Could Be Restricted—and Perhaps Overturned—This Term." *Christianity Today* 33 (April 7, 1989): 36-38. *Christianity Today* provided the most sustaining prolife coverage of the 1989 challenge to *Roe v. Wade* and its aftermath. This and Lawton's other articles provide a sample of their coverage. See Kim A. Lawton, "Confrontation's Stage Is Set: A Supreme Court Decision Marks the Beginning of a New Era in the Abortion Debate, an Era Long Awaited by Abortion Foes," *Christianity Today* 33 (August 18, 1989): 36-38, and "Taking It to the States: In Light of the Supreme Court's *Webster* Decision, Prolife Activists Focus on States as the New Abortion Battlefields," *Christianity Today* 33 (November 3, 1989): 36-38.

McGurn, William. "What the People Really Say." *National Review* 41 (December 22, 1989): 26-29. This article analyzes the situation from a neutral point of view, neither prolife nor prochoice in orientation.

Meeks, Catherine. "To Respect Life." *Sojourners* 18 (November, 1989): 22. States the prolife position with a greater degree of moral sensitivity than is normally found.

Ranck, Lee. "A Special Issue on Abortion." *Christian Social Action* 3 (April, 1990): 1-16, 25-40. Expresses the prochoice side of the debate. Written from a religious point of view.

Ann Marie B. Bahr

Cross-References

Sanger Opens the First Birth-Control Clinic in the United States (1916), p. 184; The American Civil Liberties Union Is Founded (1920), p. 327; Sanger Organizes Conferences on Birth Control (1921), p. 356; The U.N. Convention on the Political Rights of Women Is Approved (1952), p. 885; The National Organization for Women Forms to Protect Women's Rights (1966), p. 1327; The United Nations Issues a Declaration on Equality for Women (1967), p. 1391; The Family Planning Services Act Extends Reproductive Rights (1970), p. 1579; *Roe v. Wade* Expands Reproductive Choice for American Women (1973), p. 1703; Italy Legalizes Abortion (1978), p. 1988; Commission Studies Ethical and Legal Problems in Medicine and Research (1980), p. 2090; The National Organization for Women Sponsors an Abortion Rights Rally (1989), p. 2489.

SOVIET TROOPS LEAVE AFGHANISTAN

Category of event: Political freedom
Time: 1989
Locale: Afghanistan

After a decade of bloody fighting, the Soviet Union ended its occupation of Afghanistan

Principal personages:

BABRAK KARMAL (1929-   ), a leader of the People's Democratic Party of Afghanistan (PDPA), placed in control of Afghanistan after the Soviet invasion

NUR MOHAMMAD TARAKI (1917-1979), the secretary general of the PDPA who replaced Daud after the 1978 coup

HAFIZULLAH AMIN (1929-1979), the PDPA leader who ousted Taraki in September, 1979, and ruled Afghanistan until the Soviet invasion

MIKHAIL GORBACHEV (1931-   ), the president of the Soviet Union

NAJIBULLAH AHMEDZAI (1947-   ), the leader of the PDPA

MOHAMMAD DAUD (1909-1978), the first president of the Republic of Afghanistan

Summary of Event

Afghanistan, a nation about the size of Texas, has been called the "highway of conquest," because invaders have swept through the region since the time of the ancient Persians and Greeks. In fact, the very borders of Afghanistan owe less to any rational or historical nation-state development than they do to the whims of more powerful neighbors. Therefore, the citizens of Afghanistan are ethnically and culturally diverse, with most viewing themselves as members of a clan, family, village, or region rather than as Afghans.

In addition to this lack of national identity, it is important to note the country's economic underdevelopment. By the late 1970's, Afghanistan lacked a railroad system and had few paved roads. Life expectancy was around forty years, and annual per-capita income was only $168. All these factors combined to make the government in Kabul seem distant—some said as if in another world—to the average rural Afghan.

Called the "Finland of Asia," nonaligned but friendly with the Soviet Union, Afghanistan was ruled for decades by a weak king. This stable if ineffective form of government was overthrown in July, 1973, by Prince Mohammad Daud, who led a coup of leftist military officers. Although a member of the royal family, Daud abolished the monarchy and proclaimed Afghanistan a republic. There was no real democracy in this new "republic," but Daud did put forth a populist program that, at least on paper, appeared to aim at some modernization and included talk of land reform.

After a few years, however, Daud had managed to alienate much of Afghan society. Muslim fundamentalists doubted his commitment to Islam when he tried to suppress the Muslim Brotherhood, while workers were repulsed by his strikebreaking, antilabor policies. There were food shortages and increased unemployment, with hundreds of thousands of Afghans forced to go abroad to work by the late 1970's.

These factors combined with an increasingly uncertain attitude toward the Soviet Union to push the pro-Soviet People's Democratic Party of Afghanistan (PDPA) into opposition. As discontent with Daud grew, the PDPA began to prepare to overthrow him. Many new members were recruited, particularly from the ranks of the officer corps of the army and air force. Finally, in April, 1978, the armed forces overthrew Daud's government, and power passed to PDPA secretary general Nur Mohammad Taraki.

The People's Democratic Party of Afghanistan was to prove to be as riddled with factions and splits as the nation it attempted to lead. Attempts at land reform, educational expansion, introduction of women's rights, and modernization were hampered by the inexperience and the often heavy-handed methods of the mainly urban PDPA officials sent to carry them out. Although these errors certainly played a major role in fomenting conservative dissent, it is difficult to see how any government that wished to change tradition-bound Afghanistan could fail to anger the conservative rural population.

Worst of all, the new regime increasingly was seen as atheistic by the deeply religious rural masses. The growing alienation of many Afghans caused by these erroneous policies began to worry Taraki and his Soviet allies. Many of these mistaken methods came to be seen as the work of Hafizullah Amin and his faction in the PDPA.

After a visit to Moscow in September, 1979, Taraki returned to Kabul determined to change the PDPA government's course, which meant, most likely, the arrest of Amin. After a Wild-West style shootout at the People's Palace, Amin escaped, only to return with supporters and capture Taraki. On October 9, it was announced that Taraki had died from a long-standing illness. Although the details remain murky, there is little doubt the "illness" from which Taraki died was administered by Amin or on his orders.

There was little love lost between the new ruler of Afghanistan and the Soviet leadership. Amin generally was believed to be responsible for making a mess of the PDPA reform program and had embarrassed the Soviet Union severely by murdering its favorite, Taraki, only days after his widely celebrated trip to the Kremlin. If all this were not enough, Amin was making nationalist noises against the Soviet Union, on one occasion to a gathering of Communist diplomats.

Having considered military intervention for months as a possible solution to the spreading rebellion within Afghanistan, the Soviet Union struck in late December of

1979. On the evening of December 27, a special Soviet assault unit attacked the palace in Kabul and executed Amin. Four days later, Babrak Karmal arrived from the Soviet Union and was installed as new PDPA secretary general and president of Afghanistan.

Karmal attempted to backpedal on many of the most unpopular programs of his predecessors, even bringing non-Communists into his cabinet. Amnesty was offered to refugees, and major revisions were made in the land-reform legislation that had so upset feudal landlords. Karmal made great efforts to portray himself as a good Muslim. Official speeches began with a traditional Islamic incantation, while a new flag containing the old Muslim colors of black, red, and green replaced the former red flag. The new Soviet-supported government went so far as to give mullahs free tours of the Islamic areas of the Soviet Union to convince Muslims that Communism and religion were compatible.

Although Karmal's policies were much more gradual, and perhaps realistic, than those of previous PDPA governments, Karmal failed to win popular support. He was simply identified too closely with the old PDPA policies and perceived too widely as a Soviet puppet for any of these measures to have significant effect. Therefore, despite the endeavors of Karmal and the Soviets, the civil war raging at the time of the invasion continued and even intensified in light of heightened antiforeign feeling, particularly in the rural areas.

The anti-PDPA and anti-Soviet resistance movement was able to stand up to the massive force brought against it for a number of reasons. The resistance movement had the advantage that its followers were fanatically determined to fight the Soviets to the bitter end. Since the mullahs declared the struggle to be a holy war against infidels, the fight against the Kabul-based government and its Soviet allies took on an intensely religious tone.

Moreover, the cultural tradition of "blood for blood" meant that every Soviet attack left Afghan family members pledged to avenge their dead. Nor could the Red Army win by the seizure of a central command area, since the resistance was as decentralized and dispersed as the country itself. Likewise, economic measures from Kabul were of little use in a country of mainly self-sufficient farmers.

Added to this difficult situation, the Soviets found themselves fighting an enemy with powerful international backing. Rebels regularly slipped across the border to Pakistan or Iran, where pursuit by the Soviets was not politically possible. Furthermore, the rural Afghan rebels found themselves aided by the United States, which provided them with massive amounts of sophisticated weapons along with cash.

By the time Mikhail Gorbachev came to power in the Soviet Union, the war in Afghanistan was a bleeding sore for Soviet foreign policy. It seemed impossible to defeat the rebels, and the fighting was demoralizing many at home and tarnishing the Soviet image abroad. Gorbachev concluded that a settlement that allowed a Soviet withdrawal was imperative.

In May, 1986, the ineffective Karmal was replaced by Najibullah Ahmedzai, who was encouraged to seek a political compromise with the *mujahideen*. At the same time, the Soviet leader launched an intensive diplomatic campaign to find a way to end the fighting. Finally, on May 15, 1988, the Soviets announced their intention to begin removing their troops. By the time the last Soviet soldier left in 1989, the Soviets had suffered 13,310 dead and 35,478 wounded. There were no reliable estimates of the number of dead Afghans. The nation was left with countless physical and psychological scars.

Impact of Event

The Soviet military withdrawal from Afghanistan was a step toward peace in that troubled land. Sadly, however, the fighting and dying did not end with the removal of Soviet soldiers. The civil war between the Kabul-based PDPA government and the rural antigovernment rebels continued to rage.

As the Soviet Union removed its troops from Afghan soil, the antigovernment forces boasted that the days of Najibullah and the Kabul "Communists" were numbered. This prediction, which was widely supported by Western experts and echoed in the Western media, proved to be a mirage. Instead of falling into the hands of the rebels, the Kabul government shocked most observers with an unexpected show of strength.

There were a number of reasons for this surprising development. Without the unifying common enemy the Soviets provided, the anticommunist resistance began to fragment and fight among itself. Another more fundamental reason for the surprising staying power of Najibullah and for the continued fighting was that not all Afghans opposed the PDPA-imposed reforms. Among certain—particularly urban—members of Afghan society, the reforms so heavy-handedly initiated by the PDPA were, all the same, things to be defended.

For all the political intrigue and violence, the various PDPA reforms were, at least partly, motivated by a desire to modernize Afghanistan and create a more just society. Although the countless violations of human rights committed by the PDPA government helped spark the rebellion, it appears almost certain that any fundamental changes would have provoked a strong reaction. Traditionalist landlords could hardly be expected to welcome land reform even if mandated by the most devoutly Islamic government, while the education of women struck a raw nerve among the rural male population. Among rural rebels who viewed education as synonymous with atheism and often had a policy of publicly executing teachers suspected of teaching women to read, it was not only "communism" that was the enemy, it was also what in the West would be considered progress.

Thus, many urban Afghans who deplored the violations of the PDPA or even opposed socialism thought that they had little choice but to support the government, considering the possible alternative. When the element of foreign intervention by the Soviet Union was stripped away, a fundamental split between different parts of the Afghan populace was revealed.

The Soviet invasion of Afghanistan certainly contributed to the tragedy of a poor nation. The Soviet intervention was not only a violation of Afghanistan's national rights but also a failure in its own terms. Soviet troops did not and could not have defeated the antigovernment forces they sought to destroy. The result of their intervention was only to heighten the bloodshed already in progress.

Still, it is appropriate to remember that the causes behind the civil war were deeply rooted in Afghan society. The urban, educated sectors of the Afghan population had grown increasingly opposed to continuing as a backward country out of touch with the late twentieth century. For their part, the predominantly rural traditionalists saw modernization as a threat to their way of life and religion. With or without foreign meddling, the short-term prospects for peace and respect for human rights appeared dim in Afghanistan.

Bibliography

Amstutz, J. Bruce. *Afghanistan: The First Five Years of Soviet Occupation.* Washington, D.C.: National Defense University, 1986. Although dated and obviously partisan to the antigovernment forces, this book is a wealth of information on the major people and events surrounding the civil war in Afghanistan. Contains reference notes, index, and bibliography.

Gorbachev, Mikhail S. *Perestroika.* New York: Harper & Row, 1987. A useful introduction to the thinking of the Soviet leader who withdrew troops from Afghanistan, although it must be viewed as a work of public relations.

Hammond, Thomas T. *Red Flag over Afghanistan: The Communist Coup, the Soviet Invasion, and the Consequences.* Boulder, Colo.: Westview Press, 1984. While dated, this is a very worthwhile introduction to the key events of 1978 through 1981. In addition, the author provides several chapters devoted to speculation about future developments that are, surprisingly, still of use. Includes reference notes, index, and bibliography.

Rubinstein, Alvin Z. *Moscow's Third World Strategy.* Princeton, N.J.: Princeton University Press, 1988. Attempts to analyze the policy of the Soviet Union toward weaker nations. Useful, although flawed in its overreliance on a Cold-War-type analysis that, at least in the case of Gorbachev and Afghanistan, seems to fly in the face of the facts. With reference notes, index, and bibliography.

Saikal, Amin, and William Maley, eds. *The Soviet Withdrawal from Afghanistan.* Cambridge, England: Cambridge University Press, 1989. A collection of essays by notable authorities on foreign affairs, this work is indispensable for anyone wishing to study the significance of the Soviet withdrawal. Bibliography and index.

William A. Pelz

Cross-References

The Pahlavi Shahs Attempt to Modernize Iran (1925), p. 406; The French Quell an Algerian Nationalist Revolt (1945), p. 651; Indonesia's Government Retaliates Against a Failed Communist Coup (1965), p. 1305; The Brezhnev Doctrine Bans Acts of Independence in Soviet Satellites (1968), p. 1408; Soviets Invade Czechoslovakia (1968), p. 1441; The World Conference on Women Sets an International Agenda (1975), p. 1796; Khomeini Uses Executions to Establish a New Order in Iran (1979), p. 2013; Soviets Invade Afghanistan (1979), p. 2062; Gorbachev Initiates a Policy of *Glasnost* (1985), p. 2249; Muslims Riot Against Russians in Kazakhstan (1986), p. 2298; Soviet Troops Withdraw from Czechoslovakia (1990), p. 2570.

THE U.S. SURGEON GENERAL REPORTS ON TOBACCO AND HEALTH

Category of event: Health and medical rights
Time: 1989
Locale: Washington, D.C.

In its annual report on smoking and health, the surgeon general's office examined the progress made toward a smoke-free America and the health consequences of smoking

Principal personages:
CHARLES EVERETT KOOP (1916-   ), the surgeon general of the United States Public Health Service
GEORGE BUSH (1924-   ), the vice president of the United States
JIM WRIGHT (1922-   ), the Speaker of the U.S. House of Representatives

Summary of Event

On December 29, 1988, the secretary of health and human services, Otis R. Bowen, delivered to Jim Wright (Speaker of the House of Representatives) and George Bush (president of the Senate) copies of the 1989 surgeon general's report on the health consequences of smoking. Entitled *Reducing the Health Consequences of Smoking: 25 Years of Progress*, the report examined changes and developments in American smoking prevalence, as well as mortality caused by tobacco use in the United States since the first surgeon general's report in 1964. The most important change that occurred during the twenty-five-year period since the first report involved the overall prevalence of smoking, which dropped from 40 percent of the populace in 1965 to 29 percent in 1987. In addition to statistics on smoking, the report focused on possible approaches to be followed by the U.S. Public Health Service in working toward its goal of a smoke-free society by the year 2000.

The first comprehensive federal report on the health consequences of smoking was proposed in June, 1961, and approved by President John F. Kennedy in June of 1962. The selection process for the members of the committee that would prepare the report reflected the high stakes of the outcome. The names of more than 150 scientists and physicians were submitted for consideration by representatives of all the groups involved in the question of a link between smoking and health problems. These included the American Cancer Society, the American Medical Association, the Federal Trade Commission, the U.S. Food and Drug Administration, and the Tobacco Institute. The groups settled on ten members—half smokers and half non-smokers—who had never taken a public position on the question.

The completed report was delivered to the White House and then presented to the press on January 11, 1964, from a locked briefing room. It declared that "Cigarette smoking is causally related to lung cancer in men; the magnitude of the effect of cigarette smoking far outweighs all other factors. The data for women, though less extensive, point in the same direction. . . . [T]he risk of developing lung cancer increases with the length and duration of smoking and the number of cigarettes smoked per day, and is diminished by discontinuing smoking." Although the Tobacco Institute and other industry-related organizations denied the link found by the committee, the Federal Trade Commission (FTC) moved to require that warning labels appear on all cigarette packages. In 1965, Congress preempted the FTC with the passage of Public Law 89-92, the Cigarette Labeling and Advertising Act of 1965. In addition to requiring the first health warning, P.L. 89-92 also required the secretary of health, education and welfare (later the department of health and human services) to submit annual reports to Congress on the health consequences of smoking, along with any legislative recommendations resulting from new research. The 1989 report was the twentieth in the series.

In the twenty-five years since the first report, scientific research had supported and extended the original conclusions of the 1964 study. As this connection became more clear, the overall rate of smoking declined, while the number of public and private measures to prohibit and discourage smoking expanded dramatically. The 1989 report reached five conclusions regarding smoking's prevalence and consequences for mortality. First, the overall prevalence of smoking among adults declined from 40 to 29 percent, and almost half of all living adults who ever smoked had quit. Second, approximately 750,000 smoking-related deaths were avoided or postponed because of individuals' decisions to quit smoking or not to start the habit. Third, the prevalence of smoking remained higher among African Americans, blue-collar workers, and the less-educated among the population, and the rate of decline among women was significantly lower than among men. Fourth, the report found that 80 percent of smokers begin during childhood and adolescence, with the age of initiation dropping over time, especially for females. Finally, smoking remained the single most preventable cause of death in the United States, playing a role in more than one out of every six deaths.

In addition to its other conclusions, the preface to the report, written by Surgeon General C. Everett Koop, discussed the question of smoking as a matter of individual choice. Drawing from the 1988 report, *The Health Consequences of Smoking: Nicotine Addiction*, Koop rejected the frequent claim by tobacco interests that the decision to smoke constituted a reasonable and calculated decision. He cited statistics on the ages at which most smokers begin the habit—80 percent of all smokers born after 1935 started smoking before they reached their twenty-first birthday. Consistent survey data showed that when most smokers reach adulthood, when the appreciation of the health effects is significantly greater, many have great difficulty quitting because of their nicotine addiction. Specifically, more than 80 percent of all American smokers indicated that they would like to quit, and two-thirds of them had made at least one serious attempt to quit. Koop concluded that if the number of new, young smokers declined significantly from its 1987 level of three thousand per day, there would be a major effect on smoking prevalence among adults.

The 1989 report also discussed one of the fastest-growing concerns among health officials. The rate of cigarette use dropped most among the most-educated members of society, making smoking a habit of the poor and working classes. Although only 28 percent of all white-collar workers smoked in 1985, more than 40 percent of all blue-collar workers did. The report also indicated the elevated rates of smoking among certain racial and ethnic minority groups, many of which already suffered from a disproportionate share of high-risk factors and illnesses, such as hypertension.

The overall picture of cigarette smoking had changed significantly in the twenty-five years following the first surgeon general's report. The 1989 version reflected an assessment of the steps required to carry the nation toward the long-term goal of a smoke-free society.

Impact of Event

The 1989 surgeon general's report propelled the issue of smoking to the front of American consciousness. In the weeks that followed the report's release, newspapers and magazines focused on the disparities in smoking rates between men and women, whites and racial minorities, blue-collar and white-collar workers, and college graduates and those with a high school diploma or less. At the same time, a number of legislative bills were introduced throughout the country to further limit the locations where smoking was permitted. In March, 1989, two members of New York's state assembly introduced a bill designed to require local boards of education to make schools completely smoke-free as a means of reducing cigarette use among children and adolescents. Just two days after the report's release, in a highly praised move, William J. Bennett, the man George Bush picked to lead the United States' "war on drugs," declared that he would give up his own "drug habit," cigarette smoking.

Throughout the months after the report's release, tobacco companies continued campaigns that portrayed cigarette smokers as a law-abiding group under siege. The Philip Morris company, in preparation for the bicentennial of the Bill of Rights in 1991, paid for a series of television, radio, and print ads that stressed the democratic right of choice and the need to defend that right against all tyrannical invasions. At the same time, marketing for the cigarette brand "Dakota" continued. This new brand purportedly was targeted specifically at young women with a high school education or less, one of the specific groups mentioned in the report as among the most difficult to reach for health organizations. This fact made its members among the most likely to develop a cigarette habit. Later, plans were made for the sale of a brand of cigarettes specifically for African Americans, called "Uptown." When the plans became public, Secretary of Health and Human Services Louis Sullivan led a successful campaign to have the brand withdrawn.

One of the greatest losses in the fight against cigarette smoking was the departure of C. Everett Koop from the U.S. Public Health Service (PHS). During his tenure, Koop pushed the PHS into the forefront of America's health crises on a number of issues, especially the fight against Acquired Immune Deficiency Syndrome (AIDS). His outspokenness was a source of embarrassment to President Ronald Reagan's administration, which had selected Koop in part because of his work as a pediatric surgeon who opposed abortion. As a result, when his term as surgeon general expired, he was not reappointed by George Bush. Although the PHS continued to work toward reducing the use of cigarettes, the loss of the highly visible and respected Koop reduced the attention the popular press paid to the PHS's efforts.

Bibliography

Diehl, Harold S. *Tobacco and Your Health: The Smoking Controversy.* New York: McGraw-Hill, 1969. The author presents strong arguments, which are occasionally marred by the partisan tone of the work. His extensive background in public health makes this a compelling book. Appropriate for general readers. Contains a glossary, an index, and five appendices.

Goodin, Robert E. *No Smoking: The Ethical Issues.* Chicago: University of Chicago Press, 1989. Discusses the issues prompted by the existence of the tobacco industry, which produces and markets a product that is recognized as dangerous. The author treats smoking as a political issue, one with a proper moral position. Contains an index and a list of scientific studies.

Patterson, James T. "Smoking and Cancer." In *The Dread Disease: Cancer and Modern American Culture.* Cambridge, Mass.: Harvard University Press, 1987. Presents a scholarly study of cancer in America and examines the relationship between tobacco and cancer. Also discusses issues concerning cigarette advertising. Index and references.

Tollison, Robert D., ed. *Smoking and Society: Toward a More Balanced Assessment.* Lexington, Mass.: Lexington Books, 1986. Contains papers from a 1984 conference concerning the relationship between smoking and society. Examines economic, health, psychological, and social aspects of tobacco use. Valuable to readers in search of specific data; the density and technical nature of the text make it difficult for the general reader. Index and references.

Troyer, Ronald J., and Gerald E. Markle. *Cigarettes: The Battle over Smoking.* New Brunswick, N.J.: Rutgers University Press, 1983. Discusses the cultural evolution of smoking, in particular its conversion from an immoral act to a mark of social sophistication, then to a deviant behavior. Discusses the powerful groups with vested interests that are trying to destigmatize smoking. Somewhat technical. Annotations and index.

E. A. Reed

Cross-References

The Pure Food and Drug Act and Meat Inspection Act Become Law (1906), p. 64; Congress Requires Cigarette Warning Labels (1966), p. 1338; Cigarette Advertising Is Banned from American Television and Radio (1970), p. 1527; A. H. Robins Must Compensate Women Injured by the Dalkon Shield (1987), p. 2342; Canada Passes the Tobacco Products Control Act (1988), p. 2376; A Jury Awards Monetary Damages to the Estate of a Smoker (1988), p. 2381.

VIETNAMESE TROOPS WITHDRAW FROM CAMBODIA

Categories of event: Revolutions and rebellions; atrocities and war crimes
Time: 1989
Locale: Cambodia and Vietnam

Following ten years of embattled occupation, Vietnamese military forces withdrew from Cambodia in 1989, allowing political and military conflicts among Cambodia's political factions to escalate

Principal personages:

POL POT (1928-   ), the secretary-general of the Communist Party of Kampuchea from 1962, prime minister of Democratic Kampuchea (1976-1979), and leader of the Khmer Rouge

HUN SEN, a commander in the Khmer Rouge until his defection to Vietnam in 1978, became foreign minister and prime minister of the pro-Vietnamese People's Republic of Kampuchea

NORODOM SIHANOUK (1922-   ), the former king of Cambodia, who later allied himself with the Khmer Rouge after the Vietnamese invasion of Cambodia

HENG SAMRIN (1934-   ), a Khmer Rouge military commander who defected to Vietnam in 1978 and became president of the People's Republic of Kampuchea

SON SANN (1911-   ), the prime minister of Cambodia (1967-1968), became a leader of the opposition Khmer People's National Liberation Front in 1979

KHIEU SAMPHAN (1932-   ), a Khmer Rouge leader who acted as head of state of Democratic Kampuchea between 1976 and 1979; the principal spokesperson for the Khmer Rouge after the Vietnamese invasion

Summary of Event

The Communists' successful conclusion of the war for national unification in Vietnam in 1975 was accompanied by decisive military victories by local Communist organizations in both Laos and Cambodia. Although the leaderships which came to power in each of the three former states of French Indochina were Communist, each had distinct prescriptions for the postwar development and social reorganization of their countries. These dissimilar views, combined with separate links to the rival Communist superpowers, the Soviet Union and the People's Republic of China, brought the Communist Parties of Cambodia and Vietnam into political and military conflict in the late 1970's. Clashes along the Vietnam-Cambodia border and the growing cooperation between China and Cambodian Communists, known as the Khmer Rouge, prompted the militarily superior, Soviet-backed Vietnamese to launch a rapid invasion of Cambodia in late December, 1978. This military operation led to the capture of the capital city of Phnom Penh, the displacement of the Khmer Rouge government ruling what was known as Democratic Kampuchea, and the installation of a pro-Vietnamese Communist government to run the renamed People's Republic of Kampuchea.

The principal architect of Khmer Rouge policies was Saloth Sar, popularly known as Pol Pot. During the period of Khmer Rouge rule in Cambodia, from 1975 to early 1979, Pol Pot's wing of the Cambodian communist movement initiated a program of systematic political repression, the ostensible objective of which was to transform rapidly Cambodia into a self-sufficient communist state in which all distinctions of class and social status would be eliminated. To achieve this goal, the Khmer Rouge carried out forced population relocation campaigns on a mass scale and at one time contemplated the annihilation of all Cambodians over the age of twelve years so that no influences outside the control of the leadership would persist into the new era of self-sufficiency and revolutionary purity. Civil servants, teachers, professionals, and even those who were simply able to read, were singled out by the Khmer Rouge for torture and interrogation. Many of those viewed as "most dangerous" were imprisoned, tortured to obtain "confessions" of political crimes, and then executed at Tuol Sleng, formerly Phnom Penh's largest primary and secondary school. It has been estimated that at least one million Cambodians died from starvation and the repressive policies of the Khmer Rouge during the 1975-1979 period.

Although Vietnam claimed that its 1979 invasion of Cambodia was motivated by a desire to end the suffering of the Cambodian people, Vietnam's own national security concerns were most likely the decisive factor in the decision to invade. Along with Khmer Rouge contacts with the People's Republic of China, Vietnamese leaders were concerned about Khmer Rouge military incursions along Vietnam's southwestern border with Cambodia. The Vietnamese invasion drove Khmer Rouge forces from this region, and soon thereafter from the capital at Phnom Penh. The Khmer Rouge leadership and military command structure, however, survived the invasion largely intact. After establishing new positions along the border with Thailand, the Khmer Rouge continued its recruitment and political indoctrination activities throughout the decade of Vietnamese occupation while also receiving diplomatic and material assistance from both the People's Republic of China and the United States.

The military occupation was legally authorized under the terms of the February 18, 1979, Treaty of Solidarity concluded between Vietnam and the newly installed pro-Vietnamese government of Cambodia, led by Heng Samrin and Hun Sen. Official Vietnamese accounts credit its "volunteers" (soldiers) with carrying out disaster relief, resettlement, and construction projects between 1979 and 1989. Much progress was made, especially in the redevelopment of some export goods sectors, but a population growth rate of 2.8 percent per year, inflation caused by price-restructuring initiatives, and the perennial guerrilla conflict with the Khmer Rouge inhibited Cambodia's economic activity. For the 80 percent of the Cambodian people employed in agriculture, conditions continued to be harsh. A 1988 United Nations study revealed that per-capita caloric intake in Cambodia dropped during the period of Vietnamese military occupation.

The Vietnamese decision to withdraw from Cambodia emerged from an evaluation of developments in the international arena. Political changes in the Soviet Union brought into question continuance of Soviet subsidies for Vietnam and seemed to portend a reduction in Sino-Soviet military tensions, a key factor in the conflict in Indochina. Following inter-Party contacts in late 1988 between Chinese and Vietnamese Communists and the arrangement of Soviet President Mikhail Gorbachev's visit to Beijing in the spring of 1989, Vietnam announced on April 5, 1989, that its preconditions for a full troop withdrawal from Cambodia had been abandoned. Vietnam declared that all of its forces would leave Cambodia by the end of September, 1989, even if no political settlement between the Hun Sen government and the Khmer Rouge could be reached by that time.

In response, a flurry of activity developed during the summer of 1989. A major international conference was convened in Paris during August, but it failed to reach agreement on the issue of Khmer Rouge participation in any new coalition government. The negotiations were greatly complicated by the demands of the two non-Communist political factions formally allied with the Khmer Rouge, the Khmer People's National Liberation Front (KPNLF), led by Son Sann, and the forces led by former head of state Prince Norodom Sihanouk and his son, Prince Norodom Ranariddh. Soon after the Paris conference disbanded, press reports indicated that the three allied factions were preparing for an escalation of the military conflict with the Phnom Penh government. The Khmer Rouge were believed to be receiving increased deliveries of Chinese weapons, while the United States and the non-Communist Association of South East Asian Nations (ASEAN) reportedly developed covert military training and weapons supply programs aimed at strengthening the KPNLF and the Sihanoukists. Following a visit to Hanoi by a high-level delegation from Phnom Penh in early September, 1989, Vietnamese diplomats announced that the withdrawing forces would take "maximum precautions" to ameliorate the effects of an anticipated Khmer Rouge offensive against the Phnom Penh government's forces.

Beginning in mid-September, as Vietnamese forces left western Cambodia, Khmer Rouge forces based in the area launched a major offensive. The Khmer Rouge strategy appeared to be to capture substantial areas of the country as a means of securing participation in a coalition government. To this end, Khmer Rouge troops forced thousands of refugees living in camps near the Thai border to relocate to recently captured territory further inside western Cambodia. This policy continued during 1990, affecting as many as 100,000 refugees. Similar relocation programs were reportedly initiated by troops of the two non-Communist political factions, which were also active in western Cambodia.

In early September, 1989, the pro-Vietnamese party leader Heng Samrin promised that to promote national harmony, his party and the Phnom Penh government would show leniency for those people who had previously supported any of the other Cambodian political groupings. Phnom Penh, however, employed harsh methods to maintain its own military organizations in the absence of Vietnamese forces. The pro-Vietnamese government authorized military recruitment campaigns that were based upon compulsory draft regulations for both active military and auxiliary service. Recruitment tactics reportedly included surprise raids to round up urban youths, including students. Fearful of being press-ganged into the military, Phnom Penh youths were said to be going into hiding in the capital. Officials attempted to broaden the appeal of military service by changing the army's name from the Kampuchean People's Revolutionary Armed Forces to the Cambodian People's Armed Forces. Nevertheless, a steady stream of deserters, many between fifteen and nineteen years of age, sought refuge in Thailand.

For the Vietnamese forces withdrawn from Cambodia in 1989, the return to Vietnam involved difficult adjustments. Estimates (which may be conservative) put the number of Vietnamese soldiers killed during the occupation period at 23,500; another 55,000 reportedly were seriously wounded. Returning units were visited and congratulated by high-ranking Vietnamese officials, and public receptions emphasized the "victory" obtained in Cambodia. The urgency behind the withdrawal policy was suggested, however, by official reports of returning divisions being demobilized within four days of reaching Vietnam. Veterans were promised comprehensive benefits by the Vietnamese government, but reports indicated that demobilized soldiers faced numerous economic difficulties, including shrinking public welfare budgets, housing shortages, and shifting employment patterns, many of which were more salient for the veterans than were official promises of assistance.

Impact of Event

When the Vietnamese military finalized its formal withdrawal from Cambodia in late September, 1989, the official press in Vietnam marked the occasion with tributes to the troops' successful completion of their "internationalist duty." Official accounts cited the need to "respond to the Cambodian people's urgent call for help" after nearly four years of Khmer Rouge rule as the chief reason for the 1979 invasion, and referred to the need to "cope with the enemy's counter-revolutionary attack" as the chief reason for the decade-long military occupation. Nevertheless, Vietnam's withdrawal took place while the Khmer Rouge still maintained a stable organizational structure, a leadership that included such key figures from the 1975-1979 period as Pol Pot and Khieu Samphan, and a military wing estimated at around thirty thousand active soldiers. The principal effect of Vietnam's withdrawal from Cambodia was to stimulate a reescalation of the civil war between the Khmer Rouge, its non-Communist coalition partners, and the pro-Vietnamese Communist government.

The inability of the four main Cambodian political organizations to reach agreement upon a political settlement in 1989 was therefore accompanied by growing military conflict, especially in the western portion of the country. In this area, the effects of the continuing conflict were immediately apparent: youths drafted into military service, refugee families forcibly relocated, and rice fields destroyed or abandoned.

Along with new battles in western Cambodia, there remained the potential for tensions throughout the country between Cambodians and the one million ethnic Vietnamese who settled in Cambodia during the occupation period under Vietnamese government relocation programs. In official documents circulated at the United Nations, the Khmer Rouge described these settlers as being organized into multifamily units from which were drawn around sixty-thousand paramilitary forces and fifty thousand administrative and intelligence cadres. The documents predicted clashes between these Vietnamese living in Cambodia and the Cambodians themselves, and charged that since 1987 the Vietnamese occupiers had constructed an elaborate system of arms caches inside Cambodian territory, the purpose of which was to supply these informal Vietnamese forces after the September, 1989, withdrawal.

The chronic nature of the devastation in northwestern Cambodia, where most of the fighting occurred, was evident in press reports in the spring of 1991 which indicated that in that region, infant mortality rates for children under five years of age were around 20 percent, civilian injuries caused by land mine explosions led to three hundred amputations per month, and around 10 percent of the region's population had been displaced by war. The number of refugees in United Nations camps near the Thai border was estimated at 330,000, up from 250,000 in early 1990. According to observers, an unprecedented degree of despair and resignation prevailed among ordinary Cambodians, unable to conceive of a future without continued military conflict, political repression, and physical suffering.

Bibliography

Becker, Elizabeth. *When the War Was Over: The Voices of Cambodia's Revolution and Its People.* New York: Simon & Schuster, 1986. An account of the Khmer Rouge period in Cambodia, including a focus upon the cultural context and upon individual victims and Khmer Rouge officials. The author's experiences in Cambodia in the days before Vietnam's invasion make interesting additions to the well-written text, and her use of archival material from the Khmer Rouge torture complex at Tuol Sleng is especially noteworthy.

Duiker, William J. *Vietnam Since the Fall of Saigon.* Athens, Ohio: Ohio University Center for International Studies, 1989. A very useful account of Hanoi's domestic and foreign policies after 1975. Chapters 6 and 9 deal with Vietnam's invasion and occupation of Cambodia and the importance of the Chinese dimension of these policies.

Evans, Grant, and Kevin Rowley. *Red Brotherhood at War: Vietnam, Cambodia, and Laos Since 1975.* London: Verso, 1990. A detailed picture of relations between Communist organizations in Indochina after 1975, emphasizing the nationalist roots of conflicts and rivalries. Covers diplomatic and battlefield developments through the middle of 1989, when Vietnam's formal withdrawal of troops from Cambodia was announced.

Hiebert, Murray. "Standing Alone." *Far Eastern Economic Review* 43 (June 29, 1989): 17-18. A succinct presentation of the internal military situation in Cambodia as Vietnamese troops prepared for withdrawal. The same issue of this journal contains other articles by Hiebert examining political and economic aspects of Vietnam's changing policies toward Cambodia.

Kiernan, Ben. *How Pol Pot Came to Power.* London: Verso, 1985. The most detailed picture so far available in English on the origins of the Cambodian Communist movement and its long-standing links to the Vietnamese Communist organization. Provides essential background for understanding the dynamics of Vietnam's relations with both the Khmer Rouge and the government of Heng Samrin and Hun Sen.

Laura M. Calkins

Cross-References

Soviets Invade Czechoslovakia (1968), p. 1441; Khmer Rouge Take Over Cambodia (1975), p. 1791; China Publicizes and Promises to Correct Abuses of Citizens' Rights (1978), p. 1983; Soviets Invade Afghanistan (1979), p. 2062; Soviet Troops Leave Afghanistan (1989), p. 2449; Soviet Troops Withdraw from Czechoslovakia (1990), p. 2570.

PRESIDENTIAL CANDIDATES ARE KILLED
IN COLOMBIAN VIOLENCE

Category of event: Political freedom
Time: 1989-1990
Locale: Colombia

The assassination of Colombia's leading presidential candidate revealed a society increasingly at risk as it faced the violence of drug lords, paramilitary groups, leftist guerrillas, and common criminals

Principal personages:

LUIS CARLOS GALÁN (1943-1989), the Liberal presidential candidate whose call for extradition of Colombian drug lords to the United States led to his assassination

CÉSAR GAVIRIA TRUJILLO (1947-   ), the manager of Galán's campaign who won the Colombian presidency for himself

CARLOS PIZARRO LEONGÓMEZ (1952-1990), the assassinated presidential candidate of the M-19 Democratic Alliance

VIRGILIO BARCO VARGAS (1921-   ), the Liberal president of Colombia (1986-1990)

PABLO ESCOBAR (1949-   ), a leader of the Medellín drug organization

ANTONIO NAVARRO WOLFF (1949-   ), the leader of the M-19 after Pizarro's murder

GONZALO RODRÍGUEZ GACHA (1947-1989), chief in the Medellín drug world who was killed by security forces

JORGE ELIÉCER GAITÁN (1898-1948), the reform leader whose assassination thrust Colombia into the bloodiest part of *la violencia*

GUSTAVO ROJAS PINILLA (1900-1975), the dictator of Colombia from 1953 to 1957; almost won the presidential election of 1970

Summary of Event

Violence, kidnapping, banditry, bloodletting, revolts, partisan conflicts, and civil wars are all familiar in Colombia, where the geographic complexity of three mountain ranges formed the basis for the development of dissimilar economies and conflicting traditions. The resulting regional and ethnic diversity made it difficult to unify the country. Only the Catholic church and the brokered agreements between the 150-year-old Conservative and Liberal parties provided some elements of peace, national unity, and continuity. Even these arrangements depended on the acquiescence of local elites and party leaders. Periodically, these understandings broke down, especially when the dominant party's factional infighting allowed the opposition party to win. The nineteenth century saw fifty bloody conflicts, with the War of the Thousand Days (1899-1902) alone taking more than one hundred thousand lives. The twentieth century witnessed the macabre period of *la violencia* (1946-1959), when upwards of two hundred thousand people came to a violent end.

La violencia was the product of a split in the Liberal Party, in power since 1930, that allowed the minority Conservative Party to win the 1946 presidential election. The latter attempted to replace Liberal officeholders throughout the country. Liberal resistance and the assassination of their magnetic leader, Jorge Eliécer Gaitán, in 1948 led to three days of burning, looting, and death in Bogotá and wholesale human rights abuses and carnage in the countryside. It also set in motion profound forces that challenged the tradition of elite rule through the Conservative and Liberal parties. First, *la violencia* led the military to end civilian government in 1953 with the coup of General Gustavo Rojas Pinilla, who as dictator had some success in building support among the lower classes. Second, *la violencia* gave birth to guerrilla groups that matured and became an enduring force in the Colombian countryside. Finally, criminality became a major occupation in Colombia.

Faced with the prospect of losing power to the military and a persistent level of lawlessness, members of the Colombian political establishment eventually saw the wisdom of patching their differences. They did this in the historic National Front pact, whereby they agreed to rotate Liberals and Conservatives in the presidency from 1958 until 1974 and to divide political offices equally between Liberals and Conservatives. They first had to take back power from the military, which they did with the ouster of Rojas Pinilla in 1957.

To some extent the National Front achieved its goals. The Liberals and Conservatives regained control, political competition was reined in, and death in the countryside continued to drop through most of the 1960's and well into the 1970's. On the other hand, there was dissatisfaction among political groups that were not included in the power-sharing agreement. Further, the guerrilla groups spawned by *la violencia* did not disappear. They grew in numbers, experience, and ideology, so that by the 1980's Colombia had six important marxist guerrilla groups and a plethora of other types. They ruled large areas of the rugged Colombian countryside, although when challenged by the armed forces they usually moved on. Given the formidable geography, it was impossible for the military to secure all areas. The Colombian political establishment was also reluctant to give the military too much power, fearing that it would again become a threat to civilian rule, as it had in the 1950's.

The guerrilla groups generally were content to bide their time, ambush the armed forces, and live by "taxing" landowners, businesspeople, and multinational corporations in the form of demands for protection money. Some anted up and some did not. All suffered kidnappings for ransom that sometimes ended tragically. Paramilitary groups also appeared that levied their own measure of revenge against leftists and "social undesirables." Labor leaders, social activists, homosexuals, prostitutes, and others disappeared or were found abused or dead. At the same time, a criminal element flourished that astutely cloaked its entrepreneurial activities under the cover of the ongoing ideological and political struggles. One frequently did not know whom to blame for the human rights abuses that began to grow in frequency, especially after 1975.

It is in this historical context that the illegal Colombian drug trade developed and added a potent new element of money, power, organization, and weaponry to an old mix of illegality and human rights abuse. The money involved was out of proportion to the Colombian economy. The drug trade earned more in foreign exchange than Colombia's fabled mountain-grown coffee. It bought hired killers, death, protection for cocaine production and processing in guerrilla-controlled areas, immunity from military and police actions, favorable judicial rulings, legislative actions, and executive decisions. With an enormous amount of wealth and influence at every level of Colombian society, the drug lords began to pursue what they had never had and desperately wanted—acceptance, respectability, and legality.

All Colombian institutions and relationships—political, social, and economic— were at risk of being overwhelmed. Nevertheless, the drug lords were never so unified as to be a "cartel." They were too individualistic. There was a global oversupply of drugs, and the ensuing competition and turf wars led to a dangerous division in the ranks of producers, especially between the Medellín and Cali organizations. Their leaders—Pablo Escobar, Gonzalo Rodríguez Gacha, the Ochoa family, Carlos Lehder, and Gilberto and Miguel Rodríguez Orejuela—became household names.

The Medellín group in particular showed a lack of sophistication in its attempts to gain a place within the Colombian system. In its search for legitimate uses for its money and in its drive for acceptance, it created much turmoil and dislocation. Various civic leaders and newspaper editors demanded results, and the United States mistakenly viewed action in Colombia as an easy fix to its own drug problem. The Colombian government and the military began to crack down in the mid-1980's. The crackdown was haphazard at first, concentrating on the guerrillas, but became more determined and focused as time went on. On center stage was the suspended extradition treaty under which Colombian officials would try to send the more flagrant drug lords to the United States for prosecution. The Medellín "cowboys," however, brooked no restraint on their activities and responded with a reign of terror and assassination against responsible government officials. Their battle results were impressive. They made successful strikes against the police and military, especially in Medellín, on an almost daily basis. Especially intimidating, because of the rank and power of those involved, were the assassinations of Justice Minister Rodrigo Lara Bonilla in 1984 and Attorney General Carlos Hoyos in 1988. The most menacing, however, was the machine-gun slaying on August 18, 1989, of Colombia's leading presidential candidate and expected winner, the Liberal Party's Luis Carlos Galán, who had spoken out in favor of extradition. Clearly, the "extraditable ones," as the drug lords signed their declarations, had thrown down the gauntlet to the Colombian political establishment and had defined what was intolerable.

They also may have had a larger goal of capturing the Colombian state, since there is some evidence that they had created the political party MORENO and were going to field a candidate in the presidential election. By concentrating on the middle and lower Magdalena River Valley, an area in which they, especially Rodríguez Gacha, had invested heavily in land and politicians, they seemed well on their way to creating a fiefdom until the military and guerrillas resisted their efforts. The subsequent murder of two more presidential candidates appeared to be Medellín contracts. Bernardo Jaramillo, from the Patriotic Union (UP), was murdered on March 22, 1990, at the Bogotá airport. Carlos Pizarro Leongómez, from the M-19 Democratic Alliance (M-19), was killed on April 26, 1990, while on an Avianca flight. It is noteworthy that some viewed these two leftists as a more serious threat than were the drug lords.

Impact of Event

How Colombian leaders responded to the assassination of Galán and who those leaders were would offer important clues to the future direction of Colombia, including the risks of human rights abuse for different groups. Would Liberal-Conservative rule continue to survive, as it had for 150 years? Galán's murder led Liberal president Virgilio Barco to refuse to negotiate with the drug lords, to seek settlements with guerrilla groups, to collaborate closely with the United States, and to mobilize the armed forces and police in a determined attempt to exterminate or extradite the most notorious of the drug lords. By 1990, the government had succeeded in killing Rodríguez Gacha and forcing Pablo Escobar to go underground. The drug world's reaction, as noted above, did much to make Colombians think twice about the wisdom of such action.

The next president, Liberal César Gaviria Trujillo, formerly Galán's campaign manager, showed a more nuanced policy. Drug lords who turned themselves in, such as the Ochoas, were to be tried in Colombia and not extradited to the United States. President Gaviria supported the calling of a seventy-seat Constituent Congress to change the constitution. Elections to that congress got the Liberals only twenty-four seats, while the political newcomer M-19, led by the former guerrilla and ever-more-popular Antonio Navarro Wolff, made off with nineteen and was in position to challenge or to be co-opted by the political establishment. President Gaviria also made more money, weapons, and training available to the military and police, much of it coming from the United States. This would allow him to chase down both drug lords and guerrillas who continued to defy the government. For some, however, more power to the military raised the specter of greater human rights abuse. Finally, leftist guerrillas faced some painful decisions in view of the collapse of the Soviet bloc.

Human rights abuses remained significant in Colombia. The year ending in February, 1991, showed 1,451 kidnappings, of which 725 were credited to common criminals, 698 to guerrillas, and 28 to drug traffickers. Among the kidnapped victims were President Gaviria's first cousin, whose body turned up three days after his abduction, and the daughter of a former president, who was killed in a failed rescue attempt. In the months of January and February, 1991, there were more than one thousand drug-related killings in Medellín, and throughout the country thirty-one ambushes and sixty-one clashes between the security forces and guerrillas resulted in death tolls of 140 military personnel, 167 guerrillas, and 72 peasants. In 1990, there had been 313 political murders. Colombia's homicide rate was one of the highest in the world.

Nevertheless, Colombia resolutely survived. By 1980, its per-capita income was 87 percent above the 1960 level. Indices of quality of life—life expectancy, infant mortality, literacy rates, education levels, and housing conditions—had also improved substantially. The decade ending in 1990 showed Colombia as the only country in Latin America whose gross domestic product had not declined during a single year.

Bibliography

Braun, Herbert. *The Assassination of Gaitán: Public Life and Urban Violence in Colombia.* Madison: University of Wisconsin Press, 1985. Fascinating account of one of the great figures and pivotal events in Colombian history. Captures the passionate relationship between Gaitán and his followers and the breakdown of elite control. Excellent sources, bibliography, and index.

Gugliotta, Guy, and Jeff Leen. *Kings of Cocaine: Inside the Medellín Cartel—An Astonishing True Story of Murder, Money, and International Corruption.* New York: Simon & Schuster, 1989. Traces the rise of cocaine production from a cottage industry to an international operation. Good on the origins and expansion of the business. Weak on analysis and acceptance of such questionable assumptions as the industry's strong ties with marxist guerrillas and its organizational mode as a "cartel." Reads better than most suspense novels. Lots of villains. References and an index.

Hartlyn, Jonathan. *The Politics of Coalition Rule in Colombia.* Cambridge, England: Cambridge University Press, 1988. Political science analysis of National Front and coalition politics from 1958 to 1986. Concludes that bipartisan rule gave Colombia sustained economic growth and low inflation. The model building and testing of various hypotheses make for heavy going for all but political scientists. Extensive bibliography and good index.

Henderson, James D. *When Colombia Bled: A History of the* Violencia *in Tolima.* University: University of Alabama Press, 1985. Probably the best regional account of *la violencia* to date. Henderson has gone to impressive lengths to document the terrible realities that explain so much of Colombian violence and human rights abuse. His attention to the larger national context and his assessment of the various theories and explanations for *la violencia* make this an especially important work. Impressive array of local sources and a useful index.

Martz, John D. "Colombia at the Crossroads." *Current History* 90 (February, 1991): 69-72, 80-81. A perceptive overview of major happenings in 1989 and 1990, especially concerning political changes, elections, drugs, violence, and human rights. Limited references and no index.

Pearce, Jenny. *Colombia: Inside the Labyrinth.* London: Latin American Bureau, 1990. Best book-length survey of modern Colombian history available and a good read. Populist in tone and interpretation but well grounded in Colombian sources. Provides solid detail on human rights violations and labor unions, guerrilla groups, and social movements. Includes bibliography and index.

Maurice P. Brungardt

Cross-References

Panama Declares Independence from Colombia (1903), p. 25; El Salvador's Military Massacres Civilians in *La Matanza* (1932), p. 464; Gaitán's Assassination Sparks *La Violencia* in Colombia (1948), p. 737; The Declaration on the Rights and Duties of Man Is Adopted (1948), p. 755; Brazil Begins a Period of Intense Repression (1968), p. 1468; Marcos Declares Martial Law in the Philippines (1972), p. 1680; An Oppressive Military Rule Comes to Democratic Uruguay (1973), p. 1715; Allende Is Overthrown in a Chilean Military Coup (1973), p. 1725; The Argentine Military Conducts a "Dirty War" Against Leftists (1976), p. 1864; Indigenous Indians Become the Target of Guatemalan Death Squads (1978), p. 1972; The National Commission Against Torture Studies Human Rights Abuses (1983), p. 2186; Argentine Leaders Are Convicted of Human Rights Violations (1985), p. 2280.

SOVIET FARMERS ARE GIVEN CONTROL OF LAND AND SELECTION OF CROPS

Category of event: Workers' rights
Time: February 4, 1989
Locale: Estonia and elsewhere in the Union of Soviet Socialist Republics

Farmers in the Soviet Union were under tight state supervision until Mikhail Gorbachev's program of perestroika *brought about a loosening of the reins*

Principal personages:

MIKHAIL GORBACHEV (1931-   ), the president of the Soviet Union who began the basic reform of Soviet agriculture

BORIS YELTSIN (1931-   ), the president of the Russian Soviet Federated Socialist Republic, a prime mover for privatization of land ownership in Russia

ALEKSANDR NIKONOV (1918-   ), a primary theorist of agrarian *perestroika*

VLADIMIR TIKHONOV (1927-   ), a primary publicist for agrarian reform

Summary of Event

On February 4, 1989, three Estonian farmers became the first citizens of the Soviet Union to receive formal documents from the government allowing them to use land permanently and without charge for independent farming. This event represented the culmination of a fairly long and involved movement in official Soviet thinking away from an emphasis on large state and collective farms and toward an emphasis on the individual, independent peasant farmer. As such, it marked a watershed in Soviet agricultural theory and practice.

With the coming of the Bolshevik Revolution in 1917, Soviet agriculture was in dire straits. Production of food had plummeted as a result of enormous casualties of men and draft animals in World War I and widespread rural unrest in connection with the "agrarian revolution" of peasants against their landlords. Upon their accession to power, the Bolsheviks immediately issued a decree "On Land" on November 8, 1917, followed up by a more comprehensive agrarian law, "Decree Concerning the Socialization of Land," on February 19, 1918, whereby all landlord property rights were abolished and estates confiscated. In addition, all land was nationalized and was to be parceled out to local collectives, or soviets, for distribution to those who tilled it. Preference was to be given to collective farms, but the primary purpose of the legislation was to ensure the equitable distribution of land among individual peasant-farmers and thereby gain them as allies of the proletariat (under the guidance, of course, of the Bolsheviks).

This alliance, however, was not to be permanent, but was to serve as a temporary arrangement whereby the urban proletariat, which was the mainstay of the new Bolshevik state, could be assured of sufficient food. Bolshevik leader Vladimir Ilich Lenin saw the eventual outcome as the creation of a second revolution in the countryside that would set the farm laborers and poor peasantry against the more well-to-do farmers (or *kulaks*, as they came to be called).

Under War Communism (1918-1921), the Bolsheviks came to rely more and more upon forced seizures of grain and other products from the peasantry in order to ensure a minimal flow of foodstuffs to the cities. State compulsion became the order of the day, in the form of acreage goals, mandatory improvements of farming techniques, forced labor drafts, a national plan for sowing different crops, and increasing pressure on the approximately fifteen million small peasant households to join collective and state farms. As a result, by the spring of 1921 agricultural production had fallen to disastrously low levels.

Lenin's solution, in the form of the New Economic Policy (NEP), was to grant the peasantry titles in perpetuity to land that they cultivated and to restore ownership of personal property, primarily draft animals and farming implements, that had been confiscated. Although actual land ownership remained with the state, the peasants were free to choose which type of land tenure they preferred (individual, cooperative, or collective) and had the right to select which crops they wished to grow and how they chose to cultivate them. These rights were codified in the Law of Toilers' Land Tenure (or "Land Code") of May 22, 1922.

The Land Code constituted the high-water mark in terms of individual freedom for the peasantry for almost the next seventy years. Lenin's successor as head of party and government, Joseph Stalin, in pursuit of his goal of "socialism in one country," embarked upon a crash program of industrialization of the Soviet Union. This industrialization was to be financed largely by enhanced earnings generated by an increasingly rational and productive agricultural sector. Stalin and his supporters believed that the individual and small cooperative peasant holdings were both ideologically undesirable and economically backward; they believed that Soviet agriculture could be brought into the twentieth century only if such holdings were consolidated into large collective and state farms.

The ensuing period of forced collectivization, under the slogan "liquidation of the *kulaks*," was aimed ostensibly at the elimination of the remaining rural landlords. In actuality, the "middle peasantry," or individual peasant proprietors who worked their own land, were denounced as *kulaks* and forced into large collective and state farms. Those who resisted were either killed outright or exiled for long terms to Siberia. Since the middle peasantry formed the backbone of Soviet agriculture, their destruction as a group had disastrous immediate and long-term results. Even Stalin realized that something had to be done, and in 1933 he denounced local leaders for forcing the pace of collectivization, which they had done only at his insistence, and threw the peasants a sop in the form of individual plots and livestock. This meant that even though all peasants lived and worked on either collective or state farms, they were given very small plots of ground that they could cultivate in their free time and were also accorded the right to own small amounts of livestock, usually a cow and a few chickens.

This situation in terms of individual peasant rights existed relatively unchanged over the next fifty years. Under Stalin's successor, Nikita Khrushchev, an attempt was made to consolidate smaller collective and state farms and to curtail the size of individual plots, but the resulting difficulties contributed to Khrushchev's ouster from power in 1964. Soviet agriculture under Leonid Brezhnev and the short-lived regimes of his successors, Yuri Andropov and Konstantin Chernenko, was marked by enormous investments of resources in an increasingly inefficient system of state and collective farms. In this system, individually cultivated plots and individually owned livestock, although they constituted only a minuscule proportion of total cultivated land and livestock in the Soviet Union, produced an embarrassingly high percentage of the milk, eggs, and vegetables consumed in the country.

When Mikhail Gorbachev took the reins of power in 1985, the overall economy (including agriculture) had deteriorated to an almost unbearable level of stagnation and inefficiency. Gorbachev's answer to these problems involved a basic restructuring (or *perestroika*) of the economic system. An integral part of *perestroika* consisted of a series of basic changes in the agrarian sector, changes that were based largely upon the ideas of Aleksandr Nikonov, an administrator, agricultural specialist, and close personal friend and adviser to Gorbachev, and Vladimir Tikhonov, a well-known public figure and popularizer of agrarian *perestroika*. The primary ideological impetus for the Nikonov-Tikhonov reforms lay in the alienation of the peasantry from the land, an alienation born of forced collectivization and nourished by the continuing lack of any meaningful individual control over the land. In a more instrumental vein, Nikonov also alleged that the large collective or state farm was not necessarily the optimal size for modern production; he cited smaller, family-based units in the United States as a more economically efficient mode of production.

The reasoning was that if a level playing field could be created whereby individual and small cooperative farms could legally compete on an equal basis with state and collective farms, Soviet agriculture would benefit greatly. This approach was embodied in a resolution by the Estonian Council of Ministers and Communist Party Central Committee "On Individual Labor Activity in Agriculture" of March, 1988. Pursuant to this policy, on February 4, 1989, three Estonian peasant farmers (the first of more than a hundred) were granted title to their land.

Impact of Event

In terms of potential impact, granting life tenure and free usage of land to the three Estonian farmers opened up a whole new theoretical and practical vista in Soviet agriculture. Immediate consequences, however, were somewhat limited in scope.

In an immediately practical sense, Gorbachev's agrarian *perestroika* bore a remarkable resemblance to the agricultural component of Lenin's NEP. Each granted life tenure and limited inheritance, free choice of crops and methods of cultivation, and free choice to the peasantry of the mode of production—individual, cooperative, or collective—within which they desired to live and work. There existed, however, an important theoretical distinction. Lenin's NEP was designed to be a temporary measure to sate the desire for land on the part of the peasantry; eventually, through education in the principles of socialism and by the example of the more efficient operation of collective and state farms, peasants would be weaned from these petit-bourgeois proclivities. Gorbachev's agrarian *perestroika*, however, was seen as a permanent method for alleviating the alienation of the peasantry from the land and for enhancing the productivity of Soviet agriculture. Indeed, Boris Yeltsin, the President of the Russian Soviet Federated Socialist Republic (R.S.F.S.R.), stated that the peasant owner was the foundation for agrarian development.

The need for formal legislation to give individual farms legal status and protection was met by the Soviet Law on Property (passed on March 6, 1990, and based on the Principles of Land Legislation); the R.S.F.S.R. Congress Resolution on Private Ownership of the Land of December 4, 1990, and the Soviet Presidential Land Reform Decree of January 7, 1991. These documents formally allowed private ownership of land, right of inheritance, free access to land, and freedom to choose forms of farming.

Critics, however, pointed out that these laws were largely a dead letter, since managers of collective and state farms and other figures in the local agrarian apparatus dominated local legislative and administrative levels and could be expected to scuttle the actual operation of the program. Indeed, as of February 1, 1991, *Izvestia* reported that in the RSFSR there were thirty-five hundred peasant farms and four thousand small agricultural cooperatives involving a total of some fifty thousand people, a miniscule proportion of the total persons employed in the Russian agricultural sector.

The situation was paradoxical. There was a strong push from the top for the growth of individual peasant and small cooperative agricultural enterprises. The response at the grass-roots level, however, was lukewarm. This tepid response was based on at least two factors. The peasants, having been encouraged under Lenin to work hard on their own land and then denounced as *kulaks* under Stalin and forced onto collective and state farms, had no desire to be burned again. Perhaps even more important, Stalin's forced collectivization, whereby the successful middle peasants were liquidated, resulted in the destruction of the very type of people who could make agrarian *perestroika* work. The remaining peasantry, with a few shining exceptions, were largely content to continue their existence as cogs in a machine of institutionalized dependence.

Bibliography

Feinberg, Richard E., John Echeverri-Gent, and Friedemann Muller, eds. *Economic Reform in Three Giants.* New Brunswick, N.J.: Transaction Books, 1990. Compilation of articles addressing various approaches to economic (including agricultural) restructuring in the Soviet Union, China, and India. Especially useful for viewing agrarian *perestroika* in a comparative sense between the Soviet Union and China. No index or bibliography.

Gray, Kenneth R., ed. *Soviet Agriculture: Comparative Perspectives.* Ames: Iowa State University Press, 1990. This collection of articles compares recent trends in agricultural policies among the Soviet Union and other centrally planned economies in Eastern Europe. Contains an exhaustive series of figures and tables that provide graphic evidence of the downturn in Soviet agricultural production and efficiency. Also includes a comprehensive index.

McCauley, Martin. *Khrushchev and the Development of Soviet Agriculture: The Virgin Land Programme, 1953-1964.* New York: Holmes & Meier, 1976. Good overall coverage of Soviet agriculture under Khrushchev, with special emphasis on his ideas with regard to consolidation of collective farms and elimination of private plots. Contains bibliography and index.

Shaffer, Harry G., ed. *Soviet Agriculture: An Assessment of Its Contribution to Economic Development.* New York: Praeger, 1977. Compendium of four monographs, each of which addresses a different facet of Soviet agricultural policy from the rule of Stalin through the Brezhnev era. In general, the authors attribute the problems of Soviet agriculture to "natural disadvantages" of climate and geography rather than to the results of the Russian Revolution. No index or bibliography.

Shmelev, Nikolai, and Vladimir Popov. *The Turning Point: Revitalizing the Soviet Economy.* New York: Doubleday, 1989. Interesting early evaluation of Soviet economic reform by two Soviet economists who present *perestroika* as a full embodiment of the principles of socialism and as "stripping socialism of the alien veneer it has acquired." Criticizes agricultural policy under Brezhnev as one of the "black holes" that swallow resources. Index but no bibliography.

Solomon, Susan Gross. *The Soviet Agrarian Debate: A Controversy in Social Science, 1923-1929.* Boulder, Colo.: Westview Press, 1977. Despite the narrow focus implied by the title of this book, it is quite useful in providing the framework of the debate between the Organization-Production and the Agrarian-Marxist groups, a framework that outlines the dimensions of a debate that continued through the early 1990's. The views of A. V. Chaianov, the leader of the Organization-Production group, were drawn upon to provide the theoretical basis for Gorbachev's agrarian *perestroika.* Contains an exhaustive bibliography and index.

Tucker, Robert C. *Stalin in Power: The Revolution from Above, 1928-1941.* New York: W. W. Norton, 1990. Classic account of the early Stalinist period in Soviet history. Especially valuable for putting forced collectivization of Soviet agriculture into context within Stalin's overall plans for rapid industrialization of the Soviet Union. Contains an excellent index and bibliography.

Volin, Lazar. *A Century of Russian Agriculture: From Alexander II to Khrushchev.* Cambridge, Mass.: Harvard University Press, 1970. Written by a Russian-born agricultural economist who emigrated in 1915, this book is especially valuable for its pre-Bolshevik background on the enduring problems of Russian agriculture. Its exhaustive analysis of the application of Lenin's NEP to agriculture reveals some essential similarities (as well as basic differences) between Lenin and Gorbachev on the agrarian problem. Index but no bibliography.

Vidya Nadkarni

Cross-References

The International Labour Organisation Is Established (1919), p. 281; Stalin Begins Purging Political Opponents (1934), p. 503; Khrushchev Implies That Stalinist Excesses Will Cease (1956), p. 952; Soviet Jews Demand Cultural and Religious Rights (1963), p. 1177; Gorbachev Initiates a Policy of *Glasnost* (1985), p. 2249; Lithuania Declares Its Independence from the Soviet Union (1990), p. 2577; Demise of the U.S.S.R. Paves the Way for Reforms in Former Soviet Republics (1991), p. 2618.

SOLIDARITY REGAINS LEGAL STATUS IN POLAND

Category of event: Workers' rights and political freedom
Time: April, 1989
Locale: Warsaw, Poland

Seven years after having been suppressed by the Communist regime, the self-governing, independent trade union Solidarity was legalized and new, semifree elections were called in Poland

Principal personages:
LECH WAŁĘSA (1943-   ), the leader of Solidarity
WOJCIECH JARUZELSKI (1923-   ), the head of the Communist regime in Poland, who was trying to lead the country into economic and political stability
CZESŁAW KISZCZAK (1925-   ), the minister of internal affairs who had directed the suppression of Solidarity, but who later called for talks with it
TADEUSZ MAZOWIECKI (1927-   ), a Catholic journalist and Solidarity adviser who assisted Wałęsa
BRONISŁAW GEREMEK (1932-   ), a medieval historian who become Wałęsa's chief political adviser
MIKHAIL GORBACHEV (1931-   ), the president of the Soviet Union, who decided to let events in Poland be controlled by the Polish leaders
MIECZYSŁAW RAKOWSKI (1926-   ), the prime minister of Poland
ANDRZEJ GWIAZDA (1935-   ), a leading figure in Solidarity who was increasingly critical of Wałęsa's role

Summary of Event

Led by Lech Wałęsa, the independent, self-governing trade union Solidarity had emerged in the summer of 1980 as both a labor movement and a human rights movement in Poland. It attempted to promote a moral renewal and establish social justice throughout the country. Its efforts to break down barriers within society, however, challenged the privileged status of the Communist regime that had been installed in Poland by the Soviet Union after World War II. Worsening economic conditions also undermined stability in Poland. In December, 1981, General Wojciech Jaruzelski, the Polish prime minister and Communist Party leader, imposed martial law with the help and support of General Czesław Kiszczak, the minister of the interior and head of the police. Solidarity's leaders were imprisoned, and the union was outlawed.

Wałęsa and others eventually were released and martial law was lifted in July, 1983, but the economic and political situation in Poland was not really stable. Solidarity retained the support of many in Poland, and when Wałęsa was awarded the Nobel Peace Prize in 1983, the ideals of the union's struggle for freedom and justice were reinforced. Although illegal and persecuted, Solidarity kept up symbolic non-violent actions. During the 1980's, Wałęsa often spoke out against the regime and supported workers' rights. His generally moderate approach evoked opposition within Solidarity circles from those, like the former vice president of Solidarity, Andrzej Gwiazda, who wished to pursue more aggressive policies.

Within the government, the new prime minister, Mieczysław Rakowski, emerged as the leading opponent of Solidarity. As a journalist, he had edited the influential journal *Polityka* (politics) and was regarded by some, especially in the West, as a communist liberal. In negotiations with Solidarity in 1981, however, he had demonstrated his fundamental opposition to the movement, calling it a "counter-Revolution," the most pejorative term in the Communist vocabulary. By the mid-1980's, however, he was regarded as a "hard-liner" and declared to Jaruzelski that he could maintain order and stability in Poland without taking Solidarity into account.

The problems in the Polish economy were severe. Worker morale was low, industrial output was declining, inflation was skyrocketing, and strikes were increasing in frequency. In November, 1987, in a tacit admission that the economy was not working properly, the regime held a referendum on whether to carry out a new "government program for radical economic recovery," and whether to introduce a new Polish model for "democratizing political life." Although the majority of those who participated voted "yes," the percentage was far lower than the government had expected and participation fell short of the margin required by law for victory. It was an embarrassing defeat for the government and one unprecedented in a Communist state.

During 1988, conditions worsened. In a further round of serious strikes, workers demanded the reinstatement of their union and chanted, "There is no freedom without Solidarity." It was the reality that this conviction was widely held in society that led Interior Minister Kiszczak to conclude that some rapprochement with Solidarity must be made. In this decision, he and other Communist Party leaders in Poland had the tacit approval of President Mikhail Gorbachev of the Soviet Union. When he visited Warsaw in July, 1988, Gorbachev let it be known that, in light of Soviet economic problems, the question of ending the Afghan war, and the delicacy of internal reform under *glasnost* (openness) and *perestroika* (restructuring), the Poles should take charge of their own events and work out solutions which were acceptable in their own country. On August 30, 1988, Solidarity spokesman Tadeusz Mazowiecki announced that Wałęsa and Kiszczak would meet the following day to discuss possible formal talks.

There emerged from these talks an agreement that Wałęsa would be allowed to debate economic and labor issues on national television with the spokesman of the government union. In their confrontation in November, the Solidarity leader humiliated the cliché-quoting party apparatchik, Alfred Miodowicz. Wałęsa emphasized the need to legalize Solidarity in order to restore human rights in Poland and to address economic problems. In response, Prime Minister Rakowski stepped up a program of attacks upon Wałęsa and other Solidarity supporters, and compromise seemed remote. Within the party and the government, however, there were important changes taking place. It was again General Kiszczak who took the initiative. He persuaded General Jaruzelski, the party secretary and defense minister, to accept the return of Solidarity. In a stormy central committee meeting in January, it was agreed that talks would be opened with Wałęsa and Solidarity representatives.

On February 6, 1989, these dramatic round table talks began. Wałęsa was assisted by a large and capable team, which included Mazowiecki, who advised on union pluralism in Poland, and Bronisław Geremek, a historian who advised on political reform. Although the Catholic church was not formally represented, despite its generally steady support of Solidarity, its interests were protected by prominent Catholic laypeople affiliated with Catholic publications and organizations. The talks were carried on with the government deputation, headed by Kiszczak, and took place in semipublic surroundings in Warsaw as well as in more private circumstances in the nearby village of Magdalenka. It was, in many ways, a surreal atmosphere: former prisoners in formal and informal conversations with their former jailers. Most issues were hard to resolve, but, as Mazowiecki put it, it was evident that a spirit of reciprocity, which made compromise a step forward rather than a concession, prevailed on both sides. After three months of discussion, in which Wałęsa successfully resisted the more aggressive demands of Gwiazda and some other Solidarity leaders, agreements finally were reached with the regime on April 5. Taken together, these marked the climax of this stage in the recovery of political and civil rights in Poland.

The first agreement, which addressed issues of union pluralism, contained three main points. It provided for the legalization of Solidarity, for the establishment of Rural Solidarity, thus realizing the principles of trade union pluralism in the countryside, and for the reinstatement, without penalty, of those who had been fired for trade union activities during the period of martial law and after.

The second agreement, dealing with issues of political reform, went beyond anything that could have been imagined in Gdańsk in 1980. This agreement marked the beginning of the unraveling of the Communist system in Poland and elsewhere. What the government proposed, and what Solidarity accepted, was a parliamentary system in which real opposition parties would be represented. New elections were called for, to be held within two months. In the lower house of the Parliament, the Sejm, 65 percent of the seats were to be reserved for the Communist Party and its puppet coalition partners. An upper house, the Senate, was to be reestablished. In this body, all one hundred seats were to be freely contested, with none reserved for the Communists or their partners. Finally, a presidency with broad executive powers was established, with the expectation that it would be held by the regime. In related matters, opposition media were authorized, complete with a newspaper and regular television and radio programming. In addition, the government agreed to give the Catholic church full legal status, something it had not had since World War II.

Impact of Event

Elections were scheduled for June 4 and 18. The Communist regime was sure that it would win, for it doubted that Solidarity could form national slates of candidates for the open seats in only two months. Solidarity itself was, at first, in considerable confusion as to how to mount such a political campaign. After all, there had not been even the semblance of a free election in Soviet-dominated Eastern Europe in more than forty years. To the surprise of nearly everyone, the union did put together a national campaign. Its candidates campaigned on radio and television, using the access that had been granted in the April agreements. Throughout the country, there was excitement over the prospects for this election that the old-style, controlled elections under the Communists had never had.

Outside Poland, events in the weeks leading up to the election were followed closely by the Western press. Most predicted that the Communists would win. When the results were in, however, it was clear that Solidarity had won a stunning triumph: all 35 percent of the contested seats in the Sejm and ninety-nine of the hundred seats in the Senate. Bronisław Geremek emerged as the leader of the Solidarity faction in parliament. When the presidential election was held, General Jaruzelski won, but he did so by only one vote, and he needed Solidarity support. To form a government, he turned first to members of his own party. The normally docile puppet parties in the Sejm refused to support the Communists after their political humiliation in the election. By the middle of August, the president was forced to turn to Solidarity and ask it to put together the new government. Although certain crucial ministries were reserved for the Communists, the coalition which emerged under the new prime minister, Tadeusz Mazowiecki, constituted the first non-Communist government in Eastern Europe since the Communist takeover of the mid- and late 1940's. As *Newsweek* magazine noted, "the union's victory pushe[d] the Communist Party toward reform—and Poland toward democracy."

In the other countries of the Soviet bloc, the pace of reform quickened. In Hungary, a non-Communist government was established by the end of October. In the German Democratic Republic, opposition forces began calling for democracy in huge demonstrations in October, the Berlin Wall came down in November, and within a year East and West Germany were reunited. In Czechoslovakia, an opposition group was formed under Václav Havel in November, within ten days what was called "the Velvet Revolution" brought about the fall of the Communist regime, and by the middle of December the nation's first non-Communist government was sworn in. Elsewhere in the region, Communist control was radically weakened, most spectacularly in Romania, where dictator Nicolai Ceausescu was overthrown and executed in December, 1989. Thus, less than a decade after the emergence of Solidarity, limitations on human rights were disappearing throughout the region. People were learning again what it was like to live in freedom.

Bibliography

Ash, Timothy Garton. *The Magic Lantern: The Revolution of '89 Witnessed in Warsaw, Budapest, Berlin, and Prague.* New York: Random House, 1990. An account by a well-known British journalist and academic of the events which transformed

Eastern Europe in 1989. Ash knew the individuals who created the revolution personally and was on the spot as the events he described took place. His chapter on the Polish elections of June, and the immediate aftermath, is particularly insightful.

_____. *The Uses of Adversity: Essays on the Fate of Central Europe.* New York: Random House, 1989. Like his volume cited above, this book is a collection of Ash's essays published, for the most part, in *The New York Review of Books* and similar journals. The chapters in this book cover events in Eastern Europe from 1983 onward. Those which deal with Poland trace the fate of Solidarity during the period of its suppression and show how it was successful in retaining popular support.

Banta, Kenneth, and John Borrell, with John Kohan. "Poland: A Humiliation for the Party." *Time* 133, no. 25 (June 19, 1989); 24-26. Although very brief, this journalistic account provides vivid details of the legalization of Solidarity as background to the elections of June, 1989. Its narrative of events is reliable, and the observations made about the impact upon the Communist Party are especially accurate.

Goodwyn, Lawrence. *Breaking the Barrier: The Rise of Solidarity in Poland.* New York: Oxford University Press, 1991. Most of this book focuses upon the period of 1980-1981, when Solidarity emerged in Poland. The long final chapter, "The Re-Emergence of Civil Society," treats the events of 1988-1989. The author's general thesis—that Solidarity owed more to labor organizers along the Baltic coast than it did to intellectuals and the church—is a controversial one that takes issue with, for example, the views of Timothy Garton Ash. In the context of the chapter on the legalization of Solidarity, the author appears to give too little credit to the influence of intellectuals (for example, Mazowiecki and Geremek).

Kemp-Welch, A., ed. *The Birth of Solidarity.* 2d ed. New York: St. Martin's Press, 1991. The first edition of this book (1983) dealt entirely with the events of 1980 and provided a detailed analysis of the negotiations in Gdańsk. This second edition includes an excellent chapter, "From Gdańsk to Government," which puts the developments of 1988 and early 1989 into perspective very effectively. The author, a British academic, had access to very reliable sources.

Meyer, Michael. "A New Style of Socialism? A Polish Agreement Legalizes the Opposition." *Newsweek* 113, no. 15 (April 10, 1989): 36-37. Although very brief, this journalistic reporting is accurate and provides an early reliable analysis of what led to the government's decision to legalize Solidarity. The reporter is particularly good in showing opposition to Wałęsa in Solidarity and opposition within the regime to the course of action led by Kiszczak and Jaruzelski.

Staar, Richard F. "Poland: Renewal or Stagnation?" *Current History* 88 (November, 1989): 373-376, 405-407, 409. The author, an astute observer of the Polish scene, provides an analysis of the situation in Poland as of the end of August, 1989. He is particularly successful in setting the negotiations in the spring of 1989, which resulted in the legalization of Solidarity, into the context of current historical development. His cautious tone about prospects was based in his assessment of the degree to which the Polish economy had come close to collapse in the winter of 1988-1989.

Paul W. Knoll

Cross-References

The Berlin Wall Is Built (1961), p. 1125; The Brezhnev Doctrine Bans Acts of Independence in Soviet Satellites (1968), p. 1408; Soviets Invade Czechoslovakia (1968), p. 1441; Solidarity Leads Striking Polish Workers (1980), p. 2112; Gorbachev Initiates a Policy of *Glasnost* (1985), p. 2249; Hungary Adopts a Multiparty System (1989), p. 2421; Poland Forms a Non-Communist Government (1989), p. 2500; The Berlin Wall Falls (1989), p. 2523; Ceausescu Is Overthrown in Romania (1989), p. 2546; Soviet Troops Withdraw from Czechoslovakia (1990), p. 2570; Lithuania Declares Its Independence from the Soviet Union (1990), p. 2577; Gorbachev Agrees to Membership of a United Germany in NATO (1990), p. 2589; Demise of the U.S.S.R. Paves the Way for Reforms in Former Soviet Republics (1991), p. 2618.

DEMONSTRATORS GATHER IN TIANANMEN SQUARE

Categories of event: Political freedom; atrocities and war crimes
Time: April-June, 1989
Locale: Beijing, People's Republic of China

Hundreds of thousands gathered in Tiananmen Square to protest official corruption, and on June 4, 1989, the People's Liberation Army physically crushed the Democracy Movement, mainly composed of students

Principal personages:
FANG LIZHI (1936-), an internationally recognized astrophysicist who lost his party membership as a result of speeches on reform
HU YAOBANG (1915-1989), the general secretary of the Chinese Communist Party (1980-1987), whose death became a rallying point for students demonstrating for democracy
LIU BINYAN (1925-), the leading Chinese journalist who succeeded in using "investigative reporting" to criticize conservative communism
DENG XIAOPING (1904-), the dominant figure in Chinese politics after Mao Tse-tung's death in 1976
ZHAO ZIYANG (1919-), the former premier of China (1980-1987)
JIANG ZEMIN (1926-), the general secretary of the Communist Party (June 24, 1989-), chosen by the hard-line faction of the CCP to replace Zhao Ziyang

Summary of Event

The Tiananmen Square massacre on June 4, 1989, proved to be the climactic event of the massive demonstrations by the Democracy Movement, a cause backed by hundreds of thousands of student demonstrators and endorsed by millions of other Chinese. These voices were crying out for freedom of speech and better representation in their own affairs. A handbill proclaimed that the Democracy Movement's "guiding principle is to propagate democratic ideas among the people. Our slogan is to oppose bureaucracy and authoritarianism, and strive for democracy and freedom. The time has come to awaken the democratic ideas that have long been suppressed."

Decades of "suppression" led to the wave of demonstrations culminating at Tiananmen Square, but more directly, the 1986 elections sparked the human rights conflagration that left countless martyrs in its ashes and other "heroes" exiled in the summer of 1989. China's electoral laws (established in 1953) were modified in 1979 and allegedly provided a four-tier system of representative government: township congresses with two-year terms, county congresses with three-year terms, provincial congresses with five-year terms, and at the top of this hierarchy, the People's National Congress convening in Beijing. Although the Chinese Communist Party (CCP) claimed a "democracy under central leadership," it thwarted election campaigns waged by democratic factions from 1980 through 1984. The denial of appointment to elected representatives again in 1986 finally invoked public protests, beginning with students at Heifi and Wuhan and spreading to Shanghai and Beijing. Even while the demonstrators were still hammering out a workable definition of "democracy," they persisted in hanging prodemocracy banners. One factor above all others separated these uprisings from the 1989 massacre—the international free press, which was present at the latter. In January of 1987 the government created a state agency to control not only all publications and presses within the country but also the distribution of relevant supplies. Determined and undaunted, students found creative means to inform distant colleagues such as letter writing campaigns, demonstrating before foreign officials, and tireless "informative" campaigns at train stations.

Prodemocracy sentiments remained strong and became increasingly public until the June 4, 1989, showdown. One of the worst catastrophes in the history of human rights occurred when the People's Liberation Army (PLA) slaughtered hundreds of unarmed students who were only claiming what was constitutionally theirs. The duration of this debacle extends much longer than the few bloody hours in 1989, or even the three long years prior. Rather, it spans the entire era of the republic's existence.

The same constitutional support claimed by the Tiananmen Square demonstrators had been available since 1954, when Mao Tse-tung implemented the *Constitution of the People's Republic of China*. "The Fundamental Rights and Duties of Citizens" section is replete with support for open dialogue between citizens and officials. Article 35 states, "Citizens of the People's Republic of China enjoy freedom of speech, of the press, of assembly, of association, of procession and of demonstration." Articles 37 and 38 buttress this notion with the promise that the freedom and dignity of all Chinese citizens are "inviolable." Article 41 complements this theme by providing the "right to criticize and make suggestions" to state groups with the assurance that "No one [state official or representative] may suppress such complaints, charges and exposures, or retaliate against the citizens making them." These statements have proven little more than constitutional prose, and the word "inviolable" certainly pales in the face of reality.

The controversy over political standards and human rights was not new to China. The Three Principles of the People of Sun Yat-sen, the very "Father of the Chinese Revolution," were claimed by both the Chinese Communists and the Nationalists in 1949. Precedents for the Tiananmen Square demonstrations in the form of public criticism of political standards and human rights issues can be found in the Hundred Flowers Campaign (May, 1956-June, 1957) and the Democracy Wall incident (1978). In both cases, official decree abruptly stopped the citizens from voicing their right of freedom of expression. In his experiment with open criticism, Mao had invited monitored criticism of his government, but within a year he was bludgeoned with criticisms not only of easily repairable ills but also of the fundamental tenets of communism. After Mao released his essay "On the Correct Handling of Contradictions Among the People" in June, 1957, he assigned Deng Xiaoping to deal with the intellectuals who had criticized the regime and the Party. Nearly two million were questioned, with 100,000 serious sentences and several million lesser punishments given, including work in the countryside for "reeducation." Ironically, in the late 1970's Deng invoked similar consequences when he pushed for a new state constitution which included the "Great Four Freedoms" of speaking out, elaborating on personal views, holding debates, and hanging big character posters. When the collage of posters and protests at Xidan Wall in Beijing became a daily and growing challenge to Deng's policies, he abruptly ended the Democracy Wall Movement by making thousands of arrests, removing the Great Four Freedoms from the constitution, and reinforcing his March, 1979, "Four Cardinal Principles." Consequently, strict ideological party rule ensued.

On the brink of the Tiananmen Square demonstrations, Chinese universities were filled with students who had learned the lessons not only of the Hundred Flowers Campaign but also of the much-maligned Great Leap Forward and Cultural Revolution. They were entering their teen years when Chinese were last allowed to "speak out" at Xidan Wall. Most of them undoubtedly could recall Wei Jingsheng's famous anti-Deng wall poster, "Democracy, the Fifth Modernization." One 1986 Shanghai slogan was rather direct: "If you want to know what freedom is, just go and ask Wei Jingsheng."

In 1986, tolerance of open expression was once again in the air. Deng Xiaoping had miscalculated the ramifications of officially initiating debates on political reform. General secretary Hu Yaobang became the voice in the secretariat for open debate as an avenue toward reform. The liberalization cause initially received its biggest boost from party member Fang Lizhi, an astrophysicist and vice president of Hefei University in Anhui, who incited student demonstrations with his prodemocracy speeches. He blamed the CCP leaders for "the social malaise in our country today." Fang also informed the students that the CCP's "narrow propaganda seems to imply that nothing that came before us has any merit whatsoever." Propaganda, he said, could be used to praise Communist heroes but should not be used to tear down other heroes. Fueled by the Voice of America broadcast coverage of the demonstrations, students throughout China began to spread the flames of protest on their respective campuses. Once again, Deng had to extinguish a conflagration that he was instrumental in starting. The party replaced Hu Yaobang with premier Zhao Ziyang, and it stripped Fang Lizhi of his party membership. Hu's death on April 15, 1989, gave the students a pretext to demonstrate for democracy in his memory and set off the climactic events of the Beijing Spring.

Zhao Ziyang calculated his moves while making the transition from top administrator to top party member, but his reforming colors soon showed through. As an advocate for openness, he was quickly linked by party conservatives with the student unrest. Students remained vocal after the April 15 demonstrations, looking forward to the seventieth anniversary of another student movement for democracy, the May Fourth Movement. The international media present for Mikhail Gorbachev's visit on May 16 offered a forum for student demands. Three days prior, three thousand Beijing students had begun a week-long hunger strike, successfully drawing attention to reform demands. Hundreds of bureaucrats, intellectuals, and workers rallied behind these novice ascetics, and by May 17 more than one million Beijing demonstrators called for resignations from Deng Xiaoping and Premier Li Peng. After a sour May 16 meeting between abrasive hunger strike leaders and an uncompromising Li Peng, Zhao made a personal visit (apparently sincere and compassionate), trying to persuade strikers to reconsider, but to no avail. On May 20, Li invoked martial law, which proved ineffective, for the following two weeks. Reminiscent of most revolutionary movements, when the initial leaders of the student movement began to voice concern about the unruly nature of events and began dissolving the hunger strike, refocusing the protest on local campuses, new radical leadership took over. This final stage was symbolized by perhaps the most provocative development to date, erection of the thirty-foot-high Liberty statue. Peking art students had molded white plaster and Styrofoam into an Asian symbol of freedom and reform that caught the media eyes of the world. Within a few days, on June 4, their "Goddess of Freedom" was crushed to pieces by the same tanks and soldiers that had savagely claimed the lives of many of the sculptors and allied protesters.

The radical, fanatical, and militant events of late May had paved the way for the bloody massacre of June 4. When martial law was imposed on May 20, ten thousand demonstrators prevented tanks from entering Tiananmen Square, and another million demonstrators joined the cause the next day. On June 4, 1989, the PLA massacred an undetermined number of prodemocracy demonstrators and bystanders. The following day, another two hundred civilians died at the hands of the soldiers. Troops turned on each other (June 6), reflecting differences within the army leadership. At least seven officers had already publicly sided with the demonstrators. On June 7, the diplomatic community complied with orders from their respective governments to return home. Premier Li congratulated his troops for their crackdown. On June 10, the government-controlled media reported that four hundred demonstrators were arrested for inciting unrest and attacking the military. As the windows of Western media were quickly closed, the Chinese press took center stage, claiming on June 11 that no students had been killed. Pictures abound in Western print media that disprove this assertion. The rumor of stacks of student bodies burning in Tiananmen Square in an attempt to cover up evidence is believable but unsubstantiated.

The first three demonstrators sentenced to death were all male workers, not students. This would not prove to be a precedent as numerous public executions ensued, with reliable evidence of three taking place on June 21 and twenty-four the next day. Hundreds of students and intellectuals remained in jail until 1990. The Iraq crisis in 1991 took the massacre off center stage, allowing the CCP suddenly to announce the trials and verdicts on some of the most famous dissident leaders of the 1989 demonstrations.

The Western media claim evidence of more than four hundred people dying in the massacre and aftermath. The official report is much lower, and the students' accounts range in the thousands. The Western media and students' accounts fault gross violations of human (and constitutional) rights and official corruption as the main causes. Predictably, the CCP report, crafted by Deng Xiaoping, faults a "rebellious clique" and "dregs of society" whose "goal was to establish a bourgeois republic entirely dependent on the West."

Impact of Event

For the first time in China's history, the international press served as an eyewitness to the disparity between Chinese human rights and institutional prerogatives. Deng Xiaoping's "new authoritarianism," a combination of autocratic political government and liberal economic methods, runs counter to any of the hopes of the pro-democracy demonstrators. This concentration of power and money in 1991 drives an even deeper wedge between ordinary people and the privileged class than existed before 1989.

On November 13, 1989, eighty-five-year-old Deng Xiaoping made a bold attempt to prolong the dominance of the "Gang of Old" in Chinese affairs. He stepped down from his chairmanship of the Central Military Commission, handpicking his successor, Jiang Zemin. Jiang openly embraced Deng's notion of reform, with the primary concern not the subsistence needs of the Chinese people but the leadership role of the Communist Party. Deng and his cohorts boasted that the Tiananmen Square episode clearly showed that hostile force could not shake the party. Even China's most outspoken advocate of reform, Fang Lizhi, admitted that to supplant the CCP's power was impossible.

The CCP has invoked regulations, including those implemented from 1986 on, that may stifle prodemocracy uprisings for generations, or at least until key CCP leaders pass from the scene. The size of the freshman university class of 1989 was cut in half. Very few, if any, government-supported students are allowed to study the social sciences abroad. Some estimates found that less than 1 percent of the students abroad during the uprising returned to China. A thorough reindoctrination program has been instituted at every educational level. At Deng's bidding, the universities added required classes on CCP history and political ideology, seriously detracting from academic pursuits. Social science researchers were given a set list of 190 subjects on which they could publish. Most are choosing not to publish anything at all. Demonstrations have been relegated to impotency through restrictions. The names of all demonstration organizers, and even the texts of placards, are among the many details required for demonstration approval by the state security apparatus. The right of freedom of expression took a serious step backward in China after the Tiananmen Square demonstrations. How long the CCP could hold prodemocracy elements at bay, or whether these elements could be extinguished, remained the heaviest questions in 1991.

Bibliography

Falkenheim, Victor C. "The Limits of Political Reform." *Current History* 86 (September, 1987): 261-265. Falkenheim provides a good outline of the political divi-

2488 Great Events from History II

sions, personnel, and events of the Tiananmen Square ordeal.

Kwong, Julia. "The 1986 Student Demonstrations in China: A Democratic Movement?" *Asian Survey* 28 (September, 1988): 970. An account that helps to clarify the strategies, goals, and cautions of the student demonstrators. The author has written several other articles on various aspects of modern Chinese society.

Liu, Binyan. *"Tell the World" What Happened in China and Why.* New York: Pantheon Books, 1989. This is a very passionate and biased account of the Tiananmen Square demonstrations. Liu Binyan is generally considered the leading Chinese journalist sympathetic with the prodemocracy cause.

Ogden, Suzanne. *Global Studies: China.* 4th ed. Guilford, Conn.: Dushkin Publishing, 1991. A detailed account of the Tiananmen demonstrations which relies almost entirely on primary sources. The section on the People's Republic of China includes twenty-seven articles from leading journals.

Pye, Lucian W. *China: An Introduction.* 4th ed. New York: HarperCollins, 1991. This text places the modern political crises of China in a historical and cultural context. The last three chapters serve as good overviews of "The Leadership of Deng Xiaoping," "China's Bold Effort at Reforms Under Deng Xiaoping," and "China's Future Domestically and Internationally."

Stavis, Benedict. *China's Political Reforms: An Interim Report.* New York: Praeger, 1988. Stavis' account is most helpful with the details of the earliest demonstrations. He has orchestrated many quotes and incidental trivia in this exciting chronicle of the uprisings.

Warshaw, Steven. *China Emerges: A Concise History of China from Its Origin to the Present.* 7th ed. Berkeley, Calif.: Diablo Press, 1990. The last two chapters provide a useful outline of the various factors giving rise to open criticism of the CCP. The eleven indexes are filled with both primary sources and research data.

Jerry A. Pattengale

Cross-References

The Boxer Rebellion Fails to Remove Foreign Control in China (1900), p. 1; Sun Yat-sen Overthrows the Ch'ing Dynasty (1911), p. 116; Students Demonstrate for Reform in China's May Fourth Movement (1919), p. 276; Mao Delivers His "Speech of One Hundred Flowers" (1956), p. 958; Mao's Great Leap Forward Causes Famine and Social Dislocation (1958), p. 1015; The Chinese Cultural Revolution Starts a Wave of Repression (1966), p. 1332; China Publicizes and Promises to Correct Abuses of Citizens' Rights (1978), p. 1983.

THE NATIONAL ORGANIZATION FOR WOMEN SPONSORS AN ABORTION RIGHTS RALLY

Category of event: Reproductive freedom
Time: April 9, 1989
Locale: Washington, D.C.

Hundreds of thousands of people gathered in Washington to express their support for the freedom of women to control their own fertility

Principal personages:
MOLLY YARD (1912-   ), the president of the National Organization for Women (NOW)
KATE MICHELMAN, the head of the National Abortion Rights Action League
FAYE WATTLETON (1943-   ), the head of the Planned Parenthood Federation of America
NORMA McCORVEY (1948-   ), the woman whose case became the *Roe v. Wade* decision and who by the time of the march was working full-time on the prochoice cause

Summary of Event

In the 1973 *Roe v. Wade* decision, the United States Supreme Court ruled that a woman's right to privacy included the choice of abortion during the first trimester of pregnancy. After the first trimester, increasing restrictions were permissible so that, by the final trimester, abortion could be blocked unless pregnancy clearly could be shown to be a significant threat to the physical or psychological health of the mother. This compromise decision, apparently expected to settle the issue, resulted in a firestorm of protest. Based on what were at best inconsistent church traditions—the Bible contains no explicit statement about abortion—conservative Protestants and the Roman Catholic church undertook a campaign to reestablish the illegality of abortion. As emotions grew hotter, militant, sometimes violent, groups such as Operation Rescue and the Pro-Life Action League formed.

Public opinion polls in the 1970's and 1980's consistently showed that a majority of Americans favored legal abortion in at least some circumstances. In 1989, for example, a poll done by the Gallup Organization for *Newsweek* indicated that 89 percent of Americans approved of abortion to save a mother's life, 81 percent in cases of rape or incest, and 75 percent if carrying the pregnancy to term would damage the mother's health. Nevertheless, those opposed to abortion were able to chip away at the availability of the procedure. The Hyde Amendment of 1977, which limited the use of public funds for abortions, was an example. Antiabortionists were also encouraged by the shifting membership of the Supreme Court.

The *Roe* decision had been by a seven-to-two vote, but by 1989 three of the Court's majority in the decision had retired. Two of the replacements, Antonin Scalia and Anthony Kennedy, had no record regarding abortion, but both were Catholic and conservative and were expected to oppose abortion. The third new member, Sandra Day O'Connor, appeared to be a moderate. She was on record as saying that curbs on abortion would be acceptable only if they were not "an undue burden" on women. On the other side, she had also expressed the mistaken belief that medical technology was pushing the point of viability below the approximately twenty-four weeks that had underlaid the *Roe* decision. As a five-to-four decision in 1986, before Kennedy joined the Court, indicated, the prochoice majority on the high court bench was no longer dependable.

The stage was set for a showdown by the passage of a Missouri law. The legislation, written in conjunction with antiabortion activists, asserted that life began at conception and restricted the use of public money and buildings not only for actual abortions but also for counseling. Quickly challenged, this 1986 law worked its way through the federal courts, reaching the Supreme Court docket in 1989. Although legal scholars generally predicted that the case, *Webster v. Reproductive Health Services*, was unlikely to result in a decision either clearly affirming or overturning *Roe*, the Court was expected to accept increased restrictions. Jubilant antichoice forces worried mostly about how complete their victory would be, while those favoring choice began to realize that they could lose the right to abortion.

Feminists and others who favored choice had been quiescent since *Roe*. Perhaps a bit intimidated by the virulence of their opponents, they seem to have assumed that, having been recognized, the right to abortion was secure. Faced by the changed Court about to rule in the *Webster* case, they realized that, unless they could convince the justices and politicians that the public actually favored choice, that right was actually in jeopardy. The result was the March for Women's Equality and Women's Lives, sponsored by the National Organization for Women, on April 9, just seventeen days before the Court heard the *Webster* case. The goal of the march was to make clear to legislators and justices that the loudly expressed opposition to abortion was not representative of the public generally.

Coming from all over the United States and several foreign countries, an enormous crowd of demonstrators, estimated at three hundred thousand by the U.S. Park Service and twice that by the organizers, gathered in Washington, D.C. The march proceeded from the Washington Monument to the Capitol and, despite the presence of a few hundred counterdemonstrators, was conducted without serious incident. By comparison, an antiabortion gathering held earlier in 1989 drew an estimated sixty-seven thousand people. The April 9 turnout was the largest prochoice demonstration in United States history.

One impressive aspect of the march was the variety of people involved. Student groups from five hundred American colleges and universities marched. The delegation from Georgia numbered three thousand, and New York City sent one hundred fifty busloads. Other countries represented included the United Kingdom, France, Brazil, Peru, Norway, Japan, Ethiopia, and Australia.

Also impressive were the celebrities in attendance. These included entertainers such as Whoopi Goldberg, Glenn Close, Leonard Nimoy, and Judy Collins. Eighteen members of Congress addressed the gathering. The Reverend Jesse Jackson, accompanied by his son and daughter, spoke of his conversion to the prochoice side as a result of his examination of economic discrimination against women. Jackson noted that poor women had already lost access to abortion because of restrictions on public funding. It was, he said, another example of unfair social policy that gave those with wealth a freedom denied to the less fortunate.

More direct political action was also a part of prochoice plans. The Hollywood Women's Political Committee, which had raised some two million dollars for the 1986 Senate elections, pressured members of Congress who were reluctant to participate in a breakfast meeting. Five thousand marchers representing all fifty states made the rounds of representatives' offices to lobby for a variety of women's issues. In addition to abortion rights, these included the Equal Rights Amendment and the Family and Medical Leave Act. Those involved in the march were determined to make clear that, however quiescent the prochoice side had been in the past, it was going to be a major political force in the future.

One of the few disappointments for the organizers of the march was that few African Americans participated. Since minority and poor women were usually the most burdened when rights were restricted—it has been estimated that 75 percent of the deaths from illegal abortions before the *Roe* decision occurred among women of color—organizers hoped that blacks would be prominent among the demonstrators. A number of factors may have explained the low turnout: African Americans were generally less able to afford the expense of going to Washington, blacks were more divided on the question, black churches were influential and in many cases were opposed to abortion, and civil rights groups feared that involvement in the abortion debate would cost them support on other issues.

The hopes of the prochoice forces seemed to have been achieved. The large number of demonstrators showed the political potential of a prochoice stand. After an initial refusal to comment, a White House spokesperson acknowledged that the march was "very successful." Because President George Bush had courted the religious-political right with adamant opposition to abortion, his representatives were not likely to give any more credit to the march than they absolutely had to. It was left to the vice president to sneer that the demonstration was "nothing unusual."

Although the Supreme Court tended to follow the dictates of public opinion, the *Webster* decision, which came in mid-July, was of little comfort to the prochoice forces. Although *Roe* was not overturned, significant new restrictions were allowed. These included viability testing after the twentieth week (very few abortions were done past that point in a pregnancy anyway), limits on public funding, notification of and possibly required permission from parents when teenagers sought abortion, standards for clinics that would make them too expensive to operate, and informed consent that included exposure to graphic literature designed to cause women to change their minds. Ultimately, the marchers could claim only partial success.

Impact of Event

The question of a woman's right to an abortion became one of the divisive issues in American society in the late twentieth century. Abortion had, however, been a fact of life for all of recorded history. Opposition to it was rooted in centuries-old moral and ethical traditions that generally addressed the question in terms of the evils of female sexuality. The early church fathers seemed much more concerned that access to abortion would free women from the consequences of illicit sex than they were with the modern issue of fetal life. In the latter part of the nineteenth century, physicians denounced the practice as the combination of medical technology and professionalization led them to take control of gynecology. Prior to that time, the act of abortion had been mostly a woman-to-woman matter. Midwives, relatives, and friends created a network of information and aid. In a real sense, the fairly common practice of infanticide was an extension of abortion.

During the twentieth century, the demand for safe abortion grew with the availability of the technology to perform such procedures. Liberalization of the laws in New York in the early 1970's resulted in thousands of women traveling there to seek abortions. Doctors, happy to be freed of the legal ambiguities of the common practice of getting a pro forma declaration that the pregnancy was causing serious psychological problems, created very profitable and successful clinics that did nothing but abortions. Such practices declined in size when the *Roe* decision of 1973 made abortion legal all over the country.

The opposition to abortion that hinged on the necessarily arbitrary decision of when life began grew increasingly strident over the sixteen years between *Roe* and the 1989 march and rally. Norma McCorvey, the woman identified as *Roe* in the 1973 case, was in seclusion before the 1989 march because a shotgun had been fired into her Texas home the week before. At the time of the march, two clinics in Florida were firebombed, though word of this did not reach Washington in time to put a damper on the excitement caused by the tremendous success of the demonstration.

Many women and their male supporters wanted the march to sway Congress and the Supreme Court to the side of the right to choose. They hoped to force the decision makers to acknowledge the fact that decisions about procreation were made in the midst of a variety of personal and social pressures, over many of which women had little control. Whatever the factors behind a pregnancy, being forced to carry it to term meant that the quality of a woman's life could be very directly influenced for fully two decades.

The march in April, 1989, did several things. It provided a rallying point for those favoring choice to begin to make a more active defense of the right of abortion. It put elected officials on notice that there was a prochoice vote that could be ignored only at risk of losing office. It helped to redefine the choice position away from the question of population issues and toward the question of reproductive rights. The march marked a new determination of prochoice Americans to defend the right of abortion.

Bibliography

Bader, Eleanor J. "March on Washington." *The Humanist* 49 (July/August, 1989): 26-28. A clear, short account of the April 9 march by a participant who provides much detail about participants and activities. This is, perhaps, the best account of the actual event.

Hardin, Garrett J. *Mandatory Motherhood: The True Meaning of "Right to Life."* Boston: Beacon Press, 1974. This book is the definitive statement of the hard-line position concerning the importance of abortion as a response to the danger of population pressure. It should be read by anyone seeking a full understanding of the spectrum of prochoice views.

Harrison, Beverly Wildung. *Our Right to Choose: Toward a New Ethic of Abortion.* Boston: Beacon Press, 1983. Despite a disconcerting tendency to use nouns as verbs, Harrison provides an excellent survey of the religious attitudes concerning abortion. Although writing from a Christian perspective, she is critical and open-minded. She successfully argues that a prochoice position is not incompatible with Christian views.

Mohr, James. *Abortion in America: The Origins and Evolution of Public Policy.* New York: Oxford University Press, 1979. This is perhaps the best study of policy concerning abortion in the United States. It provides background essential to an understanding of the issues involved in the abortion debate. This book or something similar should be the beginning of any serious study of the question.

Tax, Meredith. "March to a Crossroads." *The Nation* 248 (May 8, 1989): 613, 631-633. The author, who participated in the April 9 march, makes a clear statement of the growing unity in the prochoice ranks and identifies the new emphasis on reproductive rights.

Fred R. van Hartesveldt

Cross-References

Sanger Opens the First Birth-Control Clinic in the United States (1916), p. 184; The National Organization for Women Forms to Protect Women's Rights (1966), p. 1327; The Family Planning Services Act Extends Reproductive Rights (1970), p. 1579; *Roe v. Wade* Expands Reproductive Choice for American Women (1973), p. 1703; Italy Legalizes Abortion (1978), p. 1988; O'Connor Becomes the First Female Supreme Court Justice (1981), p. 2141; Prolife Groups Challenge Abortion Laws (1989), p. 2443.

A HELSINKI WATCH REPORT PROPOSES REFORM OF REFUGEE LAWS

Categories of event: Refugee relief and immigrants' rights
Time: June, 1989
Locale: New York, New York

A Helsinki Watch report documented ways in which the U.S. Immigration and Naturalization Service's treatment of asylum seekers violated laws and international conventions

Principal personages:
KARIN KÖNIG, a lawyer and intern with the Helsinki Watch who wrote the organization's report on U.S. asylum policy
ARTHUR C. HELTON (1949-   ) the director of the Lawyers' Committee for Human Rights Political Asylum Project
ROBERT L. BERNSTEIN (1923-   ), a publisher and the chair of Helsinki Watch
ARYEH NEIER (1937-   ), an attorney and the executive director of Human Rights Watch

Summary of Event

Wars, dictatorial regimes, and natural disasters generated large numbers of refugees during the 1970's and 1980's. Many of the refugees sought residence in the United States. Some groups of newcomers stood an excellent chance of receiving political asylum and resettlement assistance. Others, particularly those fleeing Haiti, Guatemala, and El Salvador, faced detention, deportation, and an uncertain future in their homelands. Concerned citizens responded by forming human rights groups such as Helsinki Watch.

Helsinki Watch was founded in 1979, in the context of increased world concern for the status of refugees. New legal instruments and standards had been drafted. These included the Final Act of the Conference on Security and Cooperation in Europe (also called the Helsinki Declaration). Under its provisions, thirty-five countries pledged respect for security and human rights considerations. They also pledged that it would be their aim to "facilitate freer movement and contacts, . . . among persons, institutions and organizations of the participating States." Helsinki groups in many of the member states (including notably the Soviet Union) assumed responsibility for monitoring their governments' compliance with the Helsinki Declaration and other humanitarian standards.

Human rights increasingly came to be viewed as a global concern. The focus of rights activists was no longer solely how their governments treated their own citizens. It was extended to any government's policies which threatened the human dignity of any country's nationals. In the United States, the Helsinki Watch Committee and Americas Watch were soon joined by Asia Watch, Africa Watch, and Middle

East Watch, which all combined forces as Human Rights Watch. Human rights ideals were promoted in a pragmatic manner, with specific recommendations addressed to policymakers. Some human rights advocates were criticized for "solving" problems by issuing reports and declarations for an undefined audience, but the Watch Committees' reports were straightforward, compassionate, and subject to implementation in the near future.

Helsinki Watch was founded in 1979 by a group of publishers, lawyers, and other activists to promote domestic and international compliance with the human rights provisions of the 1975 Helsinki accords. The Watch Committees enlisted one of America's leading civil liberties attorneys, Aryeh Neier, as Human Rights Watch executive director. Random House publisher Robert Bernstein served as Helsinki Watch chair. Human Rights Watch compiled reports on human rights conditions on every continent. In particular, it advocated "continuation of a generous and humane asylum and refugee policy . . . toward all nationalities." An exemplary report was *Detained, Denied, Deported: Asylum Seekers in the United States*, dated June, 1989.

The report explores concepts which are well defined in international law. The United Nations Convention Relating to the Status of Refugees (1951) and the U.S. Refugee Act of 1980 define a "refugee" as one who is outside his or her country "because of persecution or a well-founded fear of persecution on account of race, religion, nationality, membership in a particular social group, or political opinion." Asylum is a protected status which may allow refugees into a foreign country. In the United States, refugees may apply for permanent residency after one year. Legislation in the United States provides that refugees may (not must) be granted asylum. It also provides that if there is a clear probability of persecution, an individual is not (with few exceptions) to be deported to his homeland.

Detained, Denied, Deported was the work of lawyer and Human Rights Watch intern Karin König, among others. It drew on the work of leading experts on asylum law, including Arthur Helton of the Lawyers' Committee on Human Rights. König's introduction notes that poor countries, such as Malawi and Pakistan, have assumed the biggest burden in providing asylum to refugees from neighboring countries. In contrast, such wealthy countries as the United States assert that most of those seeking asylum are not refugees entitled to protection, but "economic migrants" subject to deportation.

International standards are succinctly and accurately described in the report. The principle of *nonrefoulement* prohibits return of refugees to situations in which they would be imperiled because of their race, religion, nationality, social group, or political opinion. It applies only to refugees already present in a country—it does not create a right of entry. Article 14 of the U.N.'s Universal Declaration of Human Rights (1948) provides the right to seek and enjoy asylum. (An earlier draft included a right to seek and be granted asylum.) A United Nations High Commission for Refugees (UNHCR) conference in 1977 sought a treaty containing an individual right to asylum. The conference was adjourned indefinitely for fear that protections would be reduced rather than enhanced.

A history of U.S. asylum policies identifies a new group of "spontaneous" asylum seekers from Central America and the Caribbean. Their treatment has been less generous than that accorded refugees from southeast Asia. The Refugee Act of 1980 is associated with improvements—withholding of deportation where refugees would face a "clear probability" of persecution was declared mandatory, no longer left to the discretion of the attorney general. The report gradually shifts from dispassionate description of refugee policies to ardent advocacy of reform. It notes discrimination in treatment of refugees from different regions. Applicants for asylum from U.S. allies such as Guatemala and El Salvador had to provide more extensive evidence and establish a higher level of persecution. The claim is bolstered by citing statistics: In fiscal year 1988, Salvadorans' and Guatemalans' applications were approved at rates of only 3 and 5 percent respectively, compared to 75 percent for Iranians and 77 percent for Ethiopians. The United States Department of State claimed that Salvadorans and Guatemalans sought asylum in the United States for economic (and therefore illegitimate) reasons rather than because of persecution. The Watch Committee report includes telling case studies of government insensitivity to human feelings, drawn from immigration lawyers and nongovernmental organizations. The State Department is castigated for its analysis of asylum applicants' petitions, which is often superficial and tailored to foreign policy objectives.

The report offers five recommendations for the executive branch of the U.S. government. First is an end to policies which deter the asylum seeker from appealing negative decisions, or from applying in the first place. Specific mention is made of the Haitian Interdiction Program and of practices whereby individuals who present no threat to society are detained. The next two recommendations address the role and training of immigration agents and judges. Immigration and Naturalization Service (INS) agents should receive special training so that they can properly follow national and international law. To eliminate political bias, independent organizations' human rights reports should be given greater emphasis than State Department analyses. An agency independent from the State and Justice Departments should be involved in asylum adjudication. Although asylum seekers present in the United States receive the most extensive publicity, many more apply through the Overseas Admission Program (OAP). The Watch recommends that the OAP include a formal right of appeal, and that its activities ensure generous and nondiscriminatory admission from areas where the UNHCR determines a need. Finally, decisions of judicial and administrative bodies (many of which assure protection to the asylum applicant) need to be fully implemented.

Congress is prodded as well. It is urged to take appropriate action and to enact legislation to control the attorney general's discretion to ensure consistent and impartial application. When immigration authorities are expected to enforce and adjudicate immigration laws, the former task overshadows and distorts the latter. Although not in the Recommendations section, the text includes a specific plea for granting extended voluntary departure status (or "safe haven") to Salvadorans and Guatemalans.

Detained, Denied, and Deported is part of an ongoing research program. Helsinki Watch pays close attention to U.S. refugee issues, and Americas Watch monitors repression in El Salvador and Haiti. Human Rights Watch played a key role in another 1989 report, *Forced Out: The Agony of the Refugee in Our Time*, which sought to "awaken, alarm, shock, and horrify," in order to counter "compassion fatigue" in addressing global dimensions of the refugee issue. Efforts such as the Helsinki Watch Group's encountered opposition. Well-funded lobbies sought to limit immigration and would make exceptions for very few of those who feared persecution. It would be up to other nongovernmental groups, Congress, and the courts to promote reform.

Impact of Event

The Helsinki Watch report did not produce immediate change in U.S. policies and received minimal press coverage. By acting in combination with other advocates for the refugee, however, the Watch Committee helped encourage steps to make American policy more humane. A diverse movement advocating refugee concerns hoped to ensure humane treatment through three channels.

First are reforms instituted by the executive branch and Congress. The Immigration Act of 1990 contained important new provisions. Cognizance of the plight of Salvadoran refugees was reflected in "safe haven" provisions (they were eligible for an eighteen-month period of safe haven if they could prove their nationality and show that they had arrived in the United States prior to September 19, 1990). The justification is that during a civil war protection is justified, but not asylum. Safe haven is to be temporary—applicants are expected to return to El Salvador eventually. Immigration rights activists welcomed this step, but they criticized stiff fees for applicants, higher than for applicants under similar programs for Libyan, Liberian, and Kuwaiti refugees. They also noted other measures such as the "investor visas" which provided special access for rich would-be immigrants.

Second are court decisions and settlements. In *Orantes-Hernandez v. Meese*, a federal district court concluded that INS practices constituted coercion of Salvadoran asylum applicants. The court noted that applicants' access to counsel was often frustrated and ordered remedial steps. In another case, the Center for Constitutional Rights, a public-interest law firm, charged the United States with ideological bias in processing Guatemalan and Salvadoran asylum requests, contrary to the Refugee Act. The government agreed under a settlement to allocate $200,000 for a publicity campaign to notify refugees of their rights. The INS agreed to review 150,000 applications that it had denied in the last ten years. Another 1991 case broadened protection for children who were detained. A federal appellate court was persuaded that due process was violated by refusing to release immigrant children to nonrelatives or social service agencies.

A third area is growth of the lobby which promotes the rights of refugees. Activists are drawing connections between human rights of a country's own citizens and rights of refugees. The American Civil Liberties Union and Amnesty International have determined that important aspects of asylum and refugee issues fall within their limited mandates.

Refugee studies are drawing attention from scholars in law and the policy sciences. Many of their efforts provide data which can be used by advocates for the potential asylum applicant. Key figures in the media and entertainment industry also help call attention to the plight of refugees.

Although there have been significant victories for refugee advocates, caveats are warranted. There has been division among circuit court justices, and dissents in recent cases argue that judges should extend deference to immigration authorities. An increasingly conservative Supreme Court may rescind, in the 1990's or later, some of the protections which appellate courts have granted. Resentment of refugees has also fueled congressional attempts to limit judicial review of administrative decisions in immigration cases.

Even when courts order protection, the slow pace of implementation remains a source of anxiety. Despite judicial concern for due process protections, immigration officials are proceeding with plans to build facilities away from the areas where most potential applicants live. This would discourage asylum applicants and hamper their advocates. Further, the greatest success thus far has been achieved on behalf of refugees already present in the United States. Potential applicants from overseas still face a difficult struggle. They are often unaware of asylum procedures and of organizations which might assist them.

America is often viewed as a land with an open door to the oppressed, but that door might more aptly be described as guarded. Nongovernmental organizations such as Helsinki Watch will continue to play a major role in opening America to the persecuted. A major instrument in this effort will be the issuance of reports such as *Detained, Denied, Deported*, reports that describe U.S. obligations under national and international law and identify policies that advance human dignity.

Bibliography

Detained, Denied, Deported: Asylum Seekers in the United States. New York: U.S. Helsinki Watch Committee, 1989. Well-organized, readable description of asylum law, with application to U.S. practices. Footnotes and list of sources. Useful statistical appendix.

Frelick, Bill. *Refugees at Our Border: The U.S. Response to Asylum Seekers.* Washington, D.C.: U.S. Committee for Refugees, 1989. A brief report on a fact-finding trip which raises many of the same issues as the Helsinki Watch study. Urges improved access for asylum seekers to attorneys and nonprofit agencies. No reference features.

Human Rights Watch. *Human Rights Watch Annual Report.* New York: Human Rights Watch, 1987-   . This provides a summary of the Watch Committees' work. It reports on the variety of studies which identify and analyze human rights violations. Also monitors each U.S. administration's compliance with human rights standards.

Lawyers Committee for Human Rights and Helsinki Watch. *Mother of Exiles: Refugees Imprisoned in America.* New York: Lawyers Committee for Human Rights, 1986. A readable description of the plight of eleven detainees, published to coincide with the centenary celebrations for the Statue of Liberty. Arthur Helton's essay identifies violations of U.S. and international law. Footnotes. No index or bibliography.

Loescher, Gil, and John A. Scanlan. *Calculated Kindness: Refugees and America's Half-Open Door, 1945 to the Present.* New York: Free Press, 1986. An excellent review of the history and politics of U.S. refugee policies. Notes and explains patterns of discrimination and the "unprecedented harshness" of the Reagan Administration. Draws on extensive interviews and archival research. Index and bibliography.

MacEoin, Gary, and Nivita Riley. *No Promised Land: American Refugee Policies and the Rule of Law.* New York: OXFAM America, 1982. Thoughtful analysis conducted for a nongovernmental organization with an emphasis on refugees from Haiti, El Salvador, and Guatemala. Illuminating description of INS procedures. Concludes that the INS violates U.S. and international law. Notes and appendices, no index.

Silk, James. *Despite a Generous Spirit: Denying Asylum in the United States.* Washington, D.C.: U.S. Committee for Refugees, 1986. This pamphlet contains a description of the asylum process and analysis of growing restrictiveness of U.S. policies. It recommends that Congress play a greater role in ending programs designed to deter people from seeking asylum in the United States. Statistical table, photographs, and selective bibliography. No index.

Yarnold, Barbara M. *Refugees Without Refuge: Formation and Failed Implementation of U.S. Political Asylum Policy in the 1980's.* Lanham, Md.: University Press of America, 1990. A scholarly analysis of U.S. policies which finds bias and a failure to implement the Refugee Act. Examines nongovernmental groups which represented refugees. Concludes that nongovernmental groups have enjoyed success in widening availability of asylum. Tables and appendices report interesting data. Bibliography.

Arthur Blaser

Cross-References

The Immigration Act of 1921 Imposes a National Quota System (1921), p. 350; Congress Establishes a Border Patrol (1924), p. 377; A U.S. Immigration Act Imposes Quotas Based on National Origins (1924), p. 383; The United Nations Adopts the Universal Declaration of Human Rights (1948), p. 789; The United Nations High Commissioner for Refugees Statute Is Approved (1950), p. 855; The U.N. Convention Relating to the Status of Refugees Is Adopted (1951), p. 867; Cubans Flee to Florida and Receive Assistance (1960's), p. 1044; The Helsinki Agreement Offers Terms for International Cooperation (1975), p. 1806.

POLAND FORMS A NON-COMMUNIST GOVERNMENT

Category of event: Political freedom
Time: June-September, 1989
Locale: Warsaw, Poland

After more than forty years of Communist rule in Poland, a new government was established which was dominated and controlled by non-Communists, many coming from the Solidarity movement

Principal personages:

LECH WAŁĘSA (1943-   ), the leader of Solidarity who led the movement into the elections

WOJCIECH JARUZELSKI (1923-   ), the president of Poland who eventually turned to Solidarity to form a government

TADEUSZ MAZOWIECKI (1927-   ), a Solidarity adviser who eventually was chosen by Wałęsa and Jaruzelski to form a government

CZESŁAW KISZCZAK (1925-   ), the former minister of the interior and new party leader, who was first asked by Jaruzelski to form a new government

MIKHAIL GORBACHEV (1931-   ), the president of the Soviet Union

BRONISŁAW GEREMEK (1932-   ), a close political adviser to Wałęsa and the leader of the Solidarity faction in Parliament

JACEK KUROŃ (1934-   ), a political activist and Solidarity adviser who suggested that Solidarity try to form a government

ADAM MICHNIK (1946-   ), a historian and journalist who was a close adviser to Solidarity and supported the effort to form a government

Summary of Event

After World War II, the Soviet Union established Communist governments in the countries of Eastern Europe. Single-party systems which repressed opposition came into existence everywhere in the region. In Poland, the Communist Party officially operated in cooperation with a number of other parties to rule the country. In reality, however, these parties were puppet organizations, and Communist domination was complete. Human and civil rights of all kinds were disregarded; education, the courts, labor, and politics all were rigidly controlled. Only the Catholic church had some degree of independence, for Poland was a deeply Catholic country. Poland suffered occasional strikes and riots against the regime. Although the Soviet Union threatened to intervene to protect Communism and what it regarded as its interests, the Polish leaders were able to convince the Soviets that they could control matters on their own.

In the 1980's, however, the Polish government was faced with a different kind of challenge. An informal alliance among the Catholic church, intellectuals, and workers resulted in the creation in 1980 of an independent, self-governing trade union known as Solidarity. Led by Lech Wałęsa, it implicitly challenged Communist control, although it did so in peaceful, nonviolent ways. The union was repressed in December, 1981, and outlawed the next year.

The moral force of Solidarity, the deep support it had within the country, and an economy which was threatening to collapse completely eventually forced the regime to legalize the union in April, 1989. More important, under General Wojciech Jaruzelski, the head of the Communist Party, and General Czesław Kiszczak, the minister of the interior, and with the tacit approval of President Mikhail Gorbachev of the Soviet Union, the regime recognized that in order to ensure political, economic, and social stability and progress, it would need to make a political compromise with Solidarity.

The Communists proposed that in the lower house of Parliament, the Sejm, they and their puppet coalition partners would hold a guaranteed 65 percent of the seats, but that free elections would be allowed for the remaining 35 percent. In addition, they proposed to establish an upper house of one hundred seats, the Senate, in which all seats would be freely contested. Finally, they proposed to create a presidency with broad executive powers, to be elected by the Sejm. In return, Solidarity agreed to join the regime in a government of "national conciliation," which meant no strikes and a promise of support in implementing a radical austerity program. The election, which was set for June, was unprecedented in a Communist country. As one American diplomat in Warsaw commented, "These are breathtaking changes. If Poland succeeds, it will become the model for a wholesale restructuring of socialism in Eastern Europe."

In the election campaign which followed, the Communists were at first sure they would win. They were wrong. In less than two weeks, Solidarity candidates were nominated to contest every seat. Solidarity was also able to campaign on radio and television, for the regime had granted it access to national media in the April agreements. In addition, it also published and distributed a national paper, *Gazeta wyborcza* (the election news), edited by Jacek Kuroń, a journalist and Solidarity adviser, and printed—ironically—on the presses of the Communist Party newspaper, *Trybuna Ludu* (the tribune of the people).

Throughout the country, student activists canvassed door to door, and candidates fanned out into the countryside, promising higher farm prices, better health care, and rural schools. In addition, clergy within the Catholic church urged their faithful to support Solidarity. Although Wałęsa chose not to run for a parliamentary seat, his picture with each of the Solidarity candidates, avuncular and reassuring, was plastered throughout the country. His prestige as a Nobel laureate, national leader, and symbol of opposition to the regime was subliminally associated with the Solidarity candidates.

The magnitude of Solidarity's victory in the election was stunning. It won all 35 percent of the seats in the Sejm and ninety-nine of the hundred seats in the Senate. Equally important, virtually all the regime's thirty-five candidates, including Prime

Minister Mieczysław Rakowski, lost, even though they were running on an unopposed slate: Voters simply exercised the legal option of crossing out their names, which meant that a second round of balloting had to be held to fill these seats. Solidarity's victory was so decisive that moderate Communists, knowing that the next parliamentary election would be an entirely open one (as stipulated in the April agreements), began to seek rapprochement with Solidarity. At the same time, members of the regime's puppet parties began to suspect that their future lay with Solidarity rather than with the Communists. The morning after the election, Jaruzelski was said to have admitted, "Our defeat is total. A political solution will have to be found."

The next two months were crucial. Everyone expected that General Jaruzelski would stand for president, but on June 30, he announced that he would not do so. In the meantime, the Solidarity parliamentary faction had been organized under the leadership of Bronisław Geremek, a medieval historian and longtime close political adviser to Wałęsa. It was at this time that Kuroń proposed that Solidarity try to form a government. Wałęsa was at first opposed, arguing that it was better to remain in opposition for the time being, but Kuroń's proposal was taken up by Adam Michnik, a longtime political dissident and Solidarity adviser. In an editorial in *Gazeta wyborcza*, he suggested that Solidarity needed to take up the mandate given it by the election. Gradually, Wałęsa was won over. He let it be known that he was not opposed to Jaruzelski as president, and the general reversed his decision not to stand. On July 19, he was elected president by a margin of one vote. Solidarity's support, marshaled by Geremek, had been crucial.

Jaruzelski then resigned as Party boss and was replaced by Rakowski, who nominated Kiszczak as prime minister. It was the same old revolving door of familiar Communist faces, going nowhere. To break the impasse, Wałęsa in turn proposed that Solidarity and the former puppet parties together form a government. In the political crisis which erupted at this point, the "Polish question" became an international issue; Nicolai Ceausescu of Romania even proposed that the members of the Warsaw Pact intervene in Poland. President Gorbachev held firm to the position of noninterference he had earlier adopted. In a forty-minute telephone conversation with Rakowski, he let it be known that the Poles were on their own to work out their affairs.

On August 17, Jaruzelski and Wałęsa met, and the president identified three acceptable candidates for prime minister: Geremek, Kuroń, and Tadeusz Mazowiecki, the Solidarity adviser who had been with Wałęsa since the beginning of the movement in August, 1980. In the end, Wałęsa chose Mazowiecki, perhaps believing that Geremek's popularity was growing too fast. Within the week, the Sejm elected Mazowiecki as prime minister by an overwhelming majority. In September, he completed his cabinet. Although it contained four Communist ministers in crucial positions (Defense, the Interior, Transportation, and Foreign Economic Cooperation), it was a non-Communist government, the first to achieve power in Eastern Europe since the end of World War II. The unprecedented emergence of this government was auspicious for human rights, and Mazowiecki promised that his government would be based on the rule of law.

Impact of Event

The European consequences of the establishment of a non-Communist government in Poland were that within the next two years the system of Communist government which had dominated the "Cold War" era between East and West came to an end. Economic reforms had already proceeded very far in Hungary, but in the months of July, August, and September, a multiparty system emerged there which spelled the end of Communist control. In the German Democratic Republic, opposition forces took heart from the Polish example, and in a series of peaceful demonstrations revealed the impotence of the Communist regime there. In November, 1989, the Berlin Wall, the symbol of the Cold War, began to come down, and within a year the two Germanys had been reunited. In Czechoslovakia, an opposition group known as the "Civic Forum" was organized by the playwright and human rights activist Václav Havel, and in a matter of ten days in November, 1989, the Communist regime collapsed. Even in the Balkans, where Communist control remained to some degree, it was weakened. In violent confrontations beginning in Timişoara and spreading to Bucharest, the Romanian dictatorial regime of Nicolai Ceausescu was overthrown by year end. Although these events cannot be said to have happened entirely because of the Polish example, those who sought human dignity and the exercise of their rights throughout the region took courage from Poland's leadership. They believed that what had been wrought in Warsaw could be accomplished in their own locations.

In Poland, Mazowiecki's new government struggled to overcome the economic problems plaguing the country. A market economy was introduced, effective January 1, 1990, and had made substantial progress by the fall of that year. By that time, however, Wałęsa was critical of Mazowiecki, Geremek, and others, whom he thought to be too willing to compromise with the remnants of Communism and whose intellectual and liberal, lay outlooks contrasted sharply with his moderate and Catholic views. He forced a call for a new presidential election in the fall of 1990, and Jaruzelski retired. In a bitterly fought three-way campaign between himself, Mazowiecki, and a political outsider, Wałęsa was elected president in December, 1990. In the fall of 1991, he was able to call the first truly free and open elections to Parliament in Poland since the 1930's.

The same forces which had brought about the recovery of human rights in Poland and much of the rest of non-Soviet Eastern Europe were at work also in the Soviet Union. Communist rule, which had been weakened by Gorbachev's efforts to reform and restructure it, collapsed in the months after a failed coup by conservative hardliners in August, 1991. In December of that year, the Soviet Union ceased to exist as a state.

The events in Poland, the Soviet Union, and elsewhere do not guarantee that the future will have no new injustices, miseries, or authoritarian rulers who will individually or collectively abridge human rights. As British journalist Timothy Garton

Ash observed, however, 1989 "was the year communism in Eastern Europe died." It is clear that the possibilities for human rights were improved by that death.

Bibliography

Ash, Timothy Garton. *The Magic Lantern: The Revolution of '89 Witnessed in Warsaw, Budapest, Berlin, and Prague.* New York: Random House, 1990. An authoritative account by a British journalist and academic of the crucial developments in the region in 1989. Ash knew the major figures well, was on the spot when the events he describes took place, and has both a keen eye for detail and a fine analytical sense to make interpretations that will stand up. His chapter on the Polish election in June and his ending chapter on "the year of truth" are excellent.

Borrell, John. "An Epochal Shift: Communism Yields as Jaruzelski Asks Solidarity to Head a Government." *Time* 134, no. 9 (August 28, 1989): 16-18. Contains sound insights into events even though brief. Borrell is good at showing the internal stresses within Solidarity over the question of Wałęsa's occasional lack of democratic leadership.

Borrell, John, and James O. Jackson. "Uncharted Waters: Soviet Allies Draw Conflicting Conclusions from Gorbachev's Agenda." *Time* 134, no. 10 (September 4, 1989): 18-20. Although devoted to more than Polish affairs, this journalistic account touches upon the most crucial aspects of the Polish scene. Reports events during the crucial week when Mazowiecki was being designated as prime minister.

Kemp-Welch, A. *The Birth of Solidarity.* 2d ed. New York: St. Martin's Press, 1991. This is the second edition of a book originally published in 1983. Much of the volume is relevant to events in 1980, but the final chapter, "From Gdańsk to Government," provides a careful analysis of the events in 1988 and 1989 which led to the legalization of Solidarity and the elections. The analysis of the dynamics of Wałęsa's decision to seek to form a government and to choose Mazowiecki are excellent.

Staar, Richard F. "Poland: Renewal or Stagnation?" *Current History* 88 (November, 1989): 373-376, 405-407, 409. In his annual survey of Polish matters for this journal, the author provides a fine analysis of events, especially the economic issues facing Poland. His ability to put the narrative of events into a larger context is excellent, and the sources he used for this essay are very sound.

_____. "Transition in Poland." *Current History* 89 (December, 1990): 401-404, 426-427. Picking up where he left off in the article cited above, the author treats Polish foreign policy against the backdrop of the then-pending unification of Germany. His analysis of internal political affairs in the early months of the Mazowiecki Administration is sound and straightforward. His data for the economy suggest how difficult a set of problems Poland faced.

Weschler, Lawrence. "A Reporter at Large: A Grand Experiment." *The New Yorker* 64, no. 38 (November 13, 1989): 59-104. Building upon his previous reporting from Poland during the height of Solidarity, its suppression, and the subsequent years of illegal activity, the author provides an excellent study of the personalities and events connected with the establishment of the Mazowiecki government. His detailed narrative of the days in July and August are particularly useful, as is the flavor of his personal observations.

Paul W. Knoll

Cross-References

Soviets Take Control of Eastern Europe (1943), p. 612; The Brezhnev Doctrine Bans Acts of Independence in Soviet Satellites (1968), p. 1408; Soviets Invade Czechoslovakia (1968), p. 1441; Solidarity Leads Striking Polish Workers (1980), p. 2112; Poland Imposes Martial Law and Outlaws Solidarity (1981), p. 2152; Gorbachev Initiates a Policy of *Glasnost* (1985), p. 2249; Hungary Adopts a Multiparty System (1989), p. 2421; Solidarity Regains Legal Status in Poland (1989), p. 2477; The Berlin Wall Falls (1989), p. 2523; Ceausescu Is Overthrown in Romania (1989), p. 2546; Lithuania Declares Its Independence from the Soviet Union (1990), p. 2577; Gorbachev Agrees to Membership of a United Germany in NATO (1990), p. 2589; Demise of the U.S.S.R Paves the Way for Reforms in Former Soviet Republics (1991), p. 2618.

THE SUPREME COURT RULES ON EXECUTION OF THE MENTALLY RETARDED AND YOUNG

Category of event: Prisoners' rights
Time: June 26, 1989
Locale: United States Supreme Court, Washington, D.C.

The United States Supreme Court decided that states may execute the mentally retarded and those who were younger than eighteen when they committed murder

Principal personages:

SANDRA DAY O'CONNOR (1930-   ), an associate justice of the U.S. Supreme Court, author of the opinion in the Penry case

ANTONIN SCALIA (1936-   ), an associate justice of the U.S. Supreme Court, author of the opinion in the Stanford and Wilkins cases

JOHNNY PAUL PENRY (1957-   ), a mildly to moderately retarded man convicted of murder

KEVIN N. STANFORD (1963-   ), a man convicted of a brutal murder he committed when he was seventeen years old

HEATH WILKINS (1969-   ), a man convicted of a brutal murder he committed when he was sixteen years old

Summary of Event

A 1986 Gallup Poll found that seventy percent of Americans approved of capital punishment to deter, incapacitate, and punish violent people convicted of particularly brutal crimes. Public officials may safely predict popular support for most executions, but often have no broadly shared opinion on which to rely when designating penalties in exceptional cases. Lest they be thought soft on crime, legislators in the United States tend to authorize extensive use of the death penalty and rely on courts to disallow excesses. After a lull in executions in the 1960's and 1970's, public opinion, legislatures, and courts concurred on extensive use of the death penalty, a tendency exactly opposite to that of almost all other Western democracies.

The United States Supreme Court has mirrored majority support for the death penalty, proscribing few practices. The Court did invalidate many procedures for inflicting death because they allowed too much discretion, but soon ratified new, improved practices as constitutional. The new practices circumscribed discretion by compelling juries to assess the presence or absence of factors that ameliorated or exacerbated capital offenses. Having disciplined discretion, consistent majorities of the Court have found that death is neither cruel nor unusual punishment in most cases. The Court has been willing to ban capital punishment only if most Americans abhorred application of death to a class of offenders or if the punishment was grossly unfit to achieve any appropriate goals of punishment.

Having lost the general battles, opponents of capital punishment have tried to exempt certain classes of individuals from the death penalty. These abolitionists have argued that execution of retarded and juvenile offenders represented disproportionate and abhorrent application of the death penalty. Youths less able than adults to control their conduct or judge its consequences and retarded offenders who smile even as they are being sentenced to death should not be treated as fully cognizant defendants, abolitionists argue. Those who cannot or do not anticipate the consequences of their actions and those unable to understand what is happening to them at trial cannot assist in their own defense, these critics point out. One study found that lawyers for ninety-two percent of the retarded failed to raise competence as an issue at trial. The young and the retarded are more vulnerable to threats, coercion, tricks, false promises, and suggestions than adults. Abolitionists challenge the process that leads to death sentences as flawed and unjust when applied to either juveniles or mentally handicapped citizens.

On June 26, 1989, the Rehnquist Court rejected both challenges to capital punishment. In *Penry v. Lynaugh*, the majority declared that the Eighth Amendment permitted execution of retarded persons. In *Stanford v. Kentucky* and *Wilkins v. Missouri*, the Court similarly found that death sentences for crimes committed even by those sixteen years old were neither abhorrent nor disproportionate.

Johnny Paul Penry was convicted of the rape and murder of a Texas woman. Penry was retarded, with the ability to learn of the average child of six to seven years and the ability to function socially of a ten-year-old. Having found Penry competent to stand trial and guilty of aggravated murder, the jurors had to sentence Penry to death if they found that he had acted deliberately and constituted a continuing threat to society. These questions, created to prevent the discretion in sentencing that the Court had previously found "cruel and unusual," left jurors no opportunity to consider Penry's retardation as an ameliorating or aggravating factor. The jurors sentenced Penry to die.

Justice Sandra Day O'Connor, writing the opinion of the Court, ordered a new sentencing hearing for Penry. She reasoned that trial courts must provide juries an opportunity to consider retardation in sentencing. The trial judge should have told the jurors that they could consider retardation in answering the sentencing questions, O'Connor argued. To determine if Penry committed the murder deliberately, the jurors had to decide that Penry was truly capable of reasonable anticipation of consequences. O'Connor noted the irony that jurors were more likely to find Penry a continuing threat (the second issue) because of his inability to learn. She and the majority ruled that the Texas jury must be instructed to take Penry's mental age into account.

After awarding Penry this temporary reprieve, O'Connor held that execution of the retarded was not inherently "cruel and unusual punishment." She noted first that it would be cruel and unusual punishment to execute profoundly retarded and insane defendants. That was why, she continued, states provided hearings on competency to stand trial, as Texas had done for Penry. Acknowledging that the American Association on Mental Retardation argued that all retarded persons had reduced blameworthiness, O'Connor said that a majority of the Court did not find the capacities of most retarded people to be so diminished that the Constitution proscribed capital punishment for the whole class. "Mental age," concluded the majority, was too imprecise a measurement to exempt the retarded automatically. Thus, even retarded defendants may answer with their lives for conviction of a capital crime.

Unimpressed with mental age, the Court judged chronological age no bar to execution in *Stanford* and *Wilkins*. Kevin Stanford was seventeen years old when he robbed and raped his next-door neighbor, Baerbel Poore, and then shot her to death to prevent her from reporting him. He was tried as an adult, convicted, and sentenced to death. The Kentucky Supreme Court rejected his plea that he had any right to treatment or rehabilitation and affirmed the death sentence. Heath Wilkins committed a similar crime. He robbed Nancy Allen and, to keep her from identifying him, stabbed her eight times. Although he was sixteen and one-half years old at the time of the crime, Missouri convicted Wilkins as an adult.

Justice Antonin Scalia wrote the opinion of the Court. The only question, he said, was whether execution of convicted murderers who were under eighteen when they committed the murders was "cruel and unusual." When the Eighth Amendment was ratified, common law treated as adults accused felons over age fourteen and allowed in theory for capital punishment of those over seven. Stanford and Wilkins were unable to argue that the ban on cruel and unusual punishments originally prohibited executing sixteen- or seventeen-year-olds. Scalia noted as well that nearly three hundred offenders under eighteen had been executed in the United States since the amendment had been adopted. Scalia also reviewed policies in the states and found considerable disagreement concerning whether executing minors was cruel or unusual. Absent an original understanding or developing consensus on the point, Scalia said that the justices could disallow capital punishment in these cases only by imposing its preferences on the states. The majority, he said, refused to do so.

As O'Connor had done for the retarded in *Penry*, Scalia acknowledged that adolescents might be less mature and thus less blameworthy for their actions. He found sociological and psychological evidence on that question inconclusive. Since no scientific findings resolved the matter beyond dispute, state legislatures were free to decide the matter without judicial interference.

Impact of Event

The narrow holding in *Penry* provided opponents of executions only modest solace. In demanding that the judge make the jury fully aware of the range of extenuating, ameliorating, and aggravating circumstances that they should consider before passing sentence on convicted murderers, the majority stressed their concern that juries' discretion be disciplined carefully. The Court allowed states to execute retarded persons convicted of capital crimes if those persons are found competent to stand trial but also insisted that the possibly reduced capacity of individual defendants be considered beyond the competency hearing. The Court thus demanded that states instruct jurors to be as merciful as they reasonably can.

Beyond Johnny Penry's narrow and temporary reprieve, the decisions in *Penry*, *Stanford*, and *Wilkins* signaled death penalty abolitionists that they were running out of ways to circumscribe or delay executions. The Court made it clear that it would not restrain legislatures in most instances. This means that abolitionists would have to induce elected officials to scale back capital punishment, hardly an easy task amid growing crime and fear of crime. Had the Court legitimized greater attention to the reduced responsibility of juveniles, the mentally retarded, or both, opponents of capital punishment might have been able to find analogous instances of diminished culpability. As a result of the Court's deference to state judgment on blameworthiness, an important tactic for fending off some executions was rendered ineffectual.

In addition, the Court informed legislators and citizens alike that most justices are not interested in the actual practice of capital punishment. In these cases, as in *McCleskey v. Kemp*, a majority of the justices dismissed overwhelming statistical, sociological, psychological, and medical evidence as utterly irrelevant. *McCleskey* concerned statistical analysis showing that juries were far more likely to sentence to death blacks convicted of murdering whites than whites convicted of killing blacks. Despite such evidence, a majority of the Court continued to insist that they will look only at specific evidence of discrimination in specific cases. These justices have freed legislators to apply capital punishment to a host of situations and defendants with little or no reflection on how poorly or well the punishment suits either the crime or any legitimate purpose of the ultimate penalty.

These decisions so constricted the definition of cruel and unusual punishment that virtually any punishments selected by legislatures could pass constitutional muster. Unless penalties were proscribed at the time that the Eighth Amendment was written or have become almost universally objectionable since, the Court will find them constitutionally permissible. A majority of the justices interpret legislatures' silence on the execution of the retarded or the juvenile as acceptance, evidence to the contrary notwithstanding. Indeed, Justice Scalia insisted in *Stanford* that the only acceptable evidence of consensual abhorrence of a particular use of the death penalty was to be found in statutes. In effect, the Court has frozen the evolution of "cruel and unusual" in the Eighth Amendment.

The justices thus ratified the death penalty as a response to violent crime. The confluence of popular opinion and legislative and judicial decisions sets the United States apart from most Western, industrialized nations, in which capital punishment has grown less acceptable for decades. Justice Scalia, for example, dismissed evidence of international abhorrence for executions as having no value in assessing American policy. While polls, contentious legislative debates, and fragmented, wavering judicial decisions reveal far more ambivalence on the death penalty than *Penry*, *Stanford*, and *Wilkins* indicate, most Americans entertain doubts about capital punishment only in extraordinary cases. In most instances, the death penalty is alive and well in the United States Supreme Court.

Perhaps the most far-reaching impact of *Penry*, *Stanford*, and *Wilkins* concerns judicial instruction of popular thinking about constitutional protections and rights.

By removing themselves as a check on the use of the death penalty as a response to increases in violent crime, justices and judges deprived politicians and citizens of the benefits of sober reflection by educated individuals insulated from many of the passions that cloud judgment. The courts often follow the election returns. By following instead of leading the public and the politicians, the courts left this aspect of human rights largely within the political arena.

Bibliography

Amnesty International. *When the State Kills: The Death Penalty, A Human Rights Issue.* New York: Author, 1989. Treating capital punishment as an issue of human rights, this survey of laws and practices throughout the world is an excellent source for comparisons among national policies. It reiterates all major arguments against use of capital punishment, introducing readers to the most persuasive arguments for abolishing the death penalty.

Bedau, Hugo Adam, ed. *The Death Penalty in America.* New York: Oxford University Press, 1983. This is the encyclopedia of capital punishment in theory and practice in the United States. It features excerpts from Supreme Court landmark cases, major treatises, and statistical studies. It is designed as a sourcebook for beginners and citizens but useful as well for most students of capital punishment.

Berns, Walter. *For Capital Punishment.* New York: Basic Books, 1979. This defense of capital punishment emphasizes the importance of executions as expressions of society's moral outrage at murders and other violent crimes. Many proponents of capital punishment concede the moral high ground to abolitionists by stressing practical issues. Berns stresses the moral arguments available to proponents.

Fetzer, Philip L. "Execution of the Mentally Retarded: A Punishment Without Justification." *South Carolina Law Review* 40 (Winter, 1989): 419-447. A political scientist argues that executing mentally retarded offenders does not deter other violent crime, dramatize moral outrage, protect society, or accomplish any other legitimate social goal. This article stresses how criminal justice as practiced in the United States does not take mental retardation into account, despite judges' claims.

Johnson, Robert. *Death Work.* Pacific Grove, Calif.: Brooks/Cole, 1990. Although too graphic for delicate readers, this very readable introduction to the techniques of execution raises challenging questions about capital punishment. Even readers convinced of the deterrent or retributive benefits of the death penalty will want to ponder whether it is cruel and unusual punishment as practiced.

Streib, Victor L. *Death Penalty for Juveniles.* Bloomington: Indiana University Press, 1987. A leading opponent of executing convicted persons under age eighteen has assembled information and arguments that suggest that killing juvenile offenders advances no legitimate goal. Citizens and scholars alike can benefit from confronting the materials in this book.

Van den Haag, Ernest, and John P. Conrad. *The Death Penalty: A Debate.* New York: Plenum Press, 1983. Two experts take opposite sides of the capital punishment debate. The result is entertaining, enlightening, and a welcome respite from overwrought rhetoric on both sides of the question. This is an excellent book for beginners because it exposes myths used by both sides.

William Haltom

Cross-References

Capital Punishment Is Abolished in Sweden (1921), p. 345; The United Nations Adopts the Declaration of the Rights of the Child (1959), p. 1038; The British Parliament Votes to Abolish the Death Penalty (1965), p. 1316; The United Nations Declares Rights for the Mentally Retarded (1971), p. 1644; The Supreme Court Abolishes the Death Penalty (1972), p. 1674; The United Nations Issues a Declaration Against Torture (1975), p. 1847; An IRA Prisoner Dies in an English Prison after a Hunger Strike (1976), p. 1870; Amnesty International Exposes the Cruelty of the Death Penalty (1989), p. 2414; The United Nations Adopts the Convention on the Rights of the Child (1989), p. 2529.

TEXAS' METHOD OF FUNDING PUBLIC SCHOOLS IS RULED UNCONSTITUTIONAL

Category of event: Educational rights
Time: October 2, 1989
Locale: Austin, Texas

Large disparities in school funding between rich and poor districts in Texas were ended by a Texas Supreme Court decision and subsequent legislative action

Principal personages:

OSCAR MAUZY (1926-), the chief justice of the Texas Supreme Court who wrote the opinion declaring that the Texas system of financing schools violated the Texas constitution

F. SCOTT MCCOWN (1955-), a Texas district judge who ruled that the school finance reform legislation of 1990 did not establish sufficient equality

WILLIAM CLEMENTS (1917-), a Republican governor of Texas who insisted that a school funding bill not result in a tax increase

ANN RICHARDS (1933-), a Democrat who won the Texas governorship in 1990

GIBSON LEWIS (1936-), a Democratic speaker of the Texas House of Representatives, led the legislature to school funding reform

Summary of Event

Since the development of its public school system, Texas had financed its schools largely through local property taxes. These taxes were raised at the local level and spent on the local school system. Substantial amounts of state aid provided a minimum level of funding for every school district, but local districts were free to supplement these funds from local property taxes. Even though the level of state funding increased over the years, schools remained heavily dependent upon money raised through local property taxes. School districts could levy taxes and spend the tax money how they wished, limited only by broad state parameters.

The result of this system was that property-rich districts had a much greater ability to fund their school systems than did property-poor districts. In 1989, the one hundred wealthiest districts had twenty times the property wealth of the one hundred poorest districts. These wealthy districts could either have much lower taxes than the poor districts or could spend much more on their schools. Typically, they did both. It was not unusual for a property-rich district to have both lower taxes and ten times the amount of discretionary money per pupil possessed by a property-poor district.

This resulted in considerable disparities in the education provided to children within the state. In some of the state's poorer districts, schools lacked such ordinary aspects of a good education as science teachers and labs, gymnasiums, or cafeterias. The problem was compounded by the fact that spending on education in Texas was among the lowest in the nation. While there were great differences within the state, even the wealthiest districts tended to fall below the national average in terms of per-pupil expenditures.

Texas' system of financing education was first challenged at the federal level in the early 1970's. In 1973, the case of *San Antonio v. Rodriguez* reached the U.S. Supreme Court. In it, the Edgewood Independent School District, a property-poor district in San Antonio predominantly composed of African Americans and Mexican Americans, argued that the funding system violated the equal protection clause of the Fourteenth Amendment to the U.S. Constitution.

The high court rejected this argument, finding that the system did not violate the U.S. Constitution. The Court found that the system did guarantee to all children a minimum level of education through state-supplied aid. It held that even if education could be considered a right (which it doubted), the Court did not have the authority to guarantee people levels of education beyond the minimum. The Court also found it difficult, using its traditional "equal protection" analysis, to determine a class of people who were the object of discrimination. It pointed out that poor people often did not live in poor districts, and poor districts often contained rich people.

The heart of the Court's opinion, however, was a concern for local control of education. It praised the freedom for political participation, experimentation, innovation, and healthy competition that local school control facilitated. Centralized control of the money, it thought, would inevitably mean centralized control of education and a consequent loss of local freedom.

Having lost on the national level, the Edgewood district turned in the 1980's to the Texas state constitution for relief. Joining with other poor school districts, and represented by the Mexican American Legal Defense and Educational Fund (MALDEF), suit was brought in May, 1984, against the state of Texas. The suit alleged that the state's school finance system discriminated against students in poor districts in violation of the Texas constitution. Partly as a response to this suit, the state legislature passed a school reform law in June, 1984, that substantially increased state aid to poorer districts. The suit was reconstituted and continued, however, on the grounds that there were still large disparities between rich and poor districts.

In January, 1987, a state district judge ruled that the financing system did indeed violate the Texas constitution. This decision was overturned by the Third Court of Appeals in Texas, but its decision was in turn appealed by MALDEF to the Texas Supreme Court. On October 2, 1989, the three Republican and six Democratic judges on the Supreme Court of Texas voted unanimously that the school finance system was unconstitutional. The court ordered the legislature to design a new system in time for the 1990-1991 school year. Speaking through Chief Justice Oscar Mauzy, the court held that the Texas constitution required that there be "substantially equal opportunity to have access to educational funds." There must be equal educational opportunity for children "regardless of where they live." What had been lost on the federal level was now won on the state level.

There ensued a fierce political battle in the Texas statehouse. Republican Governor Bill Clements insisted that the funding problem posed by the court should not be met by increasing state taxes. In addition, representatives from districts which stood to gain were pitted against those who stood to lose. The legislature met in four special sessions during the spring of 1990 to hammer out a new system. After three special sessions, the legislature agreed to a bill, only to have it vetoed by the governor because it raised taxes. After the governor's veto, a court-appointed master threatened an alternative "Robin Hood" plan that would shift hundreds of millions of dollars of tax dollars from wealthy to poor school districts. Under this threat, the governor and the legislature reached a compromise which attempted to solve the problem by increasing state aid to education but left substantial discretion to local districts to raise additional funds.

MALDEF and the poor school districts, however, challenged this solution in court as not providing sufficient aid for the poor districts and failing to make expenditures in all districts equal. In September, 1990, State District Judge Scott McCown agreed, ruling that the new law was unconstitutional because it did not give all schools "substantially equal" access to funds for a similar tax effort. Rather than order a new plan, the judge gave the legislature another year to come up with a plan that met this criterion.

In the November election of 1990, Ann Richards, the Democratic gubernatorial candidate, recaptured the statehouse from the Republicans. Because the Democrats already possessed solid control of the legislature, party conflict became less of a factor when the legislature reconsidered school finance in the spring of 1991. This did not prevent another fierce political battle over who would bear the burden of the reform. The new governor took a relatively small part in the legislative negotiations that led to the passage of a variation of the "Robin Hood" plan in early April. The plan established minimum and maximum taxing levels, designed to force increased spending on schools over a four-year period. It guaranteed similar funds for similar taxing efforts by a combination of transferring property tax revenue from wealthy districts in a county to poor districts, increasing state aid for poorer districts and decreasing it for wealthier ones, and placing spending limits on the wealthiest districts. The end result of court and legislative action was a substantial change in the Texas educational system. Many suburban and city districts faced a loss of revenue; many rural and poorer districts near cities could look forward to substantially increased funding. Spending per pupil would now be roughly equal across the state.

Impact of Event

The long-term effects of the court-ordered change in Texas education would take some time to work out. The hoped-for improvement in the education in poorer districts would depend upon translating the increased dollars available into better education for children. Better teachers could be hired, and better facilities built. This seemed a likely, but by no means guaranteed, result. The plan also faced court challenges from wealthier districts, which alleged that it violated the Texas constitution by requiring shifts in property tax revenue from the district in which they were raised to other districts.

The immediate impact was felt most strongly by those school districts which faced a decrease in state aid or a transfer of their property taxes to other districts. These included middle- and upper-class suburbs and large cities. To indicate the scope of these shifts, five suburban school districts around Dallas were required to shift property tax revenue to other districts, and two additional districts, including the city of Dallas, lost substantial amounts of state aid. The districts responded by laying off teachers and constricting their curricula. Typical cuts included foreign language instruction, honors classes, and other elements of the curriculum that enabled students to advance beyond the "basics." It was clear that the "best" Texas schools would no longer be quite so outstanding.

Large cities faced particularly severe problems. The city of Dallas lost half of its state aid because of its large property base. Ironically, the city's schools were simultaneously faced with the possible loss of accreditation because of inadequacies in the system. Within the Dallas system were some of the poorest and most difficult neighborhoods for schooling in the state. The court's insistence upon equality did not consider that the complex problems of today's cities make it more expensive to provide the same quality of education delivered in a rural district.

The change also brought about a new level of bureaucracy in the state's school system. To equalize tax revenue among local school districts, new countywide taxing districts were created to supplement the local districts. These required boards to decide how to levy and distribute taxes, and staff to administer the boards' decisions. An increase in administrative costs and regulation was the inevitable result.

Thus, the decision of the Texas Supreme Court led to mixed results. On one hand, there was a prospect of improved education for children in poor districts. On the other, the best schools were hurt, local initiative was diminished, hard-pressed cities were left with decreased funds, and an already large educational bureaucracy was expanded. There was a strong possibility that the education of some would be improved, but only at the cost of dragging others down, achieving universal mediocrity.

Bibliography

Areen, Judith, and Leonard Ross. "The Rodriguez Case." *The Supreme Court Review* 1973 (1973): 33-35. An interesting analysis of the problems of wealth and equal protection, focusing on the national case involving Texas school finance.

Coons, John E., William H. Clune III, and Stephen D. Sugarman. *Private Wealth and Public Education.* Cambridge, Mass.: Harvard University Press, 1970. The seminal work advancing the view that school districts should receive a fixed amount of revenue per pupil for any particular level of tax effort regardless of the level of the property tax base.

Pritchett, C. Herman. "The New Due Process—Equal Protection." In *Constitutional Civil Liberties.* Englewood Cliffs, N.J.: Prentice-Hall, 1984. A good summary of the legal thinking about equality that lay behind the Texas Supreme Court decision about school financing, including a succinct discussion of the treatment of wealth by the U.S. Supreme Court.

Richards, David A. J. "Equal Opportunity and School Financing." *University of Chicago Law Review* 32 (1973): 41. A thorough discussion of the legal and constitutional issues that can be raised about the financing of schools through the local property tax.

Tocqueville, Alexis de. *Democracy in America.* Translated by George Lawrence and edited by J. P. Mayer. New York: Harper & Row, 1988. The best analysis of the tension between the pursuit of equality and the pursuit of freedom in America.

Glen E. Thurow

Cross-References

Spanish Becomes the Language of Instruction in Puerto Rico (1949), p. 801; *Brown v. Board of Education* Ends Public School Segregation (1954), p. 913; The United Nations Adopts the Declaration of the Rights of the Child (1959), p. 1038; Head Start Is Established (1965), p. 1284; Congress Enacts the Bilingual Education Act (1968), p. 1402; The Supreme Court Rejects Racial Quotas in College Admissions (1973), p. 1697; Congress Passes the Child Abuse Prevention and Treatment Act (1974), p. 1752; Congress Enacts the Education for All Handicapped Children Act (1975), p. 1780; Southern Schools Are Found to Be the Least Racially Segregated (1975), p. 1786; The United Nations Adopts the Convention on the Rights of the Child (1989), p. 2529.

WILDER BECOMES THE FIRST
ELECTED BLACK GOVERNOR

Category of event: Racial and ethnic rights
Time: November 7, 1989
Locale: Virginia

L. Douglas Wilder became the United States' first elected African-American governor nearly 125 years after the end of the Civil War

Principal personages:
  L. DOUGLAS WILDER (1931-   ), the governor of Virginia
  J. MARSHALL COLEMAN (1942-   ), the Republican candidate for governor
  GERALD L. BALILES (1940-   ), the incumbent Virginia governor, unable to run for reelection because of a one-term limitation
  CHARLES S. ROBB (1939-   ), the popular former governor of Virginia, U.S. senator from Virginia at the time of Wilder's election

Summary of Event

The 1989 contest for the governor's mansion in Virginia was destined to receive an unusual amount of attention both within the state and around the country. The election offered the possibility of producing the United States' first elected black governor in the former capital of the Confederacy. In addition, there were few other contests of national importance in 1989 to attract the interest of the news media. Each of the candidates spent more than $6 million in the general election campaign. History was made when, on November 7, 1989, Democrat L. Douglas Wilder was elected governor of Virginia.

Wilder, the incumbent lieutenant governor, received the Democratic nomination without challenge. He had proven his ability to win a statewide election when he became lieutenant governor in 1985, demonstrating that he could attract white voters in a state where the electorate was 80 percent white. Wilder received the full support of the state Democratic party and of outgoing governor Gerald L. Baliles, and the less-than-enthusiastic endorsement of U.S. Senator Charles S. Robb. There was friction between Wilder and Robb, but Robb did support Wilder's candidacy.

Marshall Coleman, the Republican gubernatorial candidate, had scored a come-from-behind victory in a hotly contested and often acrimonious three-man race for his party's nomination. For the first time, state Republicans employed a primary election to choose their candidate, and the Coleman campaign was noted for its strong negative content. Coleman had lost the 1981 gubernatorial election and was denied the Republican nomination for lieutenant governor in 1985, but he was resurrected politically in 1989.

By the 1980's, America had witnessed an increasing number of successful African-

American candidates at the local and state legislative levels. Many of America's largest cities had elected black mayors. The number of blacks in statewide office and at the national level, however, remained low. At the time of Wilder's election, blacks held fewer than 2 percent of the nation's elective offices. Most of those were in jurisdictions with a majority of black residents.

Wilder's candidacy was seen, then, as extremely important for civil rights in America. Wilder himself was viewed as a model for other black candidates. His campaign was not based on race. His campaign strategy was to portray himself as a moderate alternative to the extremely conservative Coleman.

Although his politics were clearly more moderate than the positions favored by former presidential candidate Jesse Jackson, Wilder may have benefited from Jackson's experience. Black candidates, who have often been dismissed by voters on the basis of their race, may have been taken more seriously after Jackson's campaigns in 1984 and, particularly, 1988. Opponents and the media, however, still struggled with the issues surrounding black candidacies. Heavy criticism of a black candidate could lead to charges of racism, while ignoring or emphasizing the race of a black candidate could be viewed as patronizing.

Blacks in 1989 faced major electoral hurdles, not the least of which was the misleading nature of public opinion polls in black-white contests. Usually reliable, polls in elections in which a black candidate faced a white candidate tended to overestimate the strength of the black candidates by several percentage points. This phenomenon was evident in the Wilder election as well as in the New York City mayoral campaign of David Dinkins and the unsuccessful California gubernatorial campaign of Los Angeles Mayor Tom Bradley. Experts speculated that the effect might be caused by racism, low turnout among black voters, fear of those polled of appearing racist, or their attempt to offer what might be perceived as the "correct answer."

Although Wilder faced many of these problems, his candidacy also posed problems for his opponent. The race factor was virtually absent from the campaigns of both candidates. Coleman's campaign was relatively negative but was careful not even to allude to the question of race. The only exception to this came late in the campaign, when Coleman complained publicly that he was the victim of a media double standard in which Wilder was not seriously questioned regarding several ethics issues raised by Coleman. Coleman, conversely, was frequently questioned about his position on abortion. The implication was that Wilder was getting preferential treatment from the press because he was black.

For his part, Wilder was equally careful not to raise the race issue. He did discuss his background, but he chose to emphasize how far Virginia had come in matters of race. His attempt to run as a moderate also prevented him from running as a "black" candidate. In his television advertisements, Wilder was usually surrounded by whites. His issue emphasis was almost solely on abortion, on which issue he endorsed a woman's right to choose. His theme was summed up by his campaign motto, "I trust the women of Virginia."

One of Wilder's most popular campaign advertisements used conservative rhetoric to take a prochoice position. In the advertisement, a narrator claimed that "Doug Wilder believes the government shouldn't interfere in your right to choose. He wants to keep politicians out of your personal life. Don't let Marshall Coleman take us back." This strategy effectively made Wilder look at least moderate, if not conservative, and it may well have been a subtle reference to the overt racism of Virginia's past.

Wilder avoided some more controversial issues. There was no discussion of funding abortions for the poor. Wilder also chose not to associate himself with Jesse Jackson or the National Organization of Women's Molly Yard, emphasizing that he had not requested any help from outside the state.

Wilder's qualifications and experience were never questioned. The grandson of slaves, Wilder grew up in a middle-class family in segregated Richmond. He excelled in the segregated schools, and he was graduated from Virginia Union College in Richmond. After winning a Bronze Star for his actions during the Korean War, he attended law school at Howard University. In 1959, Wilder was the only African-American to pass the Virginia bar exam, and he soon opened his own law practice.

He rose rapidly within his profession, and in 1969 he entered politics, winning a seat in the Virginia senate. Two white candidates split the white vote, allowing Wilder to win by a narrow margin. He worked diligently and established a reputation as a powerful individual in Virginia politics. Initially a liberal, Wilder moderated his positions and issues over time. By 1985, he was ready for a run for lieutenant governor, and some clever political maneuvering placed him on the Democratic ticket with Gerald Baliles. Successful grass-roots campaigning enabled him to win that election and position himself for the gubernatorial race in 1989.

With his election as lieutenant governor, Wilder became only the second black elected to a major statewide office since Reconstruction. (Former Republican Senator Edward Brooke of Massachusetts was the first. Pinckney Pinchback was acting governor of Louisiana for forty-three days in 1873, but he was not elected to that position.)

On November 7, 1989, Doug Wilder eked out a narrow victory over Marshall Coleman, capturing 50.1 percent of the votes cast. Nearly 1.8 million Virginians voted in the contest, which set records both for the total of voters and for the 66.5 percent of registered voters who cast a ballot. While his margin of victory was considerably more narrow than those of the Democratic nominees for lieutenant governor and attorney general, Wilder had once again fooled the political pundits and accomplished what seemed to be impossible. Many experts attributed his victory to heavy turnout among black voters and his popularity among women, but it should be remembered that Wilder took more than 40 percent of the votes cast by whites and more than 40 percent of the votes cast by men.

Impact of Event

The impact of Wilder's election was felt in three specific areas: the national stature and reputation of Wilder himself, the nation's and the state's view of Virginia, and the possible long-term effects on black candidates nationwide. Wilder's election propelled him into the national spotlight. He came to be seen by many as a national spokesperson for African Americans and as a viable candidate for the 1992 Democratic presidential nomination. Wilder welcomed this notoriety and spent much time preparing and delivering speeches around the country.

Perceptions of Virginia also changed virtually overnight. The state had changed dramatically in the previous two decades, but the changes had gone largely unnoticed. An urbanized corridor running from Northern Virginia through Richmond into Tidewater produced more than 60 percent of the voters. Many of these voters had migrated to Virginia, many from the North, and they voted disproportionately for Wilder. The rural areas of Virginia, which had dominated the state's politics, now accounted for less than one-third of the state's votes. These major demographic changes made Virginia politically more like a Middle Atlantic state than a Southern state. Virginia politics would still be considered conservative nationally, but the state had moderated considerably in twenty years.

The lessons of the election for other black candidates were mixed. Wilder's victory showed that a black willing to run as a mainstream, moderate, nonthreatening candidate could win a statewide election. This contrasted sharply with the liberal approach taken by Jesse Jackson. Jackson's philosophy was successful within the Democratic Party, where liberals wielded considerable power, but Wilder's strategy seemed much more likely to be successful in general elections.

Other lessons were drawn from the election. The journey for a minority candidate was still a long and difficult one. Wilder had many advantages in the campaign. He was the heir apparent to two popular Democratic administrations, he won the party's nomination unopposed, and he was supported by a united party. His campaign was well financed. He ran a strategic campaign, played the issues correctly, and was opposed by a relatively weak opponent. Despite all these advantages, he won by an extremely narrow margin.

Combined with the election of David Dinkins as the first black mayor of New York City, Wilder's win was seen by some as the vanguard of more political successes by blacks. Andrew Young's losing campaign for the governorship of Georgia the following year caused much of that optimism to disappear.

The effects of the Wilder victory on Virginia politics and public policy are difficult to assess. There were still relatively few black politicians in the state. Policy, too, remained largely unchanged. Governor Wilder was prevented from proposing any governmental initiatives by a continuing budget crisis that allowed him to show his fiscal conservative stripes through a steadfast refusal to raise taxes and an insistence on serious budget cuts. The consequence of these actions was a decline in Wilder's popularity within the state and a rise in his stock nationally. Wilder's legacy seemed likely to be the subject of debate for years to come.

Bibliography

Bond, Julian. *Black Candidates: Southern Campaign Experiences.* Atlanta: Southern

Regional Council, 1968. A recounting of the experiences of several candidates for state and local office in the South in the 1960's. Provides an interesting context for the Wilder election and exemplifies the changes in the South and the nation with regard to race relations.

Broh, C. Anthony. *A Horse of a Different Color: Television's Treatment of Jesse Jackson's 1984 Presidential Campaign.* Washington, D.C.: Joint Center for Political Studies, 1987. A thorough and insightful discussion of how the media covered the first serious black presidential candidate. Points out clearly the disadvantages and advantages of being a black candidate.

Edds, Margaret. *Claiming the Dream.* Chapel Hill, N.C.: Algonquin Books, 1990. A chronological journalistic recounting and analysis of the 1989 gubernatorial campaign focusing primarily on Wilder.

Lichter, S. Robert, et al. *The Video Campaign: Network Coverage of the 1988 Primaries.* Washington, D.C.: American Enterprise Institute, 1988. A brief, useful analysis of how television news covered the presidential candidates in 1988. Makes good use of statistics to present a clear and easily understood argument regarding who was treated well by the media and why.

Sabato, Larry J. "Virginia's National Election for Governor." In *Virginia Government and Politics*, edited by Thomas R. Morris and Weldon Cooper. Charlottesville: University Press of Virginia, 1990. An excellent discussion of the national and state implications of the 1989 gubernatorial election by the leading expert on Virginia state politics. Sabato provides both statistical and anecdotal analyses of the campaign and election.

Shapiro, Walter. "Breakthrough in Virginia." *Time* 134 (November 20, 1989): 54-57. Emphasizes the moderate politics and personal nature of Wilder's campaign and victory. Wilder is seen as a politician, not as a black politician.

Wilson, Harry L. "Media Treatment of Black Candidates: The 1989 Virginia Gubernatorial Campaign." *Virginia Social Science Journal* 26 (Winter, 1991): 82-90. An analysis of newspaper and television coverage in southwestern Virginia of the election. Concludes that although most news stories were neutral, those that were not were likely to be positive if about Wilder and negative if about Coleman.

Yancey, Dwayne. *When Hell Froze Over.* Dallas: Taylor, 1988. Journalist Yancey traces Wilder's rise to power from his humble beginnings in Richmond to his election to lieutenant governor in 1985. Reveals the political Wilder who seeks and uses power.

Harry L. Wilson

Cross-References

Brandeis Becomes the First Jewish Member of the Supreme Court (1916), p. 172; Robinson Breaks the Color Line in Organized Baseball (1947), p. 712; *Brown v. Board of Education* Ends Public School Segregation (1954), p. 913; The Civil Rights Act of 1957 Creates the Commission on Civil Rights (1957), p. 997; Congress Passes the Civil Rights Act (1964), p. 1251; Marshall Becomes the First Black Supreme Court Justice (1967), p. 1381; Chisholm Becomes the First Black Woman Elected to Congress (1968), p. 1451; The Supreme Court Endorses Busing as a Means to End Segregation (1971), p. 1628; Jackson Becomes the First Major Black Candidate for U.S. President (1983), p. 2209.

THE BERLIN WALL FALLS

Category of event: Political freedom
Time: November 9, 1989
Locale: Berlin, East Germany

The Berlin Wall stood as a physical and psychological barrier between East and West for twenty-eight years, until the thaw in the Cold War allowed the people to bring down the wall and reunify Germany

Principal personages:

MIKHAIL GORBACHEV (1931-   ), the president of the Soviet Union

ERICH HONECKER (1912-   ), the hard-line leader of East Germany, forced to resign in 1989 and expelled from the Communist Party in December of that year

EGON KRENZ (1937-   ), the leader of East Germany's Communist Party after Honecker fell into disfavor

HANS MODROW (1928-   ), the prime minister of East Germany

HELMUT KOHL (1930-   ), the chancellor of West Germany

Summary of Event

After World War II, relations between the main world powers—the West and the East—broke down. Repressive political policies, collectivization of land, nationalization of industry, and imprisonment of anyone opposed to the authorities became common in the East Bloc. This political disintegration reached its height on August 13, 1961, when the Soviet Union's leader, Nikita Khrushchev, ordered that the thirteen-foot-high, steel and concrete Berlin Wall be built, ostensibly to stop a "population hemorrhage"—the flight of unhappy East Germans to the West—that was draining the Eastern economy. The next twenty-eight years produced a multitude of political crises, from the Cuban Missile Crisis of 1962 to the execution of Romanian dictator Nicolae Ceausescu on December 25, 1989.

The building of the Berlin Wall effectively created a country of political prisoners. East Germans were not allowed to leave the country without going through extensive bureaucratic red tape to secure a visa. Usually such efforts were unsuccessful, even if the applicant had excellent reasons for leaving the country, such as a family emergency. In fact, application for an exit visa was likely to place the applicant under suspicion with the brutal East German state police.

Economic life in East Germany was also typical of East Bloc countries: The standard of living, although better than that of most East Bloc nations, was poor, especially in comparison with that of West Germany. East Germans suffered economic hardships typical of other Iron Curtain nations, including shortages of goods plentiful in the West. Viewed as a poor relative of West Germany, the East German government strove to prove that it was the superstar of the communist countries, usually at the expense of the rights of its people. To gain worldwide recognition, for example, the government instituted an athletic training program for children, taking them from their parents at an early age to ensure a high percentage of Olympic contenders. Increased ownership of televisions in East Germany backfired: East Germans began to receive broadcasts from the West introducing them to the most appealing sides of Western life, especially consumer goods and services that were unavailable to them.

No longer content with the broken promises of communism, the people of East Germany began to rebel against the postwar division of Berlin. When the wall was first erected down the middle of one street, people desperately tried to jump from their second-story windows to the western side. The hard-line communist government ordered that all persons trying to escape be shot on sight, and an array of machine guns was placed along the top of the wall to fulfill this order. This arrangement did not discourage everyone, however, and between 1961 and 1989, seventy-seven people were killed while trying to cross the wall (in total, 191 people were killed trying to escape from East Germany during that period), while about forty thousand escaped successfully.

The first sign of any political weakening in the wall occurred in 1983, when Erich Honecker, then leader of East Germany's Communist Party, ordered the East German troops guarding the wall to refrain from shooting people trying to escape over the border. Then, in 1985, Mikhail Gorbachev came to power in the Soviet Union, and his ensuing promise of *perestroika* ("restructuring," or economic reform) and *glasnost* ("openness") began to change the face of Eastern Europe. It was not until October of 1989, however, that the East German government began relaxing its restrictions on visas issued for trips to the West. In May of that year, Western observers began to notice signs of this new attitude, and many began to believe that a revolution of democracy was about to spread throughout Eastern Europe.

In September, 1989, Hungary opened its border with Austria to allow East German refugees to leave the East without the previously required exit visas. This group of refugees, about thirty thousand in all, became the largest single group to leave since 1961. Within days of Hungary's decision, people visiting Czechoslovakia and Poland began applying for refuge with the West German embassies in Prague and Warsaw. By the beginning of October, seven thousand East Germans had boarded trains from these cities headed for West Germany. On October 9, nearly seventy thousand people marched in Leipzig, demanding governmental reforms. In what was the first sign of the government's softening of attitude, the police did not disperse or interfere with the marchers, apparently on orders given by Egon Krenz, then chief of internal security.

On October 18, Honecker was forced to resign as head of the country, a position that he had held for eighteen years, and Krenz was chosen to replace him. It was Krenz's grasp of Gorbachev's *glasnost* aims that led to the ouster of Honecker, who had by this time angered Gorbachev with his unwillingness to accelerate the pace of reforms in East Germany. The subsequent uncovering of the corruption within Honecker's government further aroused the East German people, and civil unrest continued in cities such as Dresden, despite the announcement on October 31 that travel restrictions to Czechoslovakia were being lifted. The next day, East Germans by the thousands rushed to the West German embassy in Prague. It is estimated that between twenty and fifty thousand people fled the country within a week, and on November 5, more than 500,000 East Germans rallied in Berlin for democratic reforms. On November 7 and 8, the entire East German cabinet, or Politburo, resigned and were replaced by politicians in favor of reform.

On the evening of November 9, the East German government quite unexpectedly opened the borders to West Berlin and West Germany. As the crowds surged through, the wall became less a barrier than an architectural curiosity. Although crossing the border required a police permit, the government did not order the soldiers to resist, and throughout the night, thousands of people entered West Berlin. The border guards, faced with lines of cars three miles long filled with East Germans, did not look twice as they stamped papers and waved people through. Some of the guards even helped those who wanted to avoid the long lines to climb over the wall. Upon arrival in West Berlin, most East Germans headed for the banks, where they were given approximately fifty-four U.S. dollars as a "welcome to the West" gesture. Relatives and friends, in some cases reunited for the first time in years, hugged one another.

One of the most symbolically important acts occurred when, on November 12, a new crossing point was installed at Potsdamerplatz (a major crossroads once called by *The New York Times* the Piccadilly Circus of the German Empire), as the mayors of East and West Berlin—Walter Momper and Eberhardt Krack, respectively—shook hands. On that morning, what has been called the cruelest symbol of Europe's division and the long suffering of the people of Berlin became merely a memory.

On November 13, Hans Modrow became East Germany's new prime minister. Demonstrations in Leipzig and other cities continued despite his promise of imminent reforms. The end to the Berlin Wall came officially on December 22, when West German chancellor Helmut Kohl and East German prime minister Modrow together opened the Brandenburg Gate. Kohl became the first West German chancellor to set foot in East Berlin. The actual dismantling of the wall occurred in a matter of days, although Germany had remained divided for almost three decades. What had started as a multinational squabble over the spoils of war and had escalated into a dispute that threatened World War III would end with the reunification of Germany on October 3, 1990.

Impact of Event

The global consequences of the opening of the Berlin Wall were the reunification of Germany and the broader reconciliation between East and West. With the wall's dismantlement, the relationship between the Soviet Union and the United States moved, at least symbolically, to much firmer ground. On a personal level, the breakdown of the Berlin Wall changed people's lives overnight. Many fled to West Germany only to find that life was not miraculously better there. The deluge of refugees after the borders opened placed a considerable strain on West Germany's social services, as under West German law all East Germans were entitled to automatic citizenship. In East Germany, medical treatment was free; the burden placed on the West German infrastructure by the sudden increase in immigrants created the threat of fees for health care.

Early in 1990, the East German government implemented a system of partial state ownership of businesses to counteract economic stagnation. Foreign enterprises were then allowed to invest in businesses and to hold up to 49 percent of a venture. Significant economic restructuring commenced, and the East German people were given hope of enjoying free elections and upgraded housing. In the wake of such promises of reform, many returned to East Germany.

The flight of educated East Germans such as medical professionals, however, placed the country at risk of a shortfall of skilled workers to maintain the country's hospitals and other important elements of its infrastructure, threatening to leave the remaining East Germans with even fewer social resources. In East Germany, day-care for children under age three was available to about 60 percent of that group. In West Germany, the system had been operating at capacity before the arrival of the immigrants. One group of East Germans, however, was relatively unaffected by the political changes: the farmers. Prosperous and contented, few felt the need to re-establish themselves in West Germany.

The almost instant rejection of communism that took place in East Germany caused concerns that the people would try to take revenge for the suffering that they had experienced at the hands of their government, with its strict censorship, economic deprivation, and brutal police force. Reports were not uncommon of Communist Party officials (notably the regional chiefs of the districts of Schwerin, Halle, and Bautzen) who committed suicide rather than face an uncertain future as the reform process got under way. Old abuses of power were not going to be forgotten: The bloody revolution in Romania, followed by the execution on December 25, 1989, of President Nicolae Ceausescu, presented an object lesson in the dangers of an oppressed populace. Erich Honecker and top members of his cabinet had to be placed under house arrest to protect them while the excesses of their regime were being investigated. The fall of the communists in East Germany also led to fears of a resurgence of anti-Semitism. Ironically, as other East Germans were tasting their newfound freedom, East German Jews were living in renewed fear. The prospect of the switch from an antireligious state to a unified Germany, site of Nazism and the Holocaust, left many Jews uneasy about their future.

In East German schools, the Berlin Wall had been described as an "antifascist protection barrier," a bit of rhetoric that was tossed out with much of the Communist Party. In order to prevent new and equally damaging rhetoric from replacing it, however, the impact of German reunification on school curricula would need to be no less strong than on its political ideology. Cultures emerging from behind the Iron

Curtain began to face new economic, educational, and civic challenges in adapting to the demands and responsibilities of democracy and individual freedom.

Bibliography

Bark, Dennis L., and David R. Gress. *Democracy and Its Discontents, 1963-1988.* Vol. 2 in *A History of West Germany.* Oxford, England: Basil Blackwell, 1989. This text can be approached as one of the standard histories of West Germany in English. It focuses on the division of Germany and the Berlin Wall and discusses the link between student protests, human rights, and the German view of politics. Contains a complete list of references and an index.

Dahrendorf, Ralf. *Reflections on the Revolution in Europe: In a Letter Intended to Have Been Sent to a Gentleman in Warsaw.* New York: Times Books, 1990. This rather philosophical text is most useful for its insight into the social, political, and cultural clashes bound to result from the wholesale changes occurring in the East Bloc. Especially useful is its examination of the general mood of the East German people. Offers no reference features.

Dulles, Eleanor Lansing. *Berlin: The Wall Is Not Forever.* Chapel Hill: University of North Carolina Press, 1967. Although written in a somewhat dated style, this book is intriguing for its author's conviction, more than two decades before the fact, that the wall would "be dismantled in a meaningful period of contemporary history." Dulles' forecast of twenty years may have fallen two years short, but her vision of student protests against human rights infringements and the subsequent reunification of Germany cannot be dismissed. Includes an index and a bibliography.

Garton Ash, Timothy. *The Magic Lantern: The Revolution of '89 Witnessed in Warsaw, Budapest, Berlin, and Prague.* New York: Random House, 1990. An account of the major political upheaval that almost every Iron Curtain country experienced in 1989, including detailed information about the final days of a divided Germany and the reasons that the East Germans rebelled.

Kirchhoff, Gerhard, ed. *Views of Berlin: From a Boston Symposium.* Cambridge, Mass.: Birkhäuser Boston, 1989. This compilation of articles explores the social and cultural consequences of a divided city by discussing the cultural aspects of such a division. The periods covered by the different contributors range from that of the Weimar Republic to the late 1980's, though stopping short of the events of 1989.

Merritt, Richard L., and Anna J. Merritt, eds. *Living with the Wall: West Berlin, 1961-1985.* Durham, N.C.: Duke University Press, 1985. This collection of articles outlines the history of the wall and the methods used by the East German and West German peoples to cope with this division of their country and its violation of their basic human rights. Bibliography and index.

Waldenburg, Hermann. *The Berlin Wall Book.* London: Thames and Hudson, 1990. Although mainly useful as a pictorial overview of the wall's history, this volume also includes a brief chronology that is useful for its distillation of conditions leading to the uprising of the East German people.

Wyden, Peter. *Wall: The Inside Story of Divided Berlin*. New York: Simon & Schuster, 1989. Wyden's work is probably the most in-depth of the sources listed here. From the various methods of escape used to get across (or through or under) the wall to the history surrounding the wall's rise and fall, Wyden provides detailed discussion as well as references. Although his chronology concludes with Erich Honecker's prediction of a time "when borders will no longer divide [Germany] but unite [it]," Wyden's coverage serves as solid grounding for the events that took place on November 9, 1989.

Jo-Ellen Lipman Boon

Cross-References

The Berlin Wall Is Built (1961), p. 1125; The Brezhnev Doctrine Bans Acts of Independence in Soviet Satellites (1968), p. 1408; Soviets Invade Czechoslovakia (1968), p. 1441; Solidarity Leads Striking Polish Workers (1980), p. 2112; Poland Imposes Martial Law and Outlaws Solidarity (1981), p. 2152; Gorbachev Initiates a Policy of *Glasnost* (1985), p. 2249; Hungary Adopts a Multiparty System (1989), p. 2421; Soviet Farmers Are Given Control of Land and Selection of Crops (1989), p. 2471; Solidarity Regains Legal Status in Poland (1989), p. 2477; Poland Forms a Non-Communist Government (1989), p. 2500; Ceausescu Is Overthrown in Romania (1989), p. 2546; Soviet Troops Withdraw from Czechoslovakia (1990), p. 2570; Lithuania Declares Its Independence from the Soviet Union (1990), p. 2577; Gorbachev Agrees to Membership of a United Germany in NATO (1990), p. 2589; Demise of the U.S.S.R. Paves the Way for Reforms in Former Soviet Republics (1991), p. 2618.

THE UNITED NATIONS ADOPTS THE CONVENTION ON THE RIGHTS OF THE CHILD

Category of event: Children's rights
Time: November 20, 1989
Locale: United Nations, New York City

The Convention on the Rights of the Child was adopted by the United Nations General Assembly

Principal personages:
ADAM ŁOPATKA, the chairman of the United Nations working group which drafted the Convention on the Rights of the Child
ANDERS RÖNQUIST, the Swedish delegate to the United Nations working group during the second reading of the convention
AHMED FATHALLA, the Egyptian delegate to the United Nations working group during the second reading
NIGEL CANTWELL, the chairman of meetings of the Informal Ad Hoc NGO Group on the Drafting of the Convention on the Rights of the Child

Summary of Event

Based on reports of harsh living conditions, starvation, exploitation, and abuse of children throughout the world, the United Nations designated 1979 as the International Year of the Child (IYC). This year was chosen because it was the twentieth anniversary of the 1959 Declaration of the Rights of the Child. An important outcome of the IYC was the decision by the United Nations General Assembly to create an international treaty protecting the rights of children. The original purpose of this treaty was to put into legally binding language the ideals contained in the 1959 declaration. The convention on the Rights of the Child, however, goes far beyond the declaration's standards in protecting children's rights. Drafters of the Convention on the Rights of the Child chose to eschew the traditional protectionist approach to children's rights in favor of a text which places its emphasis on the child's human dignity.

Drafting of the Convention on the Rights of the Child was assigned to a working group set up by the United Nations Commission on Human Rights. From 1979 until 1988, drafting took place during a one-week period each year, just prior to the annual sessions of the commission. In 1988, additional drafting weeks were given to the working group in order to facilitate completion of the convention and its adoption by the General Assembly in 1989, the thirtieth anniversary of the Declaration of the Rights of the Child and the tenth anniversary of the IYC.

The working group's deliberations were based on a text presented to the Commission on Human Rights by the Polish government, which had sponsored the convention. This text contained twenty articles protecting substantive rights. During the drafting process, these articles were revised and expanded, often creating new articles and new rights. The working group was chaired by Adam Łopatka of Poland.

World interest in the Convention on the Rights of the Child, which originally had been far from enthusiastic, began to gain momentum in 1983. That year, a group of about thirty nongovernmental organizations (NGOs) established the Informal Ad Hoc NGO Group on the Drafting of the Convention on the Rights of the Child (NGO Group). In addition to participating in the deliberations of the working group, the NGO Group, chaired by Nigel Cantwell of Defence for Children International, met twice each year to review the various articles of the convention which had been either adopted or proposed by the working group. The NGO Group would then support a particular version of an article, recommend revisions, or draft entirely new articles for presentation at the next session of the working group.

When the preliminary draft of the Convention on the Rights of the Child was completed at the end of the first two-week session of the working group in 1988, the substantive portion had been expanded from the twenty articles of the original Polish model convention to a treaty containing forty-one substantive, rights-protecting articles. The implementation portion of the treaty had also been expanded from the Polish model. The implementation mechanism of the convention's preliminary draft made provisions for the establishment of a ten-member Committee on the Rights of the Child. Under its provisions, countries which ratified the convention, known as States Parties, would be bound legally to uphold the standards of the convention and would be required to submit regular reports to the committee covering their progress in implementing the rights protected by the convention. In evaluating States Parties' reports, the committee could use information from many outside sources, including nongovernmental organizations.

Members of the working group reconvened toward the end of 1988 for a second two-week session devoted to what is known as a "second reading." During this process, the preliminary draft text was subjected to a legal and linguistic review and reevaluation. To aid in their deliberations, drafters had a number of working documents. Among these was a "technical review," provided by the United Nations Centre for Human Rights, and the *Independent Commentary: United Nations Convention on the Rights of the Child* (1988), a collection of essays by legal scholars pointing out weaknesses in the convention. This collection was published by a nongovernmental organization independent of the United Nations.

Most of the preliminary draft text, including the implementation mechanism, was adopted with only minor revisions. For example, based on the recommendations of the "technical review," wording of the convention was revised carefully in order to make the text gender-neutral. There were, however, a number of articles which provoked heated debate during the reviewing process. Chairman Łopatka assigned these articles to special small drafting parties whose task it was to work out the disagreements. Since all articles of the convention were adopted on the basis of consensus, which connotes an absence of disapproval rather than active support, if even one government strongly opposed an article, it could not be adopted by the working group.

Article 14 on freedom of religion, Article 20 on foster care, and Article 21 on adoption are typical of articles which were contentious. All three of these articles were opposed by Islamic delegations on the ground that they conflicted with Islamic law. The article on freedom of religion was especially difficult to draft, since under Islamic law there can be no religious freedom before adulthood. Conversely, in the Buddhist tradition, a child as young as three or four years of age may choose to become a monk. Under threat of its deletion from the convention, the final text of this article was grudgingly agreed upon by the working group. The final text removed the right of a child to choose his or her religion.

On the other hand, deliberations over Articles 19 and 20 on foster care and adoption were brought to a satisfactory conclusion by a small drafting party headed by Ahmed Fathalla of the Egyptian delegation. These disagreements were settled by including reference to the "*kefalah* of Islamic law" as a substitute for adoption, which is prohibited in Islamic countries. In simple terms, *kefalah* is a process whereby a family assumes legal responsibility for a child, but the child is barred from taking that family's name and may not inherit from the family.

Undoubtedly the most heated debates during the second reading were those over paragraph 2 of Article 38, which sets the minimum age for participation in armed combat. A majority of government delegations supported the Swedish proposal to establish the age at eighteen, instead of the age of fifteen contained in the 1949 Geneva Conventions and 1977 protocols. This was vigorously opposed by the United States delegation on the grounds that the working group was an inappropriate forum in which to alter existing international humanitarian law. The small drafting party, headed by Anders Rönquist of the Swedish delegation, struggled valiantly to arrive at a compromise text which the United States would support. Ultimately, the United States held its ground and forced the age to be lowered to the Geneva Convention standard of fifteen.

The second reading concluded with the reordering and renumbering of the final text of the convention, with all of its fifty-four articles having been reviewed carefully and adopted by the working group. The convention then went to the plenary of the Commission on Human Rights, where it was adopted without debate. After further review by the United Nations Economic and Social Council and the Third Committee of the General Assembly, the convention was adopted by the General Assembly of the United Nations on November 20, 1989.

The final text of the Convention on the Rights of the Child is exceptional for many reasons. First, it is the most comprehensive of all the United Nations human rights treaties in that it contains the full range of human rights envisioned in the 1948 Universal Declaration of Human Rights. Second, its implementation mechanism is aimed at facilitation of States Parties' compliance rather than at approbation for failure to comply with the convention's standards. Most important, however, is that the Convention on the Rights of the Child completely alters previously accepted concepts of the child. All earlier international declarations and treaties dealing with children focused entirely on the child's need for protection. In blatant disregard of older standards, the Convention on the Rights of the Child guarantees the child's right to human dignity, which includes recognition of the standard of the child's "best interests," the child's "evolving capacities," and the child's rights of "individual personality," such as freedoms of religion, speech, association, and assembly and the right to privacy. These rights for children are not just some new dream for the future: They are rights which have already received the stamp of approval from all member states of the United Nations as the minimum set of rights which a government must guarantee to children.

Impact of Event

Even the most ardent backers of the Convention on the Rights of the Child could not have predicted the enthusiasm with which it has been embraced by the entire world community. At the signing ceremony on January 26, 1990, representatives of sixty countries brought the credentials required in order to sign the convention, a record for any human rights treaty. Moreover, while several years are usually needed before a human rights treaty acquires the necessary ratifications to go into force, the Convention on the Rights of the Child went into force on September 2, 1990, a little more than six months after the convention was opened for signature. It is probably safe to say that none of those involved in the planning of the World Summit on Children, held at the United Nations on September 29-30, 1990, would have predicted that the Convention on the Rights of the Child would already be in force at that time.

The momentum begun by the signing ceremony did not diminish. By December 1, 1991, 102 countries had ratified the Convention on the Rights of the Child. Enthusiasm for the convention was not confined to States Parties. Concerned that their governments' ratification of the convention might be merely pro forma, in many countries nongovernmental organizations formed coalitions to act as watchdogs in ensuring government compliance with the convention.

In Geneva, the NGO Group which so successfully negotiated with government delegations during the drafting of the Convention on the Rights of the Child reorganized under the new name of NGO Group for the Convention on the Rights of the Child. In its new form, it provides a conduit for information between national NGOs and the Committee on the Rights of the Child.

The ten members of the Committee on the Rights of the Child, who are to act in their personal capacities and not as government representatives, were elected in February of 1991. They held their first meetings from September 30 to October 18, 1991, and drafted their rules of procedure and their guidelines for the submission of reports by States Parties. The committee's rules of procedure generously interpreted Article 45 of the convention, allowing for the broadest possible input of information from sources other than the States Parties' reports. This procedure will help to ensure the honesty of those reports. The first States Parties' reports to the Committee on the Rights of the Child were scheduled to be submitted on September 2, 1992.

The full meaning of the Convention on the Rights of the Child and its impact on children's lives will not be felt until the committee actually applies the convention's standards to the reports from States Parties. This is an evolving process which, typically, takes years to develop. Over time, the various articles of the convention, like those of any constitution, will be interpreted and reinterpreted in view of changing world circumstances. That is not to say that the convention does not have immediate importance. Its standards are sufficiently clear, so it is unlikely that any government can ignore the rights of its children without facing censure from the world community.

Bibliography

Boulding, Elise. *Children's Rights and the Wheel of Life.* New Brunswick, N.J.: Transaction Books, 1979. Attempts to present children as active contributors to society. Compares children's rights, responsibilities, and opportunities to those of the elderly. Some discussion of the Declaration of the Rights of the Child.

Cohen, Cynthia P. "The Human Rights of Children." In *Capital University Law Review* 12 (1983): 369. This essay covers the period from the first proposal of the Convention on the Rights of the Child to the General Assembly until the end of the 1983 session of the United Nations Working Group charged with drafting the convention. It elaborates early resistance to the convention and discusses the establishment of the Informal Ad Hoc Group on the Drafting of the Convention on the Rights of the Child.

_____, ed. *Independent Commentary: United Nations Convention on the Rights of the Child.* New York: Defense for Children International-USA, 1988. A collection of essays by international legal scholars. The essays point out weaknesses in the text of the first draft of the Convention on the Rights of the Child. Among the issues discussed are the discrimination and juvenile justice provisions and the rights of indigenous peoples.

_____. "Relationships Between the Child, the Family, and the State: The United Nations Convention on the Rights of the Child." In *Perspectives on the Family*, edited by Michael D. Bayles, Robert Moffat, and Joseph Grcic. Lewiston, N.Y.: Edwin Mellen Press, 1990. The Convention on the Rights of the Child restates the relationship between the child, the family, and the state. This essay examines the way in which the convention addresses those relationships. In particular, it analyzes the interplay between the child's rights as an individual and the right to be brought up in a nurturing family environment.

_____. "The Role of Non-Governmental Organizations in the Drafting of the Convention on the Rights of the Child." *Human Rights Quarterly* 12 (February, 1990): 137-147. Nongovernmental organizations played a unique role in the drafting of the convention. This essay describes the background of the Informal Ad Hoc NGO Group on the Drafting of the Convention on the Rights of the Child, its tactics, its interactions with government delegations, and possible explanations for the success of its initiatives. Many articles of the convention exist only because of this group's efforts.

Cohen, Cynthia P., and Howard A. Davidson, eds. *Children's Rights in America: U.N. Convention on the Rights of the Child Compared with United States Law.* Chicago: American Bar Association Center on Children and the Law, 1990. These essays are divided into two sections. The first part discusses general considerations or themes of the final draft of the Convention on the Rights of the Child, such as the "child's best interests" or the "child's evolving capacities." The second section looks at clusters of articles from the convention and compares them with a general view of existing United States law relating to the clusters of rights.

Cohen, Cynthia P., and Per Miljeteig-Olssen. "Status Report: United Nations Convention on the Rights of the Child." *New York Law School Journal of Human Rights* (1991): 367. The authors examine the status of the convention after it was adopted by the General Assembly of the United Nations. They describe the ratification process and the election of members of the Committee on the Rights of the Child which will monitor compliance with the convention. Also mentioned is the relevance of the 1990 World Summit for Children.

Greaney, Vincent, ed. *Children: Needs and Rights.* New York: Irvington, 1985. Ten children's rights advocates present a multidisciplinary perspective. Includes chapters on development of children's rights in various countries. The chapter on "The United Nations and Children's Rights" contains the text of the Declaration of the Rights of the Child.

Lifton, Betty J. *King of Children.* New York: Farrar, Straus & Giroux, 1988. Discusses the life and work of Januz Korczak, who established homes for orphans in Poland prior to World War II. Korczak was known for his pedagogical theories, among them the child's "right to respect." Korczak believed that childhood was not a prehuman condition but part of life's continuum. He is revered for the fact that, rather than escaping and saving his own life, he went to the Treblinka death camp with the children from his orphanage in the Warsaw ghetto.

Cynthia Price Cohen

Cross-References

The Children's Bureau Is Founded (1912), p. 131; The United Nations Adopts Its Charter (1945), p. 657; The United Nations Children's Fund Is Established (1946), p. 689; The United Nations Adopts the Universal Declaration of Human Rights (1948), p. 789; The U.N. Convention Relating to the Status of Refugees Is Adopted (1951), p. 867; The United Nations Adopts the Declaration of the Rights of the Child (1959), p. 1038; The U.N. Covenant on Civil and Political Rights Is Adopted (1966), p. 1353; WHO Sets a Goal of Health for All by the Year 2000 (1977), p. 1893; An International Health Conference Adopts the Declaration of Alma-Ata (1978), p. 1998; The World Health Organization Adopts a Code on Breast-Milk Substitutes (1981), p. 2130.

TIBET'S DALAI LAMA IS AWARDED
THE NOBEL PEACE PRIZE

Categories of event: Peace movements and organizations; atrocities and war crimes
Time: December, 1989
Locale: Oslo, Norway

The choice of Tibet's exiled leader as recipient of the Nobel Peace Prize focused attention on the thirty-year military occupation and annexation of Tibet by the People's Republic of China

Principal personages:
> TENZIN GYATSO (1935-   ), the fourteenth Dalai Lama, the exiled spiritual and political leader of Tibet
> MAO TSE-TUNG (1893-1976), the first chairman of the People's Republic of China
> JAWAHARLAL NEHRU (1889-1964), the prime minister of India from 1947 until his death
> DENG XIAOPING (1904-   ), the Chinese Communist leader

Summary of Event

In 1940, a four-year-old peasant boy, Tenzin Gyatso, born in a cowshed in the tiny farming village of Takster in 1935, was installed by Buddhist monks as the fourteenth Dalai Lama (meaning "ocean of wisdom"). In Tibet, the Dalai Lama was the absolute spiritual and temporal head of his country. The devotion of the intensely religious Tibetan people to the Dalai Lama was for the most part unquestioning.

The Tibetans had expelled Chinese invaders in 1911, and by June, 1912, a proclamation formally reasserting Tibetan independence from China was issued. The Chinese, however, never viewed Tibet as free and independent. With the proclaimed intention of "liberating" Tibet during 1950, the People's Liberation Army of the Chinese Communist government invaded Tibet on October 7, 1950. Tibet was easy prey for the Chinese because the Tibetans had few material resources, no proper army, no arms or ammunition, and no military experience. The Chinese did not dissolve the political and religious system immediately. Although they promised Tibetan autonomy, the Chinese introduced reforms which systematically communized Tibet, weakening the religious and political authority.

Subsequent actions by the Chinese were based on a Seventeen-Point Agreement signed in April, 1951. According to the Dalai Lama, it was signed by government officials under the threat of further military operations against Tibet. The Chinese maintained that the agreement was designed to free Tibetans to return to the People's Republic of China and enjoy the same rights of national equality as all other nationalities in the country. It was never made clear from whom the Tibetans were being "freed." The Chinese repeatedly went against their own agreement and began systematically to repress, torture, and, according to Tibetans, massacre the Tibetan people.

The Dalai Lama sought and received recognition of the plight of Tibet through a resolution passed by the United Nations General Assembly in September, 1959, recognizing the violation of human rights in Tibet. The Chinese took no notice of the international resolution. In spite of the Dalai Lama's appeals, Great Britain, the United States, and India failed to provide military assistance.

Although the Dalai Lama would not lend his name to a freedom movement, some Tibetans began to fight the Chinese. By 1956, sporadic outbreaks of fighting had occurred in Lithang and Chamdo. By late 1956, refugees were streaming out of Tibet, and by mid-1958, full-scale fighting was under way. Chinese censorship was so effective, however, that virtually no news of this massive uprising appeared in the Western press.

On March 10, 1959, guerrillas led the people of Lhasa, the capital of Tibet, in an abortive uprising against the Chinese. A crowd of thirty thousand surrounded the Norbulingka, the Dalai Lama's summer palace, when they got word that he was planning to accept an invitation to attend a theatrical performance in a neighboring Chinese military camp. Their simple message was that if the Chinese insisted that the Dalai Lama go to their camp, the Tibetans would form a barricade to prevent it. If the Chinese fought, the Tibetans would fight back.

Although the Dalai Lama would have given himself up to the Chinese in order to avoid a massacre, the Tibetan people denied him this option. The Dalai Lama's life had to be saved, and he had to leave the palace and Lhasa at once. Dressed as a simple soldier, the Dalai Lama fled from Lhasa to northern India, where he was granted political asylum by Jawaharlal Nehru, the prime minister of India.

Even though the Dalai Lama had already escaped, the impasse continued until March 17, when two heavy mortar shells landed on the premises of the Norbulingka. The people quickly realized that bravery and small arms were not enough against an opponent that did not hesitate to shoot women and children hostages or to bomb a village or monastery.

Within one month of the March uprising, three million Tibetans, including religious leaders, were in prison camps. About twenty prison camps were scattered all over the mountain kingdom. Freedom of movement and speech were denied, and every Tibetan was required to carry an identity card.

Confrontation with the Chinese occurred again on March 9, 1989, when Chinese troops imposed martial law in Lhasa. Tourists reported Chinese soldiers shooting unarmed demonstrators, breaking into homes to drag people into police vans, and firing on women and children. Within days, foreigners were expelled from Tibet and the press was quieted.

Conditions in Lhasa grew worse. Asia Watch, Amnesty International, the Dalai Lama's government-in-exile in India, and several committees of the U.S. Senate and House of Representatives have documented and confirmed human rights violations. Twenty percent of the population—1.2 million people—were killed, many through armed conflict and famines resulting from collectivized farming and the diversion of Tibetan grain to China. A full-scale campaign has taken place for the destruction of Tibetan Buddhism through Communist indoctrination. Some six thousand monasteries, the centers of cultural and scholastic life, were destroyed. Tibet's forests were stripped, and some reports say that the land was used to reposit nuclear waste.

Most of the world was ignorant of China's record in Tibet, primarily because of the Chinese government's constant efforts to discredit the Dalai Lama as a political leader and its strict control of information. Although Beijing referred to him in derogatory terms, the few foreign journalists who visited the Dalai Lama have described him as warm and gently charismatic.

The Chinese government for decades managed to avoid accountability for atrocities meted out in Tibet. Its violent suppression of prodemocracy demonstrations within its own borders, in Beijing's Tiananmen Square on June 4, 1989, received international television coverage. On that date, the Chinese army turned its guns upon citizens in the streets, massacred thousands, drove student demonstrators from Tiananmen Square, and put to an end seven weeks of political protest.

Given more for idealism than for results, the Nobel Peace Prize for 1989 was awarded to the Dalai Lama, who led a government-in-exile for more than thirty years, in recognition of his nonviolent efforts to end China's forty-year control of Tibet. The Buddhist monk was praised by the Nobel Committee for advocating "peaceful solutions based upon tolerance and mutual respect in order to preserve the historical and cultural heritage of his people." One such example of his peace proposal efforts was a compromise on independence in 1988. Tibet would have become an autonomous state within China, allowing the Chinese government to continue control of defense and foreign policy.

In announcing the Dalai Lama as 1989 recipient of the Nobel Peace Prize, the committee insisted that the selection was not motivated by the crackdown of prodemocracy student demonstrations in China. Committee Chair Egil Aarvik allowed that the award could be interpreted as an encouragement to democracy-seeking Chinese students. Aarvik also stated, "If I were a Chinese student, I would be fully in support of the decision."

Impact of Event

The timing of the award was viewed as a symbol of international condemnation of the Chinese government for its crackdown on the students' democracy movement in Beijing's Tiananmen Square and the imposition of martial law in the Tibetan capital, Lhasa, following anti-Chinese riots of March, 1989. The protest movement posed new challenges to Deng Xiaoping, the leader of China, and the resulting crackdown created unprecedented anger, suspicion, and recalcitrance among the Chinese people. At home and in Tibet, the repressive tactics of the Chinese government were exposed to the world.

In the several years following the Nobel award, people made few political or economic gains. The average Chinese was a peasant, as China was still a poor, developing country. Its largely peasant population had little exposure to the concept of democracy and tended to be more protective of its recently acquired right to grow cash crops than of the human rights for which students demonstrated.

As might be expected, the Dalai Lama's selection was denounced by the Chinese embassy in Oslo as intervention into the internal affairs of the Chinese government. An embassy press attaché denounced the Dalai Lama as upsetting the unity of the nation. In contrast, when the exiled Tibetans at the Dalai Lama's headquarters in Dharmsala, India, heard the news of the Nobel Peace Prize award, a thousand of them danced in the streets. The Dalai Lama's selection was hailed by the Tibet Society of London as "the most significant international statement of support the Tibetans have ever received."

Although the Nobel Committee commended the Buddhist monk for advocating peaceful solutions, after Beijing's Tiananmen Square event, moderates in the Chinese government lost control, and willingness to talk with the Dalai Lama regarding his proposals diminished. The Dalai Lama persisted in refusing to advocate violence against the Chinese, although many young Tibetans wanted their leader to be more violent. They noted the more than three thousand political prisoners in central Tibet and the three hundred thousand troops in Tibet.

The Dalai Lama traveled internationally to publicize the continued plight of the Tibetans and to rally opposition against the unlawful occupation of Tibet. Unfortunately, many Western countries continued to support China's claim on Tibet. In a meeting with U.S. president George Bush, for example, the Dalai Lama received an audience but no more than that.

Martial law in Lhasa was lifted by the Chinese in May, 1990; however, arrests and repressive measures continued. Prisoners were tortured with cattle prods, and tourists were not allowed to leave their hotels without a Chinese guide and a military pass. More than 250,000 Chinese soldiers remained in Tibet. More than three hundred nuns and monks have been expelled from monasteries and nunneries in Lhasa. Since ethnic Chinese outnumbered Tibetans by about 7.5 million, the continued existence of the Tibetan culture seemed threatened.

Bibliography

Bilski, Andrew. "A God-King in Exile: The Dalai Lama Appeals for Democracy in Tibet." *Maclean's* 103 (October, 1990): 50-51. A rare interview with the Dalai Lama on a visit to Toronto, Canada. Topics include the impact of the violent suppression of prodemocracy, demonstrations in China's Tiananmen Square in June, 1989, the current situation in Tibet, and the monk's commitment to nonviolence.

Chopra, Pran Nath. *The Ocean of Wisdom: The Life of Dalai Lama XIV.* New Delhi: Allied Publishers, 1986. This is a comprehensive, not very objective, heart-rending biography of the Dalai Lama. Includes details of his numerous projects for his people in exile and in Tibet. Intriguing, rich details supplied by the Dalai Lama and his representatives. Rare photographs, glossary, index, and bibliography.

Hicks, Roger, and Ngakpa Chogyam. *Great Ocean: An Authorised Biography of the Buddhist Monk Tenzin Gyatso His Holiness The Fourteenth Dalai Lama.* Longmead, England: Element Books, 1984. Inspirational account of the life and works of the Dalai Lama. Includes numerous photographs and anecdotes from relatives and friends of the Dalai Lama. Index and bibliography. Supplements previous listing.

Hutheesing, Gunottam Purushottam, ed. *Tibet Fights for Freedom: The Story of the March 1959 Uprising as Recorded in Documents, Dispatches, Eye-Witness Accounts, and World-wide Reactions.* Bombay: Orient Longmans, 1961. Mainly useful as a detailed historical and chronological description of the tragic events in Tibet during the 1959 revolution from the uprising in Lhasa to the escape by the Dalai Lama, plus the international reaction and aftermath. Includes newspaper reports and published and broadcasted statements by the Indian prime minister, the Chinese, and the Dalai Lama. Rare photographs and an epilogue.

Moynihan, Maura. "Tibet's Agony: Nobel Prize, Ignoble Story." *The New Republic* 201 (November, 1989): 10-11. Identifies the Nobel Committee's decision to give the 1989 Peace Prize to the Dalai Lama as a means of exposing the Tiananmen Square massacre as well as focusing on the military occupation and annexation of Tibet by the People's Republic of China.

B. Mawiyah Clayborne

Cross-References

China Initiates a Genocide Policy Toward Tibetans (1950), p. 826; China Occupies Tibet (1950), p. 837; Mao Delivers His "Speech of One Hundred Flowers" (1956), p. 958; Mao's Great Leap Forward Causes Famine and Social Dislocation (1958), p. 1015; The Chinese Cultural Revolution Starts a Wave of Repression (1966), p. 1332; China Publicizes and Promises to Correct Abuses of Citizen's Rights (1978), p. 1983; Demonstrators Gather in Tiananmen Square (1989), p. 2483.

VOTERS IN CHILE END PINOCHET'S MILITARY RULE

Categories of event: Political freedom and voting rights
Time: December 14, 1989
Locale: Chile

After seventeen years of military rule under General Augusto Pinochet, Chileans peacefully resumed the democratic process by electing Patricio Aylwin to the presidency

Principal personages:

AUGUSTO PINOCHET (1915-   ), the staunchly anticommunist military ruler of Chile

SALVADOR ALLENDE (1908-1973), the socialist president of Chile elected in 1970 and killed during a military coup three years later

PATRICIO AYLWIN AZÓCAR (1918-   ), the leader of the Christian Democratic Party who was elected president of Chile in 1989 in the first free elections since 1970

Summary of Event

Chileans in the 1960's were justifiably proud of their long tradition of democratic rule supported by a military committed to upholding the constitution. In 1970, the candidate of a leftist coalition, Salvador Allende Gossens, was elected to the presidency in a three-way race that gave him only slightly more than one-third of the vote. His regime's attempts to redistribute national wealth caused a brief spurt in growth but soon foundered as their inflationary consequences began to be felt locally and as foreign interests searched for ways to impede Allende's success. By 1972, economic chaos reigned in Chile, yet the midterm congressional elections in 1973 did not give Allende's opposition the two-thirds majority it needed to impeach him. At that point, the military, which had supported his taking office in 1970, plotted to depose him. On September 11, 1973, it launched a well-coordinated coup. Allende died, probably by suicide, in the national palace rather than give in to the military and thus collude in the interruption of the constitutional process.

A military *junta* took control of governing the country. The national police rounded up and executed Allende supporters in what would rank among the bloodiest of military coups in twentieth century Latin America. Estimates put the number of those killed during and immediately after the coup somewhere between five thousand and fifteen thousand Chileans. Thousands of others escaped death by fleeing into exile.

The military at first insisted that it would hold power only as long as needed to restore order and prepare the way to a resumption of the democratic process. The commander in chief of the army, General Augusto Pinochet Ugarte, began to consolidate power for himself. He created the National Intelligence Directorate (Dirección

Nacional de Inteligencia, or DINA) to search out dissenters. In the purges sponsored by that organization, several hundred Chileans disappeared between 1975 and 1976. By the time Pinochet became president of Chile in 1974, he had also turned his attention to the nation's serious economic woes. Runaway inflation and nationalization of privately owned businesses had frightened away foreign capital. Chileans themselves had little confidence that investments in their homeland would provide adequate returns. Pinochet brought together a group of economic advisers to tackle these problems and devise solutions. Since several of them had completed postgraduate degrees at the University of Chicago under the tutelage of Professor Milton Friedman, an orthodox monetarist, they came to be known as the "Chicago boys."

Their policies for reducing inflation and encouraging foreign investment meant keeping a tight control on workers' wages. The resulting "economic miracle," characterized by unprecedented growth, brought benefit to a select few while most Chileans continued to find it difficult to make ends meet on their meager wages. By 1989, it was estimated that only two million out of twelve million Chileans had reaped the benefits of the boom.

In the meantime, repression by DINA mounted in order to keep discontent from surfacing. DINA did not, however, restrict its activities to Chile. On September 21, 1976, it pulled off, with the help of Cuban exiles, a car bombing in Washington, D.C., that killed Orlando Letelier, a foreign minister under the Allende regime who was living in exile, and his North American aide, Ronni Moffit. The reaction this provoked in the United States led to the dismantling of DINA in 1977. At the same time, the Vicariate of Solidarity, a Roman Catholic organization in Chile concerned with human rights abuses, kept careful count of those who were tortured by the Pinochet regime or who disappeared into the custody of the military.

In light of such outspoken opposition, and bolstered by the growth of the economy, Pinochet enacted a constitution in 1980 that appeared to point the way back to democracy in the distant future. One of the provisions of the 1980 constitution was that Chilean citizens would be given the opportunity to participate in a plebiscite on the Pinochet government in 1988. They would, at that time, vote "yes" or "no" on another term in office for the general.

Chile's "economic miracle" suffered severely with the international recession of 1981-1982. By 1983, the number of unemployed had grown from a 1973 total of 145,000 to more than one million. Resistance to the Pinochet government mounted not only among the working class but also in the middle and upper classes. Women, notably in the better neighborhoods of Santiago, demonstrated against the regime in 1983 by banging on their empty cooking pots and thus stressing the fact that it had become much more difficult to fill them. The outlawed political parties also began to regroup, and leaders discussed among themselves strategies for ousting Pinochet.

The military state, in retaliation, once again unleashed repression against protesters. Thousands of army troops patrolled the streets to keep order. When protests and strikes continued, Pinochet reinstated the state of siege he had lifted in 1979. Death squads also swung into action. Despite some of the largest demonstrations of the

1973-1988 period, Pinochet steadfastly refused to consider a rapid return to democracy, although the state of siege was lifted in June, 1985. Divisions surfaced within the military as well. The commanders in chief of the navy and air force began to discuss a transition of power with the civilian opposition. In September, 1986, after a leftist group unsuccessfully attempted to assassinate General Pinochet, the president reimposed a state of seige. Political repression tightened.

Ruling once again with a strong hand, Pinochet had little reason to believe that Chileans would find the courage to vote against him in the 1988 plebiscite. Despite the repression, however, some of the old political parties had joined together to encourage Chileans to vote "no." This sixteen-party coalition was headed by the president of the Christian Democratic party, Patricio Aylwin Azócar. Aylwin had supported the military coup against Allende in 1973, believing it necessary to keep the nation from plunging into complete economic chaos. Like so many of his fellow Chileans, he had not expected the military, and especially a single general, to control power for so long.

As they mobilized for the "no" vote, Chileans feared the worst. They expected Pinochet to react harshly against any show of dissatisfaction with his regime. They were not convinced he would accept an unfavorable vote and believed the plebiscite might be annulled and repression heightened. Apparently, however, General Pinochet firmly believed he would win.

In the October 5, 1988, plebiscite, 54.7 percent of the vote was for the "no" option. Even though Pinochet did not win, forty-three percent of the Chilean people did vote for his continuation in power. In the aftermath of the plebiscite, the general promised to abide by the 1980 constitution and prepare for presidential elections, in which he would not be a candidate. That constitution, however, allowed him to remain in command of the armed forces for eight more years and to appoint individuals to local offices and to the Congress before he stepped down. The transition was to happen on General Pinochet's terms.

Once the fear of repression faded following the October, 1988, plebiscite, Chileans flung themselves back into politics. Their long democratic tradition had not died during the Pinochet years. Realizing that many Chileans supported Pinochet's economic policies, the opposition vowed it would not dismantle the system responsible for the growth the military years had inaugurated. It would, however, attempt to distribute benefits more equitably. The coalition that had supported the "no" vote now supported the candidacy of a single opposition candidate. The man it chose to represent it was Patricio Aylwin of the Christian Democratic party.

The collapse of communist regimes in Eastern Europe took some of the wind out of Pinochet's supporters, who argued that the election of the opposition coalition's candidate could plunge Chile back into the chaotic days of Allende's socialist administration. Many who had supported those policies in the early 1970's had spent the following fifteen years in Eastern Europe, learning at first hand the pitfalls of socialist economies. Some who had fled to Poland, for example, found themselves more in sympathy with Lech Wałęsa's Solidarity movement than with the Communist party. They claimed to have returned to Chile overwhelmingly committed to liberal democracy and to a capitalist economy.

Pinochet's supporters chose as their presidential candidate Hernan Buchi, the Chilean finance minister from 1985 to 1988. They claimed he would maintain Chile's position as a rapidly developing nation. As they looked around at their Latin American neighbors, mired in economic troubles, many Chileans hoped that democracy, for them, would not mean a reversal of development.

On December 14, 1989, a majority of Chilean voters cast their ballots for Patricio Aylwin. They also elected a Congress for the first time since the military coup. The transition to democracy had been peaceful, but the military remained strong and proud of its accomplishments while in power; it was determined to oppose any attempts to call it to task for human rights abuses. General Pinochet remained in command of the army. The difficult job of governing fell to Patricio Aylwin and to the Chilean Congress.

Impact of Event

The plebiscite of October 5, 1988, followed by the presidential and congressional election fourteen months later, provided the opportunity for Chileans to resume their long democratic tradition. Exiled Chileans had been returning since 1985 and were now able to participate in the mainstream of political life. The dark days of repression had been banished to the past; yet, the joyous optimism of the majority of the population belied the existence of serious problems that had yet to be addressed.

First, there was tremendous uncertainty over how to deal with the human rights abuses carried out under the Pinochet regime. Unlike Argentina, where the military left office in 1973 in disgrace over a failed economy and a war lost to Great Britain, General Pinochet relinquished power at a time when Chile's economy was once again doing far better than those of most of its South American neighbors. The military, having witnessed the humiliation of its Argentinian counterpart, made it abundantly clear that it would not suffer rebuke placidly. Pinochet remained the commander in chief of the army. It was highly unlikely that the wounds caused by repression would be healed through justice provided by courts of law.

Second, the new Chilean leaders faced the problematic transition from opposition party to government party. The coalition organized to end Pinochet's presidency was made up of diverse parties. Many remembered the bitterness and factionalism of the last days of the Allende regime that led to the horrors accompanying the inauguration of the military dictatorship. Most were determined not to allow their differences to jeopardize democracy, but only time would tell how well the coalition members could work together once in power.

A third, and possibly the most significant, challenge facing the new regime was assuring continued economic growth along with greater attention to social justice. While the gross national product figures for Chile had grown impressively in the late 1980's, most Chilean workers, earning the minimum wage, could not support families. The coalition that had formed to oust Pinochet included parties fully committed to ensuring more equitable distribution of the nation's wealth. How to do that without frightening investors remained to be seen. A return to democracy meant that the mistakes of the regime could no longer be blamed on a strongman; they had become the responsibility of the citizenry as a whole.

Bibliography

Arriagada, Genaro. *Pinochet: The Politics of Power.* Boston: Allen & Unwin, 1988. Excellent discussion of Pinochet's consolidation of power in Chile after 1973. Written before the return to democracy, it documents the significance of the alliance of political parties against the general as well as the position of the Catholic church in its support for human rights. As late as 1987, the author was not convinced that Pinochet would relinquish power. Notes and index.

Boorstein, Edward. *Allende's Chile: An Inside View.* New York: International Publishers, 1977. An admiring account of the Allende years written by an author sympathetic to the goals of the Left. He believes socialist revolution will come again to Chile. Good view of what men like Pinochet feared in the opposition.

Loveman, Brian. *Chile: The Legacy of Hispanic Capitalism.* New York: Oxford University Press, 1988. The best overview of Chilean history in the nineteenth and twentieth centuries. Provides the continuity necessary for understanding the transitions of the 1960's and 1970's. The second edition includes an update on the Pinochet years in power. Extensive bibliography. Index.

Nunn, Frederick M. *The Military in Chilean History.* Albuquerque: University of New Mexico Press, 1976. Although most of this volume deals with the period before 1970, it is valuable to those interested in understanding why the military waited until 1973 to intervene so forcefully in politics. The last chapter, "Marxism and the Military," describes the process whereby the military came to depose Allende. Index.

Politzer, Patricia. *Fear in Chile: Lives Under Pinochet.* New York: Pantheon, 1989. Focused on the working class and based on interviews conducted in the poor neighborhoods of Santiago. The author gives insight into the lives of those who suffered most from Pinochet's political and economic policies.

Sigmund, Paul E. *The Overthrow of Allende and the Politics of Chile, 1964-1976.* Pittsburgh, Pa.: University of Pittsburgh Press, 1977. Very good discussion of the transition from reformist policies under President Eduardo Frei to radical policies under Allende, then to repressive policies under Pinochet. An essential book for understanding why Chilean politics moved so speedily from concerns with freedom and social justice to emphasis on economic growth at any expense. Notes and index.

Timerman, Jacobo. *Chile: Death in the South.* New York: Alfred A. Knopf, 1987. Written by a newspaper editor who was imprisoned by the military in Argentina during the late 1970's, this account describes the uncertainty of change in Chile in 1986. The author's own impressions of the political situation in Chile are interspersed with testimonials of individuals who had themselves experienced the state's repression.

Joan E. Meznar

Cross-References

The United Nations Adopts the Universal Declaration of Human Rights (1948), p. 789; Castro Takes Power in Cuba (1959), p. 1026; The Inter-American Commission on Human Rights Is Created (1959), p. 1032; Brazil Begins a Period of Intense Repression (1968), p. 1468; An Oppressive Military Rule Comes to Democratic Uruguay (1973), p. 1715; Allende Is Overthrown in a Chilean Military Coup (1973), p. 1725; The Argentine Military Conducts a "Dirty War" Against Leftists (1976), p. 1864; Somoza Is Forced Out of Power in Nicaragua (1979), p. 2035; The National Commission Against Torture Studies Human Rights Abuses (1983), p. 2186; Amnesty International Adopts a Program for the Prevention of Torture (1983), p. 2204; Argentine Leaders Are Convicted of Human Rights Violations (1985), p. 2280; Sandinistas Are Defeated in Nicaraguan Elections (1990), p. 2564.

CEAUSESCU IS OVERTHROWN IN ROMANIA

Categories of event: Revolutions and rebellions; civil rights
Time: December 23, 1989
Locale: Bucharest, Romania

Nicolae Ceausescu rose to power in Romania through political manipulation and a populist nationalist program, but the liberation of Eastern Europe brought the demise of the tyrannical dictator

> *Principal personages:*
> NICOLAE CEAUSESCU (1918-1989), the general-secretary of the Romanian Communist Party
> ION ILIESCU (1930-), the Communist reformer who succeeded Ceausescu as prime minister
> GHEORGHE GHEORGHIU-DEJ (1901-1965), a Romanian Communist Party leader

Summary of Event

The history of twentieth century Romania is one of class and ethnic conflict. An impoverished peasantry suffered under the oppressive rule of a brutal gentry while the leaders of the country preached the gospel of expansion, seeking to solve their land hunger by taking territory from decaying empires and their equally grasping neighbors. Modernization brought Western ideologies which added to class and national hatred in the country.

As a result of the Balkan Wars and World War I, Romania acquired Dobruja from Bulgaria, Transylvania from Austria, and Bessarabia from Russia. The populations in these lands were mixed with many nationalities besides Romanians—Hungarians, Russians, Serbs, Bulgarians, Gypsies, Ukrainians, and Turks among them. Religions also mixed in these regions—Muslims, Catholics, Orthodox, Protestants, and Jews. Ethnic and sectarian riots were common, and after the wars oppression and poverty continued. Hungarians in Transylvania and Jews in Bessarabia in particular felt the sting of Romanian law and the abuse of ultranationalistic groups and parties. Social friction in Romania worsened when, in the 1930's and during World War II, the country embraced fascism and allied itself to the German Reich.

The poverty of the masses, increased by the depression of the 1930's, and discrimination against and oppression of the minorities fueled the growth of the Communist Party in the country. Laborers in Romania's small working class were unable to organize in free unions and saw the Communist Party as an outlet. Some peasants also joined, although most preferred the various peasant parties, both democratic and fascist. Another source of Communist Party membership was the oppressed minorities, particularly Jews and Hungarians. Communists from these latter groups were chiefly intellectuals and rose rapidly to party leadership. In the 1930's, many of these intellectual leaders found their way to Moscow, where those lucky enough to survive the purges and executions of Joseph Stalin earned the patronage of the Soviet leader. World War II, however, witnessed the rise of a "native" Communist leadership among the partisans who fought fascism at home. During the war, the party kept this rivalry between the "Muscovites," led by Ana Pauker and Vasil Lucca, and the "natives," led by Gheorghe Gheorghiu-Dej, under wraps. In 1944, the "natives" were able to convince the king to give them the reins of power before the Red Army brought Lucca and Pauker back to the country.

After the war, Moscow's priority was the development of a strong security zone in the northern tier of Eastern Europe—Poland, Hungary, Czechoslovakia, and East Germany. This allowed leeway to the countries in the south. Yugoslavia's Josip Broz Tito and Albania's Enver Hoxha broke completely with Moscow. In Romania, the "native" Communists replaced the "Muscovites" without breaking from the Kremlin entirely. Gheorghiu-Dej pushed his rivals, Lucca and Pauker, off to the side but still stood shoulder to shoulder with Stalin on the international stage. Unlike the public Communist dissident Tito, Gheorghiu-Dej, similar to Mao Zedong in China, publicly remained loyal to international communism while carrying out a nationalist agenda at home.

Under Gheorghiu-Dej, Nicolae Ceausescu moved up the party ranks to the inner circles of power. He took over when Gheorghiu-Dej died. Ceausescu demonstrated his mastery of politics and rose from obscurity to supreme leadership by eliminating his major rivals. Through populism and nationalism, he built support and respect in Romania and abroad. Unlike Gheorghiu-Dej, who for all of his nationalist policies still ruled with a Stalinist iron hand, Ceausescu initiated liberal reforms in civil rights. By 1969, he had established his "cult of personality," but it was his political manipulation of party personnel rather than this cult that kept him in power.

In the 1960's and 1970's, rapid economic growth and liberalization led to improved standards of living and a foreign reputation that made Ceausescu unique among Communist leaders. He gradually changed his image from that of a hero of the proletariat to one reminiscent of the Romanian monarchs. He became an exhibitionist of extravagant wealth in the midst of poverty. Depression and foreign debt in the 1980's did not help matters. Romanians suffered a relative worsening of their living standards, even compared to their Eastern European neighbors. Rationing of food and energy meant hunger and cold for most except Ceausescu and his inner circle. His subjects' extreme hatred toward their leader replaced the popularity Ceausescu had once enjoyed.

Ceausescu increased the number and rigor of the secret police and built a large network of informers. Liberalism disappeared. Romanians found their right to travel reduced, and authorities dismissed critics from their jobs or imprisoned them. Foreigners who formerly were warmly greeted in the country now were rebuffed.

Ceausescu's attempt to industrialize his economy rapidly by razing many Romanian villages—a policy called "systemization"—brought increased disaffection. He hoped to build huge agroindustrial complexes, necessitating removal of the rural population from their traditional hearths and relocating them in communal dormitory-style apartment blocs. The program also destroyed many historic monuments, bringing condemnation upon Ceausescu from around the world. The Hungarian minority who inhabited many of the demolished villages particularly felt this oppression. Ceausescu deliberately fanned the flames of national hatred by singling out the Hungarian community for discrimination and applying the old rule of divide and conquer. Many Hungarians from Transylvania fled across the border, seeking haven in a liberalized Hungary.

Even though the new wave of democracy spreading across Eastern Europe isolated Ceausescu, he refused to change. He tried appealing to nationalism, characterizing the Hungarians who left as traitors both to Romania and to socialism. He demanded the return of the Moldavian Soviet Socialist Republic, the former Bessarabia, which was taken by Stalin from Romania in 1940. In December, 1989, the Romanian-speaking majority demonstrated there for national rights.

At the beginning of December, 1989, Ceausescu increasingly felt the pressure for reform from neighboring countries. The Romanian leader attempted to shift the blame for the country's problems by criticizing the Communist Party and by calling for improvement in living standards but no change in the political system. An international scandal broke over the treatment of Reverend Laszlo Tokes, a Protestant minister of Hungarian nationality living in Timişoara, in Transylvania. Romanian authorities had been harassing Tokes for speaking out against the discrimination suffered by Hungarians living in Romania. The authorities expelled three Hungarian journalists who came to visit him. On December 17, the Romanian police attempted to deport Tokes, but the townspeople of Timişoara, both Hungarians and Romanians, rose up in a protest that turned into a revolt. Battles between the Romanian security forces and the Timişoarians on December 19 and 20 cost thousands of casualties. Both the Western and socialist nations condemned Ceausescu. The Soviet Moldavians, who just a few weeks before had been demonstrating against cultural discrimination and Russian domination in the Soviet Union, asked Moscow to intervene in Bucharest to save their conationalists. Ceausescu angrily responded to his critics that the demonstrators were fascist agitators spurred on by Hungary.

On December 21, the demonstrations spread to the capital, where the crowd jeered and shouted Ceausescu down when he tried to deliver an address to the university. These demonstrations became riots and then a revolution. The next day, Ceausescu attempted to flee the country. A group of dissident Communist leaders whom Ceausescu earlier had expelled from the party now formed a Committee of National Salvation, led by Ion Iliescu, as an interim government. Chaos, however, continued to reign. The populace particularly sought out the hated *Securitate*, Ceausescu's fifteen-thousand-person secret police force that had held Romania in check during his dictatorship and was responsible for the Timişoara massacre.

The rebels captured Ceausescu and his wife on December 23. Two days later, a hastily assembled court-martial tried the Ceausescus on charges of genocide of the Romanian people, the destruction of the country's economy and spiritual values, and stealing more than $1 billion, which they had deposited in foreign banks. Despite their protests, the court found them guilty and ordered them shot the same day. The Ceausescus' captors filmed the grisly execution and showed it on Romanian television as proof of the dictator's death. The legacy Ceausescu left Romania was one of bitterness, poverty, and hatred. Of all the countries which in 1989 moved from authoritarian one-party rule to open societies, only Romania carried out this change through violence.

Impact of Event

Because Romanian Communism had a populist basis built up by Gheorghiu-Dej and by Ceausescu, the fall of the dictator did not lead to a dismissal of the party, as was the case in the northern-tier states. Like those in Bulgaria and Albania, Romanian socialists still had some power. Civil liberties not enjoyed since the 1930's suddenly were introduced, including freedom of speech, assembly, and religion. The Communists, however, still ruled, and economic limitations remained as opposing forces tried to come to some agreement on a new form of government. The first government replacing Ceausescu, that of Ion Iliescu, was composed chiefly of Communists and ex-Communists, some of whom the dictator had fired. This government was opposed by student and intellectual rebels in Bucharest who wanted all Communists out of power. In January, 1990, the government arranged for its supporters to break up a large demonstration in Bucharest. Freedom of speech was still respected, but the freedom to organize opposition was unofficially now severely limited. Moreover, there was little that either the new government or the opposition could do about Romania's economy, bankrupted through Ceausescu's extravagance and projects. The government gradually introduced a lessening of food and fuel restrictions and attempted to solve its food problem through plans offering state and collective land for private use. Ironically, Ceausescu's restrictions on foreign expenditures had a positive aspect, since the country's lack of large international debt made it a creditworthy customer for loans. Without a stable government, however, Romania could not take advantage even of this.

Ceausescu's fall reignited ethnic tensions in Transylvania. The Romanian Hearth association protested the government's granting of cultural autonomy to the country's Hungarians, including the establishment of schools using the Hungarian language. Romanian nationalists broke up Hungarian demonstrations for national rights, such as a peaceful march in the spring of 1990 at Tîrgu-Mureş in Transylvania. Club-wielding Romanians killed eight people and injured hundreds. Thousands of Hungarians, including some of the most educated, fled the country to avoid the turmoil and economic dislocation.

Romanian nationalists mistreated the significant Gypsy population as well. In some villages, Gypsy homes were burned. Many Gypsies were forced to relocate. Some unfortunates were lynched. Outbreaks of anti-Semitism reminiscent of the 1930's occurred as well. Although not suffering the same discrimination as the other minorities, members of Romania's centuries-old German community took advantage of the new freedom to escape the economic hardship through emigration.

Ceausescu's fall brought to light one of the cruelest aspects of his tyranny. Through his policy of forced procreation, Romanian women bore thousands of children they could not care for. Many of these were sent to orphanages and hospitals where, because of unsanitary medical conditions, a large number contracted AIDS. The plight of these infants brought a shock of horror to the world. Couples in the West desiring to adopt children sought healthy babies from Romania. There were cases of baby selling on the black market as well as cases of AIDS-infected babies offered for adoption.

In May, 1990, Iliescu and his Socialist Party (the former Communists) won a landslide election. Although observers considered the balloting honest, Bucharest dissidents claimed fraud and another violent demonstration rocked the city the following month. Unable to rely on the local police, Iliescu brought in miners loyal to him in order to crush the demonstrations. Disagreements between the government and dissidents prevented resolution of Romanian problems. By June, 1991, the cabinet still could function only on a day-by-day basis while the fate of the country remained in the balance. Civil liberties and political freedom existed, but anarchy rather than democracy remained the order of the day.

Bibliography

Ceausescu, Nicolae. *Nicolae Ceausescu: Builder of Modern Romania, International Statesman.* New York: Pergamon, 1983. A panegyric prepared for Pergamon's Leaders of the World Series, edited by Robert Maxwell. Serves as a document of the role Ceausescu played in East-West relations. Contains statements praising Ceausescu from such figures as Richard Nixon, Jimmy Carter, and Margaret Thatcher. Illustrations and bibliography of Ceausescu's works, no index.

Fischer, Mary Ellen. *Nicolae Ceausescu: A Study in Political Leadership.* Boulder, Colo.: Lynne Rienner, 1989. The best political biography and analysis of the career of the Romanian dictator up to the year before his fall. The author is a prominent American political scientist of Romanian affairs who has specialized in the role of the Ceausescu family. Documented, with bibliography and index.

Fischer-Galati, Stephen. *Twentieth Century Rumania.* New York: Columbia University Press, 1970. A standard history by a leading American scholar of Romanian studies. One of several useful volumes on modern Romanian history by the same author, this gives the background to the Communist period as well as to Ceausescu. Reveals the nationalist character of Gheorghiu-Dej's regime. Documented, with bibliography, index, and illustrations.

Fleischman, Janet. *Destroying Ethnic Identity: The Hungarians of Romania.* New York: U.S. Helsinki Watch Committee, 1989. An indictment of Ceausescu's policies toward ethnic Hungarians by the international human rights organization. Based on testimony by Hungarian émigrés from Romania and Hungary and other figures who were close to the situation. Particularly dwells on "systemization." Bibliography.

Giurescu, Dinu C. *The Razing of Romania's Past.* Washington, D.C.: U.S. Committee, International Council on Monuments and Sites, 1989. A condemnation of Ceausescu's controversial systemization policy of destroying Romanian buildings and villages for the purpose of modernization. This volume gives background material on Romanian monuments and buildings and has many photographs. Does not pay attention to the ethnic question raised by this issue. Illustrations and bibliography.

Gwertzman, Bernard M., and Michael T. Kaufman, eds. *The Collapse of Communism.* Rev. ed. New York: Times Books/Random House, 1990. One of the first books published after the Eastern European changes of 1989, this is a collection of essays, articles, and reports from *The New York Times*, with an introduction and connecting notes by the editors, who are also editors of that newspaper. The pieces are rather sketchy and simply give a chronological account of the changes in Eastern Europe. Index.

Nelson, Daniel N., ed. *Romanian Politics in the Ceausescu Era.* New York: Gordon & Breach, 1988. A specialized but excellent scholarly anthology analyzing various aspects of Ceausescu's political system. Covers the period of Ceausescu's rise to power as well as giving an introductory chapter on the Gheorghiu-Dej era. Gives details of Ceausescu's institutions in power. Contains tables and documentation; no index.

Romania: A Case of "Dynastic" Communism. New York: Freedom House, 1989. An indictment of Ceausescu's government published shortly before his fall. Contains expositions by several exiled dissidents and by Laszlo Hamos, a champion of the Hungarian minority. Index.

Tismaneanu, Vladimir. "New Masks, Old Faces: The Romanian *Junta*'s Familiar Look." *The New Republic* 202 (February 5, 1990): 17-22. A scholar's account and analysis of Ceausescu's fall, written shortly after the event. Sympathetic to the opposition. Gives a detailed account of both the overthrow of Ceausescu and the government repression of the demonstration of January, 1990.

_____. "The Revival of Politics in Romania." *Proceedings of the Academy of Political Science* 38 (January, 1991): 85-100. A scholarly article on the changes that Ceausescu's fall brought to Romanian politics.

Frederick B. Chary

Cross-References

Soviets Take Control of Eastern Europe (1943), p. 612; Gorbachev Initiates a Policy of *Glasnost* (1985), p. 2249; Ethnic Riots Erupt in Armenia (1988), p. 2348; Ethnic Unrest Breaks Out in Yugoslavian Provinces (1988), p. 2386; Hungary Adopts a Multiparty System (1989), p. 2421; Soviet Troops Leave Afghanistan (1989), p. 2449; Soviet Farmers Are Given Control of Land and Selection of Crops (1989), p. 2471; Solidarity Regains Legal Status in Poland (1989), p. 2477; Poland Forms a Non-Communist Government (1989), p. 2500; The Berlin Wall Falls (1989), p. 2523; Albania Opens Its Borders to Foreign Nationals (1990), p. 2553; Soviet Troops Withdraw from Czechoslovakia (1990), p. 2570; Lithuania Declares Its Independence from the Soviet Union (1990), p. 2577; Yugoslav Army Shells Dubrovnik (1991), p. 2612.

ALBANIA OPENS ITS BORDERS
TO FOREIGN NATIONALS

Category of event: Political freedom
Time: 1990
Locale: Tirana, Albania

After decades of isolation under its Communist government, Albania loosened its restrictions on foreign visitors and then, in 1990, joined the East European democratic revolution

Principal personages:
ENVER HOXHA (1908-1985), the general-secretary of the Albanian Communist Party and former ruler of the country
RAMIZ ALIA (1925-   ), Hoxha's successor
ISMAIL KADARE (1936-   ), the country's leading nationalist author, whose public defection sparked reform

Summary of Event

Modern Albania was formed on the eve of World War I as a result of conflict among the Balkan states and the Great Powers. The linguistic nationalism that united the Albanians belied the religious distinctions of four communities—Sunni and Shī'ite Muslims (about 70 percent of the population), Orthodox Christians (20 percent), and Roman Catholics (10 percent). Between the world wars, the country changed from a democratic republic to a fascist-style dictatorship, whose leader proclaimed himself Zog I, the king of the Albanians.

In 1939, Italian dictator Benito Mussolini turned on his ally Zog and annexed Albania to Italy. Resistance to fascist occupation began, and increased in 1940 when World War II reached the Balkans. Two main groups, the democratic, Western-oriented *Balli Kombetar* and the Albanian Party of Labor (the Communists), founded in 1942, led this resistance while fighting each other. The Communist Party arose from the nascent labor movement under the skillful leadership of Enver Hoxha, a masterful organizer from the Muslim community who, with aid from Russian ruler Joseph Stalin and Yugoslav resistance leader Josip Broz Tito, was able to put together a formidable force. Hoxha then played the major role in the resistance.

After World War II, Hoxha defeated his non-Communist rivals and became ruler of the People's Socialist Republic of Albania. The country's neighbors, both Communist Yugoslavia and Western-oriented Greece, however, still had designs on its territories. Hoxha therefore welcomed Stalin's casting Tito out of the Communist Information Bureau and became the Soviet leader's most ardent supporter.

In 1956, Stalin's successor, Nikita Khrushchev, started his program of de-Stalinization, which included modest liberalization and even rapprochement with Tito. Hoxha distanced himself from Moscow and in 1962 broke all diplomatic and cultural relations with the Kremlin. The Albanian leader steadfastly remained loyal to the memory of Stalin and emulated both his "cult of personality" and his totalitarian regime. Culture and politics in Albania recalled those of the Soviet Union in the 1930's. All art conformed to the doctrine of Socialist Realism. The leader was glorified. Nationalism was used as a unifying factor in the process of building socialism. All books praised Stalin and Hoxha as the leaders in all fields of endeavor. Hoxha himself, in imitation of Stalin, turned out volume after volume of his thoughts and memoirs. The totalitarian aspects of Stalinism also found root in Albania—strict censorship, imprisonment of lawbreakers, suspension of civil liberties, restrictions on the right to travel, and harsh penalties, including executions for minor infractions. The right of private ownership, even for personal items, was the most restrictive in Eastern Europe. The government completely banned the ownership of private automobiles. Like Stalin, Hoxha tried to control every aspect of the lives of his people. He particularly tried to prevent the influx of foreign ideas, which might lead to a lessening of what he hoped would be a national resolve to move Albania quickly and directly on the path to Communism.

There were some significant differences between Hoxha's Albania and Stalin's Soviet Union. Whereas Stalin used the Russian Orthodox church as a national unifier, Hoxha banned all public worship, citing Karl Marx's dictum that religion is the opiate of the people. Moreover, the Christian churches, with their links to Rome and Athens, were the major source of dissidence in the country, and Muslim institutions wedded to the past were an impediment to modernization. Furthermore, whereas Stalin experimented with some economic forms, Hoxha held strictly to centralized planning and a collective economy. Whereas Stalin made Russia into an international power, seeking alliances and relations with all types of foreign countries, Hoxha kept Albania relatively isolated. Albania had no diplomatic relations with either the United States or the Soviet Union, but Tirana's isolation was never complete. Although consistently denouncing both capitalist and Warsaw Pact countries, Albania maintained diplomatic and economic contacts on both sides of the Iron Curtain as well as with many Third World countries.

Many of Albania's policies reflected a nationalist rather than a Communist agenda. Albanian leaders admitted forthrightly that patriotism was one of their highest priorities, even higher than international proletarian solidarity, which they preached as well. Even the banning of religion served a national goal, as it prevented division among the communities. The economic policy of self-reliance also had a national basis. Albania had a wealth of resources, but paradoxically had one of the poorest populations in Europe, since these resources had never been used for the benefit of the people. Starting from this low base allowed Tirana to follow a program of gradual modernization and slowly rising living standards without amassing a foreign debt. The policy produced some spectacular successes, but in comparison to rapid modernization occurring elsewhere in the post-World War II world economy, the country remained far behind.

In the 1970's, Hoxha gradually reduced his power, turning the reins of government over to Ramiz Alia while he kept watch from the background. Alia made new diplomatic and commercial contacts, although relations with the Soviet Union and the United States remained closed. The government also permitted limited travel by foreign tours for citizens of those countries where diplomatic and trade missions existed. The authorities even allowed Americans of Albanian descent to visit the country. After Hoxha died in 1985 and Ramiz Alia assumed full control, even more liberalization occurred.

The changes that swept East Europe in 1989 affected Albania as well. Student demonstrations demanding liberalization began and increased during 1990. At first, Alia stood firmly against any changes and tried to suppress the growing demonstrations. He then tried to keep his system intact while seeking compromises and making concessions to the growing opposition. In March, 1990, the Communist leadership introduced its own reform program, which included economic decentralization, contested elections in factories and collective farms, and public debate on some policies such as education. Rapidly trying to end what was left of Albania's isolation, the government also reached out abroad, seeking new contacts. For the first time, direct telephone service with the West became available for ordinary Albanian citizens. In May, in the most dramatic change to that date, Alia restored the right of Albanians to practice their religions openly and to travel abroad.

In the months that followed, Alia restored other democratic political and civil rights and facilitated the ability of foreigners, including Americans and Soviets, to visit the country. For many, especially the Albanian intelligentsia, the changes were still too slow and the dismantling of the Communist system not in sight. Demonstrations and protests continued. Many, for economic as well as political reasons, attempted to leave the country, both legally and illegally. Clashes with the authorities were frequent. In October, the prominent Albanian writer Ismail Kadare publicly defected while in France as a protest against the continued totalitarian regime. His action inspired even larger demonstrations in Tirana and other Albanian cities. In the meantime, Tirana sought more contacts with foreign governments, particularly those of the United States and the Soviet Union. Alia invited United Nations Secretary-General Javier Perez de Cuellar for a state visit. In August, 1990, Albania reestablished diplomatic relations with the Soviet Union, and in March, 1991, with the United States. The following June, Secretary of State James Baker became the highest-ranking American official ever to visit the country.

Impact of Event

The restoration of civil liberties, because it was delayed, did not completely satisfy the opposition to the Communist government, led by university faculty and students. The debate over Albania's future also opened the floodgates to long-suppressed political discussion. The country was divided into two camps, those who supported Alia's slow policy of reform and those who wanted to move away from Communism as quickly as possible.

The debate turned to violence. Despite government concessions, demonstrations and riots continued. Statues of Stalin and Hoxha were toppled. Clashes between the authorities and opposition demonstrators were a daily occurrence. In March, 1991, the government declared a state of martial law in the city of Dures, the site of some of the worst violence. Opponents of the regime complained that the secret police still had free rein and that true freedom could not occur until they were curbed. Even Kadare, in exile, claimed he had been threatened. In November, 1990, Alia agreed to as complete a liberation in politics and society as was taking place elsewhere in Eastern Europe. He called for a revision of the constitution, reducing the role of the Communist Party and ending the official policy of atheism, and promised free elections and the introduction of free market principles into the economy. The parliament enacted legislation permitting foreign investment. The government freed political prisoners, and in February, 1991, a new law granted independent status to the courts, one of the main demands of the opposition. Opposition political parties and newspapers appeared. The Communists, however, retained as much support as the opposition won. The former could rely on the rural population, who mistrusted the intellectuals and urbanites, the backbone of the opposition.

Elections held in the spring of 1991 kept Alia and the Communists in power. Although international observers maintained that the elections were generally fair, the opposition claimed fraud. Demonstrations followed, leading to clashes with the authorities and further violence. In June, Alia agreed to establish a coalition government with the opposition to work out a mutually acceptable solution. Despite his problems, Alia was able to bring democracy and liberalization to his country and still remain in power a year after the changes, the only Communist leader of Eastern Europe to do so.

The upheavals that the changes brought placed the country in an even worse economic situation. Many Albanians attempted to leave, chiefly for economic reasons, although there were also some who wished to emigrate because they did not believe that the political changes were genuine or that they would last. In July, 1990, after the government introduced freedom of travel but before the easing of the visa process, thousands of Albanians trying to leave the country stormed the foreign embassies in Tirana. The authorities of both Albania and those countries whose embassies were besieged then facilitated migration and travel. A tremendous exodus followed. Many ethnic Greeks and some Albanians fled south into Greece, forcing Greece to close its border. Other Albanians fled on overloaded ships to southern Italy, where an Albanian community had lived for centuries. The Italian authorities, reluctant to accept these immigrants, sent some back and refused to feed the others in the hope that they would return of their own accord. A public outcry in Italy and abroad forced Rome to relent and to permit some of the refugees to stay. Albanians who remained in their country enjoyed complete civil and political liberties, although the country was still in economic turmoil. In mid-1991, many Albanians were still trying to flee illegally into Italy.

Bibliography

Academy of Sciences of the PSR of Albania. *The Albanians and Their Territories.*

Tirana: "8 Nentori" Publishing House, 1985. A pro-Albanian interpretation of the history and geography of the state. Makes the case for holding the present territory against greedy neighbors and emphasizes the rights of the Albanian minorities in Greece and Yugoslavia. Reveals that nationalism rather than international socialism was the main guiding force in the country under the Communists. Bibliography and index.

Bethell, Nicholas. *Betrayed*. New York: Time Books, 1987. Published in Britain in 1984 as *The Great Betrayal*. An account of the British spy Kim Philby's role in leaking to Hoxha Western plans to overthrow his government in the late 1940's. This was a key event in Hoxha's establishment of power and control of Albania. Illustrations, bibliography, and index.

Biberaj, Elez. *Albania: A Socialist Maverick*. Boulder, Colo.: Westview Press, 1990. Investigates the changes in Albania since Hoxha's death and outlines its policies under Hoxha and Alia. Biberaj concludes that Albania, despite its rhetoric, was closer to the West in the 1980's, although not necessarily to the United States, than to the Soviet Union. Bibliography and index.

_____. *Albania Between East and West*. London: Institute for the Study of Conflict, 1986. A brief synopsis of the Albanian state shortly after Hoxha's death. Describes the leadership and the country's internal and foreign policies. Concludes that Albania was drifting closer to the West, despite its rhetoric of remaining equidistant from all superpowers. Tables, documentation, bibliography, no index.

Hoxha, Enver. *The Khrushchevites: Memoirs*. Tirana: "8 Nentori" Publishing House, 1979. A volume of Hoxha's memoirs. Sheds light on his decision to move Albania out of Moscow's camp, his flirtation with China in the early 1960's, and some of the mysteries of the country's xenophobia. Undocumented, no bibliography or index.

_____. *With Stalin: Memoirs*. Tirana: "8 Nentori" Publishing House, 1979. One of Hoxha's most important volumes of memoirs. Explains his justification for remaining a Stalinist and outlines his philosophies and tactics. Very important for explaining Albania's unique place in Europe. Undocumented, no bibliography or index.

Marmullaku, Ramadan. *Albania and the Albanians*. Translated by Margot Milosavljevic and Bosko Milosavljevic. London: C. Hurst, 1975. Originally written in Serbo-Croatian by a Yugoslav Albanian. Answers the claim that Hoxha's tyrannical regime was stirring up trouble in the Kossovo region of Yugoslavia and had plans to interfere in Yugoslav domestic events. Bibliography and index.

Prifti, Peter R. *Socialist Albania Since 1944: Domestic and Foreign Developments*. Cambridge, Mass.: MIT Press, 1978. A standard history of post-World War II Albania by a leading American specialist. Written just at the time Hoxha began to give up some of his powers and Albania began its slow break with isolationism. Bibliography and index.

Schnytzer, Adi. *Stalinist Economic Strategy in Practice: The Case of Albania*. New

York: Oxford University Press, 1982. An analysis of the Albanian economic program of planning, particularly emphasizing the role of self-reliance without accepting foreign investment. Shows the achievements in steady development as well as the problems resulting from lack of outside contact. Tables, statistical appendices, bibliography, and index.

Stajka, Nika. *The Last Days of Freedom.* Translated by Jose G. Roig. New York: Vantage Press, 1980. A firsthand account of political prisons inside Hoxha's Albania. Deals particularly with the plight of national minorities in the Albanian state and the suppression of religion. The author couches the Greek cause in the language of a struggle for political civil liberties. No bibliography or index.

Frederick B. Chary

Cross-References

Soviets Take Control of Eastern Europe (1943), p. 612; Khrushchev Implies That Stalinist Excesses Will Cease (1956), p. 952; Gorbachev Initiates a Policy of *Glasnost* (1985), p. 2249; Ethnic Riots Erupt in Armenia (1988), p. 2348; Ethnic Unrest Breaks Out in Yugoslavian Provinces (1988), p. 2386; Hungary Adopts a Multiparty System (1989), p. 2421; Soviet Troops Leave Afghanistan (1989), p. 2449; Solidarity Regains Legal Status in Poland (1989), p. 2477; Poland Forms a Non-Communist Government (1989), p. 2500; The Berlin Wall Falls (1989), p. 2523; Ceausescu Is Overthrown in Romania (1989), p. 2546; Soviet Troops Withdraw from Czechoslovakia (1990), p. 2570; Lithuania Declares Its Independence from the Soviet Union (1990), p. 2577; Yugoslav Army Shells Dubrovnik (1991), p. 2612.

MANDELA IS FREED

Categories of event: Political freedom; racial and ethnic rights
Time: February 11, 1990
Locale: Cape Town, South Africa

Nelson Mandela, sentenced to life imprisonment in 1964 on charges of sabotage, was released from prison and resumed negotiations with the National Party to dismantle apartheid

> *Principal personages:*
> NELSON MANDELA (1918-   ), the deputy president of the African National Congress and a major leader in the struggle against apartheid
> FREDERIK WILLEM DE KLERK (1936-   ), a leader of the National Party and president of South Africa's minority government
> WALTER SISULU (1912-   ), a leading member of the African National Congress who had been imprisoned with Mandela in 1964
> PIETER WILLEM BOTHA (1916-   ), a leader of the National Party and prime minister from 1978 to 1989

Summary of Event

Although Europeans had practiced discrimination, taken valued lands, and waged war against the indigenous peoples of southern Africa prior to the mid-twentieth century, it was the rise to power of the Afrikaner-dominated National Party in 1948 that ushered in full-blown apartheid (an Afrikaans word meaning apartness). The Population Registration Act (1950) provided the mechanism for classifying every person into one of four "racial groups": white, colored, Indian, and African. Apartheid also controlled the movement of Africans through such measures as pass laws (requiring passports for travel within the country) and influx control laws, outlawed virtually every form of political protest through, for example, the Suppression of Communism Act (1950), and controlled the content of Africans' educations through laws such as the Bantu Education Act (1953).

Despite these draconian attempts on the part of the National Party to suppress challenges to apartheid, various organizations did indeed campaign for majority rule. One of the oldest is the African National Congress (ANC), formed in 1912. Initially, the ANC was a small organization with several thousand members from the professional and middle classes who adopted a strategy of peaceful protest, primarily through electoral politics. The growth of an African working class, the deterioration of conditions facing rural Africans, and the emergence of a new generation of activists prompted a change in ANC strategy in the 1940's.

Nelson Mandela, Oliver Tambo, and Walter Sisulu were the major ANC leaders who formed the ANC Youth League in 1944 with the purpose of reinvigorating the struggle against apartheid, made particularly necessary in the face of the National

Party victory. Mandela and others in the ANC, along with organizations such as the South African Communist Party, the South African Indian Congress, and the South African Coloured People's Organization, organized days of protests, national stay-at-homes, and a Defiance Campaign in 1952. The Defiance Campaign, a civil diso-bedience effort, was an organizational success (particularly in the Eastern Cape) and demonstrated the benefits of multiracial organization. The government responded by issuing Mandela the first of several banning orders.

Growing interorganizational coordination culminated in the Congress of the People in June, 1955, in Kliptown, a black township outside Johannesburg. It was at this congress that the Freedom Charter was discussed and one year later adopted, with some dissent, as the guiding document of the liberation movement. The Freedom Charter states that "South Africa belongs to all who live in it, black and white," and it describes a commitment to the realization of basic human rights such as equality before the laws and freedom of movement, assembly, religion, speech, and press. It remained the basic document governing the ANC's philosophy.

Before the Defiance Campaign, Mandela had been general secretary of the ANC Youth League (1947), a member of the Executive Committee of the ANC (1949), pres-ident of the Youth League (1951), president of the ANC's Transvaal branch (1952), and deputy national president of the ANC (1952). The success of the Defiance Cam-paign led to a government crackdown against all antiapartheid organizations. In 1955, Mandela, along with 155 other activists, was charged with treason. During the course of the five-year treason trial, which ended in acquittal because of insufficient evi-dence, Mandela managed to remain active within the ANC and to provide trenchant criticism of apartheid. His writings during this period deplore the conditions faced by Africans in the reserves, the decision to bar non-Europeans from attendance at European universities, and the moves toward the creation of self-governing *ban-tustans* or separate "tribal homelands" by Prime Minister Hendrik Verwoerd's gov-ernment in 1959. Mandela predicted with great prescience that "Behind the 'self-government' talk lies a grim programme of mass evictions, political persecution, and police terror. It is the last desperate gamble of a hated and doomed fascist autocracy . . ." Despite massive domestic and international condemnation of the homelands policy, four were given independence: Transkei (1976), Bophuthatswana (1977), Venda (1979), and Ciskei (1981). No government apart from South Africa recognized the sovereignty of the homelands.

Failure to end apartheid in the late 1950's produced divisions within African po-litical organizations and culminated in 1959 with the formation of the Pan-Africanist Congress (PAC). In 1960, the PAC called for a massive campaign against the pass laws, and the government responded brutally at Sharpeville (a township near Jo-hannesburg) on March 21, 1960. Approximately 69 Africans were killed and 186 wounded. A state of emergency was declared, and the ANC and PAC were banned. Shortly thereafter, Mandela went underground.

In 1961, the ANC, with some cooperation with the PAC and other antiapartheid or-ganizations, called for a strike to coincide with the government's declaration of a republic. Republic status would sever all links with Britain and thus for Europeans constituted an act of independence and defiance. Although the May 31, 1961, strike was somewhat successful in garnering African support and participation, at the same time it highlighted the government's intransigence. On December 16, 1961, Umkhonto we Sizwe (Spear of the Nation) issued its manifesto explaining the need for an organization to respond with violence against state-sponsored violence. As a founding member and commander in chief of *Umkhonto*, Mandela helped to elaborate its strategy, which focused on sabotage and destruction of property rather than violence against persons. Its activities were severely curtailed after the arrest of Mandela and other top leaders. Security forces were also able to infiltrate the group with spies.

In August, 1962, Mandela was arrested, tried, and sentenced to five years in prison for inciting an illegal strike and leaving the country without valid travel documents. In July, 1963, he was arrested for sabotage along with nine other antiapartheid activists, and in 1964 he was sentenced to life in prison. Various National Party leaders made him offers of release on the condition that he renounce violence and live in the Transkei "homeland." Mandela rejected all such offers.

By 1980, apartheid was in crisis. Neighboring states had achieved independence, the homelands policy was considered a sham by the international community, which refused to accept the homelands as separate entities, homeland leaders were viewed as illegitimate by Africans, and sharp splits within the white minority were becoming obvious. Pieter Willem Botha, who became prime minister of the National Party in 1978, embarked upon a series of reforms. For example, a three-chamber parliament providing for representation of whites, coloreds, and Indians was established in 1983, the pass laws were repealed in 1986, and elections to local councils, in which Africans could participate, were held in 1988. These reforms were rejected by most antiapartheid organizations, including the United Democratic Front (UDF), a coalition of trade unions, women's organizations, and community groups founded in 1983 to coordinate opposition to apartheid. The ANC also refused to support the reforms and encouraged Africans to boycott elections and continue to protest government policy.

Frederik Willem de Klerk, who became the leader of the National Party after Botha suffered a stroke in February, 1989, released a number of key antiapartheid activists, including Walter Sisulu, in October, 1989; met with Mandela in December, 1989; and, on February 2, 1990, legalized the ANC and thirty other previously banned antiapartheid organizations. On February 11, 1990, Nelson Mandela was released from prison and the next day gave a rousing speech at Cape Town City Hall. He called for a continuation of the armed struggle, maintenance of sanctions, and ANC-South African Communist Party collaboration in the struggle.

Impact of Event

Although the release of Nelson Mandela did not bring about the immediate abolition of apartheid, significant changes have occurred. Although groups such as the PAC continued to oppose discussions with the government, the ANC maintained a substantial amount of legitimacy. In fact, with the unbanning of the ANC, the UDF dissolved itself, thus ensuring general support for ANC efforts to engage in negotiations with the government on behalf of the majority of Africans.

After talks between the ANC and the National Party government began in May, 1990, several significant pieces of apartheid legislation were repealed, including the Separate Amenities Act (1950), the Group Areas Act (1950), and the 1913 and 1936 Native Land Acts, which had reserved 87 percent of the land for whites. Such actions were met with intense opposition by conservative organizations of whites, such as the Afrikaner Resistance Movement. The government seemed committed to continuing negotiations for a constituent assembly, a new constitution, and elections in 1994.

Negotiations were complicated by continuing violence in the townships and by Winnie Mandela's arrest, trial, and sentencing in the kidnapping, assault, and death of one of four young Africans. Between 1987 and 1991, an estimated five thousand Africans died in township violence. The ANC accused the government of favoring members of the Inkatha Freedom Party, a political movement based largely in Natal and led by Mangosuthu Gatsha Buthelezi. Although Buthelezi and Mandela signed an accord in Durban on February 4, 1991, the ANC continues to argue that government security forces have conducted violence against Africans and have prompted violence between ANC and Inkatha supporters. In May, 1991, Mandela called on the National Party government to phase out the hostel system in the Rand, which historically had separated migrant Zulu laborers and Xhosa township dwellers and had intentionally fostered enmity between them. In addition, Mandela argued that Inkatha supporters should be barred from carrying spears and other weapons to political rallies, a restriction the de Klerk government promised only partially to enforce.

As of 1991, two major issues and numerous minor ones continued to thwart smooth negotiations between the opposition and the government. The opposition called for the election of a constituent assembly based on the formula of one person, one vote prior to the adoption of a new constitution. The government wanted a new constitution written that would protect minority rights and wanted it in place before elections were held. Second, the government wanted to repeal the Native Land Acts without compensation. The opposition favored compensation and the restoration of lands to the millions of Africans who were forcibly evicted. The government announcement on June 17, 1991, that the Population Registration Act would be repealed ensured that negotiations would continue. Nelson Mandela and the ANC emphasized the need for international sanctions as long as the vestiges of apartheid continued to endanger the realization of human rights for South Africa's majority.

Bibliography

Lodge, Tom. *Black Politics in South Africa Since 1945*. New York: Longman, 1983. An excellent account of the origins and development of African opposition to apartheid. Lodge provides a wealth of detail on the different philosophies guiding the ANC, the PAC, and the Black Consciousness Movement and accounts for their varying strengths. Especially strong on resistance in the 1960's.

Mandela, Nelson. *The Struggle Is My Life.* New York: Pathfinder Press, 1986. This book provides a short introduction to Mandela's life and prints his major speeches and writings until 1985. Includes the ANC Youth League Manifesto, transcripts from the treason and Rivonia trials, and the Freedom Charter. Also contains brief and useful text on events that preceded and followed Mandela's speeches and trials.

Meer, Fatima. *Higher than Hope: The Authorized Biography of Nelson Mandela.* New York: Harper & Row, 1990. An interesting if somewhat hagiographical account of Mandela's life until the late 1980's by a sociologist and activist from South Africa who has known Mandela since the 1950's. The book is strongest in its discussion of Mandela's early years and the effects of the liberation struggle on his personal life.

Mermelstein, David, ed. *The Anti-Apartheid Reader: The Struggle Against White Racist Rule in South Africa.* New York: Grove Press, 1987. This is perhaps the most useful compendium of readings on apartheid. It contains classic accounts on, for example, forced removals, life in the Bantustans, African education, and the effects of apartheid on women. There is also a good section on apartheid in the international arena and U.S.-South African relations.

Thompson, Leonard. *A History of South Africa.* New Haven, Conn.: Yale University Press, 1990. A history of South Africa from precolonial times to the present. Thompson provides a masterful summary of the archaeological and anthropological information on South Africa prior to European settlement. He does an equally good job at chronicling the rise and fall of apartheid in the post-1948 period.

Wilson, Francis, and Mamphela Ramphele. *Uprooting Poverty: The South African Challenge.* New York: W. W. Norton, 1989. This book is absolutely essential for understanding the consequences of apartheid for South Africa's twenty-eight million Africans. The first part describes the many dimensions of life under apartheid: housing, education, hunger, and unemployment. The second part examines the causes of poverty. The last section explores the possibilities for change.

Catherine V. Scott

Cross-References

South Africa Begins a System of Separate Development (1951), p. 861; Lutuli Is Awarded the Nobel Peace Prize (1961), p. 1143; Students in Soweto Rebel Against the White Government (1976), p. 1882; Biko Is Murdered by Interrogators in South Africa (1977), p. 1887; The United Nations Issues a Declaration on South Africa (1979), p. 2008; Tutu Wins the Nobel Peace Prize (1984), p. 2244; De Klerk Promises to Topple Apartheid Legislation (1991), p. 2606.

SANDINISTAS ARE DEFEATED IN
NICARAGUAN ELECTIONS

Category of event: Voting rights
Time: February 25, 1990
Locale: Nicaragua

The Sandinistas (Frente Sandinista de Liberación Nacional), a revolutionary regime that had toppled the Somoza family dictatorship in 1979, held and lost multiparty elections in February, 1990

Principal personages:
> DANIEL ORTEGA SAAVEDRA (1945-   ), the president of Nicaragua and a *comandante* in the Sandinista front; he ceded power to UNO
> VIOLETA BARRIOS DE CHAMORRO (1929-   ), the winner of the 1990 elections and vocal opponent of the Sandinistas
> GEORGE BUSH (1924-   ), the president of the United States; he supported Chamorro and UNO

Summary of Event

The stunning electoral defeat in 1990 of the Sandinistas (Frente Sandinista de Liberación Nacional, or FSLN) by Violeta de Chamorro's diverse Unión Nicaraguense Opositora (UNO) coalition was unprecedented. Never before had a revolutionary regime run the considerable risk of submitting itself to open multiparty elections. The FSLN's crushing setback at the polls, in one of the most scrutinized elections ever held, takes its rightful place alongside all the momentous changes under way in Eastern Europe and South Africa at that time. Daniel Ortega's decision to test his party's waning popularity before the Nicaraguan electorate and to relinquish power to a fragile eleven-party union that included some of the same people who for nine years had waged a relentless war against the Sandinistas reverses the conventional wisdom about hegemonic one-party revolutionary states. Why did the FSLN dare call for elections? Why did they lose so convincingly?

The answers to these questions do not lie in glib statements such as "Nicaraguans voted with their pocketbooks" or "Soviet-style command economies do not work." Instead, the answers rest in Nicaragua's history and its often near-suicidal wish to test North American resolve in its backyard. A recognition of the symbols of this political campaign makes it evident that Nicaraguans viewed this as a referendum on war and peace.

The Sandinistas had cast themselves for eleven years as the defender of the fatherland. Their presidential candidate, Daniel Ortega Saavedra, had spent his entire life fighting the Nicaraguan establishment and its patrons in Washington. Jailed by the Somozas for seven years, a leader of the victorious insurrection of July, 1979, a member of the first *junta* of National Reconstruction (along with Violeta de

Chamorro), the winner of the presidency in the 1984 election, the chief proponent within the FSLN of the Central American peace plan, and the defender of the nation against foreign intervention during the contra war, Ortega symbolized the Sandinistas' dogged determination to create an authentic homegrown revolution in the face of United States hegemony.

Ortega's rise to power did not occur overnight. In fact, Ortega at first seemed uncomfortable in the limelight. No dogmatist like his counterpart, the formidable intellectual and fiery orator Interior Minister Tomás Borge Martínez, Ortega was awkward in public. His public speeches were long, rambling, and uninspiring. In the first heady years of the revolution, Ortega was just one among equals. A bylaw passed by the FSLN in 1979 had prohibited its militants from publicizing specific members of the nine-person National Directorate that governed the party and the nation. The *comandantes* deliberately tried to forestall the creation of a cult of personality from enveloping one leader, as had occurred in Fidel Castro's Cuba. Slowly, steadily, and perceptibly, Ortega's star began to ascend. As he became more comfortable in public, as he met all the challenges placed before him during the difficult war years, and as his moderate group within the fractious National Directorate convinced hard-liners, such as Borge and Bayardo Arce, that the FSLN had to embrace the peace accords proposed by Oscar Arias Sánchez and push ahead with the implementation of a pluralistic political process, the cult of personality grew.

Political pluralism had been one of the cornerstones of the Sandinista platform, and true to their promise, they held open multiparty elections in November, 1984. Although the elections were denounced by the Reagan Administration, which convinced a number of Nicaraguan political parties to withdraw from the campaign, various international observer teams reported that the FSLN's victory, with 67 percent of the vote, was "clean." Given the legacy of electoral fraud left by the Somoza family dynasty (1936-1979), which religiously held rigged elections every four years, the 1984 campaign, which featured political parties to the right and the left of the FSLN, was an important step toward pluralistic democracy. In 1987, a constitution was promulgated that reaffirmed the electoral process, setting the stage for the 1990 campaign.

The incumbent Sandinistas moved up the date of the elections from November to February, 1990, to give the opposition less time to organize its campaign. The FSLN had the formidable task of convincing voters to look beyond the bad times, the suffering and privation of the war years, the damaging effects of Hurricane Joan, the economic embargo, the shortages of medicines, the reappearance of malnutrition in the countryside, the high prices of no-longer-subsidized foodstuffs, the ruinous inflation, and the despised universal military draft. Sandinista rhetoric tried to convince the electorate that a vote for UNO meant a return to Somoza rule and a surrender to the contras. Throughout the campaign, Ortega blamed the country's difficulties on Washington.

Unlike many in the United States who believed that the contra strategy, backed by the Central Intelligence Agency (CIA), was a complete failure, most informed observers realized that Reagan's "freedom fighters" and the entire "low intensity" campaign had served their purpose: to destabilize the Sandinista regime, to undercut the prized social programs by diverting funds to pay for the war, and to ruin the economic well-being of the Nicaraguan people, thereby undercutting popular support for the revolution, by pressuring Western European governments to cut or suspend aid to Nicaragua while denying multilateral loans. The war had left thirty thousand dead, hundreds of thousands in exile (an estimated 175,000 alone in Miami), and families bitterly divided. Nicaraguans were tired and beaten down. It was clear that Reagan's destabilization campaign and the contra strategy had weakened the Nicaraguan economy and forced the Sandinistas to embrace the Central American peace process.

Since 1978, real wages had fallen more than 70 percent. The economy was on the verge of collapse, even though the inflation rate had been cut from an astronomical 35,000 percent in 1988 to 1,600 percent in 1989 through austerity measures such as a 50 percent cutback in government spending that would have made the International Monetary Fund proud and socialist revolutionaries cringe. Gutted in the last years were the pride and joy of the revolution, its health and education programs. In some areas of the countryside, there was precious little support for health services from Managua except for minimal neonatal care and vaccinations.

Faced with these kinds of difficulties, Ortega and the FSLN campaigned on the basis of their heroic struggle against the United States. At heart, Nicaraguans were probably the most nationalistic people in the Americas. The Sandinistas implicitly staked a claim as the rightful heir of a historic tradition of nationalistic Nicaraguan patriots. Nationalism was a strident issue at a time when, by all accounts, Nicaraguans were weary of war. Ortega's campaign staff, some imported from the French Socialist party, realized the dilemma. Ortega also had to appear to be a man of peace. He had to convince the electorate that if the FSLN won, peace was just around the corner, that the FSLN could negotiate successfully with the Bush Administration, and that the economic blockade would be lifted. *Barricada* and *El Nuevo Diario*, the Sandinista papers, were filled in the week before the election with stories that said that President George Bush was ready to recognize a Sandinista victory and that the demobilization of the hated contras was imminent.

The FSLN's attempt to convince the general public that "Yankee imperialism" was to blame for the economic collapse was only partially successful. Many Nicaraguans believed that Sandinista inefficiency, mismanagement, corruption, and privilege had also contributed to the economic malaise. The Sandinista "mixed economy" model tried to be all things to all people. Inconsistency in the application of government policies befuddled many peasants and workers. Peasants at times found it cheaper not to produce staples and instead to purchase their food at subsidized state-run stores.

Corruption and privilege were not invented by the FSLN, but one of the cornerstones of the revolution was to make sure that Somoza-style cronyism did not reappear in the new society. Although even the FSLN's biggest critics would not

propose that Sandinista largess was in the same league as that under Anastasio Somoza Debayle, there were enough government perks—houses, cars, private clubs,
and import tax exemptions—to raise eyebrows and wonder where the revolutionary
spirit had gone.

It is within this context that the FSLN's electoral promotional campaign must be
understood. Tens of thousands of T-shirts, hats, red and black scarves, posters, and
even condoms were delivered in truckloads to neighborhood campaign headquarters.
In rural communities and working class barrios, Sandinista electoral propaganda
was painted on countless homes and buildings. Even conservative estimates of the
cost of the campaign put it at more than twenty million dollars. The result was that
Nicaraguans viewed the Sandinista campaign as a cruel hoax. For years the FSLN
had been preaching austerity. Few could afford meat, and medicines were beyond
the reach of the poor. Now hats and shirts were being given away by the truckload.

If the FSLN had to run on its past as well as on Washington's war, UNO had the
same vexing problem. The coalition cobbled together in Washington included eleven
(sometimes fourteen) political "parties"—in the colorful Nicaraguan vernacular,
"couch parties," because all the members of a party could sit together on one sofa.
Many of the politicians that composed this splintered coalition had pasts that linked
them directly to the counterrevolution and Washington. Within the inner circle of
Violeta de Chamorro were Alfredo César and Alfonso Robelo, both members of the
contra directorate. César, a renegade and a son-in-law of Chamorro made things
difficult for UNO when it was discovered during the campaign that he had written a
letter to contra commander Enrique Bermudez, asking him to keep his troops in the
field until the elections to keep the pressure on the Sandinistas. Throughout the
campaign, the contras attempted to disrupt the electoral process. Numerous deaths
in Jinotega in the north and on the Atlantic Coast were attributed to contra attacks—
seven during the last week of the campaign alone. Finally, Chamorro's sensational-
istic newspaper, *La Prensa*, had been subsidized heavily by the CIA throughout the
war years.

Faced with Chamorro's obvious limitations, including lack of political experience
(she had participated briefly in the *junta* but withdrew for health reasons), her political handlers built their campaign around her strengths. At the final UNO rally
in Managua a week before the election, sixty thousand supporters cheered her call
for reconciliation. Her message was simple and direct: She alone could heal Nicaragua's extended familial body politic. In addition, she assured the crowd that upon
her election the contras would be disbanded, relations with Washington renewed,
the despised military conscription law abolished, the bloated army and bureaucracy
pared down, and the country opened to foreign investment and economic recovery.
Strikingly attractive, the silver-haired, sixty-year-old candidate wore a white lace
dress and was escorted to and from the rally in a white wagon with a matching
canopy. Six Nicaraguan cowhands rode beside her on horseback, and as she passed
by the throng in her cart, she extended her hands to the crowd as if reaching for the
sky. The message was obvious to religious Nicaraguans.

If Ortega was the nationalistic warrior, then Chamorro was the holy redeemer. Her message was peace. Economic recovery was important, but many of the economic problems were the result of war. The Nicaraguan electorate essentially believed that Ortega's confrontational style would not suffice. In retrospect, it is easy to see that the compulsory military draft was a key issue. Chamorro repudiated it, but Ortega said only that the military could be cut. Ironically, the draft was one of the few revolutionary laws the pragmatic Sandinistas had ever passed. The notion that everyone in Nicaragua had to serve in the military, not just the poor, was something truly egalitarian. Nicaraguans knew that since UNO had been created and funded by Washington, when Violeta promised peace with the *yanquis* she could deliver.

Impact of Event

With some exceptions, the electoral process was orderly and quiet on February 25. More than three thousand observers blanketed the country, including teams sent from the United Nations and the Organization of American States. A prestigious international delegation was assembled by former U.S. president Jimmy Carter. Local electoral committees charged with oversight of the election consisted of supporters from the FSLN, UNO, and other political parties. They were models of nonpartisanship. Poll watchers from all political parties checked their computerized registration rolls to make sure that there was no fraud. After the polls closed at 6 P.M., the local *juntas* painstakingly counted and recounted all the ballots for president, the assembly, and the municipal posts.

The FSLN lost the 1990 election because their nationalistic message was set aside, at least for the moment. Nicaraguans quietly stated through their vote that essentials may be delayed for a brief period as a result of war and patriotic fervor, but no society can be expected to sacrifice indefinitely. In the election's aftermath, the Chamorro Administration, which received more than 53 percent of the vote in the elections, faced a daunting task: It had to bring peace and reconciliation to a society that had been at war with itself for almost two decades, bolster a moribund economy, and continue the process of political pluralism initiated by the Sandinistas. The FSLN, which received about 40 percent of the vote, represented a formidable opposition to UNO in the National Assembly. Chamorro and her advisers were likely to find the hard-fought electoral campaign much simpler than the thorny political and economic problems facing their administration.

Bibliography

Booth, John. *The End and the Beginning.* 2d ed. Boulder, Colo.: Westview Press, 1985. This solid academic survey of the Sandinista victory in 1979 explains the forces that led to the ouster of Somoza and the first few years of FSLN rule.

Christian, Shirley. *Nicaragua: Revolution in the Family.* New York: Random House, 1985. A journalist's account of the first years of the revolution, written from a decidedly anti-Sandinista perspective.

Dodson, Michael, and Laura Nuzzi O'Shaughnessy. *Nicaragua's Other Revolution: Religious Faith and Political Struggle*. Chapel Hill: University of North Carolina Press, 1990. One of the most powerful influences on the revolutionary process in Nicaragua was religion. This solid monograph analyzes the impact of liberation theology and the split in the Catholic church.

Enriquez, Laura J. *Harvesting Change: Labor and Agrarian Reform in Nicaragua, 1979-1990*. Chapel Hill: University of North Carolina Press, 1991. A thorough, if sympathetic, analysis of the Sandinista agrarian reform efforts.

Gilbert, Dennis. *Sandinistas: The Party and the Revolution*. New York: B. B. Blackwell, 1988. A political scientist's astute analysis of the FSLN leadership and its conflictive role prior to and after 1979.

Guillermoprieto, Alma. "Letter from Managua." *The New Yorker*, March 26, 1990, 83-93. A thoughtful analysis of the Sandinista electoral defeat by an experienced journalist.

Preston, Julia. "The Defeat of the Sandinistas." *New York Review of Books* 37 (April 12, 1990): 25-29. Another detailed journalistic account of the stunning Chamorro victory.

Vilas, Carlos M. *State, Class, and Ethnicity: Capitalist Modernization and Revolutionary Change on the Atlantic Coast*. Boulder, Colo.: Lynne Rienner, 1989. One of the key problems that the Sandinistas faced was the integration of Miskito, Suma, and Rama Indian groups on the Atlantic Coast of Nicaragua. The author, an Argentine social scientist, is one of the most perceptive analysts of revolutionary Nicaragua.

Walker, Thomas, ed. *Reagan Versus the Sandinistas: The Undeclared War on Nicaragua*. Boulder, Colo.: Westview Press, 1987. An edited anthology that is unabashedly opposed to the Reagan Administration's contra policy.

Allen Wells

Cross-References

U.S. Marines Are Sent to Nicaragua to Quell Unrest (1912), p. 137; Carter Makes Human Rights a Central Theme of Foreign Policy (1977), p. 1903; Somoza Is Forced Out of Power in Nicaragua (1979), p. 2035; Arias Sánchez Is Awarded the Nobel Peace Prize (1987), p. 2336; Presidential Candidates Are Killed in Colombian Violence (1989), p. 2465; Voters in Chile End Pinochet's Military Rule (1989), p. 2540.

SOVIET TROOPS WITHDRAW FROM CZECHOSLOVAKIA

Categories of event: Political freedom; revolutions and rebellions
Time: February 26, 1990
Locale: Frenstat, Czechoslovakia

The withdrawal of Soviet troops from Czechoslovakia reestablished the independence of that nation from Soviet domination

Principal personages:
> VÁCLAV HAVEL (1936-   ), the president of Czechoslovakia and leader of the Civic Forum group that toppled the Communist regime in his country
> MIKHAIL GORBACHEV (1931-   ), the president of the Soviet Union
> ALEXANDER DUBČEK (1921-   ), a Czechoslovak political leader identified in the popular mind with the 1968 Prague Spring
> GUSTÁV HUSAK (1913-   ), the hard-line Communist leader of Czechoslovakia for twenty years, forced to resign as president in 1989
> MILOS JAKES (1922-   ), the general secretary of the Communist Party (1987-1989), ordered the use of police force to break up demonstrations in Prague in 1989
> LADISLAV ADAMEC (1926-   ), a former Communist prime minister of Czechoslovakia who prevented the introduction of martial law to end demonstrations in 1989
> JIRI DIENSTBIER (1937-   ), a former journalist and boiler stoker, named foreign minister by Václav Havel

Summary of Event

In 1955, Czechoslovakia joined the Warsaw Pact Treaty Organization that provided for a unified military command dominated by the Soviet Union. Warsaw Pact member states were not specifically required to maintain a socialist form of government. The treaty did, however, allow Pact armies to hold joint maneuvers on the territory of member nations.

In 1968, reformers within the Czechoslovak Communist Party managed to take control of the government. Led by Party Secretary Alexander Dubček and Prime Minister Oldrich Cernik, the new government attempted to create "socialism with a human face." The censorship placed upon intellectuals, travel restrictions, and centralized control over the economy were all relaxed. Freedom of the press and assembly were both discussed by the Central Committee of the Party.

Fearing that the Prague Spring would spread to other satellite nations, the Soviet Union, in cooperation with four other Warsaw Pact countries, invaded Czechoslovakia and seized control of the country. In order to ensure that the Czechoslovakian government would never again stray from orthodox Marxist-Leninism, Prime Minister Cernik was forced on October 16, 1968, to sign a treaty providing for the "temporary" stationing of Soviet troops within his nation. The treaty could be changed only with the agreement of both partners. The Soviets maintained approximately 73,500 troops in Czechoslovakia for the next twenty years.

During the process of "normalization" which followed the Soviet invasion, political associations (other than those sanctioned by the Communist Party) were banned, censorship was resumed, and a Press Law was instituted. Gustáv Husak was chosen to replace Dubček as general secretary of the Czechoslovak Communist Party. He remained the dominant figure in Czechoslovakian politics until he was replaced as secretary in 1987 by Milos Jakes. Under Husak's leadership, the government attempted to discourage popular political activity by diverting the attention of the people with increased amounts of consumer goods.

The economy of Czechoslovakia made steady improvement until 1978. In spite of the relative prosperity of the country in relation to other Eastern Bloc nations, the people of Czechoslovakia refused to accept their domination by the Soviet Union. Even as Soviet tanks had rolled into Prague on August 21, 1968, thousands of young Czechs had taken to the streets in protest. Street signs were removed to create confusion. In some areas, electricity, gas, and water supplies were mysteriously shut down. Young people confronted Soviet soldiers with words rather than weapons.

A spirit of nonviolent resistance to the Soviet-imposed system continued to permeate Czechoslovak society for the next two decades. In early 1969, a group of Czech students decided to protest Soviet occupation through self-immolation. Jan Palach and Jan Zajic became national heroes by publicly igniting their own bodies into human torches. To commemorate the first anniversary of the invasion, residents of Prague boycotted all public transportation. A group of intellectuals, led by playwright Václav Havel, also sent a ten-point declaration to the Federal Parliament in which they condemned the Soviet invasion, the government purges, censorship, and the domination of the Communist Party over the lives of citizens.

During the course of the 1970's, Havel emerged as the dissident voice of the Czech people. The son of a contractor, Havel grew up in a wealthy family and was introduced to Czech intellectuals at an early age. After the Communists seized power in 1948, the property of his family was expropriated by the state and he was denied entry into the upper levels of the educational system because of his middle-class origins. Forced to work at menial jobs during the day, he attended night classes to further his education. By 1968, he had become well known as a poet and playwright, both at home and abroad. Even though some of his works were banned in his own country, he continued to write for publishing companies in Western Europe.

On August 1, 1975, the Soviet Union and the Western powers signed the Helsinki accords, establishing specific rights that should be guaranteed to all peoples and providing a review process for the agreement. Czechoslovakia signed the accords the following year. In response to this international agreement, a group of Czechoslovak intelligentsia drew up a list of grievances known as Charter 77. The document demanded that the government comply with the Helsinki accords and listed areas where it was not in compliance. Havel, Jan Patocka, and Jiri Hajek were named as spokespersons for the group. The document was eventually signed by more than one thousand people. Havel was convicted of subversion for his Chartist activities and was sentenced to four and one-half years in prison.

Government repression was so extensive that it even included an attempt to control popular music. Viewing rock music as a challenge to its authority, the government banned many recordings. By 1983, thirty-five "new wave" bands were not allowed to perform in Czechoslovakia. In response to this action, young Czechs and Slovaks illegally circulated homemade copies of the illegal tape recordings. In 1984, the Ministry of Culture banned the Jazz Section of the Union of Czech Musicians. Some members of the Jazz Section defied the government and remained active. Several were arrested for distributing prohibited material.

As the Czechoslovakian economy began to stagnate during the 1980's, dissatisfaction with the Husak regime began to become widespread. When Mikhail Gorbachev introduced the concepts of perestroika (restructuring of the economy) and glasnost (openness) in the Soviet Union, many in Czechoslovakia hoped that their government would imitate reformers in the Soviet Union. In 1987, Milos Jakes replaced Husak as general secretary, but Husak retained his position as president of the republic. Jakes made few changes in the economy and resisted any attempt to share power with non-Communist groups.

On January 16, 1989, a group of students gathered at the base of the statue of King Wenceslas in Prague to commemorate the twentieth anniversary of Jan Palach's death. Police quickly moved in to disperse the crowd with tear gas. Havel was arrested and sentenced to nine months in prison.

Encouraged by Soviet tolerance of liberalization in Hungary and Poland, Czech dissenters became increasingly active during 1989. When fifty thousand students marched in Prague to commemorate the slaughter of their countrymen by the Nazis, the demonstration quickly turned into an antigovernment rally. Helmeted police beat the students with rubber clubs. The shock of the force used against the demonstrators rekindled memories of the Soviet invasion. The student leaders quickly found an ally for their cause among Prague's community of writers, actors, and artists, many of whom had been active in the Chartist movement. On November 19, 1989, dissidents gathered together at the Magic Lantern Theater and formed an organization known as Civic Forum. The following day, 200,000 people crowded into the main street of the capital to participate in an antigovernment rally. Jakes threatened to take action if the demonstrations continued, but Prime Minister Ladislav Adamec assured the leaders of Civic Forum that martial law would not be imposed.

Civic Forum received an emotional boost on November 24 when Alexander Dubček journeyed to Prague from Bratislava to join in the demonstrations. After meeting with the crowd assembled in Wenceslas Square, Dubček conferred with rulers of the Communist Party. Later that same evening, Jakes and the entire Politburo of the Czechoslovakian Communist Party resigned. Jakes was replaced by Karol Urbanek, a little-known functionary.

By the time of Dubček's arrival, Civic Forum had formulated an impressive series of demands. Among those demands were an investigation of police brutality against demonstrators, freedom for political prisoners, and the resignation of public officials associated with the 1968 Soviet invasion. Civic Forum demonstrated the popularity of its cause by organizing a general strike on November 27. Much to everyone's surprise, the strike was effective throughout the entire country. Even the government-controlled media covered the event.

On December 6, Adamec announced the formation of a new government with five cabinet positions being granted to non-Communists. Civic Forum rejected this compromise and Adamec was forced to resign the following day. Three days later, a new government was formed with a non-Communist majority, and Havel replaced Husak as president of the republic. Marian Calfa was named as the new prime minister. He immediately pledged to hold free elections in June, 1990. Jiri Dienstbier, a well-known dissident, was named as foreign minister.

Within days, the Havel government began negotiations with the Soviet Union to discuss the withdrawal of Soviet troops from Czechoslovakia. Deputy Foreign Minister Evzen Vacek shocked his Soviet counterpart by demanding that all Soviet troops leave his nation prior to the June, 1990, elections. On February 26, 1990, Soviet leader Gorbachev and President Havel signed an agreement providing for the phased withdrawal of Soviet troops over a period of sixteen months. A Soviet tank division departed from Czechoslovakia that very day. By May 31, 1990, more than half of the 73,500 Soviet troops were out of the country. On June 30, 1991, the last of the Soviet occupation force left the republic.

Impact of Event

The elevation of Václav Havel to the presidency of Czechoslovakia is more than a personal triumph. Havel's success in gaining the evacuation of Soviet troops from Czechoslovakian soil led to a renewed faith in the power of democratic action. The confidence engendered by this victory of the popular will against a regime kept in power by a foreign army allowed Czechoslovakia to move rapidly toward a democratization of its society.

On June 8-9, 1990, Czechoslovakia held its first free election in forty-one years. Twenty-three political parties qualified to participate in the election, although most seats were won by five major political organizations. Civic Forum-Public Against Violence won 48 percent of the vote and emerged as the largest party in Parliament.

The Czechoslovakian revolution was one of idealism but not ideology. Freedom of expression reemerged throughout the country. Bookstores replaced stale Marxist literature with a wide range of titles by authors from throughout the world. Rock music began to be played openly in Prague's Wenceslas Square and along Karluv Most. The new government ended restrictions on the practice of religion. Havel and Foreign Minister Jiri Dienstbier also hoped to bring about a revolution in the power structure of European politics. Havel proclaimed willingness to grant both the United

States and the Soviet Union a role in future European development, but he rejected the idea that any nation should dominate the continent. Czechoslovakia could emerge as a broker in any new European security arrangement.

Czechoslovakia remained in a state of transformation in 1991, and the withdrawal of Soviet troops has proven to have costs. The Soviets once maintained 132 bases in Czechoslovakia, and they proved to be poor stewards of the land they occupied. The Ministry of the Environment estimated that the Soviets polluted five thousand to eight thousand square miles of land. Diesel oil, toxic chemicals, live ammunition, land mines, and chemical weapons were all left behind by the Soviet military. The Czechoslovaks estimated that it would cost $125 million to restore the land. Since the Soviets were also withdrawing from other nations, it appeared unlikely that they would be able to contribute to the cleanup effort.

The Czechoslovakian economy was also a major concern. After years of mismanagement under the Husak regime, Czech factories faced difficulties competing against other industrialized nations for markets. Czechoslovakia was still dependent upon the Soviet Union for petroleum and as a market for its manufactured goods. German investment and American aid were expected to help the Czechoslovaks move from a state-controlled to a market-based economy. This transition led to unemployment and instability of the currency. A public opinion poll conducted in May, 1991, by the opposition Social Democratic Party (CSD) indicated that most Czechoslovaks were dissatisfied with the state of their economy. CSD official Emanuel Pluhar noted that the highest priority of the government at that time was the process of transformation to a market economy.

Freed from the hand of Soviet domination, Czechs and Slovaks could reassert their democratic heritage. Prior to World War II, Czechoslovakia was the seventh largest industrial power in the world. As Czechoslovaks cleaned the rust from their economic engine, they attempted again to become a dynamic force in the politics and economy of central Europe.

Bibliography

Bugajski, Janusz. *The Washington Papers.* Vol. 125 in *Czechoslovakia: Charter 77's Decade of Dissent.* New York: Praeger, 1977. This is the best English-language text on the Chartist movement. It contains a history of Chartist activities and short biographical sketches of leaders within the movement. It contains notes and a summary of Charter 77 documents.

Cipkowski, Peter. *Revolution in Eastern Europe: Understanding the Collapse of Communism in Poland, Hungary, East Germany, Czechoslovakia, Romania, and the Soviet Union.* John Wiley & Sons, 1991. Especially designed for young readers, this work gives a short summary of the revolutionary movements in each of the Eastern Bloc nations. Includes a selected bibliography.

Dubček, Alexander, and Andras Sugar. *Dubcek Speaks.* New York: I. B. Tauris, 1990. The original text of Andras Sugar's 1989 televised interview with Alexander Dubček which helped the revolutionary forces in Czechoslovakia gain momentum.

Garton Ash, Timothy. *The Uses of Adversity: Essays on the Fate of Central Europe.* New York: Random House, 1989. Contains a series of thoughtful essays on each of the Eastern Bloc nations. These essays were first published as magazine articles during the 1980's. Includes an index.

Gati, Charles. *The Bloc That Failed: Soviet-East European Relations in Transition.* Bloomington: Indiana University Press, 1990. This is perhaps the best analysis of the impact Gorbachev's reforms have had on the former Eastern Bloc. Gati believes that Gorbachev's efforts to encourage mild economic restructuring in Eastern Europe led to unanticipated consequences. Includes an index and an annotated bibliography.

Gwertzman, Bernard, and Michael Kaufman, eds. *The Collapse of Communism.* New York: Times Books/Random House, 1990. The work is composed of a selection of newspaper articles printed in *The New York Times* during the revolutions of 1989. Offers no reference features.

Havel, Václav. *Disturbing the Peace: A Conversation with Karel Hvizdala.* Translated by Paul Wilson. New York: Alfred A. Knopf, 1990. Based on an interview conducted in 1985, this work serves as the principal biography of Havel's life prior to his involvement in Civic Forum. Contains a glossary and an index.

Havel, Václav, et al. *The Power of the Powerless: Citizens Against the State in Central-Eastern Europe.* Armonk, N.Y.: M. E. Sharpe, 1985. Contains a series of eleven essays by leading Czech dissidents written prior to the revolution. The book gives the reader good insight into the hopes and dreams of the people who later emerged as leaders during the revolutionary movement. Includes notes on each contributor and the text of the Charter 77 declaration.

Renner, Hans. *A History of Czechoslovakia Since 1945.* London: Routledge, 1989. Broad outline of Czechoslovak history from the Communist takeover in 1948 to the rise of Milos Jakes as general secretary. The work is particularly helpful in understanding the rule of Gustav Husak. Contains notes, a bibliography, and a name index.

Riese, Hans-Peter, ed. *Since the Prague Spring: The Continuing Struggle for Human Rights in Czechoslovakia.* New York: Random House, 1979. This book is composed of protest documents written by leading Czechoslovak dissidents during the 1970's. It contains a list of 617 people who signed Charter 77 prior to 1979 as well as selected documents produced by the Chartists. Includes selected biographical notes.

Thomas David Matijasic

Cross-References

Soviets Take Control of Eastern Europe (1943), p. 612; The Brezhnev Doctrine Bans Acts of Independence in Soviet Satellites (1968), p. 1408; Soviets Invade Czechoslovakia (1968), p. 1441; The Helsinki Agreement Offers Terms for International Cooperation (1975), p. 1806; Gorbachev Initiates a Policy of *Glasnost* (1985), p. 2249;

Hungary Adopts a Multiparty System (1989), p. 2421; The Berlin Wall Falls (1989), p. 2523; Ceausescu Is Overthrown In Romania (1989), p. 2546; Lithuania Declares Its Independence from the Soviet Union (1990), p. 2577; Gorbachev Agrees to Membership of a United Germany in NATO (1990), p. 2589.

LITHUANIA DECLARES ITS INDEPENDENCE FROM THE SOVIET UNION

Categories of event: Revolutions and rebellions; indigenous peoples' rights
Time: March 11, 1990
Locale: Vilnius, Lithuania

Mikhail Gorbachev's policy of glasnost *opened the possibility for the people of Lithuania to express their desire for independence from the Soviet Union*

Principal personages:

MIKHAIL GORBACHEV (1931-   ), the president of the Soviet Union who vigorously opposed the Lithuanian movement for independence

VYTAUTAS LANDSBERGIS (1932-   ), the leader of the Sajudis movement for national independence and first parliamentary chair after independence was declared

KAZIMIERA PRUNSKIENE (1943-   ), the prime minister in the first Lithuanian government after independence was declared; resigned in 1991

Summary of Event

Lithuania, Estonia, and Latvia were the three Baltic republics of the Soviet Union. They shared a common European culture, although Estonia and Latvia had closer ties to Scandinavia and Germany while Lithuania's ties were with Poland and Central Europe. In the twentieth century, their fates were linked. All three became independent after the Russian Revolution in 1917, and each was forcibly annexed by the Soviet Union in 1940. No other of the national minorities of the Soviet Union had experienced sovereign independence during that time.

One cannot understand the enduring resentment of the Baltic peoples toward Soviet rule without a knowledge of the circumstances of their annexation and the deprivation of national and human rights that ensued. According to the Secret Protocols of the Nazi-Soviet Non-Aggression Pact of August 23 (as amended on September 28), 1939, the territory of Lithuania was put within the "sphere of interest" of the Soviet Union. Joseph Stalin wanted to incorporate the Baltic states into the Soviet Union for geopolitical reasons, particularly the fact that they provided direct access to the Baltic Sea. In the summer of 1940, immediately after the fall of France, the Soviet Union demanded the formation of new governments in each of the Baltic states in preparation for annexation. The Red Army rounded up all opponents of Soviet rule, seizing some two thousand political opponents in Lithuania beginning on the night of July 11. The compliant governments that emerged from the Soviet-controlled elections requested incorporation into the Soviet Union. During the twelve-month period of Soviet rule before Germany attacked the Soviet Union, thousands of Baltic people were executed or deported as "counterrevolutionary elements." In Lithuania, the number who died or disappeared was approximately 30,500. Popular resistance to Soviet rule emerged almost immediately after the Red Army liberated the Baltic states from German control, and it continued into the early 1950's. To pacify the region, Stalin resorted to mass repression, deporting into the interior of the Soviet Union an estimated 600,000 people from the Baltic region. The chair of the Lithuanian secret police gave as the number of Lithuanians who were deported, were convicted of state crimes, or who perished as members of the guerrilla forces at about 200,000 individuals.

After Stalin's death in 1953, conditions improved in Lithuania, as elsewhere in the Soviet Union. Nikita Khrushchev's policy of relaxation, known as the thaw, permitted a rebirth of cultural life in Lithuania, an important element of which included increased use of the Lithuanian language in the republic's educational system. Economic life improved as Lithuania developed a strong industrial sector. The industrialization of Lithuania relied largely on local labor resources rather than the massive immigration of outside (mostly Russian) workers, such as occurred in Estonia and Latvia. As a result, Lithuania had the highest percentage of indigenous population of the three Baltic republics. Almost 80 percent of the population was native Lithuanian even as late as 1991, as compared to about 60 percent of Estonians in Estonia and about 50 percent of Latvians in Latvia.

Even though Lithuania prospered, in comparison to the rest of the Soviet Union, opposition to Soviet rule never ceased. Mass demonstrations against communist rule took place in Vilnius in the fall of 1956 and in Kaunas in 1960. In 1972, the self-immolation of a young nationalist led to a full-scale riot in Kaunas. Dissident activity increased during the Leonid Brezhnev years.

Mikhail Gorbachev's accession to power in March, 1985, changed the political environment throughout the Soviet Union, but particularly in the Baltics. The new atmosphere of *glasnost* (openness) and *perestroika* (restructuring) permitted an unprecedented expression of nationalistic sentiment in Lithuania, as elsewhere. In 1988, popular fronts emerged in the Baltic republics proclaiming the idea of national sovereignty. In the summer of 1988, the Lithuanian Restructuring Movement, known as Sajudis, made its appearance. From its inception, Sajudis became a central vehicle for the promotion of the idea of Lithuanian economic autonomy, to be followed by total independence. An indication of Sajudis' growing authority was its success in the by-elections to fill five vacancies in the Lithuanian Supreme Soviet on January 15, 1989. Sajudis candidates received the most votes in each of the four districts in which they ran. The March-April republicwide elections to the newly created Soviet Congress of People's Deputies confirmed the general hold of Sajudis on the voters of the republic. Of the forty-two contested districts, thirty-six were won by Sajudis. It was a stunning defeat for the Lithuanian Communist Party and clear evidence that popular sentiment was moving away from economic autonomy within the framework of the Soviet Union to outright independence.

Public pressure moved Lithuania steadily toward a break with Moscow. On May 18, 1989, the Lithuanian Supreme Soviet declared the State of Lithuania to be "sovereign" and adopted four constitutional amendments, one of which provided that Lithuanian citizens were entitled to the social, economic, political, and personal rights and freedoms provided for in the Lithuanian constitution as well as those included in universally accepted international legal conventions. An amendment that Moscow found particularly objectionable provided that Soviet laws would be valid in Lithuania only if they were also adopted by the Lithuanian Supreme Soviet or the people in a referendum.

In August, the Baltic population dramatically expressed its resentment of Soviet rule by forming a human chain of more than one million people, from Tallinn through Riga to Vilnius, to commemorate the anniversary of the Nazi-Soviet pact that had led to the Soviet annexations. By repudiating the legality of the pact, Lithuanians rejected the legality of all the acts that followed from it. A commission formed by the Lithuanian Supreme Soviet to investigate the pact concluded that both the Lithuanian request of July 21, 1940, to join the Soviet Union and the USSR Supreme Soviet law of August 3, 1940, incorporating Lithuania into the Soviet Union were illegal.

Throughout 1989, actions were taken that inexorably pushed the country toward independence. The Lithuanian government passed a law granting Lithuanian citizenship to all persons who were citizens and residents of the Lithuanian Republic prior to June 15, 1940, and to all of their descendants living permanently in Lithuania. One of the most disturbing developments from Moscow's point of view was the separation of Lithuania's communist organizations from their ties to Moscow. This movement began with the Communist Youth Organization, the Komsomol, which formally ended its subordination to the All-Union Komsomol. Its parent organization, the Lithuanian Communist Party, did the same at a special Party Congress on December 20, voting to make itself independent of the Communist Party of the Soviet Union. No other communist party of a republic had done that before.

In an effort to head off the growing independence movement, Mikhail Gorbachev visited Lithuania in January, 1990, the first time a Soviet leader had done so in half a century. He succeeded neither in reversing the Lithuanian Communist Party's decision to break from Moscow nor in damping Lithuanian nationalism.

On February 24, 1990, Lithuania became the first Soviet republic officially to conduct multiparty elections for its highest legislative body, the Supreme Soviet. As expected, Sajudis candidates won control of the legislature and Communist candidates fared poorly. The elections demonstrated beyond a doubt that Lithuanians wanted independence outside the framework of the Soviet Union. On March 11, 1990, the Lithuanian Supreme Soviet voted 124-0 (with six abstentions) to reaffirm Lithuania's 1918 declaration of independence from the Soviet Union. The name of the state was changed to the Republic of Lithuania, dropping the words "Soviet" and "Socialist" from its title. Vytautas Landsbergis, the leader of Sajudis, was elected chair of the Supreme Council, as the new parliament was called. Along with the declaration of independence, the parliament enacted a package of acts that denied the validity of the Soviet constitution in Lithuania, reactivated the 1938 Constitution of the Lithuanian Republic, and suspended the conscription of Lithuanian youths into the Red Army.

Impact of Event

Few people had illusions that the declaration would bring quick de facto independence. Indeed, the declaration basically set the stage for a long bargaining process between Moscow and Vilnius. Landsbergis offered to negotiate with Soviet authorities the specific claims of the two sides but not to revoke, rescind, or suspend the act of independence. Gorbachev's reaction was hostile. He told the Congress of People's Deputies that he did not recognize Lithuanian independence. Moscow, on April 18, imposed a partial economic blockade on Lithuania that inflicted some economic hardship but failed to force Lithuanian compliance with Moscow's desires.

The period following the declaration of independence on March 11, 1990, was a difficult one. The Soviet blockade, although not crippling, did have a negative impact on the economy, causing shortages of goods, inflation, and economic disruption. Moscow engaged in a campaign of intimidation by increasing the presence of Soviet armed forces in the country, seizing buildings, and detaining a number of Lithuanian soldiers. Lithuania's efforts to obtain Western recognition were generally unsuccessful. Governments, such as that of the United States, that were sympathetic were reluctant to do anything that might undermine the Gorbachev Administration. Lithuania (as well as Latvia and Estonia) failed to gain admission to the Conference on Security and Cooperation in Europe (CSCE) and the Olympic movement. Under strong Soviet pressure, the Lithuanian Supreme Council on June 29 agreed to a hundred-day moratorium on its declaration of independence to go into effect after the start of formal negotiations with the Soviet Union. In June, Moscow ended its blockade.

Compounding its problems with Moscow, the government of Lithuania was divided over political differences between the parliament, headed by Landsbergis, and the Council of Ministers, headed by Prime Minister Kazimiera Prunskiene. In January, 1991, the prime minister resigned over the issue of the government's decision to raise food prices. Fundamentally, the conflict between parliament and government lay in differences over a division of duties.

While struggling with its domestic problems, the republic was confronted with a violent assault by Soviet armed forces. On January 13, 1991, Soviet troops stormed the radio and television center in Vilnius, killing fourteen people and injuring more than 150. While defending the crackdown, Gorbachev denied that he ordered it or even had advance knowledge that force was to be used. Nevertheless, the violence in Vilnius created a storm of international criticism. In an attempt to strengthen his position on the issue of holding the Soviet Union intact, Gorbachev scheduled a national referendum on March 17 on the question of whether or not the Soviet Union should survive. Lithuania refused to participate in the referendum because it did not consider itself to be a part of the Soviet Union. Instead, the government of Lithuania chose to hold a poll on February 9 in which the voters were asked: "Do you consider the Lithuanian state as an independent democratic republic?" More than 90 percent of those casting ballots voted "yes."

Unexpected political developments in the summer of 1991 led to a rapid collapse of authority in Moscow and the realization of complete independence for Lithuania. On July 29, the Russian Federation formally acknowledged Lithuania's independence. In August, an aborted coup by conservatives resulted in the collapse of the authority of the Soviet government and the transfer of de facto power to the republics. Lithuania's leaders took advantage of the situation to take control of the country's borders and domestic functions. On September 2, U.S. president George Bush, following action by the European Community, extended diplomatic recognition to the three Baltic states. Two days later, the State Council, the Soviet Union's transitional executive authority, did likewise. Formal certification of Lithuanian, Estonian, and Latvian sovereignty came in mid-September, when the three states were admitted to the United Nations.

Bibliography

Misiunas, Romuald J. "The Baltic Republics: Stagnation and Strivings for Sovereignty." In *The Nationalities Factor in Soviet Politics and Society,* edited by Lubomyr Hajda and Mark Beissinger. Boulder, Colo.: Westview Press, 1990. This is a concise analysis of the Baltic struggle for independence, with emphasis on Lithuania. The author demonstrates that the Baltic desire for autonomy is less the result of Soviet economic mismanagement, as the Baltics have been better off than the rest of the Soviet Union, than it is a popular desire to be free of Russian and Soviet domination in all spheres of life.

Misiunas, Romuald J., and Rein Taagepera. *The Baltic States: Years of Dependence, 1940-1980.* Berkeley: University of California Press, 1983. This volume treats the Baltic states as a unit. It provides a uniquely fine feel for life in Soviet Lithuania and a good description of the dissident movement. Particularly interesting are sixteen pages of photographs. Bibliography, notes, and index are included.

Nahaylo, Bohdan, and Victor Swoboda. *Soviet Disunion: A History of the Nationalities Problem in the USSR.* New York: Free Press, 1990. One of the best descriptions of the nationalities problem in the Soviet Union. It covers the entire Soviet period and all the major nationalities, providing a very fine framework for explaining developments in the Baltics. The authors make a strong indictment of the failure of Soviet leaders to observe the "national contract" made with the non-Russian nationalities when they were incorporated into the Soviet Union.

Olcott, Martha Brill. "The Lithuanian Crisis." *Foreign Affairs* 69 (Summer, 1990): 30-46. Olcott has written an eminently readable and insightful account of the reasons for and impact of Lithuania's declaration of independence. She shows that Gorbachev's opposition to independence for Lithuania was rooted in part on the destabilizing impact a breakaway of the Baltic republic would have on the rest of the country. She applauds the nonintervention policy of the Bush Administration.

Vardys, V. Stanley, ed. *Lithuania Under the Soviets: Portrait of a Nation, 1940-*

65. New York: Praeger, 1965. Here are eleven articles by Lithuanian and non-Lithuanian scholars describing twenty-five years of Soviet rule. Among the topics covered are history, the political system, the economy, education, literature, religion, and Soviet social engineering. The essays are useful even though dated. Index, notes, and a bibliography are included.

_____. "Lithuanian National Politics." *Problems of Communism* 38 (July/August, 1989): 57-76. This is an in-depth study of the interplay between Sajudis, the Lithuanian Communist Party, and the Communist Party of the Soviet Union in the Baltic struggle for independence. Within each of the institutions, there were sharp differences regarding the proper strategy to pursue. Vardys believes that Gorbachev would be hard pressed to find a formula that could reconcile Moscow's resistance to separation with the determination of the Lithuanians to have it.

Joseph L. Nogee

Cross-References

The Baltic States Fight for Independence (1917), p. 207; Soviets Take Control of Eastern Europe (1943), p. 612; Khrushchev Implies That Stalinist Excesses Will Cease (1956), p. 952; The U.N. Covenant on Civil and Political Rights Is Adopted (1966), p. 1353; The Moscow Human Rights Committee Is Founded (1970), p. 1549; Soviets Crack Down on Moscow's Helsinki Watch Group (1977), p. 1915; Gorbachev Initiates a Policy of *Glasnost* (1985), p. 2249; Soviet Troops Leave Afghanistan (1989), p. 2449; Poland Forms a Non-Communist Government (1989), p. 2500; Soviet Troops Withdraw from Czechoslovakia (1990), p. 2570; Demise of the U.S.S.R. Paves the Way for Reforms in Former Soviet Republics (1991), p. 2618.

ALGERIA HOLDS ITS FIRST FREE MULTIPARTY ELECTIONS

Categories of event: Political freedom and voting rights
Time: June 12, 1990
Locale: Algeria

Municipal elections in June, 1990, were the first permitted by the ruling party, the Front for National Liberation, since Algeria had gained independence from France in 1962

Principal personages:
ABASSI MADANI (1931-   ), the main leader of the Muslim fundamentalist Islamic Salvation Front, the main opposition party
ALI BELHAJ (1954-   ), the second-in-command of the Islamic Salvation Front
CHADLI BENJEDID (1927-   ), the head of the Front for National Liberation and president of Algeria

Summary of Event

The foundations of modern Algeria were laid by the French, who occupied the country in 1830 and declared it an integral part of France in 1848. French colonists lived mainly along the Mediterranean coast, while the indigenous Muslims—Arabs and Berbers—were largely concentrated in the interior. In November, 1954, Algerian Muslim nationalists who were organized under the Front for National Liberation (FLN) launched an armed struggle for independence against French colonialism. After nearly eight years of war that took the lives of more than one million Algerians, the FLN revolutionaries and French president Charles de Gaulle negotiated agreements which led to Algeria's independence under FLN domination. Ahmed Ben Bella, one of the revolution's leaders, was chosen president and nationalized foreign holdings. In 1965, Ben Bella was overthrown by his defense minister, Colonel Houari Boumedienne, who continued the one-party FLN socialist rule until his death in December, 1978. He was succeeded by Colonel Chadli Benjedid, known as a pragmatist and a compromise leader.

Algeria's evolution to secularism, before and after independence in 1962, is largely attributable to French cultural influence. During the colonial era (1830-1962), the French had become a dominant factor in every aspect of Algerian society. As late as 1990, French television and radio were widely seen and heard in Algeria, and numerous Algerians traveled freely to France. Nevertheless, despite French secular influence and rapid industrial growth during the 1960's and 1970's, large segments of the population had become disenchanted with the FLN under Benjedid, with the economic decline, and with the government's sociopolitical policies. In October, 1988, after large-scale riots protesting food shortages, the ruling FLN was pressured to surrender its monopoly on power and institute democratic reforms. During these riots, thousands of young protesters were wounded and at least one hundred were killed. A new constitution was approved on February 23, 1989, opening the way to a multiparty political system.

On June 12, 1990, the country's first free municipal election took place. Eleven political parties participated in this historic event, chief among which were the FLN; the religious fundamentalist Islamic Salvation Front (FIS), led by Abassi Madani, a professor of philosophy, and his second-in-command, Ali Belhaj; and the secular Rally for Culture and Democracy (RCD). The results were stunning: The FIS won a majority of the municipal seats in the country's four largest cities—Algiers, Oran, Constantine, and Annaba. The FIS received 65 percent of the popular vote and won 55 percent of fifteen thousand municipal posts throughout Algeria. It won representation in thirty-two of the forty-eight provinces.

Support for the FIS, it is argued, was part of a growing admiration in the Arab-Muslim world for Islamic fundamentalist leaders in the wake of the revolution in Iran in the late 1970's and the parliamentary victory achieved in 1990 by the Muslim Brotherhood in Jordan, not to mention political gains achieved by such forces in Turkey, Tunisia, and Morocco. On the other hand, economic factors were equally if not more crucial. When asked what motivated them to support the FIS, numerous voters responded that they backed the Islamists out of revenge against the FLN. *The New York Times* disclosed on June 25, 1990, that many voters used the vote to protest against low salaries, spiraling inflation, and promotions that were given only to those with connections to the FLN. In Algeria, they contended, the economic choices for young people during the 1980's and in 1990 were limited: to remain unemployed and celibate because jobs were unavailable and apartments in short supply; to work in the *trabendos* (black markets) and risk being arrested; to try to emigrate to France to sweep the streets of Paris and Marseilles; or to join the FIS and vote for Islam. In other words, it should not be ruled out that the vote for the fundamentalists was less a massive support for the FIS than a reaction against what voters regarded as the FLN's record of authoritarian rule and economic mismanagement and corruption. Whether they agreed with the FIS or not, many Algerians, it seems, were content in 1990 with the difference the free ballot had made in their lives. In Algiers, there was a sense of enthusiasm that is usually manifested in the wake of a national revolution.

Its electoral successes notwithstanding, the FIS was somewhat vague from the outset about its objectives. It is known, however, that Abassi Madani struck an alliance with local merchants and espoused a free market economy in lieu of the FLN's state socialism. Both Madani and Ali Belhaj described a woman's primary role as rearing a family, limiting women's employment to jobs such as nursing and teaching. The local and provincial municipal councils, which serve five-year terms, have jurisdiction over such matters as renewal of liquor licenses, the type of activities allowed at cultural centers, and the issuance of permits to build mosques. Madani and Belhaj vehemently opposed public drinking, any form of dancing, and secular programming in the media.

Ethnically, the backing of the FIS came from the Arab population, which constitutes at least 70 percent of the total Algerian Sunni Muslim population of approximately 25 million. The Berber Muslims, as well as the ethnically mixed Arab-Berber populations, were not necessarily behind the FIS. Both the FLN and FIS have been challenged by the Kabyles, members of the largest, most important Berber tribe. As French colonial rule was drawing to an end during the early 1960's, Kabyle bands carried out the most daring assaults on the French. After 1962, the Kabyles also confronted the Algerian FLN regime in the name of their Berber heritage, demanding political freedom and the kind of administrative autonomy the Kurds in Iraq sought from Saddam Hussein. Their party, the Rally for Culture and Democracy, gained 8 percent of the municipal vote in the June 12, 1990, elections, but the potential for increased electoral support among Berbers was possible once national and parliamentary elections took place. Their attachment to Berber culture and opposition to the advocacy for greater Arabization by the Arab majority threatened to increase political turmoil.

The political headway made by the FIS, Berber cultural and political reaffirmation, and the proliferation of political parties during and immediately following the 1990 elections prompted political observers in Algeria and the Arab world to speculate whether the FLN regime, which still controlled the parliament, the cabinet, the army, and the media, would react to its electoral setbacks by suppressing the freedoms it granted to the opposition between 1988 and 1990. In fact, when Madani urged the government to permit national and parliamentary elections to take place, the regime in the summer of 1990 did not rule out such a possibility but evinced concern, warning that it would reject attempts to bring Islam back to an era of political opportunism.

Impact of Event

The historic event of free elections and their outcome in Algeria hardly evoked enthusiasm in the West and in secular Algerian or other Arab circles. Quite to the contrary, there was great concern for the political and social stability of the country. In France, political extremists such as Jean-Marie Le Pen, leader of the French National Front, warned that the French government would have to contend with the integration of many more thousands of Algerians who opposed the FIS and might flee Algeria out of fear of an Islamic regime emerging there. Political moderates in Europe, too, feared that the rise of the FIS would pose a grave population problem for the Mediterranean countries of Western Europe, which in the late 1980's had struggled to absorb an estimated four million legal and illegal North African immigrants. It appeared to Western diplomats and to moderate Middle Eastern and North African regimes that the democratic movement in Algeria produced something radically different from what it had produced in Eastern Europe and Latin America: a brand of anti-Western Muslim fundamentalism. The FIS, the beneficiary of democratic elections, paradoxically did not believe in democracy and freedom.

General parliamentary elections were scheduled for June 27, 1991, one year after the municipal elections had partially reshaped Algerian political life. During that year, more political parties and movements mushroomed in the country, challenging the FLN and the FIS simultaneously. One such party was the Socialist Forces Front (FFS), led by Hocine Ait Ahmad, a hero of the 1954-1962 war of liberation against the French. Many years ago, Ait Ahmad had turned against the FLN, leading running battles against the regime. Moreover, as the campaign of strikes and demonstrations led by the FIS intensified in May and early June of 1991, martial law was imposed by the authorities on June 5. The elections did not take place as scheduled.

On Sunday, June 30, Madani and Belhaj were arrested after questioning the need for continued martial law and calling for immediate parliamentary elections. The headquarters of the FIS in Algiers were surrounded by the National Guard. Before his arrest, Madani urged his supporters to confront the authorities for having violated the basic political freedoms granted the year before.

The New York Times reported on July 2 that upon arresting Madani and Belhaj, the Algerian military charged them with "armed conspiracy against the security of the state" and said they would face trial. Since the beginning of demonstrations and clashes two months earlier, forty people had been killed and more than three hundred wounded. The army had arrested at least seven hundred people in a systematic roundup of political opponents.

Events continued to unfold, with outcomes uncertain as of mid-1991. The FLN-led government was accused by diverse factions of creating election laws favoring it, essentially for fear of additional electoral gains by the FIS. *The New York Times* also noted on July 2, 1991, that the number of troops in the streets increased and that the fundamentalists were taunting them with shouts of "infidels." Suspecting that Iran's fundamentalist spiritual leader, Ayatollah Ali Khamenei, was partly behind the chaotic situation, prodding his Algerian counterparts to bring down the secularly oriented regime, the authorities directed a sharp protest to Teheran.

Algeria's future remained an open question. Instability offered the possibility for Berbers to challenge the regime, as Iraq's Kurds had recently challenged the leadership of Saddam Hussein. Benjedid's democratization process of 1988-1990 was in peril, and it was uncertain whether elections would be rescheduled in the near future. Even with these uncertainties remaining concerning Algeria's political future, it is clear that the 1990 municipal elections raised expectations among Algeria's once-dormant political forces.

Bibliography

Beck, Eldad. "The Kabyle Factor: The 'Kurds of Algeria' Lead Parallel Bids for Berber Rights." *The Jerusalem Report Magazine* 2 (June, 1991): 32-33. An informative, though very concise, analysis of the impact of the 1990 elections and their aftermath.

Bennoune, Mahfoud. *The Making of Contemporary Algeria: 1830-1987.* New York: Cambridge University Press, 1988. This book is one of the most comprehensive histories of Algerian political, social, and industrial development. It covers thoroughly the period of French colonial rule and events since independence in 1962 until (and including) the Chadli Benjedid era. It analyzes the background to democratic reforms. Contains a complete list of references.

Entelis, John P. *Algeria: The Revolution Institutionalized.* Boulder, Colo.: Westview Press, 1986. This study focuses on the successes achieved, especially by the Houari Boumedienne regimes (1965-1978), in promoting economic and industrial expansion as well as a standard of living superior to other Arab nations. It is an overoptimistic analysis of internal domestic affairs, precluding changes in the status quo.

Gordon, David C. *The Passing of French Algeria.* London: Oxford University Press, 1966. The standard history in English of the Algerian revolution, its aftermath, and FLN rule. It analyzes the internal upheavals of the newly instituted socialist political and economic systems, and delves into major issues the young leadership grappled with during the 1960's.

Hermassi, Elbaki. *Leadership and National Development in North Africa: A Comparative Study.* Berkeley: University of California Press, 1972. An in-depth analysis of North African political systems, their shortcomings, and their degree of stability. Emphasis is placed on Algeria, Tunisia, and Morocco. The author's approach of comparative analysis is instructive for the wider understanding of the comparisons and contrasts of these three political systems. This book is a valuable resource containing a complete list of references and an index.

Knauss, Peter R. *The Persistence of Patriarchy: Class, Gender, and Ideology in Twentieth Century Algeria.* New York: Praeger, 1991. The most extensive study on Algerian internal affairs and political hierarchies relevant to the 1990 elections, providing the general context for the event. Contains a comprehensive bibliography.

Quandt, William B. *Revolution and Political Leadership: Algeria, 1954-1968.* Cambridge, Mass.: MIT Press, 1969. One of the best works in English on the Algerian political system under Ahmed Ben Bella and Houari Boumedienne, by one of the world's leading Middle East experts. This book is an important companion volume to Gordon's and Hermassi's works on FLN leadership and the single-party system policies during the 1960's. Contains an index and a comprehensive bibliography.

Tlemcani, Rachid. *State and Revolution in Algeria.* Boulder, Colo.: Westview Press, 1986. This comprehensive study is highly informative on state bureaucracy, the challenge to capitalism, and educational developments under the FLN regime during the 1970's and 1980's. Together with the works by Bennoune, Entelis, and Knauss, Tlemcani's book provides the background for the 1988-1990 events.

Michael M. Laskier

Cross-References

Japan Ends Property Restrictions on Voting Rights (1925), p. 417; The French Quell an Algerian Nationalist Revolt (1945), p. 651; Algeria Gains Independence

(1962), p. 1155; Congress Passes the Voting Rights Act (1965), p. 1296; Spain Holds Its First Free Elections Since the Civil War (1977), p. 1921; Voters in Chile End Pinochet's Military Rule (1989), p. 2540; Sandinistas Are Defeated in Nicaraguan Elections (1990), p. 2564.

GORBACHEV AGREES TO MEMBERSHIP OF A UNITED GERMANY IN NATO

Categories of event: Political freedom and civil rights
Time: July 16, 1990
Locale: Moscow, Union of Soviet Socialist Republics

The two German states achieved political reunification only after Soviet leader Mikhail Gorbachev permitted the new united Germany to remain in NATO

Principal personages:
MIKHAIL GORBACHEV (1931-   ), the president of the Soviet Union
HELMUT KOHL (1930-   ), the chancellor of West Germany who called for German unification in November, 1989
HANS-DIETRICH GENSCHER (1927-   ), the foreign minister of West Germany who insisted that Germany remain in NATO
EDUARD SHEVARDNADZE (1928-   ), the foreign minister of the Soviet Union until December, 1990
LOTHAR DE MAIZIÈRE (1940-   ), the first non-Communist prime minister of East Germany after the March, 1990, election

Summary of Event

The division of Germany into two rival states in 1949 was a result of the Cold War between the United States and the Soviet Union. Although the Western democracies created the North Atlantic Treaty Organization (NATO) in 1949, neither German state established a national army until after 1955. The Soviet Union organized the Warsaw Pact only after West Germany was rearmed and admitted to NATO in 1955. East Germany also established an army in early 1956, after having been admitted into the Warsaw Pact. The German armies were integrated into rival military organizations in large part to overcome a fear of German rearmament held by both Western and Eastern European countries.

The rearmament of the two German states after 1955 solidified the division not only of Germany but also of Europe. Until the revolution of 1989, many observers discounted the possibility of German reunification, and many argued that the division of Germany was actually "the cornerstone of a stable Europe." Neither military bloc was willing to give up its German state to the other side. Not until Mikhail Gorbachev gave Germany permission to remain in NATO in July, 1990, was it possible for Germany to complete its political reunification and terminate the special powers exercised by the four major victors of World War II.

The decision to rearm the two Germanies had a dramatic effect on both societies. Rearmament was initially opposed by a majority of Germans in West and East Germany. Although West Germany rearmed in response to American pressures, the

West German army was able to fill its ranks with almost equal numbers of draftees and volunteers. In addition, the West German government established a number of guidelines that protected the civil and constitutional rights of soldiers. Everything possible was done to prevent the emergence of a militaristic culture; the emphasis was always placed on the citizen-soldier. By the 1980's, between 10 and 15 percent of West German conscripts opted for alternative service in the military by declaring themselves conscientious objectors. Most West Germans appreciated the more than one-half million foreign troops stationed in their country as valuable allies against potential Soviet aggression. The additional demand on housing and other vital facilities in such a small country, however, was often a source of friction between West Germans and their NATO allies.

In East Germany, rearmament had a much more negative impact on society. The Communist regime did not dare to introduce conscription until 1962, a year after it had built the Berlin Wall to prevent escape from East Germany. There were few safeguards in the East German army that protected civil and religious rights. Although some conscripts were permitted to perform alternative service with military construction units after 1964, the East German army did not officially recognize the status of conscientious objector. Rainer Eppelmann, a Lutheran minister who became defense minister of East Germany after the demise of the communist government in April, 1990, was imprisoned because he declared that he was a conscientious objector. Furthermore, in 1978 the communist government introduced compulsory military studies in schools. Almost all East German officers and a majority of noncommissioned officers were members of the official Socialist Unity Party. The presence in East Germany of more than 350,000 Soviet troops ensured that any opposition would be crushed with brutal force.

Both German armies were important to the rival military blocs. The largest Soviet army in Eastern Europe was located in East Germany, and the commander of that force dominated the East German military establishment. The West German army was crucial to NATO, since it provided half of the ground forces of NATO and 60 percent of its tank units. Unfortunately for the Germans, they were in the forefront of any potential conflict between the two military alliances. Even more disturbing to many Germans was that a conflict between NATO and Warsaw Pact forces would also produce a civil war between Germans.

Although the construction of the Berlin Wall in 1961 violated the human rights of families and friends on both sides of the wall, West German leaders after 1970 decided to establish closer contacts with East Germany. Willy Brandt, the chancellor of West Germany, initiated policies that led to the signing of the Basic Treaty between East and West Germany in 1972. This treaty attempted to establish normal relations between the two German states and, at least in the opinion of West German leaders, permit closer contacts between the two peoples. By 1979, almost eight million West Germans and West Berliners were able to visit East Germany. Unfortunately for intra-German relations, in 1979 the Soviets invaded Afghanistan. Fearing the superiority of Soviet conventional forces, West German chancellor Helmut

Schmidt called for the modernization of NATO weapons. By 1983, Pershing II and cruise missiles were being deployed in West Germany. As a result of this NATO decision, significant peace movements emerged in both West and East Germany. Furthermore, Moscow attempted to prevent further German-German détente by preventing Erich Honecker, the leader of East Germany, from visiting Bonn. Not until 1987 was Honecker able to make an official visit to West Germany.

The emergence of Mikhail Gorbachev in 1985 as the leader of the Soviet Union was the most important single event affecting both Eastern European regimes and the relationship between the two German states. Gorbachev called for greater European self-reliance in 1986, and on two different occasions in 1988 he guaranteed Eastern European countries freedom of choice. In effect, he abandoned the Brezhnev Doctrine, which had threatened Soviet military intervention in the case of any East European Communist regime experiencing domestic upheaval. Gorbachev's new policy allowed the Hungarians to remove the fortifications between Hungary and Austria. The opening of the Hungarian border undermined East Germany, as thousands of East Germans fled to the West. East Germans were granted automatic citizenship in West Germany. By November 9, 1989, the Berlin Wall was opened, and the inevitable process toward German unification was launched by Helmut Kohl, the chancellor of West Germany.

Kohl and the West German foreign minister, Hans-Dietrich Genscher, assured their Western allies that a united Germany would remain in NATO. This decision, however, could never be implemented without the permission of the Soviet Union and the removal of Soviet troops from East Germany. Gorbachev had insisted in 1987 that there were two German states and that any attempt to change this historical reality would be dangerous. As late as December, 1989, in a meeting with U.S. president George Bush in Malta, Gorbachev insisted on the existence of two Germanies. Only in January, 1990, did Gorbachev change his mind and accept the inevitability of German unification. In February, 1990, he informed Kohl that the Germans could decide on the timing of unification after negotiating with France, Great Britain, the United States, and the Soviet Union. Between January and June, 1990, however, Gorbachev continued to argue that Germany could not join NATO.

The two German states moved closer to unification after the March, 1990, election in East Germany removed the communist government and established a pro-Western coalition government under Lothar de Maizière. In early July, 1990, the West German mark became the official currency in East Germany. Finally, in order to meet one of Gorbachev's key demands, NATO representatives meeting in London on July 6, 1990, agreed to change the "forward defense theory" and extend a hand of cooperation to Moscow. With this development, Gorbachev could face his domestic opposition and agree with Kohl on July 16, 1990, that a unified Germany would be permitted to remain in NATO. Kohl agreed that Germany would not acquire nuclear or chemical weapons and that the German army would be reduced to 370,000 soldiers. Furthermore, the Germans would provide massive financial assistance to help the Soviets construct housing facilities for the Soviet troops returning from East

Germany. On September 12, 1990, the four powers and the two Germanies accepted this arrangement, and on October 3, 1990, reunited Germany regained its sovereignty.

Impact of Event

Gorbachev's decision to permit Germany to remain in NATO, combined with announcements by East European countries that they intended to withdraw from military commitments to the Warsaw Pact, effectively eliminated the confrontation between the two military blocs. This development had long been demanded by peace and human rights movements in Germany. The unification of Germany also resulted in the elimination of the East German army. Only fifty thousand former members of the East German army were to be absorbed by the united German army. Although many East German officers who had belonged to the Socialist Unity Party lost their careers, the militarization of East German society and schools was abolished. The former West German army was also to feel the impact of unification, since the total size of the German armed forces was to be reduced to 370,000.

The eventual departure of Soviet forces from East Germany and the reduction of foreign troops in West Germany was expected not only to reverse environmental damage but also to make available to the Germans additional housing and other badly needed facilities. The absence of Soviet protection after 1994 will also make it impossible for Moscow to assist, as it did in the case of Erich Honecker, the escape of former East German communists from German prosecution. A number of East German party and police leaders have been indicted for human rights violations, and it is likely that further charges will be filed against other former functionaries.

Reunification is expected to pose some problems. East Germans will suffer from rising unemployment until East German industries become more competitive. They will also have to deal with the environmental destruction left behind by the departing Soviet troops. Much of the cost of unification will have to be borne by West German taxpayers.

Ironically, with increased political and civil rights, there emerged a virulent and xenophobic nationalism among some East German youths. This hostility was directed against foreigners in general and Jews and Poles in particular. On the other hand, one positive consequence of the agreement between Kohl and Gorbachev in July, 1990, was a treaty between Poland and Germany that guaranteed Poland's border. Although West Germany officially accepted the Oder-Neisse line after 1970, its constitution did not permit it to sign a final treaty with Poland until Germany had been reunified. In return, the Poles agreed to end the cultural persecution of and discrimination against ethnic Germans living in Silesia.

German reunification within the NATO alliance reassured its neighbors that Germany would not represent a threat in the future. With the demise of the Warsaw Pact, Europe was no longer confronted with rival military blocs facing each other along the German borders. That lack of hostility was expected to facilitate the expansion of tolerance and human rights on both sides of the old Iron Curtain.

Bibliography

Adomeit, Hannes. "Gorbachev and German Unification: Revision of Thinking, Realignment of Power." *Problems of Communism* 39 (July/August, 1990): 1-23. This essay offers the best short review of the evolution of Gorbachev's views on the German issue between 1985 and July, 1990. The notes are particularly helpful, since they include citations to the Russian press that reveal Gorbachev's views.

Clark, Susan L., ed. *Gorbachev's Agenda: Changes in Soviet Domestic and Foreign Policy.* Boulder, Colo.: Westview Press, 1989. Most of the contributors to this collection of essays are European scholars. Hans-Hermann Hohmann's essay on the impact of *perestroika* on Central and Eastern Europe is particularly helpful.

Frey, Eric G. *Division and Détente: The Germanies and Their Alliances.* New York: Praeger, 1987. This remarkable book, the author's senior thesis at Princeton University, offers a fine survey of the relationship between the two German states. The bibliography is particularly valuable.

Griffith, William E., ed. *Central and Eastern Europe: The Opening Curtain?* Boulder, Colo.: Westview Press, 1989. This collection of essays covers all Central and East European countries. Dale R. Herspring's chapter on "The Soviets, the Warsaw Pact, and the Eastern European Militaries" is most helpful. Herspring questions the reliability of the East European military organizations within the Warsaw Pact.

Kaplan, Lawrence S., et al., eds. *Nato After Forty Years.* Wilmington, Del.: Scholarly Resources, 1990. The chapter by Werner Kaltenfleiter on "NATO and Germany" provides basic information on Germany's role in NATO and offers intelligent interpretations. Unfortunately, the author does not provide footnotes or other bibliographical guides.

Kirchner, Emil J. "Genscher and What Lies Behind 'Genscherism.'" *West European Politics* 13 (April, 1990): 159-177. The author, a political scientist at the University of Essex, reviews Genscher's impact as German foreign minister. He argues that Genscher, a native of East Germany, quickly saw the significance of *perestroika* to German unification.

Larrabee, F. Stephen, ed. *The Two German States and European Security.* Basingstoke, England: Macmillan, 1989. This collection of essays reveals how badly some scholars misinterpreted developments in Eastern Europe. Gorbachev was pictured as a man who would never accept German unification, and James McAdams claimed that there was domestic support for Erich Honecker.

Macgregor, Douglas. *The Soviet-East German Military Alliance.* Cambridge, England: Cambridge University Press, 1989. Macgregor offers a solid history of the relationship between the Soviet and East German military, but he argues that Moscow would use force to maintain its control of Eastern Europe.

Moreton, Edwina, ed. *Germany Between East and West.* Cambridge, England: Cambridge University Press, 1987. An interesting collection of essays on the German question from the perspective of the mid-1980's. The "German plans" of the four major powers and of the two German states are examined in detail.

Turner, Henry Ashby, Jr. *The Two Germanies Since 1945.* New Haven, Conn.: Yale University Press, 1987. The most reliable short survey of the political history of the two German states between 1945 and 1987.

Johnpeter Horst Grill

Cross-References

The Berlin Wall Is Built (1961), p. 1125; The Brezhnev Doctrine Bans Acts of Independence in Soviet Satellites (1968), p. 1408; The Helsinki Agreement Offers Terms for International Cooperation (1975), p. 1806; Gorbachev Initiates a Policy of *Glasnost* (1985), p. 2249; Hungary Adopts a Multiparty System (1989), p. 2421; Soviet Troops Leave Afghanistan (1989), p. 2449; Poland Forms a Non-Communist Government (1989), p. 2500; The Berlin Wall Falls (1989), p. 2523; Ceausescu Is Overthrown in Romania (1989), p. 2546; Soviet Troops Withdraw from Czechoslovakia (1990), p. 2570; Lithuania Declares Its Independence from the Soviet Union (1990), p. 2577; Demise of the U.S.S.R. Paves the Way for Reforms in Former Soviet Republics (1991), p. 2618.

CONGRESS PASSES THE
AMERICANS WITH DISABILITIES ACT

Category of event: Disability rights
Time: July 26, 1990
Locale: Washington, D.C.

Congress extended broad civil rights protections to an estimated forty-three million Americans with disabilities through the Americans with Disabilities Act (ADA)

Principal personages:
TOM HARKIN (1939-   ), a Democratic senator from Iowa, chief sponsor of the ADA in the Senate and member of the Labor and Human Resources Committee
TONY COELHO (1942-   ), the original sponsor of the ADA who was forced to resign after congressional investigations into his finances
STENY H. HOYER (1939-   ), a Democratic member of Congress from Maryland who replaced Coelho as chief supporter of the ADA in the House
GEORGE BUSH (1924-   ), the president of the United States and a supporter of both the rights of the disabled and the ADA

Summary of Event

In 1991, the United States Census Bureau estimated that forty-three million Americans suffered from some sort of physical or mental disability. For many years, these people were not assured of the basic rights afforded nondisabled people. They often suffered from discrimination in attempting to do such simple things as get a job, see a movie, go out for dinner with family or friends, or rent an apartment. Frequently, disabled people were relegated to the status of second-class citizens.

Disabled people are confronted by two types of barriers. The first is physical barriers such as stairs and narrow doorways. People in wheelchairs cannot get in many front doors, particularly in older buildings. They cannot proceed through narrow store aisles, get into elevators or ride escalators, or use public rest rooms. The shelving in stores is often too high for their easy access, and store security systems are often too narrow for people in wheelchairs to pass through easily.

The second type of barrier is less visible and includes obstacles such as hiring practices. Many handicapped people have been victims of blatant discrimination in everyday life. In the job market, many disabled individuals face discriminatory evaluations during the application process that focus on the existence of a disability rather than on the ability to perform a job. Many times, disabled individuals are given dead-end jobs that have few opportunities for promotion.

Beginning in the 1960's, the federal government played an increased role in establishing the rights of disabled individuals. Two acts indirectly provided rights to the disabled. One was the Fair Housing Act of 1988, which required new apartments to be "adaptable" to future disabled tenants. The other act, which indirectly provided rights to the disabled, was the 1964 Civil Rights Act, which guaranteed basic rights to women, blacks, and ethnic and religious minorities. The Civil Rights Act did not specifically mention the disabled, however, and thus they were still not guaranteed all the rights accorded nondisabled people in American society.

Other federal government activities focused specifically on the rights of the disabled, including the Rehabilitation Act of 1973, which was the first milestone in the area. Section 504 of the act prohibited discrimination on the basis of handicap in any program or activity that received federal funds. This covered, for example, activities in any federal employment, in employment by federal contractors, and in programs and activities receiving federal financial assistance. If it was found that an agency denied access to the disabled, that agency could risk losing all federal funding.

The Education for All Handicapped Children Act (EHA) was another milestone for disabled rights. Passed in 1975, two years after the Rehabilitation Act, the EHA established the principle of teaching children with disabilities within the nation's mainstream school systems. The law provided that all children were entitled to a free public education, regardless of handicap. As a result of this statute, handicapped children could learn alongside other students, thus allowing disabled children to cope better with their disabilities. The number of students with disabilities who received full secondary school education grew dramatically as a direct result of the EHA.

The children who attended school under the EHA began to enter the labor market in the 1980's. They were well educated, were highly motivated, and had useful work skills. Most important, they wanted to find meaningful employment. Unfortunately, they often faced discrimination both in seeking employment and, if hired, in getting to their job sites. Many disabled people began to demand the rights afforded to nondisabled people in the work force.

Disabled people's rights groups were successful in getting members of Congress to address issues surrounding the rights of the disabled in public places. Before the ADA, there were many groups who fought for the rights of particular groups of handicapped individuals—for example, the blind or deaf. These groups all came together to support the ADA. One group that brought much public attention to the issue of disabled rights was the National Council on the Handicapped. Also working to gather support for the ADA was the Leadership Conference on Civil Rights. These groups, along with supporters in Congress, were able to garner great support for the measure.

Tom Harkin, a Democratic senator from Iowa, was the chief sponsor of the ADA in the Senate. Harkin, who had a brother who was deaf, was keenly aware of the problems handicapped people faced. He was also a member of the Labor and Human Resources Committee and chair of the Handicapped Subcommittee, to which the ADA was referred. The ADA had support from the majority of the members of the Senate, and the entire Senate passed the legislation quickly on September 7, 1989.

Tony Coelho, a Democratic representative from California and himself a sufferer of epilepsy, first introduced the ADA into the House of Representatives. Coelho was forced to resign his congressional seat in June of 1989 after investigations into his finances. He then asked Steny Hoyer, a Democratic representative from Maryland, to act as floor manager for the bill as it progressed through the House. Hoyer had been the original cosponsor of the bill and had worked closely with Coelho in the early stages of the bill.

The bill had to travel through four House committees before it could be introduced to the House for voting. This made for a much longer and more difficult route than in the Senate. The Education and Labor Committee was the only committee to approve the bill in 1989. The other three committees passed the bill in 1990. The Energy and Commerce Committee on March 13, 1990, was the second committee to approve the bill; Public Works and Transportation approved the bill on April 3, 1990; and the Judiciary Committee on May 2, 1990, became the fourth and final House committee to approve the bill. The entire House overwhelmingly passed the bill on May 22, 1990.

There were two issues that slowed the ADA on its path to becoming a law. The first had to do with an amendment that would allow employers to transfer workers with contagious diseases out of food-handling jobs, even if such diseases could not be transmitted through food. Lawmakers on both sides of the issue said the amendment was aimed at people with AIDS. Proponents of the amendment claimed that restaurant owners needed the flexibility to transfer people out of such jobs because of public perceptions that such workers would pose a danger. Opponents claimed that the law should not be based on such perceptions, which were the exact things the bill was trying to overcome.

The second issue had to do with the issue of congressional coverage. Members of both chambers of Congress agreed that Congress should be subject to the bill's ban on discrimination but disagreed on how the bill should be enforced. The House provided for an internal mechanism; the Senate bill made the provisions applicable to the Congress.

The final bill compromised on both issues. On the AIDS issue, the bill required the secretary of Health and Human Services to come up with a list of communicable diseases that could be transmitted through food. On the congressional coverage issue, the bill provided that the internal mechanism would apply in the House and that the Senate would set up its own internal procedure while also allowing for cases to go to federal court.

The ADA was passed in final form by the House on July 12 and the Senate on July 13. President George Bush, who had given strong support to the bill since 1988, when he was vice president, signed it into law at a White House ceremony on July 26.

Impact of Event

ADA was written much like the 1964 Civil Rights Act, but it was much more broad in that it included protection for any person with a mental or physical impairment that substantially limited major life activities. The ADA prohibited discrimination against the disabled in employment, public services, and public accommodations and required that telecommunications be made accessible to those with speech and hearing impairments through the use of special relay systems. The rule applied to any public facility, including office buildings, gas stations, airports, hotels, bars, restaurants, lobbies, sports facilities, libraries, parks, and more. The ADA was much broader in scope than the 1964 Civil Rights Act in that it increased the accommodations protections to include services ranging from museums, theaters, and sporting events to doctors' offices, hospitals, and pharmacies. If businesses did not comply with the new law, they might have to give back pay, front pay, attorneys' fees, and job reinstatement to people who had been the victims of discrimination.

Many people in the business communities were opposed to the ADA. They claimed they would have to spend large amounts of money to comply with the new rule. As a result of the ADA, businesses were required to install wheelchair ramps, elevators, and telephone devices for the hearing-impaired. Supporters of the ADA claimed this was not necessarily true, and that businesses had only to come up with cheap and creative solutions. The federal government also offered a construction tax credit for businesses to help them comply with the law.

The section of the law that affected the greatest number of businesses—the provisions covering hiring practices—would not cost them anything. Businesses had to rethink the way they interviewed job applicants to ensure that the questions they asked were relevant and had to examine the essential and nonessential parts of each job. Employers could face lawsuits for turning down applicants who could perform all the essential parts of a job.

Questions remained as to the very broad and vague language found in the ADA. For example, the bill required "reasonable accommodation" that did not cause "undue hardship" on businesses. The vagueness of these terms and others troubled business groups, who argued that disagreements over the definitions would lead to a high number of expensive and time-consuming lawsuits.

The ADA also forbade discrimination on public transportation. All new vehicles bought for public transit were required to be accessible to disabled people. Companies that provided intercity transportation were required to make adaptations for wheelchair users. New rail facilities were required to be accessible to handicapped persons. Also, one car per train in existing rail systems had to be made accessible.

The Department of Justice was assigned the duty of enforcing the ADA and published proposed rules to implement the ADA. The department also established a new office, within the Coordination and Review Section of the Civil Rights Division, which was made responsible for development and implementation of policy. This office was created expressly to address ADA implementation issues.

On a broader level, sponsors of the ADA hoped the bill would change the way Americans thought about and treated disabled people. Most people remained uninformed about the problems handicapped people faced. ADA supporters hoped the bill would be a first step in helping to integrate the disabled into mainstream society and that it would become common to see people with disabilities participating in activities, making nondisabled people more comfortable around them. The ADA also sent disabled people the message that they did not have to be dependent on others and that they could have greater participation in community life.

Bibliography

Gearheart, Bill R., Mel W. Weishahn, and Carol J. Gearheart. *The Exceptional Student in the Regular Classroom.* Columbus, Ohio: Merrill, 1988. Focuses on educating various handicapped students, including the hearing impaired, visually impaired, health impaired, language impaired, and learning disabled, among others. Each disabled student has particular needs that must be met by the educational system to guarantee a quality education.

Hunsicker, J. Freedley, Jr. "Ready or Not: The ADA." *Personnel Journal* 69 (August, 1990): 81-86. Provides an extremely readable summary of the provisions of the ADA for employers and in doing so predicts the effect the ADA will have on businesses. Provides legal definitions of some vague terms included in the law.

McKee, Bradford. "Achieving Access for the Disabled." *Nation's Business* 79 (June, 1991): 31-34. Provides a summary of the ADA from the business point of view. Summarizes some controversial aspects of the law and predicts how the provisions of the ADA will affect businesses. Effective dates for different parts of the bill are included.

Rovner, Julie. "Promise, Uncertainties Mark Disability-Rights Measure." *Congressional Quarterly Weekly Report* 48 (May 12, 1990): 1477-1479. Provides a legislative summary of the ADA as well as the proponent and opposing points of view on the proposed bill.

"Sweeping Law for Rights of Disabled." *1990 Congressional Quarterly Almanac* 46 (1990): 447-461. Provides a condensed summary of the ADA. After a brief background of the bill is presented, the path of the bill through Congress is described. A readable summary of the provisions of the ADA is presented.

Nancy E. Marion

Cross-References

Legislation Ushers in a New Era of Care for the Mentally Disabled (1963), p. 1206; Congress Passes the Civil Rights Act (1964), p. 1251; The United Nations Declares Rights for the Mentally Retarded (1971), p. 1644; Congress Passes the Equal Employment Opportunity Act (1972), p. 1650; Congress Responds to Demands of Persons with Disabilities (1973), p. 1731; Congress Passes the Child Abuse Prevention and Treatment Act (1974), p. 1752; Congress Enacts the Education for All Handicapped Children Act (1975), p. 1780.

IRAQ INVADES AND RAVAGES KUWAIT

Category of event: Atrocities and war crimes
Time: August 2, 1990
Locale: Iraq and Kuwait

On August 2, 1990, Iraq, motivated by a variety of factors, invaded its southern neighbor, Kuwait, thereby initiating a brutal occupation of that country and setting the stage for the Gulf War of 1991

Principal personages:
SADDAM HUSSEIN (1937-   ), the president of Iraq
GEORGE BUSH (1924-   ), the forty-first president of the United States
JABIR AS-SABAH (1926-   ), the emir of Kuwait

Summary of Event

During the early morning hours of August 2, 1990, Iraqi armed forces suddenly invaded neighboring Kuwait, resulting in the looting of that small country and the brutalization of the Kuwaiti people. This act of aggression was the result both of trends which had been developing in the upper Persian Gulf region for several years and of specific problems which, when combined, led to an escalation of Iraqi-Kuwaiti tensions and, ultimately, invasion.

In the broadest sense, three closely interconnected factors contributed to an increasingly explosive situation in the Persian Gulf region. First, throughout the 1980's, Iraqi president Saddam Hussein had systematically and often brutally eliminated all sources of rival political power in Iraq and had, simultaneously, concentrated all power and authority around himself. For example, during the late 1980's, Hussein crushed the Kurdish minority within Iraq, allegedly using chemical weapons to suppress the Kurds and sending more than sixty thousand refugees into Iran and Turkey. Furthermore, more than half a million additional Kurds were forcibly resettled away from the border in order to permit the Iraqi authorities to secure the frontier areas. Meanwhile, throughout the 1980's, Hussein effectively excluded independent elements of the ruling Baath Party from power and increasingly surrounded himself with associates disinclined to provide him with independent advice. This served to isolate the Iraqi president, a trend which was particularly dangerous in view of his lack of personal experience with the Western powers and limited experience even within the Arab world.

Second, in the aftermath of the Iraqi victory over Iran in the decade-long Iran-Iraq war, Iraq emerged as the dominant indigenous military power in the Persian Gulf region. At the conclusion of the conflict, Iraq's military consisted of more than one million men, including the sizable and well-equipped Republican Guard. In addition, during the Iran-Iraq conflict, the Iraqis had invested heavily in defense industries, particularly in chemical weapons production and the development of missile technology. Following the cessation of hostilities with Iran, the Iraqi authorities continued to emphasize the expansion of Iraq's high-tech armaments industry. In short, as Baghdad entered the 1990's, Iraq's military, backed by the Iraqi defense industrial establishment, placed Saddam Hussein in a strong position to influence Persian Gulf affairs along desired lines.

Third, against the backdrop of his monopolistic consolidation of political power domestically and Iraq's postwar military dominance in the Persian Gulf region, Hussein increasingly aspired to leadership of the entire Arab world. The Iraqi president apparently believed that the collapse of communism in Eastern Europe and the growing internal political, ethnic, and economic chaos within the Soviet Union, combined with other changes in the international power configuration, created an opportunity in which an Iraqi-led coalition of revolutionary Arab states could assert itself and emerge as a more powerful, perhaps regionally dominant, actor in the international arena. As part of his effort to assert his leadership within the Arab world, Hussein directed his rhetoric against Israel, the traditional adversary of the Arabs. On April 2, 1990, he articulated a new deterrence policy for Iraq under the terms of which, should Israel attack Iraq, as it had in 1981 when the Israelis destroyed the Iraqi Osirak nuclear reactor, Iraq would respond with a chemical attack on Israel. Later, the Iraqi president said that Iraq would extend this deterrent umbrella to any Arab state desiring Iraqi assistance. Simultaneously, the Iraqi president attempted to consolidate additional support for his effort to assert leadership throughout the Arab world by promising Iraqi support for the Palestinian cause. Hussein's bold new military deterrence doctrine directed toward Israel, combined with his encouragement of the Palestinians and other, similar measures designed to appeal to the Arab masses, allowed the Iraqi president to reap a swell of popular support throughout the entire Arab world.

Notwithstanding Iraq's regional military power, along with Hussein's effective concentration of political power within Iraq and his growing prestige as a pan-Arab leader in the aftermath of the Iran-Iraq war, Iraq was confronted by a series of serious problems which threatened to jeopardize Hussein's ambitions for himself and Iraq. The central problem was financial: Iraq emerged from its war with Iran with an estimated debt of $80 billion, $30-35 billion of which consisted of short-term loans owed to the Western powers, with the remainder owed to the oil-producing Arab states of the Persian Gulf. The debt problem was further compounded by Iraq's postwar policy of continued heavy investment in its high-tech defense industry as well as highly ambitious, visible, reconstruction projects in war-damaged areas of Iraq and the importation of consumer goods and food from abroad, all requiring additional hard currency. Finally, Iraq's already high demand for foreign exchange was further amplified by its $6-7 billion annual debt service requirements.

Iraq hoped to meet its financial requirements by increasing oil revenues. This hope was predicated upon predictions of oil price increases. Unfortunately for the Iraqis, when the price of oil declined from twenty dollars to fourteen dollars a barrel during a six-month period between January and June, 1990, they faced a serious short-term financial shortfall. Many Iraqis blamed the Western powers, arguing that the decline in oil prices was part of a larger Western conspiracy in which the West had manipulated the oil market so as to create financial hardship for Iraq and thereby force Baghdad to abandon its regional policies and ambitions. Hussein also accused Kuwait and the United Arab Emirates of "cheating" on OPEC (Organization of Petroleum Exporting Countries) production quotas, thereby further contributing to the decline in oil prices. Tensions between Iraq and Kuwait were further exacerbated by Kuwait's refusal to forgive the debt owed to it by Iraq. In short, rather than recognize the underlying sources of financial instability, adopt effective measures to reorder spending priorities, and place Iraq on a sound financial footing, Hussein instead blamed the Western powers, Kuwait, and the United Arab Emirates for Iraq's financial problems.

In addition to its financial differences with Kuwait, Iraq also had a series of territorial disputes with its southern neighbor. Prior to relinquishing claim to all of Kuwaiti territory in 1963, Iraq had, periodically, made attempts to assert full Iraqi control over the entirety of Kuwait. After 1963, although Iraqi claims against Kuwaiti territory became more limited in scope, they remained a topic of contention between the two states. One dimension of the dispute centered on the Khor Abd Allah estuary, which constitutes the maritime portion of the Iraqi-Kuwaiti border and leads to the Iraqi naval base and port at Umm Qasr as well as to the Iraqi port of Khor Zubair, further upriver. Kuwait applied the midchannel doctrine to divide the estuary, whereas Iraq claimed the entire waterway. Moreover, Baghdad sought to obtain control of Bubiyan and Warbah Islands from Kuwait, since these islands effectively controlled the estuary's entrance. Kuwait, of course, rejected Baghdad's claims, but the Iraqis thought that it was vital for Iraq's national security and the success of their political, economic, and military ambitions to obtain full Iraqi control over this important outlet to the Persian Gulf.

In addition to the Khor Abd Allah waterway dispute, the Iraqis claimed ownership of the entire Rumailah oil field, which lay on both Iraqi and Kuwaiti territory. In addition, Iraq accused Kuwait of pumping from the Rumailah oil field and selling the oil at considerable profit during the Iran-Iraq war. Baghdad demanded that the border be revised in accord with its claims to the entire Rumailah field and that Kuwait pay Iraq $2 billion for the oil allegedly pumped earlier from the disputed field. Kuwait also rejected these claims, thereby leading to a further estrangement between the Kuwaitis and Baghdad.

Finally, in the broadest sense, the Iraqi authorities capitalized upon popular Arab resentment for the wealthy, conservative monarchies of the Persian Gulf. In this sense, Baghdad was able to frame its financial and territorial disputes with Kuwait within the larger ideological rivalry between revolutionary pan-Arabism and the conservative monarchies of the Arab world.

Although relations between Iraq and Kuwait had been deteriorating for some time, tensions between the two states began to rise dramatically in late May, 1990. In mid-July, Hussein threatened action if key differences between Iraq and Kuwait were not resolved to Baghdad's satisfaction. Meanwhile, Iraqi forces concentrated along the Kuwaiti border. Then, suddenly, on August 2, 1990, Iraq invaded Kuwait. Within hours the entire country was overrun. Most of Kuwait's ruling family escaped to Saudi Arabia. Initially, the Iraqis claimed that the Kuwaiti opposition had invited Iraq into Kuwait, but Baghdad's inability to produce a cooperative Kuwaiti provisional government ultimately led the Iraqi authorities to reassert their old claim to the whole of Kuwait and simply to annex the entire country. The northern portion of Kuwait was attached to Basra, while the remainder of Kuwait became the nineteenth Iraqi province.

Impact of Event

The Iraqi invasion of Kuwait had an enormous impact upon Kuwait, the Persian Gulf region, and the entire Middle East. First, with respect to Kuwait, following the invasion, the Iraqis looted the entire country of any movable item: furniture, autos, Kuwait's gold reserves, industrial equipment, and even treasures from the Kuwaiti museum. Moreover, approximately half of Kuwait's citizenry, along with substantial numbers of Asian and Palestinian workers employed in Kuwait, fled the country. With respect to those who remained, the Iraqis ruthlessly crushed indigenous resistance. Not only did this produce a large number of brutal incidents of personal arrests, tortures, and executions, but a large portion of Kuwait's male population between the ages of eighteen and forty-five was taken back to Iraq to be held hostage by the Iraqi authorities.

Meanwhile, the international community reacted to the Iraqi aggression against Kuwait. Immediately following the invasion, U.S. president George Bush ordered an economic embargo of Iraq. The West European states and Japan also embargoed the Iraqis and, on August 6, 1991, the United Nations Security Council ordered a global economic embargo against the Baghdad regime. The following day, President Bush ordered the deployment of U.S. military forces to Saudi Arabia, thereby commencing Operation Desert Shield. The military deployment was immediately broadened to include representation from a number of Arab powers and members of the international community. On August 25, the U.N. Security Council authorized the use of military force to enforce the embargo against Iraq. Meanwhile, on August 8, the Iraqis had closed their borders to foreign nationals inside Iraq and Kuwait, thereby preventing thousands of foreigners from leaving either country. On August 28, Baghdad allowed foreign women and children to depart, but it continued to hold foreign men as hostages.

Throughout the autumn, the crisis mounted as the United States and its Desert Shield coalition partners poured troops and military equipment into Saudi Arabia. On November 29, 1991, the U.N. Security Council established January 15, 1991, as the deadline for Iraq to withdraw from Kuwait and threatened use of military force to drive the Iraqis out if the deadline was not met. Efforts by President Bush to secure an eleventh hour negotiated withdrawal and Iraq's December 6, 1990, decision to release the foreign nationals which it had been holding since early August failed to secure a peaceful settlement of the crisis. On January 12, 1991, the U.S. Congress authorized President Bush to use military force to drive the Iraqis from Kuwait, thus clearing the way for the commencement of hostilities following the expiration of the January 15 withdrawal deadline.

On January 17, 1991, at 12:50 A.M. (4:50 P.M., January 16, 1991, Eastern Standard Time), with Iraq still in possession of Kuwait, Operation Desert Storm began. Over the next five and one-half weeks, Iraqi military targets were pounded by U.S. and coalition air power. On February 23, the United States and the other members of the coalition launched ground operations against the Iraqi military forces. On February 25, Saddam Hussein ordered the withdrawal of Iraqi forces from Kuwait and, late the following day, the Kuwaiti resistance declared that it controlled Kuwait City. On February 27, 1991, President Bush announced the liberation of Kuwait and the defeat of the Iraqi armed forces. He further announced that offensive operations by the United States and its coalition partners would be suspended at midnight.

The war had a devastating impact upon Kuwait, Iraq, and the entire region. Not only was there extensive damage resulting from the air and ground operations during the conflict, but also the Iraqis took actions which will have an environmental impact upon the Gulf region for generations to come. Not only did the Iraqis ignite the Kuwaiti oil fields, but they also released a significant quantity of oil into the Persian Gulf, thereby polluting both the air and the Gulf's waters. Moreover, in their haste to withdraw, the Iraqis left within Kuwait a massive number of mines and other explosives which would require years, if not decades, to disarm. Furthermore, missiles fired by Iraq caused additional damage, particularly in Saudi Arabia and in nonbelligerent Israel, thereby compounding the devastation. Finally, in the aftermath of the war, the weakened but still powerful government of Saddam Hussein brutally crushed Kurdish and other opposition elements which emerged in the wake of Iraq's defeat. The bitter legacy of Iraq's invasion of Kuwait, the human rights violations which characterized Iraq's occupation of Kuwait and Baghdad's policies toward the people of Iraq, and the devastation caused by the Gulf War would influence the attitudes of the peoples of the Gulf region, the policies of the Middle Eastern powers, and the ecology of the area for years to come.

Bibliography

Kelly, J. B. *Arabia, the Gulf, and the West.* New York: Basic Books, 1980. This study provides a solid interpretation of the history of the Arabian Peninsula and the Persian Gulf between the mid-1960's and 1980.

Khadduri, Majid. *Socialist Iraq: A Study in Iraqi Politics Since 1968.* Washington, D.C.: Middle East Institute, 1978. This work is the continuation of Khadduri's earlier definitive studies, *Independent Iraq, 1932-1958: A Study in Iraqi Politics* (2d ed., New York: Oxford University Press, 1960) and *Republican Iraq: A Study in Iraqi Politics Since the Revolution of 1958* (London: Oxford University Press, 1969). It contains valuable information concerning the post-1968 changes in Iraqi politics and the background and rise of Saddam Hussein.

Lenczowski, George. *The Middle East in World Affairs.* 4th ed. Ithaca, N.Y.: Cornell University Press, 1980. Lenczowski's study is perhaps the best single source concerning the foreign policies of the indigenous and external powers in the Middle East since World War I. Chapter 7, focusing on Iraqi foreign policy, and Chapter 16, assessing the policies of the smaller states of the Persian Gulf, provide important background for understanding the Iraqi invasion of Kuwait.

Marr, Phebe. "Iraq's Uncertain Future." *Current History* 90 (January, 1991): 1-4, 39-42. This article is probably the best single analysis of the causes of the Iraqi invasion of Kuwait and will provide a valuable framework for analysis of the Gulf War.

_____. *The Modern History of Iraq.* Boulder, Colo.: Westview Press, 1985. Marr's study on the history of Iraq provides a valuable supplement to the works of Khadduri and Lenczowski cited above.

Miller, Judith, and Laurie Mylroie. *Saddam Hussein and the Crisis in the Gulf.* New York: Times Books, 1990. This work is a discussion of Saddam Hussein and Iraqi foreign and domestic politics leading up to the invasion of Kuwait.

Pelletiere, Stephen, Douglas V. Johnson II, and Leif R. Rosenberger. *Iraqi Power and U.S. Security in the Middle East.* Carlisle Barracks, Pa.: Strategic Studies Institute, U.S. Army War College, 1990. This monograph provides a useful discussion of the Iraqi military and political background to the Gulf War.

Smolansky, Oles M. *The USSR and Iraq.* Durham, N.C.: Duke University Press, 1991. Provides a comprehensive analysis of the Soviet Union's relationship with Iraq since the Iraqi Revolution of 1958. As such, it provides a valuable supplement to Smolansky's earlier study, *The Soviet Union and the Arab East Under Khrushchev* (Lewisburg, Pa.: Bucknell University Press, 1974).

Howard M. Hensel

Cross-References

Palestinian Refugees Flee to Neighboring Arab Countries (1948), p. 749; Israel Is Created as a Homeland for Jews (1948), p. 761; The Iraqi Government Promotes Genocide of Kurds (1960's), p. 1050; Palestinian Refugees Form the Palestine Liberation Organization (1964), p. 1241; Nations Agree to Rules on Biological Weapons (1972), p. 1662; Khomeini Uses Executions to Establish a New Order in Iran (1979), p. 2013; Iraq's Government Uses Poison Gas Against Kurdish Villagers (1988), p. 2397; Demise of the U.S.S.R. Paves the Way for Reforms in Former Soviet Republics (1991), p. 2618.

DE KLERK PROMISES TO TOPPLE
APARTHEID LEGISLATION

Categories of event: Racial and ethnic rights; civil rights
Time: 1991
Locale: Cape Town, South Africa

At the opening session of Parliament, President de Klerk announced plans to repeal the foundation laws of racial separation and domination

Principal personages:
> FREDERIK WILLEM DE KLERK (1936-   ), the president of South Africa
> since 1989
> NELSON MANDELA (1918-   ), an antiapartheid spokesman released
> from prison in 1990, elected president of the African National Congress in 1991
> MANGOSUTHU GATSHA BUTHELEZI (1928-   ), a Zulu chief and head of
> the Inkatha party

Summary of Event

At the 1991 opening session of the racially segregated parliament of South Africa, President Frederik Willem de Klerk delivered a dramatic speech in which he promised to support legislation that would scrap the remaining laws on which the system of apartheid was based. The most important of these laws was the Population Registration Act of 1950, which segregated South Africans into four racial categories: whites, blacks, Indians, and coloreds (people of mixed race). Other legislation included the Native Lands Act (1913) and the Native Land and Trust Act (1936), which reserved 87 percent of the land for the white minority, as well as the Group Areas Act (1950) and related legislation that segregated residential areas. In addition, de Klerk said that he would submit legislation to allow communities to negotiate a new system of integrated local government based on one tax base for all citizens. Finally, he proposed a multiparty conference to discuss the creation of a new constitution for the country. These ambitious proposals were outlined in a document entitled "Manifesto for the New South Africa."

De Klerk declared that these changes in law would mean that "the South African statute book will be devoid, within months, of the remnants of racially discriminatory legislation which have become known as the cornerstones of apartheid." Because de Klerk was the leader of the National Party, which had a clear majority of votes in the parliament, all observers agreed that the proposed legislation would be passed without real difficulty. Previously, the government's position had been that the Population Registration Act could not be repealed as long as the country was under the triracial constitution of 1983, with its segregated chambers for whites, coloreds, and Indians. On closer inspection, however, de Klerk explained that legal authorities had concluded that the law could be repealed with temporary transitional measures that anticipated the creation of a new constitution dispensation. Babies born after the repeal would not be classified according to race, but other South Africans would retain their racial classification until the triracial parliament voted for its own extinction in favor of a new regime.

In his address, de Klerk failed to mention three homeland laws: the Bantu Self-Government Act (1959), the Bantu Homelands Citizenship Act (1970), and the Status Acts. The first two laws had transferred limited powers of self-government to ten tribal "homelands" and had conferred all blacks with citizenship in one of these ethnic homelands. The Status Acts had recognized the "independence" of four of the homelands (Transkei, Ciskei, Bophuthatswana, and Venda), requiring that their citizens forfeit their South African nationality. A series of coups in the four homelands between 1987 and 1990 had marked the collapse of the homeland system, but a final settlement of the issue would be reached only under a new constitution.

Reaction to the speech was predictable. Rightist Afrikaner legislators were horrified, and during the speech they shouted "traitor to the nation" and "hangman of the Afrikaner." Andries Truernicht and the forty other representatives of the Conservative Party angrily marched out of Parliament. In contrast, South Africa's Democratic Party, which opposed apartheid, welcomed the proposals. In the United States, the administration of President George Bush saw de Klerk's speech as evidence that its antiapartheid policy was working. One State Department official stated, "It's the equivalent of the fall of the Berlin Wall."

As expected, de Klerk's program did not go far enough to please black organizations in South Africa, especially the African National Congress (ANC). Nelson Mandela and other ANC leaders denounced the fact that de Klerk had rejected an ANC proposal to elect a constituent assembly to draft a new constitution, meaning that the de Klerk government was determined that whites would retain a disproportionate influence in the negotiations over the constitution. Likewise, the ANC leaders were unhappy that there were no specific plans to repatriate forty thousand political refugees, to release political prisoners in the "independent" homelands, or to repeal the security laws that gave the police sweeping powers to detain political suspects. "We still do not have the vote," declared ANC leader Walter Sisulu, "and this is what our people demand today, to vote for a constituent assembly." Throughout the country, hundreds of thousands of blacks marched to demand additional changes.

Three days before de Klerk's speech, Mandela and his major black rival, Zulu chief Mangosuthu Buthelezi, had met for the first time in twenty-eight years. Following an eight-hour discussion, they had announced a peace pact for Natal province, where violent fighting between ANC supporters and Buthelezi's Inkatha party had claimed four thousand lives in five years. Despite this announcement, however, factional violence in the townships resumed within two days and continued throughout the summer and early fall of 1991. Another difficulty for the ANC was the trial and conviction of Winnie Mandela in May. While her husband had been in prison,

Mrs. Mandela had assembled some bodyguards known as the Mandela United Football Club. They were accused of abducting and beating four youths suspected of collaboration, killing one of the four. When Mrs. Mandela was sentenced to six years in prison, many ANC supporters feared that the "Winnie problem" would damage the prestige of the organization.

As Parliament prepared to pass the promised legislation, many African leaders showed evidence of a desire to reestablish ties with South Africa. At the annual summit of the Organization of African Unity (OAU) held June 3-5, the organization, after a long debate, issued a statement promising to lift sanctions if South Africa adopted measures demonstrating "profound and irreversible change toward the abolition of apartheid." In fact, a number of countries, such as Zimbabwe, were already increasing their trade with South Africa, and just after the OAU conference, Kenya and Madagascar announced that they were restoring trade and transportation ties with the country.

The same day the OAU ended its summit, the South African Parliament voted to repeal the Land Acts of 1913 and 1936 and the Group Areas Act. South Africans were thus given the legal right to buy property and live where they pleased. Even more significant, on June 17 Parliament repealed the Population Registration Act, with the white House of Assembly voting 129 to 38, with 11 abstentions. This meant that citizens would no longer be registered into racial categories at birth, although the existing racial register would be maintained until the approval of a nonracial constitution. The ANC issued a statement observing that the average black citizen was no better off than before the reforms had been enacted. Noting that discriminatory treatment in areas such as education, employment, and state pensions continued as before, the document said: "As long as such blatantly racist practices continue, the Population Registration Act will have been removed in name only."

President Bush and other Western leaders were more impressed with the reforms. Early in July, the U.S. State Department informed Bush that South Africa had fulfilled the five conditions contained in the Comprehensive Anti-Apartheid Act of 1986, and on July 10 the president formally lifted U.S. trade and investment sanctions. Bush spoke of the "profound transformation" in South Africa and expressed the opinion that "this progress is irreversible." Mandela and antiapartheid groups throughout the world criticized Bush's decision as premature; in contrast, Chief Buthelezi, who had long opposed sanctions, welcomed the action. Several countries, including Finland and Japan, soon announced that they were following the American example, and the International Olympic Committee lifted its boycott of twenty-one years after judging that South Africa had made significant advances in ending racial discrimination in sports.

Impact of Event

South African developments in 1990 and 1991 were indeed spectacular. For decades, the apartheid system had appeared to be the most flagrant example of injustice and oppression anywhere in the world. By the summer of 1991, the legal foundations for this system had come to an end. Certainly, the South African problem was far from settled, and extremely difficult negotiations would be necessary before it would be possible to arrive at a consensus for a new constitution. Even after any new constitution, socioeconomic inequalities between blacks and whites would continue to be an issue, and there did not appear to be any easy solutions to ending the ethnic violence in the townships. Nevertheless, just a few years earlier, when President Pieter Botha had stubbornly resisted fundamental reforms, few observers expected that the foundations of apartheid would be abrogated by the summer of 1991.

In the short term, the most important issue was the negotiations for a new constitution. It appeared that the constitution had to be completed before 1994, the deadline for the calling of parliamentary elections. The National party, with its popularity uncertain, had no intention of conducting another whites-only election under the old constitution. This meant that de Klerk had to operate under severe time limitations in preparing a new constitution. The ANC was determined that the new constitution would provide for majority rule based on the principle of "one person, one vote." In contrast, de Klerk and the National Party were determined to have a constitution that would include a veto and disproportionate influence for the white minority. In September, 1991, de Klerk proposed a blueprint for a constitution that would replace the presidency with an executive council made up of members of the three largest parties in Parliament's lower house and which would assign more powers to regional and local governments. Mandela, who had recently been elected president of the ANC, strongly denounced such an arrangement. White voters approved of de Klerk's efforts in a referendum on March 17, 1992. Almost 90 percent of eligible voters cast ballots, two-thirds of which stated approval of de Klerk's efforts to end apartheid.

Although nobody expected future negotiations to be settled easily, the two sides did agree on many basics, including support for a two-house legislature, the right of each citizen to have one vote, a guarantee of individual liberties, an independent judiciary, and the end of the black homelands. The ANC was less insistent on nationalizing key industries and in seeking massive redistribution of wealth, questions of major concern to whites of the country. Thus, in spite of many difficulties, there was a realistic possibility for negotiations to result in a nonracial constitution by the deadline of 1994.

Most experts believed that economic sanctions had been one of the major influences leading de Klerk's government to agree to the reforms of 1991, and continuing economic difficulties added to the urgency for seeking a political settlement as soon as possible. In 1991, the population of South Africa was almost forty-two million people, and this was expected to grow to ninety-two million by the year 2025. In 1991, black unemployment was estimated at more than 35 percent, and simply to remain at this unsatisfactory level would require an economic growth rate of 5 percent per year. During the years of the sanctions, the Gross National Product had grown by less than 1 percent per year, and it actually shrank by 1 percent in 1990.

With its resources and infrastructure, however, South Africa had the potential of becoming one of the most prosperous countries of the world, if only it could resolve its political problems.

Bibliography

Baker, Pauline. "South Africa: Old Myths and New Realities." *Current History* 90 (May, 1991): 197-200, 232-233. An excellent analysis of the crumbling of apartheid, with a useful chart of major laws. Bakers argues that sanctions had been effective, that the right wing was not a major threat, that blacks did not want a Marxist state, and that there were good reasons to hope for a peaceful settlement.

De Klerk, Frederik. "South Africa and Apartheid." *Vital Speeches* 57 (March 1, 1991): 294-300. The complete text of de Klerk's important speech before Parliament on February 1, presenting his program for the end of legal apartheid as well as other issues of South African politics.

Johnson, Shaun, ed. *South Africa: No Turning Back.* Bloomington: Indiana University Press, 1989. A collection of scholarly essays dealing with topics such as politics since 1976, internal resistance to apartheid, the police in South Africa, the Afrikaner establishment, and the history of Inkatha. The articles were written just before de Klerk came to power.

Laurence, Patrick. "Repealing the Race Laws." *Africa Report* 36 (March/April, 1991): 34-37. A clear analysis of de Klerk's parliamentary speech of February 1. Written from a pro-ANC perspective, the article emphasizes the limitations of de Klerk's policies, especially the issues of the constituent assembly and the homelands. *Africa Report* is an excellent source for up-to-date information and analysis about the continent.

Lemon, Anthony. *Apartheid in Transition.* Boulder, Colo.: Westview Press, 1987. A useful history of apartheid as well as a sociological analysis of the situation in the late 1980's, with much information about the ethnic groups of South Africa. Writing before de Klerk's election, Lemon concluded that apartheid was being dismantled and that the logical result would be for whites to have a minority share of power.

Mandela, Nelson. *The Struggle Is My Life.* New York: Pathfinder, 1991. The famous leader of the ANC provides a short autobiography in which he explains his political beliefs and his goals for South Africa. There are several editions of this book. This expanded edition includes speeches following Mandela's release from prison.

Mufson, Steven. "South Africa 1990." *Foreign Affairs* 70 (1991): 120-142. Written just before the reforms of 1991, this article provides an excellent analysis of de Klerk's policies as well as those of Inkatha and the ANC. Mufson emphasizes the uncertainty of the government's goals as well as the uncertainty of the outcome of negotiations.

Oakes, Dougie, ed. *Reader's Digest Illustrated History of South Africa: The Real Story.* Pleasantville, N.Y.: Reader's Digest Association, 1988. An interesting, readable account of the background history of South Africa, with many fascinating illustrations as well as a useful glossary. Published the year before de Klerk became president, the book does not anticipate the profound changes after 1989.

Thomas T. Lewis

Cross-References

South Africa Begins a System of Separate Development (1951), p. 861; Lutuli Is Awarded the Nobel Peace Prize (1961), p. 1143; The United Nations Issues a Declaration on Racial Discrimination (1963), p. 1212; The United Nations Votes to Suppress and Punish Apartheid (1973), p. 1736; Carter Makes Human Rights a Central Theme of Foreign Policy (1977), p. 1903; The United Nations Imposes an Arms Embargo on South Africa (1977), p. 1937; A World Conference Condemns Racial Discrimination (1978), p. 1993; The United Nations Issues a Declaration on South Africa (1979), p. 2008; The OAU Adopts the African Charter on Human and Peoples' Rights (1981), p. 2136; Tutu Wins the Nobel Peace Prize (1984), p. 2244; Mandela Is Freed (1990), p. 2559.

YUGOSLAV ARMY SHELLS DUBROVNIK

Category of event: Atrocities and war crimes
Time: 1991
Locale: Croatia

During the autumn of 1991, the city of Dubrovnik in Croatia was bombarded by Yugoslav federal forces, an assault which resulted in numerous casualties as well as significant damage to medieval structures in and around the city

Principal personages:
ANTE MAROVIC (c. 1924-   ), the prime minister of Yugoslavia
STIPE MESIC (c. 1935-   ), a Croat who became Yugoslavia's president
FRANJO TUDJMAN (c. 1922-   ), the president of Croatia
SLOBODAN MILOSEVIC (c. 1941-   ), the president of Serbia
TITO (1892-1980), the post-World War II Yugoslav leader

Summary of Event

The city of Dubrovnik, situated on the Dalmatian coast on the eastern side of the Adriatic Sea, traces its history to the end of the seventh century A.D. The city, originally called Ragusium and subsequently known as Ragusa, was founded by displaced Roman settlers from the Greek city of Epidaurus (located immediately to the southeast) after Epidaurus had been seized by Slavs. Eventually, as the Slavic and Latin communities became integrated, Dubrovnik came under the autonomous control of the Byzantine Empire. Between 1205 and 1358, Dubrovnik was controlled autonomously by Venice. Between 1358 and 1526, it fell under Hungarian protection. Subsequently, Dubrovnik came under the protection of the Ottoman Empire but retained a large measure of independence. Dubrovnik was a leading center of maritime commercial activity in the fifteenth through eighteenth centuries, second in the Adriatic only to Venice. Dubrovnik also emerged as an important intellectual center in the development of Balkan culture. Indeed, throughout its history the city has retained a strong cosmopolitan flavor which has blended Mediterranean influences with the diverse cultural characteristics of the Balkan region.

Beginning in 1272 and continuing through the seventeenth century, the city erected an elaborate series of fortifications. Dubrovnik's main city wall, approximately six thousand feet in circumference, between thirteen and twenty feet thick on the land side, five to ten feet thick on the sea side, and about eighty feet high, surrounded what has become known as the old city. Punctuating the walls are five bastions, two corner towers, twelve square towers, three round towers, and the citadel of Fort St. John (Sveti Ivan), a formidable defensive structure guarding the old harbor. Dubrovnik's medieval character has been preserved within the old city, with many of the buildings dating back to the fourteenth and fifteenth centuries. The physical characteristics of medieval Dubrovnik, combined with its rich cultural and artistic attractions, made the city Yugoslavia's principal historical tourist site, with thousands of visitors flocking to the city annually. In recognition of Dubrovnik's unique historical value, the city was placed on the United Nations World Heritage list as a site whose safety and preservation were said to be humankind's collective responsibility.

In 1808, Dubrovnik was taken by Napoleon, but in the settlement at the Congress of Vienna in 1815, the city was awarded to Austria. It remained under Vienna's control until the defeat of the Austro-Hungarian Empire in World War I. After 1918, Dubrovnik was attached to Croatia, within the framework of the newly created state of Yugoslavia, which was dominated by Serbs. Historically, Croatia and Serbia represented two different aspects of their common Balkan heritage. Whereas the Serbs were Orthodox in religious persuasion, the Croats were predominantly Catholic. Linguistically, the Serbs used the Cyrillic alphabet, and the Croats used the Latin alphabet. Eastern Ottoman Turkish influences remained strong in Serbia, whereas Croatia followed the lead of Central Europe.

During the interwar period, tensions mounted among the Serbs, the Croats, and the other nationalities within Yugoslavia. These tensions were manifested during World War II, when, under Nazi sponsorship, Yugoslavia was broken up and an independent Croatia was established. Nazi atrocities, combined with traditional Balkan hatreds, led to persecutions and massacres which, in turn, left postwar Yugoslavia deeply scarred. In the wake of the collapse of Nazi Germany in 1945, Yugoslavia was reestablished, this time under the leadership of the Communist Party, guided by the partisan leader, Marshal Tito. Tito managed to suppress the national hostilities, but, after his death in 1980, these hostilities gradually resurfaced. The collapse of communism in Eastern Europe at the end of the 1980's created the context for the disintegration of postwar Yugoslavia. Croatia and Slovenia elected governments pledged to assert independence from the Yugoslav state. On June 25, 1991, the Slovenes and Croatians declared their independence from Yugoslavia.

Slovenia moved immediately to secure its borders. Following a brief series of clashes with the Yugoslav federal army which left fifty people dead, the fighting subsided and attention shifted southward to Croatia. Approximately 600,000 of Croatia's 4.5 million citizens were ethnically Serbs. They contended that they did not wish to become an ethnic minority within an independent Croatian state. Serbian leaders outside Croatia supported these claims, asserting that Serbs left within an independent Croatia would be persecuted by the Croatian majority. Consequently, even prior to Croatia's formal declaration of independence, and with Serbian support, the Serbs within Croatia began to prepare for an armed insurgency. Following Croatia's declaration of independence, the Serbian-dominated Yugoslav federal army began operations against the rebellious Croats. Simultaneously, the federal army gradually began to coordinate its activities with the Serbian insurgents. Although the Yugoslav federal army cited a variety of goals to justify its military operations against Croatia, ranging from protecting the Serbian minority in Croatia to defending and restoring Yugoslavia, the Croatians contended that Serbia was using the federal army and the ethnic Serbs in Croatia as instruments to dismember Croatia and create a Greater Serbia. In any case, by autumn, 1991, the Yugoslav federal army and the Serbian insurgents had captured approximately one-third of Croatian territory. By that time, an estimated three to five thousand people had been killed in the intensifying Yugoslav Civil War, with as many as ten thousand wounded and more than three hundred thousand displaced from their homes.

By the beginning of October, 1991, fighting between Croatian forces and units of the Yugoslav federal army had spread to the area around Dubrovnik. On October 1, the Yugoslav army surrounded the city, laying siege to it and its sixty thousand inhabitants, 90 percent of whom were Croats. Dubrovnik's citizens, joined by refugees from outlying areas, were deprived of electric power, telephone communications, and fresh water. By late October, rationing had been introduced. Families were allocated 1.3 gallons of fresh water daily, with very small supplements sometimes collected from Dubrovnik's cisterns. People were reduced to washing and flushing toilets with water from the Adriatic Sea. Food was also rationed, with a family's weekly ration consisting of one quart of cooking oil, one pint of milk, one pound of potatoes, one pound of bread, two tins of fish, and two tins of meat. The people of Dubrovnik were concerned particularly with the prospect of disease that might result from untreated sewage and a shortage of medicine. Tensions among the population increased with the duration of the siege, as people spent long hours in basement shelters or in chambers within the walls of the old city.

By mid-October, planes from the Yugoslav federal air force had bombed the marina, and federal artillery had shelled the city, although at that point the old city remained undamaged. By October 23, units of the Yugoslav federal army had moved to positions within three miles of the old city, and the danger to Dubrovnik increased daily. As the Serbian-dominated Yugoslav military continued to increase its pressure on Dubrovnik, international efforts to prevent the situation from further deteriorating also continued. Representatives from the European Community and the United Nations, in addition to their efforts to secure a comprehensive cease-fire in the Yugoslav Civil War, appealed to both the Serbs and the Croats to honor the United Nations convention protecting historic sites and to spare Dubrovnik from further destruction. The United States condemned the Yugoslav federal army's attack on Dubrovnik as an irresponsible assault on a civilian center which was devoid of military value. For their part, Yugoslav military authorities denied that their forces had attacked the old city and pledged to keep them from doing so.

In late October, Croatian and Yugoslav army leaders agreed upon a partial evacuation of Dubrovnik, under the supervision of European Community monitors and the Red Cross. Males between the ages of eighteen and sixty, however, would not be allowed to leave the city unless they were joined by ill or elderly relatives. By the end of October, Dubrovnik's population had decreased only marginally, because refugees from outlying areas continued to arrive. The old city had sustained only light damage up to that time. As of October 28, the Red Cross reported that fifty-two people had been killed and slightly more than two hundred had been wounded in the fighting in and around the city.

In early November, 1991, Dubrovnik was subjected to its heaviest artillery and gunboat bombardment. Yugoslav federal shells hit targets inside and immediately around the old city. On November 9, the Yugoslav military intensified its joint bombardment of the old city, the surrounding tourist hotels, and adjacent civilian targets.

Impact of Event

The bombardment of Dubrovnik in early November caused significant damage to the old city and adjacent areas. Approximately fifty people reportedly were killed, and many more were wounded in the land, air, and naval bombardment which continued until November 13. Several of Dubrovnik's tourist hotels were damaged seriously or destroyed as Croatian defenders attempted to halt the advance of the Yugoslav federal forces. Federal planes attacked Croatian positions in the Napoleonic-era fort, constructed in 1808 on Brdo Srdj (Mount Sergius), which rises above Dubrovnik. Fort St. John, as well as many of the towers along the city walls, was damaged, as were a number of sites within the medieval city itself. Both the fourteenth century Dominican friary and the Franciscan friary at the opposite side of the old city were damaged, as was the seventeenth century Jesuit church. Elsewhere in the old city, such medieval architectural treasures as Dubrovnik's clock tower were hit during the shelling. Even after considering the physical damage to Dubrovnik and the suffering of its people, Croatia's new leaders vowed to defend the city against the Yugoslav federal military attacks. From their perspective, Dubrovnik had become a symbol of Croatian independence and resistance to Serbian domination.

On November 13, the Yugoslav federal shelling tapered off, and in the afternoon, a relief ship was allowed to enter Dubrovnik's harbor. Food, medical supplies, and fresh water were unloaded, and on the following day, more than two thousand refugees were evacuated from the city. This set the stage for subsequent relief efforts. Eventually, a spokesperson for the Yugoslav federal army apologized for the shelling of Dubrovnik, attributing the action to local forces that allegedly acted without permission from the central authorities.

In eastern Croatia, the eighty-six-day siege of the city of Vukovar ended on November 17 with its capture by Yugoslav federal troops and Serbian insurgents. Like Dubrovnik, Vukovar had become a symbol of Croatian resistance to Serbian efforts to suppress Croatia's spirit of independence. Unlike Dubrovnik, Vukovar was reduced to ruins, and extremely heavy civilian casualties were sustained as Serbian-dominated forces bombarded the city into submission.

At the end of 1991, as Germany led members of the European Community in formal recognition of Croatia and Slovenia, the Croatian government remained committed to recapturing those territories which it had lost at the outset of its war for independence. An internationally brokered cease-fire among the belligerents had been put in place at year's end, and many hoped that it would become permanent. Most analysts agreed, however, that the crisis in the Balkans was far from being resolved. Although it had been damaged significantly, Dubrovnik had escaped the level of destruction visited upon Vukovar. The fact that the priceless treasures of this historic medieval city were damaged at all, combined with the tragic loss of human life and the wounding of a large number of Dubrovnik's citizens, amplified the need for a common commitment by all of humankind to honor the United Nations agreements governing the protection of the irreplaceable relics of humankind's global heritage.

Bibliography

Binder, David. "Dubrovnik Diary." *The New York Times*, November 16, 1991, p. 4. This vital account provides a firsthand description of the shelling of Dubrovnik from November 10 to November 14, 1991. This article should be read in conjunction with the author's other articles published in *The New York Times* on November 9, 1991 (pp. 1 and 4), November 10, 1991 (p. 8), and November 15, 1991 (p. 3).

Engelberg, Stephen. "Brutal Impasse: The Yugoslav War." *The New York Times*, December 23, 1991, pp. 1 and 4. In this extremely concise, yet thoughtful, background report, Engelberg analyzes the causes of the Yugoslav Civil War and the situation at the time of the shelling of Dubrovnik.

Ganser, Armin. *Baedeker's Yugoslavia*. New York: Prentice-Hall, 1983. The section on the city of Dubrovnik provides useful maps and other information to assist in determining the extent of the shelling described by other writers.

Fejto, Francois. *A History of the People's Democracies: Eastern Europe Since Stalin*. New York: Praeger, 1971. A valuable history of the states of Eastern Europe since the communist takeovers following World War II. Several chapters are dedicated specifically to developments in Yugoslavia.

Krekic, Barisa. *Dubrovnik in the Fourteenth and Fifteenth Centuries: A City Between East and West*. Centers of Civilization 30. Norman: University of Oklahoma Press, 1972. This fascinating study examines the character of medieval Dubrovnik.

Nelson, Daniel N. *Balkan Imbroglio: Politics and Security in Southeastern Europe*. Boulder, Colo.: Westview Press, 1991. A series of very useful essays focusing on contemporary problems of the Balkans, with a chapter dedicated to the problems of Yugoslavia.

Shoup, Paul. *Communism and the Yugoslav National Question*. New York: Columbia University Press, 1968. A key background study necessary for understanding the complexities of the Yugoslav nationality question.

Sudetic, Chuck. "Yugoslav Army Seizes Coast Near Dubrovnik." *The New York Times*, October 23, 1991, p. 7. Like those by Binder and Engelberg, this article traces the developing story of the bombardment of Dubrovnik. This article should be read along with Sudetic's pieces published in *The New York Times* on October 27, 1991 (p. 4), November 5, 1991 (p. 3), November 13, 1991 (p. 6), and November 14, 1991 (p. 4).

Wolff, Robert L. *The Balkans in Our Time*. New York: W. W. Norton, 1967. A classic work focusing primarily on the development of the Balkans during the first half of the twentieth century.

Howard M. Hensel

Cross-References

Soviets Take Control of Eastern Europe (1943), p. 612; Solidarity Leads Striking Polish Workers (1980), p. 2112; Gorbachev Initiates a Policy of *Glasnost* (1985), p. 2249; Ethnic Unrest Breaks Out in Yugoslavian Provinces (1988), p. 2386; Solidarity Regains Legal Status in Poland (1989), p. 2477; Poland Forms a Non-Communist Government (1989), p. 2500; The Berlin Wall Falls (1989), p. 2523; Ceausescu Is Overthrown in Romania (1989), p. 2546; Albania Opens Its Borders to Foreign Nationals (1990), p. 2553; Soviet Troops Withdraw from Czechoslovakia (1990), p. 2570; Lithuania Declares Its Independence from the Soviet Union (1990), p. 2577; Demise of the U.S.S.R. Paves the Way for Reforms in Former Soviet Republics (1991), p. 2618.

DEMISE OF THE U.S.S.R. PAVES THE WAY FOR REFORMS IN FORMER SOVIET REPUBLICS

Category of event: Political freedom
Time: December, 1991
Locale: Commonwealth of Independent States (formerly the Union of Soviet Socialist Republics)

During late 1991, disastrous economic conditions, worsening quality of material life, growing nationalist separatism, and a coup attempt destroyed confidence in the central Soviet government and led to the creation of the Commonwealth of Independent States

Principal personages:
MIKHAIL GORBACHEV (1931-   ), the general secretary of the Communist Party of the Soviet Union and last president of the U.S.S.R. (1990-1991)
BORIS YELTSIN (1931-   ), the president of the Russian Republic elected in 1990
GENNADY YANAYEV (1937-   ), the vice president of the U.S.S.R. from December, 1990, to August, 1991; proclaimed acting president of the Soviet Union during the August, 1991, coup attempt
LEONID KRAVCHUK, the president of the Ukraine and one of three creators of the Commonwealth of Independent States
STANISLAV SHUSKEVICH, the chairman of the Belorussian Supreme Soviet and one of three creators of the Commonwealth of Independent States

Summary of Event

According to the 1936 constitution of the Union of Soviet Socialist Republics (U.S.S.R.), citizens of the U.S.S.R. possessed freedom of speech, press, assembly, and demonstration, as well as equality of rights, irrespective of nationality or race. The constitution also guaranteed to member republics the right of secession. The history of the Soviet Union, however, shows evidence of ongoing disregard for these rights. The social and economic consequences of that disregard prompted the dissolution of the U.S.S.R.

The year after the Bolshevik Revolution in 1917, Vladimir Ilyich Lenin established the Soviet Republic of Russia. At first, the government declared that all land, housing, and large factories were public property, to be managed by the central government. In 1921, however, Lenin combined privatized small industries and retail trade with state-controlled large industry, banking, and foreign trade. When the Union of Soviet Socialist Republics was founded in 1922, however, its agricultural, industrial, and other economic resources already were exhausted.

Joseph Stalin took over the Communist Party of the Soviet Union in 1924 and inaugurated highly centralized economic planning. He created collective farms and launched his country into rapid industrial development. Unfortunately, the Soviet people suffered from a neglect of both agriculture and production of consumer goods, declining living standards, and increasing political coercion. In the 1930's, Stalin eliminated political opposition with mass arrests, forced labor, and executions. He also extended Soviet domination in Europe, beginning with annexation of the Baltic states on the eve of World War II and continuing with the establishment of the Iron Curtain in the postwar period. In the mid-1950's, the U.S.S.R.'s economic growth began to slow, worker productivity fell, and consumption of goods declined.

Nikita Khrushchev, who emerged as the new Party leader in 1953 and became premier in 1958, eased Stalinist restrictions, but his attempts to reform the Soviet economy were unsuccessful. When his farm program collapsed in 1964, he was forced into retirement.

Leonid Brezhnev, who succeeded Khrushchev as Party leader and later became president of the U.S.S.R., stifled political reform. As economic growth slowed further in the 1960's and 1970's, Brezhnev continued to use central economic planning and attempted to improve living conditions. With gains in agricultural production barely matching population growth, food importation became necessary. After 1979, Soviet productivity declined dramatically, living standards fell, and shortages of goods and services became severe.

In 1986, Mikhail Gorbachev (party secretary since 1985) launched a radical economic reform program known as *perestroika* (restructuring), accompanied by *glasnost* (openness) in Soviet society. In a general loosening of central economic control, in 1987 Gorbachev removed industrial subsidies and moved industry into partial free-market operation. He decentralized economic management, allowed individual farmers to work private plots and sell produce on a free-market basis, and ordered payment of workers according to productivity. Gorbachev also restructured prices, generally upward, to ease consumer shortages. An obstructionist bureaucracy, however, implemented these reforms slowly.

Many Soviets initially supported the 1987 reforms, but by late 1989 most considered the economic situation to be deteriorating and blamed the deterioration on Gorbachev's reforms. The reforms had caused workers to work longer, harder, and often for lower wages. They faced higher prices in state stores, where goods were increasingly difficult to find. Supplies were more plentiful in privatized markets and on the black market, but prices were even higher. *Perestroika* had resulted in frustration, erosion of support for Gorbachev, Party defection, and work stoppages.

In 1988, Gorbachev began restructuring the Soviet government. His democratic reforms resulted in the first free, multicandidate election in the U.S.S.R. since 1917 being held in 1989. With the economy and living standards worsening, however, the Party spiraled into decline. Soviet satellite states swept away their Communist regimes, and Soviet republics declared sovereignty (Azerbaijan, 1989) and independence (Lithuania, 1990). Having legalized opposition parties early in 1990, the Communist Party relinquished formal control over the Soviet Union. Separatist sentiments and activity increased in the Soviet republics. In May, 1990, anti-Communist nationalist Zviad Gamsakhurdia of Georgia and radical populist reformer Boris Yeltsin of Russia won the presidencies of their republics in popular elections.

In mid-1991, Gorbachev formulated a new Union Treaty to transform the U.S.S.R. into a confederated "Union of Sovereign Soviet Republics." The proposed treaty called for a new constitution that would allow national elections and diminish the power of the Party and the Soviet central government. The signing of the treaty was scheduled for August 20, 1991.

Instead, on Sunday, August 18, 1991, a coup d'état began with Gorbachev's arrest. Involving all but two of Gorbachev's own ministers, the coup sought to overthrow Gorbachev, prevent the signing of the treaty, and return the U.S.S.R. to strong centralized Party rule. On Monday, August 19, vice president Gennady Yanayev was proclaimed acting president, and an emergency committee assumed power. The Soviet military commander in the Baltics took control of the three secessionist Baltic republics, Lithuania, Latvia, and Estonia. In Moscow, Yeltsin persuaded a unit of Soviet tanks to protect the Russian government. He called for nationwide resistance, the return of Gorbachev as Soviet president, and a general strike.

On August 20, Soviet tanks moved to within one mile of Yeltsin's headquarters. Fearing attack, tens of thousands of resisters erected barricades to protect Yeltsin and his democratically elected government. Strong protests against the coup and other scattered Soviet military activity erupted in Moldavia, the Ukraine, and Kazakhstan. Shaken by intense, widespread anticoup sentiments, three members of the emergency committee resigned. The coup began to fall apart.

On August 21, coup opponents gained ground. Soviet tanks withdrew from Moscow, and in the Baltics, Soviet troops began returning to their bases. In Moscow, the Party denounced the coup, the Congress of People's Deputies demanded Gorbachev's reinstatement, and crowds celebrated outside the Russian parliament. Latvia and Estonia, where military crackdowns had been severe, declared immediate independence. Gorbachev returned to Moscow on August 22. With most coup leaders under arrest, Gorbachev and his ally, Yeltsin, began rebuilding the Soviet government. Even as Gorbachev proclaimed his devotion to socialism and the Communist Party, the Lithuanian government banned the Party and confiscated its property.

The August, 1991, coup attempt had several effects. It elevated Yeltsin to the forefront of Soviet and world affairs, where he became a symbol of Western democracy. Defeat of the coup also removed high-level obstructions to Gorbachev's reforms, the very reforms coup instigators had tried to prevent. The coup also fanned republican independence movements and precipitated the dissolution of both the Communist Party and the U.S.S.R.

While Gorbachev set Soviet political and economic reforms in motion on August 23, Yeltsin began chipping away at Soviet authority in the U.S.S.R. Latvia banned the Party, and republican governments seized Party property. Across the Soviet Union, citizens turned on Party bosses and organizations, and crowds vandalized statues of Communist heroes.

Gorbachev's proposed new union grew shakier. Late in August, more Soviet republics declared independence, ignoring Gorbachev's exhortations to preserve a modified union. On August 26, leaders of the breakaway republics firmly declared central authority to be dead. Three days later, the Communist Party ceased to exist. On September 5, the Congress of People's Deputies transferred power to the republics. The next day, the Baltic states' independence was approved.

As central power crumbled, republican leaders took political and economic control. On December 7, 1991, Yeltsin, Ukrainian president Leonid Kravchuk, and Belorussian chairman Stanislav Shuskevich met to discuss a trade agreement. Deciding that it was impossible to reform the economy within the Soviet structure, the three leaders formed a "Commonwealth of Independent States" on December 8 and proclaimed the Soviet Union's end. According to their agreement, Commonwealth republics would launch coordinated economic reforms and jointly move toward free-market prices, beginning on January 2, 1992. Other articles of the agreement concerned liquidating nuclear arms, respecting the territorial integrity of other republics, and guaranteeing every citizen equal rights and freedoms.

On December 17, 1991, Gorbachev agreed to dissolve the Soviet Union. Five days later, Russia, Ukraine, Armenia, Belorussia, Kazakhstan, Kyrgyzstan, Moldavia, Turkmenistan, Azerbaijan, Tadzhikistan, and Uzbekistan approved the Commonwealth pact and sealed the fate of the U.S.S.R. On December 25, 1991, Gorbachev formally resigned as president, the first Soviet leader ever to leave office voluntarily. Six days later, the Soviet Union, the world's first communist state, officially ceased to exist. Into its place came an ill-defined but optimistic Commonwealth of Independent States.

Impact of Event

The U.S.S.R. had collapsed as a result of poor economic conditions, worsening quality of life, and growing nationalist separatism. The political and economic health of its successor, the Commonwealth, was very poor at its beginning. One political result of the dissolution of the U.S.S.R. was increased potential for ethnic and nationalist ferment. After the dissolution, fears that the new republics would follow the course that Romania and Yugoslavia had taken after their break from the U.S.S.R. were borne out. Georgia came close to civil war within weeks, and within one week ethnic strife led to violence in Armenia and Azerbaijan. Fear also arose that political upheaval might come at the hands of ill-provisioned and disgruntled Soviet military personnel.

Popular uncertainty about the future also increased following the dissolution. The example of Eastern Europe was not encouraging. When Communist Party control in the Soviet Bloc collapsed in 1989, it brought suffering to the people. Following the implementation of free-market economic reforms, unemployment rose, production decreased, shortages became more common, and inflation raged at rates as high as seven hundred percent per year. Consumer goods became too expensive for purchase by many potential buyers. In Albania, starvation loomed as a threat. Although economists in the U.S.S.R. predicted that within months the cost of goods would stabilize and more products would become available, in the Russian republic families prepared for the worst, stockpiling food in preparation for famine.

That the disintegration of the U.S.S.R. freed the former Soviet republics to move toward economic reform was most apparent in Russia. After the dissolution, President Yeltsin quickly began privatization of state-owned property, agriculture, and industry. He also introduced new monetary and fiscal policies, the most important of which was the elimination of price controls early in January, 1992. The prices of basic commodities (bread and gasoline, for example) remained controlled, but all other prices were set free for the first time in more than seventy years. The hope was that this would stimulate manufacturing, yield the production of more goods, bring supply in line with consumer demand, and thus moderate inflation.

The early effect of these reforms on the economy and on material conditions of life was worse than the Russian populace expected. Unemployment soared, and more was likely to come as the huge Soviet bureaucracy and military were disassembled. In addition, the ruble lost value. In Russia at the time prices were freed, 100 rubles were worth sixty-three dollars. Two weeks later, 110 rubles brought one dollar. By late February, however, the Russian government had moved to stabilize the ruble, and its value appeared to be rising. Even so, at that time the Ukraine, Belorussia, Moldavia, and Kazakhstan planned to begin printing their own currency. Hand in hand with the devaluation of the ruble, inflation soared. In the first month without price controls, Russian prices increased an average of two hundred percent. In St. Petersburg, food costs soared to ten times their previous level, while salaries remained the same. There were no significant increases in available supplies of goods. During the winter of 1992, St. Petersburg faced real hunger. Supplies there had become scarce at the end of the summer, after the neighboring Baltic states had lifted price controls and Baltic shoppers had flooded into Russia, where goods were cheaper, to buy supplies. Rationing was begun in St. Petersburg in the fall of 1991, but when Yeltsin freed prices, almost everything disappeared from the store shelves.

Standing out among the immediate effects of the disintegration of the Union of Soviet Socialist Republics was popular discontent in both political and economic realms. Within months of the formation of the Commonwealth of Independent States, ethnic and nationalist violence had erupted. In the face of shortages of crucial foodstuffs and supplies, there was fear that bread riots, another coup, or the dissolution of the Commonwealth might be on the horizon.

Bibliography

Church, George J. "Postmortem: Anatomy of a Coup." *Time* 138 (September 2, 1991): 32-44. This excellent article presents a detailed, play-by-play account of the coup, its major players, and their motivations.

Goldman, Marshall I. "The Consumer." In *The Soviet Union Today: An Interpretive Guide*, edited by James Cracraft. 2d ed. Chicago: The University of Chicago Press, 1988. This article, in an excellent collection of concise pieces on the Soviet Union from its beginnings to 1988, provides a broad look at agriculture, housing, and the availability of consumer goods between the 1940's and the 1980's. It alludes to increasing popular discontent.

Johnson, D. Gale. "Agriculture." In *The Soviet Union Today: An Interpretive Guide*, edited by James Cracraft. 2d ed. Chicago: The University of Chicago Press, 1988. Johnson gives a brief but detailed overview of Soviet agricultural production from the 1950's to 1985, compares it with U.S. production, and explains factors that led to the U.S.S.R.'s poor agricultural performance and increasing costs.

Matthews, Mervyn. *Patterns of Deprivation in the Soviet Union Under Brezhnev and Gorbachev*. Stanford, Calif.: Hoover Institution Press, 1989. This study of material conditions in the Soviet Union presents and analyzes sociological surveys done in the Soviet Union from the 1960's to the mid-1980's. Although a bit heavy with statistics, Matthews' work contains detailed information on food, clothing, and household goods; public desires to obtain consumer goods; and the popular assessment of living conditions in 1985.

Millar, James R. "An Overview." In *The Soviet Union Today: An Interpretive Guide*, edited by James Cracraft. 2d ed. Chicago: The University of Chicago Press, 1988. Millar surveys the Soviet economy, includes information on its consumer impact, and analyzes the potential of various reforms.

Shelton, Judy. *The Coming Soviet Crash: Gorbachev's Desperate Pursuit of Credit in Western Financial Markets*. New York: Free Press, 1989. Unlike several other sources noted here, Shelton predicted an economic crash in the U.S.S.R. Generally a macro analysis of the Soviet economy and East-West relations as of 1988, the book contains informative sections on consumer conditions in chapter 2. Chapter 3 details Gorbachev's economic reform plans.

Smith, Gordon B. *Soviet Politics: Struggling with Change*. 2d ed. New York: St. Martin's Press, 1992. Smith's work is an indispensable source of information on the U.S.S.R. immediately prior to its disintegration. Chapter 10 treats the Soviet economic system and chapter 11 outlines social policy and problems. An appendix includes "The Constitution of the U.S.S.R." and a draft of Gorbachev's "Treaty on the Union of Sovereign Republics."

Martha Ellen Webb

Cross-References

The Baltic States Fight for Independence (1917), p. 207; Lenin Leads the Russian Revolution (1917), p. 225; Khrushchev Implies That Stalinist Excesses Will Cease (1956), p. 952; Gorbachev Initiates a Policy of *Glasnost* (1985), p. 2249; Ethnic Unrest Breaks Out in Yugoslavian Provinces (1988), p. 2386; Soviet Farmers Are Given Control of Land and Selection of Crops (1989), p. 2471; Ceausescu Is Overthrown in Romania (1989), p. 2546; Gorbachev Agrees to Membership of a United Germany in NATO (1990), p. 2589.

GREAT EVENTS
FROM
HISTORY II

CHRONOLOGICAL LIST OF EVENTS

VOLUME I

VOLUME II

VOLUME III

VOLUME IV

VOLUME V

ALPHABETICAL LIST OF EVENTS

C

KEY WORD INDEX

CATEGORY INDEX

CATEGORY INDEX

INTERNATIONAL NORMS

NUTRITION

OLDER PERSONS' RIGHTS

PEACE MOVEMENTS AND ORGANIZATIONS

POLITICAL FREEDOM

CATEGORY INDEX

REFUGEE RELIEF

VOTING RIGHTS

WOMEN'S RIGHTS

CATEGORY INDEX

GEOGRAPHICAL INDEX

PRINCIPAL PERSONAGES